CW00346256

Enchantress of Nations

Enchantress of Nations

Pauline Viardot: Soprano, Muse and Lover

MICHAEL STEEN

ICON BOOKS

Published in the UK in 2007 by
Icon Books Ltd, The Old Dairy, Brook Road,
Thriplow,
Cambridge SG8 7RG
email: info@iconbooks.co.uk
www.iconbooks.co.uk

Sold in the UK, Europe, South Africa and Asia
by Faber & Faber Ltd, 3 Queen Square,
London WC1N 3AU or their agents

Distributed in the UK, Europe, South Africa and Asia
by TBS Ltd, TBS Distribution Centre, Colchester Road
Frating Green, Colchester CO7 7DW

This edition published in Australia in 2007
by Allen & Unwin Pty Ltd,
PO Box 8500, 83 Alexander Street, Crows Nest, NSW 2065

Distributed in Canada by
Penguin Books Canada, 90 Eglinton Avenue East,
Suite 700, Toronto, Ontario M4P 2YE

ISBN: 978-1840468-43-4

Typesetting in 11 on 14pt Adobe Garamond by Wayzgoose

Printed and bound in Slovenia

Contents

ABOUT THE AUTHOR

Michael Steen OBE Hon RCM was born in Dublin. He was organ scholar at Oriel College, Oxford, having previously been at the Royal College of Music and Eton. He then spent 30 years in a successful career in the City of London. He was chairman of the Royal College of Music Society and is chairman of the trustees of the Friends of the Victoria and Albert Museum. He is a trustee of the Gerald Coke Handel Foundation and the Anvil Trust, and a member of the Council of the Open University. His very well received *Lives and Times of the Great Composers* was published in 2003 by Icon Books and subsequently in the USA by Oxford University Press.

List of Colour Plates

1. Louis Viardot out shooting (1847) – a water-colour by Carl Schulz
2. Pauline Viardot, a portrait around 1844 by Maurice Sand
3. Vasily Polenov, *The Moscow Courtyard* (1878)
4. Vasily Perov, *The Last Tavern by the Town Gate* (1868)
5. Pierre-Auguste Renoir, *Les Grands Boulevards* (1875)
6. Pierre-Auguste Renoir, *View of Bougival* (1873)
7. Francisco Goya, *Portrait of a Man*, traditionally said to be of Manuel Garcia, Pauline Viardot's father.
8. John Singer Sargent's portrait of Manuel Garcia, Pauline Viardot's brother (1905)
9. Ary Scheffer's portrait of Franz Liszt (1837)
10. Ary Scheffer's portrait of Dickens (1855)
11. Les Frênes
12. Watercolour sketch of the Viardot theatre (1869)
13. Watercolour sketch of Turgenev's house in Baden-Baden (1875)
14. Louise Héritte-Viardot's watercolour of Courtavenel

Author's Note

The sources, upon which this book is wholly dependent, are listed in the section entitled 'Sources'.

I am grateful for the considerable assistance which I received at the British Library, the Bodleian Library, the Corporation of London Libraries, the City of Westminster Library, the Wellcome Trust Library and the Royal College of Music Library. Whereas the content of libraries may be different, their staff displays a similar degree of courtesy, helpfulness and speed of response which is both exceptional and exemplary.

I have been particularly fortunate to have had considerable advice, assistance and some most helpful direction from the experts in this field, Patrick Waddington (Emeritus Professor of Russian Literature at Victoria University of Wellington) and Alexandre Zviguilsky (Chairman of the Association des Amis d'Ivan Tourguéniev, Pauline Viardot et Maria Malibran, and curator of the Museum at Bougival). Among other matters, they have indicated the considerable pitfalls and inaccuracies to be found in many ostensibly reliable and distinguished sources on Turgenev. Others to whom I am most grateful for advice and assistance on specific topics are Dr Paul Banks, Paula Best, Lord Donald Graham, Professor Hugh Macdonald, Sarah Batchelor, Dr Richard Joyce, Barbara Kendall-Davies, Jonathan Price, Richard Todd, Professor Anton Seljak and Professor Nicholas Žekulin. These are just some of those with whom I have corresponded. I was particularly fortunate to meet the nonagenarian Mr Kyril FitzLyon (whose great-uncle was one of the Four Paws) and his son, Mr Justin FitzLyon. They allowed me access to Mrs FitzLyon's papers and, among other aspects, amplified the background in Russia.

I am most grateful to M and Mme Gérard Vigneron for their warm welcome and permission to wander around the site of Courtavenel, on more than one occasion.

I am deeply grateful to those who commented on early drafts either in full or in part: Dr Guy Deutscher, David Vaughan, Grant Meekings, Dr Janie Steen and the late Clive Ryder Runton. Because I did not act on all their suggestions, none of those mentioned can be assumed to agree with the final text, let alone my opinions. The responsibility for any errors that remain is entirely mine. However, without their input, whatever shortcomings the book may have would have been more considerable.

The team at Icon, led by Peter Pugh, has been tremendously helpful, and I must especially thank Duncan Heath, Andrew Furlow and Sarah Higgins. The book could not have been written without considerable effort by, and encouragement from, Professor Robert Steen and Mrs Elizabeth Steen, and Sir Stanley Cochrane, Bart. But I owe Rosemary my wife a special word of thanks for her unswerving support, patience and tolerance.

PRESENT-DAY EUROPE SHOWING KEY PLACES

FINLAND
St Petersburg
ESTONIA
RUSSIA
Pskov
LATVIA
Riga
Moscow
LITHUANIA
Serpukhov
River Niemen
Optina Pustyn
Königsberg
Tula
Yasnaya Polyana
Astapovo
Spasskoye
Mtsensk
BELARUS
Oryol
Varsaw
UKRAINE
KIA
HUNGARY
MOLDOVA
apest
ROMANIA

Preface

The great Russian author, Mikhail Lermontov, regretted that he had to provide a preface, both to explain the purpose of his book and to defend it against its critics. He realised that his reader usually 'doesn't care a damn' about such matters and probably cannot be bothered to read it.[1] However, he berated his reader for being ignorant, humourless, badly educated and, not least, 'a country bumpkin'. I do not, so I shall press on.

First, the purpose. Pauline Viardot, the soprano, has been called one of the most remarkable women of the 19th century.[2] A book about her, her admirer Ivan Turgenev and, to a lesser extent, Charles Gounod, enables the general reader to appreciate not only their considerable achievement, but also to hear about the times in which they lived and to meet their families and many of their distinguished acquaintances.

An opera star, a writer of international repute and a significant composer make a formidable combination when it comes to networking. By the time Pauline died in 1910, aged nearly 90, her life had encompassed virtually the whole of the century after Napoleon. It had touched the lives of many interesting people. Besides, she came from a family of stars, the best-known being her elder sister and role model, Maria Malibran, a top soprano of the 1820s. Turgenev, of course, knew everybody of significance in literary circles in London, Paris, St Petersburg and other European centres.[3] Gounod, an odd man, had some odd friends, as we shall see.

The lives of the protagonists, besides being fascinating in themselves, provide a means through which the general reader can also dip into the rich artistic world of 19th-century literature and music, the world of George Sand, Dickens, Flaubert, Tolstoy and Dostoyevsky; the world of Rossini, Berlioz, Chopin, Liszt, Saint-Saëns, Fauré and the other Paris-based composers and artists of the time. Our odyssey takes us around Europe, to the New World, but most especially to Russia whose particularities we need to understand. We learn of some of the unhappy experiences of the children of successful parents. Backstage in the workplace, we encounter competition and bitchiness. We hear of seduction, duels, violence, of mock executions and real ones, of prison in Siberia. In Mexico, we experience a robbery. Inevitably, we hear of appalling disease and shocking poverty.

We discover that even though in our world today everything is supposed to be new and superlative, little that is fundamental changes. The degree of 'change' that each generation experiences is very similar. We may also be surprised by the insignificance and fragility of mortals, however successful at the time they may appear, or indeed important they consider themselves to be. Many of the people in this book, many of those included in the pen-portraits of Some of the Others in the Cast, would in their time have been regarded as 'celebrities'. Indeed, the first printed use of the word as applied to a person arose in the middle of our period, in the late 1840s, around the same time that tinned food became good and cheap enough for general use.[4] Ordinary people of limited intelligence easily 'imagine themselves exceptional and original and revel in that delusion', as Dostoyevsky pointed out in *The Idiot*.[5]

Clearly, there is much to fit on the canvas. So, I have had to be selective. For example, I have been very brief about Pauline's long tours in Germany and the British Isles, and Turgenev's travels around Europe. I have viewed the scene from Dover, so I have tended to concentrate on the French and Russian friends, acquaintances and rivals, at the expense of the English.[6] There is no room for an appraisal of Turgenev's individual works, let alone Gounod's. I touch on Turgenev's. I quote extracts, if only because he once said 'You will find my whole biography in my works'.[7] This carries some risk because, whereas people and events may have provided him with the bricks with which to build, his stories were fiction. I quote extracts from his contemporaries if only because they, especially the other Realists, paint the scenery far better than I can possibly do.

Many of my sources have also provided quotations which it would be foolish to try to paraphrase. To them I am also most grateful. Their attribution in the narrative would break the continuity. To find the source, readers should turn to the back. Many of my sources are letters. In our age of telecommunication, we can easily forget that, for the first half of the nineteenth century, the only means of distant communication was the letter. One contemporary claimed that fashionable and ambitious Parisians wrote twenty letters an hour,[8] an estimate which perhaps will come as no surprise to users of 'mobiles'. However, unlike today, the author could not necessarily be sure where the recipient was to be found and to which address to send the communication.[9] The volume of letters is immense. Over 6,250 letters survived to be included in the major edition of Turgenev's works.[10]

The dates in this book are those given in the Gregorian calendar. Most countries had adopted this calendar by 1752, when England, sensibly cautious about unnecessary acts of harmonisation, at last fell in line, after holding out for 170 years. Ireland stood firm for a further 30, but Russia remained an odd-man-out until February 1918. Thus, during the nineteenth century, Russia was always twelve days adrift.[11] Because of this, it was often the custom to date letters with both old-style and new-style dates. For example, Turgenev's important entry in his record, 'on 14/26 I first time with P', referred to the 14th of the month in the Russian calendar, and the 26th in the calendar to which we are accustomed. It should be assumed that I have used the new-style dates.

As regards translations, especially from Russian, I have often picked and chosen, mixed and matched, in order to develop text that I consider best suits my purpose. Sometimes I just trust that the French words, especially in their context, will be obvious to my readers, so I do not translate at all.

At the risk of annoying those who properly prefer consistency of language, I have deliberately transliterated names in the way in which I would use them in conversation, or, as a general reader, find unexceptionable to see in print. Thus, I refer to Tsar Nicholas I, yet call Turgenev's cousin, or Anton Rubinstein's brother, Nikolay. And I find Maria Tolstoy easier on the eye than the technically correct Mariya. Besides, I contentedly talk about Rossini's *The Barber of Seville*, but Bellini's *La Sonnambula*. Who wouldn't? This is how ordinary people refer to them. For all this, I plead the wisdom of Ralph Waldo Emerson who so famously wrote, 'A foolish consistency is the hobgoblin of little minds, adored by little statesmen and philosophers and divines.'[12] I fortunately do not fall into any of these categories.

My book, I reiterate, is especially for the general reader. A truly academic study could not possibly risk being so casual, or even so irreverent – except of course about colleagues – as I sometimes am. Some readers may regard it as unsatisfactory for a male to purport to interpret the emotions of a female with a character as complex as that of Pauline Viardot. A man is at least given the opportunity to be gallant, to defend the lady's honour, which I have tried to do, I trust, in a reasonably balanced way.

This book is to be enjoyed. I also hope that it may whet the appetite and encourage the reader to avoid the sad fate of one of Turgenev's characters, a naval lieutenant who 'read no books, because he was afraid of a flow of blood to the head'.[13] He was seduced, robbed and deposited in a ditch.

Michael Steen, Mattingley

Pauline in middle age

Overture

London, mid-July 1849. The temperature had reached nearly 29°C in the shade and 43° in the sun, and *The Times* reported 339 deaths from cholera during the previous week.[1] As its reader consumed his enormous breakfast, he was probably not too concerned. The reports of disease came from the East End and those other insalubrious areas south of the river, such as Kennington, where England had only recently seen off an alarming political demonstration, the largest 'in history'. This could now be dismissed lightly as 'a fussy and futile demonstration of low-class cads'.[2]

The outlook was indeed calmer than previously. Four Irish rebel leaders were lucky to be transported to Tasmania, to join the deluge of convicts descending on the colonies, instead of being hanged, drawn and quartered as the treason law stipulated. 'Ireland' anyway was old news. There was always some trouble, famine, rebellion or something else there. Nobody had a clue what to do about it and nobody ever would.[3] Of course, there was still trouble across the Channel. The French were restoring the Pope to Rome from whence he had fled ignominiously. That was interesting. Fifteen notorious 'communists' had been arrested somewhere in France. There was also something in the newspaper about an insurrection in a tiny German principality called Baden. Yet, despite a shipwreck, a terrific storm, and a murder in a bawdy house near Waterloo,[4] London was calm, prosperous and recovering its due sense of self-satisfaction.

The Times, of course, reported news about royalty. Queen Victoria was to pay a state visit to Ireland which would hopefully provide the 'tonic for trade'[5] that the country so badly needed. The papers were full of drawings of the beautiful countryside which she would see. Hopefully, nobody would take a pot-shot at her, as had that mad terrorist in Hyde Park,[6] a couple of months before. The Court Circular, however, was reassuringly informative, even if stylistically clumsy. 'The Queen and Prince walked this morning at an early hour in Osborne', it recorded. 'And the younger branches of the Royal family walked and rode as usual'.[7]

There was little news of sport in the newspapers to provide a distraction, although there were lengthy reports of theatre and opera. And even if the reader might be more interested in advertisements for rustic stools at two shillings* and rustic seats at three,[8] he could not have failed to notice how an 'anxiously anticipated new opera',[9] *Le Prophète*, was being heralded. It was to be 'the grand event of the season'. 'The mise-en-scène', *The Times* had heard, 'was likely to surpass the splendour of all that has hitherto been presented at the Royal Italian Opera'. The show was 'now performing at the Grand Opera in Paris with unprecedented success'.[10] The reader seemed to recall seeing that, in Paris, it cost the equivalent of £8 to buy a ticket for a seat in the stalls. A box with four seats cost £40.[11]

On Wednesday 11 July came the official announcement, pompously addressed 'to the Nobility, the Subscribers, and the Public':

> Madame VIARDOT-GARCIA has ARRIVED in town from Paris. The first appearance of this eminent artiste will take place in the course of next week in Meyerbeer's new opera of LE PROPHETE which has been for some time in active preparation, with new scenery, dresses and decorations.[12]

The Covent Garden première of *Le Prophète* was a resounding success. The *Illustrated London News* declared that Pauline Viardot's 'histrionic and vocal genius has soared to sublimity'.[13] *The Times* said that her acting represented 'one of the highest exhibitions of dramatic art that has been witnessed on the lyric stage'.[14] Camille Saint-Saëns, the composer, extolled her 'burning maternal passion … this maternal love more fierce than the flames of Eros himself'. The composer Hector Berlioz, who wrote a column in the *Journal des débats*, was ecstatic. Charles Dickens thought it worthwhile to attend several performances. One fellow novelist, W. M. Thackeray, praised Pauline as the 'sublime *mater dolorosa*'. Another, George Eliot, later featured her in a poem.[15]

Pauline Viardot, the prima donna, the celebrity, is hardly known today.

*A shilling was twelve pence, £0.05.

So too, the opera *Le Prophète* and its composer, Giacomo Meyerbeer, whose hits such as *Les Huguenots* and *Robert le Diable* are only occasionally heard. On the strength of them, Meyerbeer, who had an amazing 'facility for feeling the pulse of the public', managed to become, in his time, 'one of the richest men in Europe'.[16] Today, it is difficult to appreciate the exalted and influential position he occupied. It has even been suggested that 'the modern press conference with refreshments' was his invention.[17] Georges Bizet, the composer of *Carmen*, called him 'the Michelangelo of Music'.[18] Berlioz, for once without exaggeration, coined the aphorism that Meyerbeer not only had the luck to be talented, but the talent to be lucky.[19]

Pauline Viardot starred from Madrid to St Petersburg. The distinguished French novelist George Sand may have exaggerated when she claimed that Pauline was both the greatest singer of the nineteenth century and 'the greatest female genius of our age'.[20] Dickens considered that it was worth making the considerable effort to journey to Paris just to see her perform in Berlioz's adaptation of Gluck's *Orphée*.[21] 'Madame, je vous présente une fontaine',[22] said the producer when he showed Dickens into Pauline's dressing-room. Dickens, who in his own words, was 'disfigured with crying', regarded her as 'one of the greatest actresses of any time'. Her performance in *Orphée* was 'the finest presentation of grief' that he could imagine. In case we are unconvinced, Dickens's opinion about Pauline's acting was also shared by someone who is reputedly the most famous actress ever, Sarah Bernhardt.[23]

For all her stardom, Pauline did not have a faultless voice and she was not always associated with success. Her appearance in *Sapho*, Gounod's first opera, was little short of a fiasco. However, her singing seems to have had some intangible quality, indicating powers of interpretation which we possibly miss today, when we are so programmed to 'piped' music, whether by wireless or on disc. For Liszt, Pauline 'belonged to the most brilliant dramatic stars of our time'. But he went further and, at a time long before feminism, declared that she would 'always be differentiated by the variety of her talents, her equal mastery of Italian, French and German Art, her extraordinary cultural accomplishments, the nobility of her character and the purity of her private life'.[24] 'Never has there been a woman composer of genius – finally here is one', he proclaimed.[25] However, his expectations were unfulfilled. Her operettas, songs and many other compositions never justified her being awarded this accolade.

The London première of *Le Prophète* took place on Pauline's 28th birthday. She had been born in Paris in 1821 into a family of glittering musical stars, the Garcias, who came from Spain. Her father starred in the operas of Mozart and Rossini. Her elder sister was the legendary soprano Maria Garcia, La Malibran. Her brother was one of the most highly regarded singing teachers of the 19th century. Divas such as Nellie Melba and Joan Sutherland can be directly traced from the generation of stars taught by him.[26]

While still eighteen, she was married to the *littérateur* Louis Viardot, then the Director of the Théâtre-Italien, which was one of the great opera companies of Paris. As a consequence of professional jealousy and bitchiness backstage she was eased off the Paris stage, into St Petersburg, to the British Isles and elsewhere in Europe. She toured extensively and performed and promoted her art to which she was almost obsessively devoted, believing, as Daniel Barenboim tells us today, that music should be 'something that is used not only to escape from the world but rather to understand it'.[27] At a professional level, Pauline was the first foreigner to sing Italian and Russian music in Russian. And by making Russian music known to the West, it is likely that, 'after Liszt and Berlioz, no foreigner did more valuable work for Russian music'.[28] She also provided the model for a character in two of George Sand's novels.

She is no exception to the rule that 'celebrities' are, with few exceptions, but grains of sand on the seashore, albeit grains which momentarily glint in the sun. Lyric artists bequeath little that endures beyond the memory. Her claim to the attention of posterity arises not so much from her own art, and reputation as a teacher, as from her friendship with the 19th century Russian novelist and playwright, Ivan Turgenev.* She became his muse.

Turgenev was a successor to Pushkin, before whom there was no significant Russian literature and, in particular, no Russian novel of any importance. Pushkin's *Eugene Onegin*, a verse novel written during the 1820s, was the first 'to expose the realities of Russian social life, its virtues and its vices'.[30] Turgenev, building upon the foundation of his own numerous short stories, created six novels, the most enduringly famous of which was *Fathers and Sons*, which was published in 1862. Bazarov, its central character,

*The French spelling 'Tourguénieff', or Turguénieff (as *The Times* used in its obituary), gives a helpful indication of how his name might best be pronounced in English.[29] The spelling varies in both French and English, and in this book it has been used as it has been found.

affected the small but influential élite of the liberal and radical Russian youth, in the same way as Goethe's Werther influenced the Romantics of the previous century.[31] Turgenev leads us towards, and led, both Tolstoy and Dostoyevsky, with whom he sparred.

Turgenev's stories and novels are shorter and are written using a softer palette of colour, with more delicate treatment, than that which Tolstoy and Dostoyevsky used in their epics. Turgenev's works seem cleverer and more subtle than those of the 'two self-centred, angry literary giants'.[32] He 'was not a preacher and did not wish to thunder at his generation'.[33] His stories, so simple in outline, yet 'rich in detail and subtle characterisation',[34] are more accessible than the works of many other novelists who often published their lengthy tales in countless instalments, each episode structured so that the reader would want to buy the next edition of the magazine. Despite the artistry of those novelists, their distended text was often more designed to fit the publisher's business plan and the printers' pagination requirements than the aims of the author.

Henry James, the American-born author of the masterpiece *The Portrait of a Lady*, said that Turgenev 'is particularly a favourite with people of cultivated taste; and nothing, in our opinion, cultivates the taste more than to read him'.[35] James claimed that 'no romancer has created a greater number of the figures that breathe and move and speak in their habits as they might have lived; none on the whole, seems to us to have had such a masterly touch in portraiture, none has mingled so much ideal beauty with so much unsparing reality'.

Henry James was initially worried about the 'picturesque gloom' which he found in much of Turgenev's output. James was another Realist and so could justify this. 'Life is, in fact, a battle', James wrote. 'On this point optimists and pessimists agree. Evil is insolent and strong; beauty enchanting but rare; goodness very apt to be weak; folly very apt to be deficient; wickedness to carry the day; imbeciles to be in great places, people of sense in small places, and mankind generally unhappy'.[36]

Turgenev, who was two and a half years older than Pauline, was born in 1818, with a silver spoon in his mouth. He was brought up on a large estate just over 200 miles to the south of Moscow. The mansion was replete with around 40 house-serfs. On the estate, there were 5,000 other souls tilling the fields.[37] Serfs provided an orchestra and a source for rampant sex. And victims and culprits for murder. Turgenev's grandmother is reputed to have smothered a serf boy who irritated her, whether intentionally or by accident is not entirely clear.[38] Violence was prevalent in Russian society. Dostoyevsky's father, who came from a *nouveau* and junior section of the 'nobility', was almost certainly murdered by his serfs in revenge for his habit of flogging them.[39]

Turgenev's friendship with the Viardots began in November 1843, when he was 25. It lasted until his death almost 40 years later. For long stretches of time, he stayed in the Viardots' château, Courtavenel, near Paris.

Two years after Turgenev met Pauline, she allowed the relationship between them to intensify. This first phase continued on and off.[40] It ended in 1850, around the time that Turgenev completed his play *A Month in the Country*. At that time, Pauline was working with Charles Gounod on his first opera, *Sapho*. Significantly, in that year Turgenev's short story, *The Diary of a Superfluous Man*, first appeared in print. Many of the heroes, or anti-heroes who run through his fiction, are 'superfluous men', 'birds of no account'.[41] Turgenev may have thought he was one. He returned home to Russia.

Turgenev's liberal attitudes displeased the Russian authorities. He was briefly imprisoned and subsequently held under house arrest. After he was eventually allowed to return to France, there was a recrudescence of Pauline's friendship with him in the summers of 1856, 1859 and 1860. The final phase of their relationship lasted for the remaining twenty years of Turgenev's life.

The Viardots, who found the Second Empire of Napoleon III corrupt and distasteful, emigrated. They were not alone in thinking that France was becoming a whorehouse and a sink of iniquity.[42] Turgenev joined them in Baden-Baden and built a house next door. Later, after the collapse of the Empire, he lodged on the top floor of the Viardots' house in Paris. Also, he built himself a villa next to the Viardot's house at Bougival, an attractive setting for the Impressionist painters, to be found a few miles down the Seine from the city.

In the 21st century, no biographer of either Pauline or Turgenev can avoid considering the nature of their 'affair', which lasted almost 40 years, during which Pauline remained almost always contentedly, if not particularly passionately, married to Louis, her husband. That Turgenev was deeply in love with her, there can be no doubt. She was spiritually unfaithful to Louis, in the sense that he did not possess her undivided love: one soul being dedicated exclusively to another.

Pauline was no beauty. It was said that Meyerbeer insisted on her having a protuberant tooth extracted before he would let her sing in *Le Prophète.* If this improbable tale is indeed true, she must have been one of the first celebrities to avail herself of cosmetic surgery.

Despite her looks, Pauline must have radiated considerable sex appeal, at least enough for the promiscuous poet Alfred de Musset to fancy her. Some biographers have presented her as a brazen, loose woman who was in and out of bed with several men as well as Turgenev. George Sand's son Maurice, Hector Berlioz and the prominent Paris artist Ary Scheffer, even the Grand-Duke of Baden, are among the candidates to seek with Pauline between the sheets. And a colourful lady-friend of the composer Charles Gounod insinuated, in a single, subtle, skilful, sentence that 'it is nobody's business if she has or has not been Gounod's mistress'.[43]

The Russians regarded Pauline as a Circe who ensnared one of their greatest writers and lured him away from the Mother Country. A satirical magazine, the Paris equivalent of *Private Eye,* observed that Turgenev 'was tied to the petticoats of a tramp-singer'.[44]

It would be a mistake to jump to hasty conclusions about their relationship. A large proportion of today's communications business would have one believe that copulation is the purpose of life, more especially for singers and other celebrities. In a biological sense it is. Yet fidelity is deeply embedded in the human psyche. Even in recent years of apparently rampant sex, a survey conducted in the UK showed that fewer than one in twenty men and one in fifty women admitted having more than one sexual partner while married. It also showed that around 80 per cent of men and a slightly larger percentage of women believed extra-marital sex to be always or mostly wrong.[45] Even if these figures, whatever they may say, are adjusted for the inevitable bias of the respondents, their implication regarding physical behaviour is clear. The male of the species deludes himself if he believes that the married or otherwise committed female will automatically comply with his wishes.

Unless some new information comes to light, say some correspondence which has lain hidden, we shall never know for certain whether Pauline was physically unfaithful to her husband. For the moment, let it be said that the circumstantial evidence for Pauline having cohabited with Turgenev is mixed.* It will be my contention that it is far from adequate to 'convict'.

*There is some circumstantial but uncorroborated evidence that he cohabited with her daughter.

It is therefore even more improbable that she had an affair with Gounod or the others.

To appreciate the tone of Pauline's relationship with Turgenev, it is only necessary to hear the following dialogue from Turgenev's well-known play *A Month in the Country*. A young man says that 'it must be sheer bliss to be loved by the woman you love'. 'May you long preserve such a pleasant illusion!', retorts an older man. 'Love, whether happy or unhappy, is genuine misery when you surrender to it. You just wait! You will learn what it means to be tied to a skirt, to experience the shameful and tormenting slavery of Love, and to drink its poison.'[46]

The older man sounds like some crusty old codger or male 'chauvinist'. No, he is aged only 30, around the age at which Turgenev wrote the play. His disillusionment and rejection reflect Turgenev's state of mind only a few years after he had begun his relationship with Pauline Viardot, whatever its nature was.

Act One

CHAPTER 1

THE GARCIAS

PAULINE GARCIA WAS born at 83 rue de Richelieu, Paris 2^{e}, on 18 July 1821. Six weeks later, she was christened Michelle-Pauline-Ferdinande-Laurence in the nearby church of Saint-Roch, a medieval pilgrim who protected the people from pestilence.[1]

Today, an office block which houses financial institutions occupies her birthplace. It is close to the Paris Bourse and around the corner from the Boulevard des Italiens. That district was once the hub of operatic and theatrical life, where Donizetti would stroll, where Rossini could enjoy the excellent ice-cream at Tortoni's, and where the best food could be obtained at the Café Hardy.[2]

It would be over sixteen years before Pauline would make her début on the Paris opera stage. In those years, she grew up within a prominent theatrical family and spent her childhood in the shadow of her successful and famous sister Maria.

'Music was in the air the Garcias breathed', according to Saint-Saëns.[3] Pauline's father, Manuel, was arguably the leading tenor and baritone of the first decades of the 19th century (Plate 7). His reputation was formidable. 'The great Garcia never demeaned himself so far as to sing falsetto like the present-day miserable little tenors', wrote Turgenev in one of his stories, 'No Sir, he sang with a full chest. And what an actor! A volcano.'[4]

Manuel Garcia. See also Plate 7

Manuel's two wives were singers. His elder daughter Maria soared to fame as a brilliant mezzo-soprano. She is remembered by posterity as *La Malibran* who Rossini said was 'unique'.

Manuel Rodriguez, who assumed the name 'Garcia', had been a chorister at Seville Cathedral. He did not know his father.[5] According to various accounts, his family had been Moors, Jews or perhaps gypsies, somewhere along the line.[6]

Manuel created the role of Count Almaviva in Rossini's *The Barber of Seville.* He had all the right attributes for a count, being carefree, tactless and often sadistic. He was handsome, wild, charming, an ideal Almaviva*. He was also an exceptionally talented musician. It has been suggested that Rossini, who was short of time, got him to compose the serenade with guitar accompaniment 'Se il mio nome' in the first Act. Manuel is also said to have written out 'from memory' the entire orchestral score of the *Barber* and of Mozart's *Don Giovanni.*[7] Whether or not we believe this claim, Manuel did compose songs and several operettas with enticing titles such

*The Count woos Rosina, the ward of an old doctor. With the assistance of Figaro the barber, he disguises himself as a music teacher and arranges to elope with her.

as *El seductor arrepentido, El poeta calculista,* and *L'amante astuto.*[8] He also wrote a book on singing and was a good cook.[9]

Manuel was his own man. In Naples, then the centre of entertainment and the equivalent to the modern Hollywood, he was asked to sing in a new opera which he thoroughly disliked. He attended the rehearsals and listened very carefully, but still refused to sing. This appalled his co-star, Rossini's wife, who feared that in performance the singers would be hissed off the stage. She need not have worried. On the night, Manuel improvised his own part to accompany hers. Thus he avoided singing 'so much as one note of the composer's music'.[10]

Manuel was a bigamist.[11] He caused a scandal by appearing on stage with both his first wife, who was a *bolero* dancer, and his mistress. Although he did not get divorced, he proceeded to marry the mistress. She was Maria Joaquina Sitges, a young widow whose name was later gallicised to Sitchès. She bore him two other surviving children as well as Pauline. Manuel 'junior' was born in 1805. Maria was born three years later in March 1808. Pauline, born thirteen years after Maria, was something of an afterthought.[12]

Longevity was a feature of Pauline's generation. She lived until she was almost 90. Not only did her brother Manuel (Plate 8) live until he was 101, but, an example to us all, he remarried when he was 70 and then had several children.[13] Maria's life was unfortunately cut short by a riding accident.

The Garcias moved from Spain to Paris in the year before Maria was born, but, being theatre people, they were never settled. Maria made her first appearance in Naples aged five or six, when she sang in an opera composed by Ferdinando Paër, a family friend, a protégé of Napoleon, and a rival of Rossini at the Théâtre-Italien.[14] She was educated at a convent school in Hammersmith, a few miles to the west of London.

Maria's musical education came from her father, a very hard taskmaster. Pauline's godfather Paër walked past the Garcia house, heard shrieks. He told his companion not to worry. 'It's only Garcia walloping his daughter to encourage her to warble her trill', he is reputed to have said.[15]

Maria made her formal début, aged seventeen, at His Majesty's Theatre in London in a performance of Rossini's *Barber.* She made an immediate impact both vocally and visually. At a time when singers wore 'a hearse of feathers' or enormous hats, she wore a simple circlet.[16]

After a tour around England, the Garcia troupe, including the four-year-old Pauline, set off for the 'other world', to New York for a Rossini season. This, the first season of Italian opera ever to be held there, was at the invitation of a wealthy wine merchant, one Dominick Lynch.

It took about five weeks to cross the Atlantic from Liverpool. This provided ample rehearsal and teaching time. The troupe would rehearse on deck, when the weather permitted. The passengers and the crew doted on little Pauline. She amused them with a stunt in which she replied in French, German, Italian and Spanish to questions, presumably pre-arranged, which were asked by the troupe.[17]

Time aboard was also whiled away by writing a newspaper. One edition included a song, the words written by a London architect. The music, 'graceful and spirited', was composed by Garcia; it was later published in New York.

Manuel Garcia's teaching methods took the other passengers by surprise. Among those on board was a group led by the outspoken Welsh philanthropist and co-operative socialist, Robert Owen, who was travelling to Indiana to visit New Harmony, the utopian community which he had founded a few months earlier. This failed to live up to its name. Differences about the form of government and the role of religion emerged. Owen withdrew from it a few years later, having invested and lost most of his considerable fortune.

During the Atlantic crossing, Maria captivated a Captain McDonald who was from Owen's party. She also played chess with Owen's son. Owen, who believed strongly in the importance of early influences in the formation of a person's character, must have been appalled by Garcia's foul language and uncouth behaviour. One day, after Garcia had knocked down his twenty-year-old son, the captain was called. 'If you lay a finger again on a single passenger here, or on your son, or on your daughter, or on any other soul on board,' he declared, 'I'll have you below in irons, Sir, – in irons. Do you understand that?'[18]

The country to which Manuel's family were travelling was seething with activity. It was about to explode into the nation we recognise today. A couple of years before, President Monroe had announced his Doctrine that Europe should keep its hands off the Americas. The interior was opened up. The Erie Canal, 'The Big Ditch', was completed, thus extending trade to the Great Lakes. Despite the threat of the torch and scalping knife, wagons piled high with furniture and children, accompanied by cattle, horses, sheep and hogs, headed for the frontier, where plots of 80 acres were obtainable for $100. As the country expanded, politicians sought to maintain a balance between the northern Free states and the southern states whose cotton, sugar and tobacco trades depended on slave labour.[19]

New York, which was also expanding fast, was then 'a small but promising city which clustered about the Battery and overlooked the Bay, and of which the uppermost boundary was indicated by the grassy way-sides of Canal Street', just to the north of the suspension bridge which was later built across to Brooklyn. Beyond, was a 'region where the extension of the city began to assume a theoretic air, where the poplars grew beside the pavement (when there was one), and mingled their shade with the steep roofs of the desultory Dutch houses, and where pigs and chickens disported themselves in the gutter'.[20]

When they arrived, the Garcias received help from the colourful Lorenzo da Ponte, the librettist of Mozart's *The Marriage of Figaro, Don Giovanni* and *Così fan tutte.* Da Ponte was in New York escaping his creditors. He was a former priest who had been banned from Venice for adultery. After the death of his patron Emperor Joseph II, he wandered around Europe until he moved to the USA, first as a grocer, then as a teacher of Italian. In the year in which the Garcias arrived, he was appointed professor at Columbia College, the institution which later became the University.[21]

The season in New York began at the end of November 1825 and comprised *Figaro, Don Giovanni,* five Rossini operas and Zingarelli's *Romeo.* The opening performance of Rossini's *Barber* in the Park Theatre was a great success. It yielded $3,000, a sum which a fashionable doctor could take nearly two months to earn.[22] Maria appeared as Rosina with her father as Almaviva. Her brother Manuel made his début as Figaro. The audience was distinguished. It included Joseph Bonaparte who had been King of Naples and Spain, and Fenimore Cooper whose novel *The Last of the Mohicans* would be published in the following year. Later, the actor Edmund Kean, wild, unpredictable, alcoholic, was in the wings to congratulate Garcia on his rendering of Rossini's Othello, the role in Shakespeare's play in which he himself triumphed and in which, a few years later, he would collapse, before being carried away to die.[23]

Garcia needed to retain Maria as his prima donna, so took steps to nip her love affairs in the bud. However, she was determined to escape the claustrophobia surrounding her father and she sought a protector. She experimented with several amours, found a suitable one within four months, and married him. She was still just under eighteen.

Maria had hooked Eugène Malibran, an American citizen, half-Spanish and half-French in origin. At 45, he was over twice Maria's age. He was ostensibly a 'decent middle-aged man'. His correspondence indicates that he was a somewhat reluctant suitor.[24]

Eugène Malibran's entrepreneurial activities as a merchant and banker did not succeed. He was forced to compromise with his creditors. His financial predicament would have attracted little sympathy, because, at that time, he and his fellow capitalists were regarded as no better than leeches and bloodsuckers.[25] Presumably, he no longer seemed quite such a good catch. Because Maria's earning power was not as good in the United States as in Europe, she returned alone to Paris, where she arrived at the end of November 1827.

The timing of Maria's return to Paris from the United States was excellent. This was the moment when the new French Romantic movement burst forth. It was the time when Berlioz's head was turned by Harriet Smithson's performance of Ophelia in Shakespeare's *Hamlet*. It was the time when the young Théophile Gautier, the poet, novelist and influential journalist known for his long hair and his crimson waistcoats, danced mockingly around a statue of Racine, the great classical playwright.[26]

The French Romantics wanted to jettison the strict rules with which classical French drama complied. Shakespeare had not kept to rules whereby the action of a play had to take place on the same day and in the same place, and where the events in the story had to comprise a single chain of cause and effect. The French Romantics saw no reason why such stringent and antiquated rules should apply to them. In February 1830, there was uproar during the first performance of Victor Hugo's play *Hernani*, at which a group of students and artists was assembled six hours before the curtain went up. They had been recruited in order to drown with applause the jeers of the traditionalists who they labelled 'grocers', the equivalent of Philistines.[27] Many of the students probably had little notion of what they were supporting and Hugo was rejecting.

Maria Malibran, née Garcia

The time was opportune for Maria Malibran to assume the role of high priestess in the new Romantic culture. With her appearance in Paris, in Rossini's *Semiramide*, she 'set the world on fire'.[28] And the audience watching the last act of his *Otello* was bowled over by her emotional performances of Desdemona's mournful 'Willow Song', in which she accompanied herself on the harp.[29] We may be sure that her performance, while full of grace and charm, would have seemed to us 'more artificial than natural'.[30] This was something people would later say of Pauline. But it was typical of the acting style at the time, conditioned as it was by the traditions of the classical masters, such as Racine. Much of the action in his great dramas took place off-stage and was reported in lengthy monologues, which were punctuated by invocations and exclamations such as Ô Ciel! Ah, Dieux! (O Heaven! O Gods!) This dramatic style assumed and necessitated histrionics from the cast.

The precocious Charles Gounod was taken at the age of thirteen to hear Maria in *Otello*. This was a reward for good schoolwork.[31] He said that when he entered the theatre he felt as if he was in a temple. Something divine was about to be revealed to him. Gounod left the theatre in a state in which he felt totally uplifted emotionally. His sententious description is of particular interest, because the temple and the priestly power of the artist to reveal beauty and generate an emotional, virtually spiritual, uplift were aspects which would feature strongly in Pauline's mission as a singer.[32]

Maria was exorbitantly remunerated. In London, she reputedly charged 75 guineas* a night and she was entitled to the proceeds of a benefit performance as well. She charged 70 guineas for a concert at Bath or Bristol. Her fee for singing at a private party was 25 guineas; a few years later, at Drury Lane, she was paid 150 guineas a night. This was at a time when starving field labourers in southern England were hanged, or transported to Australia, for rioting in protest at their daily wage of half-a-crown.[34]

Meanwhile, when the New York season ended in September 1826, the rest of the Garcia troupe went to Mexico City where, nine months later, they opened with the *Barber*, sung in Italian. Pauline, who was still only aged five, had piano lessons from the cathedral organist.[35]

The Garcias did not stay long in Mexico. It was an unstable place 'with scenes of conflict dreadful to witness'.[36] It had long been ruled by an increasingly loathed Spanish élite which had exploited its mineral wealth. After a series of revolts, upheavals and guerrilla war, the last viceroy withdrew and independence was proclaimed. This was followed by a civil war. Between 1828 and 1830, there were three contested presidencies. Indeed, from 1821 to 1868, over 50 persons succeeded each other as presidents, dictators or emperors.[37]

This was not a place in which to linger. So, during 1828, Manuel decided to convert his wealth into gold and set out with it for France.

The first leg of the journey was the 300 miles through the mountains to the seaport of Vera Cruz on the Gulf of Mexico. The family travelled in a convoy of around 30 people, including twenty women and children.

*A guinea was 21s (£1.05), and half-a-crown was 2/6d (£0.125). Reports of Maria's fees vary, but despite inconsistencies, they were stratospheric. Her fees at the Théâtre-Italien were 1,175 francs per performance. Towards the end of her short life, she was said to be worth 600,000 francs. One might purchase a large mansion in the fashionable Faubourg Saint-Germain for around half that sum.[33]

With them, so the story goes, was the cart containing the Garcia fortune which, according to one account, amounted to 600,000 francs (then around £24,000), clearly a very large sum. Security was provided by a convoy of guards. In a gorge,[38] the guards suddenly transformed themselves into brigands. They ordered the men to lie face downwards on the ground; the women were told to go with the children into the forest.

Pauline, who was wrapped by her mother in her large coat of Scottish tartan,[39] several times asked whether they were going to be killed. To this her mother gave the comforting reply, 'Oui, oui. Tais-toi, tais-toi'. Yes, but shut up! The brigands took a couple of hours to break open the trunks and seize the loot. After they had made off, their victims seem to have sat down and had a party, even though they had been robbed of all their possessions, including Pauline's own much-prized coat. Or, at least, this was how Pauline recalled the experience, some 30 years later.[40] According to another account, the brigands forced Manuel Garcia to sing. They enjoyed his performance so much that they returned to him some of his gold and gave him an escort to the coast.[41]

During the long sea journey home, Pauline was taught singing by her father. Later, she recalled his mixture of passion and kindness, his childish naïveté and insane daring. She remembered his unquenchable exuberance. He 'was built like an Apollo, a trifle stout, his hair was naturally wavy and fell in white orderly curls. In his every pose, he was a model for painters or sculptors'.[42] She obviously adored him.

We have seen that Manuel had a fearsome reputation for whipping his children to make them sing. However, with Pauline, he seems to have been more gentle, and she was only once chastised for not concentrating. Maybe a single wallop was sufficient. Later, Pauline would object to the stories which represented her father as a tyrant.[43] Perhaps she was Daddy's darling, perhaps he recognised that she 'was equally gifted but not as lazy* as Maria',[45] or simply that he had not handled his elder daughter well and had better treat the younger one differently. 'Pauline can be guided by a thread of silk', he said. 'Maria needs a hand of iron.'[46]

*As an adult, Maria was hardly lazy: a typical working day might comprise an hour at the piano, a 10am rehearsal, a concert from 1–4pm, and an opera from 7–10pm, besides the socialising that was expected afterwards. She called it 'a galley slave's life'. Pauline took a similar view of her tours in England which she described as 'travail de nègre'.[44]

Maria had been back in Paris for over a year by the time the rest of her family arrived from Mexico in the spring of 1829. Pauline was aged seven. Maria, already a star, advanced the family some cash to keep them going. She appeared with her father in *Don Giovanni*, in which she sang the part of Zerlina, the peasant girl who the Don almost succeeds in seducing. However Manuel was aged 55 and a 'has been'. He retired from the stage in January 1830. From then on, he earned his living by teaching. He has been described as 'the father of modern singing'.[47]

Pauline accompanied the pupils when her father was giving lessons. Of course, she continued to receive instruction from him. He soon realised that in her he had another star. Indeed, he is reputed to have said of Maria 'there is a younger sister who is a greater genius than she'.[48]

Garcia also used to say 'It is only by learning the secret of practising that there is any possibility of learning to sing well'. Rather than concentrating on songs, he taught his pupils solfeggio – do, re, mi, fa – which the governess teaches the children in *The Sound of Music.* He also made them repeat phrases with exactly the same embellishment time after time. This method paid off for Maria on at least one occasion early in her career. It was normal for stars to reserve their embellishments until the actual performance in order to avoid giving their game away to the other singers. On the night, the leading tenor duly stepped forward and warbled his opening aria, fully ornamented. He then turned condescendingly to Maria who simply echoed what he had just sung, much to the amusement, delight and derision of the audience.[49]

Manuel's lessons soon came to an end. He died in June 1832, after a short lung illness. His death was little noticed in the press. Paris was rather more concerned with a cholera epidemic which by the end of May 1832 had claimed over 18,400 lives, including that of the Prime Minister.[50] This was the time of the disturbances which were later immortalised in Hugo's *Les Misérables.*

After Manuel died, the family at first resided with Adolphe Nourrit, one of Garcia's eminent pupils. He tried to arrange for Pauline to be taught by Rossini.[51] But nothing came of this.[52]

Pauline was still aged only ten when her father died. She had not been old enough to obtain much benefit from his tuition. For composition, she was sent to the elderly Czech teacher, Antoine Reicha, who had taught Berlioz and Liszt, and had known Beethoven, Haydn and Salieri. For piano, at which Pauline was already showing great promise, Manuel had already sent her to Charles Meysenberg, a distinguished teacher.[53] He was once a piano prizewinner at the Conservatoire. Like many of his colleagues, he also ran his own music business.

Pauline's mother was a friend of Liszt's mother. Liszt also gave Pauline piano lessons and she developed a teenage crush on him.[54] Although she claimed that she studied with him for a couple of years, her studies with him did not actually last long.[55] In June 1835, he was off to Basle to rendezvous with the Comtesse Marie d'Agoult who for the next five years was his mistress and bore his three children. One of these became Wagner's second wife, Cosima.

Liszt

Franz Liszt (see plate 9), who was possibly the greatest pianist ever, was born about 30 miles south of Vienna, just inside Hungary, in 1811. He was brought up on the estate of the wealthy Esterházy family, where Haydn had been in charge of the music.

Liszt's parents whisked the infant prodigy off to Paris, where his technique, musicianship and, not least, showmanship made a sensation. He began to cultivate his taste for religion and women. He settled in Italy with the Comtesse d'Agoult. Then he left her and, between 1840 and 1847, he toured Europe relentlessly. He toured afar to Ireland and Gibraltar, the Urals and Constantinople. He was in St Petersburg a few months before Pauline went there.

At the end of the 1840s, Liszt settled in Weimar with his second long-term mistress, Princess Carolyne von Sayn-Wittgenstein. There, at the small grand-ducal court, he created a centre for the 'New German School' which was represented especially by the music of himself, Wagner and Berlioz. His later years were spent between Weimar, and Rome, where he became an Abbé, and Pest, where he supported the cause of Hungarian music. In his extraordinary life, he combined being a virtuoso, a composer, a teacher, a supporter of Hungarian nationalism, a womaniser and a practitioner of deeply felt religion. He died in 1886.

Pauline always regarded Liszt as a colossus. Twenty years later, she would say, 'After him, I shall not for a long time be able to listen to anyone else playing the piano'.[56] She also commented, somewhat cryptically 'I assure you that he is infinitely better than his reputation, and his music too'.[57]

When Maria returned to Paris, she received considerable help from Comtesse Merlin, who was a pupil of Pauline's father. She was another Hispanic, having been born in Cuba. She was reputedly an excellent singer, although her position in 'society' meant that she could not venture beyond charity concerts and salon performances.[58] This Countess invited Maria to her own salon. She helped her find her feet.

Comtesse Merlin tells a tale of how Maria acquired a friend and adviser who would prove to be of great assistance at a difficult time. Maria was appearing in a salon. She was showing off. Everybody applauded except for a man with an enormous nose who stayed in a corner and took little notice. No pretty woman likes to be ignored, so Maria sauntered up and enquired what he thought of her performance. 'Not much', he replied quietly. He added 'but because I respect you, I prefer to say this to your face even if it annoys you'.[59] The man's name was Louis Viardot.

Whether this story is true or not, it illustrates what people thought of Louis. He was reserved and a bit dull; however, he would always be totally frank. Essentially, he was reliable, a safe pair of hands.[60]

When Maria, who was in Rome, read of her father's death in the newspaper, it was to Louis Viardot that she turned to find out if it was true,[61] particularly as she was concerned that her father might have been caught up in the political upheavals of that year. She was performing Desdemona at the time. So, perhaps not surprisingly, she wrote 'Mon pauvre ami!!! What terrible grief. I feel as if my heart is being pierced by a dagger a thousand times.'[62]

The transatlantic marriage of Maria and Eugène Malibran could not be resuscitated. Besides, for a celebrity, the pressures against fidelity can be irresistible. Soon after returning to Paris, Maria had an affair with the handsome and talented Belgian violinist, Charles-Auguste de Bériot. When they had an illegitimate child, she was regarded in Paris as a fallen woman. Her father refused to see her. Even her best friend, to whose château she would escape for relaxation, closed her doors to her.[63]

Charles-Auguste de Bériot

Maria was having a difficult time professionally as well. The box-office of the Théâtre-Italien was suffering from the success at the Opéra of Meyerbeer's new work, *Robert le Diable*, which was premièred in 1831. At twenty-two, Maria found that she had lost her Paris audience. Her star had fallen like a meteorite, just as it had risen like a rocket. Bériot's position was not much better. He was being eclipsed by the Italian violin virtuoso, Niccolò Paganini, a wild and exciting pop star.[64]

Maria moved with Bériot back to Brussels. She never went back to Paris, except to have her baby which sadly did not survive. For this, she went clandestinely, disguised with a wig.[65]

Maria continued to support the family, so Pauline found herself based in Brussels. Her sister was almost always away, often in Italy. Occasionally

Pauline went with Maria and Bériot when they toured Belgium and Germany. Those who showered Maria with gifts would also present a small one to the little sister.[66]

Maria's relationship with Bériot fluctuated. The couple quarrelled. Bériot, a somewhat dull man, wanted a conventional middle class life and doubtless admired the needlework at which Maria excelled. He applauded her charitable nature and generosity. She was said to be 'generous to excess, mean in trifles'. Less appealing to him were her tantrums, her excessive exuberance and unconventional behaviour. Maria provided a 'mixture of the frivolous and the serious'. She would enjoy the smart, high life, fast horses and shooting. Equally, she was quite capable of stuffing a whole orange into her mouth.[67]

Maria was unpretentious yet strong-willed. Carlo Severini, the boss of the Théâtre-Italien, once called her bluff, after she said that she would cancel her engagement. He brought in the exceptionally beautiful[68] Giulia Grisi, about whom we shall hear much more. Rossini told him that this action would lose him 100,000 francs a year; 'That may be' he said. 'But I prefer to secure my peace of mind'.[69]

In 1833 in London, Maria appeared in an English-language production of Bellini's *La Sonnambula.* She took the lead role, Amina, the fiancée who is prone to sleepwalking and who is accused of being seduced by a Count while on one of her nocturnal promenades. Maria then became the leading interpreter of Bellini's operas. Thus, her star rose again, particularly in Italy. Once, at La Scala, there were sixteen curtain calls after the first Act of *Norma* and thirty at the end. The police often had to intervene to quell the hysteria. On Maria's arrival in Venice, that 'pearl in a sewer' as Gounod would call it, the city is said to have stopped work and turned out to greet her.[70] Bellini became infatuated with her. He had a locket containing a self-portrait of her among his possessions when he died.*[71]

Maria's remuneration reflected her status as a celebrity. In London in 1835, she received £2,775 for 24 performances. Around the same time, an ambitious 23-year-old parliamentary reporter with the name of Charles Dickens, 'the rapidest and most accurate shorthand-writer in the Gallery',[72] was paid 5 guineas (£5.25) a week. This represented a considerable improvement on the 6 or 7 shillings which he had earned as an eleven-year-old worker in a factory manufacturing boot-blacking.[73]

*Despite the locket, some biographers doubt whether she had an affair with Bellini.

A second child was born to Maria and Bériot in January 1833. They were finally able to marry once her marriage to Eugène Malibran was annulled by a Paris court two years later; the negotiations leading up to this were handled by Louis Viardot. Yet her second marriage was short-lived. In early July 1836, pregnant once more, Maria went out riding in Regent's Park, London, with her friends. She adored riding. She was a fine horsewoman, even if she was a bit wild and inclined to take unnecessary risks.[74] Her horse bolted around the inner circle of the Park. Someone tried to grab the bridle and stop the horse. The result was that she was catapulted onto the paling. Despite being severely bruised on the head, and against the advice of her 'Italian', 'foreign' homeopathic doctor, Dr Belluomini,[75] she carried on with her programme of performances and returned to Belgium. She never recovered fully from her accident.

On 14 August, Maria took part in a concert in Liège, the first at which she appeared on the platform together with her fifteen-year-old sister Pauline. A fortnight later Pauline accompanied Bériot on the piano in a concert in Lille. In early September, after a brief stay in her country house at Roissy not far from Paris, Maria went to Manchester for a tour which was also to include Norwich, Worcester, Liverpool and Dublin. One of her rivals was performing with her. Their ornamentation became increasingly elaborate, indeed sensational, as they competed for the audience's applause. In the encore, Maria insisted on a repeat which she intended to use to 'crush' her rival. She said to the conductor: 'If I sing it again, it will kill me'. She did; and it did. She collapsed on leaving the stage.[76]

There was considerable controversy about exactly what happened next, the reports being aggravated by a recent high-profile dispute between doctors of conventional medicine and 'homœopathy'. The conventional doctors, whose profession was founded on 'the discovery of the seat and cause of the disease', felt threatened by the homeopathic doctors whose system used tiny doses of drugs to induce similar symptoms to those manifested by the illness. The conventional doctors openly described 'homœopathy' as 'quackery' and 'a system of knavery and deception'. One doctor said in the *Lancet* that the facts that he had heard about homeopathy 'could scarcely be exceeded in wonder by the resurrection of the dead'. He reported that 'coffee diluted a millionth is an excellent sleeping potion, but is effective only in those cases which arise from restlessness of the mind'. He added that he 'had given it to a young clergyman', but discovered that 'coffee is of no use in procuring sleep when the brain itself is diseased'.[77]

Maria, prostrate in her room in the Moseley Arms in Manchester, was at first attended by conventional doctors. She continued to deteriorate. Dr Belluomini, who was called from London, treated her for 'nervous fever'. After a while, she became senseless. Doctor Lewis, a 'conventional' doctor, was brought in. He said that there was no hope. He prescribed frequent but small quantities of 'equal portions of port-wine and fresh yeast', 5–10 grains of camphor every two hours, anodyne fomentations to be applied to the abdomen, injections of strong chicken broth to be used, the feet to be kept very warm, the hair to be cut off, and cold vinegar and water applied to the head'.[78] Later, he prescribed a draught of carbonate of ammonia, tincture of opium and cinnamon water. Nineteenth-century medicine was primitive whatever variety was applied.

In Lewis's absence, Belluomini induced a miscarriage, whereupon Maria died. It was 23 September, a year to the day after Bellini had died. She was only 28. Her first husband, whose name she had immortalised, died almost three weeks later.[79]

Maria was temporarily buried in what is now Manchester Cathedral. Bériot wanted her to lie in Belgium. After much argument, she was exhumed and reburied in the cemetery in Laeken.[80]

The French who regarded Malibran as an icon of the Romantic Age, blamed the English for her loss. England killed her, said Jules Janin, a leading music critic. He blamed the fog. 'She killed herself because she wanted to animate that statue of iron and coal, which is called England'.[81]

Maria Malibran had become a legend in her time. In the Hon. Mr Sucklethumbkin's Story, one of *The Ingoldsby Legends*, published in the year after her death, Lord Tomnoddy got up at half after two; he had nothing to do:

> My Lord Tomnoddy he raised his head
> And thus to Tiger Tim he said,
> 'Malibran's dead, Duvernay's fled.
> Taglioni* has not yet arrived in her stead;
> Tiger Tim, come tell me true,
> What may a Nobleman find to do?[83]

*Taglioni was a very popular ballerina, renowned for her diaphanous costumes and her lead role in the

With infinitely greater artistry, Alfred de Musset published a poem of 27 stanzas as a tribute to his Marietta, the flower of her age, who had captivated Europe with a lyre in her hand.[84]

More objective commentators, some years later, expressed doubts about the quality of Maria's mezzo-soprano voice. It was 'not naturally a voice of first-rate quality', said one. Perhaps her father had forced her in the upper registers – she had a range of two-and-a-half octaves. Critics also said that she could not dance in time.[85]

Maria passed over the stage like a meteor; she did not leave 'her mantle behind for others to take up and wear'.[86] Because she died young, she left no legacy. She did not establish any one new opera, nor did she create a style which others would follow. Liszt perhaps put his finger on it when he observed a few years later that the premature death of Malibran helped her posthumous reputation. Had she lived, 'who knows, she might very well have finished up by going to St Petersburg and singing out of tune like la Pasta'.[87]

Meanwhile, the Staffordshire potteries produced statuettes of her. Celebrities fade. However the surplus stock was easily adapted into statuettes of Queen Victoria to mark her accession in the following year.[88]

What of Maria's younger sister, Pauline? Despite her talent and wish to be a virtuoso pianist, and the support of Liszt, her mother insisted that she follow in her sister's footsteps and become a singer.[89] This meant going on the stage.

sensational Nun's Ballet in Meyerbeer's *Robert le Diable*. Mademoiselle Duvernay was a famous French opera dancer who had introduced a *pas seul* called the Cachuca, which was the rage in London at the time.[82]

CHAPTER 2

The Stage

Paris ranks among the most magnetic of capital cities. As we continue to set the scene for Pauline's début, we shall see how astonishingly vibrant it was in the early 1830s. At this time, Chopin arrived from Poland; Heinrich Heine, the German poet, settled there. Culturally, it poured forth riches. Victor Hugo published *The Hunchback of Notre-Dame* and Balzac *La Peau de Chagrin.* Musset had just published his *Contes d'Espagne et d'Italie* and Stendhal his *Le Rouge et le Noir.* In 1831, Eugène Delacroix, the leading Romantic artist, submitted six paintings at the Paris Salon, the regular exhibition of art arranged by the Académie des Beaux-Arts in the Grand Salon of the Louvre.[1]

Musically, Paris was in the process of becoming the opera capital of the world. The Italian castrati, who had delighted audiences in London and Vienna, were a thing of the past. The prima donnas, especially those who sang beautifully rather than 'howled'*, now reigned supreme. They gravitated to the Opéra and the Opéra-Comique where the works of Cherubini, Halévy, Auber and Meyerbeer were being staged; or to the Théâtre-Italien which presented operas by Rossini, Bellini and Donizetti.[2]

The standard was high, but the intense rivalry between the stars provided a 'barrier to entry'. New talent, up-and-coming singers such as Pauline, would have great difficulty entering, let alone prospering in, this

*Emperor Napoleon I particularly disliked the yellers and howlers, although this did not prevent him taking a substantial one to his bed. This presumably stopped her yelling.

environment. Two divas, Stoltz and Grisi, were so exceptional that they could hold the management of the Opéra and Théâtre-Italien in an armlock. It was not for nothing that Maréchal de Saxe, a great-grandfather of George Sand, once said 'I would rather command an army of 100,000 men than attempt to direct an opera corps'.[3] We shall see later that it was not very different in London.

Opera was show-business, grand in name, style and in the extent of its success. 'Grand opera' was fantastic, sensational. Fourteen circus horses took part in the cavalry charge scene in one of Spontini's operas.[4] In Auber's *La Muette*, the prima donna did not sing a word. She was a ballet dancer. At the end, she threw herself into the crater of Vesuvius which belched flames of coal-gas.

No one was better placed to exploit the public demand and the increasing technical potential than Meyerbeer.[5] He drew on his considerable personal wealth to ensure that the critics regarded his operas as a success. Meyerbeer teamed up with the successful librettist Eugène Scribe, who has been called 'a one-man factory geared to the mass-production of plays', and with Dr Véron who was then the Director of the Opéra. They devised a formula for extracting a return from the purses of the new and rich bourgeois class, the nouveaux-riches.[6]

Meyerbeer was expert at manipulating the 'claque', which was made up of those who hired their services to applaud or hiss, as requested. The investment was colossal. It cost 160,000 francs to stage Meyerbeer's *Les Huguenots.* His *Robert le Diable*, with its large crowd scenes and an ostensibly historical subject, was a hit. The yield was commensurate. Less than three years after its première, the Opéra had staged the hundredth performance of *Robert* and the show had appeared on the programmes of 77 theatres in 10 countries.[7]

Stanford, who was regarded as a distinguished composer later in the century, described Meyerbeer's 'innate desire for popularity at all costs' and called his works as 'an amazing conglomeration of fine music, trivial detail, masterly orchestration, and a striving (so obvious as to be often silly) after effect'. His products were never ugly, yet 'vulgarity hobnobs with nobility on equal terms everywhere'.[9] As a consequence, Meyerbeer was loaded, not just with cash, but with royal honours.

Giacomo Meyerbeer, born in Berlin, was less than six months older than Rossini. He was a talented pianist and a fellow student of Weber in Darmstadt. As the son of Jakob Beer, a rich Jewish banker, he could afford to tour Europe to complete his studies. The Paris production of *Il crociato* made his reputation. He demonstrated his flair for producing lucrative grand opera with *Robert le Diable* and *Les Huguenots.* The style of these had an enormous influence on the development of 19th-century opera. In the early 1840s, he worked in Berlin, but this was not a success. He returned to Paris. According to the poet Heine, Meyerbeer thought he had been a mouse in a previous existence and had a horror of cats. Possibly because cats dislike water, he always dressed for rain. Apart from his passion for money, he had a mania for tidiness and secrecy. He burnt all the letters he received.[8] He died in 1864.

The royal family itself was not particularly interested in music. Louis XVIII preferred food. His brother and successor, King Charles X, preferred religion. He went to sleep during *Il viaggio a Reims* which Rossini composed for his coronation. (But he was in his sixties.) Louis-Philippe, the King of the French, preferred reading romances while his wife did the knitting.[10]

Even if unmusical, the King of France was concerned about what went on in theatres and opera houses in his realm. Governments worry that any gathering of people facilitates protest and fosters sedition, or, in modern parlance, raises issues of 'security'. Thus, then as now, any sizable group, whether at the opera or elsewhere, needs to be regulated and, if necessary, policed. Theatre and opera were considered 'a school for scandal and an abyss of turpitude'.[11] As a consequence, they were closely controlled by the state, through the use of government subsidy and patronage. The government also exercised a tight grip on content.

Gaetano Donizetti was born into a poor family in Bergamo in the north of Italy in 1797. After an uncertain début, he settled in Naples. He composed at a frantic pace, 50 operas in 20 years, sometimes at the rate of 5 a year, and around 70 in all. He had composed 30 by the time *Anna Bolena* made his name internationally in 1830. This was followed by *L'Elisir d'amore, Lucia di Lammermoor, La Favorite, Don Pasquale* and many others no longer remembered. He never really recovered from the early death of his wife and their young children. He moved to Paris and later took a post in Vienna. He began to show symptoms of syphilis and acute sexual depravity. He was incarcerated in an asylum near Paris before being allowed to return, in an appalling state, to Bergamo for the nine months before his death in April 1848.

The authorities insisted that opera in Paris be carefully parcelled out between three opera houses. Foreign imports, such as works by Bellini and Donizetti, which were sung in Italian, were assigned to the Théâtre-Italien. Well-born young ladies could safely attend these performances, because they were unlikely to understand fully the love scenes when they were sung in a foreign language.

The Théâtre-Italien received relatively little subsidy from the government[12] compared to the Opéra and the Opéra-Comique. These possessed both the right and the obligation to perform works in the French language. Although the Opéra-Comique generally performed lighter works, the distinction related to the use of the spoken word, which was permitted at the Opéra-Comique but absolutely prohibited at the Opéra, where the entire work had to be set to music.

The content was censored by the authorities. The libretto was reviewed; if it was acceptable, the composer was invited to play the score. After this, the Minister of Police scrutinised the work for moral and political aspects.[13]

There was one long-standing tradition, which was tantamount to a regulation. All operatic works performed at the Opéra had to include at least one ballet. The appearance of the delicious ballerinas displaying their lovely feet was regarded, particularly by the dandies of the Jockey Club, as the most exciting moment of the evening. Although this convention exasperated composers such as Verdi and Wagner,[14] it contributed to the development of the graceful ballets we see, such as *Giselle* and *Les Sylphides.* It led, not least, to the delightful pictures by artists such as Edgar Degas.

Opera provided, especially for the well-heeled fans and the young, a means of escape, just as cinema and television do today. It had many of the attributes of the television show. It provided 'a source of hit tunes; a magnificent spectacle; an escapist dream world'.[15] New operas were being staged at a rate which would amaze us today, when a new opera is an unusual event and received with some justifiable apprehension.

For the fans, the opportunity to see their idols and the ballet dancers supplied the principal attraction. And the tediously extended recitatives provided an excellent chance to chat and to 'quiz' with lorgnette or monocle the occupants of the other seats and boxes. Anyway, so long as the music and the story were pleasing, they were of little importance. Indeed, if the star wanted to show off, or if it better suited the vocal range, a popular number from an unconnected work might easily be substituted anywhere in the show. Alternatively or additionally, such hits could be used for encores during the performance. Imagine the effect if Pavarotti had broken into *Nessun dorma* every time he took an ovation! Such disruptions did not trouble the audience, which was really interested in the people, the fashions, the latest gossip and scandal, the legs and other attributes of the dancers. Of course it was important to have heard that the critics and those who knew about these things had actually recommended the show.

The audience's attention was, however, inevitably caught once the stars began their vocal gymnastics. The singers embellished the music with their own elaborate ornamentation, which was much more exciting than artistic.[16] A London critic disliked the habit. 'The garniture may overlay, as much as it sets off, the material which it is meant to decorate', he complained.[17]

In the early years, Pauline was specifically criticised for excessive use of ornamentation. Indeed, Schumann complained that, as Rosina in the *Barber*, Pauline 'transformed the whole opera into a great variation. She scarcely left one melody untouched.' By contrast, her arch-rival Giulia Grisi was reputed to keep closer to the original.[18]

The exaggerated, artificial style in which these stars performed would not be to our taste, but it captivated the audience then.[19] It called for an extrovert character. A Russian aristocrat said that the shouting and the bodily contortions are 'in a melodramatic genre in which passion is replaced by delirium, anger by rage, and love by something whose name cannot yet be found, as far as I know, in any dictionary'. Berlioz fell for his first wife after he had seen her sensationally histrionic performance in the role of Ophelia. The English, however, did not really approve of this style. Mendelssohn, from Berlin, disliked it.[20]

Sex was then, as now, an important attraction for the audience. In the mind of an ordinary man, especially a lusty one, 'une charmante fille de théâtre' was easy and natural prey.[21] The stage and sin, whether exemplified by extra-marital sex or prostitution, were closely linked, not least in the opinion of the Church. For 1,500 years, it withheld the sacraments from actors and actresses. They were denied Communion, marriage, absolution and a Christian burial. This applied until 1849, when the Council of Soissons revoked earlier decisions dating back to the 4th and 5th century. There had been a temporary respite during the Revolution; however this was removed in 1816, soon after the Restoration. A celebrated victim of this age-old practice was Molière, the 17th-century comic playwright. When he died, his funeral was at night; the Archbishop of Paris forbade his clergy to be present at the burial.[22]

The treatment of opera singers was generally more tolerant than that of actors. Yet, although they were not officially condemned by the Church and state, their profession was frowned upon. For example, the son of a Piedmontese general, the Cavaliere Giovanni Matteo di Candia, 'a lyric tenor of great sweetness and beauty', assumed the stage-name 'Mario' so as not to sully his family name by associating it with the stage. When the diva Henriette Sontag, who was once Bériot's mistress, wed Napoleon's relative Count Rossi, the marriage had to be hushed up so as not to compromise his diplomatic career.[23] In one of his tales, Maupassant refers to a student from the Conservatoire who had just made her brilliant début at the Odéon; it would have been contrary to etiquette for a baron to marry her. There was, and is, a considerable difference between having a mistress and marrying her.

It would be unwise to underestimate the social disadvantage that Pauline would experience as a young performer. Even late in the 19th century, a provincial woman told Pauline's son, a leading violinist, that she was surprised that his wife looked so distinguished considering she was the spouse of an artist.[24] He was also refused entry to a provincial hotel whose management declared 'we don't take artists here'.

The attitude to singers and actresses was broadly similar across the Channel in England. In the 1860s, Dickens did not want his daughter to go on the stage, because there were people in the theatrical profession 'who would make your hair stand on end'.[25] Some people, of course, might say the same today.

As La Malibran exemplified, the rivalry between singers was intense. Berlioz marvelled at the opera world, its intrigues, the hatred which was generated.[26] 'I am exhausted and disgusted by the harassment these ladies subject me to,' declared the manager of one opera house. 'My patience is at an end.'[27]

George Sand described some of the tricks of the trade which the stars adopted. A rival might be induced to miss an entry. Or, in the middle of a duet, the rival's part might be sung so as to give the condescending impression that she needed a lesson in how to sing correctly. The rival could be confused by stage directions being ignored, moving right instead of left, or she could simply be tripped up. Perhaps lead her in among the chorus, thus making it difficult for her to emerge with dignity? Or, just spread, or, worse, deny, salacious stories about her virtue.[28]

Some of the worst excesses* were exemplified by Rosine Stoltz, a prize bitch. There was one notorious occasion, at a performance of Fromental Halévy's *Le Lazzarone, The street boy.* Stoltz deliberately disrupted the ovation being given to the other diva who she thought might be encroaching on her turf.[30] In the middle of the applause for Rosine's rival, titters began to be heard. They became a peal of mirth. What was happening? Stoltz was strutting across the front of the stage, dressed as a street-boy. Her head was back, her arms were in the air and she was unrolling a large skein of macaroni above her mouth. When the librettist expostulated, Stoltz replied that the stage is a free-for-all,[31] and stalked back to her *loge* which, conveniently for this *canard,* can be used to designate a theatre box, a dressing-room, or merely a hovel.[32] A *loge,* said her detractors, was her natural homing ground, because she was said to have been born in one.[33]

A couple of years after the incident with the macaroni, the première of a new *pasticcio*† entitled *Robert Bruce* was cancelled at 5pm on the first night, ostensibly because Stoltz had a cold, but actually because the advance publicity was appalling.[34] Once under way, after a brilliant start, Stoltz suddenly sang flat at the words 'Ah! Que de larmes (What tears!)'. The public gasped as it thought that she was fainting. After some further histrionics, she pulled out her handkerchief and stormed off the stage issuing a volley of unprintable abuse, words 'qui ne sont tolérables que sur un champ de bataille'.[35]

*There are more recent examples, of course. Birgit Nilsson, the twentieth-century soprano, was bitten in the neck during a love scene by a tenor who was enraged by not being able to sustain his top note for as long as her. Nilsson subsequently pulled out, complaining 'I have rabies'.[29]

†This was a pot-pourri of favourite melodies from three Rossini operas, *La Donna del Lago, Zelmira,* and *Armida.* Such pasticcios were normal at the time, but today are largely only concocted for gala performances attended by royalty, politicians, celebrities and donors.

Rosine Stoltz, born Victoire Noël in 1815, made her stage début in Brussels at the Theâtre de la Monnaie and married its Director. In that year, she also made her Paris Opéra debut in *La Juive*, and, for ten years remained there. The Director at the Opéra, Léon Pillet, became her lover. He was a liberal whose main claim to the position was that he had supported the winning side in the 1830 Revolution and had written a biography of the King's sister. Stoltz later made enormous sums performing in Brazil, but when she died in 1903, she left hardly enough money to buy a proper funeral.[36]

Stoltz's celebrity behaviour continued at the same level. She was the subject of a libel in which it was stated that she had sold her children to a Jewess to make candle grease.[37] The libeller was fined and was imprisoned for a year. She persuaded the octogenarian and down-at-heel Marquis d'Altavilla to admit that he was her father. On his death-bed, a few years later, he gasped when the rattle subsided, 'Madame Stoltz never paid me my annuity'. She also claimed to have married, on his deathbed, a Duke who did not exist. She then married the grandson of the Great Godoy, the parvenu politician and lover of the Spanish Queen around the time of Napoleon. Like many political families, the Godoys had no money. His grandson, Rosine's bridegroom, was a croupier in San Sebastian. Rosine promised him a pension, provided he stayed there.[38]

Such intrigue can lead to complications. After the Marquis's death, Godoy claimed in court that the Altavilla titles were his by right of his wife. However, court cases and appearances are grist to the mill of celebrities. It did not bother Rosine that she had to depose that the marriage with Godoy had never taken place.[39]

Many celebrities, especially those from poor backgrounds, long for titles to be conferred upon them. Rosine's were said to be phoney, although she did turn down marriage with the King of Württemberg because he was blind. When her illegitimate son was ennobled by her lover, who was the brother of the English Prince Consort, Rosine thought that his titles might be inherited backwards. So, she styled herself with her son's. Some wags suggested that, since her parents had been concierges, her coat of arms should include a broom. Unfortunately Rosine's claim to be a godchild of Pope Pius IX carried no title. That did not deter her. At the end of her career, she signed herself with the mouthful 'Comtesse de Ketchendorf, Baronne de Stoltzenau, Princesse du Lesignano, Duchesse de Bassano, Princesse de la Paix, née d'Altavilla (Rosine Stoltz)'.[40]

Rosine also had, or thought she had, a role as an international ambassador. She claimed to have warned the Tsar on behalf of Emperor Napoleon III that the Crimean War was about to break out. She provoked the evacuation of Rome in 1870. She spoke psychically with Marie-Antoinette. The antics of many modern celebrities pale into insignificance beside Rosine. She was quite simply 'excessive en tout'.[41]

At the time when Malibran died, the beautiful Giulia Grisi, for whom Bellini had composed the lead part in *I Puritani*, was becoming a considerable rival. The British Princess Victoria already regarded her as Malibran's superior.[42] After a leading English critic saw Grisi in Rossini's *The Thieving Magpie*, he wrote that her 'voice is deliciously pure and young'. To the critic, her execution was 'brilliant and fearless – sometimes a little too florid – her arms like sculpture, but used in a thousand ways which would make any sculptor's fortune … her hair magnificent, her action easy, passionate and never extravagant'.[43]

George Sand said that Grisi's face, the face of a classical Greek beauty, was sheer perfection.[49] Others were not so complimentary and said that although 'her head was very beautiful, her figure was not good, for her

Giulia Grisi, the niece of Napoleon's mistress and favourite contralto, Josephina Grassini, was born in Milan in 1811 and died in Berlin in 1869. After her début in Bologna, Grisi was signed up for six years at a very low fee by a Florentine impresario who then moved her to La Scala for a handsome transfer fee. At the première of *Norma* in December 1831, Grisi sang the part of Adalgisa, the friend of the druid princess and her rival in love. Grisi was said to have saved the performance from disaster. Later, in the title role, she was without rival. To avoid her onerous Italian contract, Grisi escaped, using her maid's passport, through the Swiss mountains.[44] She could never again perform in Italy.[45] For almost all of the next twelve years, she appeared every winter in Paris and every summer in London. She had so many farewell performances that it was said 'her career may be said to have been remarkable in the length of its autumn'. When in 1866 the curtain came down on her 'final' performance at Covent Garden, it knocked her to the floor.[46]

Mario, who became Grisi's lover, was exiled for his political connections with the cause of Italian nationalism. He was born in 1810. He made his début at the Opéra in *Robert le Diable* in December 1838. His London début was in the following year in *Lucrezia Borgia* opposite Giulia Grisi. Mario had a considerable range and could sing a high falsetto.[47] He was very generous, to such an extent that he had not much to retire on when he left the stage in 1871.[48]

legs were too short'.[50] The poet Musset regarded her as 'insupportably common, vulgar'.[51] She had the reputation for being ignorant, uneducated and having a fiery temper.

Grisi tired of her husband, a French Count who was famous for his duelling exploits. She became the long-term mistress of Mario. As she could not get a divorce, she was unable to wed him. He was the leading tenor of the time. Surprisingly, he combined his brilliant singing career with being a chain smoker. 'Except at meals I never saw him without a cigar' wrote one impresario.[52]

Recently, it has been suggested that 'Grisi and Mario were the most romantic couple of the Romantic Age'. They constituted 'a fairytale partnership that had no equal before the arrival of movies'.[53] Second only to Grisi was Fanny Persiani. Her father, a distinguished Italian Othello, was so ugly that he would ask composers to write parts for him which he could start to sing in the wings; so, the sound of his voice would precede his appearance. No beauty herself, Fanny 'was singularly tasteless in her dress'. Her one good point was her hair.[54] For her, Donizetti wrote the title role of *Lucia di Lammermoor*. Turgenev said that she fitted perfectly into the role of the naughty woman.[55] A gesture that she made as Adina, the soubrette village girl in Donizetti's *L'Elisir d'Amore*, reminded him exactly of one of his mother's chamber-maids.[56]

Importantly for Pauline, Fanny was typical of a new and increasingly popular breed of soprano who, like song-birds, could excel in purity of tone and accuracy of pitch, especially in the high registers, where Pauline was weakest.[57]

The stage demanded a very tough, competitive, extrovert character.

Pauline drawn by her sister

CHAPTER 3

Musset

Pauline made her first formal public appearance as a singer in the Hôtel de Ville in Brussels on 13 December 1837, with her sister's widower, Charles de Bériot. After another appearance with him in Louvain, she went on a concert tour of Germany. Ten months later, there were rumours that they might get married.

Around this time, a Belgian banker was desperately trying to launch his son onto a similar career as a pianist. The boy was César Franck who was a year or so younger than Pauline. He met Pauline and played before Malibran and Bériot. The shy, self-effacing boy rapidly disappeared behind the scenes. He was insufficiently extrovert to succeed as a virtuoso. Rather touchingly, about ten years later, he dedicated to Pauline the song 'Combien j'ai douce souvenance' (How sweet my memories are).[1]

Pauline was more successful. She started to gather riches, both pecuniary and cultural. The Queen of Prussia sent her a gift of emeralds.[2] As well as meeting Mendelssohn, she also got in touch with Clara Wieck, the virtuoso pianist who was almost two years older than her. A few months before, Clara had tried to become engaged to a lodger in her home, Robert Schumann. The engagement was so vehemently resisted by her father, a formidable man and distinguished piano teacher, that it would require a bitter and protracted court case before Robert and Clara could get married. The two girls began a friendship which lasted, with its ups and downs, almost 60 years. At this time, they saw each other virtually every day, and we can only guess at their gossip. Robert later dedicated some songs to

Pauline. He also asked her to compose a short piece which could be published as a supplement to one of the issues of his journal, the *Neue Zeitschrift für Musik.* Clara found herself overawed and almost overwhelmed by the talent, personality and not least bossiness of Pauline.[3]

Clara Schumann, née Wieck

Pauline's touring continued. In August, when she was in Wiesbaden, Meyerbeer took the opportunity to hear her perform. He said he was delighted with her and would compose an opera especially for her. After a short visit to northern Italy, Pauline, now aged about seventeen-and-a-half, returned to Paris where she appeared at the Théâtre de la Renaissance. This was on 15 December 1838, in a concert led by Bériot.[4] She sang three rather second-rate songs, including one showy piece which had been written specially for Malibran by the leading conductor in London, Michael Costa.

Pauline's début in opera took place, however, at Her Majesty's Theatre in London five months later on 9 May 1839. She sang the role of

Desdemona, in Rossini's *Otello*, a part which nobody today would dream of giving to a girl who was not yet eighteen. Half an hour elapses before Desdemona appears. While Pauline waited behind stage and heard the characteristic Rossini climax in the overture and the interminable singing of the men and chorus, she must have wondered how she would fare in the technically difficult finale to the second act, when she has to deal with the conflicting claims of her suitors. In this number she would be right at the top of her range. She will have comforted herself with the fact that that the *pièce de resistance* in the third act, the sad 'Willow Song', would be a success because it would enable her to show off the acting at which she was supreme.

Pauline duly obliged by opening with her piece by Costa, despite it having no connection with the opera. As we have seen, this was normal practice, and enabled the artiste to parade her talent whereas the opera itself was typically only of secondary interest. Besides, Desdemona's first appearance is not very dramatic and she may have felt that her début needed spicing up and more impact. She started nervously, but later in the performance her passionate acting, coming straight from the heart, pleased the audience, even if some thought her style was exaggerated.[5]

Desdemona when played by Maria Malibran had been received rapturously. So there was an inevitable attempt to compare the abilities of the two sisters. The London critic, writer and poet[6] Henry Fothergill Chorley, who for several years had written in a periodical called the *Athenaeum*, recalled that the performance contained 'all the Malibran fire, courage and accomplishment, but something else besides, and (some of us fancied) beyond these'.[7] Chorley recognised Pauline's considerable potential, while noting her poor presentation and some deficiencies in her voice. For praise, he singled out 'her instinct for acting, experience of music, knowledge of how to sing, and consummate intelligence'.[8]

Pauline was so exhausted after this début that she had to cancel a concert organised for the following day.[9] But she did find the energy to drop Clara a line telling her of her great success and her plans for the future.

After the London opera season, Pauline had a holiday in Boulogne. On 8 October, she made her Paris operatic début, again in *Otello.* This was at Théâtre de l'Odéon which was then the residence of the Théâtre-Italien. To lead off her performance, she substituted an aria from a different opera by Rossini.[10]

Henry Fothergill Chorley

In Paris, life for an adolescent girl moving among stage and artistic celebrities was bound to be very exciting. Equally, it was dangerous.

Pauline moved in the salon society. In the Faubourgs Saint-Honoré and Saint-Germain, each night after dinner, members of the affluent classes would visit one of the many salons, each presided over by an influential and almost certainly formidable lady. There, refreshed with coffee, tea, even punch, the Parisians could converse about politics and culture (but not normally sport)[11] and possibly listen to music. The salon would end, perhaps, by nine o'clock, or at least by midnight.[12] In the aristocratic houses the musicians, even Rossini and those who he had assembled, would enter by a side door. After their performance, they would be suitably thanked and shown out. The fee would be sent over on the following day.[13]

In less grand establishments, the musician could have a greater rapport with the hostess and her guests.[14] One such hostess was Caroline, the wife of Councillor Maxime Jaubert. She was a tiny woman, but a veritable ball of fire. Her salons matched her lively character and she herself was a good musician. Pauline attended her salon.[15]

Caroline Jaubert's brother was one of a group of dissipated rakes which included a golden-haired, 29-year-old dandy, Alfred de Musset.

When still a teenager, this scion of a 12th-century family was hailed by the leading critic Sainte-Beuve as a genius and had translated De Quincey's *Confessions of an English Opium-Eater.* A year later, Musset wrote the controversial, but successful, *Contes d'Espagne et d'Italie.* Before long, he was recognised as one of the leading writers of 'the 1830 period', a poet of the first rank and a master of character and language in his prose. His plays are less well-known outside France and were less successful, although his *Les Caprices de Marianne*, for example, was subsequently considered 'one of the finest pieces in the repertory of the Théâtre Français'. Eventually, as befitted him, he died of an affliction of the heart. One contemporary suggested that 'the symptoms of the heart disease which caused his death in 1857 may sometimes have been mistaken for the symptoms of intoxication'.[16]

At the time he met Pauline, Musset's profession necessitated him behaving as a suffering poet, and experiencing romantically fashionable fits of madness. Musset was high risk. A few years earlier, he had eloped to Venice with the novelist George Sand. When they both fell ill, Sand sent Musset packing after she had made off with the attractive doctor who was treating them both. On Musset's return from Venice, Caroline consoled him in her bed, before rapidly passing him on to others, including her cousin who frightened him off when she made a particularly novel suggestion, marriage.[17]

Alfred de Musset

Meanwhile, Musset's relationship with Caroline stabilised. She became a remarkable influence on him, his muse, his Titania, his Faerie Queen. He called her his Godmother; she called him her Godchild.

At Caroline's salon, Pauline met the hostess's former bedmate.[18] To the young and still impressionable Pauline, his immediate attentions must, at first, have been thrilling. The fact that Musset was also flirting with her mother was, for the moment, beside the point.[19]

After Musset heard Pauline sing, he dreamt of a renaissance in Art. When not in his cups, he wanted to blend the classical conventions with the best features of the Romantic 'déluge'. Out would go the admirable, yet so restrictive, rules of classicism, but also the excessive effusions of romanticism. The yoke would be smashed, the fever passed.[20] This initiative would be led by 'Paulette', who he then called 'l'aimable Paolita',[21] jointly with an actress who he had also met recently, Elisa Félix.

This seventeen-year-old Swiss-born Jewish girl was known then and to posterity simply as 'Rachel'. She was to become one of the greatest actresses there has ever been. She had recently made a sensational début at the Comédie-Française in Corneille's *Horace*.[22]

Rachel

Rachel* had a perfect, almond-shaped face, and was fascinating if not beautiful. Despite being less than five feet tall, she dominated the Paris stage for seventeen years, particularly in tragic and dramatic parts such Racine's Phèdre, a role which has been likened to that of Shakespeare's Lady Macbeth.[24] Phèdre is the incestuous and suicidal queen, and Racine's tragedy lays bare the complexity of love. A critic described Rachel's style, her 'horror-stricken countenance' and the 'quivering play of her hands, every fibre listening and yielding and struggling with despair'.[25] 'Whoever has not heard and seen Mlle Rachel in a salon can only have an incomplete idea of her feminine attractiveness and of her talent as an actress', said a rival, a top English actress. 'Her features, a little too delicate for the stage, gained much by being seen nearer. Her voice was a little hard, but her accent was enchanting, and she modulated it to suit the limits of a salon with marvellous instinct. Her deportment was in irreproachable taste. Deferential with dignity, modest, natural and easy ... her success in society was immense'.[26]

The realism of Pauline and Rachel, the purity of their style, had brought, for Musset, a breath of pure fresh air into the artistic world. 'Le retour à la vérité est la mission de ces deux filles', he wrote.[27]

Musset, who disliked Bériot, did not actually attend Pauline's first Paris concert. He anyway felt that she was too young for it. She repeated to him, in more private surroundings, what she had sung.[28] He then wrote a long eulogy in the periodical, the *Revue des Deux Mondes*, in which he concluded with his poem 'Sur les débuts de Mesdemoiselles Rachel et Pauline Garcia'.[29]

As we already know, Musset had published a poem as a tribute to Maria Malibran. Although he preferred Pauline's interpretation of the 'Willow Song', he did not want to rate the performances of Maria and Pauline. 'On ne surpasse pas la perfection',[30] he wrote in a subsequent article in the *Revue des Deux Mondes*. He explained that they each had interpreted Desdemona in a different way. For Maria, Desdemona was a heroine. 'Love, anger, terror, everything about her was exuberant; even her melancholy was emphatic'. Pauline, by contrast, played the part of Othello's wife almost as

*Rachel died of TB aggravated by overwork, travel, including a tour of the United States, and her racy private life. Coming from a poor background, on first being introduced into 'society', she was 'greatly embarrassed by the conventions of the table'. At a grand dinner, she found that 'the question as to the proper use of the knife and fork in the consumption of asparagus was infinitely embarrassing'. History presumes that Pauline knew better.[23]

a virgin in love, with a presentiment of her fate. She was 'brave only at the moment of death'.[31]

We know that early 19th-century opera singers declaimed their parts in a wooden and highly stylised fashion. They adopted conventional attitudes and made stilted gestures which some have likened to the giving of semaphore signals. Maria and Pauline also seemed to have posed, but were much more fluid and natural in their attitudes. They allowed the music to suffuse and support the image which they were communicating. When Pauline died on stage, she executed it in a romantic and beautiful way. It was this that appealed to the romantic Musset. But this was far removed from the realism with which modern audiences are provided. Pauline would perhaps have gone dreamily to sleep, or dropped down dead gracefully as in a ballet. There would have been no grunts, let alone death rattles or rigor mortis. The naturalistic, preferably shocking, style which we associate with a whore such as Carmen only developed later in the century.[32]

So Pauline, despite the poor design of her costumes, was a hundred times better than all those bawlers Musset spent so much time having to listen to. 'She began her career as others would be content to finish', he declared.[33]

Musset's praise was genuine. And while it may have resulted in him dreaming of a renaissance in art, he was also dreaming of something else besides. 'Je ne sais laquelle des deux, Pauline ou Rachel ...', 'I don't know which of the two to have, Pauline or Rachel', he told Madame Jaubert.[34] Pauline had progressed a long way from her crush on Liszt, when she was so excited on the days of her piano lessons that she could hardly do up her boots.[35]

Of course, Musset thought that he was entitled to gratitude. He expected women to fall at his feet. However Pauline, who particularly disliked his habit of ogling her with his bloodshot eyes, would not. She overheard what he had confided to Madame Jaubert. She was disgusted. Her discomfort with his arrogance probably gave him a kick; the fact that she found him physically repellent provided him with a more galling series of problems which even he did not know how to resolve.[36]

Something happened in early January 1839 which cut this vain dandy to the quick and brought him down to earth. Pauline seems to have joked in English, that 'devilish' language, with George Osborne, a virtuoso pianist from Ireland, who looked like Rossini's double. They seem to have laughed at Musset's florid appearance not realising that, despite Osborne's speaking with a 'creamy Irish brogue',[37] Musset understood every word that was being said. The poet later explained that his flushed look was a symptom of fever caused by a toothache. It was also attributable to his wrapping himself up in his fur coat. It had nothing to do with alcohol.[38]

Shocked by the rebuff, Musset consoled himself with Rachel, with whom he had 'regular and frequent relations'. He also undertook to write a five-act tragedy for her. However, as he confessed to his 'Godmother', he could not prevent himself thinking of Pauline while he was in Rachel's arms.[39]

Musset's experience led him to publish a poem in which he described how a fair lady's smile has the fatal power to send him who aspires to her love into transports of rapture, or the depths of despair. Yes, a few words, or just none, indeed the unconcerned or mocking look, can feel like the thrust of a dagger straight through the heart. Here are two beautiful verses from it:

Oui, femmes, quoi qu'on puisse dire,
Vous avez le fatal pouvoir
De nous jeter par un sourire
Dans l'ivresse ou le désespoir.

Oui, deux mots, le silence même,
Un regard distrait ou moqueur
Peuvent donner à qui vous aime
Un coup de poignard dans le coeur.[40]

What was this teenager like who Musset was trying to seduce? She had developed into an excellent pianist, organist and composer, as well as singer. She was obviously intelligent and outstandingly talented. She could read and speak Spanish, Italian, French, German and English, even if her accent was sometimes imperfect;[41] and she liked reading the works of the German authors, such as Schiller and Goethe. She was a very good landscape painter. She could draw caricatures very well, a particularly useful skill in an age when letters, embellished with the occasional cartoon, were such an important means of communication. Her conversation was delightful.

She was a person of great warmth, although less wild than her sister. Clara Schumann also took to her warm and outgoing personality.[42]

Musset identified Pauline's trump card. He observed that she 'possesses in a word the great secret of artists. Before expressing something, she feels it. She does not listen to her voice, but to her heart'.[43] She was always most concerned with the dramatic effect of a performance. Despite introducing irrelevant numbers at her début, once she had found her feet Pauline no longer treated opera as a kind of concert performance in costume. She generally refused to break the flow of action to give the encores the audience wanted. In this she differed from other singers.[44]

Unlike so many prodigies whose virtuosity is all technique and little music, Pauline was truly musical. When Clara Wieck saw her again in Paris,[45] she recorded in her diary that she 'sings very dramatically, always without notes. She accompanies herself without looking at the piano. She can play anything by ear.' It would be particularly fitting that the opera which Gounod wrote for Pauline would be about Sappho, who was considered in mythology to be the tenth Muse.[46]

Most of Pauline's admirers, even Turgenev, agreed that she was very plain, or perhaps grew to be very plain. 'Richement laide (ugly)' was the phrase used.[47] In her teens, 'the ant' may have been an apposite way of describing the tightly-waisted, black-haired Pauline, who was so unusually hardworking and industrious for a middle-class girl of her time. We hear of her large nose and thick lips. Her neck was too long.[48] We have only to look at the pictures of her to see what was meant; the big mouth, the almost protruding black eyes. She seemed rather masculine.[49] She was in complete contrast to Rachel, the feminine little Rachel. When told that Rachel would welcome a visit, the King's son salivated with anticipation. 'Where? When? How much?' he demanded. We can easily understand that the English actress quoted earlier found she could no longer meet Rachel, 'her conduct having for some time excluded her from the circles in which they had formerly met'.[50]

Yet, when Pauline was a virgin aged seventeen, Musset wrote that she was 'décidément jolie à la scène',[51] pretty on the stage. And later, this Garcia, this gypsy, radiated some kind of captivating charm and exuberance which the pictures cannot convey, the despair of painters and the delight of poets. 'What made her even more captivating than her talent as a singer was her personality – one of the most amazing I have ever known', said Saint-Saëns, who later knew Pauline very well. Pauline reminds us that personality is such an important component of human magnetism. She was similar to the novelist George Eliot, who radiated an extraordinary attraction, despite it being said that she was so ugly that, like Medusa, one look from her would turn you to stone. Little personal nuances, ability and individuality are what really create human attraction, and music.[52]

Marie d'Agoult, Liszt's lover, was not always taken with Pauline's performances, but conceded that she gave one the impression that she had 'l'air d'une demoiselle du très grand monde',[53] who looks on her audience with a kind of disdain. She was classy. She also radiated a sort of magic. It seems to have been something to do with her smile and her 'wonderful infectious laugh'.[54] Heine, the poet, was delighted by the moments 'when she opens wide her large mouth with its dazzling white teeth and smiles with such savage sweetness and delightful ferocity'. She had an attractive mannerism in which she would raise her right shoulder and incline her head to the same side.[55]

Her voice had 'the velvetness of the peach and youth', Musset claimed. It combined bitterness and sweetness, as in the taste of wild fruit.[56] Saint-Saëns, referring to a more mature Pauline a decade or so later, took a rather less complimentary view. 'This marvellous voice did not please everyone', he said, 'because it was by no means smooth and velvety'. He suggested that the fruit was a bitter orange.[57] Her 'voice grows unconsciously upon you until at last you are blind to its imperfections', wrote another contemporary. Indeed, like that sultry, sexual voice of Callas a century later, Pauline's voice seems to have been amazingly powerful but a little harsh; Saint-Saëns felt that it was more suited for the superhuman, rather than the human role. We can understand why she triumphed in the role of Orpheus, the legendary Greek hero. Perhaps it is not surprising that she never sang in public in Italy.[58]

Rossini thought that Pauline's voice was far superior to Maria's. Saint-Saëns drew attention to its tremendous power and its prodigious range in which, unusually, she could unite contralto, mezzo soprano and soprano, a combination which is very rarely heard.[59] It must have been incredible to hear her, for example, as Angelina (Cinderella) in the Quintet from Act I of Rossini's *La Cenerentola*. In a modern analogy, it must have been like Concorde surging through, indeed soaring far beyond, the sound barrier, while the four Jumbos competing with her plodded behind.

Pauline could dazzle audiences with her range* which, like her sister's, stretched over almost three octaves, from a cello-like F sharp below middle C, to a flute-like top D.[61] On one occasion, this versatility enabled her to resolve a problem when her opposite number was ill. Pauline sang both the mezzo-soprano and soprano part in the same performance of Meyerbeer's *Robert le Diable*. Fortunately, Robert's half-sister Alice and Princess Isabelle, who he loves, need not appear on the stage at the same time.[62] Pauline's achievement was rightly regarded as a tour de force.

The voice sounded naturally deep, like her sister's. It was best in those lower notes, that rich, deep chocolatey sound of the contralto, the deep sound which was much favoured at the time, before Verdi pushed voices to a higher pitch.[63] And, one imagines that, as with Kathleen Ferrier whose unique sound we recall in recordings of *Dido's Lament* by Purcell, there was a depth beneath the high notes 'giving them an added richness'.[64] We can feel the quality of Pauline's voice when we listen to the luscious and lascivious sounds of Dalila in Saint-Saëns' *Samson*. He created Dalila with Pauline in mind.

If indeed Pauline's voice combined the deep purity of Ferrier with the eroticism of Callas, it is not surprising that Musset, like Samson, was captivated. However, Pauline's distinctive style, very different from her sister's, was possibly disadvantageous when it came to the perception of the general public. Her purity and freshness meant that, in her early years, she made an ideal Cinderella. Although the part of Rosina in Rossini's *Barber* enabled her to display some of her luscious mezzo notes, she was perhaps insufficiently pert for the role, at least to start with. She was too innocent and virginal, and she lacked the soubrette's hint of sexual potential. Listeners considered that she would in due course make an excellent Countess in *The Marriage of Figaro*, characterised by those pure and glorious arias, 'Porgi amor' and 'Dove sono'.[65]

She soon took great care over her costumes. At this time, the singers provided their clothes themselves. The Italians, in particular, took little trouble with production, design, costume or appearance. The costumes then were grotesque, the decor miserable. In order to ensure that hers were right, Pauline would visit libraries and make sketches.[66]

*The Prière from Act IV of *Le Prophète*, written specially for Pauline, concludes with arpeggio from top B flat down to bottom G below middle C.[60]

For the gypsy girl, the omens were very propitious indeed. Yet the competition and rivalry were intense, and her physical disadvantages were considerable. Despite her suitability for the superhuman role, she was mortal. She was very nervous when performing, particularly on first nights. In her first performance as Rosina in Paris, she had a memory failure which she successfully covered up by some deft improvisation. Even at the Royal Italian Opera in 1848 in London, her trembling was apparent in all parts of the house.[67]

Noticeably plain, if not ugly; an unusual, even imperfect voice; virginal. Could she compete against the machinations of the Paris stars, particularly that Grecian beauty, the divine Grisi? She would be Pauline's 'implacable enemy and rival for many years to come'. Grisi and her lover Mario, who Chorley years later described as 'the best operatic tenor actor who has been seen in our time',[68] constituted a formidable partnership, formidable competition. We shall see.

Meanwhile someone, possibly Musset, possibly Louis Viardot, introduced Pauline to the novelist George Sand.[69] They struck up an exceptional friendship.

Pauline Garcia

CHAPTER 4

GEORGE

ONE OF THE more bizarre, but lasting friendships which the pure and demure Pauline developed at this time was that of Aurore Dudevant who by then used the *nom de plume* George Sand, and who for convenience we shall call George. The writer of over a hundred novels and plays, she was the leading *littératrice* of 19th-century France.

Sand was a novelist of far-reaching influence. Turgenev ranked her with Dickens and George Eliot. She was widely read in Russia where her works, despite their radical and feminist content, got past the censors, who did not consider that they constituted an assault on the Russian government. A prominent Russian critic compared her to Homer, Shakespeare and to Cervantes, the author of *Don Quixote.* These comparisons sadly have not stood the test of time.[1]

Sand particularly liked writing about women, because Woman's destiny interested her. Her new-found friend Pauline Garcia provided an ideal subject to depict in her novels *Consuelo* and *La Comtesse de Rudolstadt.*

The notorious, sexually insatiable novelist had been the mistress of Musset. They had eloped to the Hotel Danieli in Venice. At the time when Pauline first met her, she had recently returned from an unfortunate escapade to Majorca with her latest conquest, the increasingly sickly Frédéric Chopin. That relationship was beginning to lose impetus.[2]

Pauline met the swarthy and black-eyed George Sand around October 1839. Her influence on Pauline's life was to be immense. In the following ten years there was to be a continuous flow of correspondence, often undated, between them. Pauline was occasionally ticked off for dilatoriness in replying. In later years, they wrote fewer, but still numerous, letters to each other.[3]

The correspondence began with Sand, at 35 and nearly twice Pauline's age, addressing her as 'Reine du monde', Queen of the World. However extrovert the Garcias may have been, one wonders what they made of that; and also what they thought of Sand's grandiose comparison of Madame Garcia with Cornelia, the daughter of the Roman general who defeated Hannibal. She was fabled for being the 'highest type of Roman matron'.[4] George continues by writing, this time about Pauline, 'I admire genius, but when it comes with goodness, I prostrate myself before it'. This style seems to support the opinion of a recent biographer that 'there is something wonderfully exaggerated about George Sand's life and writing'.[5]

George, who was born on 1 July 1804, now entered Pauline's life. George had been sired by a nobleman on a Parisian 'dancer'. Her mother was made an honest woman a month before her birth. The nobleman played the violin and believed that he was a composer comparable to Haydn. He was descended from the Maréchal de Saxe, one of the 400-odd illegitimate children of the Elector of Saxony, Augustus the Strong, in this case by the fabulously beautiful Aurore de Königsmarck. George Sand inherited the name Aurore, the goddess of the dawn, but not the looks, apart from the velvety eyes.[6]

George smoked cigars; through the haze she would penetrate you, Sphinx-like, with those jet black eyes.[7] She had a reputation for wearing trousers, a man's hat and a coat of black velvet which considerably disguised her feminine curves. Her outfit emphasised her smallness and lent her a kind of youthful virility. Although it might sound as if she was a kind of intrepid amazon, she 'was essentially a self-centred woman who wanted to have her own way'. The Comtesse d'Agoult wondered whether she was a man, a woman, an angel or a demon.[8]

Dickens had a far from flattering impression of Sand when he met her, albeit some years later, at the Viardots'. He said that she looked like Queen Victoria's monthly nurse. 'A singularly ordinary woman in appearance and manner', was how he described her.[9]

When not in Paris, George Sand occupied the Château de Nohant, near Bourges in the middle of France. In 1840, the journey there took eighteen hours from Paris on the mail coach. It took longer if the traveller was not prepared to bed down in the coach and insisted on spending the night in Orléans. It was quite normal for the coaches to roll onwards at a steady pace through the darkness of the night, with 'the lantern, hanging from the postillion's seat, lighting up the horses' cruppers'.[10]

George lived in the lovely château which she had inherited from her paternal grandmother who looked after her when her father was killed in a riding accident. Her mother had been despatched back to the netherworld whence she came.

Nohant may indeed qualify to be called a château. However, the size and period of what George called her 'modest residence', which had been rebuilt in the late 18th century,[11] could easily disappoint the modern tourist who is in search of antiquity, or just intent on divesting cash in a grand château hotel. Equally the description 'a large bourgeois mansion',[12] while accurate, totally fails to convey the charm of this large country house, its delightful park and, it would seem, its deliberate lack of pretension to grandeur. Adjacent to the 'quasi-château' are its outbuildings and a tiny church. France is full of lovely houses, but this is a perfect one.

When she was only eighteen Aurore Dupin, as she then was, married Casimir, the 27-year-old illegitimate son of the Baron Dudevant. The initial experience was seemingly not a success. Years later, she wrote to her inebriated half-brother: 'Take care that your son-in-law does not brutalise your daughter on their wedding night. Men seem oblivious to the fact that what is mere fun for them is martyrdom for us. Tell him to control himself and to take it slowly and gently. Nothing is worse than the fright, the pain and the distaste of a poor child who knows nothing and finds herself raped by a brute.' She added, 'we try to bring them up like saints and then we hand them over like fillies'.[13] For Aurore, this experience had no long term harmful effects. Nine-and-a-half months later, she gave birth to her son.

Casimir drank heavily, was mainly concerned with hunting and shooting, and was unfaithful. Three years after her wedding, while on a family holiday in the Pyrenees, Aurore herself began an affair with a magistrate who was there to serenade his fiancée. In the following year, she renewed an earlier friendship with a boyfriend who almost certainly became the father of her daughter Solange, who was born on 13 September 1828.[14]

A drawing of George in 1833 by Alfred de Musset

A few years after that, having been aroused by games of hide-and-seek with Jules Sandeau, who was seven years her junior, Aurore absconded from Nohant to Paris. The couple collaborated on a book which was published under the pseudonym J. Sand. She worked as a journalist for *Le Figaro*, and by the spring of 1832 she had written her first novel, *Indiana*, which she published under her new name as George Sand. Overnight, she became 'famous'.[15]

Sandeau found the pace rather fast. He fell by the wayside, especially after George caught him with the washerwoman. Ever inventive, George became passionate about a leading actress, the small, fragile Marie Dorval. With 'liquid eyes and delicate yet sensuous features', Dorval was at the time also in bed with Alfred de Vigny, the poet and author who had created a specific role for her in his play *Chatterton*.[16] Officially, Dorval was also married to her second husband. Sand wrote 'Everything was passion with her, motherhood, art, friendship, love, indignation, religious yearning; and as she neither knew how nor wished to practise moderation and restraint, her whole existence was lived at a terrifying pitch and at an intensity which seemed impossible to sustain'.[17]

The affair with Dorval was punctuated by a brief affair with Prosper Mérimée, the short-story writer, expert in depicting local colour and later the author of the novella *Carmen.* George then eloped with Musset to Venice. As we know, she went off with the doctor who was treating them. The poet Robert Browning replied, when asked who was Sand's latest lover, 'I can't say, since she has a new one every day'.[18] Seemingly insatiable, she became the lover of the Bourges lawyer handling her separation from Dudevant; next, she became the lover of her children's tutor, the lover of another writer and, of course, the lover of Chopin. 'She gazed deep into my eyes while I played', wrote Chopin. 'Such dark strange eyes she had ... her face was masculine, its features heavy, almost coarse, but those sad, strange eyes. I longed for them ... my heart was conquered ... She loves me! Aurore! What a charming name! Like the dawn it banishes the darkness!'[19]

Pauline and this remarkable woman were very quickly on intimate terms. George, whose tone of writing is nothing less than gushing, calls Pauline 'fifille', little daughter. Pauline, however, continues to address her as Madame Sand, long after the young singer has referred to Chopin as Mr Fritz, or le bon Fritz, or Chip-chop, or even Chip-chip.[20]

However, it is not too long before Pauline's letters are signed off 'Votre fifille' and Pauline addresses Madame Sand as 'Chère Ninounne', a standard term of endearment for an older woman. Yet all this familiarity runs alongside a sophistication in letter-writing style that is quite extraordinary for a nineteen-year-old. And we find Sand sharing with this teenager confidences about her daughter Solange, about her education and her difficult adolescence.[21]

One might infer that there was something improper, perhaps sexual, in the relationship between the two somewhat masculine women, one much older than the other. Liszt's mistress the Comtesse Marie d'Agoult seems to have suspected that the relationship was a lesbian one.[22] However, it seems more probable that, because Solange and her mother were increasingly at odds, George needed someone to whom she could transfer her maternal affection. She confessed that she loved Pauline with the same sacred love which she had for her own children.[23] Indeed, when Pauline's career took her from the novelist's orbit, Sand transferred her affection to Augustine

Brault, a cousin who she adopted and brought up at Nohant. Meanwhile, invocations such as 'If only you were like Pauline' were hardly designed to solve the growing-up problems of an adolescent daughter, whose unhappy life we shall later explore.[24]

George in 1841, by Pauline

George was probably jealous of Musset's attention to Pauline. She warned Pauline's mother that her daughter should be careful of Musset. This Pauline succeeded in doing, such that Musset's brother would say that there were three women who inspired Alfred with his finest verses; George Sand, Rachel and the ungrateful, 'l'ingrate, l'absurde', Pauline, as he used to call her.[25]

George widened Pauline's circle of friends. Within a couple of years, we read of Pauline inviting the novelist to dinner at 5.30pm followed by a visit to the vaudeville, in a party which included Delacroix, who was a regular guest at Nohant and arguably the greatest French Romantic painter.[26] Apart from the friendship with Chopin, other visitors to Nohant were Liszt and Marie d'Agoult. Sand's circle also included Meyerbeer, the German poet Heinrich Heine and the Polish poet Adam Mickiewicz.

George ensured that Pauline's career was well and truly launched.

A couple of years after she met Pauline, George began to write *Consuelo*, a novel which occupied her, when not suffering from chronic migraine,[27] for the two years between December 1841 and February 1844. During 1843, this came out in instalments in the *Revue Indépendante*. Pauline later told a great friend and confidant, Julius Rietz, the conductor at the Leipzig Gewandhaus, to read *Consuelo* if he wanted to get to know her.[28] This could have been a practical joke. The novel runs to 103 chapters. In its conclusion, the reader, after being informed that the book 'already has become too long and discursive',[29] is told that there is going to be a second part, a sequel. This duly appeared as *La Comtesse de Rudolstadt* which provides a further 41 chapters before an Epilogue. *Consuelo* represents a formidable challenge to any reader, let alone Rietz who had far more important things to do than reading novels.

The length and rambling style of *Consuelo* may be due to its being written, as was the custom at the time, in instalments of minimum length, for publication in a magazine. Some of these were already on sale before the work was complete. Dickens's novels also suffer from a similar genesis,[30] although he had the advantage of writing during the day, whereas Sand would work through the night.

Because the story of Consuelo is supposed to tell us about Pauline's character, we need to dwell on it. However, we must remember that it was fiction. Also, Sand is said to have based aspects of her novel, not just on Pauline, but also around a German soprano, long since dead, whom Mozart thoroughly disliked.*[31]

The historical novel is set in the 1750s. It features a talented opera star

*Mozart said of Gertrude Mara, one of the great sopranos of the eighteenth century, and her husband: 'If you only knew these people you would at once see conceit, arrogance, and unblushing *effronterie* written on their faces'. Madame Mara made a scene in Mannheim when her husband, a 'wretched cellist', was not allowed to accompany her. Her husband then assaulted the court conductor whose daughter Mozart was fond of. Madame Mara's characteristics are similar to those of Corilla, Consuelo's rival in Sand's novel.

aged eighteen, who happens to be ugly. Beneath a 'torrent de cheveux noirs', she has a large mouth, beautiful eyes and teeth.[32] She also has a large bosom, a narrow waist, small feet and pretty hands. This person, who sounds so like Pauline, escapes from the lascivious clutches of a Venetian impresario and from the importunate demands of Anzoleto, her childhood sweetheart, a successful tenor. The escape is arranged by her teacher, Nicola Porpora, in real life a rival to Handel and 'probably the most famous singing teacher of the eighteenth century'.[33] Porpora criticises Anzoleto because he does not worship Art, 'but glory and his own glory', a familiar failing. His 'destiny will be as the flash of a meteor', in contrast, we may assume, to that of Consuelo whose destiny will be lasting.[34]

In the middle of a thunderstorm Consuelo, using a pseudonym, arrives at the haunted, gothic Castle of the Giants, the seat of the Counts of Rudolstadt, located in the Bohemian Forest 300 miles to the north of Venice. The last of the Rudolstadt line, Count Albert, who Turgenev would later describe as insufferable,[35] seems eccentric, possibly mad. He seems to be under the impression that he is the reincarnation of one of his forebears from the time of the religious 'Hussite' wars which divided Bohemia in the early 17th century.

When Albert hears Consuelo sing, he cries out in Spanish, 'O Consuelo, Consuelo [remember, she is still incognito] I have now found thee'.[36] He knows Spanish from his time in the Crusades, centuries earlier. He calls her Consuelo because she will provide consolation. For him, her Language of Music manifests a higher order of ideas and sentiments than the Language of Words. Music expresses all that the mind dreams of mystery and grandeur. It is the revelation of the Infinite.[37]

Albert falls in love with Consuelo. Her former boyfriend, the tenor, turns up and causes some disruption in the castle, especially as his presence reminds the Rudolstadts that their son is falling for an actress. Consuelo decides that she had better leave, especially after she finds a freshly dug grave.[38]

In the night, Consuelo flees in the direction of Vienna, penniless. She collapses by a fountain, exhausted. She wakes to find a boy tending her. The youth turns out to be Haydn. Remember, this is fiction. The pair set off together, with Consuelo definitely 'wearing the trousers', into which she changes.[39]

Maurice Sand's illustration of Haydn and Consuelo sharing his picnic at the fountain

Amid various and considerable adventures, Consuelo and Haydn spend the night in the lodgings of a jolly prelate who, in a nice touch, says he was one of the 400 natural children of King Augustus the Strong. While enjoying his hospitality, who should turn up, in the last stages of pregnancy? Consuelo's chief rival from her days in Venice, the loose-living, celebrated prima donna Corilla. She bears a striking resemblance to Giulia Grisi, and is 'a theatrical singer who says she is famous but has the air and tones of a low drab'. Consuelo delivers Corilla's baby whose father is Consuelo's boyfriend, the tenor. Consuelo then adopts the child.[40] As we shall see, Pauline will later adopt the child of another woman, fathered by a man she loves. She will do it for Turgenev.

Consuelo and Haydn reach Vienna, where she is eclipsed by Corilla whose 'coquetry turned the heads of those simple German lords, no-one observing that her voice was rather hoarse. Every handsome woman on the stage seemed a great artist to them'.[41] Franco-German entente is, of course, a recent phenomenon.

A letter arrives from Count Albert professing his love. Consuelo's positive response is suppressed by Porpora who does not want her diverted from her destiny in life, which is to be an evangelist for her art. In the event, she is whisked off to the Giants' Castle where Albert is dying of grief, having heard from Porpora that Consuelo would never marry him. On his deathbed, Albert marries Consuelo. She wants to be neither rich nor a countess, and resumes her career.[42]

It is timely to remind ourselves why we are at all concerned with this curious tale. There are two important reasons. George Sand wrote about Albert's philosophising and about Consuelo's destiny at the time that Pauline had begun to accept that her destiny was indeed to tour abroad to proclaim her art. This was also a destiny which Liszt in his relentless travels was exemplifying, *par excellence.* In their actions, all three were embodying the role of the artist which had earlier been advocated by the Saint-Simonian movement, which was very influential at the time.[43] To this we shall return. Had Pauline not faced such intense competition on the Paris stage, we may reasonably wonder whether George would have concocted this role for Consuelo, or whether Pauline would have accepted it. In Liszt's case, there was no ulterior motive; in Pauline's, there could have been an element of 'needs must'.

In the second place, we are interested because Pauline has said that the character of Consuelo, this 'fille charmante et vertueuse', is the key to her own character, which, so far, has appeared to be almost tediously goody-goody.[44] We are told that she does not have a lover. 'Elle n'a pas d'amant'.[45] Despite her back-packing with Haydn and her marriage to the dying Albert, Consuelo is still a virgin.

The sequel *La Comtesse de Rudolstadt* begins a year later, in Berlin. Consuelo has pursued her career at the court of Frederick the Great. The tastes of the tough and self-centred King are 'subordonnés à une logique si glacée' such that his attention to the opera performance has a paralysing effect on the performers.[46]

Consuelo annoys the King who incarcerates her* in Spandau prison where she spends three months. In an exciting sequence, one of her jailers tries to rape her when she attempts to escape. However, she is sprung. She finds herself in a coach with a mysterious masked man to whom she snuggles up close, even though their proximity does not feel to her as if it compromises her chastity.[47]

She finds herself in an idyllic baroque park where she is held virtually as a prisoner by a kind of Masonic Order, reminiscent, to us, of *The Magic Flute*. She is told that she has to choose between the masked man and Albert. This option comes as a surprise, because Albert is supposed to be dead; however, we now learn that he only appeared to die. He was, in fact, alive. No wonder Turgenev expressed considerable distaste for the lack of realism in Sand's novels.[48]

Albert now turns his vast intelligence to the advantage of the Order, into which Consuelo is initiated after undergoing various demanding proofs. It transpires, as no doubt the reader by now suspects, that Albert and the masked man are one and the same. Consuelo and Albert marry. The happy couple are last seen on the site of the Castle of Giants which has been dismantled and sold. Consuelo wears a gypsy costume; she lives a rustic life. Albert looks and talks like an oriental sage.[49]

Some biographers of Sand seem convinced that this fantasy of epic proportions is her finest and her most popular novel.[50] Turgenev however found Consuelo, especially in *La Comtesse de Rudolstadt*, somewhat 'pédante', as he found Sand's other heroines.[51] Tolstoy thoroughly disliked the book. He regarded it as a 'mixed up rigmarole'.[52] What Pauline's friend and correspondent Julius Rietz made of it, history does not record.

The novel is replete with Liberty, Equality, Fraternity and other 'revolutionary' themes. It lambastes the monarchy and the Church as dragons of monarchical and clerical despotism. It includes much that might be

*Gertrude Mara had been imprisoned by Frederick the Great when she married the cellist who the King did not like.

regarded as Women's Lib, and describes most marriages as 'tombs of love' and 'legalised prostitution'.[53]

It has been said that 'the heroine is composed partly of what Pauline Viardot was, and partly of what George wanted her to become. She is modest, gentle, noble, selfless and generous. She is "a pure and holy girl, a Saint Cecilia returned to this world", a person "with whom the world fell in love as soon as they heard her sing" '. Pauline entirely approved of her portrait. She dutifully strove to copy it and to realise George's fictional concept of her.[54] Whether she succeeded or not, and for how long, we shall see.

Pauline's friends and supporters were troubled by George's influence on her. One evening, Pauline was at a dinner in London at which Liszt was also a guest. He took her on one side and had a quiet but firm conversation with her about George, her love of intrigue and gossip and her 'deplorable lack of sincerity'. Pauline, while first defending George, protested that she was not particularly tied up with her.[55]

Indeed, if one wanted to protect one's reputation, one would not choose the notoriously promiscuous novelist as one's best friend. The following dialogue, reported, as one might expect, by the scurrilous Edmond de Goncourt, illustrates the kind of reputation she developed. Sand furiously told her son-in-law, who was a sculptor, that she would make public his appalling conduct. He casually replied that, if so, he would do a sculpture of her (at very best) arse, with which the public was already well familiar.[56]

Later in life, George Sand seems, to her friends at least, to have radiated wonderful qualities. She had charm and a love of humanity, even goodness which Turgenev would later call 'saintliness'.[57] However, before mid-century, by no stretch of the imagination was Sand a suitable confessor for a girl half her age.

By the time George Sand wrote *Consuelo*, Pauline had found her Albert and had married Louis Viardot. In the next chapter we must turn to him and his 'best friend', the distinguished and fashionable painter Ary Scheffer.

CHAPTER 5

Louis

Maybe the person who introduced Pauline to George Sand was Louis Viardot. (Plate 1). He was a 'Garcia' enthusiast who, when aged nineteen, had gone without food in order to afford the 30 sous* for the ticket to see Pauline's father performing in *Don Giovanni*.[1]

Louis had been Maria Malibran's confidant. When she tried to break off an engagement at the Théâtre-Italien, claiming poor health, he had been asked 'to use his influence with the capricious cantatrice' to persuade her to relent. George Sand also found Louis an ideal person to turn to for help when her husband tried to seize possession of the children.[2] George encouraged Louis to marry Pauline.

Louis was small in height. He had none of the good looks of Consuelo's first boyfriend, Anzoleto. Apart from Saint-Saëns, who sported a similarly large hooked nose, nobody thought that Louis was handsome. Wags suggested that his large nose might actually cause him to tip over at any moment.[3]

Louis has been described as 'an old young man'. But there was nothing young about Louis. He was 21 years older than Pauline. He was possibly rather similar to Councillor Jaubert who was 24 years older than his wife. Louis's erudition, his left-wing politics, his agnosticism, and not least his obsession with shooting and his secondary role in life have left the image of someone who was pedantic, priggish and rather absurd. Two years before his engagement to Pauline, he had been engaged to another girl, but had

*There were 20 sous to a franc.

broken off the engagement when he found that her political views were 'wrong'. She was a supporter of the restoration of the Bourbons.[4]

Louis's republican reputation and his tendency to shun high society would rebound on Pauline. The combination of Louis as a husband and George Sand as a confidante was unlikely to further Pauline's career which, to a great extent, was dependent on support from the establishment. Some writers think the effect was disastrous.[5]

Louis's eldest daughter found her father cold, strict and frightening. Yet he was no more so perhaps than any other 'Victorian' father. Pauline said that although he appeared 'very cold, he is not so. His heart is warm and good, and his mind is far superior to mine.' She went on, 'his sole fault is that he lacks the childlike element, the impressionable mood'.[6]

Yet Louis did not lack a sense of humour. He could laugh and joke till he cried, according to his daughter Louise, especially when he was observing the mannerisms of those across the Channel. His description of the stuffy English, their women who are determined to go out into the rain in unsuitably flimsy dresses, their unspeakable Chinese tea, their slavish obedience to regulations[7] of which no sensible self-respecting European takes any notice, is in several respects modern.

In later life, Louis struggled with lumbago, which may have given the impression that he was somewhat fuddy-duddy. However, Dickens regarded him as 'an extremely good fellow'.[8] And he was certainly no prude. He participated to the full in lively 'after dinner' male conversation.

For example, in the 1850s Louis wrote to Turgenev about the chamberlain of the notoriously oversexed Napoleon III who had importuned an actress on behalf of his master. The actress skittishly said she would need to be paid six times her normal price because she would need to acquire some special lingerie. To encourage the chamberlain to agree her fee, which he did, she said she would show him the three fish. When she came out of the Emperor's room, the chamberlain asked her to comply with her undertaking. She lifted her skirts in front and said 'brill' (a bearded fish), then, displaying her back-side, said 'ray' (the word in French also means furrow); then she led the aristocrat to the mirror where she pointed at him with her finger and said 'mackerel'. 'Maquereau' is slang for a pimp. In politer usage, it denotes an oily fish associated with lubricity.[9]

This very French story may seem unnecessarily crude and lewd for a man who was a conscientious and successful author. Louis had already published *The History of the Moors in Spain* and translations of *Don Quixote* and of Cervantes's short stories. Louis's two volumes of Cervantes's hilariously funny novel ran to nearly 1,500 pages or 700,000 words, as did the German translation published around the same time. Later, he translated a Pushkin novel from Russian.[10] His *Apology of an Unbeliever*, a short book, 'drawn from numerous ancient and modern classical sources',[11] went into three editions and was translated and published in London, surely an indication of both quality and commerciality.

Because of Pauline's later relationship with Turgenev, Louis's literary skills are sometimes compared with those of the Russian; even more so, because Louis wrote *Souvenirs de Chasse* and Turgenev wrote *Sketches from a Hunter's Album*. This comparison is bad luck on Louis; moreover, it is unfair. *Souvenirs de Chasse* is a travel book which tells of Louis's own hunting experiences in countries such as Spain, Hungary, Russia, Prussia and England. Turgenev's *Sketches* are a series of realistic short stories about characters and situations.

Louis, whether up to his knees in the River Guadalquivir escaping from a herd of *toros*, or describing the Spanish priesthood at work sponging off the agricultural labourers, wrote fluently in a rather jolly, hearty style. He also writes with considerable humour, especially when again describing the oddities of the English, or the military approach to shooting in Prussia, where everything is done precisely as if by order.[12]

Louis himself was a shrewd businessman, and George Sand sought his advice from time to time. His business interests seem to have ranged from the manufacture of tricycles to the publication of pocket-size books which could easily be read on the railways. Louis was also an art connoisseur and even the English, whose art he much disparaged, recognised him as a well-known art critic and published his work.[13] He wrote a series of books about museums in Europe, in which he observed that the pictures at Hampton Court were second-rate, and that those in the Hermitage and the National Gallery were a hotchpotch of masterpieces and mediocrities. He suggested that the pile of royal gifts in the Prado should be reorganised. He particularly liked fifteenth-century Florentine art.[14] He assembled his own 'small, but choice, collection of pictures'. His Rembrandt, *The Butcher's Shop*, he later presented to the Louvre.[15]

Turgenev once wrote to Louis saying that he had found the original of one of his pictures. This was a painting by José de Ribera, the Spanish baroque painter who settled in Naples and whose style was marked by dramatic realism of the kind which was likely to appeal to both Louis and Turgenev. When confronted with the suggestion that his was a mere copy, Louis exploded and expostulated that his picture was of course the original.[16] No doubt the Louvre checked out the provenance of his Rembrandt.

Louis had a 'passion, amounting almost to a mania, for shooting', or hunting, as it is called on the Continent. According to Pauline, all his dreams were of this obsession, which he had enjoyed since going out with his father at the age of five.[17] At least Louis's dreams were of conventional game, in contrast to those of another great sportsman Giacomo Puccini whose taste in quarry was more rounded. Puccini was a notorious womaniser as well as an excellent shot.

Louis genuinely cared about the countryside and wildlife. He enjoyed fresh air, the country way of life, going into fields and forests, over rivers and mountains, sleeping rough in a cabin, and eating black bread. Shooting enabled him, like Turgenev, to indulge his passion for gun dogs whose bravery and tenacity he admired. The sport also enabled him to get away from the beaten track and the towns and to meet all classes of society.[18]

When we read of Louis participating in the slaughter of a bear and four young ones, personally killing two fifteen-month-old cubs, one stabbed with his poignard, we can admire him for his daring. Equally, we may raise an eyebrow with surprise. We can wonder how a man as obviously sensitive as Louis could, with no compassion, fell a stag surrounded by hinds and fawns.[19]

It is difficult for many people today to tune in to someone who regarded Russian moose and bears, Hungarian wolves, Prussian boar and English partridge and pheasants just as objects created for his destruction. For Louis, the number slaughtered was a measure of 'sporting' success. He could jest at the success of a friend who shot 1,600 grouse in one year being comparable to the *mille e tre* women who, Leporello claims, were bedded '*in Ispagna*' by Don Giovanni.[20]

Louis was born in 1800. He came from that solid provincial professional background which had produced some of the leaders in the French Revolution. Louis's father was a leading, somewhat too liberal, lawyer in Dijon. He died when he was young, leaving Louis's mother and her five children in considerable poverty. Opportunities for liberal-minded people were not enhanced by the restoration of the monarchy in 1814–15.[21] It was a difficult time. Louis set out to follow in his father's career, but soon turned to journalism.

In 1823, a French army restored the King of Spain who returned to Madrid 'sitting on a chariot twenty-five feet high drawn by a hundred men in green and pink livery'.[22] Louis, who was doing his compulsory military service at the time, was sent to Spain, where he had always wanted to go. As an anti-monarchist, he was relieved to find himself assigned to the supply train. He was in charge of the stores in a Seville munitions factory.[23]

When he returned to Paris, Louis became a journalist. He supported republicanism. He advocated the granting of more rights to the workers who, despite their aspirations, had not seen much improvement in their lot. He participated in the July Revolution of 1830, 'Les trois glorieuses', when the last of the three Bourbon brothers, the excessively conservative and religious King Charles X, was expelled and replaced with King Louis-Philippe. Louis Viardot was in charge of the occupation of the Préfecture de Police. During the July Monarchy, he was on the left wing of politics and journalism. He held various minor positions, such as secretary of the revolutionary committee for Spain.[24]

The July Monarchy rapidly became extremely unpopular, as the money-grubbing bourgeoisie got richer, while at least two-thirds of the population remained on or below the breadline.[26] Louis Viardot worked on various journals; the *Globe*, the *National* and the *Revue républicaine*. Some of his colleagues would later become influential, such as Adolphe Thiers, who later became President of France, Pierre Leroux, the writer on philosophy and politics, and Sainte-Beuve, the outstanding critic and literary historian. In 1837, Louis stood as a candidate for the legislature, but he was not elected. However, there was no let-up in his activity. Shortly after his wedding, he published a paper on food tariffs in England, the so-called 'corn laws', as hot a topic in politics as the European common agricultural policy today and not dissimilar in subject matter.[27]

Les Trois Glorieuses and the July Monarchy

Charles X was the younger brother of the guillotined King Louis XVI. He was also a brother of King Louis XVIII who replaced Napoleon at the time of the Restoration and the Battle of Waterloo. When he came to the throne in 1824, Charles was aged almost 67.[25] By then, he was a reformed libertine and a religious bigot. He was an incompetent ruler and was served by very bad advisers. He abdicated in 1830 following the uprising of 27–29 July, *Les trois glorieuses.* He was succeeded by a distant cousin, Louis-Philippe, a descendant of Philippe Duc d'Orléans, the brother of Louis XIV. Louis-Philippe, who was proclaimed King by Lafayette, the general who in 1781 had defeated the British at Yorktown in Virginia, had impeccable credentials. He was the son of 'Philippe Egalité' who had voted for the death of Louis XVI, and who later himself went to the guillotine. Louis-Philippe called himself King of the French, and was ridiculed for his pear-shaped head, his bourgeois attitudes and tendency to carry an umbrella.

By the mid- to late 1830s, the régime in Paris had lost all semblance of control. The authorities closed down several newspapers and magazines, and discouraged demonstrators by using the newly-invented technique of drenching them with water. There were several attempts at assassinating the King. The first of these was in July 1835, when the terrorist used an 'infernal machine' of 25 linked rifle barrels. The King got away. However, fourteen were killed including a twelve-year-old girl. Within a year there was another attempt, again unsuccessful.[28] Louis Viardot would quip that the only time he would say 'Vive le Roi' was when he got an invitation to a royal shoot.[29]

On 14 January 1838 the Salle Favart, which housed the Théâtre-Italien at the time, was engulfed in flames and burnt down. Fire was a chronic hazard in theatres. The blaze had illuminated most of Paris when the Théâtre de l'Odéon went on fire, at the turn of the century. The introduction of gaslight, at first at the Opéra in 1822, increased the risk.[30]

The fire of 1838 broke out during a performance of *Don Giovanni*, in which Grisi was starring. The cause was possibly the fireworks used to illuminate 'the infernal gulf into which the commandant hurls the profligate'.[31] The director of the theatre, Carlo Severini, was killed when he tried to jump from a window to escape from his flat, which was up at the top of the theatre.[32]

A new director was needed. It comes as a surprise that Louis Viardot was selected, because he was 'a reactionary in music', at least according to Saint-Saëns. Although he had written some lyrics for songs, he found the music of Beethoven 'too advanced'. He did not get much beyond Mozart. Louis would later say that music festivals in England gave him terrible musical indigestion,[33] which provides an interesting measure of his musicality.

However, Louis's appointment may have been a commercially astute move. He possessed considerable business acumen. He had good connections, especially with Spaniards. It seems probable that his appointment was required by a Spanish banker who shared Louis's taste for pictures. This banker was an important donor for the Théâtre-Italien. Such sponsors expect the objects of their patronage to be run properly and efficiently. Louis would be a reliable administrator for the Théâtre-Italien.[34]

Louis's first task was to find somewhere for the company to go, and he selected the Théâtre de l'Odéon, down the Boulevard Saint-Germain on the Left Bank. George Sand thought it highly regrettable that the Théâtre-Italien should be relegated to the Latin Quarter. Louis needed to provide a specific attraction in order to bring in the audience, so he decided to engage Pauline to perform. When the Garcias were in London, they were called upon by him for this purpose.[35]

This was the worthy yet complex man who George Sand intended for the girl she described as her 'reine du monde'. Despite her recent celebrity Pauline, a professional musician, an actress, could well find it difficult to lead 'to the altar', as opposed to bed, anyone more exciting.[36] In any event, Louis made a far preferable alternative to Musset. The poet promptly drew a hilarious and lengthy comic strip in which he depicted the bridegroom, with his enormous toucan-like proboscis, endeavouring to win acceptance for his proposal from the bride and her family.[37] That Musset went to such trouble is, in itself, telling.

Pauline, according to the custom of the time, could theoretically choose whether or not to marry Louis. Pauline's mother thought Louis was too old, but Madame Sand ensured that her protégée took a positive approach to the proposal.[38]

The marriage took place on 18 April 1840, after the Paris opera season had ended. The ceremony was held at the Mairie of the Second Arrondissement, in which Pauline was born.[39] Weddings were then relatively quiet family events. Victor Hugo tells us that the French had not yet imported English habits such as 'exposing the bridal couple to a hailstorm of worn-out slippers and old shoes, in imitation of Marlborough's wedding at which a ferocious aunt assailed the bridal pair in this way as a gesture of good luck'.

WALPURGISNACTSTRAUM ou noces d'or d'Obéron
et de Titania.

Musset's cartoon: Louis leads his three sisters in to the registry for his marriage to Pauline

The normal routine was for a banquet to be held after the civil ceremony. The union was consummated in the domestic nuptial chamber. In those days, the French did not head straight off on honeymoon. They did not yet appreciate 'the sheer bliss, on that most mysterious and sacred of all nights, of clattering and bumping along to an inn, to consummate one's marriage while in an adjacent chamber the cabman tries to seduce the serving wench'.[40]

Given that neither the bride nor bridegroom was religious, we can assume that the Viardots did not adopt the usual routine of attending a church service alone on the following morning.[41]

That the couple were then hardly in love was to be expected and normal. However, it was not long before even George Sand, the expert in the secrets of the four-poster, found Pauline's 'love' for Louis hard to fathom. It was 'tendre, chaste, généreuse, grande sans orage (unstormy), sans enivrement (without intoxication), sans souffrance (suffering), sans passion en un mot'.[42] Pauline considered that no emotion at all was better than emotion which might be painful, inconvenient or, in particular, which might interfere with the smooth running of her career and her mission to use her art as a medium through which to reveal the great truths of life. This was the central tenet of her life.

George attributed this characteristic of Pauline's to 'the profound egoism of the first-class artist'. She began to wonder whether Pauline was capable of much love at all.[43] But more of that later.

Louis now became Pauline's business manager. He devoted himself to her, rather as she devoted herself to him.[44] He had assumed a considerable task. He was responsible by law for the administration of his wife's property. In this era, she owed him obedience, whereas he owed her only protection.[45]

The unusual feature in the Viardot match was that Pauline provided the potential to generate enormous earnings from her work. Unlike the relatively passive yield from an heiress, this source of income needed active exploitation if the cash was to flow. To avoid any conflict of interest between fulfilling his duties at the Théâtre-Italien and managing the commercial interests of his wife, Louis resigned his post and was 'charged with an important mission by the Minister of the Interior relative to the fine arts'.[46]

The Viardots went on a trip to Italy. In Rome they visited the Villa Medici, where all those laureates who had won the coveted Prix de Rome were required to spend a couple of years. The French Government had established this prize under the auspices of the Académie Royale des Beaux-Arts, a section of the Institut de France which also included other academies, such as the Académie Française and academies for sciences, moral and political science, and belles-lettres. The prize was awarded* in music, painting, architecture, sculpture and engraving, and was intended to enable young French artists, aged below 30, to study for five years without financial worry. The prizewinners received 3,000 francs for each of five years, and were required to spend their first two years in Rome and their third year in Germany.[47]

Young Gounod playing Don Juan de Mozart:
from a drawing by Ingres

The director who presided at the Villa Medici was the prominent painter Jean-Auguste-Dominique Ingres. He asked Pauline to sing an aria from Weber's opera *Der Freischütz.* In this, she was accompanied by a young laureate by the name of Charles Gounod, who condescendingly recorded in his memoirs that he 'was amazed at the wonderful talent of that child'. We may assume Gounod shared with Pauline his views on Italy. Rome, he thought, was a 'veritable provincial city, ordinary, colourless and

*The examination included various set works. The musicians first had to work up a vocal fugue. If they got through that round, they were required to compose a cantata for two voices and orchestra. For the short-listed landscape painters, a tree had to be painted; after that, a historical subject. Surprisingly, some great artists actually won it, although, as in the case of Berlioz, generally not without difficulty or contention.

dirty almost everywhere'. It 'invites to meditation, Venice to dissipation. Venice is a passion, not a love, Naples is a smile'.[48] The precious Gounod never lacked charm, as we shall see.

Back in Paris, Pauline had to accustom herself to organising the linen and housework, and also to integrate with Louis's sisters, 'les pas trop belles soeurs',* Jenny, Nanine and Berthe. Perhaps with these, particularly the spinsterish Berthe, in mind, Turgenev later described a typical maiden aunt who had a wrinkled face. She 'came rolling in on her fat little feet'. 'An old maid, she smelt of camphor, like a piece of clothing that has been lying for a long time in moth balls'. The Viardot sisters had a passion for birds and dogs. In their apartment, there was a shrieking parrot and a pair of turtle-doves which flew around leaving their visiting cards; there was also a small, but smelly and grossly overweight dog, like a Pekinese. There were also mice for which saucers of bread soaked in milk were strewn around the floor.[49] It must all have seemed very unfamiliar to the young singer who was not yet nineteen years old.

Had Louis stayed in his post at the Théâtre-Italien, he would have had a rocky ride. It was the preserve of Giulia Grisi who was not going to allow anyone else, let alone the director's wife, to elbow her way in and displace her. Grisi sang many of the roles which Pauline also sang, such as Desdemona from *Otello* and Donna Anna and Zerlina from *Don Giovanni.*

Grisi was, as we know, outstandingly beautiful. She had a superb and even voice. She therefore dominated, and deserved to dominate, the Paris and London opera stage in the mid-thirties and mid-forties.

There was no room for Pauline as well. If Grisi and Persiani ensured that the Théâtre-Italien was a closed shop, or if Pauline's fee was too demanding, perhaps there was always the Opéra? No; the incomparably bitchy Rosine Stoltz saw to that. The besotted director sacrificed everything; actors, musicians, and eventually himself for Rosine.[50]

The opera world of Paris, then the musical, literary, intellectual and scientific capital of Europe,[51] was essentially closed to Pauline. So, Pauline did occasional work. Thus we find the Viardots organising a charity concert for the benefit of victims of the terrible floods around Lyon. It was

*This ambiguity was used by Pauline in a letter to George Sand. A 'belle soeur' is a beautiful sister; a 'belle-soeur' is a sister-in law.

badly attended. It competed with similar charity concerts, including one organised by the now elderly Madame Récamier, the doyenne of the salon hostesses. Pauline also sang in salons and at court before the King.[52]

The only place for her to reach her potential and perform her art was in London, and by singing in concerts and going on tour. This is what she did. Meanwhile, Louis had introduced her to his 'best friend',[53] Ary Scheffer.

Years later, Pauline herself would describe how, before their engagement, Louis asked Scheffer what he thought of Mademoiselle Garcia. 'Dreadfully ugly', was the response; 'but if I were to see her again, I should fall madly in love with her'.[54] Pauline must have radiated an irresistible magnetism.

At this time, Scheffer was in his late forties, five-and-a-half years older than Louis. He was a painter of 'lachrymose and sugary pictures', who was then acknowledged as 'the most effective living painter' in religious art,[55] in which 'leaving dogma for morality, and restoring sacred history with the ideas of his own century, he endeavoured to found a fresh school of religious philosophy'.[56] At least, that is what Louis Viardot said, whatever it may mean. Today, two flights above the *Venus de Milo*, the visitor to the Louvre obtains some insight into this as he faces Scheffer's vast canvas *La Tentation du Christ.* The gallery is worth a visit because, as well as other Scheffer pictures, nearby there is Delacroix's own self-portrait and his evocative, well-known picture of Chopin. In the adjoining gallery are several works by Ingres, including *Cherubini and his Muse.*

Scheffer's mother Cornélia, who was Dutch, came from a line of painters; his father was German.[57] Ary took an active part in the revolution of July 1830. He served under Lafayette, the kingmaker of Louis-Philippe, to whose children Ary taught drawing. Apparently Ary rode through the barricades with the message asking Louis-Philippe to accept the throne. As the July Monarchy progressed, Scheffer became disillusioned with the bourgeois King. One therefore wonders whether to believe a nineteenth-century writer and friend of Scheffer who claimed that, when the King fled in 1848, Scheffer hailed some cabs to get the King and his family away.[58] Scheffer had exhibited in Amsterdam before he was twelve years old. He had moved to Paris around 1811. There, he had been a fellow-student with Delacroix, although their styles were completely different.[59] Scheffer's

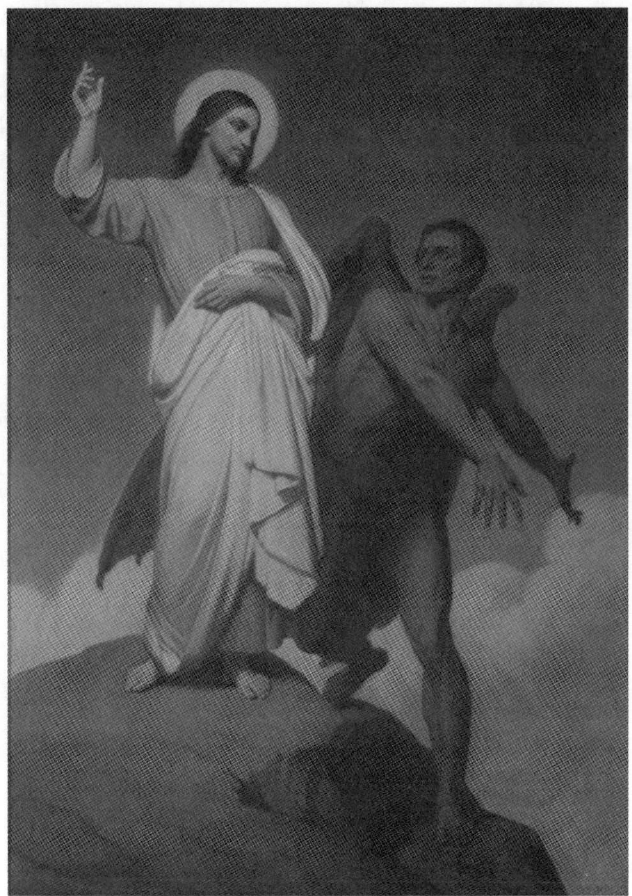

Ary Scheffer, *La Tentation du Christ*

series of paintings illustrating *Faust*, such as *Margaret at the Spinning Wheel*, were particularly popular, as was *The First Kiss* and *Francesca da Rimini*. Later in life Scheffer turned to religious subjects. It has been said of his works that 'the charm and facility of their composition could not save them from the condemnation provoked by their vapid sentiment'.[60] However, Scheffer's vision was far wider. In the 1830s, he made his atelier available to the young Théodore Rousseau, whose influential works were consistently and contentiously rejected by the selectors for the Paris Salon. Rousseau was responsible for bringing the study of nature, realistic rather than stylised, back into landscape painting.[61]

Scheffer's studio in the Rue Chaptal attracted leading politicians and celebrities. His pictures commanded enormous prices. A copy which he made of *Francesca* was bought for 1,100 guineas.* The purchaser, an English peer, thought that it was the original.[62]

Pauline's drawing of Ary Scheffer

Scheffer was a workaholic who also loved music. In 1843, Pauline published a book of her own compositions illustrated with lithographs by him. He became her spiritual mentor, a father figure for her.[63] Pauline would also play the piano at his dinner parties. After one, the writer Jules Janin told his daughter that she played Mozart and Beethoven until midnight.[64]

*By way of comparison, the annual salary of the editor of a daily newspaper could be around £1,000 in the mid 1840s. Patrick O'Connor, murdered in the Bermondsey murders in 1849, at the time of *Le Prophète*, was paid an annual salary of £300 as a gauger, a Customs and Excise officer who measured the contents of casks.

In the next eighteen years, Scheffer was someone upon whom Pauline could lean. They became so close, indeed, that some people suspected that they had an affair. She had lost her father, and was married to a husband who was more than twenty years older than her. Scheffer would always provide Pauline with 'the sustaining and kind love of a father'.[65] She came to adore him like a daughter.

CHAPTER 6

TOURS

PAULINE WAS VIRTUALLY ostracised from the opera stage in Paris. She set forth on a life of relentless touring, a long hard slog. She did this for two reasons. First, she was the income-provider for both herself and Louis; and secondly, she had an urge to be an evangelist for her art. The tours took the newly married couple first to England and then to Spain.

The slog would be made considerably easier by new technology. The pace of change in the 1830s and 1840s was phenomenal. Those years saw the widespread introduction of the railways, photography and the electric telegraph. While Pauline travelled around, teams of men were building embankments, tunnels, bridges and viaducts. Evidence of railway construction was to be seen everywhere. As we would expect, this caused delay and disruption, but it would enable travel to places which would not have been accessible before, and in a reasonable time.

Louis marvelled at this miracle. He could be 'hurled into space' on the Manchester to London Railway.[1] On the line into Bristol, which had just opened, he could sit in a vast armchair and watch the world go by, without being jogged up and down or pitching and rolling. He wondered, as do all generations, where new technology, these 'huge horses of civilisation devouring coal and spewing flame', would lead.[2]

Rail travel was a rather different experience from that with which we are familiar. Until 1844, trains going out of the terminus in Euston Square in north London had to be winched on a hawser up to Camden Town; those going in had to be lowered down by brakemen.[3] An 'express' might travel at around 26 mph although, later in the century, the non-stop journey from Paddington to Swindon, on the way to Gloucester, could be travelled in less than an hour and a half at a speed of over 50 mph.[4] For Louis, this technology would indeed open up new vistas. Soon, he could be hunting on a Friday morning near Paris; on the Saturday night, he could be in Thetford, Norfolk, on a shoot with the Baring banking family.[5]

New Technology

The railway was 'England's gift to the world'. The 'miraculous railroads, that are the talk of all nations',[6] evolved from the trams used in the English coalmines. The Stockton and Darlington Railway opened in 1825, and the Liverpool to Manchester line five years later. Planning for railways in France began in the early 1830s, and the first line opened in Prussia in 1835. By the early 1880s, 17,000 miles of railway were open in France.[7] Steam power also accelerated the Atlantic crossing. In April 1838, the Great Western steamship did the New York run in fifteen days, half the time it took sailing boats. Many felt that mankind was growing too noisy and commercial and there was no room left for spiritual peace.[8]

Photographs, or daguerreotypes, began to circulate in Paris around 1839, the year in which the first camera was made in England. In that year, Fox Talbot presented his photographic process to the Royal Society.[9] By 1850, a gentleman in Cumberland could use sun-pictures to copy his art collection. By 1870, Pauline had already assembled a collection of photographs of celebrities.[10]

Telegrams began to be available in mid-century. In May 1844 Morse's message, 'What hath God wrought!' was transmitted between Washington D.C. and Baltimore. Four years later, the lines between Paris and Calais, and Dover and London, were used to alert Louis-Napoléon about news of the 1848 uprising in Paris. For Pauline, the telegram became an everyday and convenient means of communication.[11]

Rail travel could however be fraught, so much so that some people, such as Rossini, refused to use it as a means of transport.[12] Accidents happened frequently.[13] The soprano Henriette Sontag and her troupe were proceeding from Glasgow to Aberdeen when they collided with a snowdrift near

Laurencekirk. Fortunately, the party found its way through the snow to the house of 'a hospitable farmer'.[14] In a modern twist, Pauline's daughter joined an action group to sue the Belgian state for damages she incurred in a crash between Brussels and Paris.[15] She received no compensation. Dickens was amazingly fortunate to find his coach suspended in mid-air when the 7am boat-train from Paris was derailed on a viaduct at Staplehurst in Kent. He thus avoided being among the ten killed and many injured. According to the *Illustrated London News*, the scene was 'a sight perfectly appalling'. Some of those killed were smothered by the 'liquid mud' in the 'ditch' into which the coaches were precipitated. Pauline, who some years later was involved in a railway accident, wrote to Dickens to commiserate; he told her that whenever he was in a train travelling at speed, he now felt as if the carriage was going to tip over. He also said he would arrange for her to be sent a complimentary copy of *Our Mutual Friend*, when it was ready.[16]

Back to February 1841. The Viardots took the sea-sickening four-hour journey across the Channel on a steamboat.[17] Pauline spent five months in England performing in operas by composers such as Rossini, Bellini and Cimarosa. According to Liszt, the quality of the music in London that year was unexceptional. Even there, Pauline could not leave opera politics entirely behind. She looked forward to her 'duel' in which she would play the masculine Romeo opposite a Juliette played by the exquisite Grisi. Nobody else, apart from Pauline, seemed too excited about this.[18]

Pauline was well-received and she had Louis with her. Nevertheless, the teenager was lonely and unhappy, emotions still familiar to many a foreigner or provincial who moves to London for the first time.

The poet Shelley compared Hell to London. 'Reeking London's smoky cauldron'[19] was indeed a miserable place, as portrayed by Dickens. 'Fog everywhere. Fog up the river, where it flows among green eyots and meadows; fog down the river, where it rolls defiled among the tiers of shipping, and waterside pollutions of a great (and dirty) city ... Gas looming through the fog in divers places in the streets.'[20] Or no fog, but the 'flat-fish, oyster, and fruit vendors linger hopelessly in the gutter, in vain endeavouring to attract customers; and the ragged boys, who usually disport themselves about the streets, stand crouched in little knots in some projecting doorway, or under the canvas blind of the cheesemonger's.'

We can read what it would have been like, when Pauline left the world of fantasy and emerged from the stage door to return to her lodgings at 184 Regent Street. 'It is nearly eleven o'clock, and the cold thin rain, which has been drizzling for so long, is beginning to pour down in good earnest; the baked-potato man has departed – the kidney-pie man has just walked away with his warehouse on his arm – the cheesemonger has drawn in his blind, and the boys have disappeared ... The little chandler's shop with the cracked bell behind the door, whose melancholy tinkling has been regulated by the demand for quarterns of sugar and half-ounces of coffee, is shutting up.'[21]

London was grim, ghastly. Foreigners noticed that the place smelt of horse-dung; however, the odour was often worse. The graveyards overflowed and emitted a horrible stench. In the slums, an average of 30 people crowded into small and decrepit houses, sometimes seven or eight families dwelling in one room.[22] So, we should beware of being too sorry for a young French opera singer in Dickens's London. While Pauline was receiving bursts of applause from the affluent audience, 'that wretched woman with the infant in her arms, round whose meagre form the remnant of her own scanty shawl is carefully wrapped, has been attempting to sing some popular ballad, in the hope of wringing a few pence from the compassionate passer-by. A brutal laugh at her weak voice is all she has gained. The tears fall thick and fast down her own pale face; the child is cold and hungry, and its low half-stifled wailing adds to the misery of its wretched mother, as she moans aloud and sinks despairingly down on a cold damp doorstep. The weak and tremulous voice tells a fearful tale of want and famishing; and the feeble singer of this roaring song may turn away, only to die of cold and hunger'.[23]

Pauline's self-indulgent loneliness manifested itself in an outburst to George Sand about how much she disliked the English, an indictment so stinging that one wonders whether it was driven by homesickness, or by self-pity induced by the realisation that, banished from Paris, this drudgery was what the world now had in store for her. Or perhaps Pauline's dislike of England was stoked by Ary Scheffer whose anglophobia was considerable, or possibly by her memories of her sister whose life the English had taken. Or maybe it was just that the French habitually disliked the English, then 'such a proud, insolent, scornful, conceited people, looking upon themselves as superior to all the rest of the world'.[24] The feeling was reciprocated. Since then, the mantle has been passed on.

Pauline would have liked George Sand to join her in London. However, George suggested that Pauline should visit her instead. Pauline did not make her invitation particularly attractive. She described, less graphically than Dickens, how London is a black, sad place, where the inhabitants are cold and unwelcoming, and where bad taste is pervasive.[25] Louis, contemptuous of the English stiffness and by their inflexibility about when shooting was permitted and when it was not,[26] was perhaps more tolerant. However, he continued to derive supercilious amusement from the English obsession with rules and regulations[27] and by the London season being held at the height of summer. During the months when everyone else leaves the town for the country, the English, 'toujours excentriques et seuls de leur espèce', quit the country for the town.*[28]

Chip-Chip with Pauline at the piano

*The English were generally the butt of much ridicule from Continentals, motivated partly by jealousy at English commercial and industrial success. Turgenev, having attended a farce in London at which the audience split their sides laughing, said that an Englishman laughing was not a pretty sight; he sounded like some machinery grinding to a halt. In Russia, the English were often called the Eyseyki, because of their frequent repetition of 'I say'.

Pauline was by now five months pregnant. However, she managed to spend a fortnight at Nohant with George Sand during August. Chopin wrote 'Madame Viardot was here for two weeks. We did all sorts of things other than music making'. They went for picnics and swam in the river. Pauline and Chopin would also spend hours together at the piano; commentators observe her influence on Chopin's music. Chopin's *Prelude in C sharp* opus 45 is said to be inspired by the broad melodic line of Pauline's mezzo-soprano voice.[29]

Soon, Pauline had to return to England to sing at the Three Choirs Festival. The Viardots travelled from London by train on the new railway line to 'Glocester', as Louis spelt it. He had some difficulty with English places. For him, Derby was famous for its race course, a fact which residents of Epsom might well contest.[30]

Pauline was still negative. She complained that, even in Gloucester, the air was so unhealthy that almost everyone was ill. 'England is a country which must be seen, but not lived in', declared Louis. Pauline could be contemptuous of the English audience. 'The audience this evening, for instance, knew that I am a "celebrity", so it applauded everything that I did with equal warmth. Had I sung not quite so well, it would have been no less satisfied'.[31]

Louis would later become more appreciative of England, at least when it was a question of shooting. And there is no doubt that, following behind his wife, he could visit places, museums and galleries where he would otherwise never have gone. He was interested to visit the schoolroom where 'Horace Nelson', the most hated name in France after William Pitt, carved his name before going to sea.[32]

Pauline knew that she had to keep going. As well as being the breadwinner, she believed that she was entrusted with a genuine mission to perform her art. In accepting this obligation, the role of Consuelo, she was responding to principles enunciated a decade earlier by the extremely influential Saint-Simonian movement.[33]

To achieve their utopia, the disciples of the eccentric Comte de Saint-Simon advocated change far more drastic than similar movements such as that led by Robert Owen, the Garcias's acquaintance from their Atlantic crossing. The Saint-Simonians called for a wholesale reorganisation of society which, in their view, should be led by prominent industrialists and scientists.

Although they were structured hierarchically, the original Saint-Simonians were 'way out' and hippy.[34] They permitted unorthodox personal relationships, provided that the union resulted in progress for the individual and society, a matter to be determined by their leader Barthélemy Enfantin.

Several of George Sand's friends, such as her colleague on the *Revue indépendante*, Pierre Leroux,[35] were involved with the movement, as were many musicians, notably Franz Liszt and the leading tenor Adolphe Nourrit. Bizet's wife's family, the Halévys, were at the top of the hierarchy.

The movement peaked around 1830. The authorities cracked down on it two years later, but its influence was enduring and considerable.

The Saint-Simonian philosophy evolved in the vacuum left by the French Revolution which annihilated, for many, the stabilising influence of state and Church. The state had provided an institutional framework to which human beings had to relate. The Church had said what their objectives should be, the values to which they should aspire.

Essentially, the Saint-Simonians argued that science can indicate what has to be done in order to achieve a *particular* objective. But only through feeling and emotion can the *appropriate* objective be revealed. Who creates feeling and emotion? The artist. Thus – and here is the big leap – the artist has a role similar to that of a priest in creating the ambiance in which people can identify the values to which they should aspire. Music, being the most communicative of the arts, with its potential to exalt people to higher ideals and to beautify their existence and surroundings, has a special role to play.*[36]

As George Sand had explained, Pauline's chosen profession, a 'priestess of perfection in music', was sacred, the loftiest which a woman could embrace. She was charged with a mission to convert the ignorant to beauty. Her art was light years distant from the sordid world, the 'dens of corruption', frequented by such as Rosine Stoltz. Pauline was stepping back in time to the dawn of religion, when the theatre and the church were one

*The Saint-Simonians would be intrigued by the use of music today as a means of educating and galvanising a mass audience so as to apply political pressure.

and the same sanctuary. That was when the Arts were born at the foot of the altar, the altar at which Pauline was expected to officiate.[37]

This elaborate philosophy was all very well. However, the Paris opera stage remained closed to Pauline. When there, she performed in concerts.

She was chosen to be among the soloists at the ceremony when Napoleon's remains were at last returned to Paris from St Helena. There was a magnificent state funeral, with the procession, pomp and circumstance that characterises such occasions. A vast orchestra and chorus performed the Mozart *Requiem.* With her on the platform were Grisi, Persiani, Stoltz, Rubini, Lablache and Tamburini, among others – the élite singers in Paris at the time.[38] The route began at the Arc de Triomphe which had been inaugurated four years before.[39] The massive arch was topped with a vast plaster statue of the Emperor. The procession passed along the Champs Elysées which was thronged with over half a million people; it then crossed the Seine to Les Invalides. Pauline was probably relieved to be inside, because the temperature outside was said to be 'fourteen degrees below zero'.[40]

At the end of October 1841, Pauline sang in the first performance of Rossini's *Stabat Mater*. The performance was held in private, in the home of the virtuoso pianist and piano manufacturer Henri Herz. She was not on stage at the public performance on 7 January 1842, when she was replaced by Grisi, 'that goose', as Sand called her.[41]

The replacement of Pauline was probably not intended as a slap in the face. She had more important things to occupy her. Her first daughter whose full name was Louise-Pauline-Marie, but who they called Louise or Louisette, was born on 14 December 1841. George, who was in the middle of writing *Consuelo,* suggested that if the air in Paris was poor, the child should be brought by her nurse to stay at Nohant.[42]

Childbirth was particularly disruptive for an opera singer. The Viardots did not have another baby for over ten years.[43]

By the end of February 1842 Pauline was back, performing at a concert at the Conservatoire. She sang an excerpt from Gluck's *Orphée*, a psalm by Marcello and an aria from *La Cenerentola.* On the following day, she took part in a concert given by Chopin. At this, she sang her own setting of La

Fontaine's *Le Chêne et le Roseau* with Chopin accompanying. Pauline, as we shall see, was a very competent composer. For Saint-Saëns, her compositions were 'highly creditable' and 'extremely original'. 'Her tastes were strongly futuristic', he said. Yet she was very self-effacing. Once she sang a Spanish popular song, 'a wild haunting thing with which one of the Rubinstein brothers fell madly in love'. It was several years before Pauline would admit that she wrote it herself. 'This admirable artist had a horror of publicity', wrote Saint-Saëns.[44]

In April 1842, Pauline and Louis set off for Madrid via Bordeaux. From there, they went south to Andalusia, to Granada. Pauline had some difficulty putting together a cast. The opera company had been disbanded and the tenor was in mourning for a relative. So the company Pauline assembled was half-professional, half-amateur. The audience in Madrid was captivated when, responding to yet another call for an encore, Pauline asked for the piano to be brought onto the stage. She then accompanied herself in a French Romance and some Spanish songs.[45]

Pauline was happy in Spain, the land of her forebears. She enjoyed the sunshine. It helped that Louis had friends there whom he had met while on national service some twenty years earlier. Several were now in high places. Spanish politics had swung violently and bloodily backwards and forwards between the liberal supporters of the young Queen Isabella II on the one hand, and the Carlist* and Basque supporters of absolutism on the other.[46]

At the time of the Viardots' tour, the supporters of Queen Isabella were in the ascendancy. Pauline sang before the Regent who gave her some jewellery and tried to shock her with dirty stories.[47] She also sang before the eleven-year-old Queen who presented her with some diamonds. Pauline's frosty relations with the British continued after Pauline attended an opera at the Embassy. Tired and bored, she left before the performance was over. A Mrs Scott, who fancied her vocal prowess and was the lady of a prominent official, felt snubbed, even though the clock had struck one. Besides, Pauline was due to attend a rehearsal at 10am.[48]

*The three-year-old Isabella succeeded her father in 1833. Don Carlos, the Queen's uncle, had laid claim to the throne under the original Salic Law which excluded females from the succession. There was almost continuous civil strife. The Queen later became notorious for her depravity. She was exiled in 1868 and died in Paris in 1904 as 'the Countess of Toledo'.

Soon after the Spanish tour, the Viardots went to George's château at Nohant. They arrived in time to celebrate Solange Sand's fourteenth birthday, when they danced until one in the morning. Here, Pauline found her fans. George, Chopin and Delacroix had been discussing her unique and marvellous qualities. They had predicted how, one day, the public as well as the experts would come to appreciate them.[49]

Nohant

Real success still eluded Pauline. When she was at last engaged by the Théâtre-Italien for the 1842–3 season, her contract was mainly to perform secondary roles.[50] She was to be a foil to Grisi; she was to sing trouser parts which the feminine Grisi did not want. So, in October 1842, Pauline appeared in Paris as Arsace, the son and fiancé of Semiramide, Queen of Babylon, in Rossini's opera. Grisi was in the tragic title role. Pauline also appeared in *La Cenerentola*, *Tancredi*, *The Thieving Magpie* and Fioravanti's *Le Cantatrici Villane*.[51]

For Pauline, this Paris season was not a success. She rapidly learnt to face up to tough, wounding criticism. Critics did not like her tendency to embroider the music, not always with perfect notes. They criticised her prolonged trills which, wobbling both as to pitch and rhythm, were considered unattractive from a dramatic point of view.[52] In the December 1842 edition of the periodical, the *Revue des Deux Mondes*, the critic Henri Blaze de Bury seized the opportunity to finish off, once and for all, this aspiring opera singer. In a regular feature article, he declared that Pauline had failed to fulfil the great expectations which her supporters had held out for her. While he lavished praise on her rivals, he complained of Pauline's pathetic performance in *Semiramide* and of her petulance and puerility in *La Cenerentola*. Although her style might suit some literary salons, it had no place at the 'Bouffes'; that is, the Théâtre-Italien, he wrote. The critic then added a bowlful of salt to the wounds which he had inflicted. He recommended that Pauline take a leaf out of the book of Grisi and Lablache.

The knock-out blow was a recommendation that Pauline should stop seeking inspiration from cheap novels, where the characterisation is about as superficial as those 'vapoureuses nuances' which one encounters in the 'miniaturistic' piano works of 'Monsieur Chopin'.[53]

The Square d'Orléans in Paris, where Sand and Chopin had two separate but interconnecting apartments, erupted. There was an ulterior motive behind Blaze de Bury's attack. Louis Viardot, together with George Sand and one of her mentors, the thinker and writer Pierre Leroux,[54] had recently started up the *Revue indépendante*, a journal with socialist and republican leanings. This publication, for which Louis provided the financial acumen, created undesirable and increasing competition for the relatively bourgeois *Revue des Deux Mondes* which they considered had deserted the 'democratic' cause. The attack on Pauline provoked Louis to respond in a letter on 7 December 1842 to *Le Siècle*. He accused the critics of striking a woman in order to wound a man.[55]

The atmosphere when these protagonists came together at a soirée at the Rothschilds in January must have been entertainingly frosty. Pauline, Grisi, Mario and Lablache sang at this; Chopin played the piano. The audience of overdressed, slightly vulgar, super-rich Parisians, who we see in the portraits of Ingres,[56] must have felt they had got particularly good value that evening.

For Pauline, the message continued to be clear: stay away from Paris. So in April 1843, after a concert in Dijon, we find her in Vienna where, as in

Madrid, she was a colossal success as Rosina in the *Barber*. The scene with the music lesson gave Pauline the opportunity to dazzle the audience with her brilliant technique and also to feast them with her gorgeous lower notes.

However, the enormous personal cost of the Paris rejection can be gleaned from the correspondence with George Sand. Pauline's daughter, aged sixteen months, had been parked with George at Nohant, where her nurse was enjoying the attentions of Chopin's valet. George reported that Louise was teething, that she and Chip-Chip adored each other and, something that surely must have tugged at Pauline's heartstrings, that Louise was already calling George Sand 'Maman'. Pauline asked George's son Maurice to provide a sketch of her little child because she and her husband were beginning to forget what their daughter looked like.[57] Louise herself never quite recovered from her upbringing, as we shall see.

Even in Vienna, all was not plain sailing. The Italians did not like the way that Pauline was displacing their diva Tadolini in *La Sonnambula*. The public had split into two factions; the Italians on the one hand, and the Germans, who supported Pauline, on the other. The first Act was disrupted; in the second, the tenor unfortunately hit a wrong note which led to even more disruption; all this put Pauline off to the extent that her second aria was not sung well. She omits to say how she managed to get through the evening. Fortunately, she recovered, and at her last performance (yet again in the *Barber*), she was called out twelve times.[58]

Meanwhile Louis, in 'purgatory' because shooting was out of season, wisely escaped on a trip down the Danube, where he sagely observed that the roughest work was done by women.[59]

Pauline then laid on a benefit concert to raise money for a poor artist. The stars associated themselves with 'good works'. Grisi was made an honorary governor of Westminster Hospital in recognition of her charitable works.[60] Stoltz, of all people, was reputed to have founded a 'Maison de retraite' for repentant women.[61] A charitable image was perhaps in the course of a day's work.

At the beginning of July,[62] Pauline moved on to Prague where she sang in the *Barber* on three successive nights. She then went straight to Berlin, well known as another hotbed of intrigue and infighting. There, Meyerbeer had been appointed as the Prussian Generalmusikdirektor in the previous year.[63] This was a truly fraught position to hold. His distinguished predecessor, Gaspare Spontini, had long been locked in dispute with the opera management. Recently, Spontini had been howled off his rostrum and had received a nine-month prison sentence, after being convicted of slandering the King. Fortunately for the composer, the sentence was remitted.[64]

Pauline, however, received a tremendous welcome in Berlin. Meyerbeer was most impressed. He declared that he would do nothing for the Paris Opéra until she was engaged there. Like Liszt, he toyed with the idea of an opera based on *Consuelo*, for which the Château des Géants could be an ideal setting. Then, in August, Pauline went on to Leipzig.[65]

Not surprisingly, George wanted Pauline to come to Nohant to join Louise. She sent her directions about taking the train from Paris to Orléans and travelling onwards to Nohant by diligence. The journey now took less than twenty-four hours. It was even quicker if one gave 10 francs to the conductor to induce the postillions to shorten the stop for dinner. Later, with Sand's own solid and well-sprung charabanc, the journey could be done in eleven hours.[66]

Pauline Viardot by Henriette Legrand

On 25 August 1843, after five days and five nights travelling from Leipzig, the Viardots arrived in Paris. Pauline went down to Nohant with her mother, leaving Louis behind to fix up some important business.[67] The weather was good. Chopin said that there was hardly any singing at the piano, because they were out of doors most of the time.[68] It was a very short stay. On 10 September, Pauline, her mother and Louisette returned to Paris. They were accompanied at least as far as Orléans by Bouli, the nickname used for George's son Maurice, who was just under two years younger than Pauline.

Ten days later, Pauline was able to write to George that she had signed a contract with the Imperial Theatres at St Petersburg.[69]

Act Two

CHAPTER 7

RUSSIA

IN ST PETERSBURG during 1843, 'everyone' went to hear the performances of Giovanni Battista Rubini. Although said to be 'the greatest Italian tenor of the age', he was in his forties and rather past his prime. He was attempting to prolong his career.[1] When planning the next season with the Director of the Imperial Theatres, Rubini lit upon the idea of inviting young Pauline to provide the star attraction. The cast would also feature Tamburini, a well-worn baritone,[2] who had recently sung Doctor Malatesta in the première of Donizetti's comic opera *Don Pasquale* at the Théâtre-Italien. He was so much admired by Pauline that subsequently she kept a bust of him on the great chimneypiece in her château at Courtavenel.[3]

St Petersburg had recently attracted superannuated stars, such as the top soprano Giuditta Pasta. And over the years, there had been a trickle of distinguished musicians flowing into the city, such as the composers Domenico Cimarosa and John Field. Muzio Clementi went there to sell his pianos. The much younger Liszt, who was always a special case, had also performed there a few months before, as part of a self-imposed programme of relentless, far-reaching European tours.[4]

Pauline would be well compensated for agreeing to dilute the average age of the clutch of rather threadbare opera celebrities. At around 50,000 paper roubles,[5] just above 50,000 francs,[6] her fee was slightly less than the 60,000 roubles paid to Rubini, and the fee which Tolstoy tells us was paid to a star ballet dancer described in *War and Peace*.*[7]

*The tangible wealth of a middle-ranking merchant could be in the order of 56,500 roubles. All rouble

Pauline was also entitled to half the proceeds of a benefit performance. Later, this was increased to the full proceeds. Her fee was also raised to 65,000 roubles,[8] a little bit more than the annual salary which perhaps someone equivalent to a company director might expect to be paid.[9]

The signing of the contract for St Petersburg was a moment for some celebration. Equally, it could be interpreted as a confirmation of failure. Pauline's rival stars must have been delighted to hear that she was being rusticated to Russia for the winter. Even for Louis, who can only have been satisfied with the fee which he had negotiated, the winter weather restricted the scope for shooting.

What would Pauline have known of this far-flung place, apart from talking to her brother-in-law, Bériot, about his experiences there some four years before?[10] By the time that she signed her contract, the Paris bookshelves were well stocked with the Marquis de Custine's best-seller *La Russie en 1839* which was very topical, having caused an immediate sensation when published earlier in the year.[11]

The Marquis was a contentious and sad figure. He was the grandson of a general who waged war in the Rhineland on behalf of the Revolution and was subsequently guillotined. Almost twenty years before the book was published, the author was found unconscious in a muddy road having been mugged, ostensibly by a common soldier whom he had propositioned. Thereafter, he had the reputation of being 'France's most distinguished and notorious homosexual'. Tsar Nicholas I, outraged by the ingratitude demonstrated by his highly critical book, regarded him as a scoundrel, and several pamphleteers were assigned to expose his book's inconsistencies, inaccuracies and tactlessness. Custine was portrayed as a cad, and a pathetic one at that.[12] This reaction was neither surprising nor unique. A few months earlier, Dickens's critical *American Notes*, which were published following a tour in the United States, led the *New York Herald* to describe the English author's mind as 'coarse, vulgar, impudent and superficial'.[13] These are odd adjectives with which to describe the man who was to be England's pre-eminent novelist.[14]

figures and comparisons are exceptionally tentative for the reasons outlined in the Note on Money on page 511.

Whether Custine had some hidden agenda to support Polish nationalism,[15] or whether his contentious account of Russia and its peoples was accurate, does not really matter to us. His version represented the latest popular view circulating in Paris at the time that Pauline was about to go to Russia. Of course, like travel reports old and new, the book was full of wild generalisations.[16] We should not complain, because few travellers are guiltless of generalising as a national characteristic something which they chanced to see in a hotel or restaurant or on a street, or heard about from a taxi-driver. Thank goodness, especially when the comment is critical. Tales of others' travels would be even more insufferably boring without this aspect to leaven the dough.

Drawing upon Custine and various Russian novelists, we shall look at Russia: wintry, cold, vast and authoritarian. Its isolation and its obsession with secrecy did nothing to dilute its appalling image. The Russians were 'not yet civilised'. It was a country of 'regimented tartars'.[17]

It was a chilly prospect to be incarcerated for the winter in St Petersburg, a city frozen and blasted by icy winds. There was no question of taking Louise; St Petersburg was unhealthy. The city had a very high incidence of chest diseases,[18] and thus was a particularly unsuitable destination for an aspiring opera singer. 'Headcolds, cold sores, sore throats, fevers of all possible types' were normal in November, the time when Pauline would make her début.[19]

The average temperature in January was –10°C, whereas in Paris it was just above the freezing level. The last ship left St Petersburg for Le Havre in the first week of November.[20] From then until early April, the Neva in St Petersburg and the Moscow River were ice-bound,[21] which at least provided the advantage that residents could get to the other side by walking on planks.[22] Even in May, there could be snow. Usually the summer was roasting, yet we hear of the temperature around Midsummer's Day being 4°C. At that time of year, the white nights, the white starless sky, simply got on some people's nerves, as did the absence of sunlight, the dark days, in winter.[23]

Pauline would remember that the Seine had partially frozen during the cold winter of 1840–41. However, she had to think back well over ten years, to the time when her family had just returned to Paris from Mexico, to remember when the Seine was completely frozen.[24]

Without the dark, cold, freezing winter, Pauline might not have been invited to St Petersburg. It was a Court city, into which the Russian 'nobility' crowded in winter in order to escape from the boredom of their estates. Once there, they were effectively besieged by the weather for six months.[25]

The courtiers needed something 'in their luxurious setting of idleness' to occupy them, something to dispel boredom and to enable them to while away 'the long and unendurable day'. Opera and ballet, balls, dinner parties and even skating provided the smart set with a pretext for dressing up and meeting friends.[26]

During the opera performance, which was after they had dined at around half past four, the 'nobility' could tittle-tattle about 'the latest piece of news, the theatre and ill-natured gossip', provided they were not overtaken by sleep. They had no particular reason to expect Pauline's voice to be any different from that of any chorus-girl. After a couple of Acts, they would have seen everybody it was necessary to see. There would be no point in staying longer.[27] They would go home to eat, drink and gamble.

In some drawing-room, there might perhaps be a supper party in honour of the latest diva, such as Pauline. Tea would be taken from the samovar, a Russian ritual. (Some thought that the people were becoming noticeably feebler as a consequence of the growing popularity of this Chinese herb.) After the samovar, those present might be served from a table on which stood 'several kinds of vodka and as many kinds of cheese'. There would be 'several varieties of caviar and pickled herrings, preserves, and plates of French bread cut in very thin slices'. This was far more exotic and palatable than the dishes of jams and jellies, and glasses of bilberry wine, to be had at home in the manor house.[28]

How were the Viardots going to get there? Although St Petersburg was only 400 miles from Moscow, the distances in Russia seemed to be boundless. By the middle of the century, the empire covered one sixth of the land surface of the planet.[29] To Louis Viardot the Russian horses, going at 10 mph, seemed very fast and strong. They could do 35 miles in one stage, whereas in England a typical stage might be, say, 15 miles.[30] A troika of three horses, the equivalent of a sports car, travelling at high speed, might average twelve miles an hour.[31]

With the advent of the railways, transport would become appreciably better. By 1846, steamer and railway would put St Petersburg six days from Paris. Meanwhile, the Viardots faced the prospect of an arduous journey. The difficulties of getting into this isolated place were notorious, paralysed as it was with 'useless formalities', something which may not surprise those who apply for a visa today. The Viardots originally planned to travel via Lübeck and then take the steamer to St Petersburg. However, despite Custine's talk of 'the ruses and knavish tricks of the postmasters at every stage' and the customary habit of swindling foreigners,[32] the Viardots took the overland route via Berlin and Riga. Entry by land was said to be easier than by sea.[33]

The Schumanns, who arrived at St Petersburg towards the end of Pauline's first visit, also went by land, using the coach and sleigh. For them, the hotel accommodation on the way was appalling. In one room they dared not sit down because of the bugs and dirt. Robert Schumann's wife Clara wrote to her children 'We have driven in carriages and sleighs, across the ice of three rivers, all larger than the Elbe. There are many wolves in the forests here. They often appear beside the highway and watch the travellers as they pass, quite quietly.' Just as well. There were tales, probably exaggerated, of wolves gobbling up whole battalions of soldiers during Napoleon's 1812 campaign.[34]

Berlioz did the trip a few years later. His description of his four weary days and four weary nights does not sound encouraging. Never known for understatement in any means of communication, he described his sleigh-ride: 'In this hermetically sealed metal box, into which the snow dust succeeds in penetrating and powdering your face, you are ceaselessly and violently shaken, like shot in a bottle, the result of which is a great many contusions on the head and limbs, caused by perpetual shocks from the sides of the sledge.' He added 'I also suffered from an unspeakable discomfort and nausea that may fairly be called snow-sickness on account of its likeness to that produced by the sea.' Berlioz complained of the unbearable cold, 'towards the middle of the night, notwithstanding all one's fur bags, cloaks and pelisses, and the hay stuffed into the sledge'.[35] Fortunately, the Viardots' journey was in October when the weather might have been more slushy than icy. Before setting off, Pauline would have been well advised to go to the shops to buy herself some very warm clothes, including a full-length sheepskin-lined overcoat in which to travel.

Once in the country, the visitor was allowed nowhere without a guide. 'They refuse you nothing but accompany you everywhere; indeed, courtesy becomes a means of surveillance here', wrote Custine. If getting in was uncomfortable, getting out could be impossible. Nobody could leave unless their creditors had been warned by means of three newspaper advertisements inserted at weekly intervals. Post horses were not supplied unless an official certificate was provided to show that all bills had been paid.[36]

The Viardots must have visited the routine tourist spots. They went to the wooden cabin in which Peter the Great lived when he started to build the city, 140 years before. They were impressed by the contrast between the cabin and the opulent, vast Winter Palace in which the Tsar now lived.[37]

To Custine, the relatively modern city of St Petersburg was not particularly attractive. Significant buildings in the new capital, such as St Isaac's Cathedral, were still under construction. Custine's travel reports would not be read if they were wholly negative, so he did concede that there was something 'picturesque' about St Petersburg. However, for him it was 'a city without character, more grandiose than impressive, more vast than beautiful'. It was 'full of buildings without style, taste or historic interest'. He referred to 'the poor taste of its borrowed architecture' and he disliked the surrounding flat, marshy countryside. His jaundiced opinion shows how taste has totally changed, when contrasted with the glowing reports from the tourists who flock to St Petersburg today. 'Petersburg is Russian, but not Russia', Custine was told by Tsar Nicholas.[38]

Although for over 500 years the ancient Moscow had been a centre of power in its own right, it was from St Petersburg that the Tsar, the autocratic monarch, now dominated his vast and expanding realm. As Father of the People, god-like and far above criticism, everything depended on his Supreme Will.[39]

Like most royalty, the Tsar was egocentric.[40] 'It is easy to see that he cannot forget for a single instant who he is or the constant attention he excites', wrote Custine. The consequences are familiar. 'Bad news is suppressed, bad things are hidden, papered over or whitewashed. The obsequious courtiers continually conspire to pull the wool over the eyes of their master.' Those with any sense kept their mouths shut.[41]

Tsar Nicholas I

Beneath the Tsar, the country was administered with military discipline by the 'nobility'. Peter the Great had specified that the 'nobility' must be literate and must serve the state, either in the army or in the civil service, 'where the lack of practical knowledge was almost the highest qualification'. The 'nobility' was regimented into two Tables of Ranks, a military one and a parallel one for civilians. There were fourteen different classes. At this time, Classes I to V in the civil table constituted the hereditary 'nobility'. It was possible for a free man to be promoted up the ranks and thus achieve personal 'nobility' (for life) or even hereditary 'nobility'.[42]

Dostoyevsky's father, a doctor in Moscow's Maryinsky Hospital for the Poor, was promoted into the 'nobility'. He managed to buy 1,000 acres of poor quality land 100 miles south of Moscow, where the Dostoyevskys lived in a small thatched shack.[43]

As was customary in many countries, and still applies, the state and the

Church, 'the handmaid of despotism',[44] mutually reinforced each other in order to support their own spheres of power. Nearly 70 per cent of the population were Russian Orthodox. Less than ten per cent were Roman Catholic.[45] The Orthodox Church was fiercely jealous of its position, as it showed later when excommunicating Tolstoy who, in his later years,* opposed and criticised institutional Christianity.

As in any autocratic society, the penalties for infringing the rules were considerable. Pauline's great friend would soon discover this. The Tsar might exile you if, say, he heard that you had taken part in a duel or were reluctant to serve in his army. Exile to one's estates was a fearsome, lonely prospect.

It could be far worse. Criminals might be sentenced to imprisonment in Siberia, 'the graveyard of the living',[46] followed by a period of compulsory military service. In the prison, heads half-shaved, under threat of being flogged for any infringement, they were 'jammed like herrings in a barrel'.[47] In due course, we shall hear of Dostoyevsky's ghastly Siberian experience.

Custine's reports can only have caused considerable alarm in the Viardot household. He told of a Frenchman who was arrested at midnight; he was held for four days in solitary confinement and then languished for three weeks in prison with nobody daring to help him. Had it not been for a compatriot alerting the French ambassador, he might still have been there![48]

The 'nobility', who Pauline was in Russia to entertain, comprised about 600,000 persons of both sexes. This class constituted the top one per cent of the population.[49] Even then, the phrase 'landed gentry' may convey more to us than 'nobility', which sounds too exclusive and aristocratic. The wealth was very unevenly spread. Eighty per cent of this class owned fewer than 100 serfs, whereas Liszt's mistress, Princess Carolyne, had 30,000.[50]

There were, indeed, the grandees; great aristocrats such as the forebears of Tolstoy's mother who was a Princess Volkonsky. There were the fashionable classes, such as the Moscow ladies who shopped in the Tverskaya and Kuznetsky-Most, and the men who frequented the St Petersburg Yacht Club or the English Club in Moscow, where they could savour the atmosphere of 'repose, comfort and propriety' and 'leave their cares and anxieties

*The clergy were strictly prohibited from attending his burial in the grounds of his home. Institutionalised religion finds dissent difficult to cope with.

with their hats in the porter's room'. There were also the landed gentry in the provincial towns, who congregated in their local county council which was chaired by their local Marshal. His cockade of office and his cap with a red band belied his responsibility for mundane matters such as roads, schools and hygiene.[51]

Pauline will have been relieved to hear that the top layer of this upper class conversed in a just-about-intelligible French. The smartly-dressed wives wore French gowns. The upper classes drank their champagne suitably chilled, and their Château d'Yquem was carefully chambré. Indeed, the hero of Pushkin's poem *Eugene Onegin* had a French valet. 'The French are our Gods ... French dresses, French ideas, French feelings', it was said. Thankfully, there were also more Russian activities. There were 'trotting races and pancakes, bear-hunts and troikas and gypsies and carousals to the accompaniment of breaking glass'.[52] The neighbours might arrive in their sledges for a name-day celebration, have a great party, play cards, dance the waltz, the mazurka and the cotillion, and then doss down in the hall, the saloon, the maids' quarters or wherever else they fell.

Life in St Petersburg was of course not a succession of grand balls like the one depicted in the third act of Tchaikovsky's opera *Eugene Onegin*, or as portrayed in Tolstoy's *War and Peace*. However, Custine sensed that in the capital, despite much superficial grandeur and magnificence, there was hardly any joy. Beneath the surface, there was widespread corruption and sleaze.[53] Between the lines in *War and Peace*, we can read of discreet abortions carried out by a 'society' doctor.[54] Some members of the upper class were rich and powerful enough, as today, to use their wealth to screen the irregularity of their behaviour.[55]

For many of them, life was an uphill struggle. They found it very hard to make ends meet and to convert the value of their crops into the hard cash which was essential to exist in either of the capitals.[56] By contrast, the yield from 300 serfs was sufficient, at least for a time, to finance a totally idle life and 'lie about like a piece of dough'.[57]

The young gentry dreaded the lonely existence on their estates.[58] Those well-off enough headed to Moscow (Plate 3, *The Moscow Courtyard* by Polenov) and St Petersburg. The dough-like character had not been back to his estate for twelve years. Absentee landlordism and the failure to maintain and invest resulted in inevitable decline. The economy of an estate was reasonably self-sufficient when the owner resided on it. However, when he drew his income in cash to pay for his lifestyle in Moscow, St Petersburg, or indeed abroad, there were often insufficient resources to reinvest and maintain the country estate.[59]

We hear of an obviously down-at-heel princess. 'They have no carriage of their own, ma'am', says a servant, always the best connoisseur of class, 'and their furniture is very cheap'.[60] We hear of an elderly couple, living in a provincial town, stuck in a time warp. 'They were not rich but several times a year their peasants came to bring them poultry and provisions. On a certain day, the headman of their village came to present the rent and a brace of grouse.'[61]

The struggle to sustain the lifestyle did not prevent 'almost all Russian gentry being convinced of the exclusivity of their class, which was blessed with characteristics peculiar to them alone'.[62] The most typical might well be idleness. One fictional character declared 'Never in my life, thank God, have I had to pull a sock on my foot myself'. Indeed, if the sock was put on clumsily one just kicked the serf on his nose.[63] A novelist defined a new gentleman as 'the sort of master who puts on his socks and takes off his boots himself'.[64] Yet, despite their snobbery and loutish behaviour, the 'nobility' depended on the domestic serfs to operate the household, even to act as a bush telegraph to tell one part of the house what was going on in the other.[65]

Sandwiched beneath the 'nobility' and the serfs was an intermediate class. There were priests, who were almost a separate caste, and the progenitors of a large proportion of the intelligensia. There were merchants and tradesmen of varying degrees of affluence. At the top end of the scale there were the seriously rich, who acquired status by marrying their daughters into the 'nobility', and thereby provided a necessary injection of cash. Some of the merchants and tradesmen were, however, appallingly impoverished. There were also the threadbare urban immigrants and itinerants, the Germans, Poles, Finns and Jews. And although Pauline will have been insulated from them, we must not forget the twilight world of those living in tenement slum buildings or on the hay barges, as depicted by Dostoyevsky in *Crime and Punishment.* In that novel, a central character is a teenager licensed with the prostitute's 'yellow card', the sole source of income on which her downwardly mobile family, headed by her drunken father and mortally tubercular stepmother, fail to subsist.[66]

The urban merchants included a large group of small shopkeepers and artisans, the *meshchane.* Pauline was intrigued to see them in action at the end of the St Petersburg season. Because the merchants were not allowed to participate in the 'nobility''s formal vote of thanks to her, they came in their own deputation to present the homage of the Russian people. Even the rich merchants displayed cringing servility. There was no self-standing bourgeois class in the western European sense.[67]

The serfs comprised about 80 per cent of the population. They were regarded by many gentry as being 'in the transitional stage between monkey and man'. The serf 'was no better than a pig' and needed the stick. There are countless stories of floggings, conscription to the army or deportation to Siberia for the most trivial of offences – such as not working hard, looking surly or doffing one's cap reluctantly. However, not all serfs were treated cruelly, and the structure was remarkably resistant to change.[68] The serfs were conservative, male-orientated, and, like all country people of the time, especially hide-bound by superstition. God forbid a yokel walking along a country lane should encounter a 'black monk' or see a hare run across the field.[69]

The serfs were regimented by their own communal tribunal and their village elder.[70] The Russian peasant was no fool. He knew how to manipulate the system to his advantage. Novels are full of stories of peasants and their elders taking toffee-nosed gentry for a ride. There was a saying that 'the Russian peasant would even fleece God himself'.[71]

If all else failed, Louis Viardot heard that the murdering of nobles by peasants was a routine event, with about one case a week being reported. Also common was the sacking and firing of the manor house. Turgenev's sister-in-law was such a nasty piece of work that her serfs tried to kill her. It seems probable that Dostoyevsky's drunken, lecherous and sadistic father was smothered by his serfs with the cushions from his carriage. He was greatly disliked because he flogged so much. Such a dénouement was not without precedent, even at the top of the hierarchy. The father of Tsar Nicholas I had been assassinated by being strangled with the sash which he wore to signify his Order of Chivalry.[72]

Women were at the bottom of the pile. The 'Katyas and Mashas', with their 'short fat figures', were considered by Custine to be plain, even ugly.

He described their 'voluntary deformity', their dresses which were belted 'at the shoulders, a little above the bosom, which wobbles underneath. It is hideous.'[73] He was not alone in his opinion. 'In Russia, a well-shaped nose is rarer than a tiny foot', wrote one Russian novelist.[74] However, one girl in a hundred was spectacularly attractive,[75] a statistic which, if reliable, indicates that, on an estate of reasonable size, there was considerable scope for the young bloods.

The house-serfs were fair game, as the older men also found. Dostoyevsky's venomous character, old Karamazov, rejoiced at the class structure because 'there will always be some lovely scullery maid for her master to take'. House-serfs were preferable to yokels working on the land. They had more class and were less smelly. Sex with serfs revolted Tolstoy, yet it did not stop him seducing them. He got his aunt's maid pregnant and, during his engagement, he released his pent-up passion by going to the village and seducing a serf girl.[76]

However repellent this may seem, it can be hypocritical to make self-righteous comparisons between Russian serfdom and 19th-century western society. Slavery and its traffic were widespread in the first half of the 19th century, and Britain had been the leading slave-trading nation. In 1807, British shipping and subjects were prohibited from participating in the trade, but 'the remaining trade was even more atrocious in the conditions it imposed on its victims than before'.[77] Slavery was only phased out in the British colonies in the 1830s, and the slaves only achieved full freedom in Jamaica around five years before the Viardots first went to Russia.[78] In France, slavery was only finally abolished in 1848, and in the USA after the Civil War in the 1860s. Even today, there could be up to 30 million people who are forced to work for nothing, and who are deprived of their freedom and the fruit of their labour by violence or the threat of violence.[79]

Also, at home in France, life provided no bed of roses, except for the fat, lecherous and self-indulgent bourgeoisie who, with the remains of the aristocracy, took the place of Russia's nobility at the top of society. Underneath, in France, the destitution was terrible. In the 1820s, 80 per cent of those who died in Bordeaux were penniless.[80] In Paris, around fifteen per cent of babies were abandoned. There were nearly 150,000 children aged below fourteen working in the cotton industry, in terrible conditions. We hear of 'large numbers of thin, pale women, walking barefoot through the sludge'. And of a still larger number of young children, 'equally dirty and haggard, dressed in rags which are thick with oil that has fallen on them while working'.[81] Pauline would not have been surprised to hear that, in one large town in France, two-thirds of the men, half of the women and a quarter of children were ill.[82] Even the efforts of the hard-working to better their lot could be annihilated by a disaster such as the death or injury of a breadwinner.

In Russia, by the middle of the century, many people recognised that social reform was necessary. Pressure had built up after the Napoleonic Wars, particularly from those officers who had returned from fighting in western Europe where they had seen more liberal régimes. An opportunity for concerted action arose in late 1825 when Tsar Alexander I died suddenly. His younger brother Nicholas I ascended the throne, bypassing, with royal family consent, their brother Konstantin whose marriage was morganatic. On 26 December 1825, 3,000 people demonstrated in St Petersburg's Senate Square. The Tsar had six of the 'Decembrists' executed; he sent 31 to Siberia for life and 85 for specified periods.[83] This put a stop to political protest for a considerable time.

Underneath, there was an element of social reform. Some of the 'nobility', such as Prince Andrew in *War and Peace*, freed their serfs, or perhaps put them on a 'Quit-rent' system whereby the serfs paid an annual sum for the privilege of being released from the obligation of agricultural labour. This, in substance, meant that their tenure was not too different from that of a tenant farmer.

Some of the typical arguments for 'no change' which were heard elsewhere were voiced in Russia. The economic consequences of reform would be dire and social chaos would ensue. Louis Viardot, whose radical social conscience twinged sharply when he was in Russia, was told that it was just a matter of the Tsar, in his infinite wisdom, choosing a suitable moment for implementing the Emancipation.[84] Even after the death of the despotic Nicholas I, his omnipotent successor was paralysed by fear of upsetting the equilibrium with which the mass of the population, in the countryside, was actually quite content. However, in the late 1850s, the process of developing a policy for Emancipation was put in hand. The legislation was promulgated in 1861.

Pauline would, rightly or wrongly, have heard that Russia was fundamentally a violent society in which 'ill treatment is as formally regulated as a customs duty'. Violence was institutionalised. An ordinary mortal could beat anyone, so long as he was in a class below. Rakes would tie a policeman back-to-back to a bear and throw them both into the canal. The Tsar decreed that two Jews, guilty of a minor infraction, should run the gauntlet twelve times through a thousand soldiers who flogged them as they ran.[85]

Some of the worst anti-social behaviour was evinced by the despatch riders of some minister, glorified flunkey or aide-de-camp of the Tsar. They barged their way around.[86]

We also read of many duels and of two in particular which severely depleted Russia's literary talent. Less than seven years before Pauline's début in St Petersburg, Alexander Pushkin could not tolerate his brother-in-law's behaviour towards his wife. After a normal day's work, on a freezing winter's evening, Pushkin faced his adversary in a duel to the death. The first shot went through Pushkin's groin into the base of his spine. As he lay in the snow, the poet took two minutes to return the fire. He wounded his opponent, although not fatally. Pushkin was taken home, where he died almost 48 hours later after suffering torturous agony.[87]

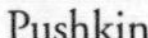
Pushkin

Lermontov

Pushkin, from the landed gentry near Pskov, was among the first intake at the school at Tsarskoe Selo opened by the Tsar in 1811. His maternal great-grandfather was Abyssinian. He was greatly influenced by the romanticism of Byron. After being banished for his political writings, he wrote *The Prisoner in the Caucasus*. He became involved with the conspirators who evolved into the Decembrists and was fortunate to avoid being implicated. Music-lovers may associate him with his fairytale epic *Ruslan and Lyudmila*, with his historical tragedy *Boris Godunov* and with *Eugene Onegin*, each the basis of an opera by Glinka, Mussorgsky and Tchaikovsky respectively. His masterpiece *Eugene Onegin*, which Belinsky described as an encyclopaedia of Russian life,[88] was published in 1831. Pushkin died on 10 February 1837, aged 37.

Lermontov was from a military family. After briefly studying at Moscow University he joined the Guards. For his poem *The Death of a Poet*, which followed Pushkin's death, he was cashiered and sent to serve in the Caucasus. When back in St Petersburg, he had a duel with the son of the French ambassador. He was again rusticated to the Caucasus, this time in a regiment which was undertaking particularly dangerous duties, which he performed with conspicuous bravery. After a brief return to the capital, he returned to the Caucasus where, on 27 July 1841, the duel took place in which he was killed. He was 26. The duel imitated the one described in *A Hero of our Time*. This was held, at only six paces, on a ledge jutting over a cliff where even a slight wound would result in the loser being dashed to pieces below. The contestants drew lots to decide who would fire first.[89]

Four years after that, Mikhail Lermontov, the poet who had publicly demanded vengeance for Pushkin's death, and who, some say, inherited his crown, was himself killed in a duel. At the time, he was serving in the army in the area around Chechnya, fighting tribesmen whose leader today might seem like an Islamic fundamentalist. The challenge to Lermontov came from a poseur whom he had mocked and possibly caricatured. It seems that Lermontov drew his opponent's deadly fire with his infuriating last words: 'I shall not fire on that fool'.[90]

We hear of blind drunkenness which, 'absurde, impitoyable, folle', was the scourge of Russia.[91] Dostoyevsky tells of the ubiquitous drinking dens with their 'unbearable stench'. The death rate from drunkenness was four to five times that of the countries to the west. The many holy days provided an opportunity for heavy drinking. The drunkard who stumbled and fell on the way home during winter would die in the cold, unless picked up by the police which some towns employed for just this purpose.[92]

We hear of crazy gambling. Bets might be laid on whether a loaded pistol pointed to the head would fire when the trigger was pulled. The more conventional gaming was less horrifying than Russian roulette, but was still shockingly reckless. In *War and Peace*, during just one night, Count Rostov loses over four times his annual pay as a lieutenant, while over a long period his father's resources are gradually and relentlessly plundered by his neighbours as a result of his poor play at cards. Dostoyevsky was convinced he had an infallible 'system' which would make his fortune. As is the case with such people, he found himself down to pawning his trousers. On another day, when he won, he brought his newly-wed wife flowers and fruit.[93]

Despite all the disadvantages, Mother Russia is a beautiful country and, then as now, was much revered and loved by its population who were deeply patriotic. We hear the sound of the peasant strumming the balalaika. Despite 'the intolerable midday heat', we hear of the cool river water, 'the soft plash of the little waves caressing the ear'. We see 'a young girl, in a broad-rimmed straw hat, with a rose-coloured parasol over her shoulder'.[94] The scene reminds us again of the start of Tchaikovsky's *Eugene Onegin*, or the setting for Turgenev's play *A Month in the Country*. Or of Chekhov's *Uncle Vanya*, with its garden seats and the table set for tea.

The winter could be extraordinarily beautiful.[95] Pushkin described the 'cold perfection of the sky, the hoar-frost and sun in freezing weather, the sledges, and tardy dawns together with the pink glow the snows assume'. Louis Viardot also observed the marvellous combination of moonlight and snow.[96] The beauty of Russia, its flatness, the boundless steppe which merges into the infinite sky, the changing seasons, were aspects which were captured, later in the century, by the great school of Russian landscape painters.

Turgenev describes how, in winter, one could go walking through the deep snowdrifts. One would 'look up at the blue sky above the reddish woods so as to relieve one's eyes from being being completely dazzled by the bright, sparkling surface surrounding one everywhere.' Spring then comes like a violent explosion, as the country shakes off the snow and ice which has encumbered her for five months. 'The skylarks sing trustingly under the sun's oblique rays on patches where the snow has thawed, and with a gay noise, a gay roaring, the torrents go whirling from ravine to ravine'.[97]

There was dawn rising in summer, when the sky begins to turn crimson. 'The crows wake up and flutter clumsily around. Sparrows twitter on the haycocks. The road becomes clearer, the clouds grow white, the fields become green. You can see a village with a white church and through the mist the blue line of a river winding serpent-like through six or seven miles of country. The air is impregnated with the fresh bitterness of wormwood and the honeyed fragrance of the buckwheat and the clover. In the distance an oak grove, lit by the red rays of the morning sun, rises like a wall. You hear the sound of a cart. The peasant slowly leads his horse, helping him stay in the shade. You say "Good morning". Soon you hear the metallic sound of him sharpening his scythe. The clouds grow larger and form a dark vault overhead. The grass, the bushes, everything suddenly dims. Quick! There's a shed, there. You run to it and shelter. What a downpour, what lightening! The thatched roof lets in the rain and moistens the fragrant hay. But, the storm passes over and the sun comes out again. How brightly everything sparkles. How fresh and clear is the air. You scent the soft fragrance of the wild strawberries and mushrooms.'[98] Such is the beauty of the Russian countryside. Such is the beauty of its prose. All that it lacks is the soft music of its spoken word.

As the century wore on, the countryside was scarred by increasing industrialisation and railway building. The nobles were desperate to extract more value from their estates. So they built factories; they needed the money. However, 'gentry aren't accustomed to that sort of occupation', wrote the novelist we are about to meet. 'Commercial acumen is needed to succeed. Gentry don't have that. We see them everywhere building cloth, paper and cotton factories, but in the long run all these will fall into the hands of merchants. It's a pity, for the merchants are nothing but leeches.'[99]

Turgenev predicted that the middle class of urban merchants would displace the gentry by the turn of the century. 'By that time, the land will have come into the hands of owners, without distinction of rank'; a new class of merchant, who will exploit the people, will have evolved. However, 'the people will be none the happier for it', said some.[100] Greed would predominate. Indeed, Chekhov's cherry orchard would be bought from the impecunious nobility by just such a merchant, and be hacked down to enable the development of summer villas.[101]

Even in 1840, to the Marquis de Custine it was obvious that the present society was doomed. 'I seem to see the shadow of death hovering over this part of the globe', he wrote. 'Russia is a pot of boiling water tightly closed but sitting on a fire which is growing steadily hotter – I fear an explosion'. 'Explosion is inevitable, although we cannot predict when.'[102]

The Russian intelligentsia, which mushroomed from enlightened opinion in Moscow University circles in the 1830s, was very conscious of its situation and knew that something had to be done. However, they did not know what to do. 'Russia has fallen behind Europe', wrote Turgenev. 'We must catch up; but we lack inventiveness. We did not even invent the mousetrap'.[103]

It was not as simple as catching up. Which way should it go? In the past, Russia had looked to the East. Once Russians began to turn to the West, as they did during the Napoleonic Wars, the edifice became unstable. The Russian nation suffered from a kind of schizophrenia. Did it tilt towards the East or West? Was it Byzantine, Tartar and Asian; or was it European? Was it sclerotic and moribund, or did it have the potential to be efficient?[104]

The Russian educated classes were divided; the privileged French-speaking élite, such as the Turgenev family, tended to look westwards. However, ranged against the Westernisers were those who preferred the Eastern Slav traditions and those of the Orthodox Church.[105] Neighbours living in remote provinces might be French-speaking and pro-West, or Russian-speaking, in which case they were likely to be Slavophile. All the arts reflected this division, whether music, architecture, painting, sculpture, or writing. With 'literature the laboratory of society', Turgenev and his contemporaries, such as Goncharov, found themselves at the centre of this increasingly desperate and contentious search for a solution. Educated Russians hungered for roots which only Russia had to offer; however, 'Russia was a wilderness'.[106]

There were few other options open to Pauline at this time other than to accept the invitation to Russia. And it represented a great opportunity not to be missed.

On 3 November 1843, Pauline appeared for the first time on a Russian stage. She was Rosina in Rossini's *Barber*. The build-up was such that one journalist reported her performance before it had actually taken place.[107] It had been said, with some exaggeration perhaps, that she was 'the most talked-of opera singer in Europe'. St Petersburg 'society' was bowled over by the Rubini, Tamburini, Viardot trio. It was 'overwhelmed with an enthusiasm for Italian opera which bordered on hysteria.'[108] Pauline also sang the role of Desdemona, and appeared in *La Sonnambula* and *Lucia di Lammermoor*. She was at last receiving the ovation that she desired, not just from the crowd, but even from the high priest of Russian music himself, Glinka.

It must have been splendid. As in other European capitals, St Petersburg 'society' went to the opera to attend a fashionable, rather than musical, occasion,[109] at least more so than today. The auditorium was large and magnificently lit with thousands of candles. The Tsar, accompanied by the Tsarina, his family and court, entered. When he approached the front of his box, the entire audience rose. Tsar Nicholas I, 'a militaristic martinet, imposingly tall, with the powerful voice of a man born to command',[110] was in dress uniform of bright red. Each member of the audience was thus appropriately reminded of the social and hierarchical structure and his exact position in it.

Pauline's first performance of *La Sonnambula* was an unprecedented success. She was recalled fifteen times. Afterwards, she was given a 'shake-hands *à l'anglaise*' by the Tsar, himself. The handshake of 'the drill-master of Europe' was probably a painful, even frightening, experience. In common with many leaders, the Tsar found it difficult to smile with his eyes and his mouth at the same time.[111] It was said that 'he poses incessantly', with the result that 'he is never natural, even when he is sincere'.[112] It is surprising that he paid any attention to Pauline. However, we may suppose that he had to occupy himself somehow.

Outside, as Pauline made her way from the theatre in her droshky, it was a murky November St Petersburg night, pitch black at twenty paces. Rain and snow seemed to fall all at once. The rain jetted horizontally as if from a fire hose and streamed down from the buildings onto the granite pavement. In the deserted streets the wind howled and the streetlights creaked. Then the snow would fall even heavier, in bigger and thicker flakes; the streetlights would creak even more piercingly, and the wind would sound still more mournful, more pitiful, 'like an importunate beggar pleading for a copper coin for sustenance'.[113]

As the season progressed, Pauline continued to receive rave reviews. However, the adulation has to be placed in context. Despite Russian imperial glory and the court being 'much the grandest thing in Europe', Russians were regarded as somewhat provincial in their musical appreciation, so reports of her successes did not carry much weight in Paris and London. The Russian audience chattered through the overture,[114] and the staging could be 'grotesque ... pretentiously false and unnatural'. The scenery was often made of crudely painted cardboard. Indeed, with the actors waving their arms in the air, opera seemed faintly absurd to Tolstoy.[115]

Pauline had the prescience to realise how much people appreciate it when visiting VIPs use the local language, a ploy familiar to the modern politician. The applause thus reached fever pitch when she sang, as an encore, a well-known song in Russian.[116]

Pauline felt understandably homesick without Louisette and her good friends. She had to be cautious when writing to a 'suspect' person such as the radical George Sand. Correspondence was routed via George's son, ostensibly to avoid alerting Russian censorship to its actual destination.[117]

It was ironical that the Viardots, radical republicans as they were, sought employment in this extraordinary, authoritarian place. Pauline was critical of the suffocating political atmosphere in Vienna, which she could not stand. Yet neither she nor Louis seems to have been unduly concerned about Russia and its politics. Of course they would never have settled there, whereas they might have settled in Vienna. The irony of their predicament was one which the perspicacious George Sand could not miss.[118]

At a more prosaic level, it was not long before Louis was invited to go shooting. He would have to wait for the moose and wolves. Before the winter set in, the quarry was limited to foxes and hares. He was told that, in order to increase St Petersburg's population of hares, which were much larger than the French ones, the keepers had imported Muscovite rodents. These had somehow made their way back to Moscow and seemed to have taken the St Petersburg ones with them.[119]

When Louis, wearing the customary long waterproof boots, went away shooting, there was no question of going alone. A guide was necessary so as to avoid getting totally lost in the dense forest where there were no rides or paths. His efforts about fifteen miles from the city yielded little compared to the terrific noise created by the regiment of about 200 beaters, and the considerable expense.[120]

The shoot could be quite an undertaking. In 30 hours, they travelled 170 miles, exhausted 80 horses, employed 250 people and spent 1,500 roubles. However, Louis found that he could relax on the divan-like seat of the sledge and be rocked gently to sleep. Two dashboards of skin, like bats' wings, protected him from the hard snow that was thrown up by the horses' hooves.

A feature of these shoots was the Rabelaisian lunch. This included a vast pâté de foie gras, some cutlets, and also the national dish, the cabbage soup which was iced like sugar candy. This was washed down with bottles of Madeira and champagne.[121] 'Voilà une chasse russe', Louis declared.

The shooting lunch was probably better in quality than the usual Russian food which, on the whole, was tasty but dull. Russian cutlets comprised boiled beef which was minced and fried in cakes, something akin to a rissole or hamburger. The Russians would eat curd fritters, sour cucumber soups, salt cabbage, pickles, jelly puddings, syrups, jugged poultry with saffron, and custards made with honey.[122] In an inn, the guest might be served with the inevitable 'soupe Julienne' and 'cutlets, with peas and hazel-hens dried to blackness'. As today, dishes were enlivened with pretentious French names – or by adding the name of a slashing military hero, as in 'Skobelev cutlets' – in order to make the basic ingredient sound appetising.[123]

Possibly it was during lunch that Louis was introduced to a little-known poet, who had just seen his wife performing Rosina. It was the poet's 25th birthday. He was conspicuously tall and good-looking. He had chestnut hair and blue eyes the colour of the sky. Like Louis, he loved shooting.[124] He was a patrician and looked like one.

Four days later, on 13 November, just ten days after her début, Ivan Turgenev walked into a flat in Nevsky Prospect, opposite the Alexandra Theatre, and into Pauline's life. He was three years older than her. For many years to come, he would recall this anniversary in his correspondence with her.[125]

'First love is like a revolution', he later wrote. 'The established course of everyday life is instantly smashed in smithereens. Youth stands at the barricades, its flag fluttering far above, ready to greet enthusiastically whatever may lie ahead, death or a new life.'

As Robert Burns wrote in that 'Song' which was particularly loved by Turgenev, Pauline and Ivan would 'clamb the hill thegither; And mony a canty day' they would have 'wi' ane anither'.[126]

Pauline's sketch of the handsome Turgenev

CHAPTER 8

FIRST LOVE

IVAN SERGEYEVICH TURGENEV was introduced to Pauline as 'a young Russian landowner, a good shot, an agreeable conversationalist and a bad poet'. He was very charming, always a fund of good stories. He also had a naivety about him which was very engaging. Like many Russians of his class, his family spoke French, except to the serfs.[1]

A few months before they met, Turgenev had obtained a minor unpaid post in the Ministry of the Interior, where he worked under a celebrated linguist and ethnographer. There, he spent most of his time reading the novels of George Sand and writing verse. Perhaps this was not surprising. One, albeit fictional, character exclaimed: 'Thank heavens my job in the civil service doesn't require my presence at the office'.[2]

By the time Turgenev met Pauline he had, earlier in the year, obtained some recognition which followed the publication, at his own expense, of his poem entitled 'Parasha'.[3]

Surprisingly, this initiative pleased Turgenev's mother. Normally, she tended to find fault with much that he did. It is said that she thought his voice 'common'. As well as having the fashionable lisp, Turgenev had a hearty, unnaturally high and shrill laugh. Indeed, his voice was 'almost feminine', particularly when he became excited, according to the pianist Anton Rubinstein.[4]

Turgenev dutifully respected, but disliked, his mother. He and his brother got on very badly with her. Varvara Petrovna Lutovinova, 'a brow-beating old bitch', as we may assume that the house-serfs called her, was very rich. She had refinanced his father, a handsome, but penniless aristocratic cavalry officer, an excellent horseman.*[5]

The conventional picture of Varvara Petrovna is, as we shall see, so dislikeable that one wonders whether it can possibly be true. Turgenev himself described her directly as a 'capricious and power-loving woman who alone gave us – and sometimes even took from us – our means of survival.'[6]

Of his father, now dead, Turgenev might have thought, 'I have never seen a man more exquisitely calm, self-confident and self-controlled'. 'I loved him, I admired him', Turgenev said of a similar character, but he found him distant. 'He seemed to me to be the embodiment of manhood – and, oh how I'd have worshipped him if only I'd not been constantly aware of being strictly kept at arm's length.' His father's main passion was spent in chasing women who were doubtless attracted by his appearance in his white uniform replete with stars and medals. He had a nineteen-year-old Princess for a mistress. As Turgenev later indicated, it was acceptable for a man to take a mistress, provided he was not so foolish as to give her a present of horses from his wife's stud.[7]

Varvara Petrovna

* It was a hallowed principle that an impecunious army officer should marry a rich wife. Tolstoy's father married the heiress of Prince Nicholas Volkonsky, and the principle pervades *War and Peace*. The father in Turgenev's *On the Eve* also had married a rich wife; and the father's great-uncle, a retired officer, lived on the inheritance from his wife who came from the merchant class.

Turgenev's father had the class; his mother, the money. She reared her two sons and her illegitimate daughter at Spasskoye-Lutovinovo, her vast country estates. Her third son was partially paralysed and died aged sixteen.[8]

Turgenev had been born a somewhat delicate child, on 9 November 1818. His birthplace was the family's house in Oryol, some 220 miles to the south of Moscow. He had the necessary pedigree. His father's family was descended from a Tartar prince. An ancestor had been beheaded, a fate which can be far from disadvantageous when descendants seek to make progress in life. Turgenev's father was decorated for his action at Borodino, the battle fought to the west of Moscow, in which Napoleon's army was considerably weakened as it approached the city.[9]

Oryol, which was built along a river, was then a regional market town. Near the Governor's residence, with its striped sentry boxes at the gates, there was a leafy promenade. There was the wide marketplace which stank of rush mats and cabbages. The place was full of peasant carts, harnessed to shaggy, potbellied nags which stood with their unkempt heads hanging down submissively. Crowded taverns emitted the acrid smell of alcohol and the noise of peasants hoarsely singing drunken songs. It was, however, sufficiently pleasant for Tolstoy to choose it as the place for Pierre, the principal character in *War and Peace*, to recuperate after his captivity.[10] Today, it is virtually featureless. Turgenev said that it was a place of which he had no fond memories.[11]

Turgenev's mother, Varvara Petrovna, was 'of untameable disposition and harsh of hand' as a consequence of her family background. Like one of Turgenev's characters, her grandfather used to 'hang his serfs on hooks by their ribs'. It is said that when a farmer threatened to sue him for seizing some land, he had the farmer flogged until he agreed to surrender it.[12] He told the farmer to be grateful to him for only taking his land and not his life.[13]

Varvara Petrovna herself had experienced a hard upbringing. Her stepfather had tried to rape her when she was sixteen. Her mother apparently smothered a serf boy who irritated her, whether accidentally or intentionally we do not know. Turgenev would echo this episode in his story of *The Brigadier*. In this, a lady hurls her pageboy down the stairs. She allows him to die in the lumber room, before having him buried secretly.[14]

As well as owning houses in Oryol and Moscow, Varvara Petrovna possessed the enormous and agriculturally rich estate at Spasskoye.* Its setting is idyllic rather than scenic. It is located some 35 miles on the Moscow side of Oryol, before the undulating country turns into the flat, dreary landscape south of the capital. The estate is only a few miles from Mtsensk, the typical middle-Russian town featured by Leskov†[15] in his *The Lady Macbeth of the Mtsensk District*, the story used in Shostakovich's opera which Stalin seized upon as a pretext for persecution. Today, Mtsensk is conspicuously run down, although it still boasts a statue of Lenin. Some of its factories are sadly rusty and derelict.

Spasskoye

The mansion at Spasskoye was a large rambling manor house, made of timber with an iron roof. Three years before Turgenev met Pauline, it had been destroyed in a fire seemingly caused by a serf who was fumigating a sick cow. Fire was a familiar hazard. The timber houses, heated by stoves and lit by candles, were a considerable risk. 'Everyone knows that our county towns burn down every five years', Turgenev later wrote. The Turgenev family now occupied a wing which had remained.[16]

*Spasskoye should be scanned with the emphasis on the first syllable, rather like 'William'.

†Turgenev was slightly over twelve years older than the novelist and short story writer, Nikolay Semyonovich Leskov. At first, Leskov worked as a legal clerk in Oryol and Kiev. *Lady Macbeth*, whose heroine lives and dies by violence, was published in 1865, and *The Steel Flea* in 1881.

The rich black soil around Spasskoye grew hemp, rye, wheat and tobacco. The region was well known for the quality of its horses and cattle. Spasskoye was also an excellent estate on which to go shooting. The estate's 5,000 souls and twenty villages provided Varvara Petrovna with a considerable income. Her household was presided over by its chamberlain and order was maintained by her private guard. Varvara Petrovna was attended by her ladies and around 40 house serfs. There were butlers and footmen. As well as the kitchen staff, there were laundresses, seamstresses, tailors and dressmakers. There were carpenters. There was the drunken shoemaker, and the saddler who acted as both a vet and as a doctor for the servants. There was a serf orchestra. Some similar houses also employed a serf portrait painter,* although there is no record of one at Spasskoye.[17]

Varvara Petrovna's 'adopted' daughter acted as her secretary and occasionally forwarded Turgenev his meagre allowance. This girl, with her mixture of infantile bonhomie and devilish wile, Turgenev regarded as a female Tartuffe, a religious hypocrite. She was in fact Varvara Petrovna's own illegitimate child, sired by Dr Andrey Behrs, her physician. Varvara Petrovna went abroad to hide the scandal; she could return the following year because fortunately her husband had died. One of her beau's legitimate children would, in due course, marry Leo Tolstoy.[18]

It has been suggested that Varvara Petrovna organised her son's first experience of sex, when he was only fifteen. If so, it was shrewd of her to do this in a controlled way. The fourteen-year-old Tolstoy caught gonorrhoea after being taken by his elder brother to a brothel, possibly in a room set apart for the purpose in one of the monasteries of Kazan to the east of Moscow. Turgenev would later tell how, on a damp, drizzly day, he was walking in the garden; a pretty chambermaid took hold of him by the hair at the back of his head and said 'Come'.[19]

The day was erotic, he said; the setting beautiful and natural. Today, the wild flowers, the yellow dandelions, the blue forget-me-nots in among the unmown grass are magnificent. The garden at Spasskoye has lime tree walks and lilac, acacia, honeysuckle, birches and maples. All in all, there are twelve species of trees. We can hear the sound of the birds which Turgenev

*For example, G. V. Soroka, the distinguished landscape painter, was a serf. He was refused freedom by his master, although he did encourage his talent. Soroka was involved with the uprisings which followed the Emancipation. He wrote to the Tsar to complain about the arrangements for land purchase. For this, he was sentenced to be flogged, but committed suicide first.

loved. Turtle-doves and orioles chatter, chirp and sing, as do chaffinches, thrushes, cuckoo and woodpecker.[20]

At Spasskoye one can see an oak and some apple trees planted by Turgenev. However, the visitor stands in awe before the larch which actually presided over the dreaded Varvara Petrovna herself. She was a truly formidable woman, normally sombre and sour, 'solitarily living through the final years of avaricious and boring old age'. If, as is reasonably supposed, Turgenev's short story *Mumu* portrays features of his mother, she was an insomniac and utterly selfish. When she was in a good mood, she was furious if everyone else did not display radiant pleasure. Her family had 'flogged their way forward' and she was no exception. When she personally birched Ivan's elder brother, she apparently beat him so hard that she fainted from the exertion; the small boy had to rush and get water to revive his tormentor. Doubtless, she then carried on.[21]

When he was nine, Turgenev was sent to a boarding school in Moscow and, two years later, he moved to a secondary school. However, he was only there for a few months before his mother brought him home to finish his studies and to enjoy the shooting for which he was developing a passion.[22]

Before his fifteenth birthday, Turgenev went to Moscow University, where he was known as 'the American' because of his 'democratic' tendencies and interest in the United States. When he was sixteen, he moved to the philosophy department at St Petersburg University, where he shared rooms with his elder brother who by then was at the Cadet School. Around this time, Turgenev wrote his first literary work, *Steno*, which was unpublished. When still in his teens, he wrote an unfinished poem 'The Old Man's Story'. He translated parts of Shakespeare's *King Lear* and *Othello*, and Byron's *Manfred*. He also wrote poems of his own which were published only later. From 1838, some short works of his began to appear in print.[23]

Just before he was twenty, Turgenev moved to Berlin which was then 'something of a philosophical and cultural Mecca for young Russians'. On the way to Germany, from St Petersburg to Lübeck, the ship caught fire. Turgenev seems to have behaved less than heroically; he was accused of elbowing his way past the women and children. Whatever may have happened, he referred to this event periodically throughout his life. His behaviour weighed on his conscience, even to the time of his death.[24]

In Berlin, Turgenev lived in style. He took with him his valet Porfiry who was an illegitimate son of his father and thus his half-brother.*[25] This was perhaps not unusual, because, in one of his stories, he tells of a youth aged sixteen who is attended by his own manservant who sleeps on the floor.[26]

Turgenev was to be seen at cafés, concerts and theatres. On board ship, he had met the wife of a Russian poet. He then proceeded to have a love affair with her when they reached Berlin.[27]

Turgenev's fellow students included the historian Granovsky and the philosopher Stankevich who were 'perhaps the leading minds in Russian intellectual life of the 1840s and 1830s respectively'. Granovsky gave Turgenev an edition of Shakespeare's works, with the inscription 'Approach with Fear and with Faith'. Stankevich embodied 'altruistic service to the cause of enlightenment and humanity'. After he died of tuberculosis in Rome in mid-summer 1840, aged only 27, Turgenev felt that he should carry his baton forward.[28]

Berlin at the time was almost overwhelmingly rich in culture and provided a wonderful opportunity for a young man who had an entrée to the salons, where artists, musicians, scholars and statesmen met. These were presided over by rich ladies such as Lea Mendelssohn and Amalia Beer, both mothers of great composers. In salons such as these, Turgenev could encounter extraordinary and outstanding people, for example Goethe's 'lover' Bettina von Arnim, whose husband, the folklorist, once joked that she was 'half witch, half angel, half seeress, half liar, half child, half actress, half adventuress, half nun, half sleepwalker, half coquette'. Turgenev could meet others of colossal distinction such as Alexander von Humboldt, the internationally-renowned naturalist and explorer who had put Latin America onto the scientific map. Humboldt had been part of Schiller's coterie in Weimar and has been called 'the last man who knew everything'. He wrote some 35,000 letters in the course of his life. His brother Wilhelm, recently deceased, had established Berlin University.[29] Also in Berlin at the time was Karl August Varnhagen von Ense, the widower of one of Berlin's leading salon hostesses until her death five years earlier. Varnhagen had fought against Napoleon at Wagram, had attended the Congress of Vienna and had been dismissed from the diplomatic service on account of his liberalism.[30] What an experience for a young man to move in such circles! What an education!

*Porfiry later became a doctor in Mtsensk.

Turgenev had a quick visit home to Russia, and then visited Italy. On a May evening in Sorrento, his heart was momentarily captured by 'Chouchou', a beautiful seventeen-year-old Russian with enormous almond-shaped eyes. But he returned to Prussia via Lucerne where he picked up a tart on the bridge and had a fantastic experience taking her on a large tomb in the town cemetery.[31]

In Berlin, Turgenev shared lodgings for a whole year with Mikhail Bakunin who he had met a week or so after Stankevich died. Bakunin, a noble from the province of Tver, was studying the works of the German philosophers. He was four years older than Turgenev. He had left the army without permission.[32] He would soon become a by-word as an anarchist and agitator, arguing that the existing order should be overthrown by violent means; the Russian peasant, with his tradition of violent revolt, would have the key role in this.

In 1841, Turgenev spent Christmas at the Bakunin estate. He seems to have been caught up in a 'metaphysical entanglement', 'platonic, nevertheless intense', with Bakunin's sister Tatyana. However, this blue-stocking and 'fervid virgin', became far too passionate, and Turgenev was put off when she tried to borrow money from him to help her brother. She and her sister had fallen in love with the chaste and self-denying journalist Belinsky when he came to stay some five years earlier.[33] The girls were again out of luck.

Turgenev's relationship with Tatyana was the prototype of a relationship which he would introduce throughout his fiction. On the one hand, there is a loving and wholly devoted woman who is ready to surrender life and honour; on the other, there is a man who would like to reciprocate her love, but cannot. Thus the man loses 'the happiness that could be his because he cannot bring himself to grasp it, to commit himself, yet, no sooner lost than bitterly repenting his folly'.[34]

After his time in Berlin, Turgenev went back to Russia where he sat for his degree in philosophy. He then visited Dresden and Berlin before again returning to St Petersburg in order to get a job in the civil service.

Turgenev was at this time on good terms with his mother, so far as this was possible. However, he was kept on a tight financial rein and so, in St Petersburg, he lived the dandified, bohemian existence led by many impecunious noblemen at the time.[35]

This brings us back to the year 1843, a crucial one for Turgenev, not just because it was at the end of that year that he first met Pauline. In that year, he also met Vissarion Belinsky, the journalist. Belinsky was the first to understand the importance of literature as an engine of social change, and thus became the pioneer of Russian socialism. In his short career of only fourteen years, this enthusiastic Westerniser also shook up an apathetic literary public and made it demand an authentic Russian national literature. Although Belinsky was a very serious character compared to the somewhat frivolous Turgenev, he became his friend and father figure, a man whose work Turgenev always admired. Belinsky's favourable review of Turgenev's poem 'Parasha' launched him. It provided him with the confidence to throw up the civil service job and to develop his literary career.[36]

Meanwhile, Turgenev had sired a little daughter by a seamstress from Spasskoye. By the time he first met Pauline, the little girl was aged eighteen months.[37] Unlike his brother who married the German governess and consequently was cut off by his mother, Turgenev did not make the mistake of marrying the seamstress. At this stage, he seems to have been completely unaware of his daughter's existence.

After Pauline made her début in St Petersburg, Turgenev went night after night to hear her perform. His ostentatious applause caused some irritation,[38] which was aggravated when he sponged his way into his friends' boxes because he could not afford a box of his own. After the performance, he joined the group of young fans who congregated in Pauline's dressing-room. There is no evidence that Pauline fancied him particularly. However, she displayed the exaggerated exuberance and warmth that she inherited from her Spanish father, so Turgenev may well have got the impression that she did. The story goes that her four principal admirers were expected to sit on the paws of a bear skin on which she would recline. They became known as the Four Paws.*[39] 'Love is an illness', Turgenev would later write in one of his stories, 'in love, one person is the slave, the other the master. Not without reason do poets speak of the chains of love.'[40] This aspect will probably not have crossed Pauline's mind. She was no doubt greatly relieved to be serenaded by some men who were less than double her own age.

*One seems to have been Pyotr Vasilevich Zinoviev, whose great-nephew married, and worked closely with, April FitzLyon, the distinguished biographer of Pauline Viardot in the 1960s.

In Pauline, Turgenev immediately recognised 'the glamour of things European, the epitome of civilisation and culture, and a living symbol of the free flight of music, detached and remote from terrestrial cares'. Thus, she was to become 'the poetic ideal of his Art'.[41]

Meanwhile, when the opera season ended, Pauline performed at various concerts. At one held in the University she sang in Russian and was acclaimed for her pronunciation, so she had clearly been receiving tuition, although it seems improbable that Turgenev was yet her teacher.[42]

Just as this tour was coming to an end, the Schumanns arrived in St Petersburg and were warmly welcomed by Pauline. 'I am leaving you Clara Schumann; her singing on the piano is better than mine', Pauline told the press when she left at the end of the season.[43]

Despite the discomforts, the Russian appearance had been a colossal success. It was announced that the Italian opera, including Pauline, would appear in the following year.[44] However, for the moment it was a matter of packing bags and moving onto the next location, Vienna. Pauline doubtless experienced the considerable relief felt by those leaving Russia for the West. She was leaving what Custine had described as 'this Empire of deep silence, of great empty spaces, of barren fields, of solitary cities, of cautious countenances whose lack of sincerity makes society itself seem empty'.[45] Whether she felt, as he did, that 'a bird escaped from its cage could not have been more joyous', we do not know.[46]

While Pauline was performing in Vienna, Louis went to Paris where George Sand showed him his daughter Louise, who had grown bigger and spoke Spanish like her father and mother. Pauline, however, remained in Vienna in April 1844, and was so dilatory in her correspondence that she had to apologise to George for not writing.[47]

Vienna was still in the grip of the tight controls exercised by the chancellor, Prince Metternich, once doyen of the Congress of Vienna. He was absolutely obsessed with security. Even during the previous visit to Vienna, the Viardots had had to be wary on account of this. There, 'George Sand' was a suspect name to write on an envelope which might well have found its way onto Metternich's desk and into the Emperor's study. If this did indeed happen, history does not record what they thought of the letter in which Pauline referred to the inadequate Emperor, in whose presence she had sung. She described him as 'that unfortunate half-wit they call emperor, who has to be treated like a child'.[48]

Perhaps the Austrians had read further into *Consuelo* and come across passages which even today conjure up thoughts of Women's Lib. The later pages of this novel, ostensibly about the purest and most virginal singer, were sprinkled with seditious phrases. Royalty and clergy were said to be the source of iniquity. Sentiments such as these would have made the vain and repressive Metternich apoplectic, and a small amount of research would have uncovered Pauline's husband's political affiliations. Maybe we should not be surprised that, whereas she was welcomed by Viennese high society in 1843, doors were closed in 1844.[49]

Around May 1844, Pauline received a letter from Turgenev. He had been ill in Moscow with a chest complaint.[50] He was always suffering from some or other medical complaint, a combination of actual illness and hypochondria. He would frequently resort to pastilles, and mixtures such as milk mixed with Seltzer water.[51]

Turgenev had read the notices in the *Allgemeine Theater Zeitung* announcing Pauline's arrival in Vienna. He duly praised the album of songs which she had composed. He told her that he would spend the summer hunting around St Petersburg, with his memories.[52]

After the 1844 Vienna appearances the Viardots did not go to Nohant, despite attempts by George to lure them there.[53] They had another interest to divert them. Stars buy stately homes; and French ones buy châteaux.

CHAPTER 9

From Courtavenel to Moscow

When Pauline moved to Vienna after the first Russian season, Louis had gone to Paris to complete the purchase of Courtavenel, a château located in the Brie countryside. It had two pepper-pot turrets, a moat and drawbridge. Together with the ornamental gardens, hothouses, orchards and park, the estate comprised around 100 acres. Pauline's mother had bid at auction for it on the Viardots' behalf. To the hammer price of 100,200 francs should be added around 30,000 francs for the urgent repairs that were needed to furnish and modernise the château, which was in a considerable state of disrepair. This outlay, financed by Pauline, absorbed all her savings so far. It represented only about a quarter of the total capital which she would eventually have to invest in the place, including extending the estate to take in neighbouring fields and farms.[1]

George Sand had kept an eye out for a suitable place for the Viardots in Berry, her part of the country. She had also obtained details of property in the Sologne area between Paris and Nohant, south of the Loire, where the marshland, lakes and ponds would have provided Louis with excellent shooting. However, the stagnant water, infested with insects, would have been bad for the family's health.[2] Ironically, the Sologne was a place to which those who would unsuccessfully man the barricades in 1848, men and women with whom Sand and the Viardots had great affinity, would be deported, there to contract fever and die.[3]

Instead the Viardots chose Courtavenel, a sixteenth-century castle. In some ways rather forbidding, it also had an elegance and charm. The gardens had an ornamental lake and were full of roses, dahlias, mignonettes, pansies, geraniums. Ancient poplars and chestnut trees lined its allées. It even had a miraculous fountain, the Fontaine Saint-Martin, nearby. Of course, the shooting was good. The fields, streams, copses and woods provided good cover for game.[4]

Pauline now was the châtelaine and had to furnish and run the place. However, she had little time before she had to return to St Petersburg and Moscow and earn the money necessary to finance her new lifestyle. She would have liked to squeeze in a visit to the Sand family at Nohant. She would have liked to see Maurice, whom she found particularly good fun, even though his attention to her was causing Louis Viardot increasing concern. Besides, she was booked to perform at the celebrations to unveil the Beethoven memorial in Bonn.

Pauline's sketch of Courtavenel from the main entrance

Courtavenel was convenient. It was little more than 30 miles to the east of Paris. The traveller taking the 9.30am diligence from Paris reached it at 3pm. The Bériots had once lived in a country house on the way. Today, it is not easy to find the exact location of the Viardots' château. It is close to Rozay-en-Brie, a charming walled town which was prominent in the religious wars which were raging[5] at the time when the castle was built, the period in which Meyerbeer's grand opera *Les Huguenots* is set. Just short of

Pécy, the persistent traveller will suddenly come upon the remains of the moat, for the château itself is no more. The ruin now consists of just part of the cellar and the foundations of the two towers, in one of which Pauline's study was located. Even in her time, the water in the moat was covered with green slime, its surface broken only by the antics of a multitude of frogs.[6] It is still choked with weeds, descendants of those which Turgenev much enjoyed clearing. The moat demonstrates that vegetable eventually triumphs over animal, however famous and celebrated it may be.

George pestered Pauline to come and stay at Nohant. However, she was busy arranging the furnishings for her own château. Their friendship cooled, even chilled, especially when Chopin's sister, who he had not seen for fourteen years, hung around in Paris for ten days waiting for Pauline to bring her to join him at Nohant. Because her passport from Poland to France would soon expire, her time was particularly precious. George wrote Pauline a stinker of a letter in which she accused her of having politically incorrect delusions of grandeur. George said that she was obsessed with her celebrity status, with crowns, jewels, Russians and roubles. Someone with all this new-found wealth could easily make appropriate arrangements to travel, George sarcastically suggested.[7]

Unfortunately, the Viardot carriage had broken down. There were no seats available on the diligence. So Pauline suggested that George should come to her, rather than vice versa. The relationship between George and her protégée was strained. George anyway was irritated that Louis had not spoken out forcefully against Russian despotism. Now she had no idea where Pauline was, and had to write to two addresses, one in the country and one in Paris.[8]

To be fair, Pauline could not possibly spare the time. She had only a few months before returning to St Petersburg, and Louis was plying backwards and forwards between Paris and Courtavenel. To appease George, Louis rather absurdly, and wholly incorrectly, played down the size of the house. It was 'a modest little country house', he said, 'not to be compared in size or grandeur to Nohant', which he said was four or five times bigger. He painted a rustic picture of the Viardot family existence. Apparently they lived very simply with a cook and a gardener, and enjoyed the milk from their cow, the eggs from their chickens and vegetables from their garden. In fact they were being ripped off, as frequently happens to urban dwellers when they set up as landed gentry.[9]

Pauline's sketch of Courtavenel – the garden front

This agricultural simplicity would not last long. As a consequence of relatively slow transport, country houses in those days were virtually hotels in which people of a similar class to the owners, sometimes just hangers-on, could come, go and stay, even when the owners were away. With no telephones to presage arrival, there was sometimes no warning at all. Soon, Courtavenel would be full of visitors. Turgenev would often be one of these.

The regular visitors also included Pauline's mother, her chain-smoking uncle Pablo Sitchès and Mariquita his wife. There was the Sitchès's daughter Antonia who was about to sing some minor roles with Pauline at St Petersburg and be launched on her own career as a prima donna. There was Manuel Garcia, Pauline's impetuous, impatient and charming brother, a fund of naughty stories. The distinguished horn-player Eugène Vivier kept the household amused with his pranks. He would sound chords on his horn. He would also somehow enclose smoke in soap-bubbles.[10]

Louis's brother Léon was also a visitor, and he painted portraits of both Pauline and Louis. Not to be forgotten were Jenny, Nanine, and Berthe, Louis's three sisters. There was also Louise's governess, presumably 'an elderly dry old thing of about 60, with a black hair-piece under a colourful mob cap, and cotton wool stuffed in her ears'. Usually, there were around eight hunting dogs lolling on the floor of the drawing room. And, last but not least, there was a menagerie of cats, monkeys, and Manon the goat.[11]

Manuel, Pauline's Distinguished Brother (Plate 8)

At Courtavenel, Manuel Garcia had the reputation for being wild, for fooling around, and for sharing lavatorial jokes and pranks with Turgenev. They also played chess together. Manuel gave up a singing career because his voice lacked the necessary power.[12] He was, however, one of the greatest singing teachers ever, and thus to be described as the 'Nicola Porpora of the nineteenth century'.[13] One of his most famous pupils was the 21-year-old Jenny Lind whose voice he recreated. He settled in England in the middle of the century. By the end of it, he lived in Cricklewood. His first wife, Eugénie, who he divorced, was a pupil who made a career first in Italy, then in Paris. Manuel wanted to discover the source of register and timbre. Using a small dentist's mirror, he discovered that voice is produced by vocal chords, not in the chest or throat as had originally been thought. His paper *Observations on the Human Voice* was presented to the Royal Society. He also invented the laryngoscope,[14] with which to look at the vocal chords. An example of this can be seen at the excellent Turgenev museum in Bougival.

Soon, Louis would have time to go shooting; Pauline would admire the flat but wooded countryside from a small knoll. Other distractions included billiards and riding. Pauline had her white stallion which her mother, fearing that she might have an accident like Maria, made her stop riding. This may have been wise. On one occasion, Manuel fell off his horse and broke his right arm.[15]

A central feature at Courtavenel was the little theatre which was constructed in the attic above the Great Hall. It had a real stage and footlights. It was here that the Viardot amateur dramatics took place; the servants provided the audience. The theatre was called the Théâtre des Pommes de Terre, because a ticket for admission was one potato.[16]

The cuisine seems to have left something to be desired by Russian, if not French, standards, at least so far as quantity was concerned. A visitor somewhat later, Afanasy Fet, the poet and translator, found the watery soup and wafer-thin slices of ham inadequate to his appetite.[17] He was a soldier, however, so he may not have been keen on modern cuisine.

George's adored son Maurice, with the nickname of Bouli, came to stay briefly. At twenty, he was nearly two years younger than Pauline. It must have been fun for her to have someone around of a similar age, although, with all the work which Pauline had to do at her new château, there can have been little time for canoodling, had she been so inclined.[18]

Maurice was a talented painter. He had sent her, via Louis Viardot, for whom he had long had an avuncular affection, a picture of a place in a forest near Nohant where he and Pauline had been on walks with his sister Solange. He was 'obsessed with' Pauline and he has been described as 'laying siege to the singer in her country house near Paris while her husband was away'. Another author talks of Maurice's 'brief clandestine affair'. Certainly, a few years later spice, if not support, for this canard was added by the publication of a somewhat incoherent six-page pamphlet. This sanctimoniously accused Sand of being corrupt, hypocritical, irreligious and lesbian. Replete with innuendo, the pamphlet implicates both Maurice and Turgenev. Maurice, who has had an affair with Pauline, is said to be sick with jealousy about the Russian who has replaced him in the bed; Pauline is accused of deceiving not only her husband, but also her lover, Maurice.[19]

Circumstantial evidence, such as an occasional *double entendre* in George's letters, is sometimes adduced to confirm that Pauline did have an affair with Maurice, even though Louis was party to this correspondence.[20] Although the wider aspects regarding her relationship with Turgenev call for fuller examination later, it seems appropriate to consider and dispose of Maurice now.

Custom required that, for the year following a wedding, the young bourgeois wife should be accompanied by her husband, or chaperoned by her mother or mother-in-law. However, after the year was over, 'the gates of freedom opened wide'. Both husband and wife might have an affair, provided it was done discreetly and the wife continued to run the domestic establishment. The husband should behave with dignity. Suitably managed, an appropriate liaison could actually 'add lustre to the salon of a wife'.[21] Pauline had been married for some time. She already had a child. She was extremely fond of Maurice. According to the rules, hide-and-seek would have not been necessary. But an extra-marital affair would require Louis to be complaisant.

It is probable that George Sand – who at the time was very possibly in a four-poster with the politician Louis Blanc, perhaps discussing socialism[22]

Maurice dressed up as a Spanish girl

– saw an opportunity, lots of fun, nothing particularly wrong, if her darling son obtained some risk-free education by having an affair with her young married protégée. By giving her blue-eyed boy, the apple of her eye,[23] Pauline on a plate, George could also establish whether her Consuelo was indeed capable of passion. This assumes that George did not want to keep Pauline for herself.* The hitch was that Louis was not going to tolerate it.

During Pauline's visit to Nohant in the previous year Louis was feeling

*George had had the affair with the actress Marie Dorval. Gautier and Goncourt speculated whether Pauline and George were hermaphrodites. George's correspondence makes it absolutely clear that she did not think that Pauline was a lesbian.[24]

fed up, possibly because Pauline was having a high old time with Maurice and getting carried away romping and pirouetting through the woods. Maurice had fallen for her. He complained to his mother that the Paris winter would be unbearable without Pauline, who by then had returned to Russia.[25] In August 1844, Maurice is 'yearning' for her. George writes that she will stop suggesting that Maurice should accompany Pauline, as her squire, jockey or rider, on the way to or from Nohant. To say so would only make Louis get up on his high horse again.[26]

Reading between the lines, it seems that Louis was justifiably concerned that Pauline's reputation might be becoming compromised; she needed chaperoning. Indeed, it was subsequently thought best for Pauline to keep away from Nohant for a bit.[27] Whether this was at the instigation of Louis or whether Pauline thought it best, we cannot tell. The relationship between the Sand and Viardot households came under further strain, there is no doubt.

Meanwhile, Maurice went to Courtavenel at the end of September 1844. It also seems that he was in Paris at the time when Pauline was there, just before she left for Russia.[28] She went via Brussels, from where she wrote hurriedly to George an unwise and incriminating letter, asking after Maurice: 'Comment se trouve Maurice après son petit voyage?' 'We promised each other to be courageous', she adds. She says that she cannot write more at the moment.[29] The letter continues: 'Je l'aime très sérieusement.' In a suitably conspiratorial way, she concludes, 'Write to me soon, care of the management of the Imperial theatres at St Petersburg. Encode the letter with *double-entendres* where possible'.[30]

On the face of it, this letter, addressed to a recipient who Liszt had said relished gossip and intrigue,[31] is naive, crass and compromising. With it, the surviving correspondence with Maurice halts.

Some commentators seize upon Pauline's letter as cast-iron evidence of an affair, although it can at most have been something like a 'one-night stand'. However, arguably, the letter supports a wholly contrary point of view. Pauline, in her early twenties, was an international prima donna and châtelaine of a large castle and its demesne, and with an extremely forceful and determined character. She was not a naughty teenager, let alone some kind of object or plaything George could manipulate or use to entertain herself. Besides, is it conceivable that anyone, teenager or adult, would correspond in such terms with her lover's mother if she were actually having an affair? And if she really was so immature, would she not have written something more romantic, more tabloid than 'très sérieusement'? Perhaps 'Je l'aime avec passion' or 'Je l'adore'?

Is it not more probable that Pauline, feminine, young, nubile and even in love at last, was trying to keep that interfering and irresponsible woman at bay? She turned to Ary Scheffer, her father-figure and her husband's best friend, for help and advice. For the moment, the advice was to let both George and her rampant son think that she really did love the youth seriously rather than in some sort of flighty, teasing way. To avoid confusion, letters on the subject should be sent through different channels because Louis was normally a party to her correspondence. One might also conjecture that by 'très sérieusement' Pauline simply meant that she loved Maurice with something she would later describe as 'the most heart-felt deepest, truest, warmest, sunshine-clearest love that ever woman felt as friend for friend'.[32]

There are lots of possibilities. To this writer it seems probable that Maurice was the equivalent of the ardent, youthful lover, the tenor Anzoleto, who was Consuelo's first love and who wanted to seduce her. Although sorely tempted, Consuelo resisted his advances just before she escaped from Venice. Pauline would later confide: 'As for an *Anzoleto*, without Ary Scheffer I would have made a gigantic mistake. I had lost my willpower. I recovered it in time to get a grip of my heart and do my duty. ... I wanted to kill myself. Out of sheer cowardice. I was almost senseless, but Scheffer, who watched over me like a father, prevented me and fetched me away. I gradually came to my senses and when my willpower returned, I was that much stronger. I committed no sin.'[33]

Some experts think that she was talking of Gounod in this reference to Anzoleto. But it must be equally if not more probable that the reference was to Maurice, who was probably the first young man Pauline really loved. However, she knew that her marriage and her loyalty to her husband prevented her from consummating that love. It would seem that she underwent a considerable crisis and, in the circumstances, it is not difficult to imagine her standing on a bridge over the Seine and looking at the murky waters below. Pauline had experienced a bit of a fling and had experienced much pain.

The crisis passed. In the following spring, when the Russian 1844–5 season was over, Turgenev was back banging on Pauline's door. In the late summer, Maurice*[34] was away chasing George Sand's ward Augustine Brault. So far as *that* relationship was concerned, Sand assured Pauline that Maurice was not prepared to be accused of seducing his mother's 'adopted daughter'.[35] This assurance is particularly relevant, because it is unlikely that George would have have given it, had Maurice seduced Augustine's predecessor in that role, that is, Pauline herself.

Besides, however damaging her Brussels letter to Sand may seem, it does not prove that Pauline and Maurice consummated their dalliance. As Pauline herself put it, a few years later, 'J'aime Maurice comme un frère',[36] perhaps with that love which Debussy would later portray so perfectly in *Pelléas et Mélisande.* 'Ils s'étaient embrassés comme des petits enfants', they kissed each other like little children.†[37] Maurice went on to pursue his career as a minor painter and poet, a country gentleman at Nohant where he assembled his collection of puppets and butterflies.[38]

For the St Petersburg 1844–5 season, Pauline took on the title role, the druid priestess, in Bellini's *Norma*, a part to which she would attach great significance and found challenging. She was somewhat apprehensive for fear of reviving memories of Pasta four years before. Once a great Norma, Pasta had botched her runs, shrieked her top notes and made an unpleasant sound in the low notes which were often wrong or off-pitch. This gave rise to Liszt's remark, to which reference has already been made that, had Malibran not died prematurely, she might have finished up singing out of tune like Pasta.[39] Pasta was not the last opera singer to discover the importance of choosing the appropriate time to retire.

The young Pauline of course performed magnificently in *Norma.* Then she started preparing for the role of Norina, the attractive young widow, in *Don Pasquale* which Donizetti had composed a couple of years earlier.[40] Her season in Russia was a tremendous success. The last night, which saw

*Maurice eventually, in 1862, married Lina, daughter of Luigi Calamatta, a distinguished painter and printmaker who, like Scheffer, had been involved in the 1830 Revolution and thus gained considerable support from King Louis-Philippe. Augustine was destined, by George, for the distinguished landscape painter Théodore Rousseau, but their engagement was wrecked after an anonymous letter was received. Apparently Solange, George's daughter, was responsible for stirring up the old story about Maurice and Augustine. Rousseau was devastated.

†Experts regret that Pauline's letter of condolence on Maurice's death in 1889 has not survived.

the final 'retirement' of Rubini, verged on the ridiculous. There were coronations with golden crowns, tears and showers of jewels.

Pauline then rushed off to Moscow for a few days before 'escaping back as quickly as possible to France'. Going the 400 miles from St Petersburg to Moscow may seem straightforward today. Then, it would be another six years before the railway line opened.[41]

A few years before, Custine had travelled the four days over the 'steppes, the marshes with their spiry pines and their stunted birches'. He compared the experience to going on the roller-coaster in Paris. The Russians, however, thought this was the best road in all Europe, despite the missing bridges and the holes in the road. At a hard gallop, they could travel on it at twelve to fifteen miles an hour, while the Tsar's suite could average about twenty. Travellers could expect breakdowns every 50 to 60 miles.[42]

The Viardots may have recalled Custine's description. 'The uneven plain, thinly inhabited and only half cultivated, is dotted with a few stunted firs. It was out of the midst of the swirling dust-cloud that I saw, as it were suddenly spring up, thousands of pointed steeples, star-spangled belfries, strangely shaped towers, palaces and old convents.' White-stone, golden-domed Holy Mother Moscow rose from the earth as if by magic.[43]

No doubt, the Viardots found unforgettable this first view of Moscow and were intrigued by 'the bizarre shapes of the towers', and by the vast commercial city, 'dusty, ill- paved, poorly constructed, thinly populated ... the chaos of plaster bricks and boards that is called Moscow'.[44]

Pauline's success at the Bolshoi was tremendous. On one evening, she was recalled 30 times and had to repeat every item. Even Varvara Petrovna, who attended a concert with her son, was forced to concede that 'that damned gypsy does sing well'.[45]

Although there were concerts every night, Moscow was relatively quiet compared to the buzz of St Petersburg because, 'in spite of its *cafés chantants* and its omnibuses, Moscow was still a backwater'. Turgenev showed the Viardots the Kremlin, the sights. They then returned together to St Petersburg, where Pauline gave a charity concert in aid of a children's hospital. She pleased everyone by again singing in Russian. She went on to France.[46]

For the second half of June, Pauline was again at Nohant for three weeks with George and her family.[47] This visit was welcomed by Chopin who found her a source of inspiration, and a distraction from Maurice.

The mutual dislike between Chopin and Maurice, which had recently germinated, was developing fast.

Chopin much enjoyed a Spanish song which Pauline composed. He wrote to his family in Poland 'I have always listened to it with rapturous pleasure. I doubt whether one could hear or think of anything better of its kind.'[48] He added that Pauline would bring it to them on her way back to St Petersburg. 'This song will bring you and me together.'

The weather in June 1845 was atrocious. The roads to the nearby town, Châteauroux, were under water. Bridges were down and buildings destroyed. When Louis set out to fetch Pauline home, he had to turn back.[49]

After this, Pauline spent a few days at the seaside before setting off to perform at the unveiling of the Beethoven memorial in Bonn. Meyerbeer was responsible for organising the celebrations. 'Everybody' was in the Rhineland for this, including Queen Victoria and Prince Albert. Pauline found herself mingling with the British and Prussian aristocracy. She performed at a reception given by the King of Prussia in the Cardinal Archbishop's magnificent baroque castle of Brühl, near Bonn.[50]

Meyerbeer and Liszt had gathered together a large group of musicians. This included Chopin, and Berlioz who was impressed by Pauline's 'poetic expression' and 'exquisite method'.[51] She sang some extracts from Gluck's *Orphée*, a work on which she and Berlioz would work together about fifteen years later.

Also present was the music teacher and critic Fétis,* who for some reason had omitted Pauline from his *Biographie universelle des musiciens*, 'the most comprehensive biographical dictionary of musicians of its time', the last volume of which had come out in the previous year.[52] Pauline was still, it seems, not regarded as *persona grata* in Paris.

Chopin was much amused by the amount of merchandise being sold at the Beethoven event. Beethoven cigars were for sale, although Beethoven only smoked a pipe. Lots of other memorabilia were available. There was so much junk that Chopin reckoned 'that the wretched composer of the *Pastoral Symphony* must have had a vast furniture business'.[53]

*François-Joseph Fétis, writer and, later, director of the Brussels Conservatoire, had taught harmony to Pauline's brother Manuel. He included the rest of the Garcia family in his *Biographie*. An entry on Pauline eventually appeared in 1881, after the death of Fétis, in the supplement with the Second Edition. It was only with a bit of pressure that an entry about her was put in *Larousse*.

CHAPTER 10

Circe

In the summer following Pauline's incriminating letter about Maurice Sand, Turgenev stayed at Courtavenel. He later wrote that he had spent the happiest days of his life there.[1] Even though he had claimed poor eyesight as the reason for his obtaining permission to leave the civil service, he and Pauline now sat together under the trees and read the works of Goethe and the great classical writers. He paddled around the moat, looked up and saw the evening sunset illuminating the black hair of George Sand who had come to visit.[2]

We can only speculate as to what emotions Pauline felt during Turgenev's visit in 1845. According to one biographer 'he not only loved, but was loved in return'. However, this assertion was qualified by saying that 'they had not even exchanged kisses. Everything lay ahead of them'. Others, rightly or wrongly, are less confident. They say that he 'was apparently quite unable to break through her indifference'.[3]

Turgenev got along very well with Louis. They saw eye-to-eye on politics; they had their literary interests in common. They were both absurdly keen on shooting;[4] Louis was writing a book about his shooting exploits; Turgenev was contemplating writing some short stories with shooting as the common theme. They worked together on translating and publishing some short stories by Gogol.[5]

After going off on a short trip to the Pyrenees, Turgenev returned in October for eight days. Pauline's mother acted as his hostess because, by then, Pauline had left for her third and final annual tour to St Petersburg.[6]

Her career was going from strength to strength, particularly in Germany where she had the invaluable support of Meyerbeer. Turgenev, however, was a rolling stone at this stage. His career as a writer had still to take off. Besides, he was perennially short of cash.

Pauline's 1845–6 tour to St Petersburg was not the success which she had experienced in previous years; indeed, it developed into a disaster. To start with, the Italian opera had lost its novelty and fashionableness. Verdi's *I Lombardi* was received badly. More worrying for Pauline, she nearly lost both husband and daughter. Louis caught cholera and then whooping cough. Young girls are particularly prone to whooping cough, an alarming disease with dangerous side-effects, which is still notifiable today. Louisette, who was in Russia with her parents for the first time, caught it. She was a tough little piece. She was more concerned by the Russian nurse who stole her breakfast and beat her. Luckily, she survived with no complications; however, she passed her illness on to Pauline.[7]

Even treatment by the attractive Dr Andrey Behrs could not prevent the whooping cough putting an end to the Russian trip at a most inconvenient time. It was no easy thing to go home from Russia during mid-February. The frozen season was actually the easiest time to travel on Russia's dreadful roads. But when the thaw, 'le dégel', began, the countryside degenerated into a sea of mud.[8] One traveller portrayed some of the difficulties experienced in a tarantass, the clumsy four-wheeled vehicle with a leather top. 'The exhausted little nags from the posting-station dragged us through the dissolving black loam of the highway',[9] he said. 'Three times we stuck fast in the mud up to the hubs; my postillion kept abandoning one wheel, and crawling to the other with a hoot and a howl; but it was no easier than the first.' On reaching the post-house, the traveller was assigned to 'a room with a battered wooden couch, a sagging floor, and tattered paper on the walls; it reeked of small beer, bast-mats, onions and even turpentine'. There, he could enjoy the company of the fleas and the bedbugs.[10]

When the Viardots reached the River Niemen, in modern Lithuania, the countryside was in flood like a sea. They were given a lift in a boat, and they travelled on an amazing kind of amphibious vehicle, half-boat, half-sledge. Once free of Tilsit, on the border with East Prussia, they went hell for leather. They did not stop at Königsberg, but went straight on to Vienna.[11]

Pauline had seen something of Turgenev in St Petersburg. On the Western New Year's Eve, a time of lively celebration in French households, a supremely happy Turgenev and his exuberant Franco-Spanish hostess exchanged kisses for the first time. That evening, he had been to an opera at which Pauline was performing; it was by Nicolai, the composer of *The Merry Wives of Windsor.* A few months later, Turgenev sent her, via a captain in the horse-guards who was also a Viardot admirer,[12] two letters ostensibly about whether she would be returning to St Petersburg. He thanked her for sending him details of the arrangement of her room. He wanted her to remind herself of him when she was walking around Courtavenel, going into the greenhouse for example.[13] A few days later, he sent her an article which he had written. He added that that he imagined her in her little closet.[14] 'It is three months since you left, how many will it be until your return? Will you return?' he wondered.

When Turgenev wrote to Pauline, he would occasionally break into other languages, such as English, Spanish, and particularly German which he used especially when he wanted to express endearment.[15] It has been suggested that German, the language of Goethe's supremely romantic *The Sorrows of Young Werther*, was a language which Louis was incapable of understanding.[16] This is improbable. Louis went hunting in Prussia, he wrote a book on German museums, and his lengthy introduction to his translation of *Don Quixote* was translated into German.[17]

In May of the following year, Louis was away in Paris. Pauline was relieved to have some time to herself at Courtavenel; she relaxed and read works by Dante and Byron. Pauline, who had been a regular visitor in and out of the Sand household in Paris,[18] was, on the one hand, upbraiding George for her 'glacial silence'. 'If I have done something wrong, chastise me', she wrote. On the other hand, she had sorted things out for herself, including matters of the heart.[19] 'I think I see more clearly, feel more clearly and breathe more clearly', she told George.[20] A crisis, perhaps relating to the need to manage the attentions of Maurice, the blandishments of Turgenev and, not least, the reasonable demands of her husband, seemed to have passed, for the moment.

Turgenev did not go to France for that summer. Instead, he went shooting. Pauline remained in the forefront of his mind. In October, when he knew that she was in Berlin, he wrote saying that he had been to the latest performance of *Norma* in St Petersburg. 'I felt a tug at my heart-strings when I entered the theatre, you can imagine why'. He criticised the singers and wrote that there were all sorts of rumours about her returning. The Tsar had apparently ordered that she be engaged, regardless of cost, and had sent an offer of 80,000 roubles. Turgenev sent her his address just in case she came. He added that it was cruel of her not to write. His friendship with Pauline, which had developed with so much promise, looked as if it might be fizzling out, much to his distress.[21]

The 1845–6 tour proved to be Pauline's last long winter tour to St Petersburg. For the next few years, she did not return to Russia. From the end of January until May 1847 she was on stage, immensely successfully, in Berlin. She was made very welcome; she was invited to visit the royal palace. Pauline toured other German cities such as Hamburg, Dresden and Munich.[22] She would later say that she found that the reception which German audiences gave to new performers was cold to start with. The ice melted slowly, but rapidly turned into boiling water.[23]

Pauline sang Beethoven's *Fidelio*, Gluck's *Iphigénie* and Bellini's *Norma.* She starred as Rachel, the Jew's daughter, in Halévy's *La Juive.* Some of the performances were sung in German. In Berlin, she performed the feat which was widely acclaimed. In the same performance of Meyerbeer's *Robert le Diable*, she sang her own part and also that of the other lead role, for which the prima donna was indisposed.[24]

During these visits, Louis took the opportunity to go shooting. He discovered that in Germany, where everyone is musical, those who arranged shoots could usefully be 'bribed' with opera tickets.[25] In case his hosts might think a single invitation was sufficient, he let it be known that, while it was a great pleasure to shoot in a place where one had not shot before, it was even more pleasurable to return to a shoot one knew. Louis's correspondence implies that he was accompanied by a friend from Moscow. Had he not suggested that this Muscovite was not a very good shot,[26] we might immediately assume that it was Turgenev.

Turgenev, at this stage, was still of relatively little consequence. He was known and respected for his poetry and criticism; however, his literary career was not assured. Indeed, he was somewhat concerned about this. The only practical means of publishing a work in Russia was to get it included, or serialised, in one of the periodic journals. One of these was *The Contemporary*, a paper which had been founded by Pushkin who had even worked on it on the day of his death.[27] This journal was revived by the radical poet Nikolay Nekrasov, a flamboyant bon vivant, who one critic has said 'wrote in what seems a patronising and sentimental way about the unhappy lot of the peasant'.[28] Other contributors to the journal were Ivan Goncharov, the author of *Oblomov*, the great dramatist Alexander Ostrovsky, who wrote *The Snow Maiden*, and the highly influential critic Vissarion Belinsky, Turgenev's mentor.

Turgenev deposited the short story 'Khor & Kalinych' at the office of *The Contemporary*. In about ten pages, this tale contrasted two serfs, one who was pragmatic and practical, the other an idealist. It was published at the beginning of 1847. The acclaim which it received reinvigorated its author.[29]

'Khor & Kalinych' would form the first of a series which was later entitled *Sketches from a Hunter's Album*. Turgenev wrote some more of these short stories during the summer of 1847. Between 1847 and 1851, 21 of them appeared in *The Contemporary*.[30] Stories such as 'Yermolay and the Miller's Wife' acquainted many, who should surely have known already, of the iniquity of serfdom in practice. In this story, the miller's wife had earlier served as a chambermaid. After ten years' excellent service, she was sacked because she became pregnant, one may assume by the son of the house. Her hair was cut off, she was dressed in the shabbiest clothes and sent to the country, where, fortunately for her, a miller was pleased to take her and make her his chattel. She was now ill and dying of tuberculosis.

According to Turgenev, Tsar Alexander II indicated that these *Sketches* provided an important stimulus for him to initiate the emancipation legislation of 1861. 'If I were vain about such matters, I should ask that my tomb should bear an inscription recording what *Sketches from a Hunter's Album* did for the Emancipation of the Serfs', he later said. 'Tsar Alexander let me know that they provided him with a considerable stimulus to institute the reform.'[31] Turgenev's *Sketches* presented the serfs as individual human beings, a concept not recognised by many landowners. They also depicted the arbitrariness, cruelty, hypocrisy and incompetence of the landowning class. The stories portrayed other themes as well, such as the native shrewdness of the serf and, not least, the great beauty of the Russian countryside.[32]

When the Viardots were on tour in Germany, the correspondence between Pauline and Turgenev was revived. He became increasingly obsessed by her. He subsequently gave us an indication of the emotion he felt. A character in one of his novels pressed himself against the hands of his 'sovereign mistress' and exclaimed 'I will go wherever you are and remain with you until you drive me away'.[33]

In May 1847, at a time when Pauline was singing in Dresden, Turgenev, Belinsky and the Viardots found themselves at the same hotel. They also met briefly in the museum. After the Viardots left for Frankfurt, Belinsky and Turgenev went to a spa, where Belinsky was due to take a cure. There, they were joined by Turgenev's great friend, the corpulent Pavel Vasilyevich Annenkov, who was a prominent literary critic and editor of Pushkin's works. Turgenev absconded to Courtavenel, leaving Annenkov to cope.[34]

Turgenev spent most of the rest of the summer at Courtavenel, where he was welcomed as part of the family. He went shooting and arranged Louis's library. For the next three years Turgenev followed Pauline, plodding and padding along after her when he could. Occasionally he broke leash, as he did when he went on a trip to the Mediterranean. Sometimes, he could not follow her because he had run out of cash, for which he was dependent on the whim of his unpredictable and domineering mother. There were some romantic moments, or at least Turgenev interpreted them as such. On one occasion, he walked with Pauline through the woods at Courtavenel. 'Do you remember that day when we saw the sky so blue through the golden leaves of the aspens? Do you remember?' he would later ask.[35]

Turgenev's friends thought that Pauline had cast a spell over him – indeed one biographer has described her as 'the Courtavenel Circe'.[36] However, another has pointed out that 'If Turgenev was a prisoner, he was in a prison of his own making'.[37]

In autumn 1847, Pauline left with Louis and Louise for Dresden, Hamburg and Berlin again.[38] While in Berlin, she got in touch with some of Turgenev's colleagues. One was Turgenev's new-found friend Ludwig Pietsch, a German artist, illustrator and journalist.[39] Another was Hermann Müller-Strübing, who taught her Greek. This hard-drinking, fast-living classicist became 'one of her closest friends and admirers' and, briefly, a suitor of George Sand. He was another radical democrat; indeed, at one stage he had already been condemned to death. Müller-Strübing was a character. In Pauline's drawing-room, he ate all the cakes intended for ten guests before their arrival.[40]

When the Viardots were on tour and Turgenev could not afford to accompany them, he moved to Paris and lodged with Pauline's mother. There he worked relentlessly at his writing. Indeed, he told Pauline that he was swamped by ideas, rather like an innkeeper is overwhelmed by a sudden avalanche of guests. He continued to follow Pauline's progress around Europe by reading articles in papers such as the *Illustrated London News*. He wrote to her almost every day. He was able to inform her, proudly but confidentially, that he had heard that Gogol had spoken complimentarily about his work. Pauline's replies were usually just contained within letters written home to her mother, nothing much more.[41]

Pauline seems, at this stage, to have been mainly concerned with her own success. Her voice had matured and she was being acclaimed in a variety of roles.*[42]

Clara Schumann

*Her repertoire included Rossini's Desdemona, Angelina and Rosina; Bellini's Arsace, Norma, Ninette, Amina and Romeo; Donizetti's Lucia; Mozart's Zerlina and Donna Anna; Gluck's Iphigénie; Halévy's Rachel and Meyerbeer's Alice and Valentine.

When in Berlin, Pauline received a request from Clara Schumann to sing in Robert Schumann's lovely secular oratorio *Das Paradies und die Peri.*[43] She refused. She may have been wise to steer clear. Schumann was unwell at the time and a previous performance had been an utter disaster. However, to the fraught Clara, it seemed that success was going to Pauline's head. She had sold her soul to Meyerbeer who, for the Schumanns not least, was definitely a second-rate composer.

Meyerbeer had not produced a new work for thirteen years, and his new opera *Le Prophète* was nearing completion and was awaited with great interest.[44] We may recall that, a few years before, he had rather grandly promised that he would not have a new work performed at the Paris Opéra without Pauline in it. However, he was a slippery character and he also had Jenny Lind, a soprano who was much admired by Mendelssohn, in mind for one of the parts.[45] Rosine Stoltz may even have been at the top of his list. However, after Rosine and her lover the Director were 'sacked' from the Paris Opéra, Meyerbeer gave the part of Fidès to Pauline. He modelled it specifically for her voice.[46]

In February 1848, negotiations were completed for Pauline at last to appear at the Opéra, for the September 1848 to May 1849 season. *Le Prophète* was not expected to be ready until January 1849 and, in the event, was delayed by three months. In the meantime, Pauline would perform in other productions such as *Les Huguenots, Don Giovanni* and *Norma.*[47]

Before all this, there would be the London summer season of 1848.

CHAPTER 11

London and Paris

Approaches had been made to Pauline back in 1846 to entice her back to London. These, according to the Director of Her Majesty's Theatre, 'did not succeed on account of the exigencies of her repertoire'.[1] Whatever this may mean, we may surmise that she was too busy in Germany at the time, or, alternatively, that she considered an offer to appear in the 'Promenade' concerts was inconsistent with the image which she wished to project.

The London opera stage was no less 'political' than Paris. The rivalries were intense. However, Pauline had an attribute which few others possessed: Consuelo's purity. She would, in due course, be identified as suitable to field against the virginal Jenny Lind who was adulated by the London audiences. Jenny was the cause of what became known as the 'Opera Fuss'.[2]

Pauline's engagements in England at this time kept her away from Paris when the barricades went up and down during 1848. The Viardots, however, returned there periodically and were active supporters of the newly-established Second Republic.

First, Pauline turned down an offer of 100 guineas a night for 40 performances during the London season of 1847.[3] This came from a particularly colourful impresario. Louis Jullien was a Frenchman, 'a musical speculator of great daring',[4] who was based in the West End, where he was married to a flower-seller. Jullien boasted 36 Christian names, those of the members of the Philharmonic Society in the Alpine town in which he was born.[5] He provides a suitable introduction to the commercial musical scene in London, around ten years after Pauline's first visit.

As a boy, Jullien was nearly carried off by an eagle; he nearly got lost in an ophicleide, a brass instrument which has since been replaced by the tuba; also, he nearly died from phonophobia (he could not bear the sound of music, especially the flute). He was a hero of a battle in the Greek War of Independence, and survived several duels. He was also the sole survivor of the Swiss Guards who were massacred when defending the Tuileries at the time that the monarchy was overthrown in August 1792; the reader is invited to ignore the fact that this event took place twenty years before Jullien was born. He died in a lunatic asylum.[6]

At the Coliseum in London's Regent's Park, Jullien had created 'Promenade'* concerts along the lines of those founded in Paris in 1830. Jullien's market, the same as that of the elder Johann Strauss in Vienna, comprised the ordinary uncultured person, the one-shilling public who wanted a pleasant evening out; that is, as the industry might say today, an entertainment rather than an art experience. So, his performances began with him being handed his jewelled baton on a silver salver. A high moment was Jullien's own arrangement of 'God Save the Queen'.[8]

The booming guns of Tchaikovsky's *1812* were for the future: the overture was not yet composed. However, Jullien found a suitable warhorse in Bellini's *Suona la Tromba* from *I Puritani*. This he arranged for cornets, trumpets, trombones and ophicleides and serpents, twenty of each. Beethoven's *Fifth Symphony* was augmented with four ophicleides, saxophone and side drums. A tin full of peas was rattled to enhance the storm effects in the *Sixth*.[9]

The Royal Albert Hall had still to be built. Jullien's 'Concerts Monstres' were held in places such as Exeter Hall, in the Strand. This hall had a capacity of 3,000 people. It was actually intended for religious and charitable purposes. A seat in the stalls could be obtained for 10/6d (£0.525); in the Western Gallery, it would cost half-a-crown (£0.125p).[10]

It was fortunate that Pauline did not take Jullien's bait. Berlioz, who did, was not paid. Jullien went bankrupt.[11]

*Jullien gave up his Promenade concerts in 1859. Between then and 1895, when Henry Wood started his series, the Promenade tradition in London was continued sporadically by various people, including Jullien's son.[7]

Opera in London, both backstage and frontstage, had many of the same features as in Paris. In any case, the stars were imported. The impresario who ran Her Majesty's Theatre spoke of 'the constant insubordination, the incessant annoyances, and the wear and tear of mind, occasioned by the habitual conflicts between manager and artists'. He claimed that these characteristics had hastened the death of his predecessor, who at one time was forced into bankruptcy. There were opportune 'colds' and 'indispositions'. The expression 'a singer's illness', so he said, became part of the vocabulary.[12]

Occasionally, there was a real crisis. We have already encountered Antonio Tamburini, the well-known Italian baritone who was nearing the end of his career. Three years before Pauline appeared with him in St Petersburg,[13] the manager at Her Majesty's had tried to lay him off. This annoyed Grisi and her pack of supporters, which was headed by a Viscount. The peer had a soft spot for Giulia and had duelled with her first husband.

So when Tamburini's replacement appeared, he was greeted with hisses and howls. On the next evening, the performance ground to a halt. The peer packed the boxes full of people shouting 'Tamburini, no intimidation'. Tamburini had to be re-engaged immediately. Of course, when he made his reappearance, he wept bitterly. 'If those tears could but be analysed' said the impresario in a rather clumsy metaphor, 'their component parts would be found to be of gold and silver'.[14]

The 'Tamburini riots', as they were called, were but an aperitif. The disruption went on, much to the delight of the public. 'There had never been such acrimony, such furious disputes, or such an unscrupulous paper war as marked the commencement of the operatic year 1847 in London', said the then Director of Her Majesty's, Benjamin Lumley. His conductor, Michael Costa, had walked out, or was sent out, either because Lumley had refused to stage an opera composed by him, or because Lumley had criticised him for devoting too much time to other activities.[15] Grisi and Mario left without notice. They were soon joined by Tamburini and Persiani, who relied upon the excuse that they had been slighted by not being re-engaged. 'The chief enemies of my management decamped', complained Lumley. Only the comic actor Lablache, whose 'delightful lessons' and anecdotes were for around twenty years 'the high point' of Queen Victoria's week,[16] stayed loyal to Lumley.

The 'Royal Italian Opera' was duly established in the theatre at Covent Garden. It was financed by Persiani's husband. He engaged the artists at cut-price rates. Lumley hit back in the courts, claiming that his theatre, formerly the King's Theatre,* possessed a legal monopoly of Italian opera production. Unluckily for Lumley, 'the age was one when it was the policy of Government to discountenance monopolies of every kind'.[17]

To continue in business, Lumley had quickly to find some competitive talent and a new show, a hit. For conductor, he hired Michael Balfe, an Irishman who is today remembered for his ballad 'Come into the Garden, Maud', and by 'I dreamt that I dwelt in Marble Halls'. For talent, Lumley identified Jenny Lind who was slender, graceful and 'very fair with a profusion of auburn tresses'. Jenny's eyes showed she was a truly great artiste. 'The feeling and intelligence of those bright orbs are unmistakeable', wrote her Victorian biographers.[18]

For the show, Lumley had in mind an opera to be composed by Felix Mendelssohn, whose music was very popular in England. He had agreed to write *The Tempest* to words by Eugène Scribe, the supremely successful Parisian librettist. This must have seemed a rather odd combination to Turgenev for whom Scribe was the epitome of bourgeois decadence.[19]

Perhaps therefore it is not surprising that Mendelssohn ground to a halt halfway through composing the opera. But this was not the only problem which Lumley faced. The trouble was that Bunn, the manager of Drury Lane, had already tracked down Jenny and pressed her into signing a contract to appear at his theatre for 50 louis d'or (1,000 francs) per performance. Byron had observed,

> But then, no doubt, it equally as true is,
> A good deal may be bought for fifty Louis.[20]

Lind's fee, the equivalent of £40, was not particularly high. Malibran had been engaged there, fifteen years before, for £125 per night.[21]

Lumley explained to Lind that the proper place for her to star was at Her Majesty's, rather than in Drury Lane. He set about persuading her to break her contract. At first, she resisted. However, with Mendelssohn's encouragement, she eventually agreed to £4,800 for the season at Her Majesty's. She would start as Alice in Meyerbeer's *Robert le Diable.* Lumley

*Today, the site of Lumley's theatre is to be found between the Haymarket and the suitably named Royal Opera Arcade, the oldest shopping arcade in London.

Jenny Lind was passionate about Mendelssohn. It is said that, had he been less honourable, he could easily have had an affair with her.[22] She was born in Stockholm in 1820. Her career nearly came to a premature halt through overwork. 'Madame, vous n'avez plus de voix', Manuel Garcia told the 'Swedish Nightingale', and advised her to take six weeks' complete rest. When he first taught her, she was 'a thin, pale, plain-featured girl looking awkward and nervous, and like a very shy country school-girl'.[23] She recovered completely. She starred in many countries in Europe. At the end of the 1849 season in London, she made a tour of the provinces; it was her swan-song, as she sensibly retired from the stage in the following year, before her 29th birthday. She went on a recital tour of the US. She married her accompanist Otto Goldschmidt in 1852 and later became professor of singing at the Royal College of Music. She was renowned for her charity. Pauline disliked her, especially as she thought her career and her charity were really just puff.[24]

told her he would settle Drury Lane's claim for compensation which, at that time, could have been liquidated by a payment of £500.[25]

Lumley pompously announced that Lind was coming. However, she was slow in arriving, probably quite sensibly. Bunn had warned her that Lumley was unreliable. She was also worried that she would be put in prison for breaking her contract. Although the London impresarios may have thought that Lind 'was as inexperienced in all such matters as a child', she was not stupid. Besides, the Covent Garden opera did everything it could to dissuade her, even to the extent of purchasing Bunn's contract.[26]

The season opened at Her Majesty's with a charity performance that raised £2,000 for the victims of the Irish famine. However, Lind still did not appear. She refused to come unless the Drury Lane claims were dropped. When Lumley's announcement was said to be a lie, he sued for defamation.[27] He even went the considerable distance to Vienna to fetch Lind. Meanwhile, his patrons delayed buying seats until she came. For the time being, his theatre was deserted. The press called this sensation 'the Opera Fuss'.

Jenny Lind came once Mendelssohn was established in England which he was visiting for a gruelling schedule of performances of *Elijah*.* The nightingale was 'caught and caged', it is true; however, Lumley knew that 'it did not necessarily follow that the caged bird would sing'.[29] Eventually the bird did. After Lumley had jumped a few more hurdles, Jenny made her London début as Alice in Meyerbeer's *Robert* on 4 May 1847.

'Nothing like her voice had been heard before', it was reported. The box office was besieged. Jenny Lind's appearances were so popular that a new expression took root, 'a Jenny Lind crush'. 'It was not possible to obtain stalls for a single performance at which she appeared for less than five guineas. The sums paid for boxes ranged from 50 to 80 guineas, so that it will readily be understood that librarians and enterprising ticket dealers realised for once small fortunes'.[30] Parliamentary business ground to a halt as the MPs deserted Westminster to hear her. The Duke of Wellington was obsessed by her. The Queen, accompanied by the Prince Consort, exclaimed 'What a beautiful singer. What an actress!' '"How charming! How delightful" … These were the exclamations that fell from the lips of Her Majesty, who I had never before seen thus moved to enthusiasm',

*The soprano solo was written with Lind in mind, but she dared not turn up in time for the Birmingham première in the year before.[28]

reported a self-satisfied Lumley. Lind's operatic season in 1847, was 'one unbroken series of triumphs'.*[31]

Lumley's self-satisfaction was shortlived. He also staged a new opera, *I Masnadieri*, by Verdi whose successful reputation was by no means established in London at this time. Even Lumley had to admit that this work, which was based on Schiller's story *Die Räuber*, 'could not be considered a success'.[32] He was not alone. Turgenev saw it and told Pauline about 'l'attitude glaciale et ennuyée (bored) du public' towards it. He thought the opera was 'mauvais, mauvais et archi-mauvais'.[33] Since Lablache, renowned as he was for his 'colossal girth and thundering voice', was cast in the role of a starving prisoner released from a dungeon, this tragedy had its hilarious moments.[34]

Turgenev, writing to Pauline from London, said that Lind, for whose voice the music of *I Masnadieri* was not suited, had sung badly and hoarsely. However, perhaps mindful of Lind being a pupil of Manuel Garcia, he excused her on the grounds that her role required a singer who could roar.[35] Jenny was suitable for angelic roles. He was more enthusiastic about her performances in *La Sonnambula* and *Robert.*

The Viardot family were never Lind enthusiasts. Pauline's daughter Louise later wrote that she saw and heard Jenny Lind on several occasions. 'I will not dwell on her personality', she wrote. 'As a singer she seems to me overrated in spite of her fame. She was cold, terribly cold, as cold as her nature'. Coldness was never a characteristic of Pauline's performance; she seems to have been a better actress, although she lacked Jenny's prettiness.[36]

It was against this background that Pauline was signed up at Covent Garden for 1848, where a rival capable of taking on Lind was required. Notice of the re-opening of the Royal Italian Opera was given in the *Illustrated London News* of 29 January 1848 which also announced Pauline Viardot's appearance.[37] The press build-up was necessary because, meanwhile, 'the vast space of Her Majesty's Theatre was filled to suffocation on every night when the Swedish Nightingale appeared'. 'Overcrowded houses could not be crowded more'.[38]

*Because of Lind's eventual success, Bunn claimed £10,000 in damages. Although he had originally claimed only £500, he was awarded £2,500 in a 'sensational' case.

Why Pauline? It must have been clear that the Italians, with their soiled reputations, were not ideal to field against Jenny in the high noon of Albertine England. Reports of Lind's private life referred to 'her unblemished character, of her unbounded charities, and of her modesty'. There was even rumour that she was becoming religious, getting married and leaving the stage.[39] Who better to field against this paragon of virtue than the pure and virginal Consuelo herself?

Pauline's appearance on 9 May 1848 in Bellini's *La Sonnambula* was awaited with excitement. One Lind adherent prophesied that the combat would be bloody. Within a few hundred yards, an opera-goer could hear Jenny and, a few days later, Pauline in the same opera.[40]

However, the squib was damp. Pauline failed to eclipse Lind. The contest which actually took place was between Pauline and her Italian colleagues. One might reasonably have thought that the two teams at Her Majesty's and Covent Garden respectively would have pulled together and fought a good match against the other; Lind, Tadolini and Lablache versus Viardot, Grisi, Persiani and Mario. No such luck for Pauline! The incorrigible and idiotic Italians in Pauline's team were up to their old tricks. They fought among themselves.

On Pauline's first night, Mario was 'off sick'. His understudy 'did not feel up to it'.[41] Pauline had to appear opposite Flavio, a tenor who had only arrived in London on that day. She complained to Sand that she felt as if she were in a battle confronting one of those armies which were then marching around Italy in the cause of Italian nationalism and reunification.[42]

As a consequence, the quality of the performance was badly affected. Chopin, who was in London at the time, recognised that Pauline faced stiff competition. He did not think that she was particularly outstanding.[43] And the press was hardly complimentary about her. 'Had we not, from Continental Experience, been well acquainted with her musical and histrionic genius', said the *Illustrated London News*, 'we should not have recognised Viardot-Garcia until her finale.' However, the periodical provided a feature column on Pauline. This duly noted her respectability. 'In every relation of her private life Madame Pauline Garcia Viardot is endeared to her family and friends', reported the journal. It added that her husband had recently been offered the post of French *chargé d'affaires* in Madrid.[44] Pauline might equal Lind in virtue, but not in voice.

Fortunately, Pauline quickly recovered from her 'stage fright' and, a week later, the reporter wrote that 'it was difficult to recognise in the Viardot of Saturday the Viardot of the preceding Tuesday'. She was now receiving the ovations which she deserved.[45]

Pauline also appeared to great acclaim as Romeo in Bellini's *I Capuleti* and also in Mozart's *Don Giovanni.* The *Illustrated London News* regarded Pauline's Romeo as 'a triumph of mind over matter. It was the creation of Shakespeare's Romeo out of the flimsiest materials provided by the composer'.[46] Pauline was also a great success in the Italian version of *Les Huguenots.* She sang the part of Valentine, the daughter of the Catholic leader, and the lover of the Huguenot Raoul, a part sung by Mario. Meyerbeer, ever sensitive to his market, had given Costa *carte blanche* to adapt *Les Huguenots* for the London audience which was unlikely to take kindly to four hours of serious music. The three female stars, Viardot, Castellan and Alboni, sang 'God Save the Queen' when the Queen and Prince Albert came in to attend the première.[47]

Of course, Pauline's success rattled Grisi. When it came to Pauline's benefit performance, Mario claimed he was again indisposed. Grisi offered to sing extracts from Bellini's *Norma.* As Norma, Grisi had no rival. Her beauty and voice would easily eclipse Pauline's. Pauline, sensibly, was having none of it and retorted that she could quite well sing the part of Norma herself.[48] In the event, she appeared in *Les Huguenots.*[49]

Against the grubby activity behind the scenes, Lind's reputation could only flourish. Pauline will have read in the papers about her arrival at Blackwall, when 15–20,000 people lined the quay.[50] Even if the figures were almost certainly exaggerated by the journalist, this piece of publicity would have irritated Pauline considerably. Jenny had outclassed her.

It comes as some surprise that newspapers and their readers were at all interested in operatic 'star-wars' at this time. There was so much else to distract them. At the time of the press build-up for Pauline's début in *La Sonnambula,* some 15,000 people had demonstrated, on Kennington Common in south London, to support 'The People's Charter' for parliamentary and voting reform. The government was sufficiently worried that it asked the ancient Duke of Wellington to command the defence of Westminster. A force of 150,000 special constables was enrolled. The authorities had feared a much larger turnout of demonstrators because 300,000 had been summoned.[51] They were relieved that the whole affair fizzled out.

There was also agitation in Ireland. In Dublin, several men were arrested under the Drilling Act 'while performing military evolutions in a large room in the city'. During the summer, a rising was fomented by William Smith O'Brien, an aristocrat descended from Brian Boru, the 11th-century High King of Ireland.[52] However, 19th-century life in London generally went on as normal. The Prince of Wales bought a twenty-foot sculling boat which, judging by subsequent photographs, did not get much use. Among other items in the news were the Paris fashions and the appointment of a new Archbishop of Canterbury. And, of course, there was the Derby.[53]

On the Continent, events proved to be far more revolutionary. The *Illustrated London News* was pleased to report that Paris had narrowly escaped being again 'the theatre of a sanguinary tumult arising out of the wicked designs of the Communists and ultra-Republicans'.[54] The paper provided lurid pictures of the violence at the barricades. It printed headlines such as 'Civil War in France'. The journal reported how Rachel had sung the 'Marseillaise' during a performance at the Théâtre-Français. And it told of the death of the Archbishop of Paris, shot through the loins from behind as he tried to mediate at the barricades.[55]

While Pauline was singing on the London stage, Europe was aflame. The violence had begun in February. An uprising in Sicily ignited virtually every capital on the Continent. Although events took their own particular course in each country, the pattern was fairly similar everywhere. At first, monarchs were expelled; however, the middle classes disliked the vacuum and the chaos, so counter-revolution followed. This was enforced with a brutality which left scars across Europe, from Paris to Vienna, from Venice to Buda and Pest.

In France, King Louis-Philippe's régime, which had been inaugurated in 1830, was sitting on a powder keg. It was deeply unpopular. The Prime Minister François Guizot was 'compared to an honest woman running a brothel'. Not even in 1789 had the French monarchy been surrounded 'by such an aura of doom and discredit'. The Citizen King, who had already survived several assassination attempts, tried to avoid Paris. However, his absence just increased his unpopularity. The government's reputation was not helped by particularly poor harvests in 1845 and 1846. Also, January 1848 was appallingly cold and the Seine froze.[56] More than that, Revolution was 'in the air'.

In February 1848, the citizens of Paris took to the streets. The barricades went up, the Palace of the Tuileries was invaded, and Louis-Philippe, 'the epitome of all that was dull and commonplace, a grocer in a cotton nightcap', was sent packing. His throne was burnt on the Place de la Bastille. The fall of the monarchy had been so rapid that 'as soon as the first stupefaction that succeeded it had passed away, the middle classes felt a feeling of astonishment at the fact that they were still alive'.[57]

When the 1848 uprising began, the English rushed back home and business came to a halt. There was a run on the Bank of France. George Sand and her friends, such as Louis Blanc, the socialist thinker, were deeply involved. He set up workshops; she used her journalistic skill to support the provisional government, which was led at first by Alphonse de Lamartine, the romantic poet. She wrote inflammatory articles which were designed to rally the slumbering rural and provincial population. She also used her influence in the new corridors of power to help friends, such as Mazzini who led the Republic in Rome.[58] Turgenev, however, was in Brussels when the barricades went up. And Louis Viardot, a more probable revolutionary, was hunting in Prussia.[59] There was considerable confusion. At one stage, a desperately worried Pauline wrote to George to say that she could not find Maurice.[60]

Louis Viardot returned to Paris during a lull in the storm. He angled to be a candidate for the elections to the Assemblée Nationale. He sent his *curriculum vitae* to George. She replied that there was no chance of his nomination, because there was such a long queue of applicants. There was a chance, which came to nothing, that Louis or Pauline's brother might be appointed Director of the Opéra.[61]

George wanted Pauline to compose a new 'Marseillaise' which could be sung alongside the original one at the opening of the Théâtre de la République. In the event, Pauline composed a cantata, *La Jeune République*, which was among the 33 submissions that were awarded a bronze medal. Around 800 compositions had been sent in. Because she was suffering from an attack of migraine and neuralgia, Pauline could not take part in the official performance at the beginning of April. It was a big occasion attended by many VIPs including Lamartine himself. The solo parts were performed by Gustave-Hippolyte Roger* who was accompanied by 50 Conservatoire maidens, wearing white muslin trimmed with tricolour ribbons. The cantata then went on sale. Its profits went to the Fund for Patriotic Gifts. Putting aside any views people might have had about Pauline's musical skill, her radical political orientation, which matched that of her husband, was clear to all.[62]

In the event the counter-revolution, induced by the conservative middle classes, prevailed; George Sand felt ashamed of being French. When the 'Revolution' collapsed, Pauline offered George a sanctuary at Courtavenel. George's friends told her to make a run for Italy. However, she remained at Nohant where she had fended off the local people who shouted 'Down with Madame Dudevant', 'A bas Madame Dudevant, A bas les Communistes'. Although they raised their hats to her, they also threatened to burn her château.[63]

During the upheavals, Pauline's main professional work was still centred on London, where she made many appearances with Berlioz. Like Mario, she also sang songs at Chopin's London concerts. One was held at Lord Falmouth's on 12 July.[64]

She had arranged her own transcription of several of Chopin's mazurkas. For these, she used Spanish words, and the arrangements were popular items in her programmes. Chopin felt some justifiable irritation when they were billed without any reference to the fact that he was the original composer. Chopin, who was such a sensitive man, echoed Clara Schumann's concern that success was going to Pauline's head. 'It is all the same to me', he wrote about the transcriptions, 'but there is a pettiness behind it'.[65]

For Pauline, the season in London had had its happy and unhappy moments, its intrigue. In a nutshell, she said, it was 'full of the ups and downs in the good life which only performers can understand'.[66]

On returning to Paris in the autumn, the Viardots spent 75,000 francs[67] buying a town house. Thus, in early December, we find Pauline heading her letter to George Sand 'Rue de Douai, 16'.

*Roger had already appeared with Pauline in London. Later, he sang opposite her in *Le Prophète.* As a result of his gun exploding when he was out shooting, his arm had to be amputated. His career was finished; he became professor of singing at the Paris Conservatoire. He was a visitor to Courtavenel.

'Où diable est située la rue de Douai?', George asked Louis. She might well ask where it was. It was in 'le nouveau Paris', close to the Barrière Blanche, and was sandwiched between the disreputable area to the north of the river and the equally disreputable area around Montmartre.[68] Going northwards from the Seine, 'that lovely, smooth, variegated, and stinking river filled with visions and with filth', one passed 'through the smell of the gaslights and the noise of the omnibuses', and went past the brothels which infested the area behind the recently consecrated church of Notre-Dame-de-Lorette.[69] The rue de Douai, a property development, would then be found in a respectable 'arty' area, a veritable oasis.

This was just before one reached 'the drab slope of Montmartre' whose hill was topped with windmills. The large Benedictine abbey whose abbess had been guillotined during the 1789 Revolution had been razed, and replaced by tall yellow and grey houses 'among clusters of sparse greenery'. At the foot of the hill was the desolate city outskirt, where steam and smoke spewed from a tall forest of factory chimneys, the roads were black with coal dust and the ruts brimmed with stagnant water. 'Le Château Rouge', the pleasure gardens for those with three francs to spare, had recently opened for a few years, but mostly the area was full of drinking dens where the wretched population, for many of whom three francs represented more than a day's wage, solaced and soaked themselves in alcohol.[70] Beyond were the building sites and then the fortifications of Paris, where the working classes could at last find fresh air in which to disport themselves.[71]

The Viardots' house in the rue de Douai, like Courtavenel, is no more to be seen. Today, the building located on its site looks over a square in which there is a modern statue, which for those in the know is just recognisably one of Berlioz. The new building comprises flats above and a baker's shop below. It is a stone's throw from the Moulin Rouge, the dance hall which was opened 40 years after the Viardots moved into their house.[72] There, the cabaret performed the cancan. There, one might find the characters which were portrayed so famously in the work of Toulouse-Lautrec. Today, one can see the towers of the Basilica of Sacré-Coeur peeping above the houses and sex shops.

The Viardot residence in this oasis was a 'pretty little house with a triangular garden'. It was surrounded by trees, and 'separated from the street by a small wall with railings and a wrought iron gate, with a small courtyard in front and a garden behind'.[73] The garden was at the back of the house, at the junction of the rues de Douai and de Bruxelles. From the courtyard, there were steps up to the main entrance, with a basement and 'offices' below. At the side of the courtyard, there was a stable and staff quarters.[74]

The Viardots' son Paul would later write that the location was chosen because it was well away from the centre and the air was clean. It was also 'on ground suitable for the cultivation of artichokes'.[75] Scheffer's delightful villa, built in the Italian style, was very close by in a parallel street. It still stands, and gives an indication of how pleasant and leafy these prosperous suburban residences must have been at the time.

The Viardots probably spent as much as the purchase price on doing up the house.[76] They built a conservatory out into the garden, which was later turned into a picture gallery. They also added a further storey between the second floor and the attic.

As staunch radicals, the Viardots were somewhat self-conscious about their acquisition. Pierre-Joseph Proudhon, the socialist, was preaching that 'All Property is Theft'.[77] However, with the success of the counter-revolution, the bourgeois values of the middle class were back in vogue. 'Property rose to the level of Religion and was confounded with God.'[78] Louis's journal, the *Revue indépendante*, was a casualty of this time.

The Viardots searched for justification for their house purchase, as prosperous radicals often do in such circumstances. They soon found that, at their residence, they were providing a commendable amount of employment to all sorts of workmen who would otherwise be unemployed.

In George Sand's view, Louis had chosen an excellent time to buy because, with all the upheavals in Paris, house prices had halved. She bemoaned the fact that her daughter Solange had been forced to sell her property at the bottom of the market. Indeed she tried to interest Pauline in investing in this property, a straight chance to double one's capital, so she calculated. Was this a curious suggestion for a 'socialist' to make? Maybe not. Whatever the politics of George Sand and the Viardots, they had all worked very hard for their living. Why should they not enjoy the fruits of their endeavour?[79]

THE SECOND REPUBLIC AND THE SECOND EMPIRE: KEY EVENTS

The Second Republic was proclaimed at the end of February 1848. King Louis-Philippe fled, so 'the July Monarchy' came to an end.

The new government set up workshops to provide employment. However, this initiative failed. An uprising from 23–26 June ('the June Days') was crushed with the help of the National Guard, a middle-class militia whose role was to maintain order. The barricades went up and down. The government was utterly ruthless in its suppression. Around 1,500 were killed, 15,000 arrested and 4,000 deported.[80]

The disruption enabled Louis-Napoléon, the leader of the Bonaparte faction and nephew of the former Emperor, to step in and, in December 1848, be elected as President of the Republic for a single four-year term. He had the overwhelming support of 74 per cent of those voting. The comparable figure for Paris was 58 per cent.[81]

In December 1851, Louis-Napoléon staged a coup in order to extend his four-year term of office. The coup was immediately approved by a plebiscite in which over 90 per cent were in favour.[82] The Prince-President gradually consolidated his position.

In November 1852 the Senate, in a decision which was ratified by 80 per cent of the electorate of around 10 million,[83] re-established the Empire as the 'Second Empire'.

The 'Great' Napoleon had died in May 1821 on St Helena. His heir presumptive was his son, the King of Rome, later Duke of Reichstadt, who was born in 1811. He died of tuberculosis in 1832 at his grandfather's palace, Schönbrunn, near Vienna. The new Emperor therefore styled himself 'Napoléon III'.

In January 1853, Napoleon III married a Spaniard who became Empress Eugénie. Their son, the Prince Imperial, was killed in the Anglo-Zulu War in 1879.

The Second Empire lasted until the defeat in the Franco-Prussian War. This began on 19 July 1870. Napoleon III was captured at Sedan on 2 September. Paris was besieged; it capitulated on 28 January.[84] This led to the Commune which collapsed on 28 May 1871. The Third Republic, which emerged from the defeat by Prussia, succumbed in 1940.

CHAPTER 12

Le Prophète

Chopin's reservations about Pauline's reception in London were possibly coloured by his irritation at the way success seemed to be going to her head. Even if, for him, she was not yet in the first rank, she was about to perform a role for which, at least at the time, she would be renowned.

Throughout the winter of 1848–9, preparations were made for Pauline's first appearance at the Paris Opéra, in *Le Prophète*.[1] Meyerbeer, as usual, adapted his 'concoction made to order' to exploit her 'uncommon voice'.[2] In order to ensure wider use, he specified in the score that 'every time the vocal line, written to show off Mme Viardot's exceptional compass, rises or falls above or below the normal mezzo-soprano range, a way to avoid this extension will be found, written in small notes'.[3] At the final rehearsal, Meyerbeer sat down with Père David, the 'chef de claque', the paid cheerleader. Together, they amended passages to optimise the potential for applause.[4]

The composer Sir Charles Stanford heard that, during the final rehearsals, Meyerbeer threatened Pauline that if she did not have a protuberant tooth removed he would give the part to somebody else. Even though we may think this improbable, the existence of the anecdote underlines Meyerbeer's reputation for hard-headed commercialism. It also reminds us of Pauline's reputation so far as her appearance was concerned.

There was a considerable publicity build-up, as we heard at the beginning of this book. Leaks in the press were deliberately orchestrated to keep the public informed and salivating. There was talk of the 150,000 franc production,[5] and of the new technology, electric light, which was in use for the first time at the Opéra. This would be used to portray the rising sun.[6]

The ticket touts had a field day. Three days before the première on 16 April 1849, the mortally ill Chopin had heard it said that Madame Viardot in the part of the mother was expected to make everyone cry. Chopin was in the audience, as was Richard Wagner who walked out ostentatiously at the end of the first Act.[7] Wagner thus missed Meyerbeer's spectacular dénouement, of the variety which the Paris audience had come to expect.

Le Prophète is set at the time of the Reformation. It is about a mother's love for her son. John of Leyden, whose appearance makes him look like the biblical King David, is chosen to be the leader of the Anabaptists, a heretical Protestant sect. Before this, John has to choose between surrendering his fiancée into the clutches of the local count, or letting him seize and imprison his elderly mother Fidès, a part played by Pauline. He chooses to surrender his fiancée, whereupon Fidès sings the beautiful aria 'Ah mon fils' and John receives her blessing.

Meyerbeer provided a *coup de spectacle* for the ballet which was compulsory in grand opera at the Opéra. In the 'Pas des Patineurs', the Anabaptist insurgents make merry with the local peasants on a frozen lake near their camp. The dancers used roller-skates on artificial ice.

At John's coronation Fidès, who by now is a beggar, recognises her son and approaches him. However, his 'divine' reputation will be questionable if his followers see that he is merely the son of a beggar and not a reincarnation of King David after all. So, he has to disown his mother who is taken away in chains. He begs her forgiveness and she sings the second well-known aria 'O prêtres de Baal'. However, the Anabaptist leaders have lost confidence in John and conspire to betray him.

So, after a bacchanalian scene in the palace, John has the whole place blown up, including himself and his mother.[8] The curtain falls. As with much of grand opera, the audience can expect an explosive dénouement.

The start of the world première was described by the correspondent of the *Illustrated London News*. Three knocks from the prompter quelled the buzz of conversation. Then, 'as the curtain rose, a pin might have been heard to drop'.[9]

Pauline began somewhat nervously, although she soon settled into the part. The reporter described the fifth act as 'Siddonian in dignity and Kean-like in burst of feeling'. He added, 'this scene of Viardot was electrical in its effect'. The house rose en masse three times to applaud. The critic said that 'whether for the alternate use of the soprano and contralto registers, whether for the daring vocal intervals, her prolonged shakes, and finished intricacies, and whether for the histrionic genius which illumed the conception, never within my recollection, at home or abroad, have I witnessed a grander display of consummate lyric Art.' Pauline could not have asked for much more praise.[10]

After the performance, Meyerbeer told his mother that he had never seen any actor reach such tragic heights and declared that 'Madame Viardot is one of the greatest artists who comes to mind in the past and present history of music'. Also, if one believes the story, the composer went to Pauline's dressing-room and presented her with a bracelet. In its centre, set in costly jewels, was a piece of white enamel. It was Pauline's front tooth.*[11]

'What can I say to you?', Meyerbeer was reputed to have said to Pauline. 'There were the tears of thousands to prove the effect of your singing'. To this, he added, wholly improbably, 'I totally forgot that I was the composer of the opera'.[12]

However, this show was not going to last long, if only because, as one writer explained with commendable succinctness, 'in no other opera, to my knowledge, is the heroine an old woman'.[13] Delacroix described the work as the 'awful *Prophète* ... the annihilation of Art'. Some years later, Saint-Saëns deplored its 'musical marquetry' and described the opera as 'a mosaic without colours, a garden without flowers, a practical course in musical theology without true faith'. To Chorley, the London critic, 'the charm of Madame Viardot's splendid personification wore itself out because of the stilted and untruthful nature of the situations'.[14] It was a measure of her achievement that she surmounted these obstacles and earned such praise.

The religious subject matter of this opera, the glorification of anti-Roman Catholic heresy, was unfortunate in its timing. During the 1848 upheavals, the Pope was toppled from the throne of the extensive Papal

*When Stanford visited Pauline, in the early 1900s, he was tempted to ask to see the bracelet, but was too polite to do so.

States which then comprised the centre of the Italian peninsula. He was kicked out of Rome, which became a Republic under the leadership of the republican propagandist Giuseppi Mazzini and the patriot and soldier of fortune Giuseppi Garibaldi. French political leaders were split about what to do in Italy. In March, the Assemblée Nationale had voted to send a force to support Mazzini and Garibaldi. However, the Prince-President, who attended *Le Prophète*, was now more interested in supporting Catholicism and restoring the Pope to his throne. In the event, the Pope was reinstated after the French came to his assistance. His exile only lasted for around three months.

The temperature in Paris, both political and physical, was very high. Around the time of the Assembly elections in May, the Opéra had to close because of a riot. Added to this, an epidemic of cholera broke out.[15] With yet more revolution on the horizon, the correspondent of the *Illustrated London News* took the opportunity to remind its readers that, in 1535, the real John of Leyden and his followers had 'committed every excess and every horror, promulgating socialism, the community of goods and the abolition of all distinctions'. The correspondent was pleased to point out that, in reality rather than in fiction, John was captured and made to suffer slow torture, before being despatched.[16]

The show, which Meyerbeer sensibly truncated so as to be acceptable to a London audience, moved across the Channel.[17] There, Pauline's stellar position had already been established. In late May, she appeared as Valentine in *Les Huguenots. The Times*, recollecting her eventual success a year before, reported that in this role she 'may be said to have gained her reputation in this country as an actress and as a singer'.[18]

The PR build-up went well, whether by accident or design. In his Concert Monstre held in Exeter Hall on Friday 1 June, Monsieur Jullien advertised excerpts from *Le Prophète* 'now performing at the Grand Opera in Paris with unprecedented success'. A few weeks later, a notice appeared in the press stating that the 'Pas des Patineurs' advertised 'by a rival establishment' was not the original. That was 'in rehearsal at the Royal Italian Opera'. It emphasised that 'any other performance of this *Pas* or any part of it can only be executed in an imperfect form'. Four days after this, the directors of the Royal Italian Opera were pleased to announce that Madame Viardot-Garcia was engaged to perform in *Le Prophète* early in July. Four days after that, it was announced that *Le Prophète* was to be 'the grand event of the season'.[19]

On Wednesday 11 July, *The Times* announced that Pauline had arrived in London. 'As a spectacle, the *Prophète* in Paris surpassed every opera ever before produced at the Grand Opera; and it is to be brought out here, it is asserted, on an even grander scale', trumpeted another newspaper.[20]

When the curtain rose on the scene in Dordrecht, the superb set looked like a Dutch painting. The critics were ecstatic. The critic praised Pauline's 'rich contralto register' and 'wondrous soprano compass, executing at the close a shake on the high notes of consummate skill and power'.[21] Despite her having a cold, 'a finer piece of acting and more surprising and accomplished singing were never before witnessed on the lyric stage. She seemed on Tuesday night at times to be inspired; and the excitement created in the house by her bursts of lofty enthusiasm was unexampled. In the third and fourth acts, the house rang with acclamations at her great points;* and the showers of bouquets and recalls were incessant.'[22]

Mario was not overlooked. 'His Prophet was one of the most picturesque and forceable of his impersonations', said one report.

The media's use of superlatives seems almost to have excelled modern usage, and has to be treated with caution. When Pauline was triumphing at the Royal Italian Opera, Henriette Sontag, one of the professional and bedtime rivals of Malibran,[23] was down the road at Her Majesty's singing 'each note bright, limpid and polished in the extreme'.[24] Sontag's performance in *Linda* would alone 'be worth a pilgrimage', the papers also claimed. The blonde Venus, 'the Nightingale of the North',[25] had been sufficiently attractive for HM Ambassador in Vienna to stalk, and consequently earn the nickname Lord Montag (because, for a German, Montag follows Sontag). She was now well-worn and into her forties.[26]

The season ended in mid-August, when the normally flat period for news was enlivened by the reports of Lola Montes, the King of Bavaria's notorious Irish mistress, being tried in London for bigamy. Also a corpse was found under the flagstones in a house south of the Thames, in Bermondsey.[27]

*A 'point' here is a vocal flourish or an elaborately decorated cadenza, usually at the end; so that, as the composer of 'Jerusalem' noted, 'the audience might have the impression of astonishment in their minds to urge them to applause'.

Sontag

Pauline had been lodging in Maida Vale, the new estate of magnificent mansions on the northern outskirts of London. She left her residence there to go to perform at the Liverpool Festival. In the winter of 1849–50, she was back in Paris, where she gave 34 performances singing in *Le Prophète*, and in spring 1850 she performed in Berlin before handing the role over to a former pupil, Wagner's niece Johanna.[28]

Pauline was at last achieving greatness, not just international stardom. She was singing like 'une harpe du ciel'.[29] However, for Turgenev in France, things seemed less rosy. We shall shortly look at what was happening to Pauline's child Louise and the other children caught up in Pauline's success story. Meanwhile Turgenev was adrift, with no money.

For him the outlook was equally unpromising back home in Russia. In April 1849 the Russian authorities, their weather eye towards western Europe, cracked down on a network of radical discussion groups made up mainly of civil servants, junior officers, teachers and students. The organisation was known, after its leader, as the Petrashevtsy circle. Of the 40 arrested, fifteen were sentenced to death, including Dostoyevsky. This repression put the wind up many writers at the time.[30]

Turgenev stayed in France. There he became ill, possibly from his recurrent hypochondria, possibly from the cholera, a disease which terrified him throughout his life, as did the fear of death. Or maybe he was suffering from the bladder complaint which he had experienced in the previous year. Whether it was actually venereal or merely psychosomatic, his condition was a tell-tale sign of his activities.[31]

The lease on Turgenev's apartment expired. He was about to leave Paris when serious illness struck. He had, many times, been casually in and out of the flat belonging to his friend Alexander Herzen, the left wing thinker and publicist. Herzen was, by now, disillusioned with the failure of the 1848 insurrection. He and his wife regarded Turgenev as a bit of an old woman and Natalya Herzen was bored with his 'limp and weary gaze'.[32] Turgenev needed a bed for the night and came to stay. Herzen recalled how, after dinner, he complained of the heat. Herzen suggested he took a bath. Turgenev came back, unwell. He drank some soda water with a little wine and sugar in it, and then went to bed. In the night, he woke Herzen and exclaimed, 'I'm finished; it's cholera'. 'He really was suffering from sickness and spasms', said Herzen who looked after him for ten days.[33]

It was against the unpropitious backdrop of poor health, physical and mental, that Turgenev worked on his play* *A Month in the Country.* He also wrote the short story *The Diary of a Superfluous Man.* These two works show how down in the dumps he was. They also give a good indication of how matters stood between him and Pauline at the time.[35]

---

*At this time, some of Turgenev's plays were running successfully in St Petersburg: *A Provincial Lady* ran successfully in Moscow in early 1851.[34]

Turgenev started writing *A Month in the Country* in early 1849 and had completed the fourth of its five acts by Christmas. The play was completed by the end of March in the following year.[36] However, it was not published until January 1855, when it appeared in *The Contemporary.* It was only staged seventeen years later, and even then the censor insisted that various passages were excised. However, when Turgenev first wrote it, it had considerable success in private readings in the salons.[37]

The play is set on a country estate in Russia. The apparent tranquility of a triangular relationship between a rich nobleman, his discontented wife and their resident family friend of four years is plunged into chaos. A young tutor arrives to teach her son. 'Everything's destroyed, scattered, gone.'

Natalya Petrovna, the wife, is just under 30. She is clever, beautiful, bored and provincial. 'Uncertain of her feelings and racked by guilt', she 'wreaks havoc upon all who surround her, until she has no alternative left but to return in a mood of bleak humiliation to her troubled and unloved husband'.[38] Meanwhile, her jealousy prompts her to wreck the love of her seventeen-year-old ward Verochka who falls for the tutor.

At one moment, Natalya Petrovna asks the young Verochka whether she wants to marry for love rather than convenience. Her ward replies, 'Yes, but you … Didn't you marry for love?' Natalya Petrovna's hesitation implies considerable doubt, although she tartly responds 'Yes, for love, of course.' Later, *à propos* the tutor, she says 'I'm in love for the first time in my life'.

Turgenev identified himself with Rakitin, the unsatisfied and aimless family friend. A distinguished commentator has said that 'he tended towards this kind of self-conscious caricature all his life'.[39] And, of course, it is not difficult to construct an analogy between Natalya Petrovna and Pauline. The rich, cuckolded husband can be interpreted as Louis Viardot. It seems wholly improbable, however tempting it may be, that the young tutor can have been based upon Charles Gounod who, as we shall soon hear, Pauline only began to collaborate with from the autumn of that year. 'Much of the play had been completed and therefore the main outlines of it already planned before Gounod came into Pauline's life.'[40]

There is no suggestion that the story of *A Month in the Country* is anything other than fiction. Turgenev invariably based his characters on real-life people who inspired or just interested him. However, his characters were 'a synthesis of many observations',[41] rather than a portrait of any one specific person. Yet the tone of this play certainly reflects the dramatist's depressed, jilted mood. It is also a surprising premonition of things to come.

This mood is also apparent from *The Diary of a Superfluous Man*. This short story is about 'a man of often real talent, who can find no place for himself in the society of his time', a man who is 'superfluous by virtue of his own failings as well as by virtue of the indifference of society to his personal inadequacy and his personal fate'. He is the 'the bird of no account', and 'the living embodiment of the sickness at the heart of Russian society'. Sometimes, at best, he is a misfit.[42]

The story of *The Diary* concerns the recollections of a dying 33-year-old. 'I've been completely superfluous in this world of ours', he writes. 'People are bad, good, clever, stupid, pleasant and unpleasant; but superfluous ... no. But in my case nothing else can be said about me. I'm superfluous and that's all there is to it'. The man dies during the night of 1–2 April. It would have been too definite if he had actually died on April Fools' Day.[43]

The 'superfluous man' pervades Russian literature of the period. Pushkin's Eugene Onegin, also the subject of Tchaikovsky's great opera, became one of the first. The 'superfluous man' appears in Turgenev's novels right up to his final one, *Virgin Soil*. At the end of this, the leading character shoots himself. When for a moment he regains consciousness, he has just the time to exclaim 'Failed again'.[44]

In mid-June, around the time that Pauline arrived in London for *Le Prophète*, a run-down, depressed and superfluous Turgenev moved to Courtavenel. He had no choice. He had no money with which to lease another flat in Paris; he was in debt to his publisher. His mother had cut off his cash flow and it was not long before he was scrounging a loan of 400 francs off Louis, and money off Pauline's aunt. While Pauline triumphed, Turgenev's circumstances must have seemed very bleak. But he did have the pleasure of living in *un château enchanté*, his enchanted castle.[45]

Pauline, when not taking part in one of the 25 performances of *Le*

Prophète which took place at the Opéra before 6 July, could go home to Courtavenel. There, the two of them would relax and read together. Perhaps they would read works by Goethe, or Thackeray's *Vanity Fair*, which had been published very recently. This was a vintage time for English literature, with the publication of Charlotte Brontë's *Jane Eyre* and Emily Brontë's *Wuthering Heights* as well.[46]

Then, all of a sudden, something seems to have taken place which may have given Turgenev some grounds for hope, even optimism. Something happened between him and Pauline. We know this from a cryptic note which he subsequently made in his papers relating to that June: 'on 14/26 I first time with P'.* What he meant by this has been the subject of much speculation. Whether it denoted something more significant than just flirtation on his part, or compassion on hers, we will return to later. Maybe there was some physical expression of sympathy from a caring Pauline, the 'sister of charity' who regarded it as 'her destiny to care for wounded hearts'.[47] Maybe there was something more. Whatever did take place, Turgenev became far more upbeat.

When, a few days afterwards, Pauline went to London for the production of *Le Prophète*, Turgenev remained in Courtavenel. He wrote to her, effusively and lengthily, sometimes twice a day. He kept Louis informed of things which needed to be done about the place. He set about reorganising the library and reading the books. He took Louis's dog Sultan for walks. He cleared the rushes out of the moat.

He went out coarse-fishing before dawn with Pauline's uncle. On one such occasion, they caught 118 fish. During the day, Turgenev scratched off the harvest bugs. He reported a violent hailstorm which destroyed the crops. He also wrote to Pauline about his experience at the local fête. Listening to the village band, a clarinettist, trumpeter and two violins, had been rather like suffering under a dentist's drill.[48]

Turgenev's correspondence was irrepressible. He followed closely the reports of Pauline's success in the London première of *Le Prophète*. He could not afford the English newspapers and periodicals such as the *Illustrated London News* and the *Athenaeum*, so he had to scrounge a franc from Pauline's aunt in order to go and read them in Paris library. He managed

* Russia still used the old style 'Julian' calendar, which, in the nineteenth century, was twelve days behind the Gregorian calendar adopted in Western Europe. Turgenev often adhered to the convention of giving both dates in this way in relation to an occurrence outside Russia.

to get the *Musical World* sent to Courtavenel.[49] On writing paper embossed with a bouquet of flowers, he told Pauline how he read about her. At the moment when he knew she was on stage, he followed the performance in his mind, applauded her bows, threw bouquets of flowers, and imagined the encores. He wrote to her 'My dear one, my darling. Every moment I am thinking of you ... I have called out your name so rapturously, stretched out my arms to you so lovingly, that you surely must have heard and seen'.[50]

While Turgenev was emerging from his depression, a tragedy was unfolding in Paris; Chopin was dying. Pauline had rather lost touch with her friend from Nohant who had so doted on her daughter Louise. Nevertheless, she recorded his last hours. 'All the great ladies of Paris thought themselves obliged to come and faint in his room.' A photographer, making daguerreotypes, asked for the bed to be put closer to the window 'so that the dying man should be in the light'.[51]

Pauline was asked to sing in the performance of Mozart's *Requiem* at Chopin's funeral which was held almost a fortnight after his death on 17 October. The congregation in La Madeleine was very distinguished. It included Meyerbeer, Delacroix and Turgenev.[52] George Sand, of course, was not there. She had last seen her lover eighteen months earlier, when she was going to a reception which followed a service held for those killed on the barricades. She encountered Chopin on the staircase, going in the opposite direction to her. As they passed, he was able to tell her that her daughter Solange had given birth to her baby.

The quality of the singing at Chopin's funeral must have seemed very poor and muffled. Pauline had to be hidden from view behind a black velvet curtain. With some difficulty, special permission had been obtained from the ecclesiastical authorities to allow female voices, despite St Paul's categorical prohibition of women either speaking or singing in church.[53]

Pauline insisted on a fee of 2,000 francs for that appearance behind the curtain. The cost was borne by Chopin's admirer from Scotland who financed the funeral. Pauline applied a principle: Never Sing for Nothing. 'You are not going to make yourself into an artist just for pleasure', she told a pupil. 'I hope that it will give you pleasure, but you must also earn your living'.[54] One of Chopin's old friends expressed his shock at the mercenary attitude shown by all the soloists, a sign of the times in which they lived. He thought that the singers' own self-respect should have impelled them to offer their services as a gesture of homage to Chopin and 'not to sell to his memory'.[55]

One doubts if this commentator was alone in thinking that success seemed to have gone not just to Pauline's head, but to her pocket as well.

Act Three

CHAPTER 13

Gounod and *Sapho*

Meyerbeer's *Le Prophète* propelled Pauline to the top of her profession and enhanced her prestige enormously. The opera itself may not have been first-rate, but her performance unquestionably was. It might not be unreasonable to suppose that, after this triumph, she felt sufficiently confident of her upward momentum to transfer her affection wholeheartedly to Turgenev. That is, if they were lovers and she truly wanted to. She did not. Instead, Turgenev felt a considerable draught.

Even if such a notion so much as crossed her mind, and she knew how to overcome the considerable practical difficulties which she would face, along came Charles Gounod. He became a keen participant in the fun and games at Courtavenel. He might have stepped straight into *A Month in the Country*, in the role of the tutor. Like Turgenev, he was personable, handsome, well-spoken, a good conversationalist. He was also attractive to women.[1] Pauline and Gounod worked on *Sapho* which she performed in Paris and London, around the time of further upheavals in France. Then all of a sudden Gounod's own loyalty, if it ever existed, became suspect. He announced he was off to get married.

Gounod was one of the more improbable personalities in music, so much so that, as Pauline herself would find, it was impossible to believe much that he said. He was a mass of contradictions. Perpetually torn between the church and the theatre, he was 'the scholar who read and learnedly annotated Saint Augustine, yet was ready to set to music the trashiest libretti if he thought they would bring him success on the stage'. On the one hand, he had a mother fixation; on the other, he also liked young and pretty girls, at times the 'the younger the better'.[2]

Gounod

Pauline, as we have seen, had first met Gounod in Rome when on her honeymoon. The Prix de Rome laureate accompanied her in an aria which Ingres, the distinguished painter, had asked her to sing.[3]

Gounod came from a family of sword-cutlers whose home was in the Louvre building, on the Seine side, where several craftsmen lived and had their workshops. His father was an art teacher in the Ecole Polytechnique, who married a lawyer's daughter, from Rouen. She, at 26, was almost half his age. She eked out a living giving piano lessons.[4]

Gounod's father knew Carle Vernet, the court painter to Louis XVIII, and son of the landscape painter Joseph Vernet. This contact possibly helped Gounod *père*, at the Restoration, to become the official artist to the

Duc de Berry* and drawing-master to the pages of the King's Chamber. As a perquisite of this office, old Gounod was provided with an official lodging at Versailles, where he built up his own art collection of works by Michelangelo, Jordaens, Poussin, Rembrandt and Van Dyck.[6]

Charles-François, the Gounods' second son, was born on 17 June 1818. He was three years older than Pauline and a few months older than Turgenev. By the time that his father died, which was when he was four, Charles could, so it was said, distinguish between the major and minor key, recognise intervals and appreciate modulation. This was no mean feat, although it would later be eclipsed by that spectacular prodigy Camille Saint-Saëns who by the time he reached a similar age had already begun to write music, and was on the way to being an expert on fossils and the life cycle of butterflies.[7]

Charles Gounod's mother, like many ambitious mothers, wanted her son to become a lawyer. However, in 1836 he went to the Conservatoire. There, he won the second prize in the Prix de Rome. Three years later he won the first prize, whereas Saint-Saëns did not win the Prix de Rome at all.[8]

Gounod was an ideal person to be a student at the Villa Medici in Rome, where all the laureates, whether musicians, painters or sculptors, spent two years. Ingres, who was a friend of Gounod's father, was so impressed with the young man's drawing skills that he offered to arrange for him to return to Rome as a laureate in painting. Although this offer was not taken up, young Gounod helped Ingres with his work. The hands in Ingres's well-known portrait of the grumpy, pedantic Cherubini were modelled by Gounod. As one author describes it, 'the composer of *Ali Baba* confronts posterity with the hands of *Faust*'s creator'.[9] This possibly explains why Cherubini's fingers seem more realistic than the usual boneless sausages (or worse) which substitute for fingers in many of Ingres's otherwise great portraits.

Gounod was a loner and he showed early signs of religiosity. He attended the services of a Dominican friar Henri Lacordaire who was a fashionable preacher in Rome at the time. This reinforced his enthusiasm for the Renaissance polyphonic music sung in the Sistine Chapel. He became passionate about the wonderful masses and motets of Palestrina and Lassus.[10]

*The Duc de Berry, nephew of Louis XVIII and son of Charles X, was assassinated in 1820 outside the Opéra. At the time, as well as being in search of his mistress, he was an heir presumptive to his throne.[5]

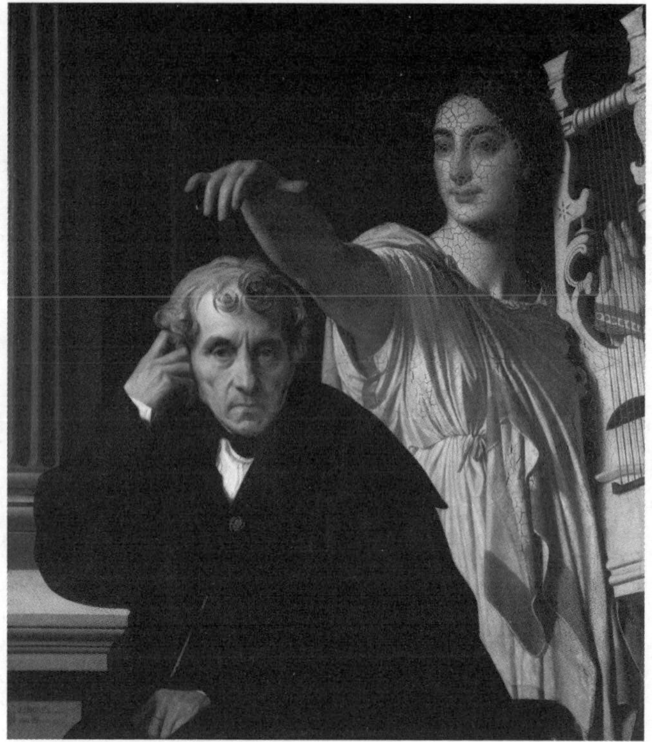

Cherubini with Gounod's hands?

The students were required to send back to Paris examples of their work. When Gounod's *Te Deum* arrived in Paris, the distinguished composer Gaspare Spontini condemned it as clumsy and badly worked out. Still, undeterred and undismayed, Gounod headed off to Vienna for the German stage of his Prix de Rome. In Berlin, he caught up with Fanny Mendelssohn, whom he had met in Rome. Then, she had been somewhat disconcerted by his wild enthusiasm. Now, she gave him an introduction to her brother. They spent four days in Leipzig together.[11]

After his stay in Germany, where he composed some masses, Gounod returned to Paris to become organist at the Eglise des Missions Etrangères for which he was paid a salary of 1,200 francs per annum. This church is on the Left Bank, close to the Boulevard Saint-Germain.* There, he tried

*The church is on the corner of the rue du Bac and the rue de Babylone, to the south of the Musée d'Orsay.

to introduce the music of Bach and of Palestrina, two composers who he believed shared a spiritual unity with Michelangelo. The congregation was less enthusiastic about this. When the matter was raised at a 'counselling session', Gounod gave a response which all organists might care to memorise for their dealings with clergy. 'Monsieur le Curé', he retorted. 'I am here not to consult your parishioners, but to edify them'. The Curé sacked him. However, an hour later, the cleric regretted his decision and began to negotiate. Gounod's response was commendably uncompromising. 'If I must listen to everybody's objections, there will be no way of getting along', he affirmed. 'Either I remain independent, or I go.' To this the Curé sighed, 'Ah, Mon Dieu, what a dreadful man you are'. He promptly re-engaged Gounod, who stayed for five years. Gounod and his mother shared lodgings with the Curé.[12]

Gounod remained under the influence of the Dominican who had returned from Rome to Paris. In October 1847, Gounod was authorised to live with the Carmelites and, as a day pupil, to take courses at the Seminary of Saint-Sulpice. He had already begun to style himself 'Abbé', although he never actually took holy orders. However, consistent with his tendency to fluctuate between 'the poles of sacred and profane love', it was now opportune for him to turn to the theatre, where fortunes were made. To do this, however, he needed a libretto.[13]

In the summer of 1849, through a mutual friend, Gounod was introduced to Pauline and was among many potential musicians who sought to 'leverage' her prestige following her success in *Le Prophète.* She told him to see Emile Augier, a prominent dramatist who Turgenev regarded as a 'premature old bore'. Gounod, as a boy, had played 'at rolling-hoop in the Luxembourg Gardens' with him.[14]

Pauline said she would perform his leading role, provided that Augier would write the libretto and provided that the Director of the Opéra – a colourful character who was reputed to have exclaimed 'My dream is to die insolvent and in style' – would stage it. Pauline had sufficient stature that she could make the commissioning of such a work a condition of the renewal of her contract at the Opéra. She could also insist, against the Director's inclination, that the work should be a full-length opera rather than just a 'one-act curtain-raiser'.[15] This opera would be *Sapho*. The story about the poetess from Lesbos must have seemed an interesting choice for those who may have wondered if there was something sexual in Pauline's relationship with George Sand.[16]

Gounod was given until the end of September 1850 to have the opera ready. In early April, just after he signed the contract with the Opéra, his elder brother, an architect, died suddenly at the age of 43. He left behind a two-year-old child and a pregnant widow. Both Pauline and Louis provided great moral support to Gounod at this difficult time. Although Pauline was away on tour, she suggested that he and his mother should recuperate from their bereavement at Courtavenel. Also, with time running out, he should get on with the composing the opera. The Gounods duly went to Courtavenel and stayed there with Pauline's mother and Turgenev.[17]

Turgenev pottered in and out during May. When Pauline was away touring, he wrote to her to tell her about the dogs and give her other news. The gardener, who he thought rather lazy, needed help as the work was getting on top of him. Louise had got through an attack of measles. He informed her about what Gounod was up to. He ventured his opinion that Gounod's music was too rarefied, too idealistic.[18]

When Pauline returned, she was fed up with singing 'the eternal *Prophète*', so it came as a relief to her to work with Gounod in the château and in its arbours. She made music with this new Mozart 'from morning to evening, and dreamt about it from evening to morning'. 'Daily contact with this musical genius', she told George Sand somewhat affectedly, had clarified her taste 'in an unbelievable manner'. George Sand responded in kind. This new Mozart would be 'the foremost composer of the century, a musical genius who will open a new era'.[19]

The enthusiasm was also mutual between Pauline and Gounod. He was astonished with the way that, within a few days, she knew the score of *Sapho* sufficiently well to accompany herself on the piano, 'almost from memory'. He later described this as 'the most extraordinary feat of musical memorising' that he had ever witnessed. Her involvement at this stage was crucial. Although Gounod was a very good tenor and a reasonably competent pianist, he 'lacked virtuosity and had a certain amount of trouble performing his own scores'. This was according to the somewhat acid judgement of Saint-Saëns.[20]

Pauline and Gounod found time to draw this joint sketch of Turgenev

For the moment, even Turgenev was captivated by 'le bon Gounod',[21] and derived considerable amusement from listening to his sighs as he wandered around the woods in search of inspiration. Equally, Gounod was quite content to carry the eight-year-old Louise on his shoulders, and to jog over to Rozay in the tilbury, in order to collect Turgenev on his way back from Paris.[22]

Gounod fitted comfortably into the light-hearted atmosphere. He composed canons for four voices which they sang when paddling the boats on the moat in the evenings. In the Théâtre des Pommes de Terre, the production of Beaumarchais's *Le Mariage de Figaro* starred Gounod in the title role. Turgenev was the Count, Pauline's pupil Désirée Artôt the Countess, Pauline herself was Suzanne and Louise was Chérubin. Granny Garcia, the wardrobe mistress and guardian of splendid robes once worn by her husband Manuel and her elder daughter, completed the cast* as Don Bazile. Louis sat in the audience.[23]

*Désirée Artôt is chiefly remembered today because Tchaikovsky, surprisingly and unsuccessfully, proposed to her.

Granny Garcia

Louise said that her happiest days were connected with Courtavenel and 'the merry life we led there'. She recounted several tales about the practical jokes which seem to have been a particular speciality of Pauline. A guest might perhaps get into a bed which immediately collapsed; or emerge from his bedroom to be showered with a cascade of water from a bucket high above; or be invited to shoot at a magpie which refused to fall, because it was only a stuffed one which had been tied to a tree.[24]

Turgenev, who must have been becoming increasingly jaundiced by the presence of the composer and Pauline's manifest enthusiasm for him, was a participant if not a victim in the pranks which Louise recalled. Once, we are told, he woke at dawn to hear cocks, hens and ducks cackling in his cupboard. On another occasion, a skeleton was put in his bed. At least, this was rather less slippery than the objects which a Russian officer apparently found in his bed, his pockets and his cupboard. It was known that he could not abide frogs.[25]

String attached to Turgenev's furniture was strung along the walls to the billiard room next door. Later, when he went to bed, the string was tugged and the furniture moved. On yet another occasion, he found someone in his bed with a hat on; he thought it was old Berthe, Louis's sister, although it was actually the bearskin. Next day, when he came in from shooting, Pauline dressed up in the same outfit and lay on the sofa. When Turgenev approached, she leapt up and boxed his ears.[26]

There was the day when a rat apparently got into the kitchen and ate the cook's slipper. A rat-hunt was immediately organised. Armed with staves, the hunters found the rat which managed to escape. Turgenev was greatly impressed with the rat's survival instinct and ability. Unfortunately for the rat, the cook discovered it later, hidden up the sleeve of her coat. That was the end of it.[27]

Berlioz was invited to stay. However, maybe wisely, he said that he was too busy to accept. The shooting did not tempt him. He told Pauline that 'If Monsieur Viardot had wolves and bears to hunt in his woods, all well and good'. But he was 'willing to bet that there's nothing there except titmice … if that'.[28]

During this time, many of Turgenev's *Sketches from a Hunter's Album* were gradually being published in *The Contemporary.* That they were regarded as contentious is evidenced by the fact that when a collected edition was published,[29] not only was the book an 'instantaneous success', but a countess declared 'C'est un livre incendiaire'.[30] The old Tsar had the censor who passed it dismissed.

Turgenev's mother then demanded he come back to Russia. She sent him his annual allowance of around 1,700 silver roubles to enable him to clear his debts, and the money for the journey as well.[31] Before he set out he was tipped off, probably by his friend Annenkov, that the authorities were expected to pounce on dissidents. Although Turgenev was increasingly unpopular with the authorities, his name had not yet come up. Nevertheless, it would have been foolish to rush back. So he returned to Courtavenel and spent the first part of June there, enjoying the usual jollifications. He saw the Viardots off from the Gare du Nord to London on 17 June. Afterwards, he wrote to them to say he must return to Russia as otherwise he might be put on the list of exiles, with potentially adverse consequences to his work and his property. Besides, his principal paymaster, his mother, called.[32]

Five days after the Viardots left, Turgenev departed for Berlin and Russia. He soon bemoaned his homesickness for Courtavenel. Impatient with the fifteen days it took for news to reach Moscow, he compared his departure to that of a Roman peasant girl he had once overheard saying *Addio*, farewell, to her lover. When he reached the estate at Spasskoye, there was little to relieve his renewed sense of depression.[33]

Turgenev's brother Nicholas had ignored his mother's injunction and married the German girl who she employed to look after her illegitimate 'adopted' daughter. As a consequence, Nicholas had been thrown out and had taken up residence ten miles away at Turgenevo, a property which he had inherited from his father. It was not long before Turgenev also had a violent row with his ferocious mother, and departed to join his brother.[34]

Suddenly everything changed, in a material sense. Less than six months after his return, on 28 November, Varvara Petrovna died in Moscow. It is said that she went out in style; she made her exit to the accompaniment of her serf orchestra playing the polka in the adjacent room. At this performance, those present included her illegitimate daughter and her son Nicholas with his wife. Turgenev was not there; he only arrived in Moscow four days later.[35]

Turgenev had come into a fortune. His estates of around 15,000 acres at Spasskoye and elsewhere should have yielded some 20–27,000 francs (6,200 silver roubles) per annum.[36] He was a man of independent means, rich even. However, this was not as good as it sounded because of his absenteeism and his laid-back attitude to money. He probably would have preferred his brother's inheritance of less land and fewer debts.[37] But, for the moment, a new life seemed to have dawned.

If he was to receive a reasonable return from his estates, he would need to manage them. He would also have to do something about his serfs. Only at the end of the decade did he begin to anticipate the provisions of the Edict which was eventually issued in 1861. At the cost of about a quarter of his income, Turgenev then freed the domestic serfs. He put the estate serfs onto the quit-rent system at around 3 roubles per 2.7 acres; he also supplied them with building materials. The peasants, conservative as ever, were reluctant participants in all this reorganisation.[38]

Although he had some grounds for optimism when he returned home,

Annenkov's premonitions about the government crackdown proved to be correct. When Turgenev left Paris in that June of 1850, little did he realise that he would not see France again for six years.[39]

—

Meanwhile, back in the bowers and glades of Courtavenel, Gounod and Pauline continued to work together to put on *Sapho.* Louis chipped in with suggestions, usually to ensure that Pauline's part in the title role would be sufficiently prominent.[40]

The real Sappho lived in around 600 BC on the island of Lesbos, off the west coast of Turkey. She has been described as 'incomparably the greatest poetess the world has ever seen',[41] even if our generation may be more inclined to associate her with something different. In the myth as told by Ovid, the dark-skinned lady, who possessed more talent than beauty, could no longer be satisfied by the Lesbian maidens. She fell passionately in love with Phaon, a 'toyboy' from Etna, who was as beautiful as Apollo. After Phaon deserted her, she leapt from a cliff into the sea.[42]

Act I of Gounod's opera features a poetry contest at the Olympic Games, on the west coast of Greece, between Sapho and another poet. Sapho, who sings of Love, is acclaimed the winner. Phaon falls for her and jilts his previous mistress, Glycère.

By the beginning of Act 2, all key players have flown the 250 miles to Lesbos, where Phaon leads a conspiracy to overthrow the local tyrant. It is not the conspirators' Bacchanalian drunkenness which is their undoing. No, the jealous Glycère uses her feminine charms to obtain their names which she then threatens to disclose, unless two conditions are met. Sapho must appear to be unfaithful and swear to reject Phaon, but must not disclose why; secondly, Phaon must take her, Glycère, with him into exile.

The blackmail works, the conditions are to be implemented. In the third and final act, Phaon awaits exile by the pounding sea. He longs for Sapho, who overhears him cursing her on account of her (apparent) infidelity. Having sung 'O ma lyre immortelle', Sapho sees no solution other than to leap from the cliff. 'Ouvre-toi, gouffre amer, ouvre-toi. Je vais dormir pour toujours dans la mer.'

Even compared to most opera librettos, this story, with its wet dénouement, is dire. The critics revelled in demonstrating their classical prowess by identifying inaccuracies in the telling of the myth. Like the audience, they found the work boring, 'ennuyeux'.[43] This is not surprising. There is little drama and not much to capture the imagination; the characters are wooden.[44] The first and second acts are wearisome. However, the opera occasionally provides Gounod, who believed that 'melody alone counts in music',[45] with the opportunity to supply some of his incomparably beautiful tunes. These are 'O ma lyre' itself, 'Ma vie en ce séjour est un ruisseau limpide' (My life in this place is a limpid stream), and, in the third act, Phaon's self-pitying lament 'O jours heureux'. All of these seem to be taken straight out of a delicious box of chocolates. And the cat-fight between Sapho and Glycère will particularly please those who have a penchant for duets sung by high sopranos.

As with *Le Prophète*, the timing of the production of *Sapho* was unfortunate. Although France was nominally a republic at this time, its president, Louis-Napoléon, who had been elected at the end of 1848 with overwhelming support, was 'an imperial cuckoo in the republican nest'.[46] The constitution provided that the president could only serve for a single four-year term. Given the massive support for Louis-Napoléon, there was bound to be a crisis in 1852 when his term came to an end.[47] The crescendo had been orchestrated in 1851. By the time of the première of *Sapho* on 16 April 1851, the president was already locked in a struggle with the Assemblée about his re-election, among other matters.[48]

As the Bonapartist political drama, one of the greatest in 19th-century France, evolved, the prospect of an opera star being applauded for singing 'Tremblez tyrans, forgeurs de chaînes' was hardly likely to put the censor at ease. The censor was in any case concerned by more mundane 'immoral' features of the draft submitted to him, such as the sexual decadence of the Greeks, and Glycère's offer of her favours so as to obtain the list of the conspirators. The libretto had to be toned down.[49] Even then, sentiments such as those expressed in the song 'O liberté, déesse austere', in which revenge was invoked,[50] were at the very least inopportune. They invited circumspection rather than applause from the audience. As if these aspects were not enough to worry the civil servants, the conspirators depart for exile expressing their patriotism and threatening to return and avenge their wrongs. It is hardly surprising that, on that first night in mid-April, the libretto was withheld from sale.[51]

So, the première at the Opéra, exactly two years after *Le Prophète*, was not a success. It was produced together with two insignificant works; one by a German, Rosenhain, another by Auber. There was little advance publicity.[52] Some critics were favourable, at least about Pauline's performance. Théophile Gautier, the poet, novelist, influential critic and journalist, said that Pauline had conceived the role 'in a sculptural and wholly classical manner'. He added that each of her poses looked 'like a Greek statue come to life'.[53] However, receipts on the first night were below half* the normal level for a successful opera and remained poor. Pauline only gave six performances; her replacement, who could not carry the part, gave only three. Wisely, the conspiratorial material was cut from a couple of revivals later in the year, in which Pauline did not participate. According to Berlioz, the opera was also torn apart so that its length became compatible with a ballet being staged on the same evening.[55]

In London, the opera, sung in Italian, fared no better. *Saffo*, as it was called, was performed at Covent Garden in Italian on 9 August 1851. Two days later, *The Times* gave it a devastating review. The newspaper started by condemning some of Gounod's religious works which had been foisted on London recently; they were described as 'crude and indigested efforts'. The critic then launched into the opera. 'A more uninteresting libretto could not well be imagined,' he declared, 'nor one less suited to music'. Gounod's music was 'flat, dull and wholly devoid of rhythmical tune'. The big trio was 'passion torn to tatters without a vestige of expression or gleam of sentiment'. The reviewer praised the performance of Michael Costa, the conductor, and the London stalwarts Enrico Tamberlik and Jeanne Castellan who sang the parts of Phaon and Glycère. He was distinctly lukewarm about Pauline's role and her performance. 'We never saw Madame Viardot in a more lengthy or fatiguing part' he said. 'The continual strain for effect lessened the chance of achieving it. Her movements and poses were more than usually studied and artificial'. However, the librettist and the composer, so said the critic, should take the blame for the fiasco.

The Times was not alone in its views. *The Musical World*, a magazine published every Saturday, consigned *Saffo* to oblivion. Its critic found himself compelled by duty 'to the unpleasant task of condemning the music of

*Receipts were of the order of 4,000 francs. Normal receipts were 8–9,000 francs for a good night. The box office returns automatically assumed 100 per cent attendance from 'season ticket' holders, so the actual attendance level may have been rather less.[54]

Sapho without reserve'. He added 'we shall never forget the dullness that folded the house in its embraces on Saturday night. Almost every one appeared to be dozing'. To ram the point home, *The Musical World* appended the negative review from *The Times*.[56]

The *Sapho* adventure illustrates Pauline's well-intentioned desire to patronise, promote and support a relatively obscure composer. For this, as we shall see, she got little thanks. Her involvement also calls into question her judgement. Top artistes cannot endorse with impunity products which are perceived as poor.

The critics began to turn on Pauline and question the quality of her voice. Léon Escudier, the music publisher and editor of the journal *La France Musicale*, led the pack. 'Madame Viardot does not sing any more; each note which emerges from her intelligent voice is an ear-splitting shriek'.[57] Possibly the cat-fight was too much for Pauline. Perhaps, when she was a child, her father had forced her voice in the upper registers as he had done with Maria Malibran.[58]

Relations between the participants became distinctly strained. Gounod, who only a few weeks earlier had been gushing 'Je vous aime' and 'Je vous embrasse comme je vous aime',[59] rounded on Pauline for being a bad singer 'already nearing her end, and always singing out of tune'.[60] The tap which normally spouted charm was suddenly turned off.

At the end of August 1851, it was announced that Pauline was in need of rest. It was said that she was withdrawing from the stage for a year. As it turned out, she was by then pregnant with her daughter Claudie.[61]

The Viardots went to recuperate at Duns Castle, near Berwick on the Scottish borders. There they stayed with Louis's friends, the Hays. Louis enjoyed the shooting and the romance of Sir Walter Scott, the land of *The Lady of the Lake.* His excitement and good humour were considerable when he found himself shooting grouse on Lammermoor itself, only to discover that there was no gothic castle, no house, indeed not a rock, nor a tree, but they were 'au milieu d'un désert'. There, he got soaked in a storm. However, he discovered that 'wisky' demonstrated that, contrary to the laws of physics, fire can quench a storm. The Viardots' fellow guests in Scotland were unusual, at least by French standards. One lady had the reputation of taking her chickens with her to bed.[62]

Louis was being criticised in the Paris press for his association with radical political activists such as Louis Blanc and the former Interior Minister Alexandre-Auguste Ledru-Rollin. This minister had, in mid-1849, been brave enough to demand the impeachment of Louis-Napoléon. Following a demonstration against French foreign policy in Italy, he had led the government in June 1849. After his premiership of around two hours,[63] surely the shortest 'in history', he was soon heading off into exile in England. There, with other exiles, he was entertained to dinner by the Viardots at their residence, 27 Clifton Villas in Maida Vale, ironically a suburb which had been named to commemorate a British defeat of the French around forty years earlier.[64] Some critics described the Viardots' dinner as a political 'banquet', a cover used in France for a political meeting.[65] The Viardots' affiliations were by now thoroughly suspect. Besides, Pauline, a friend and protégée of George Sand, had been the composer of *La Jeune République*.[66]

On the night of 1 December 1851, Louis-Napoléon staged his coup and had himself declared president for life. Some activists at first sought sanctuary in the Viardots' house. The police turned up and thoroughly searched the place. They pulled out every drawer. Letters from foreign revolutionaries such as Manin and Kossuth, the Venetian and Hungarian leaders, were seized. The correspondence with George Sand might also have been taken, were it not for George's habit of signing her letters to Pauline, 'Ninounne'. This had no significance for those doing the search.[67]

The crackdown had begun. Anyone remotely radical was wise to get out of France immediately, unless they wanted to be locked up. Nearly 27,000 people were arrested or prosecuted in default; some 15,000 were condemned to various sentences and some 9,000 deported to Algeria.[68] Eighty-eight deputies from the Assemblée, including Victor Hugo, were expelled from French territory. Pierre Leroux, the Viardots' friend and publishing colleague, headed to exile in Jersey. Turgenev was naturally very worried for the safety of his friends and of his recently-discovered daughter Paulinette who, as we shall shortly see, the Viardots had agreed to foster. Late in December, the Viardots themselves thought it best to seek sanctuary in Scotland again.[69] Berwickshire was a useful bolt hole from arrest.

For Louis, the return to Scotland provided the opportunity to go fox-hunting. However, being a 'mediocre cavalier', he only followed on foot. He was not encouraged by what he was told. Recently, one knight got contusions in his kidneys, another 'Sir' was killed, and a captain was badly injured when his horse lashed out at him. Despite these forebodings, the hunt enjoyed a capital day in ideal weather. It was foggy and there was drizzle. The fox got away after a run of four or five hours.[70] Pauline took the opportunity to compose. Around this time, she worked on transcriptions of Spanish popular songs. She also planned a comic opera based on George Sand's *La Mare au diable*. Louis continued to dream of the chase.[71]

Pauline did not reappear on the operatic stage for the whole of 1852, although she sang at the Birmingham and Norwich festivals.[72] On 21 May 1852, in Paris, she gave birth to 'a jewel of a child', Claudie-Pauline-Marie. The baby, like her elder sister, was named after her father whose full name was Louis-Claude.[73] On the next day he joyfully announced the happy event to Pauline's old friend Clara Schumann who expressed considerable surprise and reproached her for not keeping in touch. Claudie's arrival did 'Loulou a great deal of good'.[74]

Pauline had served Gounod's ambitions by creating *Sapho*. His opera had been performed at the Opéra, on the most prestigious stage in Paris. It was a shame that it had not been a success, but his name was known; he was established.[75]

At the Conservatoire there was a professor of piano, Pierre-Joseph-Guillaume Zimmermann, son of the piano manufacturer. He was distinguished and highly influential. His pupils included a teenager called Georges Bizet who would later compose *The Pearl Fishers* and *Carmen*. Zimmermann was not infallible as a musician. He is said to have had the temerity to suggest that the perfect pitch of the young Saint-Saëns was not perfect at all. However, Saint-Saëns quickly demonstrated that he was talking rubbish.[76]

Gounod would visit the Zimmermann apartment and meet the four daughters. When with the Viardots, he would joke about them as the dreary daughters. However, in the Zimmermann household, Gounod's 'gushing manner' went down well. He seemed a good catch.[77]

Madame Zimmermann knew that she needed to force the pace if she was to get even one of her brood off her hands. She demanded that Gounod either marry their daughter Anna, whose portrait shows her looking extraordinarily like Pauline, or stay away. Gounod wrote a letter saying

Anna Gounod, 1859, by Ingres

that he should not aspire to Anna's hand. When Gounod went to the Zimmermann house to deliver the letter, Anna's mother presumed that he had come to propose. She welcomed him as her daughter's fiancé. Gounod had not the gumption to hand over the letter; maybe he never intended to do so.

A month before Claudie Viardot was born, Gounod visited the Viardots and announced both his engagement and his forthcoming appointment to the important position of Director of the Orphéon de la Ville de Paris. This was a choral society for young people which had been founded about twenty years earlier, to provide a harmless form of recreation for the working classes and to keep them out of mischief.[78]

Over dinner, Gounod assured Pauline that the wedding would be postponed until after her child was born so as to enable her to attend. However, five days after the birth of Claudie, a leading prelate solemnised the matrimony of Charles and Anna at the church of La Trinité. The Viardots had been informed that nobody was being invited to the wedding. The relationship with the Viardots had chilled rapidly.

Events moved very quickly. The Viardots sent an inkstand as a wedding present. Pauline sent Anna a personal gift of a bracelet. This was returned two days later by Gounod who wrote that he himself was giving his bride a bracelet and it was the only one she wished to wear. Louis Viardot was furious at the insult and, on 1 June, he wrote a letter to Gounod closing his doors to him. 'You will be no doubt a great musician, and you will have admirers', he wrote, 'but I doubt you will keep any friends'.[79]

Gounod dashed round to Ary Scheffer to seek advice. He told the painter that the Zimmermanns had been alarmed by gossip about his friendship with Pauline; indeed, they had received an anonymous note about it. Whether Anna had furiously declared that 'she did not accept presents from her husband's mistresses', as was subsequently suggested, we cannot be sure.[80]

Scheffer told Gounod to send an apology and insisted that the Gounods' first official call after their marriage should be paid to Pauline; if this did not happen, then Louis would alert Zimmermann to his son-in-law's behaviour. Gounod did write an apology. However, as the visit did not take place, Louis seems to have notified Zimmermann, although without any particular consequences. This is not surprising if, as one of Gounod's detractors has claimed, the marriage was 'in the nature of a business arrangement'.[81]

Pauline told George Sand that Gounod was a religious hypocrite, bogus, another 'Tartuffe'. Sand sympathised and also laid into Gounod; Turgenev, writing from Russia, was incensed, but said that his fury was not such as to stop him enjoying Gounod's music.[82]

A few days after the wedding, Gounod received his appointment to the Orphéon.*[83] Perhaps this prize came with the bride, or maybe Gounod was awarded it for writing the incidental music for *Ulysse*, a drama by Ponsard, which was first performed a few weeks later.

Possibly, the fracas over Gounod's marriage arose from the suspicion that Pauline was carrying Gounod's child.[84] Before looking at this allegation, we may equally postulate that the Viardots were simply furious at the insult

*Gounod was busy conducting the Orphéon at the moment Anna's first child was born. The child did not survive.

implicit in Gounod's behaviour. They were incensed by the implication that the Zimmermanns entertained such a canard about Pauline and regarded her as an unsuitable person for their daughter to have as a friend. If there had been any serious belief that Gounod was actually the father of Pauline's baby, the Zimmermanns, however desperate they were to marry off their numerous daughters, would surely have deferred or cancelled the marriage.

That Gounod was 'besotted' with Pauline could well have been true. We have seen how Pauline helped to launch and create him as a composer of operas.[85] *Sapho* took them both to London at the same time in August 1851, around the time that Claudie was conceived.

Over the years, there has been a determined, almost desperate, attempt to show that Claudie, called Didie, was not the child of Louis. At one time, the child's paternity was imputed to Turgenev who later was conspicuously, indeed passionately, fond of her.[86] However, it has been shown that it is most improbable that he could have been in London at the relevant time. He was in Russia at least until 8 August and Pauline left London during the second week of September. Although there is a blank in Turgenev's diary between the end of July and the beginning of October,[87] the notion that he could have fitted in a clandestine sex holiday to London, timed to fecundate Pauline, seems sufficiently preposterous for the 'voyeurs' to turn their attention elsewhere.

Their spotlight immediately focuses upon Gounod. They observe that the baby Claudie grew into a competent painter, like Gounod's father.

Gounod, who by now styled himself 'Abbé', was indeed a consummate womaniser. Turgenev called him a 'prêtre érotique'.[88] His reputation would eventually become so tarnished that Bizet could jest, when it was suggested that Gounod should be appointed Director of the Conservatoire, that it would be unsafe to assign to him the direction of a school for young girls.[89]

Sapho was, without question, one of the great operatic disasters, and not just in Paris. The Covent Garden production had been a fiasco.[90] As a consequence, Gounod badmouthed Pauline. What more propitious circumstances could one imagine for them both to find solace from each other in bed and beget a child?

Proponents of Gounod's paternity of Claudie cite the testimony of his subsequent lady-friend who is also the source of Anna's reported outburst on receiving the Viardots' wedding present. This woman insinuated, in a single sentence which a modern tabloid would find hard to surpass for

Lovers? Gounod's and Pauline's drawings of each other

content yet brevity, that 'it is nobody's business if she, Pauline, has or has not been Gounod's mistress'.[91]

The lady-friend was Georgina Weldon, who we shall soon see was a more bizarre character even than Gounod. She raises the matter in but a few lines in her voluminous, enjoyably self-serving writings. She acknowledged that Pauline had launched Gounod, although she did not think much of her. 'As for her talent and her person, they are in the "public domain". I never admired her in any way'. However, she claimed that she was 'quite impartial when she spoke of Madame Viardot'.

The tone of Pauline's correspondence with George Sand about Gounod does not support Weldon's impartial insinuation.[92] And in assessing its significance, we need at least to be aware of Georgina's character. She received a four-month sentence as a common felon convicted of criminal libel; five years after that, she received a six-month sentence on a similar charge; and she was the subject of a civil action for assault.[93] Indeed, in the case of Pauline's relationship with Gounod, this technicolor inmate of Newgate and Holloway jails shows a surprising and commendable lack of self-confidence.

Given that it is simply conjectural that Gounod was the father of Claudie, we may surely postulate an alternative scenario. This is equally conjectural, less romantic and more conventional. Pauline had turned 30; it had been around ten years since Louise was born. If she was going to expand the family, it was opportune to do so. She had built her career. The reviews of *Sapho* had criticised her voice severely,[94] and it would appear that she had passed her peak.

The birth of Claudie, known affectionately as Didie, was followed less than two years later by the birth* on 15 March 1854 of Maria-Anne-Félicité. The paternity of this baby, who was known simply as Marianne, has not been seriously challenged.

Until Gounod's marriage fiasco, Louis and Gounod were on very good terms. Louis even wrote to Gounod from Scotland to say that he had written the scenario for an opera which Gounod could compose after Augier had written the libretto.[95] However complaisant a husband Louis may have been, or may be thought to have been, he surely could not have written such a letter had he thought that his wife was five months pregnant with Gounod's baby. Her condition must have been apparent to all.

The Viardots' relations with Gounod were not resumed until they met him again, in circumstances outside their control, in London in 1870.

*Marianne's birth was tinged with sadness, because news had very recently come in regarding Robert Schumann's attempted suicide.

CHAPTER 14

Children

Turgenev has gone away to Russia and Gounod has gone off to get married. This seems a convenient point to have an interlude and catch up with three sad girls, two of whom have featured so far in this story, and one who is still to come. They were victims, veritable case studies in adolescent and parental disaster. The two were George Sand's daughter Solange, who was by now married and in her twenties, and Pauline's eldest daughter Louise, who was now aged around nine. The third was the child by the seamstress at Spasskoye, Paulinette Bruère, as she became. She would be Turgenev's only acknowledged child. She was around the same age as Louise. All three were unfortunate in their parents.

Solange Dudevant was born to George Sand on 13 September 1828. It is probable that her father was not Casimir Dudevant, George's increasingly estranged husband, but a medical student who the novelist had first known when she was in her teens. She subsequently had a rendezvous with him in Paris nine months before Solange was born.[1]

Within a couple of years of the birth, Solange was in Paris with her mother who by then had embarked on her notable literary career. Sand was living with the nineteen-year-old Jules Sandeau. Thereafter, she took a succession of men. Solange, the child of a notorious mother who had taken to wearing men's clothes, can hardly be said to have received a conventional upbringing. Yet when Comtesse Marie d'Agoult saw her as a nine-year-old, she found a delightfully beautiful blonde, a kind of 'wood-nymph which has escaped from the forests, on whom God smiles and all nature applauds'. Liszt's mistress could see that this loving, passionate, indomitable girl was destined for a life of struggle and combat which would either be a disaster or a great success. She was in complete contrast to her relatively straitlaced elder brother Maurice.[2] George thought he was suited to become a businessman; that is, unless his attempts to become a painter came to anything. Why a businessman? Well, 'a certain dullness of mind seems an almost necessary qualification for everyone seriously engaged in making money', wrote one novelist.[3]

When Solange was nine, Casimir, her legal father, abducted her. George wrested her back. The child was returned 'like a princess at the border between two states'.[4] In the following year, her mother and Chopin decamped for their winter in Majorca, taking Solange and Maurice with them. By the time she was in her teens Solange, who George dressed up like herself, as a boy, was being moved from one *pension* to another, where she was being educated. She was already showing herself to be a difficult and rebellious child. Added to this, George 'adopted' Pauline Viardot. When Pauline went off to live her own life, she 'adopted' Augustine Brault, a cousin. She seemed to prefer anybody other than her daughter on whom to bestow her maternal affection. In later years, she transferred it to Maurice's wife, Lina.[5]

It is no wonder that when the Sand family were walking with Pauline in the garden at Courtavenel, their hostess turned round and saw the frustrated teenager chopping off the heads of the flowers by slashing them with her riding crop. A ticking-off from Pauline can only have made the adolescent yet more resentful.[6]

When she was eighteen, Solange was betrothed to a nice country gentleman. At last, all seemed set fair, until she and her mother went to Paris to have busts made of them by the handsome up-and-coming sculptor Jean-Baptiste-Auguste Clésinger. He had met George a couple of years before.

Around the time of the sitting, Clésinger exhibited at the Salon a piece which depicted with great and unusual realism a woman bitten by a snake. It was suggested that this outrageous sculpture, a brilliant piece which can only be appreciated three-dimensionally, displayed the most interesting parts of the anatomy of Apollonie Sabatier, known as La Présidente, a courtesan who belonged, at the time, to a Belgian industrialist. Later, she would be used by Flaubert as a model for one of his characters. The combination of pain and ecstasy leaves little doubt as to what, and the precise moment, the beautiful sculpture of this 'rather vulgar creature endowed with classical beauty' depicts.[7]

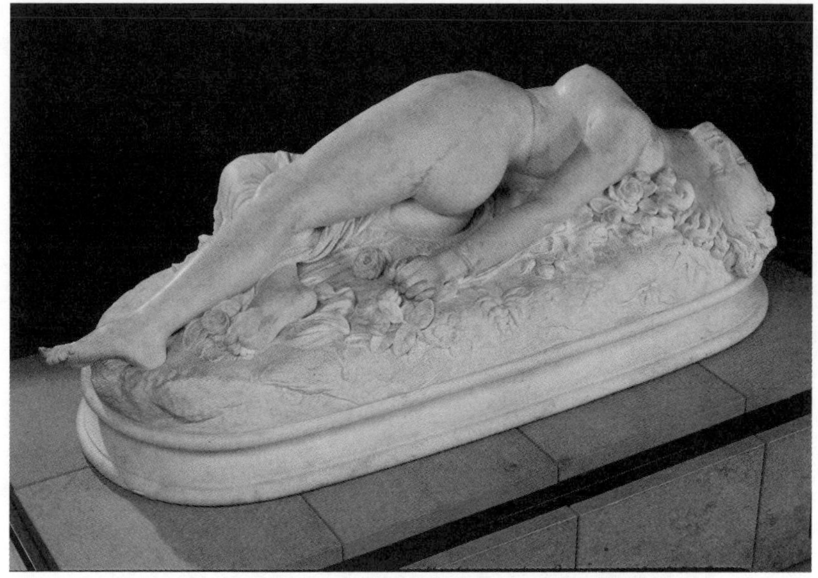

Clésinger, *Woman bitten by a snake*

We return, however reluctantly, to the sitting in Clésinger's studio. The expert on the naked female body seems to have explored Solange there and then. Very possibly he explored her mother as well. The wedding to the country gentleman was called off. Within weeks, on 21 May 1847, Solange and Clésinger were married in the tiny church next to the château at Nohant. The relationship between mother and daughter deteriorated further. It was exacerbated by the fact that Clésinger raided Solange's considerable dowry in order to liquidate his enormous debts. This should perhaps not have been surprising, because it seems improbable that Clésinger could possibly have had any other reason to enter the state of matrimony.

A moment of crisis was reached in the château at Nohant. Clésinger wielded a hammer and Maurice pointed a pistol. Before either came to harm, the Clésingers were ejected and took refuge in a nearby village. Chopin came to Solange's aid. She was pregnant and she borrowed his coach to get back to Paris. Chopin,[8] whose position in the Nohant household was anyway becoming untenable because Maurice was fed up with him, continued to support Solange. This was a noble gesture which virtually ensured his final separation from her mother. Whether George interpreted this as disloyalty to her, or whether, as a woman, she was consumed with jealousy, we can only speculate.

Solange

Solange's first baby died within a week.[9] Three years later, with her second daughter, also called Jeanne-Gabrielle, but known as Nini, she returned to her mother who made it clear that she was welcome to visit although not to stay.[10]

The Clésinger marriage was doomed from the outset; when it collapsed, Solange took shelter in a convent. She bemoaned her fate. She warned her mother that she might turn to vice. George retorted that she should try 'a little vice and prostitution', although she doubted that her daughter possessed the requisite selling skills. This letter, in which she told her daughter to pull herself together, is lengthy and extremely critical.[11] A rocket like this was probably the right thing to fire off in the circumstances, even if a modern parent would not presume to write in such a peremptory and critical tone. Sand put her finger on the crux of Solange's difficulties when she told her that her real problem was to be George Sand's daughter. About that, absolutely nothing could be done. 'Alors le grand malheur de ta position, c'est d'être ma fille, mais je ne'y peux rien changer'.[12]

Poor child. Solange was fundamentally a decent girl. This unfortunate victim of a self-centred mother actually preferred religion to vice. With her latest lover in tow, Sand looked after Solange's child. The baby was reclaimed by Clésinger. However, after being sent back and forth like a shuttlecock, the little girl died in 1855; Sand took the opportunity to write her story.[13] Solange had no more children. She settled in a château some two miles from Nohant, where George made it absolutely clear she was not welcome. She died in 1899.[14]

The Viardots tended to support the Clésingers' and Chopin's side of the argument. Louis Viardot gave Sand some help and advice with her finances, which the Clésinger affair threw into considerable disarray. But he also told her bluntly that she herself had been a contributory to the Solange fiasco. The Solange situation also contributed to a long-lasting 'period of relative coolness' between Pauline and George which endured during the 1850s and 1860s.[15]

Is it surprising that Louise Viardot, Pauline's first child, also had an unhappy childhood? Louise, who was thirteen years younger than Solange, was born on 14 December 1841. She said in her memoirs that the Viardots were very disappointed that she was not a boy.[16]

She remained an only child until her sister Claudie arrived, some ten years later. Unlike many only children who are doted upon by their parents, Louise was parked out while her mother pursued her career and travelled Europe. At first, as a baby, she was deposited with George Sand. Not surprisingly, Louise started calling George 'Maman', as we have heard. Chopin loved her too.[17]

Later, when the Viardots were abroad, the painter Ary Scheffer acted *in loco parentis.* His 'niece' Cornélie* became Louise's best friend. Cornélie's mother, whoever she may have been, had died shortly after she was born. Cornélie was brought up in the country until she was aged seven, when Scheffer's mother took her under her wing.[19]

From the age of six to nine, Louise was boarded out. Madame Renard, a 'charming' Englishwoman who had passed all her life in France, provided the service. Pauline thought Louise would benefit from this arrangement, although Louise, in retrospect, said that she did not. Like many children whose home is far away, she was deeply unhappy. 'Nobody looked after me and I had to stay at school when the other boarders went home on holidays and Sundays', she subsequently complained.[20]

She was taken on the 1845–6 tour to St Petersburg where, we recall, she caught whooping cough and passed it on to her mother. Divas with whooping cough do not make good performers. So, the Viardot ménage had to set off for home earlier than planned. One might guess that Pauline would have been infuriated that her child's illness disrupted her tour.

However, Louise had occasional moments of fun. Meyerbeer bought her a chocolate cow in a sweet shop. In a scene reminiscent of Mozart playing with the infant Marie-Antoinette, Louise played hide-and-seek with Prince Fritz, who later married Queen Victoria's daughter and briefly ruled as Kaiser before his early death. Rather less relaxing was her performance of duets with her mother before the Prussian royal family.[21]

Louise was about eight when Gounod came to Courtavenel for the first time, and carried her on his shoulders when going for walks. There were the practical jokes played on Turgenev, and the fun and games held in the Théâtre des Pommes de Terre. However, there was also the normal routine for a little girl. At 8pm, having sung a little ditty with her mother, she was marched up to bed.[22]

As Louise grew up, she developed into a difficult child. Meyerbeer called her 'Napoléon-Louise', and he foresaw problems.[23] Turgenev thought

*Cornélie, when fifteen, married M Marjolin, 'a physician of repute' and surgeon at the Sainte-Eugénie hospital. He was doctor to the Empress. Ary Scheffer's brother also had a daughter called Cornélie, who married Ernest Renan, the philosopher and friend of the Viardots, in 1856.[18]

at heart she was a nice girl despite her tendency not to care a damn about anything or anyone. Pauline thought Louise's character was beginning to resemble that of her aunt Maria. 'Elle est difficile à élever', she said. Pauline was very strict with her. She reduced her to tears in lessons.[24] It was not an easy or cosy relationship.

Louise – the young woman

Later when she was sixteen, Louise joined the operatic tours to England and Ireland. She sometimes helped to coach the cast. Previously, she had been prevented from seeing her mother singing parts in which she came to a grisly or sad conclusion. Usually, when she was taken to the opera, she was not allowed to stay to the end.[25]

In the 1860s, soon after the family moved from Paris to live in Baden-Baden, Louise married Ernest Héritte who was twenty years older. This union was 'in accordance with her parents' wishes'.[26] Little was known of Ernest Héritte at the time, Louise said, except that he was in the diplomatic service.[27]

She had a baby son, Loulou, born on 17 April 1864 following a difficult confinement.[28]

Poor Louise. After first being stationed in Berne, the 'young marrieds' were transferred to Cape Town for three years. Louise's departure may have been a great relief for her parents; however, to her, it must have seemed like going to another world. The journey from Southampton lasted 48 days.[29] At this time, before the diamonds were discovered, the place was hardly enticing or glamorous. The British in the Cape Colony had, only ten years before, driven the rebellious Dutch farming community north over the Vaal River into the Transvaal; five years before, some 50,000 members of a tribe perished in a bloody collective suicide which was committed in the confidence that they would rise again as a glorious warrior nation.[30]

Louise, however, was intrepid; she was unfeminine for her time. She went leopard hunting. She rode out to visit the British admiral at Simonstown. She climbed Table Mountain, got lost in the dark, and had to be rescued by soldiers from the garrison, after spending two nights on the mountain among the wild animals.[31]

During her return to the northern hemisphere, Louise's ship hit a dreadful storm in the Bay of Biscay. She survived this; however, she could not survive the fact that, while in the Cape, Ernest Héritte had transferred his affections to a Miss Stephens. Consequently the marriage broke down. The whole family rounded on Louise who had moved with her child to stay with her parents in Baden-Baden. Her father was particularly upset.[32] Pauline, who was away on tour in Berlin and Breslau, wrote her a long letter accusing her of throwing a black veil over the happiness of the family. Turgenev, who had no doubt that Louise's character was the cause of the marriage breakdown, tried desperately to be diplomatic.[33]

To Turgenev, Louise seemed surprisingly unmaternal. She was uninterested in and rough with Loulou. Turgenev thought that Louise was destined to be unhappy, and also to make unhappy all with whom she came into contact. She was sometimes violent, sometimes gloomy. She almost always did the opposite of what she was advised to do, especially when the advice was given by her sanctimonious Aunt Berthe. Turgenev could not imagine how Louise could be Pauline's daughter.[34] To us, this may indicate how myopic even a leading novelist can be in his assessment of human characteristics.

Through the auspices of Rubinstein, Louise got a job in St Petersburg, where she went in 1867, the year after her separation, having left little Loulou behind for Pauline to look after. For a time, she gave up her musical career and took up studying medicine. However, by 1880 she had returned to music, and she settled in Heidelberg. She composed an opera, *Lindora.* Her works included a cantata, *Das Bacchusfest*, which was staged in Stockholm in 1880. She also composed a quartet for piano and strings, a vocal trio, and numerous songs.[35]

Louise – in later years

Liszt, who for all his wildness was never less than shrewd, could appreciate the difference between Louise and her mother, 'the illustrious Pauline Viardot who has always had an excellent home life* with her husband'. Louise had separated from hers, said Liszt, and composed, 'with all the bravura of genius, great musical works such as *Fire of Heaven*, and *The God and the Dancing Girl*'. Liszt wrote that he had 'never come across a female composer possessing a talent so vigorously frenzied'.[37]

While in St Petersburg, in the 1860s, Turgenev worked with Louise on a publication. This gave him the opportunity to study her character and to write about it to Pauline, who despaired of her. He told her that Louise cut

*Liszt's seemingly gratuitous, but important, point about the Viardots' happy marriage was also made by one of Sand's early biographers.[36]

her hair short like a boy, something which may well reveal the underlying reason behind the breakdown of her marriage. She was lonely, bitter, scornful and contemptuous of society; she did not really enjoy teaching, and she had not a bean to live on. Yet she had established herself as an intelligent and excellent musician of integrity, while at the same time being eccentric, impossible and off-hand.[38] He thought she was sick and was very sorry for her. One wonders whether it remotely crossed Pauline's mind that she might be responsible.[39]

Louise's son Loulou eventually became French consul in Istanbul, where he embezzled the funds; he committed suicide in 1923.[40] Louise, perhaps fortunately, had died in her mid-seventies, five years before.

It is difficult to imagine Pauline's emotions back in the summer of 1850, when Turgenev wrote from Moscow, around four months before his mother died, to say that he had discovered a love-child of his. The child was called Pelageya, a name which was normally and entirely coincidentally gallicised as Paulinette. This eight-year-old, sired on his mother's seamstress in 1842, looked unmistakably like her father.[41] Turgenev felt that he had to do something about her. His mother would have 'the young lady', as the other serfs called her, dressed up and brought into the drawing-room, where the old termagant would ask her visitors who they thought she looked like. After a good cackle, she would despatch the girl back to her serfs' quarters.

After his mother died, Turgenev wrote to Pauline to ask her advice on what he should do about Paulinette. In *Consuelo*, George Sand's heroine adopts the child of another woman, fathered by the man whom she herself has loved. Almost by analogy, Pauline offered to have Turgenev's child in France as a companion for Louise who was five months older. Turgenev agreed to pay 1,200 francs per annum to Louis Viardot for the child's upkeep, although at times he got behind with his payments. He also arranged to pay Paulinette's mother an allowance.[42]

So, in early November 1850, when Pauline was busy working with Gounod on *Sapho*, Pelageya was sent to Paris in company of a Madame Robert, a French woman who was returning to Paris with her daughter. The party embarked at St Petersburg on the 6pm steamer, which set out into the Baltic for the fifteen-day journey to Paris. The wife of Turgenev's agent had provided the child with some warm clothes. There was not much else in her little bag. A brief letter, for Madame Robert to give Pauline, introduced the child. 'Voici, chère Madame Viardot, la petite Pauline'; in the envelope there was a 50-franc tip for Madame Robert.[43] Pauline urgently wrote back asking for details; whether the child had been vaccinated, for her baptismal certificate and so forth.

The Viardots' adoption of Paulinette was an extraordinary step, not least because Pauline and Turgenev would both have been well aware of Solange's jealousy when the distant cousin Augustine was imported into Nohant. Lou,[44] already showing signs of being a difficult child, long ignored by her parents, could surely be expected to react adversely to a competitor arriving on the scene. Turgenev would later mirror Paulinette's emotions when he conjured up the fictional experience of a similar figure. 'Imagine what the little girl must have felt when she was was taken, aged nine, into the big bleak house to live there with the master'.[45]

Maybe the Viardots were already contemplating enlarging their own family. Once the baby arrived, Paulinette could provide a companion for Louise. Claudie would indeed be conceived in the following year, but the companionship role did not turn out at all as planned.

For the moment, Turgenev seems to have regarded Paulinette as a substitute for the offspring which he and Pauline were precluded from conceiving. He called her '*notre* fille', '*our* daughter', in the letter which he wrote to Pauline only days after Paulinette's departure.[46] However, Turgenev did not warm to Paulinette when he formed his initial view of her on the journey to St Petersburg. Nervously, he described her as untamed, timid and badly brought up.[47]

The eight-year-old serf girl was tough; indeed, she horrified her father when she told him that she was pitiless because nobody had ever shown her any pity. She did have one good point at this time; she seemed keen on music.[48] One is reminded of Victor Hugo's description of Cosette, the little orphan in *Les Misérables*. 'The ominous thing was that at the age of eight her heart was ice cold. This was not her fault. It was not that she was incapable of love, she simply had never had the opportunity to love anyone.'[49]

As a consequence, Paulinette shows signs of having had a massive chip on her shoulder throughout her life. Louis adored her and Granny Garcia was particularly kind to her and wrote to her. However, it seems that

Paulinette could not get round to replying. She seems to have found it very difficult to return affection. Instead of repaying the Viardots with gratitude, she developed a veritable loathing for them.[50]

Eighteen months after Paulinette arrived in France, Pauline felt obliged to scold her for her sulks and her gargantuan appetite, characteristics which Turgenev conceded that he had displayed in his own character at a similar age. She had a character of iron smelted in serfdom. She would need to be handled firmly. Turgenev was, besides, appalled at her ingratitude to Pauline. At one stage, there was talk of the child being sent back to Russia; however, he would not have it.[51] He tried to think positively. 'She is warm-hearted', he wrote later, 'and I often think of her with great affection'.[52] He sent her a present of some earrings from Rome. Also, he wrote to her often, sometimes in a tone which today seems surprisingly harsh. It is only matched in severity by Sand's letters to her daughter.[53]

There was not much affection between Louise and Paulinette. They loathed each other. They were parked together with Mademoiselle Renard;[54] as might be expected, this did not work. In early 1854, Turgenev insisted that Paulinette be removed and sent to an establishment under the direction of a Madame Harang.[55] Paulinette by now was a particularly unattractive-looking adolescent, a Turgenev in a skirt.[56]

Five years later, Turgenev deduced from her letters that Paulinette, who was then aged seventeen, no longer thought as a child. He insisted that Madame Harang should not let her go out too much, as it would not be good for her. However, it seems that things got no better. Pauline, later in the year, wanted Turgenev to write an admonishing letter to Paulinette.[57]

He despaired that his daughter was by now in many ways so unlike him. From the start, he had been very keen that she should be good at music. However, she liked neither music, nor poetry, nor nature, nor dogs. He liked nothing else. When she was eighteen, he despaired at her poor grammar when writing French.[58]

Turgenev had some distant relatives living in Paris, the family of Nikolay Ivanovich Turgenev, a writer and exile who had been implicated in developing the philosophy for the Decembrist rising. These Turgenevs took a keen and kindly interest in Paulinette and wanted to introduce her into 'society'. Turgenev was reluctant to allow this on account of the former serf girl's origins.[59]

A Mrs Innis, who was a devout and rather intolerant widow from

Preston in Lancashire, was engaged as Paulinette's governess and companion. In 1863, the two of them came to live in Baden-Baden.[60] However, after Paulinette had a colossal row with Pauline, they retreated to Passy, near Paris, where she and Mrs Innis lived in a tiny flat which Turgenev said was no bigger than a cabin on a boat.[61]

Shortly thereafter, in January 1864, Turgenev asked Pauline to get the low-down on a young man, an insolvency official who was ardently wooing Paulinette. However, this came to nothing, it seems, because the lady rejected his advances as she did those of other suitors.[62]

However, a year later, at the end of February 1865, no doubt to the relief of the older generation, Paulinette was received into the Roman Catholic Church and married Gaston Bruère, the son of a retired notary. Gaston was aged almost 30. Outwardly, he was said to look rather like the Prince Consort. Underneath, he lacked refinement. He ran a glass and porcelain factory in Rougemont. This is around 40 miles beyond Chartres, a city with a magnificent cathedral renowned for the beauty of its stained glass.[63]

The glass works, which were established shortly after the Revolution, employed around 50 glassblowers.[64] The factory was attached to an early 17th-century château. This was located on a wooded hill looking over the small Loir river which provided the power to mill the corn which was grown in the fields around. It is a very attractive and rustic location. Today it is still somewhat remote. Although glassmaking was one of the industries of the region,[65] Rougemont is no 'zone industrielle', but may be found in the middle of nowhere.

'He combines being both bourgeois and distinguished, bourgeois in the simple sense',[66] said the bride's father, making the best of it. Like all in his position, Turgenev was relieved that his daughter looked radiant; indeed, she received Gaston with a smile which he had never seen her give before. Turgenev took the legal steps necessary to have her declared legitimate and provided a dowry comprising an initial sum of 100,000 francs, followed by a further 50,000 francs. He also gave the couple a piano, an essential means of entertainment in their lonely dwelling.[67] The dowry was a very substantial sum indeed. The annual wages of a farm girl 'who did the work of the house', the role Paulinette might have expected to perform in Russia had her father not come to her rescue, was 250 francs.[68]

Once the happy couple went away, Mrs Innis, who loved Paulinette like a mother, broke into floods of tears.[69]

Paulinette

Turgenev's friends in Paris had promoted this match. Gaston's landlord, a Marquis and the owner of the factory building, was the son-in-law of a salon hostess, the Comtesse de Laborde, now Madame Delessert. The Countess, probably encouraged by the author Prosper Mérimée who was her confidant, was another of those Parisians who took a particular interest in, if not pity on, Paulinette. Turgenev visited the young couple at Rougemont, paid his respects to the Marquis and enjoyed shooting there. This was an expense which the Bruères could well have done without.[70]

The marriage was unhappy and Paulinette's situation was not helped by her interfering mother-in-law who, from the outset, detested her. Paulinette, who was usually pregnant, had several miscarriages. She lost a child who was born prematurely in October 1865. The next child also died. However, her daughter Jeanne, born in 1872, survived, as did a son, Georges-Albert who was born three years later.[71] Turgenev adored his grandchildren.

Gaston's business was wrecked by the Franco-Prussian War.* He could not resolve his commercial problems. Paulinette's dowry was used to finance the losses. Turgenev's correspondence with his daughter becomes more strident as he resists her insistent demands for financial support which he knew would just go down the drain and which he could not afford. He became particularly worried when Gaston accessed part of her dowry which was settled in trust for the children. Indeed, the last two years of his life were overshadowed by having to deal with the increasing financial embarrassment of Paulinette. Meanwhile, Gaston drowned his sorrows in alcohol, threatened her physically, and talked of suicide.[72]

Eventually, Paulinette had to escape from her husband, with her two children. Because of the risk that Gaston would reclaim her, the escape to Solothurn, about twenty miles from Berne in Switzerland, had to be kept an absolute secret. Turgenev and the Viardots' governess, Madame Arnholt, seem to have whisked Paulinette away in a cloak-and-dagger operation. Paulinette underestimated the need for secrecy once she was there. 'Cache-toi et sois muette' was the watchword, Turgenev insisted. He expressed great concern that Paulinette's tryst with an admirer by the name of 'Karl' would bring the whole venture and her hiding place to light, with the consequence that Gaston would descend, and exercise his right to seize her and take her back.[73]

In the year before he died, Turgenev arranged for Paulinette to be paid an allowance which amounted to 5,000 francs per annum. One can never accuse Turgenev of lack of financial generosity towards his daughter.[74] However, the money was to be channelled through Pauline, presumably so that Gaston could not get his hands on it. Turgenev also stipulated that if Paulinette raised any objection, the 'deal' would be off. Paulinette did not appreciate the reason for this and resented her dependence on the goodwill of Pauline. There was no love lost between them. Paulinette spread rumours about her father being in the pocket of the Viardots. At the time of his death, relations between her and her father were severed. He omitted her from his will and her estranged husband set about contesting it, but that is for later.[75]

*The commercial rationale for this, the usual explanation, is not entirely clear. After it was captured on 21 October 1870, Chartres was an important centre of operations for the Germans for the remaining three months of the war. But one might have expected Gaston's business to have recovered thereafter.

After Gaston died, Paulinette settled in Paris with her two children. She died in 1919.[76]

These three unhappy stories illustrate the difficulties of being the child of an outstanding parent. They may also say something about the egocentric character of the parents concerned. Pauline recognised that she herself had a very forceful character. 'I will do what I think I ought to do in spite of water, fire, society, the whole world', she said.[77] One suspects that she became more difficult, increasingly determined and autocratic as she got older. Many people do.

CHAPTER 15

ARREST

WE MUST RETURN to the time when we last left Turgenev at Spasskoye, parted from his beloved Pauline, who appeared to have transferred her attentions to Gounod. He was taking stock of his inheritance after his mother died; he now had considerable responsibilities as a landowner. His experience on taking possession must have been similar to that of one of his characters who 'went into the garden and was well pleased. It was overgrown with steppe grass, with dandelions and with gooseberry and raspberry bushes. But there was plenty of shade, and there were several tall lime trees with curiously twisted boughs.'[1]

Turgenev then spent much of 1851 tidying up his family affairs.[2] When he went through his mother's papers and found her diary, he was appalled. What a woman! 'Dieu lui pardonne tout … mais quelle vie'.[3]

The Viardots, out of the blue, received a letter in which Turgenev said that he was in prison. An earlier letter, which he had sent the week before, had merely indicated that unforeseen circumstances had detained him in St Petersburg for longer than he had originally planned.[4]

The information about his incarceration was written in mid-May, after Turgenev had already been in prison for a fortnight. Perhaps because he knew of Pauline's imminent confinement, or because he was not allowed to say so, he withheld the news. This arrived almost certainly after Claudie was born.

His imprisonment at the end of April followed his publication of an obituary, in the form of a 'Letter', to mark the death of Nikolay Gogol, the dramatist and novelist, who had died on 4 March 1852. The circumstances of Gogol's death, in his 43rd year, were somewhat unclear.[5]

Gogol's satire and criticism were not forgiven in Government circles. His play *The Government Inspector* lampooned the corrupt bureaucracy. Worse perhaps, it was a considerable stage success. His entertaining novel *Dead Souls* ridiculed serfdom and much else in Russian society. The authorities decided to suppress any eulogies about the man who, some said, was the leading Russian writer to follow Pushkin.[6] Gogol's name was not to be mentioned, and he most certainly was not to be praised.

Turgenev took no notice of the prohibition. If the authorities had been looking for a pretext to stamp down on him, they now found it. His 'Letter' gave Gogol due praise. He lamented 'the death of a man who we now have the right, the bitter right, to call great, a man whose name signified an epoch in the history of our literature, a man of who we are proud as one of our glories.'[7] 'Only thoughtless and short-sighted people do not feel the presence of a living flame in everything uttered by him', he wrote.[8]

The St Petersburg censor banned publication of the 'Letter'. However, Turgenev persuaded the Moscow censor to pass it. The Tsar was infuriated by this attempt to bypass his authority. He sacked the Muscovite and ordered Turgenev to be arrested for 'manifest disobedience', a very serious sin which the autocratic monarch did not easily forgive.[9] Modern rights of free speech aside, Turgenev's behaviour must have looked like flagrant disobedience. His position was not helped when the police intercepted a letter in which he wrote that a high-ranking and highly-regarded official, who had denigrated Gogol, was up to his neck in filth. Today, the compliant official would doubtless be honoured for being politically correct.

Turgenev, who had been contemplating going on a hunting trip to the back of beyond,[10] found himself instead languishing in a police cell. Although this might sound an unpleasant experience, Turgenev enjoyed good food and drink. He could read books and receive visitors. He amused himself by getting the chief of police drunk on champagne. Together they toasted the memory of Robespierre.[11]

The prisoner whiled away his time by writing 'Mumu', a short story which featured an unpleasant woman, not unlike Turgenev's mother, who maltreats a deaf-mute serf. This did not prevent the English critic Thomas Carlyle describing it as the most beautiful and most touching story he had ever read. Turgenev also took the opportunity to examine the police archives which were stored in the room in which he was detained. Much later, he told Gustave Flaubert that he kept fit by carrying two packs of 52 cards, one card at a time, the eight steps from one corner of the room to the other, twice a day. This involved 416 trips in a day, during which he took about 3,300 steps, which he calculated was tantamount to walking about two kilometres.[12]

Turgenev tried to appeal to the Tsar through his rather less autocratic son. He pleaded that he was not disobedient. He submitted that he had sent the letter to the Moscow censor not so as to bypass the St Petersburg one, but to obtain a permission which he knew would be necessary in due course anyway.[13] However, the Tsar's original instructions were unchanged. After one month in prison, at the end of May 1852, Turgenev was exiled to his estates. He was required to stay within 40 miles of Spasskoye.

With the help of an occasional 10-rouble note, Turgenev got on reasonably well with the local policeman who was sent to check up on him. The story is told how another plainclothes officer, deputed to follow Turgenev out shooting, had a rougher ride. He irritated Turgenev who struck him on one occasion with his riding whip.[14]

A letter sent to the Tsarevich on the anniversary of his arrest was waylaid by the chief of the political police. Only after three fruitless applications was Turgenev allowed to leave Spasskoye. He could then return to the capital cities, consort with literary friends and indulge in champagne, women and song. That was in mid-December 1853, eighteen months after he had been exiled. Even then, his movements were restricted, and he was not allowed to leave Russia until an amnesty from the new Tsar Alexander II enabled him to go abroad in August 1856.[15]

Much of Turgenev's time during his confinement at Spasskoye was spent shooting. On one occasion his bag was more than 300 pieces. There were 69 woodcock, 66 great snipe, 39 jacksnipe, 33 capercaillie, 31 partridge, 25 quail, 16 hare, 11 waterrail, 8 moorhen, 4 duck and a curlew.[16]

The main house at Spasskoye was occupied by his agent; that is, his estate manager and steward. Turgenev himself lived in the small wooden bungalow at the back. The agent had been a member of Belinsky's circle, and he and his family seem to have been congenial. Turgenev shared a birthday party with him. All went reasonably well, at least until Turgenev discovered that everyone's wages had been increased and the equivalent of 100,000 francs had gone down the drain.[17] It seems likely that Turgenev and his agent both made a hash of it. Two literary men do not necessarily make one good businessman.[18]

Christmas was livened up by a fancy dress party for the serfs. For the remaining time, Turgenev found that a good way to avoid boredom was to divide up his day into various tasks such as eating, walking, writing, working and playing billiards with the doctor. The same routine was repeated daily.

Turgenev really missed music. He was similar to one of his characters in *On the Eve* who 'like all Russian nobles, had studied music in his childhood, and, like most Russian nobles, played very badly; but he was passionately fond of it'.[19] Although Turgenev could tinkle on the square piano in the dining-room, that was no substitute. Nor were the renderings of Beethoven's *Coriolan* and pieces by Mozart, played as duets by the agent's wife and her sister.[20]

Kindred spirits lived miles away. Occasionally visitors came to stay, such as his friend Vassily Petrovich Botkin,[21] who was a critic and writer about Spain. 'Oh, if only it's some nice person I can talk to a little',[22] no doubt Turgenev thought to himself when a carriage came in sight. When he had visitors, he could play a game of chess which he loved. He and his guests would also organise amateur theatricals.[23] Botkin was a bon vivant and gourmand, so we may assume that they also feasted themselves on bread and butter, smoked goose and pickled mushrooms, nettle soup and little pies, chicken in white sauce and Crimean white wine.[24] A few years later, they both travelled to Italy together.

Life for the nobility on their estates at any time, especially in winter, could be indescribably tedious. So, Turgenev was bored and lonely. However, around the summer of 1854, he became infatuated with Olga, an eighteen-year-old cousin whom he almost married. To warm his bed, however, he was solaced by Feoktista, one of his house-serfs. Their 'affair' lasted a couple of years.[25] She had been purchased from a relative[26] for 700 roubles, a premium compared to the normal 50 roubles paid for a serf. This has given rise to the allegation that she was some kind of sex slave. More likely, the arrangement was along the lines of that which he later described in his *Fathers and Sons.* In that novel, the landowner lives with a serf girl, Fenechka, with whom he had already had a boy.[27]

At the end of 1852, Turgenev heard that Pauline was about to visit St Petersburg. She performed in the *Barber* on 15 January 1853. After a rather shaky start, she was rapturously received. She also appeared in a version of *Le Prophète* which had been adapted to pass the Russian censor. Its title was changed to *The Siege of Ghent.* And Anton Rubinstein accompanied her in an aria from one of his operas. Louis went to considerable trouble to enable Turgenev to come and see them in St Petersburg, although he was unsuccessful.[28]

The St Petersburg to Moscow railway line had opened a couple of years earlier, so Moscow was now far more accessible. Nevertheless, Pauline went by road when she made the 400-mile journey from St Petersburg. She was without Louis, who was not well and had to leave Russia.[29]

As it was Lent, there were no opera performances. Besides, the Moscow opera house had recently burnt down. So Pauline gave concerts in which she sang works by local nationalist composers.[30]

Even if Pauline could have spared the time, it would have been improper for her to visit Turgenev at Spasskoye without Louis. However, Turgenev did succeed in making a clandestine visit to Moscow, for just under a week in early April.[31] Whatever may or may not have happened on this occasion is unknown. If Turgenev fantasised about a delightfully romantic tryst beforehand, he may have been deeply disappointed and frustrated. At this time, Pauline was dutifully writing to Louis saying how much she missed him and loved him.[32]

Once she was outside Russia, Pauline did not feel that Turgenev's visit needed to be treated as clandestine in any way. She mentioned it to Herzen when she saw him later in London. Her behaviour during the escapade to Moscow is possibly encapsulated in a sentence which she wrote a few years later. 'What interior happiness one has each time that willpower has gained a victory over passion, over instinct.'[33]

Their lives now separated. By the time they next met, Turgenev was quite grey-haired,[34] prematurely aged. As he himself would say, 'there is no denying that the years disfigure beauty, no matter of what grade'.[35]

Pauline returned to France. After a very quick stop in Paris, she went to London where she sang in a concert virtually every day (excluding, of course, Sundays) for 42 days. Her life now centred around touring and, in particular, the London opera season. In the summer of 1854, she was in London, and later in the year sang at the Three Choirs Festival in Worcester.[36]

Until her final assault on the Paris opera world with *Orphée* at the end of the decade, Pauline did not feature on the Paris stage.[37] There was a notable exception when, in February 1855, she stood in at the Théâtre-Italien for the prima donna who was indisposed by the untimely arrival of a baby. Pauline had three days and one orchestral rehearsal in which to prepare for the part of Azucena, the vengeful gypsy in *Il Trovatore.*[38] For this, Verdi sought a character 'torn between maternal and filial love',[39] so the part suited the creator of Fidès in *Le Prophète.*

Pauline was again cast as Azucena in the London première in May. The *Illustrated London News* then noted that the role 'is a creation entirely of her own; full of individuality and truthfulness ... nothing can be more artistic than her singing, though the extraordinary power of her acting throws it into the shade'.[40] Elsewhere, her performance was described by the critic Chorley as one of the most remarkable interpretations of the period.[41] The London première coincided with the state visit of Napoleon and Eugénie.[42] Queen Victoria and the imperial party attended on the first night. The production 'continued to be repeated to immense houses and with unabated applause' for several weeks.[43]

Soon Pauline was off to Birmingham, Manchester, Liverpool and Dublin. In the following year, she was in Baden-Baden, Gloucester and Bradford.[44]

When not on tour, the Viardots fitted neatly into the Paris musical scene. On 25 January 1856, with other leading people in the musical world, they attended Berlioz's concert, the 'crowning concert of his Paris career', at which *L'Enfance du Christ* was performed.[45]

Meanwhile, our principal performers found themselves not only at different ends of Europe, but on the opposite sides of the first major European war since the Battle of Waterloo a generation earlier. The French and British formed a coalition to fight the Russians.

The Crimean War was a consequence of the decline of the increasingly moribund Turkish Ottoman Empire. It was precipitated by 'miscalculation and muddle, rather than deliberate aggression'. Russia claimed the right of the Orthodox Church to custody of the holy places in Palestine, a right which has been disputed since the First Crusade and before, and is still a source of great friction today. Russia also asserted her right to protect the Orthodox Slavs from being persecuted and terrorised by Muslims in the Balkans, a grievance whose lingering effects we also still see today. As Turgenev made a character say in *On the Eve*, 'the accursed Turks drive us like a flock, they cut our throats; they have taken from us everything, everything, our rights, our lands.'[46] The circumstances were not helped by the mutual dislike of Napoleon III and Tsar Nicholas I. British concerns about Russia's expansion and her ambitions, particularly with respect to the overland route to India, also contributed to the hostilities. The origins of war are never as straightforward as they seem to be.

Turgenev was bullish at the start of the Crimean War. He said that all 65 million Russians were fully behind their government.[47] Although the hostilities had begun in the summer of 1853, the heroic events selected for teaching to British schoolchildren only began in September 1854, when the British and French landed in the Crimea. There was an allied victory at the Alma River. The allies laid siege to the city of Sebastopol, a Russian naval base. An attempt by the Russians to take the allies' supply port at Balaclava was defeated. This was the scene of the Charge of the Light Brigade on 25 October. It was followed ten days later by the Battle of Inkerman.

The coalition forces then dug in for the freezing winter. The British army was fortunate that the charity administered by Florence Nightingale and her associates mitigated the appalling consequences of the scandalous incompetence of the British military command.

When there was talk in Russia of mass conscription, Turgenev said that he would do his bit, if necessary.[48] However, he was not called upon to do so. A Russian victory spoilt the best laid plans of the coalition command to mark with a glorious victory the 40th anniversary of the Battle of Waterloo. Yet eventually Sebastopol succumbed to its siege. As it had held out for 349 days, the Russians could claim great heroism; and the coalition forces, who had taken it, could claim a famous victory. British schools do not normally emphasise that the Russian evacuation was eventually secured by the French under General MacMahon, taking the land defences on the Malakoff Heights.[49]

While the war continued, Turgenev was stuck in Russia with all the time in the world to read and write. When not shooting, this was what he did. He had long been considering how best to write a novel. Just as Brahms deferred completing his *First Symphony* until he felt he could compose one properly, so Turgenev did not write a novel until he felt skilled enough to do so. He first experimented with a lengthy work, entitled 'Two Generations', which never saw the light of day.[50]

Then a cholera outbreak in mid-summer 1855 made it sensible to stay inside the house. During seven weeks, around the time of Botkin's visit, Turgenev set about writing his first proper novel. He drew up a list of the characters and their characteristics.[51] The novel, *Rudin*, was published in the following January and February issues of *The Contemporary*. A French translation of it was published in 1862.

A few words about the central plot do poor justice to Turgenev's skill, his superb portraiture, etching, landscaping and characterisation; but they also indicate the novel's fragility. The scene is the provincial estate of a wealthy widow, a 'grande dame who imagines herself a patroness of the Arts and an intellectual and God knows what, while in fact she's no more than an old, High Society crone'.[52] She is surrounded by sycophants. Onto this stage arrives, out of the blue, the 35-year-old Mr Dmitry Rudin. This visitor creates a considerable impression and 'within a quarter of an hour his voice alone filled the room'. Rudin can seem truly insufferable. 'You sneeze, and he'll at once start proving to you why you sneezed and didn't cough', it was said.[53] One of the leading experts on Turgenev puts it graphically, 'An English Rudin would have gone into the Church and become famous for his eloquence'.[54]

Rudin 'soon stopped talking about his adventures in foreign parts' and reflected 'on the aims of civilisation and science, on universities and on university life in general'. 'Vous êtes un poète', declares the hostess, after

Rudin 'standing by the window, not looking at anyone, soared eloquently, even to poetry'.[55]

All this enchants and arouses Natalya, the intense daughter of the house who 'was not fully developed, was thin, sallow, and had poor deportment'. However, her 'pale face was beautiful' and she 'knew all Pushkin by heart'. When with Rudin, her pulse beat feverishly 'and many a disturbed sigh escaped from her perturbed breast'.[56] She had not experienced these emotions when in the presence of the man who her mother actually intended for her. She was now in love.

Rudin is made welcome and stays sponging for more than two months. When Natalya's mother hears of a clandestine meeting between Rudin and Natalya in the arbour, she quickly changes tack and shows her displeasure. She would rather see her daughter dead than married to the impecunious and largely unknown visitor.[57]

Natalya arranges to elope. However, Rudin, a 'superfluous man' if ever there was one, funks it at the last minute. Natalya, who is fully prepared to leave, feels utterly deceived. She asks what she should do, to which he responds 'We must submit, we must submit to our fate'. 'For God's sake, why didn't you stop me?' she not unreasonably asks. She accuses him of being a coward. He shrieks, as she runs away, 'You're the coward, not me'.[58] She marries the original man whom her mother intended her to marry.

The text of *Rudin* underwent considerable change to reflect the comments of friends.[59] The character of Rudin was altered, it is has been said, to dilute its resemblance to Mikhail Bakunin, who in autumn 1855 was handed over by the Austrians to the Russians and imprisoned. A sequel was added.[60] Rudin, increasingly disenchanted, moves on like the Flying Dutchman, eternally wandering 'through business failures, teaching, indefatigably striving towards an ideal'. Appropriately, he dies on the 1848 barricades in Paris.[61]

Around the time when Turgenev was at Spasskoye writing his first novel, the Viardots, in Paris, made friends with a more established novelist, Charles Dickens.

In the mid-1850s, Ary Scheffer, possibly Louis's closest friend,[62] painted Dickens's portrait, although the sitter did not regard it as a good likeness

(Plate 10). Indeed, the sittings were so 'interminable' that they delayed his work on *Little Dorrit*.[63]

Dickens stayed in Paris, a city he loved, during the winter and spring of 1855–6. He saw a great deal of both Scheffer and Pauline. Dickens also had recently arranged for some of Turgenev's *Sketches from a Hunter's Album* to be published in England.[64]

It must have been an amazing experience to meet the English novelist; he was a good raconteur and very good company. He would sing, do conjuring tricks, and even dance the hornpipe. He also shared the Viardot passion for amateur theatricals. When with Pauline, Dickens cannot have failed to recall that his sister Fanny, who had died of tuberculosis, had been a silver medallist at the Royal Academy of Music, where she studied singing and piano and later taught harmony. When her improvident father could not afford the annual fee of 38 guineas, she had had to be taken away.[65]

The Viardots were present in Scheffer's studio, as was the poet Robert Browning,[66] when Dickens read his folksy fable *The Cricket on the Hearth*. This, like *A Christmas Carol*, was one of the tales he would declaim before vast audiences, although his own relentless and exhausting tours and readings of his works were still in the future.

The theatrical and oratorical skills of the great English novelist, his almost vulgar flamboyance, the hand movements, the expressiveness, the histrionics and the slight lisp[67] would on their own have provided a memorable experience. To Louise, aged thirteen, he seemed 'tall, slender, upright with keen eyes, sparse beard and grave face'. Louise said that he did not speak much; however, 'what he said was always interesting'.[68] She must have been rather overwhelmed, because Dickens was actually a little less than middle height. Others, however, would have agreed that he looked like a cavalry officer, even if an unusually extrovert one, rather than an author.[69]

The Cricket on the Hearth is a curious title for a Christmas book. We are told that having such a chirping insect on the hearth 'is the luckiest thing in all the world'. While the gist of Dickens's folksy tale unfolded, it is difficult to imagine quite what went through the minds of at least two out of the 60 people in the audience. The little wife tells her husband, a ponderous carrier, a parcel delivery man who is at least twice her age, that she 'used to fear that ours might prove to be an ill-assorted marriage, I being such a child, and you being more like my guardian than my husband'.

What did the Viardots think when they realised that the crux of the story was the carrier's dreadful suspicion that his wife has fallen for a younger man, with whom he has seen her? 'Did I consider how little suited I was to her sprightly humour, and how wearisome a plodding man like me must be to one of her quick spirit?', he wonders as he broods on his apparent misfortune and tries to console himself.[70] Imagine the Viardots' relief when they heard that the supposition that she was faithless was completely unfounded, her virtue is assured, and everyone lives happily ever after.

At the very least, this tale, which was described as 'sentimental twaddle' by one contemporary,[71] had the potential to embarrass the Viardots. It would make anyone sitting in the audience who suspected that Louis had been cuckolded feel either excruciatingly awkward or hilariously entertained. The starched collars would have concealed the sniggers. Was the Viardots' presence and the choice of reading on that afternoon a coincidence, or was the event deliberately contrived by Scheffer with some ulterior purpose? The subject matter lay most uneasily with any suspicions Parisians might have had about Pauline's fidelity to her husband.

After the reading, Pauline was asked to sing. She first had to overcome her tears of emotion.[72] As to whether they were tears of shame, or deserved to be, we shall shortly consider.

Early in the new year, the Viardots invited Dickens to dinner. We may wonder whether the novelist, who was a stickler for punctuality, turned up, as usual, a quarter of an hour early.[73] Did he also comb his hair at the table, as he was wont to do? The purpose of the dinner was for Dickens to meet George Sand, who by now was 'chubby and matronly'. Dickens told his companion Wilkie Collins, the master of mystery stories, the author of *The Woman in White*, that 'there was 'nothing of the blue-stocking about her, except a little final way of settling all your opinions with her, which I take to have been acquired in the country where she lives, and in the domination of a small circle'. So much expressed in so few words![74]

Dickens, who had an obsession about tidiness, observed that there was a great deal of coming and going. He could usually recall the exact position of every piece of furniture in any room in which he had stayed, so he found troubling all this bustle and apparent disorder. 'The Viardots have a house away in the new part of Paris', he wrote, 'which looks exactly as if they had moved into it last week and were going away next. Notwithstanding which, they have lived in it eight years'.[75]

Dickens's other comments are surprising, given the Viardots' reputation. 'The opera is the very last thing on earth you would associate with the family' he said. 'Piano not even opened. Her husband is an extremely good fellow, and she is as natural as it is possible to be.'[76] One may assume that Dickens's visit coincided with some of the considerable alterations being made to the rue de Douai house, such as the additional storey which was added.[77]

Having heard about the episode in which the Viardots were asked to hear Dickens read *The Cricket on the Hearth*, we can treat with incredulity the suggestion that Pauline, up to the mid-1850s, had been unfaithful to Louis, her husband. While suspicion might have fallen on Maurice Sand, Gounod or Turgenev, the suggestion that she had also had an affair with Ary Scheffer seems particularly absurd. To the disadvantage of his reputation, however, Scheffer made the mistake of writing to her: 'Thank you a thousand times for … you know why … the happiness you gave me.'[78] Those who believe Pauline was just a tart, people who regard all women as nymphomaniacs unless proved otherwise, leap to the conclusion that she must have been in and out of bed with him.[79] The moral of the tale is never to write a cryptic phrase or sentence, at least about love.

The timing of the affair is said to have been in the mid-1850s, just when Scheffer was painting portraits of Pauline and of Dickens. An artist's studio is ideal territory for the voyeur, especially if the artist, like Pauline's father's friend Francisco Goya, wishes to portray the subject in the nude.[80] However, the notion that Pauline and Scheffer had an affair seems improbable. For long he had assumed the role of a father to her.[81] They had worked together for years: in 1843, she published a book of her own compositions illustrated with lithographs by him.

In one recent exhibition guide, it is reported that Pauline, 'to Turgenev's great indignation, carried on a love affair with him [Scheffer] for several years'.[82] One such writer says that, in the mid-1850s, 'all Paris knew about it, and Turgenev endured his disgrace with impotent fury'.[83] Towards the end of his life, 'when there was no danger of her knowing it', Scheffer indeed admitted to Pauline that, for years, he had loved her 'with all his soul'. Maybe, he would have liked that love to extend beyond spiritual and paternal love. He was not the first, nor the last, to find himself in this situation. However, there is no evidence whatsoever to support the idea that he actually abused his paternal role.[84] Since 'all Paris' was notably uninterested in Pauline, it seems improbable that her bedroom was the talk of the town.[85]

Scheffer had, at the beginning of the decade, married the widow of a general, an important official in the household of King Louis-Philippe. This 'lady of English descent' was said to be beautiful, albeit slightly past her prime. She also seems to have been a shrew who resented her husband's friends and 'fell into the deplorable error, of which many, otherwise estimable, women have been the victims; viz. of requiring that her husband should not only love her above all things, but should love nothing besides'.[86]

Madame Scheffer's death in the middle of the decade, following the recent death of his brother, plunged Ary into black depression, almost prostration. 'His whole being was unstrung as it were', said a contemporary. His daughter Cornélie said that her father felt thoroughly weary of life.[87]

A good meal with the Viardots in a London restaurant seems to have been too much for Scheffer. He had a heart attack in the night. He managed to get home to his country house at Argenteuil, where he died on 15 June 1858. Pauline ministered to him on his deathbed.[88] The likelihood that he had an affair with her in his last decade surely seems most improbable in the circumstances which have been described.

We will look later in more depth at the possibility that Pauline had an affair with Turgenev. However, if we take stock at this stage, in the mid-1850s, we can say with some confidence that it is highly improbable that Pauline had been physically unfaithful to her husband Louis. In arriving at that view, the circumstantial evidence, not least Dickens and his *Cricket*, has been very helpful.

gentle. However, there is no evidence whatsoever to support the idea that [illegible] actually [illegible] after all [illegible] [illegible] probable that her [illegible] was the talk of the town.[illegible]

[illegible] had [illegible] of the [illegible] the widow of a [illegible] an important official in the Household of King Louis Philippe [illegible]

[illegible]

[illegible] did [illegible] [illegible] have been [illegible]

We shall look later in more detail at the possibility [illegible] with [illegible]. However, [illegible] such [illegible] in the [illegible] 1840s [illegible] [illegible] that [illegible] highly improbable that [illegible] had been physically intimate [illegible] that [illegible]

CHAPTER 16

Tolstoy

By the end of the Crimean War, Tsar Nicholas I was dead. He was so depressed that it was even rumoured that he had committed suicide. Russia had fallen from the pinnacle it had reached in 1815, when it was the strongest power on the continent. However, for Turgenev, the succession of Alexander II and the subsequent Peace of Paris in March 1856 facilitated his eventual return to France and to Courtavenel.[1]

Turgenev first had to make the difficult choice between settling in Russia, or leaving it to return to the land of his dreams. His life had moved on; he was a respectable landowner. He must have wondered whether he should recognise that his chances with Pauline were very low, especially as Louis was still around. Perhaps he should settle down.

There had recently been other women in his life. We have already heard of his honourable intentions towards his cousin Olga and the possibly less honourable behaviour with his serf girl Feoktista.* The Russian girl from Sorrento[3] whom he had fallen for all those years ago was now married, but she seems to have come back into his life and may even have made a pass at him. He also became infatuated with Leo Tolstoy's younger and only sister Maria who lived not far from Spasskoye. Her brother's large estate at Yasnaya Polyana was only 60 or 70 miles away from Turgenev's estate. Turgenev went past it when he went from there to Moscow. Sometimes he would stay the night and sleep on a plain iron bedstead downstairs.[4]

*Feoktista, the serf girl who he had freed, had a son, although probably not by Turgenev who gave her money to marry and continued to help her financially.[2]

We must look at the 'animated, attractive'[5] Maria Tolstoy who Turgenev might well have married, if matters had turned out differently. Maria also provides a pretext for digressing to consider the turbulent relationship between the two great writers. We might have expected that a warm personal and professional friendship would have endured. That was not to be; it was only towards the end of Turgenev's life that an attempt was made to heal the wounds that had opened and festered.

First, Maria. She was unhappily married to her distant cousin, Valerian Petrovich Tolstoy, who was in the government service in Siberia.[6] She is supposed to have inspired Turgenev's story *Faust* which was written in the summer of 1856.

Faust is a curious tale, one which Pauline did not like.[7] It is about the devastatingly destructive power of love, a subject about which Turgenev had an obsession. The downfall and death of Gretchen (Marguerite) in Goethe's great drama is a direct consequence of her seduction by Faust. Turgenev's story concerns a girl whose mother deliberately deprived her of Art for fear that it would release 'those pent-up emotional forces which play havoc with people's lives'. The girl remains under the spell of her deceased mother and has not read a novel, a poem or any 'invented work'.[8] She lives quietly with her husband and a child. Turgenev's narrator invades this settled yet uninspiring scene. He introduces her to literature, in particular to Goethe's *Faust.* She and the narrator fall in love. This destroys her. Within a few days, she dies.

Much of the book seems to reflect Turgenev's repressed attitude at the time. The narrator observes that 'Life is not a joke and not an amusement, life is not even a pleasure. … life is hard labour. Renunciation, constant renunciation – that is its secret meaning, its solution'.[9]

The girl in Turgenev's depressing story, with her good figure, her golden hair, her unfussy character, seems to have looked very like Maria Tolstoy. Both were indifferent to poetry.[10] When the girl's mother says to her, 'You're like ice, until you melt, you're as strong as stone, but when you melt, not even a trace of you will be left',[11] we may wonder whether Turgenev was thinking of Maria or Pauline.

Maria Tolstoy

In reality, Maria was far from icy. Rather, she was 'passionate'. At one moment, she announced that she was going to stay at Spasskoye with Turgenev, alone. Some years after her tryst with Turgenev, which was probably no more than a flirtation, she 'was pursuing the most extraordinarily romantic adventures, having brought an end to her unsatisfactory marriage'. Indeed her subsequent *curriculum vitae* may well have influenced Tolstoy's *Anna Karenina*, his novel about a married woman disgraced by sexual scandal. In the early 1860s, in her mid-thirties, Maria became the lover of a Swedish viscount, by whom she became pregnant. She stayed in Scandinavia while the scandal died down.[12]

As sometimes happens in such circumstances, Maria subsequently became a nun. She settled in the austere convent attached to the well-known Optina Pustyn' monastery, located two miles outside Kozyolsk, not far from Moscow.[13] This monastery housed magnetic spiritual leaders who also attracted Gogol and Dostoyevsky.

This might have been the end of Maria so far as posterity is concerned. However, she reappears around the night of 9/10 November 1910, a moment of high drama in literary history. It was to her that Leo Tolstoy fled, having secretly packed up and left home. His six-hour train journey ended what had become 'one of the most miserable marriages in history'.[14]

During the following day, Maria and her brother decided that he should rent a small place in the monastery grounds. However, for some unknown reason, Tolstoy set off again in the early hours of the next morning.

Because he needed medical attention, the train stopped at a remote railway-halt called Astapovo, around 125 miles (as the crow flies) to the east of Spasskoye. Soon it was clear that he was too ill to proceed any further. Police and press, the *Pathé News*, and family caught up. Leo Tolstoy died there, aged 82, on 20 November 1910.[15]

For many, including the 20th-century novelist Virginia Woolf, Leo Tolstoy is 'supreme among the novelists of the world'.[16] Born on 9 September 1828, he was the fourth son. When he was eleven, his father dropped dead in a street in Tula. He and his siblings were eventually moved to the care of his father's sister in Kazan, 'that formidable fortress of Islam',[17] 500 miles to the east of Moscow. His grandfather had been governor there. There, Leo went to university.[18]

When he was eighteen, he obtained possession of the house and estates at Yasnaya Polyana with its 4,000 acres of land and 330 serfs. As a general rule, the youngest son inherited the estate where the family had grown up.[19]

Four years later, Tolstoy joined the army in the Caucasus, the region which includes Chechnya. Later, he was with the Russian armies when they reached Bucharest. He also took part in the defence of Sebastopol during the Crimean War. In Sebastopol, and subsequently in brothels of St Petersburg, his wild and loose living, heavy drinking and hard gambling took on epic proportions. He caught venereal disease.[20]

To pay his debts, which were largely incurred when gambling, the centre of the house at Yasnaya Polyana was dismantled. Its timber and valuable bricks were sold to someone who wanted to build elsewhere. Just the two wings were left, in one of which Tolstoy lived. In the other, he set up a school to educate his peasants. This was an illegal activity which prompted a police raid by the 'Third Section'. They even dredged the lake when searching for incriminating documents.[21]

During his wild bachelorhood, Tolstoy often saw Turgenev. The two authors frequently met up in Paris, although they found it best to occupy separate flats. They saw the sights together. Even though their programme included respectable activities such as attending a couple of Pauline's concerts, it is not difficult to imagine what 'seeing the sights' really meant. At one stage, Turgenev came to Tolstoy's lodging to confide his worries that he was suffering from genital trouble.[22] 'He wont have treatment and gads about', Tolstoy observed.[23]

In 1862, Tolstoy married Sofya Behrs, known as Sonya. They had thirteen children. Three daughters and five sons survived beyond childhood.[24] Sonya was the legitimate daughter of Andrey Behrs, the prominent Moscow physician and lover of Turgenev's mother. After Tolstoy proposed to Sonya, he gave her his diaries which chronicled his exploits with women.[25] One of his principal characters in the novel *Anna Karenina* felt compelled to make a similar gesture.[26]

Tolstoy soon transferred all his energies to the composition of *War and Peace*. However, he had to fulfil the duties of a local landowner as well. He was appointed as a magistrate with special responsibility for implementing the Emancipation legislation.[27] The announcement regarding this followed the accession of Tsar Alexander II in February 1855 and the end of the Crimean War in the following year. In late 1857, provincial committees were asked to formulate proposals. They reported back two years later. The Edict was promulgated on 3 March 1861. This was rightly regarded as a major event, so Turgenev was criticised by Herzen for being in Paris at the time.[28]

The provisions of the legislation and its practical implementation were complicated, too much so for the former serfs to understand. In principle, they could buy their master's interest in the land, at a price which was calculated using a formula which was tilted against them. There was much to argue about, not least land valuation. The government loans provided to assist the purchase saddled the ex-serfs with debt. Subsequently, the increase in the population meant that the serfs' allotments were insufficient to provide for both subsistence and redemption of the loans. Many thought that they had been cheated; hence the sense of grievance and the consequent violence. Tolstoy's arbitration decisions were often in favour of the serfs, yet they were mostly overturned on appeal.

Meanwhile, back in the mid-1850s, Tolstoy did not welcome Turgenev's attentions to Maria.[29] Tolstoy had developed a dislike for Turgenev. He was jealous of Turgenev's literary success. He may also have been jealous of Turgenev's success with a St Petersburg tart whom he also fancied. Other than joining in binges together, they had next to nothing in common. Turgenev, the smooth and Europeanised liberal, was clean and tidy, took great pains with his clothes and linen, used quantities of eau-de-cologne and enjoyed charming the ladies. One might have expected this description to fit the highly-born and well-connected Tolstoy. One of his cousins was Minister for Education and Procurator of the Holy Synod; two were ladies-in-waiting to the Tsar's only daughter. Tolstoy, however, did not care about his appearance. He was untidy, smelled of tobacco and preferred gypsy cabarets and whorehouses to drawing-rooms.[30]

At first, the two writers co-existed somehow. On his return from the Crimean War, Tolstoy stayed in St Petersburg with Turgenev. He 'painted the town red' with 'debaucheries, gypsies, cards, and then slept like a log till two o'clock in the afternoon'.[31] This may seem to us today to be normal behaviour for a casual visitor to a bachelor flat. However, in his diary, Tolstoy refers to the quarrels which arose almost daily. There was a particularly unpleasant incident at a dinner party when Turgenev praised George Sand; Tolstoy, who, somewhat surprisingly, deplored her morals, shouted angrily that her heroines were only fit to be tied to a hangman's cart and dragged through the streets.[32]

The two authors spent much time analysing their opposing temperaments. Not surprisingly, the relationship between them deteriorated inexorably. 'You are the only man with whom I have had any serious misunderstandings', Turgenev informed Tolstoy. However, he also regarded Tolstoy as the great hope for Russian literature.[33]

In the late spring of 1861, Tolstoy came to stay with Turgenev at Spasskoye.

The visit got off to a bad start when Turgenev let him read the manuscript of the novel on which he was working at the time. It was *Fathers and Sons.* Tolstoy promptly dozed off on Turgenev's large sofa.

On the following day they both went to visit Fet, the poet who lived nearby. Fet's wife was the sister of Turgenev's friend Botkin, the critic and writer. To make conversation, she asked some innocuous question about how Paulinette was getting on with her English governess. Turgenev responded that Mrs Innis was rather pedantic. She had asked him to specify the amount he wanted Paulinette to donate to charity. She also made the girl fetch and mend the clothes of the poor. Tolstoy considered that this charity was hypocritical. He took exception to her father's pomposity; it was all a farce, he said. Turgenev, who had 'a nagging sense of guilt' about Paulinette's illegitimacy, exploded at this criticism of how he was having his daughter educated. He threatened to smash Tolstoy's face.[34]

Tolstoy stormed out. He demanded a duel or an apology. The apology failed to reach him. Still in a fury, he called out Turgenev to duel with him, even unto death. Turgenev again apologised. He offered to duel, as requested, according to the established conventions. Tolstoy responded that he despised Turgenev and wanted no more to do with him. Once Tolstoy had made known to his friends and acquaintances what he had said, there was another challenge, this time from Turgenev which Tolstoy refused. After some further vitriolic correspondence, they broke off relations completely for seventeen years.[35] This was just as well. Pushkin and Lermontov had been killed in duels; Russian literature could ill afford to lose another two of its talented writers.

In the meantime, Tolstoy's fame began to eclipse that of Turgenev. *War and Peace*, written in 1865–9, made him into a celebrity, a national hero. Initially, Turgenev found *War and Peace* 'a boring failure of a novel'. Later, he helped to promote the French translation of it. 'I should be very happy to assist the French public to appreciate the best story written in our language', he said.[36]

Turgenev disliked Tolstoy's philosophising. For Tolstoy, leaders such as Napoleon were mere pawns in a predestined series of events, despite all their posture and pretence otherwise.[37]

After Tolstoy had written *Anna Karenina* in 1873–7, his philosophising increased. He adopted what has been described as 'the dreary and narrowing view that an artist's function was to tell the world how to behave.' Shortsighted, refusing spectacles, seated on a chair with legs which were shortened to help him work at his desk, he worked on his new-found religious philosophy. A novel about the Decembrists was abandoned for *What I believe*, which was finished in autumn 1883.[38]

Tolstoy grew a long white beard and wore a peasant's cap, shoes and belted shirt. Like one of his own fictional characters, he did menial work on the estate, where he would go ploughing for hours. Although summers were spent in Yasnaya Polyana, between 1882 and 1901 he spent winters at a house which he acquired in Moscow. He bought this for the sake of the children's education. Also, Sonya preferred the bright lights and some socialising to being stuck with an eccentric in the country.

Tolstoy's activities in his Moscow house were no less odd. In winter, he would enjoy his hobby as a cobbler. He took up bicycling aged 67, a sure sign of eccentricity. In the Moscow museum, we can see the boots which he cobbled and the bicycle. He also became a vegetarian, teetotaller and non-smoker. He would eat no dairy products or white bread. More conventionally perhaps, music was his passion, and sometimes he would play the piano for three or four hours a day.[39]

In his religious thinking, Tolstoy drifted away from Russian Orthodoxy. He was a very 'good' man. In the 1891 famine, in which around 400,000 people died, the Tolstoy family ran soup kitchens on their estates in the Samara district. The Orthodox Church however took a different view of his opinions; he was excommunicated by the Holy Synod in 1901.[40]

His views and possibly his celibacy also exasperated his wife, as did the arrival of a new friend and confidant, Chertkov, the son of a rich general who was an aide-de-camp to the Tsar. Chertkov took Tolstoy's writings to England. For Tolstoy, England, the land of the free, was a kind of utopia. Indeed, he dreamt of living in Bournemouth, possibly another sign of his unusual character. Had he gone, he might not have been allowed back to Russia, because the authorities regarded him as a considerable nuisance, even seditious. Tolstoy's trenchant opposition to government had been overlooked, at first because he was so well connected to people of influence, and later because of his enormous distinction.[41]

Sonya had to live with Tolstoy from day to day. She found his behaviour and views increasingly difficult to tolerate. She had been the commercial brains behind *War and Peace* and *Anna Karenina.* She acted as his secretary and devoted business manager. It is said that, as his amanuensis, she wrote out the equivalent of seven fair copies of *War and Peace.* 'He starts rewriting it as soon as I have the final copy ready, and this is for the umpteenth time', she despaired. Although married for 48 years and devoted to him, the more he wrote about religion, the more they quarrelled.[42]

When Sonya accused Tolstoy of having a homosexual relationship with Chertkov, he exploded. The relationship was spiritual rather than sexual, apparently. His wretched wife became 'seriously mentally sick'[43] and began firing at a picture of Chertkov with a toy pistol.[44]

A sketch of Tolstoy by Pauline

Meanwhile, in spring 1878, Tolstoy wrote to Turgenev saying 'Forgive me if I have been at fault in any way in regard to you'. This letter was the kind which 'a postulant nun might have written to a school-friend before going into the cloister'. Turgenev replied that he no longer had any animosity towards him; he hoped they would meet again while he was visiting Spasskoye.[45]

Turgenev stayed with Tolstoy at Yasnaya Polyana later that summer and again a few years afterwards. Their reconciliation was not entirely successful. There was little common ground. Although Tolstoy was grateful for Turgenev's support,[46] he still could not warm to him as a person. He could not tolerate Turgenev's elegant, suave, superficial European manners.

Tolstoy was also irritated by Turgenev's light-hearted fooling around with the children, his mimicking a chicken, his dancing the cancan. Turgenev 'was a fountain spouting imported water and gave one the feeling that the jet might cease playing', Tolstoy said. On the other hand, Turgenev thought that Tolstoy was going mad.[47]

Turgenev at one stage had written that any attempt 'to bring together two such conflicting personalities as yours and mine is doomed to fail'.[48] Turgenev visited Tolstoy several times again. They went shooting together. However, a real rapprochement was unlikely. Their personalities and their outlook on life were just incompatible.

When, in May 1882, Turgenev was very ill, Tolstoy wrote him a compassionate letter, to which Turgenev responded that he intended to live for a long while yet. We shall see later that when Turgenev lay on his deathbed, he finally wrote to Tolstoy and encouraged him to return to his art.

Tolstoy was supposed to have delivered an oration at a memorial to Turgenev. However, the government called it off.[49] This was probably a fitting end to one of the stormiest relationships between prominent authors that there has ever been.

CHAPTER 17

Reunion?

We now go back to the mid-summer of 1856, when Turgenev was granted permission to leave Russia. He decided to go to France, and immediately started organising his visit.

In early September, Turgenev met the Viardots in London, where they were based in Highgate.[1] Turgenev had warned the Viardots that he was greying. It was, after all, six years since he had left Paris. He had not seen Pauline for three years since her brief visit to Moscow.

When in London, we may surmise that, like royalty and everyone else, they visited the shell of the Covent Garden theatre, scene of many of Pauline's performances, which fire had 'reduced to a shapeless mass of ruins'. The theatre, with all the sets and archives, had been destroyed in March 1856, in a fire which appears to have started in the carpenters' shop above the gas-lit candelabra. A masked ball was just coming to an end at the time; amazingly, the only two people who had been missing turned up later.[2]

Soon the Viardots and Turgenev were all together again at Courtavenel, where Turgenev spent the autumn, idling away the time shooting and participating in amateur dramatics. The château was, as usual, crowded with visitors.[3]

In some ways, it was idyllic. They paddled around the moat; Pauline played the guitar on the lawns in the evenings. Louise would accompany her mother on the piano, or sing with Paulinette. They had concerts. In the theatre, they acted plays by Racine, with Paulinette as Iphigénie. Turgenev played the fool and told stories. They played his favourite game, the 'portrait game'. At the top of a sheet of paper, he would sketch a profile, sometimes grotesque, and write a character description underneath. The written bit would be folded over and the page passed to the next person who would write a character sketch, sometimes at considerable length, fold it over and pass it on. After this, Turgenev would read out what everybody had written, and call for a vote for the booby prize. The winner was then obliged to disclose his or her identity, much to the derision and perhaps relief of the others.[4]

Claudie Viardot ('Didie')

Turgenev adored Didie who was aged four. He played with her and her little sister Marianne. He told them stories. However, as we know, his own daughter Paulinette, now fourteen, was a disappointment. She 'could not lay claim to any beauty',[5] and the sparks which were generated between her, Louise and Pauline continued to fly.

On the surface, the atmosphere was jolly. Underneath, however, Turgenev was far from happy. Regardless of whatever dreams he may have had about the bliss awaiting him there, the château at Courtavenel was the home of Louis and Pauline Viardot. It was not his. His friend and neighbour, the poet Fet, visited him there in September and found him perched on the edge of another man's nest, frustrated to the point of desperation by Pauline, who presumably was not responding to his advances.[6] Turgenev felt that Pauline must exercise some sort of hypnotic power over him, 'some kind of sorcery, just like witchcraft'.[7] He is said to have told Fet that it seemed that he was only happy when a woman has her heel on his neck and is rubbing his nose in the mud. 'How fortunate it is for a woman to be ugly',[8] he exclaimed in an almost insane moment of disloyalty. Perhaps Pauline found his attentions too demanding and wearying.[9] There was some crisis, some rupture. Whatever happened, she told him to lay off.

When the Viardots went to Paris for the winter, Turgenev moved to a flat at 206, rue de Rivoli, then to 11, rue de l'Arcade. This was one of the occasions when he lived it up with Tolstoy.

In the following month,[10] Turgenev began to spin like a top and launched himself on an odyssey in search of medical treatment. He went to London where he put up in a hotel in Leicester Square. The letters with which he bombarded Pauline may just reveal his hectic diary. Alternatively, he may have wanted Pauline to think that he was fully employed without her.

He visited his friend the radical writer Alexander Herzen who had moved to London. Turgenev was admitted to the Athenaeum Club and went to the Geographical Society. He met Thackeray, the author of *Vanity Fair*, and Macaulay,[11] who was working on his fifth and final volume of *The History of England*. He also met the thundering Scot, Thomas Carlyle, who was an influential essayist and historian, and possibly 'the single most important writer in England during the 1840s'.[12] This latter encounter was unlikely to be easy. Carlyle disapproved of novels and 'prating story-tellers',[13] regarding those who read fiction as idle and frivolous. Turgenev, for his part, was by no means unusual in having considerable difficulty reconciling Carlyle's support for both obedience and liberty.

Turgenev met other Victorian characters, one who would shortly ride on horseback from Vienna to Constantinople; and another, surely the epitome of 'muscular Christianity', a clergyman who had rowed in the first Boat Race and had walked from Cambridge to London in a single day.[14]

Turgenev visited the Houses of Parliament. He must have been fascinated to see the building which had been formally opened four years earlier. But much of it, including the clock tower, was still incomplete. The chimes of Big Ben had not yet been heard.[15] Turgenev encountered the torpid atmosphere in the place which Dickens refused to visit because of his 'hatred of the falseness of talk, of bombastic eloquence'.[16] In the Commons, where the law respecting lunatics in Scotland was being discussed, Turgenev saw the Prime Minister, Palmerston, his hat down to his nose, ostensibly asleep, rousing himself only to mumble the occasional answer. He thought Disraeli behaved like a first tenor or a fashionable author.[17] He sat on the steps of the throne in the House of Lords,[18] where he will have missed the wisdom of the Archbishop of Canterbury because, according to the official report, his remarks were inaudible.

At the time, British politicians should have been concerned with the ferocious Indian Mutiny, in which troops in the Bengal army rose and massacred the British officers, their women and children. The British responded in kind, by shooting hundreds of sepoys from guns. However, the London government kept its head down and the news was slow to break.[19] There was a straw in the wind. On the day Turgenev was in Westminster, a peer complained that the Governor-General in India was personally supporting charities which aimed to convert the 'natives', a very pertinent matter since the Mutiny was prompted by concern that the British were undermining the Muslim and Hindu religious traditions. His Lordship's request for an assurance that the 'natives' would be allowed to practice their religion was irritably, even angrily, dismissed on the grounds that his information had been supplied by the telegraph. 'There is no doubt', the Minister bizarrely asserted, 'that it is impossible to rely upon the exact truth of any information which is forwarded merely by telegraph'. What Turgenev made of this altercation is not recorded; one doubts that he appreciated its significance.

Pauline's brother Manuel Garcia introduced Turgenev to Charles Hallé, whom Turgenev found improbably phlegmatic and gentleman-like for an artist. A year later, Hallé founded the orchestra which was to be called after him. Turgenev went to the annual concert given in St Paul's by the charity children. He also bought a gun from the top gunmaker, Lang; and he went to the Derby.[20]

Turgenev stayed in Wiltshire with the Nightingale family. He described his visit in a letter to Pauline. The gathering included, among many others, Sir Charles Trevelyan who had been knighted for his rigid efficiency, some might say 'brutal complacency',[21] as the head of the Treasury during the Irish famine. The haughty Captain of the Royal Yacht was also present, as was a colonel who seemed to come straight out of *Vanity Fair*. Florence Nightingale however was up in London, preparing evidence for a Royal Commission on the Health of the Army, which followed the revelation of the scandalous inadequacies during the Crimean War.[22]

Not surprisingly Turgenev found Trevelyan* a bit dull. He had no small talk. His brother-in-law Macaulay once said that his 'topics, even in courtship, are steam navigation, the education of the natives, the equalisation of the sugar duties, and the substitution of the Roman for the Arabic alphabet in Oriental languages'.[24]

The house party went on an excursion to Salisbury Cathedral which Turgenev thought was one of the most beautiful he had ever seen.[25] He told Pauline about the 'Long service. Sermon encore plus long, prononcé in a whining tone par un clergyman à cheveux plats'.[26] One is reminded of the Reverend Obadiah Slope; Anthony Trollope's *Barchester Towers* was published in that year.[27]

Turgenev, the atheist, was impressed by the family evening prayers, a ritual which was attended by the servants. Prayers were read by Mrs Nightingale, presumably taking due precedence over Trevelyan who normally 'delighted in reading chapters from the Bible aloud in a deep sonorous voice'. Of different sonority was a rendition by the wife of the Captain of the Royal Yacht who sang like a typical industrial machine, with the others joining in the refrain, squawking like parrots.[28]

Turgenev found that he had to admire the sheer respectability of the

*Shortly before this, Trevelyan was responsible for recommending the reforms which made the Treasury supreme in the civil service. Subsequently, as Governor of Madras, he leaked to the press his views on financial policy. These differed from the policy of the central government, thus setting a precedent from the highest level for a procedure which has become commonplace today.[23]

English, whereas a decade earlier he had been wont to disparage them. He could see that there was something durable about England's empire, although he was writing almost twenty years before Disraeli styled the Queen an Empress.[29]

From London, Turgenev moved on to Sinzig, a spa on the Rhine, a few miles downstream from Coblenz.[30] There, nine months after that time when he had experienced so much pleasure, yet so much frustration, he heard that Pauline had been delivered of her son Paul who was born at Courtavenel on 20 July 1857.

It was now that Turgenev wrote his short story, 'Asya'. He had come to realise that 'there are turning points in life, when the past dies and something new is born; woe to the man who cannot sense them and either holds on stubbornly to a dead past or seeks prematurely to summon to life what has not yet fully ripened'.[31] He makes several bitter references to the 'treacherous', 'cruel and beautiful widow' who had 'just broken his heart'.[32] He must have sensed that the birth of Paul provided confirmation that his relationship with Pauline had hit the buffers.

What is the story of 'Asya' otherwise about? The narrator encounters a Russian painter and his seventeen-year-old half-sister. It transpires that she is the daughter of a serf girl in the painter's home.[33] Did Turgenev, when constructing this character, perhaps think of his own daughter Paulinette? Not so stodgy, however. The sylph-like Asya has a 'half-savage charm that irradiated her slender body'.[34] Her chameleon-like character fascinates the writer and distracts him from his regular nocturnal recollection of his 'unhappy love affair'.[35]

Asya falls in love with the narrator. 'You've gone into a beam of moonlight, you've broken it,' she says. 'I've grown wings but I've nowhere to fly.' However, this will-o'-the-wisp is whisked away to London by her brother, and the narrator never sees her again. He has failed to declare his love for her until it is too late. He has failed to utter those three crucial words that he loves her. He never again experiences that 'burning, tender profound feeling'.[36] He is doomed to the 'solitary life of a lonely bachelor, living out the tedious years', and preserving as sacred relics her notes and a dried geranium flower.[37]

We may read this apparently harmless, but beautifully poetic tale of less than 50 pages as some evocation by Turgenev of his mental state and his relationship with Pauline. Not so his audience in Russia. 'Asya' exploded a disproportionate[38] public row which Turgenev cannot have anticipated. The question at issue concerned the direction in which Russia and Russian literature should head. As the 1850s progressed, the new guard at *The Contemporary*, who paraded themselves as 'men of the sixties', became more outspoken. For example, they questioned the potential of the nobility to provide any useful moral leadership. Not surprisingly, the censors gave the journal increasing trouble, and it was eventually suppressed.[39]

This increasingly radical faction, with Nikolay Chernyshevsky as its leading light, opposed the men of the forties, that 'decade of high ideals and grand illusions',[40] who maintained that orderly change could best be achieved through the efforts and influence of liberals, rather than by revolutionaries.[41] These 'out-of-touch and out-of-date' reactionaries included the prominent literary critic Pavel Vasilyevich Annenkov who championed Turgenev.

The 'men of the sixties' were hoping for some thundering polemic from Turgenev. They were severely disappointed; 'Asya' did not provide the clarion call that they expected from an aspiring author. Turgenev was condemned as an epicurean aristocrat and obsolete,[42] indeed superfluous, as a writer. It was an image he would never live down.

Meanwhile, Turgenev continued to spin. The waters at Sinzig did not agree with him. He headed for Baden-Baden. There Tolstoy, who was gambling recklessly, told him that he disliked 'Asya', and borrowed 500 francs from him. Turgenev bought himself another gun dog.[43] He was 'incorrigible', he said it himself. He despatched the animal to Courtavenel to join Louis's pack of dogs lolling in the great hall.

He went off for a cure to Boulogne. In the middle of the century, this was a 'popular' resort, being easily within reach of Paris and close to England. It was often visited by Dickens, who appreciated that a bottle of excellent wine could be obtained there for 10 pence (less than 5p) a bottle. Dickens also found it a convenient place to lodge a lady-friend.[44]

In the autumn Turgenev returned to Paris, where he saw Paulinette and took her to the opera.[45] He next went to the South of France and Italy. On the Corniche, he thought that the women were stunningly beautiful. He wrote to Pauline about 'the most ravishing creature he had ever seen'. Genoa was different, the women were repulsive.[46] Was Pauline bothered, we may well wonder.

Having travelled around Italy, he left for Vienna, still in search of further medical treatment.[47] His schedule seems quite breathless.

Pauline too was never still. However, she perhaps had a less medical reason to be on the move. She performed in Warsaw, Berlin, Leipzig, Stettin and Dresden. She was in London for the summer season. She was in Hungary[48] for the autumn. From Pest, a droll Louis wrote to Turgenev that they had visited nobody, nobody had visited them and they felt they were quarantined because of the pest.

After Christmas, she was again in London where she gave a large number of concerts. In the following year, there were 50 concerts, she said. Pauline began to regard this relentless touring as a form of slavery.[49]

It comes as a surprise that Pauline's former rivals Grisi and Mario were sometimes on the boards with her as well. Among the motley company, Pauline was the only one who spoke English well. She must have found it satisfactory when her former rivals had to rely on her to act as an interpreter between them and the costume-makers, the machinists, the chorus, everybody. Indeed, at times, Pauline seems to have virtually been the stage manager.[50]

As well as performing opera, Pauline sang oratorio which was particularly popular in England in the provincial cities such as Birmingham and Norwich. Her repertoire included popular works such as Mendelssohn's *Elijah*, and Handel's *Samson* and *Messiah*.[51] The distinguished singer Sir Charles Santley said that Pauline was the only singer whom he had ever heard performing Jezebel in *Elijah* 'with true dramatic fire'.[52]

She enjoyed appearing in Dublin, where 'there was not a trace of English starchiness'. She could relish the great applause when she created Lady Macbeth, 'with prodigious fire',[53] and enjoy pleasant walks in Dublin's Phoenix Park. However, she found somewhat disconcerting the Irish habit of whistling their applause instead of clapping. We may wonder whether the dinner laid on by the 'ministre de la justice' was really much fun.[54]

There were the occasional moments of sheer hilarity. To create the atmosphere for the 'Gran Scena del Sonnambulismo', Lady Macbeth's sleep-walking scene, Verdi provides a protracted orchestral introduction followed by a confabulation between the doctor and the lady-in-waiting. Almost five minutes elapse before the Queen appears, her mad utterances punctuated by questions 'She sighs?', 'This too?' from the doctor and gentlewoman. Pauline was waiting in the wings, with her lamp, when some frustrated Irishman in the Gods, who did not understand Italian, yelled out, 'Sher, is ut a boy or a gurl?' The audience started laughing. Pauline feared that this diversion would wreck the dramatic impact. Whether or not it did, *she* brought the house down.[55]

On another occasion, Orpheus rushed forward during 'J'ai perdu', slid on the slippery floor, and was fortunate to fall on 'his' knees at the footlights. There were the last moments of *Rigoletto* in Liverpool, when the jester's murdered daughter was carried on with policeman's boots sticking out of the sack. Everyone thought this was hilarious except the audience who were seriously and 'deeply moved, thinking all was as it should be'.[56]

Still, why did Pauline do all this touring, and submit to this slavery? Actors have an extraordinary loyalty to their profession. Today, in the West End, stars perform night after night, night after matinée. Some are actors who ostensibly have no financial need so to do, yet are drawn by a magnetic force to tread the boards. Many conductors, instrumentalists and indeed some opera singers never retire, even though they have had their 'last performance'. Some may enjoy it. Some may get a particular buzz from the applause. Some may regard the propagation of their art, the gift with which they have been endowed, as a fundamental duty. Some may feel they cannot do without it. When Adolphe Nourrit, the leading tenor at the Opéra in the mid-1830s, thought his career was coming to an end,[57] he became increasingly depressed. His voice and memory deteriorated. He committed suicide.

Pauline seems to have got a buzz from having a large audience captured, laughing with her, weeping with her, completely in thrall. However, for her, this was not some trite, tabloid emotion that goes with the adulation of a celebrity. For her, this process was the essence of Art as revealed through her.[58] Art was much more than entertainment, terms which many people today seem to think are synonymous. It was, is, and should be, a revelation which raises us onto another plane.

Pauline grew up in the early 1830s at a time when the 'role of the artist' was very topical. We have seen that the Saint-Simonian sect maintained that the artist was a kind of evangelist 'for the holy cause of Art'.[59] By going forth and performing his art, society would come to understand the ideals to which it should be striving. In this sense the artist, they held, also had a sacramental role similar to that of the priest who reveals his religion to his congregation. The Saint-Simonians were enormously influential. Thus Franz Liszt, for example, genuinely believed, however pompous it may seem to us, that by performing his art he was facilitating the appreciation by his audience of inner truths and ethical values.[60] Much that was good came from this. Hence, his relentless concert tours around Europe. Hence, his later interest in teaching.

George Sand saw Pauline, her Consuelo, in this role. Pauline was the ideal artist, a Priestess of Art.[61] 'It has been truly said that the object of music is the awakening of the emotions', declares Albert in *Consuelo*. For George, no other art but music can so sublimely penetrate the innermost heart of man; 'no other can reveal to the soul the splendours of nature, the delights of contemplation, the character of nations, the tumult of their passions, the languor of their sufferings, as music can. Regret, Hope, Terror, Meditation, Consternation, Enthusiasm, Faith, Doubt, Glory, Tranquillity, all these are given to us and taken from us by Music'.[62]

The notions of the Saint-Simonians, Liszt, Pauline, are all gone. It is difficult for us ordinary mortals, who anyway are addicted to screen and recorded performance, to grasp how an artist's performance has the power to transport us into an unknown mystical realm and 'penetrate the vaporous veil which aggrandises and renders divine all that is seen through it'. It takes a great leap to say that this facilitates the understanding of the ethical objectives to which we as mortals should be striving.[63] We shall probably get no further than the supremely uplifting emotion which we may experience when, with the sound of superb music or voice ringing in our ears, we walk into the street from hall or theatre, or even during those all-too-rare church services which uplift us into another dimension. Then, we are 'seized by one of those shuddering sensations of the soul in which one seems transported into a higher world'.[64] We may also experience this emotion when we gaze at a great painting or finish a novel which displays exceptional insight or sensitivity. In a more down-to-earth way, we perhaps have a similar feeling when we see something incredibly beautiful, for example, the countryside on a spring day. It is heavenly, not worldly; it is the sound of music, not noise; it is a form of culture, not sport; it is a privilege, not a right.

Turgenev experienced this and encapsulated it in a 'Prose Poem'. 'Stay! A mystery is revealed, the mystery of poetry, life and love. This is immortality'. After the prima donna has sung her last note, is dead and has 'escaped above from all that is transient and temporal', still her moment will endure. She would, he wrote, remain for ever in his memory. 'Let me partake in your immortality; let the reflections of your eternity fill my soul.'[65]

So, even if this experience did not take Pauline the next step into the realm of ethics, there was a philosophical, even poetical, reason for her slavery. There was also a commercial and practical reason for it. Pauline will have known that, for singers, Nature brings their duties to a very early close. Pasta had illustrated that point for her a few years before. Pauline had heard Pasta for the only time in 1850 in Donizetti's *Anna Bolena*, the role which Pasta had originally created.[66] By then, her broken hoarse voice was in 'a state of utter ruin'. Pauline said that she was like a wreck of a picture, although the picture was the greatest picture in the world.[67]

This experience forcibly reminded Pauline that she must advance her public career and provide for her retirement while her voice permitted.

One of Pauline's letters reveals that there may have been a still further motive. 'These little journeys which I have made alone this winter have been very salutary holidays for me', we find her writing from Dublin. 'On the one hand, they have been reposeful for my heart somewhat fatigued by the expression of a love which it cannot share; and on the other, absence can only fortify my friendship, my esteem and my great respect for this man who is so noble and devoted and who would give his life to gratify the least of my caprices, if I had any.'[68] She was deeply devoted to Louis. However, she needed space.

Even when at home at Courtavenel, she needed solitude. Her favourite spot was a quarter of an hour from the house, where she would sit alone on a great rock at the foot of a magnificent elm which stood on an elevation in the middle of the wheat. From there, she could see at least twenty miles all around. On one side, the horizon was limited by a dense wood, through which a lane led straight to the château. She hears a distant bell. It is already five o'clock and they are ringing for dinner. Down that narrow lane she must return.[69]

Sometimes Pauline's tours kept her in touch with old friends. One who she met on her tours was Dickens. They were both in Dublin staying in the same hotel, Morrison's.[70] He was there to perform a reading of his works at the Rotunda.

Pauline in middle age

During Pauline's visits to Weimar, where she sang Norma, she would practise on the instruments at the Altenburg, the house above Weimar where the 'utterly unhappy', 'even childlike' Liszt was ensconced with his second long-term mistress, Princess Carolyne. At this time, the princess was trying to obtain consent from the Tsar for a divorce from her estranged husband so that she could marry her reluctant fiancé. Pauline seems to have divined his views on their marital problems. 'If I were in his place, I should greatly fear that the Emperor of Russia might consent', she wrote. 'I think that, in Liszt's own mind, this idea is not particularly attractive'.[71]

1

Louis Viardot out shooting (1847) – a watercolour by Carl Schulz.

Pauline Viardot, a portrait around 1844 by Maurice Sand.

3

4

The Moscow Courtyard (1878), by Vasily Polenov (3), a picture once owned by Turgenev, and *The Last Tavern by the Town Gate* (1868), by Vasily Perov (4), evoke the atmosphere of Russia in the 19th century.

5

6

Pierre-Auguste Renoir's *Les Grands Boulevards* (1875) evokes the excitement of fashionable Paris (5). This contrasts with the idyllic serenity of his *View of Bougival* (1873), where the languid and calm pace of life, which the dog enjoys, is enlivened only by two lovers embracing (6). Les Frênes is located in the trees above the Seine.

7

Manuel Garcia, Pauline's father: this portrait, which has been attributed to Francisco Goya, has traditionally been said to be of Manuel Garcia. It belonged to the artist's sons.

8

Manuel Garcia, Pauline's brother: John Singer Sargent painted this portrait of Manuel in 1905. The sitter died on 1 July 1906, aged 101.

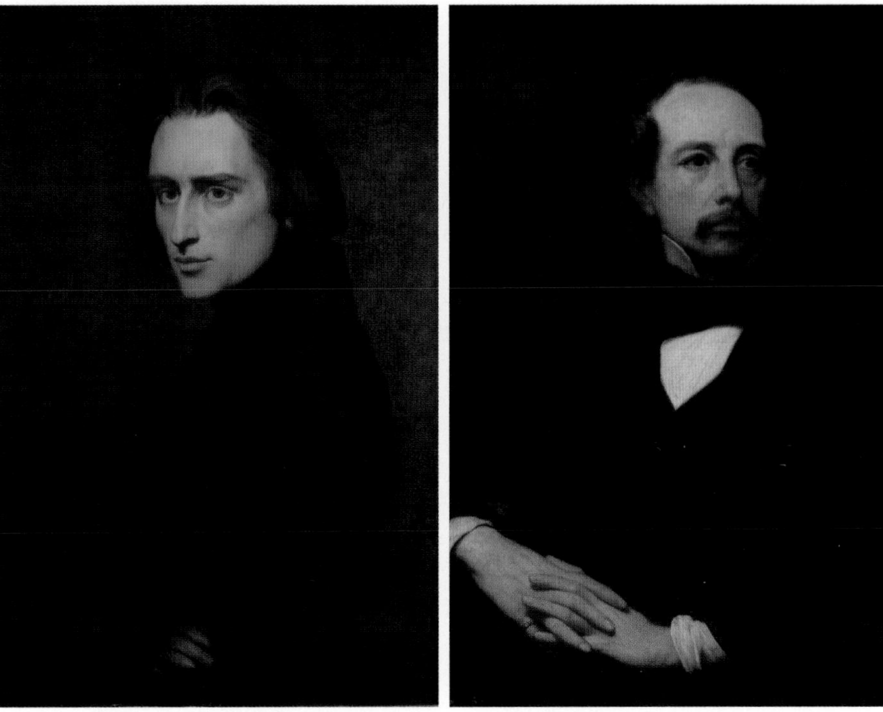

9  10

Two portraits by Ary Scheffer: Franz Liszt (1837), the lady-killer, in his twenties (9), and the unusual portrait of Dickens (1855) (10) painted during 'interminable' sittings around the time of the Paris reading of *The Cricket on the Hearth* (chapter 15, page 230).

11

Les Frênes has recently been threatened by development.

12

13

14

Residences: Watercolour sketches of the Viardot theatre (1869) (12) and Turgenev's house in Baden-Baden (1875) (13) have suffered from the passage of time. Louise painted the watercolour of Courtavenel (14).

At the end of a tour, Pauline experienced the joy of returning home to her family. We can see her being greeted at the station by Louis and Louise. Then home, where the younger girls who were already tucked up in bed would jump out with excitement when she went into their room. This was, for her, 'a lovelier reception than any success on the stage'. She would join the crowds and she would try to avoid the pickpockets when she went to buy their New Year presents.*

Pauline, in her later thirties, needed not just space, but also someone to lean on, other than her husband who was approaching the age of 60. In the early years, George Sand had provided this support. During the forties and fifties, Ary Scheffer also provided rock-solid moral support.[72] Pauline also had less conspicuous confidants and correspondents, people who were very important to her, such as Count Matthew Wielhorsky, an able amateur cellist in St Petersburg, a fan who was possibly one of the 'Four Paws' back at the time of her début in St Petersburg.[73] She frequently corresponded with him.

After Scheffer's death, Pauline particularly relied on Julius Rietz.[74] Although unromantic, austere, unfunny and middle-aged,[75] Rietz was a highly-regarded cellist, conductor and composer, a musician of great talent. He had worked closely with Mendelssohn and had been a colleague of the Schumanns in Leipzig, where he became the conductor at the Gewandhaus, the concert hall.[76] He was also prominent in the revival of the music of J.S. Bach whose works had mainly lain dormant during the century since his death. Back in 1829, with his elder brother Eduard, who was a leading violinist, Julius had copied out the parts for Mendelssohn's historic revival of Bach's *St Matthew Passion.* He subsequently edited the *B minor Mass* and the *St Matthew Passion* for the Bach-Gesellschaft Edition. He also edited works by Handel, Mozart and Haydn. He was a distinguished, worthy German. Pauline must have found it a pleasure to converse with him.

Rietz and Pauline got to know each other properly in the spring of 1858, when she sang in Leipzig. That tour was very successful. The journal,

*In France, New Year rather than Christmas was the focus for particular celebration.

the *Neue Zeitshrift für Musik*, called her 'the greatest singer of our time'. Rietz gave her the gift of the manuscript of one of Bach's cantatas.[77]

During her subsequent tours of England and Ireland, Pauline sent Rietz long letters, sometimes almost illegible. During 1859, they wrote to each other almost every day. After writing a long letter to her 'bear', as she called him, she picked up the pen again to him at 11pm at night. At one stage, she was writing to him at 2am in the morning from Nottingham, while she was tending her maid who was sick.[78]

Julius Rietz

Pauline wrote to him from Wolverhampton, also in the English Midlands: 'I love you with the most heart-felt deepest, truest, warmest, sunshine-clearest love that ever woman felt as friend for friend'.[79] Statements such as this have given rise to the suggestion that they were lovers. They may have been. Anything is possible if one wishes to assume the improbable premise that she was a nymphomaniac. He could presumably be a candidate from her time in Germany. As relatively little is known about their relationship compared to the other candidates, he is the most difficult to dismiss with any reasonable certainty.

However, there is no reason to suppose that they were lovers. Why is she any more likely to have allowed him into her bed than any of the others? Especially as her bed was in the English Midlands at the time she expressed these sentiments, and he was in Leipzig.

Rietz seems to have found his exuberant and enthusiastic correspondent exhausting, if not overwhelming. The correspondence became rather one-sided and Pauline regularly had to admonish *him* for being dilatory in replying, a complaint which Turgenev would frequently level against *her*. 'This correspondence, bursting forth so suddenly, seems to have collapsed just as suddenly.'[80] It dried up.

Turgenev also needed an emotional prop at this time. This was provided by the 'charmante', 'très sympathique, bonne et spirituelle',[81] Countess Elizabeth Lambert.

Countess Lambert

Countess Lambert was the daughter of a former finance minister. Her husband had been a friend of Tsar Alexander II when he was a boy. He later became an aide-de-camp. Turgenev probably first met the Countess, who was in her mid-thirties, in the winter of 1855–6. She wrote him very long letters. She almost alarmed him with the intensity of her pursuit. She received him in a room lined with icons and piled high with books. He had to endure her attempts to convert him to religion; she had to put up with hearing about his obsession for an opera star in a distant land.[82]

Although the grey-haired Countess Lambert was actually the same age as Pauline, Turgenev thought her 'aged' and sickly.[83] She was unlikely to provide an outlet for Turgenev's lusts and appetites. He had an eye for beautiful women and, as we know, was always immaculately turned out, a bit of a dandy.[84]

Many years later, Turgenev told his friends in Paris about one of his women who refused all presents until, when pressed, she surprised him by asking for soap. He gave it to her; she went away, washed her hands, came back and asked him to kiss them in the same way that he kissed the hands of the ladies in the St Petersburg drawing-rooms. 'Love alone produces a particular flowering of the personality,' he said.[85]

Countess Lambert provided something different. When, in 1858, Turgenev went back to Russia, he resumed his friendship with her. 'She has become a great friend – I spend all my evenings with her',[86] he wrote to Pauline, whether merely by way of information or to arouse her jealousy. It had no ostensible effect. In that year, he only saw Pauline when he saw her performing in Leipzig in April. The correspondence spluttered on for a bit. He sent her an operetta libretto which he had written for her. She did not answer his letters, and he even had to rely on Paulinette for information about her.[87]

In mid-July 1859, Turgenev called at Courtavenel, before returning to Spasskoye two months later.[88] However, his relationship with the Viardots was to all intents and purposes now limited to business correspondence with Louis about paying for the upkeep of Paulinette.

CHAPTER 18

CONSUMMATION?

IN THE SUMMER of 1857, Pauline gave birth to Paul. This was around nine months after the crisis, the rupture with Turgenev. Paul has been said to look like Turgenev. Although Turgenev never took much interest in him,[1] he was sufficiently vocal that he was Turgenev's child that he created a bitter and enduring rift in the family, with his two sisters taking the opposite view. So this is an opportune moment to digress and to focus on Pauline's private life. It is a suitable time to consider the contentious question as to whether anything untoward may have happened between the sheets, or in the arbours and greenhouses of Courtavenel, or the woods of Brie.

Without question, Turgenev adored Pauline. He was obsessed by her and was always thinking about her, not merely as one might love a close member of the family, but much more.[2] At times, he felt that he was her protector, and responsible for her welfare and happiness. He told one of his friends that he loved her so much that he would dance on the roof, stark naked and covered in yellow paint, if she asked him to do so.[3] 'I love her more than ever, and more than anyone in the world', he told Tolstoy.[4] 'There is not a night when I don't dream of you',[5] he wrote to her in that hot steamy summer of 1850. On his deathbed, he wore a locket with her picture on one side and his initials on the other.[6] 'How gloriously her large dark eyes had flashed in the light', he wrote, in a short story, possibly thinking of Pauline. 'How beautifully her heavy black hair cascaded over her raised head and shoulders'.[7]

The extent of their relationship is very hard to assess. On the one hand,

Turgenev writes something ostensibly erotic; on the other, he includes it with a letter which is going to be shown to Louis. He wrote from Russia thanking Pauline for the description of her room which she had sent him. He had drawn its shape on a sheet of paper so that he could imagine it more easily. Yet this same letter, written at the time of Pauline's infatuation with Gounod, was addressed to them all. It contains a specific word of thanks to Louis for his letter.[8] Thus, something which at first seems like a personal love letter cannot actually have been one.

For Pauline, at times, the relationship was probably erotic. Her parentage was Spanish; she had some of the characteristics of Carmen. She was exuberant, possessive, dominant. She was jealous of other women in Turgenev's life. She wrote that she spent much time thinking of him and she sent him dried flowers with her letters. She was, at least occasionally, mentally unfaithful to Louis.[9] Whether she shared love which was consummated with anyone other than her husband, we will never know for certain. We can only speculate, based on circumstantial evidence. She said that, had it not been for Ary Scheffer pulling her back, she might have fallen into the abyss.

Much turns on Pauline's character. If it were shown that she was prepared to offer herself to men other than Louis, we can be virtually certain that Turgenev will have been one of them. That is why it has been so important to consider the other candidates for her favours, Maurice Sand and Charles Gounod, Ary Scheffer and Julius Rietz. We have done so; and we have found insufficient reason to entertain them. Hector Berlioz, who is sometimes cited, we shall easily dismiss in a later chapter.

In weighing the evidence for and against Pauline having had a physical affair with Turgenev, we must try to avoid applying modern 'standards' to earlier periods, when the environment was so different. The behavioural standards applicable at the time have a considerable bearing on the probability that she would be physically unfaithful to her husband. We will also need to consider where Louis himself stood in all this. And of course we need to consider Turgenev's own attitude to women.

Ways of satisfying love change in their acceptability and sufficiency. Once upon a time, a glimpse of the female foot, even the bare elbows,* had the potential both to arouse and satisfy, in a way which is unimaginable today.[11] And the kiss: 'For God's sake, one kiss as a pledge of ineffable hap-

*Homer celebrated women for their ankles and cheeks rather than for their legs or breasts. Pushkin seems to have found the foot more stimulating than lip, cheek or breast. Victor Hugo described a prim piness', a character whispered as in a delirium. His object of desire instantly drew back. 'The triumphant radiance, the colour left her face. Her gentle eyes blazed sternly. "Never! Never! Don't come near me!" she said in alarm, almost in horror.' He sobered up suddenly.[12]

The allegation that Pauline and Ivan consummated sexual relations[13] is unsubstantiated. Pauline's case is not helped, however, by her and her heirs having destroyed much of the correspondence which would provide an authoritative view and possibly even a cast-iron defence. Shredding, as we well know, can do irreparable harm to a reputation.[14]

Before taking our speculations further, we should first remind ourselves of how the roller-coaster friendship between Pauline and Turgenev evolved.

Their relationship, which began with him as one of the fawning admirers, the 'Four Paws', back in 1843, was unexceptionable in the early years. There were then three-and-a-half years, from January 1847 until June 1850, when Turgenev followed Pauline around like a lap-dog, with 'unquestioning, submissive, undemanding devotion'.[15] During these years, there were some specific *moments intimes*, to which we shall return later.

In 1850 the relationship cooled abruptly, a few months after Turgenev had completed *A Month in the Country*. On 22 June 1850, Turgenev set off for Russia. After the end of the year, correspondence between Pauline and Turgenev seems to have halted, although one biographer suggests that maybe it was so intimate that it did need to be shredded.[16] Another jumps to a diametrically opposite conclusion, that 'it was Pauline Viardot's affairs with other men, or at least with one particular man, that finally made him decide to leave her and return home.'[17] Here, the innuendo refers, of course, to Gounod.

There was then the long six-year period when Turgenev could not leave Russia. He was either in prison, under house arrest, or otherwise confined. He wrote a short story about an unattainable woman. It was entitled 'Three Encounters'. This possibly reflects an erotic dream which he had in that hot summer of 1849.[18] 'I looked up and there she was soaring through the air, all in white, with long white wings, beckoning me to come to her.

spinster who 'could have given points to an English miss. Her life was haunted by a dreadful memory: her garter had once been seen by a man.'[10]

I raced after her, but she flew swiftly. In vain I stretched my arms eagerly to her … *'Addio'* she said, flying away from me'.[19]

During April 1853, Turgenev took the opportunity to slip quietly into Moscow in order to meet Pauline. However, nothing came of it.

The close friendship was revived in August 1856. Turgenev was let out of Russia and rejoined the Viardots. He and Pauline were together at Courtavenel in September. They seem to have been particularly happy. It has been alleged that he 'hunted with the husband and probably slept with the wife', and sired Paul who was born on 20 July 1857, some nine months later. However, within a few weeks of Paul's conception, the relationship went sufficiently sour that, in November, our Romeo set up on his own in a flat in the rue de Rivoli. A chronic bladder complaint returned, probably trouble with his prostate which possibly left him impotent.[20] It was sufficiently unpleasant that it caused him, a person who disliked religion, to write a prayer craving relief.[21] He also suffered from acute depression,[22] and proceeded, as we have seen, to whizz around France and Italy in desperate search of a cure.

Turgenev went away to the Rhine. In his disillusionment, he wrote 'Asya', the tale of another superfluous man who had just had his heart broken by a 'cruel and beautiful widow'.[23] 'She was extremely handsome and intelligent and flirted with everyone including me', he wrote. 'When she ditched me, she wounded me cruelly.' He added, to console himself: 'I must admit that the wound was not so very deep. But I considered myself bound to wallow for a while in melancholy and solitude.'[24]

Then, apart from a brief visit to Courtavenel in 1857, for the next three years the relationship between Pauline and Turgenev was cool. In early 1859, she told Rietz: 'I have committed no sin'.[25] However, she also said that she needed space and getting away on tour provided this.[26]

In July and August 1859, Turgenev spent two fortnights at Courtavenel. He published *On the Eve* in 1859. In this, a man who is disappointed in love raises the question, the one which Turgenev had earlier raised when the poet Fet came to see him at Courtavenel around the time of Paul's conception: what was the use 'of clinging to the edge of another person's nest'?[27] Turgenev was again at Courtavenel in the summer of 1860. By early autumn, his relations with Pauline were at a low ebb. There was another breach at that time; what caused it we do not know.[28]

In the second twenty years, which we shall soon reach, the years between 1863 and his death twenty years later, Turgenev lived next door to, or with, the Viardots. However, it is rarely suggested that his relationship with Pauline in those years went beyond being a very good friend of the family.[29]

To help us assess the likelihood that Pauline would have consented to a sexual relationship with Turgenev, we need to look at the customs of the time. It has to be said, at the outset, that this background does not particularly assist her case. Paris reeked of sex. It has been said that more women were sold there than in Constantinople. At the lower end of the French social scale, there was no incentive to marry, so casual unions were frequent. However, in the bourgeois classes, the dowry made it attractive to get married and adopt the accepted code of behaviour, which, so long as there was compliance, was not in itself very strict.[30]

Adultery, for women, was a crime; not so, of course, for men. However, in practice, a year or so after marriage an affair was acceptable, provided it was done by consent,[31] discreetly and with dignity. Had Louis acquiesced, had he not 'got up on his high horse', Pauline could have enjoyed an affair with Maurice Sand. It was not acceptable, however, to flaunt a passion or abandon children. Thus, when Musset and Sand eloped to Venice, and when Marie d'Agoult eloped with Liszt to Switzerland, 'society' was suitably outraged.

Pauline started life from a 'bohemian' background.[32] She came from a profession which both in fact and in many men's minds was associated with prostitution, or, at best, sex for money.[33] For many, the oldest profession was the only escape from economic desperation and starvation, as Fantine in Hugo's *Les Misérables* and Gervaise in Zola's *L'Assommoir* found out. As one would expect in France, the official trade was regulated. By the time Pauline came of age, there were 240 registered brothels.[34] Prostitutes, apart from the 3,800 who were officially registered, ran the risk of imprisonment in the Saint-Lazare. Quotations varied from 50 centimes for a visit with the common prostitute who walked the streets with a bare bum under her silk skirt, to 40 francs for the 'standard time' of 12–20 minutes for a visit to a very high class tart, or even 100 francs when more adventurous tastes were catered for. It is not hard to find shocking stories. The

Goncourts told of a little girl who offered her fourteen-year-old sister, her own role being 'to breathe on the windows of the carriage so that the police could not see inside'.[35]

Infinitely superior, at least in their own view, were the courtesans, the *grandes horizontales*. In contrast to the prostitute, the courtesan could exercise choice. The courtesans had the beauty, character, or opportunity to choose the buyers to whom they would sell their warmth and award the trophy; the cash flow would be used to finance the luxury they craved. One of the courtesans best known to us is the tinker's daughter Marie Duplessis, portrayed in Dumas's popular novel *La Dame aux Camélias*,[36] and thus the Violetta of Verdi's *La Traviata*. Her promotion from prostitution came when she was picked up by a Duc, then by a Vicomte; in the year before she died, aged 23, she married a Comte.

Many of the stars were 'kept women', perhaps just a little less mobile than courtesans. Pauline's sister 'lived in sin' with Charles de Bériot; her rival Giulia Grisi cohabited with the tenor Mario. Perhaps Musset had this relationship and little more in mind when he made a pass at Pauline.

Musset was not being unreasonable. There were many others around who were prepared to cohabit. Madame Jaubert and her cousin Aimée are examples, as is Rachel. There were Flaubert's conquests, such as Louise Colet, and Louise Pradier, whose salon reached its climax when the hostess entered clad as Venus in a diaphanous tunic held in place by a large diamond.[37]

Of course, hypocrisy about immorality was regnant. In 1857, Flaubert was prosecuted for his sexually explicit *Madame Bovary*. A few months later, Charles Baudelaire was also prosecuted for obscenity and fined for publishing *Les Fleurs du mal*.[38] The pictures of bourgeois in tall hats in the Jardin de Paris or in Montmartre, and the works of Toulouse-Lautrec later in the century, tell it all.

The easy attitude to 'morality' seems consonant with the British view of the French. The country had a reputation for sexual freedom,[39] particularly towards the end of the 19th century, when it became imperative to arrest its population decline.

We cannot rely on Parisian moral standards to defend Pauline against the charge that she cohabited with Turgenev. However, we can rely on her common sense.

Despite the lax atmosphere and what the novelist Maupassant called 'the mad longing',[40] whereby even a mother who normally led a life of blameless respectability can crave 'to run the risk of incurring eternal damnation, by flinging herself, just once, into the full tide of Parisian vice',[41] we should not underestimate the practical difficulties and the considerable risks. These included conception and the appalling consequences, particularly disease, which accompanied extra-marital sex.

For a woman, the deal was often bad. Even in a seedy little provincial hotel in Rouen, the overheated yet sexually frustrated Emma Bovary failed to obtain satisfaction, though she savagely stripped off, tore at the delicate laces of her corset, 'which slithered down over her hips with a serpentine hiss', and flung herself stark naked into her lover's arms. She then felt nothing exceptional.[42] However, her rancid enthusiasm surprised her lover with a slight feeling of distaste.

It is hard to imagine unrestrained and fully satisfied passion in a drawing-room over-furnished with fragile porcelain and silk-upholstered sofas. It is hard to imagine lovers who were so dependent on ladies' maids and valets for their appearance and much else, ripping off their unsuitable, clumsy and starchy clothing.[43] Satisfaction must have been difficult to obtain, despite the stories in the novels.

There was a limit to the number of times that the butler could credibly say that the chaise-longue had been sent away to be re-upholstered, or the cushions needed cleaning. On the other hand, 'it' was achievable by the skilled. After all, in the 18th century, François Boucher painted a picture of his mistress Louise O'Murphy in just such circumstances, before he passed her on to King Louis XV.[44] And, a century later, Edward, Prince of Wales* could presumably unfix his fly-buttons with a flourish.

Provided a woman could afford to avoid having sexual relations, there were however very good reasons why she would choose to do so. Sex was a far cry from the casual, easy activity which is so often promoted on the screen today. It was more a matter for fear than kicks.

There was the risk of conception. Childbirth was frighteningly dangerous, not just the event itself, agonising and often fatal, but also because of complications.[46] For ten days thereafter, there was a high risk of puerperal

*At least he did not have to restrict his visits to tea time. For him alone, it was permissible to entertain a lady to lunch or a midnight supper in seclusion. An alternative, the English house party, could be hazardous as the Bishop of Chester and his wife found, when Lord Charles Beresford groped his way into their bed in the dark, exclaiming 'Cock-a-doodle-do'.[45]

Boucher's pornographic picture of Louise O'Murphy

fever, caused by infection of the genital tract. This 'scourge of childbirth' was considered to be fatal in 99 per cent of cases.[47]

Forty per cent of the time, a woman would be fertile.[48] The safe period and *coitus interruptus* were seemingly inconsistent with the lifestyle of the woman's lover or protector. One may surmise that Caroline Jaubert had good reason to keep her trysts with Alfred de Musset to two sessions, one of three weeks and one of two.[49]

Barrier methods of contraception had been available since the mid-16th century, becoming known in France as *'la capote anglaise'* and, in England, as 'the French letter'. By the 1850s, rubber condoms retailed in the USA for $5 per dozen.[50] However, the 'device' was very crude. A two-penny leaflet warned that 'accidents in its use cause it to be somewhat unsafe,' and added the observation that 'it is in every way inconvenient'.[51] We prefer not to have to imagine Turgenev in the greenhouse, or lying on the ground looking up through the leaves of the golden aspen, or for that matter in Pauline's boudoir, complying with the recommendation[52] that the products should first be tested by inflating with air or filling with water.

Contraceptive devices were mainly used in order to avoid infection, which was the other major risk. Turgenev did not manage this particularly well. He was reckless in his purchase of prostitutes, of which St Petersburg was full.[53] It seems probable that a Berlin girl who sued him for defloration also gave him the urethritis which troubled him for the rest of his life. In 1850, he experimented with a new and fashionable variety of girl, a colonial import, perhaps 'as noxious and as putrid as the muddy liquid of a Sahara oasis'.[54] He then had another attack of his recurrent urinary trouble. There is a reasonable probability that he contracted syphilis in the mid-fifties. A few years later, in St Petersburg, he became infatuated with a Polish tart called Nadezhda. She may well have provided him with a particularly nasty and suspicious carbuncle which subsequently had to be cut away from his groin.[55]

By the end of the century, syphilis was rampant. It is infectious in its early stages, and it was estimated that a fifth of the population of Paris had it at this time. After a long latent period, there was a close to even chance of the disease being lethal, in the most unpleasant way. So the consequences of an occasional aberration, let alone of sexual profligacy, could be appalling. It may be that the novelist Thomas Hardy could have contaminated his first wife, condemning her to two decades of the mental and physical deterioration which eventually killed her. Edmond de Goncourt described his brother's galloping and horrifying experience in the final stage: within a few weeks of developing a minor speech defect, he was totally incoherent.[56] The composers Donizetti and Schumann, the novelist Guy de Maupassant and the painter Manet are just a few of those who paid the price, 'all raving in their various insane asylums'.[57] Flaubert caught the disease and it may well have hastened his death. In his last novel, one of the characters bemoans catching venereal disease from the housemaid who was not 'without experience'. 'She should have warned me', complains the foolish victim, apportioning the blame in an almost 21st-century way. Women are 'hell beneath a skirt'.[58] One imagines that Mrs Hardy might have talked about men and trousers.

Turgenev's friend Maupassant, whose stories depicting Paris of the 1880s are obsessed with sex, knew the implications of male sexual incontinence. 'Beware of love!' he cautioned. 'It is out to ambush you at every corner. Its traps are laid, its arrows sharpened, its tricks prepared. It is more dangerous than a cold, bronchitis or pleurisy. It is merciless, and leads to irreparable folly.' He adds, 'It will get you. I am bound to tell you so, just as in Russia it's ones duty to point out to someone that his nose is frozen.'[59] And Zola's Nana, a low-class tart, was transformed from a stunningly beautiful young woman to a rotting syphilitic, her work of death and destruction complete. 'The fly which had taken off from the cesspit of the slums with its germs capable of putrefying society had poisoned those men merely by settling on them'.[60]

Besides the risk of babies and sexually transmitted diseases, the social, civil, religious and domestic consequences of extra-marital sex were discouraging. Divorce, legalised briefly at the time of the Revolution, became illegal at the time of the Restoration in 1815, so was unavailable. And, a law enacted in the 1880s which allowed legal separation was used sparingly.[61] The heat which agitation for liberalisation could generate is evidenced by the trouble in one town when an advocate of divorce law reform came to speak. There was a riot.[62]

The fallen, discarded woman was nobody's wife; she was 'lost'. There was the sense of shame, humiliation, remorse, bitterness and pain which Tolstoy described with such taste and characteristic economy in a powerful two-page chapter of *Anna Karenina.* 'What for nearly a year had been the sole desire of Vronsky's life, replacing all his former desires; what for Anna had seemed so impossible, terrible, yet so fascinating, had at last come to pass. He stood over her, begging her to calm herself yet not knowing himself why or how. "Anna! Anna!" he implored in a trembling voice. "Anna, for Heaven's sake!" But the louder he spoke, the lower she hung her once proud, gay, but now humiliated head, and sank from the sofa. She would have fallen onto the carpet had he not held her. "My God, forgive me!" she sobbed and pressed his hand to her breast. She felt like a criminal with nothing left but to humiliate herself and crave forgiveness'.[63] No hysteria; just shame, abject shame.[64] Unless one was shameless.

For Anna, from now on, it was downhill all the way. She was pregnant, condemned to increasing deceit, 'a bad woman', whom no 'respectable woman' could receive. Her character inexorably decomposed and degraded. Precisely because of her womanhood, she was isolated, rejected, snubbed, denied access to her darling son.[65] There was no future. Her insecurity became intense. Her consequent self-induced jealousy drove her to insanity and to death.

Maupassant, no prude himself, tells us how this sense of shame extended across the social spectrum. One of his characters, a bourgeois woman, having yielded, rushed out into the street and, seeing the street-cleaners at work, 'felt as though her own overheated dreams had just been sluiced down into the sewers'.[66] A farm girl who realised she was pregnant 'felt as though she were at the bottom of a pit whose walls were impossible to climb and from which she could never escape, with disaster ready to descend on her like rocks from above'.[67] Turgenev, normally no hypocrite, had no hesitation himself in regarding a fallen woman as disgraced. When his friend Botkin seduced his cousin Elizabeth, Turgenev approved of her expulsion from his brother's house where she lived.[68]

Behind the superficial sexual free-for-all, the psychological pressure to 'behave' was immense. That is, provided the woman could afford to do so.

How, if at all, does this reflect on Pauline, extremely intelligent woman that she was?

First of all, as Tolstoy's Anna discovered, the spotlight shone on the woman. All the social consequences, all the blame, would fall on her. Pauline had seen this. When her sister Maria, as a married woman, had conceived an illegitimate child, she was outcast by 'society'. Her best friend Comtesse Sparre, a daughter of Naldi, the *buffa* singer whose château she used to visit regularly, closed her doors to her.[69]

There is plenty of evidence that Pauline was not rebuffed in this way. We shall see that the Baden and Prussian royal families were visitors at Pauline's salons in the 1860s. They would surely not have been so welcoming, nor honoured her, had they suspected that she was a 'bad woman'. Aristocrats such as Princess Trubetskoy, to whom Turgenev would send the Viardot family 'regards' when writing, would have distanced themselves had they not been content with Pauline's morals. Equally, Turgenev was welcomed by Pauline's extended family, including her mother.[70] They would surely have taken a different attitude had they been uncomfortable about his behaviour with Pauline.

Secondly, many practical difficulties would arise from an unplanned pregnancy. There is no reason to suppose that Pauline expected any difficulty in conceiving, once the demands of her professional schedule permitted her to do so. Even though it was accepted that married opera stars might become pregnant,* a breakdown in family planning would disrupt Pauline's 'superior passion' which was to sing in order that her audience would appreciate the deeper truths.[72] If she had gone along with George Sand's plans, irresponsible as they were, the effect on her income and on her reputation could have been very damaging. She took the trouble to lecture her fertile friend Clara Schumann on the need for restraint, a matter to which Clara, whose love for Robert was infinitely more romantic than Pauline's love of Louis, took great exception. Clara told her to mind her own business.

Thirdly, Turgenev was unreliable. Pelageya, now Paulinette, was living evidence of his potency, fertility and, not least, his sexual incontinence. Pauline must have known, or at least suspected, what he did in Paris to gratify his lusts. Thus, the risk of contagion was considerable. Pauline may not have known of the prostitutes of St Petersburg, of the foreign immigrants in Paris. Possibly she did not know of the action for defloration brought, when he was only twenty, by the girl who claimed for the expense of burying their dead child.[73] However, she might have discovered the carbuncle caused by the Polish tart, had she looked.

Fourthly, Pauline came under a great deal of pressure from Louis who adored her, worshipped her and depended on her emotionally and financially. She knew this. 'My husband and Scheffer have always been my dearest friends', she wrote from Dublin. 'I have never been able to return another feeling in exchange for Louis's keen and deep love, despite the best will in the world ... the human will has only a negative effect on the heart – it can force it to be silent but not to speak'.[74] She was hardly oblivious to 'the traditional decencies and sanctities of marriage'. Besides, even if she could not reciprocate his keen and deep love emotionally, she would hardly have wanted to return it by infecting him.[75]

Fifthly, she may not have suffered the sexual frustration that would

*Law in Italy required singers to inform management of their pregnant condition prior to contract. This was partly because pregnancy, like menstruation, was thought to affect the voice, but also because of the inevitable commercial disruption to which it led. Verdi's second wife, in an earlier incarnation, found herself concealing her condition, falsifying medical certificates, giving birth in secret, and abandoning the child.[71]

have motivated her to be unfaithful to Louis; it may not have mattered that he did not turn her on. Despite the large eyes and Spanish warmth, she had resisted Musset's advances, to which the actress Rachel, her more highly-sexed and compliant colleague, had yielded.[76] George Sand told Delacroix that Pauline was her 'modèle primitif pour Consuelo', although she did add that the Consuelo whom she was talking about was Consuelo, the 'enfant et débutante'.[77] Pauline herself said that Consuelo provided the key to her own character. In the novel, Consuelo's childhood boyfriend exclaims, with a mixture of rage and despair, 'how calm, pure, cold you are', 'O Consuelo, que tu es calme, que tu es pure, et que tu es froide!'[78] Consuelo's virginity lasts more than a thousand pages.

That purity is why Pauline's admirers saw her as France's answer to Jenny Lind, one of whose 'unique selling propositions' was her almost wearisome virginity. Pauline herself much later said that despite being of Latin origin, her strange upbringing so far in the north had endowed 'her heart with constancy and steadfastness'.[79]

Outwardly, Pauline was a warm-hearted, enthusiastic, impulsive person. Of course, she enjoyed being surrounded by adoring men, like the 'Four Paws' in those first days in Russia. Her Spanish exuberance might even be described as gushing.[80] She would greet women with a 'salvo of kisses'. In a letter to one of the 'Four', Count Wielhorsky, she wrote saying that she would jump at his throat and kiss him 'violently'.[81] Her effusive approach, particularly to those she knew very well, may easily have misled men about her intentions.

What of Turgenev and Louis? Their friendship seems wholly incompatible between a wife's lover and her husband. The two men got on particularly well. Louis regarded Turgenev as a big baby, 'un gros innocent'. They had politics and literature in common. They worked together on translations. They went shooting together. In the early 1850s, Louis suggested that Turgenev might be interested in buying a property very close to Courtavenel. Later, Louis encouraged him to move to Baden-Baden.[82] Apart from sponging off Louis by residing at his expense, Turgenev often borrowed money from him, whether for day-to-day expenses as in the late 1840s, for lending on to a friend in the 1850s,[83] or for capital projects as in the 1860s.[84] In what sounds a familiarly modern piece of refinancing and risk management, Turgenev sold his Baden-Baden house to Louis and leased it back at five per cent.[85]

Had Turgenev really been having an affair with Pauline, Louis could surely never have sat in the audience while the Courtavenel household staged *Le Mariage de Figaro*, the play by Beaumarchais. In this, Pauline 'married' Gounod, while Turgenev 'tried to exercise his *droit de seigneur*'.[86] The only part which Louis himself would act was that of Arnolphe in Molière's *Ecole des Femmes*, a hilarious comedy in which it is said 'if you don't want to be cuckolded, don't take a wife'.*[87] Louis must have had a most unusual sense of humour, or tolerance, if there really was hanky-panky between his wife and his friend.

Louis shared naughty stories with Turgenev. At the beginning of 1853, he sent him a scurrilous letter full of *double entendres*. Louis recounted how, for variety, the notoriously sportive Emperor had wanted to take one of his mistresses in the rear, to 'chasser au faucon'. The actress objected saying 'No Prince, that's the artist's entrance' (the other being the public one).[88]

Is it conceivable that a husband would write in such a way to a man who had recently been having his wife? Or who he expected might do so? Or who was the father of his daughter Claudie, born around eight months earlier? Maupassant later described the usual reaction of the cuckold. 'The thought that the woman you have loved – whether wife or mistress – has given herself to another, has taken his kisses as she once took yours, is something so horrible, so appalling, that, after but one day of such torment, you will stop at nothing.'[89]

Louis was no fool. His books radiate a high, perhaps too high, sense of integrity. Even though he was financially dependent on Pauline, it is hardly conceivable that he would either have allowed himself to be cuckolded, or remained such a good friend of his rival, had he suspected that his wife might be cohabiting with him.

Occasionally, Louis felt that he needed to lodge a protest. In the early years of the *ménage à trois* in Baden-Baden in the 1860s, when Turgenev was no longer a visitor but a next-door neighbour, Louis was concerned

* In *Ecole des Femmes*, the middle-aged roué is so fearful that his young ward might be unfaithful to him when she becomes his bride that he has her educated in complete ignorance. Needless to say, she falls head over heels for a handsome fair-haired youth.

about the impression given to respectable people. He advised Pauline to be cautious and sensitive to gossip. He also regretted that another seemed to be taking on the paternal role, whether in relation to conversation, music or the children, which should naturally belong to him. There appears to have been some particularly affectionate correspondence in 1871 to which Louis seems to have taken exception.[90] Sadly, this has not survived.

Against this background in which seduction was so unpropitious and so unlikely, what are we to make of a number of specific moments, apparently intimate, between Turgenev and Pauline?

There seems to have been one such moment in 1847 when they were in the woods together. It was summer. They lay on the grass and looked up at the sky through the golden leaves.[91] Some words in a short story written at this time may evoke their experience. 'The wood was filled with sunlight. The sky shone through the jubilantly rustling foliage and sparkled like diamonds. The clouds had vanished, dispersed by the wind; the weather had cleared, and in the air could be felt that special dry freshness, imbuing the heart with a feeling of elation.'[92] We cannot just assume that Turgenev and Pauline made love because they lay on the grass beside each other. In the story, the narrator awakes to see nearby a one-time lover heartlessly telling a serf girl that he is abandoning her. For Turgenev, lasting love is an illusion.

Turgenev spent much of the summer of 1849 at Courtavenel, when, as we have seen, he and Pauline would read together, and when she was away he would write her voluminous letters.[93] Three years afterwards, he made the cryptic entry in his Memorial recalling this time: 'on 14/26 I first time with P', indicating that something significant happened on the 14th day of the Julian calendar, which was the 26th in the Gregorian.[94] One can speculate what this something was. We have already noted that they had exchanged kisses – whether sensual or merely celebratory, it is not clear[95] – at the annual New Year festivities, so this must have been something more. In a 'Prose Poem' addressed to Pauline a few years before he died, he asked that she should not visit his tomb, but should remember him by reading a favourite passage from a book which they used to read together.[96] They would sit under the trees, gaze at each other and read the works of Goethe.

Turgenev named trees after their favourite works, such as Hermann the chestnut tree which was called after Goethe's *Hermann and Dorothea*.[97] Reading together, and the pleasure and physical closeness that went with it, may have been the limit of their romance.

As Gladstone illustrates, men have an irrepressible urge to enter sexual information in their records.*[98] However, unless the information is explicit, the note regarding 14/26 is as inconclusive as Pauline's injudicious letter to Maurice Sand. The entry might just mean that they had managed to avoid the prying eyes of Berthe[99] and had a good fruity kiss, full of passion. Whatever it was, it was brief and did not endure. Until ten days before 26 June, Maurice Sand had been at Courtavenel, in the way. *Le Prophète* had been running in Paris. A fortnight afterwards, Pauline was needed in London.[100] Despite their correspondence in the following months being particularly warm, even poetic,[101] in the absence of a verb one can conclude nothing from Turgenev's cryptic entry. It might mean many different things.

After *Le Prophète*, Pauline worked with Gounod on *Sapho*. This was the time when *A Month in the Country* was completed and *The Diary of a Superfluous Man* first appeared.[102] 'I'm superfluous and that's all there is to it', Turgenev makes the Man exclaim.[103] This hardly implies a rip-roaring affair; it is perhaps more indicative of unfulfilled expectations.

It will also help us to assess the likelihood of Turgenev having successfully consummated his love for Pauline, if we look more closely at Turgenev's own attitude to sex and love.

It need not surprise us that Turgenev[104] frequented brothels. It was far simpler to purchase sexual release from the market than to obtain it by seduction. 'That's why the majority of us prefer our Claras, the women of the *demi-monde*', wrote Tolstoy. Besides, 'they're only concerned whether we have enough cash; but the others also weigh our merits in the balance'. For a man, purchased sex, despite its risks, was physically and emotionally far simpler than the more reputable variety.[105]

*Gladstone, the British Prime Minister, had a mission to rescue prostitutes, as did Dickens with 'unmarried mothers'. Their philanthropy took them on nocturnal wanderings into strange places. Gladstone periodically entered the sign of a whip in his diary, an indication which has bemused biographers and enthralled their readers.

Turgenev was 'in love with the Viardot like an eighteen-year-old' during the Baden-Baden period, according to Herzen.[106] However, when it came to the physical consummation of spiritual love, there is much in Turgenev's writings to suggest that he would back off at the last minute. He did not wish to let the carnal aspects spoil the spiritual and emotional.

It has been suggested that he found consummation less important than the emotions which preceded it. Sometimes it was an 'onerous duty', even 'an isolated occurrence never to be repeated'. In his works, Turgenev consistently presents passionate love as a disaster. He is horrified by its potential to destroy and enslave. Indeed, for him, happy or lasting love is an unattainable illusion.[107]

In Turgenev's *Smoke*, the narrator is engaged to be married. However, he is seduced by another woman, with devastating consequences for himself. In *Spring Torrents*, the hero is seduced on a wild and romantic ride. He has become just the latest of the conquests and chattels of the beautiful predatress. Once fallen, he is quickly shelved; meanwhile, he has lost his true love. In another story, *Faust*, love is an illness. Taken against your will, you are suddenly stricken. The heroine falls sick and dies the moment she admits love. In *A Month in the Country*, we hear Turgenev's jaundiced opinion of women. A woman's love is portrayed as being 'like a brook in spring. On one day it rushes, the next day it scarcely moves; it is like a thin, fresh little trickle along the dried up bed of the stream'.[108]

We shall see later that when he became infatuated with a respectable woman who actually appears to have wanted him, Baroness Vrevskaya, Turgenev backed away.[109] This, it appears, was his style.

We should return to the point at which this chapter began, with Paul. Although Louis's paternity of Marianne is usually not doubted,[110] this is not so with her brother. Paul, who eventually fell out with his mother, is reported to have said that he was Turgenev's son. Paulinette seems to have accepted him as a half-brother. They had axes to grind. It is improbable that Turgenev was Paul's father,[111] if only because by the time of his conception the relationship between Pauline and Turgenev had deteriorated. One suspects that if, as might be suggested, Paul was conceived in Turgenev's Paris flat, his bladder complaint would have cramped his style, and possibly Pauline's.

On the day after Paul's birth, Louis sent the news to Turgenev who was on the Rhine writing 'Asya'. Immediately, Turgenev sent Louis his congratulations, particularly on his having a son. He also thanked him for having thought of notifying him. 'The skylarks sing to you in your heart' he wrote, using a Russian saying. At the same time, he wrote to Pauline asking for details of the baby and its birth. He predicted a great and radical future for the boy. His *Who's Who* entry would describe him as the son of 'la célèbre Pauline Garcia, etc etc. et de l'ingénieux écrivain et traducteur de *Don Quichotte*', that is Louis.[112] One would have to be very cynical to think that Turgenev, who was fundamentally a decent person, was being insincere when he wrote this. Yet the tone of the letter is so effusive as almost to be a 'cover' to hide his deep disappointment that the boy was not the consequence of his own love for Pauline.[113]

Soon after Paul's birth, Turgenev returned to Courtavenel. However, he knew that this was a mistake and that he should go away. For another three-year period, the relationship of Turgenev and Pauline went into cold storage.[114]

As the years went by, Turgenev was relatively uninterested in Paul. His attention was focussed on the young girls, particularly Claudie,* for whom he provided a dowry and wrote letters in exceedingly fond terms. It seems probable that Louis's fathering of Paul represented the end of all Turgenev's hopes and dreams. This perhaps contributed to the severe depression from which he suffered.[115]

Around ten years later, Turgenev wrote to congratulate his great friend Annenkov who he said had become 'the father of a child given to you by the woman you love'. Had he thought he was the father of Pauline's son, would he have added, as he did: 'I have never experienced that happiness'?[116]

Unless some hidden correspondence is unearthed, we are most unlikely ever to know the extent of Turgenev's relationship with Pauline.[117]

*There is circumstantial evidence that Turgenev had an affair with Claudie, although we must assume that she also might have been discouraged by some of the disadvantages referred to earlier in this chapter. Mr Kyril FitzLyon recalls his wife being struck with how much Claudie's daughter looked like Turgenev. Because Claudie herself could not be Turgenev's daughter (see page 201 at end of chapter 13), Mrs FitzLyon inferred that Turgenev and Claudie must have cohabited. Apparently, Mrs FitzLyon only met the daughter at a stage when she felt that it was too late to change the text of *The Price of Genius* to develop this theory.

However, the public display of the *ménage à trois* would have been under great strain had Turgenev actually been cuckolding a complaisant Louis. 'One must get out of the humiliating position in which one is placed. One can't live *à trois*', said one cuckold, Tolstoy's Karenin.[118] That Turgenev could do so with the Viardots, publicly, points towards the strength and integrity of the Viardots' relationship. We shall see this as we read on.

We cannot doubt that, by the end of Pauline's life, she absolutely adored both her husband and Turgenev. Had Turgenev been a tree, she would have been 'both his roots and his crown'.[119] She adored and loved, in her exuberant way, several other men along the way.

So, why should we assume that Pauline was physically unfaithful to Louis? She was neither whore, harlot nor courtesan. Even the occasional one night stand, whether with Turgenev or Maurice Sand, simply would not have been 'worth it' for her. The idea is wholly inconsistent with her character. She said, almost enigmatically, that she could admire Liszt's relationship with his mistress Princess Carolyne. She infinitely preferred that 'to the hypocritical virtue of an unfaithful wife'.[120] For Pauline, there was 'passion but no friendship' in George Sand's relationship with Chopin which reinvigorated Chopin but asphyxiated George. Pauline believed that friendship was 'a passion which cannot wane. It is the finest of all'.[121] And what really mattered to her was her art. For Turgenev, 'happiness was never to be fully attained, love never fully requited',[122] and, as a result of Pauline, this concept became the essence of his art.

None of this can be conclusive. However, the evidence creates a picture. Pauline's accusers must explain why, exceptionally in Parisian 'society', she did not obtain Louis's permission and have a fling with Turgenev openly. It would have been so much easier than the clandestine one we are encouraged by some Anglo-Saxon authors to suspect. Why did she take so much trouble to destroy correspondence that she feared might be construed as incriminating? Why did her daughter Louise so resolutely deny,[123] as she did, that there had ever been an affair? Pauline's accusers have an uphill task.

As one would expect, Pauline's detractors have to question the veracity of Louise. She dictated her memoirs when she was over 70 and, as a consequence, is never regarded as an accurate historian. In case readers are inclined to believe Paul's testimony but disbelieve Louise's, it needs to be said that it is equally easy to find inaccuracies in Paul's writings.[124]

Perhaps we should try to imagine Pauline, the rather plain and swarthy

Pauline, 'souple et forte', 'lithe and strong', being taken in the arbour or upstairs. 'L'acte fut silencieux et brutal'. 'Lips moist and eyes gleaming', she then abandons herself to lust. Sinuous, surging, her nerves stretch like strings. She diffuses an aura of steamy passion, penetrating and acrid, 'pénétrant et acre'.[125] We then see her entering the great hall of Courtavenel, her once proud but now shame-stricken head drooping on her ample bosom. She quakes before a complaisant and forgiving Louis and declares 'Je l'aime sérieusement'. This flight of fancy would make great fiction which, with Emile Zola's help,*[126] it is.

Consider the passage in 'Phantoms', Turgenev's fantasy published in 1863. Transported to Italy, the narrator encounters Julius Caesar's legions marching on Rome. He describes how the 'innumerable throng suddenly begins to stir, and rise, rise, undulating and exchanging barely audible shouts; the throng moves nearer and nearer, grows greater, surges mightily; an indescribable effort, a tense effort sufficient to lift the whole world, could be felt'.[127] This description, analogous perhaps to the orgasmic third movement of Tchaikovsky's *Pathétique* Symphony, is suddenly terminated with the narrator crying out: 'I do not wish it, I cannot, I do not want Rome, coarse, menacing Rome. Away, away from here'.[128]

Turgenev also wrote that 'it is a well-known fact that walking on the edge, on the very brink of an abyss, is a favourite feminine occupation'. With Pauline, he seems to have taken himself to the edge of the abyss.[129] However, Turgenev never jumped. That, of course, is precisely why the friendship could and would endure forever. They both realised this.

*Edmond de Goncourt said that although he, like a homeopathic doctor, supplied eroticism in miniscule quantities, Zola doled it out in bucketfuls.

CHAPTER 19

TURGENEV TRIUMPHANT

THE PHILOSOPHER IN Turgenev's *On the Eve* despairs 'What's the use of clinging to the edge of another person's nest?' He provides his own answer. 'Gird your leather apron, tailor, and go to your work bench in your dark work-shop', he declares. 'Let the sun shine on others!'[1]

Following the rupture with Pauline in 1856–7, that is what Turgenev, aged almost 40, now did. He knew that, as yet, he had not achieved anything like greatness. He had criticised Tolstoy for his dilettante approach to Art and felt that the same charge could be made against him. He needed to do something about it. He launched himself, or possibly was launched, into a period of intense activity. He became the great author who we now know.

His novels poured forth. In 1859, he published *Nest of the Gentry* which he had begun to plan three years earlier. It was a major success and yielded 4,000 silver roubles. *On the Eve*, for which he was offered double the 4,300 silver roubles he asked, followed in 1860. *Fathers and Sons* was published in 1862.[2] His considerable output in this very short space of time comprises an astonishing achievement.

Turgenev wrote 'Asya' when on the Rhine. He then returned to France and spent some time at Courtavenel, where he went shooting with Louis. Pauline was away. Turgenev then moved on to Rome where he made progress on his next work which he had begun shortly after *Rudin.* His novel *Nest of the Gentry,* sometimes translated as *Home of the Gentry,* or *Gentlefolk,* was finished at Spasskoye in October 1858. Its underlying theme is yet again disappointment in love.[3]

In this novel, which is set most probably in Turgenev's home town of Oryol, a civil servant courts Liza, a girl who possesses the qualities of a Madonna. Into the quiet provincial scene steps one of Turgenev's great figures, Lavretsky. He is estranged from his exceptionally beautiful, intelligent wife. She had deserted him when they were resident in Paris. Lavretsky falls in love with Liza who wants him to forgive his wife and return to her. After he reads a newspaper report that his wife is dead, a future seems to open up for both of them.[4] Liza and Lavretsky meet in the garden and fall in love with each other. It was 'that happiest of nights' when they had 'a few never-to-be-repeated moments'.[5] However, the newspaper report turns out to have been false. Suddenly the wife reappears. The incipient romance is shattered. Liza insists that Lavretsky be reconciled with his wife, and she herself withdraws to a convent which is located in one of the remotest parts of Russia.[6]

Some years later, Lavretsky returns to Liza's house where her younger sister and her family are now happily living. He recalls the night in the garden. Meanwhile, he had 'really learned how to till the soil, and he toiled not just for himself', but for the good of his serfs as well.[7] Lavretsky has apparently visited Liza in the remote nunnery. She scarcely looked at him. 'What did they both think? What did they both feel? Who can know? Who shall tell?[8] Life has its moments – has its feelings – to which we may be allowed to allude, but on which it is not good to dwell.' One can but point to them and pass on. Cast a cold eye on Life, on Death, Horseman, pass by![9]

Countess Lambert, Turgenev's confidante, on whom the character of Liza may well have been based in part,[10] disliked *Nest of the Gentry.* For her, it was 'written by a pagan who had not yet renounced the cult of Venus, but already understands the sterner call of duty towards which his sick soul is drawn, rather against his will'. However, the novel was a tremendous success. It was the most universally acclaimed work which Turgenev ever wrote.[11]

After the success of *Nest of the Gentry*, Turgenev went to St Petersburg and on to the spa at Vichy. He began work on his next novel *On the Eve*, which is set in the Balkans in the 1850s, on the eve of revolution.

A twenty-year-old heiress – 'she had relatives who were very poor, the poor ones on her father's side, the wealthy ones on her mother's' – falls in love and elopes with a 26-year-old Bulgarian partisan. This 'obscure Montenegrin' dies of consumption in Venice, on the way to war. We are told that the heiress is either lost in a shipwreck while taking his coffin to Bulgaria, or disappears into the army to serve as a nurse.[12] Coincidentally, two decades later, an 'aging, weary, morose and gout-ridden' Turgenev dithered about a 33-year-old baroness. When he would not have her, she went off to volunteer as a nurse in the Russo-Turkish War. She died of typhus while serving at the front.[13]

The novel is, again, relatively short. The economy of style is used to great effect, whether in the description of an outing and picnic to a castle, or in the picture of Venice, or in the erotic love scenes.[14]

We read some interesting comments on attitudes at the time. 'At the theatre Verdi's *Traviata* was being staged, a decidedly commonplace affair, to tell the truth, but which had already managed to make the round of all the stages in Europe.'[15] There is some excellent irony. At the height of the heiresse's monumental row with her parents over her secret marriage, her father's mistress turns up.[16]

However, a novel about an ineffectual Bulgarian patriot raised the stakes considerably. Turgenev again annoyed his Russian colleagues and fell between Right and Left, as he had done in earlier works. It seems that there could be no real reconciliation between his brand of liberalism and the aspirations of the younger intelligentsia. He annoyed the revolutionaries by apparently supporting the Establishment; he annoyed the Establishment by seeming to endorse régime change. It was a no-win situation. The crack in his reputation, which already had begun to open when *Rudin* was published, widened and 'later became a gulf'. He was regarded as 'a European in Russia and a Russian in Europe'.[17]

In a bizarre twist, Ivan Goncharov, who was the author of *Oblomov* and one of Turgenev's literary colleagues, accused him of stealing a scene from his own novel *The Precipice*. Turgenev demanded that the matter be settled either by arbitration or by a duel. The arbitrators thankfully decided that both authors had drawn their ideas from Russian sources, so some similarities were inevitable.[18] Yet another duel, in which a Russian author might have been killed, was thus avoided.

Next Turgenev, in early 1860, wrote *First Love.* This 'undisputed masterpiece'[19] is, like 'Asya', a long 'short story'. A sixteen-year-old develops a crush, which for him is intense love, on the beautiful but down-at-heel Princess Zinaida,[20] who is five years older. 'She mocked at my passion, teased me, petted me and tormented me', and 'played with me as a cat plays with a mouse', he says. When on a midnight search for her, he detects someone stalking through the garden towards her house. He had set out for a rendezvous, but had 'walked past someone else's happiness'.[21]

The nocturnal predator is the youth's father, who has only married his wife for her money. The princess has become his father's mistress. Turgenev leaves the reader wondering whether the princess has fallen to the father as a *quid pro quo* for his financial support for her louche, technically noble, mother. Or is she a masochist who gets kicks from being struck with the father's riding crop?[22] The young princess's reputation is of course destroyed.

We have already heard that Turgenev once declared that the reader would find his whole biography in his works.[23] He went so far as to say that '*First Love* is part of my experience'.[24] However, we must be careful. While individual characters in his works can draw on experience, or be inspired by individuals, the books are not biographies, but fiction. Yet the author himself never seems too far away from all these tales; and when the father dies of a stroke, having warned his son to 'beware a woman's love, beware that happiness, that poison', we are unlikely to miss his personal point. Similarly, when the heroine in *On the Eve* discovers that 'the happiness of every mortal is founded on the unhappiness of another', just as a statue demands a pedestal,[25] we can appreciate just how lacerated Turgenev was by his own personal circumstances, and how unfulfilled he was.

Turgenev's readership was unaware of his emotions. *First Love* shocked Countess Lambert and Turgenev's other friends. Chorley, the English critic who combined personal friendship with Napoleon III with a Quaker background, was appalled.[26] Louis Viardot, in language remote from that of a cuckold, wrote a letter admonishing Turgenev for glorifying an adulterer who had only married his wife for her money. He thought that Turgenev was drifting into the sewer of the modern novel. It was 'adultery and yet more adultery, unbridled, glorified!' The princess and her parvenu tobacco-reeking mother were odious.[27]

In the summer of 1860, Turgenev took a holiday in Ventnor on the south coast of the Isle of Wight and stayed in a house by the sandy beach. This beautiful resort, sometimes called 'England's Madeira', was in that period also a place where consumptives went in the hope of a cure.[28] The large gorse-covered downs rose superbly above as Turgenev looked out to 'the glittering ocean shimmering at moments with blue and silver'. He could inhale the fresh bracing salty air and walk along the lush and verdant coastline to beauty spots such as the Blackgang Chine, which an earlier novelist had called 'a druid scene of wilderness and ruin'.[29] He could admire the stunning views to The Needles and the Dorset coast far beyond. At the same time, he must have been reminded of all the friends he had lost through tuberculosis; Stankevich, Belinsky, Chopin and others.

In Ventnor, Turgenev conceived *Fathers and Sons.* He also discussed with a number of prominent Russians who were also staying there how education should be spread among the serfs, after Emancipation. He toyed with a programme which would call for the Emancipation to be accompanied by other social change. His programme would call for public hearings and accountability, the abolition of corporal punishment, the emancipation of religious dissenters, and the shortening of the period of military service. Nothing came of Turgenev's good intentions. If proposals as radical as these had reached the authorities, he might have been in very deep trouble.[30]

Fathers and Sons was written in Paris in the months which followed. Today, it is regarded as the perfection of the novel form.[31] When it was published, it 'caused the greatest storm among its Russian readers of any novel before or, indeed, since'.[32] At Turgenev's request, his publisher, who was anyway perturbed by the content, had delayed publication because of the uncertain situation which followed the Edict of Emancipation. The novel's publication in the following March coincided with violent political demonstrations and the imposition of a ban on newspapers such as *The Contemporary.*[33]

Turgenev again drew the fire of both the radicals and the traditionalists. The controversy centred round the figure of Bazarov, who, it has been suggested, was the first Bolshevik. He called himself a 'nihilist'. This was not a new word.[34] It denoted someone who would 'submit to no authority, and accept nothing without question regardless of whether a principle is generally accepted', and who 'rejects everything that cannot be established by the rational methods of natural science'.[35] Bazarov became an inspirational character for the younger generation, in a somewhat similar way to that in which Goethe's Werther, as a source of romanticism, had influenced previous generations.[36]

The novel is set at the end of the 1850s. Arkady, recently graduated, returns to his family's run-down 200-serf estate. He is accompanied by his radical friend Bazarov, 'a country doctor in the making', 'un jeune homme d'opinions avancées'.[37] Bazarov drives a wedge between father and son, and particularly irritates the uncle, a sophisticated ex-guards officer, a westernised martinet.

Bazarov was fond of women and appreciated beauty. But he regarded love 'in its ideal or, as he called it, romantic sense, as unpardonable nonsense, as folly. For him, chivalry was a type of disease or deformity'. To the father, however, it is incomprehensible that Bazarov can 'disdain poetry, and have no sympathy with Art, with Nature'.[38]

Unfortunately, human will is at the mercy of powers far stronger than itself.[39] Bazarov falls for, although is spurned by, a rich widow who lives nearby in a 'sumptuous, luxuriously furnished house'. She admires his character, but does not reciprocate his emotions.[40]

Bazarov rejects his parents whose way of life he finds asphyxiating. He dies. The cause is not the duel which he has with Arkady's uncle who finds him with his hands on the father's serf mistress. It was far less 'romantic'. He becomes infected by doing a mundane autopsy on a peasant who had died of typhus. The book concludes with the sad and emotional picture of Bazarov's doting parents tending his grave.

It is not difficult to see how the picture of the dilapidated gentry and their foibles irritated the traditionalists, while the character weaknesses and ultimate failure, even waste, of the nihilist infuriated the radicals. The former objected that Turgenev had made a hero of a long-haired, contemptible individual. The latter were furious, because Bazarov was portrayed as less than perfect, an anti-hero; and, besides, Turgenev had vilified the 'children' and extolled the 'fathers'.[41] Herzen, who was disillusioned with the West, poured vitriol on the novel in eight letters published in his magazine *The Bell. The Contemporary* became more abusive. It also took the opportunity to cast a slur on Turgenev's supposed relations with Pauline.[42]

At a time 'when the politically minded called for polemic and propaganda', the apolitical Turgenev, who sat on the fence, was in an impossible position.[43]

This description of *Fathers and Sons*, of course, does scant justice to this classic. What is it that makes Turgenev, appearing as he did between Pushkin, Lermontov and Gogol on the one hand, and Tolstoy and Dostoyevsky on the other, such an important writer?

In the early 19th century, Russian literature was still in its infancy, with virtually no established tradition. Pushkin, 'the beginning of beginnings' as Maxim Gorky called him, was only born as the 18th century turned into the 19th. His *Eugene Onegin* was completed in 1831, about five years before his fatal duel. Shortly after that tragedy, there was the other when Lermontov was killed in his twenties. His five tales, which he claimed portrayed the 'vices of his whole generation in their ultimate development', appeared in 1840 as *A Hero of Our Time.* Soon after that, Gogol's *Dead Souls* was published. It was arguably 'the first generically Russian prose novel'.[44] However, it was never finished.

Belinsky, whose life was cut so short, had called for an authentic Russian literature. Turgenev, 'the enlightened, big-city gentleman, glittering with foreign polish',[45] duly appeared and nailed his flag to the mast which fluttered westwards. His outlook enraged his contemporaries, including Dostoyevsky who would deride him as the typical well-off Russian liberal of the 1840s and 1850s; the type who enjoyed recounting his experiences during the February Revolution of 1848, 'pretending that he himself had taken part in it, just short, perhaps, of manning the barricades'.[46]

Turgenev was a realist. But his realism is not the technicolour of, say, Émile Zola. His real-life pictures are painted in soft shades, sometimes in pastel. They illustrate the rapid development of Russian society. He tells us 'about the human condition, about human relationships, about life and the way people live it'. This is not just some cinema show expressed in words. Turgenev thought that Art should itself be an instrument of change.[47]

Contemporary Realism in Painting

It is not surprising that Turgenev acquired paintings by George Sand's friend Théodore Rousseau. He was a leader of the 'Realistic' group of landscape painters which was greatly influenced by the scenes painted by John Constable. They tended to congregate in the hamlet of Barbizon on the edge of the Forest of Fontainebleau. There, they found peace, natural scenes for painting and cheap lodging. Jean-François Millet whose scenes from peasant life are typified by his famous picture *The Gleaners*, was also in this group. These artists were the precursors of the Impressionists.

Gustave Courbet, the painter of *Bonjour, Monsieur Courbet*, was a leading Realist, as was Camille Corot who was a friend of the Viardots. Courbet entitled his exhibition of 1855 'Le Réalisme, G Courbet'. He had a sad end. He supported the Commune and was accused of instigating the destruction of the column in the Place Vendôme. He had to go into exile to avoid the enormous fine imposed on him. Corot was a very versatile artist. His work has been forged many times: he is said to have painted 3,000 paintings of which 10,000 have been sold in America.[51]

Because Turgenev's characters are real people, it follows that none of his heroes are at all heroic. Real life is rarely epic. Some of his contemporaries, Chorley for example, found Turgenev's realism rather depressing and mournful. He observed that Turgenev's stories are 'in the minor key'. This aspect, while making them 'faithful to national life and character, does not make them more cheerful'.[48] Chorley was a bit of a depressive and needed cheering up,[49] yet he was not alone in his assessment. Henry James, the American-born novelist and a great admirer of Turgenev, observed that his work moved 'in an atmosphere of unrelieved sadness', and felt that he was 'a cold-blooded pessimist, caring for nothing in life than its misery, for nothing in misery but its picturesqueness'.[50]

Turgenev's works are notably short compared to those of his contemporaries. Visitors to art museums can be surprised by how small are some of the world's greatest paintings. The photographic reproduction, say in some book about the artist, gives little notion of size. In a gallery, we can find we have walked past some masterpiece, simply because it is so small. Turgenev's picture frame was comparatively small, his style delicate and sensitive.

In the gallery of Russian literature, the far larger, garish canvasses of his contemporaries tend to eclipse his. They detract from him,[52] such that we can even lose him. Not for Turgenev the great Russian blockbusters, *War and Peace, Anna Karenina, Crime & Punishment, The Devils, The Brothers Karamazov.* From works such as these, Turgenev's contemporaries in France obtained a preconceived, exaggerated yet simplistic impression of the universal coarseness, uncouthness and harshness of Russian life. They were disappointed that they could not hear these aspects resonating fortissimo in Turgenev's works. Edmond de Goncourt, who had admired Turgenev as a raconteur, dismissed him as a landscape painter who had ended up in the court of Louis XIV.[53] He even had a row about this with Flaubert, who came to Turgenev's defence.

We can see that, from the earliest of Turgenev's *Sketches from a Hunter's Album*, his skill lay in realistic portraiture presented with the greatest economy of style, an approach adopted by Chekhov* in the decades following Turgenev's death. Turgenev told Henry James that when evolving his fiction he tended to start with a picture of a person or persons and then construct the story, the scene and the secondary characters around the key person or persons. The material that envelopes his central figure, the natural scenes and the minor characters, even the love story itself, merely evoke the atmosphere, or provide the setting, or the necessary contrast.[54] That Turgenev then wholly succeeds in welding his characters together constitutes an amazing achievement.

Like it or not, Goncourt's over-simplification has prevailed. Tolstoy and Dostoyevsky are names which, for the generality of the English-speaking public, stand larger than Turgenev in the annals of Russian literature. One can easily find Dostoyevsky being described as 'the other genius of the age',

*Anton Chekhov's exquisite short stories such as 'Lady with Lapdog' and his plays such as *The Seagull* began to appear in the 1890s. Chekhov, whose father had been a serf, was born in Taganrog, on the Sea of Azov by the Crimea, on 29 January 1860. After the failure of his father's business, the family moved to Moscow where Chekhov graduated as a doctor, wrote sketches for magazines and provided for his family. In the last years of his short life, he suffered from tuberculosis and spent much time in Yalta or on the French Riviera. He died in July 1904, within six months of the first performance of *The Cherry Orchard.*

that is, apart from Tolstoy. Turgenev does not get a look-in.[55] Yet, for the same English-speaking public, Pushkin does not get much recognition, and he was arguably the greatest of them all.

Turgenev was a founder and innovator. He was one of the few among the writers of his generation who foresaw the emergence of social forces which would reshape the nation. In a way, he was 'the forerunner, even in a sense the guide' of Tolstoy and Dostoyevsky. In this sense, he is what Henry James described as the novelist's novelist.[56] It has been suggested that he was 'incontestably the cleverest and most cultured of the great Russian writers'. One leading commentator suggests that 'beside his clear-sighted genius, Tolstoy and Dostoyevsky were mere ignoramuses'.[57] Maybe this is going too far.

It is perhaps appropriate that Tolstoy met Turgenev, and Dostoyevsky met Turgenev, yet Tolstoy and Dostoyevsky never met.[58] Turgenev was the filling in the sandwich, between the two chunky pieces of bread on either side. Or, depending on one's point of view, they were the two halves of the cake, with Turgenev the icing on the top.

CHAPTER 20

PAULINE TRIUMPHANT, *ORPHÉE*

WHILE TURGENEV'S REPUTATION was rising or falling, depending on the viewpoint of his contemporary, Pauline was in the doldrums. However, she was about to experience a renaissance.

Pauline's winters were spent in Paris in the house in the rue de Douai. In the other seasons, the Viardots enjoyed country life at Courtavenel. She did not appear on the Paris stage for seven years after *Sapho*,[1] and, being a highly principled person, took a dim view of both Paris musicianship and the standards that prevailed there. 'You have no idea of the baseness which rules here now in Art and in every sphere of public life', she said. 'Nearly all the woman singers are *courtisanes*.' Pauline observed that bribery and racketeering were rampant.[2] 'Everything is accomplished now through protection but woe to him who must beg for it!', she recorded. 'He must usually purchase this needful exalted favour with his honour. God be praised, we do not need it; we have never debased our freedom, soiled our honour'.[3]

This was the Second Empire, led by the disarmingly absurd Napoleon III and his excessively influential and interfering wife Eugénie. 'The Spanish Beauty' was the granddaughter of a wholesale fruit and wine merchant in Malaga. The arriviste régime seemed, on its surface, to be a success. The Exhibition of 1867 presented Paris as London's rival as a centre of industrial progress. Baron Haussmann, the prefect of the Seine, rebuilt a charming higgledy-piggledy city into the glorious capital which we now know.[4]

There were lavish receptions and balls. There was glitz and gloss at the top. It was boom time for businessmen and *nouveaux riches.* Superficially, there was a great deal of 'change' and buckets of money. It succeeded, of course, because people just wanted money and fun.

This was a smart, sleazy society, a 'steamy orgy of men in black suits and women in crinolines', 'where a duke rubbed shoulders with a crook'. The Duc de Morny, a bastard son of the Emperor's mother,[5] neatly combined *le chic et le chèque.*[6] While people at the top could be flattered by satire, such as that provided by Offenbach, others saw it differently. Émile Zola later would thunder that there was 'filth at the top, filth down below, there's nothing but filth and more filth'.[7]

La Païva, the former mistress of the piano virtuoso and composer Henri Herz, cramponned her way from the Moscow ghetto to a Paris palace with an alabaster staircase valued at a million francs. She was now a marquise and was lucky. Outside her foetid bedroom, furnished with its bed for business which was said to have cost 100,000 francs, the average wage for a Parisian who worked an eleven-hour day was 3.81 francs. A skilled laundry-girl, who might carry on work until three in the morning, was paid 3 francs and an unskilled one, or a flower girl, 2 francs.[8] A skilled sign-painter might be paid 15 or 20 francs a day, but a blacksmith might only get 7 francs a day, his wage having been recently cut by 40 per cent because of the introduction of new machinery. Out of their income, 30 francs a month would be needed to give a child a basic education and training in a church school.[9]

Haussmann, a Lutheran who was addicted to figures and detail, estimated that almost three-quarters of Parisians lived in poverty.[10] As Victor Hugo illustrates in *Les Misérables,* numerous families dwelled in tenements of 'sparse and congested squalor, with a packing-case as a cupboard, a pail for the water supply, a straw mattress for a bed'. The floor took the place of table and chairs in a room where one might find 'seated in a corner on a thread-bare and tattered piece of carpet, a thin woman surrounded by a huddle of children'.[11] Next to the stove there would be no coal. On the shelf above, there was probably just a bundle of pawn tickets.[12] Other authors talk of the stench of families piled into one tiny airless room, the fumes of unhealthy trades, the greasy steam from cooking meat out on the landing, the stink of rags and the humid reek of clothes drying on strings. The maid on annual wages of 300 francs whose upkeep was paid for by her employer, would live in a tiny attic a few feet square. Her furniture comprised the bed, a chair and a little rickety washstand with a broken basin. There was no fireplace, but there was a skylight which let in the cold in winter and the heat in summer.[13]

Somewhere above the middle of this society were to be found the Viardots; rich, radical, republican and respectable.

At home in Paris, Pauline set herself up in comfort with a Pleyel piano and a selection of her favourite books in the languages she knew. Her bookshelves contained works by Dante, Tasso, Shakespeare, Byron, Goethe and Schiller. Her favourite author was Homer. Her children said that they knew the stories from *The Iliad* and *The Odyssey* better than their fairy tales.[14]

With the proceeds from the sale of some of the jewels which she had been given in Russia, Pauline bought a two-manual salon organ which had been built by Aristide Cavaillé-Coll, the most distinguished organ builder in France in the 19th century. It had been on display at the Exhibition of 1855 and it cost over 10,000 francs.[15]

During the 1850s, when in Paris, Pauline's salon provided a crucible in which prominent musicians, artists and writers living in Paris could mix. Her Thursday salons were attended by the cultural élite. Her guests could listen to wonderful music and readings in the drawing-room where her portrait by Scheffer hung. They could wander down the steps through her husband's picture gallery and towards the organ room. They could admire his collection, his Rembrandt, his Velasquez.[16]

Those who attended included artists such as Corot. Louise recalls meeting Liszt's 'first' mistress, the Comtesse Marie d'Agoult who now wrote successfully under the pseudonym Daniel Stern. George Sand was often present. Louise noticed that 'this small woman with her beautiful observant eyes spoke little and sat quietly smoking her cigarette. If anyone entered who she did not know, she never opened her mouth.' Others at Pauline's salon were refugee politicians such as the Polish Prince Czartoryski and Ary Scheffer's great friend Daniele Manin, 'the last doge of Venice',[17] the President of the Venetian Republic during the rebellion in 1848. Manin had led the defence of Venice when it was bombarded by the Austrians before its capitulation in August 1849.[18] Louise said that he was 'now eking out a living by giving Italian lessons'. He taught Dickens's daughters.[19]

Of course many musicians attended the salons, such as Rossini, Berlioz, Ambroise Thomas, Massenet, Lalo, and the Rubinsteins. Wagner came when he was visiting Paris. César Franck might play the organ. Louise sometimes found the evenings torture because she was expected to sight-read parts in trios and quartets which were led by top artists. However, the visitors were occasionally less awesome. Some even provided light entertainment, such as a countess 'who fell asleep as soon as the music began, and who would suddenly wake up and clap violently'.[20]

The organ which Aristide Cavaillé-Coll built for Pauline

Rossini, who carried his 60 years and 'his great paunch with sprightly good humour', also provided considerable amusement.[21] Pauline claimed that she was the only person he ever kissed. He must have been a comical sight, provided that one was not troubled by the slight nervous tic which he had in one eye.[22] His choice of wig was usually a cause of some amusement – sometimes he wore several. 'He always has a diabolical wit', wrote Pauline. He was asked how to prevent bad breath after eating onions. 'Eat garlic', was his response.[23] 'Do you know what Wagner's music sounds like to me?', he asked Louise on one occasion. He promptly lifted the lid of the piano and sat down on the keyboard.[24] The impact on the instrument of the large and portly bon vivant is not recorded.

The Viardots dined at the Rossinis' and attended Olympe Rossini's soirées. Pauline was caustic about the quality of the performers at these. 'A crowd of dreadful little tuppenny half-pfennig musicians', she called them. She added, 'As for Rossini, all this crowd that passes through his salons as though through a street, amuses him'.[25] Olympe, a quondam courtesan who was once enjoyed by the novelist Balzac, dressed up to the nines in her fabulous jewellery and took her position far more seriously.

At her own soirées, Pauline could show her guests her latest, amazing, acquisition. This was her 'bijou le plus précieux', Mozart's manuscript of *Don Giovanni.* When it was shown to Rossini, he lowered his bulky frame to the floor and prostrated himself in deepest reverence.[26]

In 1855, with the proceeds of some more beautiful diamonds, Pauline bought the *Don Giovanni* autograph from the piano manufacturer Streicher. She paid £180.[27] The manuscript had been available for many years. The Viennese would not stump up the 5,000 francs cash (about £200) for it, nor would the British Museum. 'That the powers directing our own gloomy shrine of antiquities in Bloomsbury rejected the offer was at that date perhaps not very surprising', wrote one London-based critic, near the end of the century.[28]

In 1892, Pauline gave the priceless manuscript to the Paris Conservatoire. She had originally intended to bequeath it in her will. But during her long old age many people wanted to gain access to it. In view of its importance, she would never risk it being taken away for display in exhibitions. She must have felt that some sensible arrangements for access were desirable, so she decided to present it to the Conservatoire during her lifetime. She stipulated that the manuscript should never leave its library.[29]

On Sundays, Pauline held soirées which were very different. There were charades, forfeits, impromptu musical performances and Turgenev would recite stories. On one occasion Saint-Saëns, then organist of La Madeleine, the fashionable church, acted the temptations featured in Meyerbeer's *Robert le Diable*. The prop for the vice of drunkenness was a fashionable cup of the alcoholic drink 'coco'. The guests also performed the notorious 'Nuns' Dance' clad in white sheets. Pauline accompanied them on the piano while they beat the rhythms on saucepans with wooden spoons.[30] Music can be fun.

One of Rossini's quips was to say 'Wagner has some good moments, but bad quarters of an hour'. Although Wagner's music would not obviously be an immediate choice to perform at a soirée, the house in the rue de Douai was the setting for what was probably the first ever performance of the superb central 'Love Scene' from Act II of Wagner's *Tristan*. This event, in May 1860, was carried out at the composer's request. Wagner himself sang Tristan; Pauline sight-read Isolde, and Wagner's friend, the pianist and conductor Karl Klindworth, was at the piano.[31] According to Pauline's son, the audience was limited to Liszt's then mistress, Princess Carolyne Sayn-Wittgenstein, and Comtesse Kalergis, the niece of the Russian Foreign Minister. Marie Kalergis, who was estranged from her husband, a diplomat of Greek origin, had recently provided Wagner with 10,000 francs to relieve him of his debt. She was part of the fixtures and fittings in Paris, a patron of Berlioz and an *amoureuse* of Musset.[32] On account of her lily-white complexion, Gautier called her 'la symphonie en blanc majeur'. For unsuccessful gentlemen however she was known as the 'White Elephant'.[33]

Pauline, on the whole, disliked Wagner's music, and the style of music championed by Liszt. The 19th-century musical world was sharply divided. On the one hand, there were those who supported Liszt's 'New German School' which was generally flamboyant and unconstrained. On the other, there were those who took the side of its fierce and implacable critic, the usually more sedate and 'classical' Brahms. When Saint-Saëns ran through the first Act of Wagner's *Lohengrin* for Pauline, she declared 'what deadly monotony! what wearisome ugliness. It is ugly, it is doleful, it is sadly inflated! What pompous nullity and what extravagant insignificance'.[34] Turgenev was also unenthusiastic about Wagner's music; at heart he was a conservative, and did not like to make the intellectual effort that modern music demanded. Louis found himself appropriately apoplectic, and, after hearing *Lohengrin*, they had to play some works of J. S. Bach in order to clear the air.[35]

However, Pauline's views mellowed and she came to like *Lohengrin.* She went to the first performance of *Die Meistersinger* in Munich, and she continued to see it frequently. She was by no means wedded to Italian music which she thought was often charming, but little more.[36]

We may surmise that Wagner told those present in Pauline's music room that the central love duet of *Tristan* is introduced with a hectic, breathtaking, passionate section, which today has the audience 'on the edge of their seats'. The Irish princess and Cornish knight then sink down together in love. The duet is concluded when their love-making is interrupted in the very act, *in offener Tat*, by Isolde's husband the king and his entourage. We may be sure that Wagner will also have explained, possibly at length, that the duet encapsulates his philosophy, influenced by Schopenhauer, of lovers being bound together in death, heart to heart, mouth to mouth, undivided, unified in endless night, the *Liebestod.*

It is not clear who sang the part of Isolde's lady-in-waiting, whose warnings from the tower that the night is passing are ignored by the lovers. Whether Pauline and Wagner really sight-read the wild introduction, in which she reaches top B flat as her fourth note, we may doubt. The erotic music depicts the hectic embraces and kisses. The passionate Isolde continues at the top of her register, hitting top C several times. The tempo accelerates with a *molto accelerando* from a *molto vivace.* In the printed score, a page only lasts around six seconds, and this pace continues for about fifteen minutes. Besides the challenge for Pauline's voice, the accompaniment would have been a test for Klindworth. It seems more likely that the performance consisted only of the slow, soft, tender, supremely beautiful section, in which the lovers invoke the Night of Love to enfold them, *O sink hernieder.*

As a consequence of her early dislike of Wagner's music, Pauline apparently gave what Klindworth called a lukewarm performance.[37] Possibly the story, the cuckolding and betrayal of King Mark by his great friend, may have seemed too close to the bone. At any rate, Pauline's voice did not have the 'wind-pressure' or stamina for Wagner's roles such as Isolde.

The gathering must have been truly astonished by the gripping and

sensuous music, which is one of the most evocative pieces ever written. Pauline will never have participated in anything like it before. This was a historic milestone in the history of music, but a performance of which Pauline could not be particularly proud. That is sad. Wagner's Tristan has outlasted Rossini's Desdemona and will continue do so for many years to come.

But Pauline was about to expunge her guilt.

In May 1859, Pauline sang at a benefit performance for Caroline Miolan-Carvalho who in that year, so it was said, received greater acclaim in London than any new soprano since Pauline's own début. Caroline had married Léon Carvalho, the Mauritius-born founder-proprietor of the Théâtre-Lyrique, the fourth opera house in Paris.[38] Carvalho had the idea of Pauline singing in a revival of Gluck's *Orphée.*

In Gluck's original Viennese version, the title role Orfeo had been sung in Italian by a castrato. Gluck arranged it for a tenor for the 1774 French-language version which was staged in Paris twelve years later. Almost a hundred years after the première of this great work, Carvalho, an innovator, wanted it sung by a contralto. This represented a commercial and artistic gamble which some thought bound to fail.[39]

To achieve the necessary compromise between the two existing versions, the Vienna and Paris productions respectively, Carvalho turned to Berlioz.

His choice was surprising because Berlioz was an arch-purist when it came to performing classical works.[40]

Pauline had known Berlioz for years. To start with, he was frosty. Early in her career, he had said that her voice was too low for Gluck's Eurydice. However, at the time of the Beethoven memorial festival in Bonn in 1845, he was more complimentary. His attitude softened. He discussed her songs with her, and was a guest at her soirées.[41]

Working with Saint-Saëns, Berlioz made several amendments in order to enliven Gluck's somewhat stately and static opera into something which would appeal to a mid-19th century Paris audience. An air, for a long time (incorrectly) thought to be composed by someone other than Gluck, was inserted. Pauline was let loose, at its conclusion, to sing her own elaborate cadenza.[42]

Hector Berlioz, drawn above by Pauline, represented the epitome of French romantic music and colour. He was born in 1803, in a small country town near Grenoble, in southeast France. He studied in Paris to become, like his father, a doctor. To his family's horror, he decided to devote his life to music. He composed the *Symphonie fantastique* soon after he became obsessed with the Irish actress Harriet Smithson who made a tremendous impact in the Paris production of *Hamlet* in 1827. She took no notice of him; yet, eventually, she married him after she had fallen from grace. He had returned from Italy, where he studied after winning the Prix de Rome. Harriet went progressively downhill and died. Berlioz then married his mistress, a minor opera singer.

The Paris establishment disliked the romanticism of Berlioz and his lack of conformity. He had to make his living from working outside France and from the journalism which he disliked, but at which he was very successful. He became increasingly despondent. His much-loved works include his symphony *Harold en Italie*; his overtures such as *Les Francs-juges* and *Le Carnaval romain*; his songs such as 'Les Nuits d'Eté', and works such as *La Damnation de Faust, L'Enfance du Christ*, the *Requiem, Roméo et Juliette* and *Les Troyens.* He also published an influential compendium on orchestration. Berlioz died in Paris in 1869, two years after his son had succumbed to yellow fever when serving with the navy in the Caribbean.

The team was also concerned that Eurydice's music in the Elysian Fields made her appear far too content, even happy, for one who had died. She sang 'Cet asile aimable et tranquille' at a time when the wretched Orpheus was struggling to retrieve her and bring her back to Earth. So Berlioz and his assistants invented another role, that of an *Ombre heureuse*, a 'happy shade', to sing this aria.[43]

Berlioz never did things by halves. He had plans that Pauline would be an 'admirable Cassandra' or Dido in his own massive opera *Les Troyens*, on which he was working. While the rehearsals for *Orphée* went on, Pauline helped Berlioz, who did not play the piano, with the piano reduction of *Les Troyens*. Saint-Saëns recalled seeing her, 'pen in hand, eyes alight, the manuscript on her piano, doing the transcription of the 'Royal Hunt and Storm', the ballet in Act IV. Paul, her son, claimed that she made technical improvements to Berlioz's harmonies.[44]

Pauline performed various items sung by Cassandra and Dido at the Baden Festival in August 1859. She sent Liszt an invitation to attend. Although he particularly wanted to hear Dido's duet from the fourth act, he did not think the performance justified his making the journey.[45] Pauline's performance got good reviews. However, as Liszt rightly reckoned, there was little chance of *Les Troyens* being staged in full anywhere. This was because of Berlioz's 'singular position vis-à-vis, or rather opposite, as they say in English, the Grand Opera'.[46] The musical establishment in Paris had always distrusted, even disliked, Berlioz.

Orphée was staged in Paris on 18 November 1859. The production was, to everyone's surprise, an outstanding success. Meyerbeer attended the third performance; after the sixth, Prince Jérome presented Pauline with a bracelet.[47] Pauline, who wore a costume designed by Delacroix,[48] thought that 'the role of Orphée suits me as if it had been written for me'. Particularly in the very popular 'J'ai perdu mon Eurydice', she 'reached tragic heights rarely seen on the stage'. She sang the motif, which appears three times, in three different ways. First she sang it almost still, quietly, sadly, expressing sorrowful amazement; secondly, she was choked, wracked with tears. Then, she fell on Eurydice's corpse; she rose and threw herself across the stage and sang the third section in a state of total despair.[49] By our modern standards, this may sound overacted and exaggerated. However, today we sometimes hear jaunty and rollicking performances which could benefit from a far greater understanding of the dramatic setting.

Pauline in Berlioz, *Orphée*

The audience was at first stunned. It then erupted for two minutes between the second and third sections. Chorley, the London critic, wrote that 'it is something to have lived to see such an event in musical days during which Signor Verdi is King. It may be doubted whether such a perfect representative of Orpheus ever trod the stage as Madame Viardot. Her want of regularity of feature, and of prettiness – helped instead of impaired the sadness and solemnity of the mourner's countenance'. Chorley described how her voice, 'its unevenness, its occasional harshness and feebleness – consistent with the tones of the gentlest sweetness – was turned by her to account with rare felicity'. He suggested that 'a more perfect and honeyed voice' might have been unsuitably feminine for a male such as Orpheus. He concluded that 'her musical handling of so peculiar an instrument will take place in the highest annals of Art'.[50]

Berlioz wrote that Pauline 'united an irrepressibly impetuous and imperious verve with a profound sensibility and with an almost deplorable facility for expressing immense grief'.[51] Comtesse Marie d'Agoult said that Pauline's acting had surpassed that of Rachel. Throughout the performance, the countess felt that the pictures on a Greek vase had come to life.[52]

There were some light-hearted aspects. The Eurydice, who Berlioz thought was 'as ignorant as a carp of everything to do with Art', was heading towards stardom, having begun her career at the popular café-concerts. At a rehearsal, Berlioz kept stopping the orchestra to coach the chorus. The budding soprano disapprovingly asked Pauline 'That's Monsieur Gluck, isn't it?' 'No, it's one of his friends', came the response. 'Well, he's got a nerve – *in his absence*.' During the performance, Eurydice complained 'Ooh, I do wish the applause did not last so long'.[53]

Louise was highly amused by the thought that some members of the audience would find themselves listening to Gluck, whereas they had thought that they were going to see a different show, *Orpheus in the Underworld*. The press rumpus accusing Offenbach of desecrating antiquity had assured the success of his operetta with both public and Court, as had its famous *Galop infernal*, the cancan. It was all the rage in Paris around the same time.[54]

Carvalho's production of *Orphée* ran to 124 performances in two seasons. At first, it alternated with Gounod's *Faust*. By mid-June 1861, Pauline had sung her part 121 times, even during a time when Paul, who was now almost four, was worryingly ill with broncho-pneumonia. The doctors had assured her that her duty was to her public, while theirs was to the patient; she should carry on. Lord Dudley requested a special performance in the private theatre of his house. No doubt he made it worthwhile, because Pauline made a lightning trip to London just for this. And there was hardly a concert in which Pauline appeared, whether in Birmingham, Liverpool, Manchester or Dublin, when she did not include the 'grand aria'.[55]

Meanwhile, Berlioz was lobbying hard to get *Les Troyens* performed in Paris, but without success. There was a run-through, for the benefit of Princess Carolyne, in the Viardots' salon at the end of October 1859.[56]

During the preparations for *Orphée,* Berlioz came to stay for a couple of days at Courtavenel to go through *Les Troyens* with her. He had been invited earlier, but declined because his son, who was in the navy, was coming home on leave.[57]

It has been said that Pauline was the first woman 'with whom he was on completely equal terms' to capture Berlioz's heart.[58] There was not much competition. His first wife, Harriet Smithson, was for a very brief moment a celebrity actress before she began an inexorable descent. This was ameliorated, temporarily for her, but certainly not for her husband, with brandy. His home life with Marie, his long-term mistress who became his second wife when Harriet died, was also a nightmare. By most accounts, she was a ghastly woman. Her character is said to have prompted Wagner to ask Liszt 'whether the Almighty would not have done better to leave women out of the scheme of creation'.[59] Since neither Liszt nor Wagner would have lasted long without the opposite sex, Wagner's exasperation must have been considerable.

In September 1859, Pauline wrote that Berlioz had fallen in love with her, 'but I hope that this fever of my poor friend B will pass by without untoward incident or violent scenes.' 'He is in such an infirm condition that any emotion kills him', she said.[60] Berlioz was then aged 55 and Pauline had turned 38. As Berlioz, whose second wife had still got three years to live, is sometimes considered a candidate for Pauline's charms, we had better consider the circumstances.

When Berlioz reached Courtavenel, he was clearly ill. Louis comforted him at his bedside.[61] When Berlioz managed to get up, he went for a long walk with Pauline in the grounds of the château and poured out his heart to her. She had become his ideal, he said. Berlioz begged Pauline not to refuse to come and see him if he became seriously ill and called for her.[62] Berlioz was never one to hide his emotions; and Pauline may well have been flattered by the attentions of an exceptional composer, despite the fact that few of his contemporaries were prepared to recognise his genius. Pauline thought it best to give the bizarre undertaking for which he asked.

During the autumn and winter Berlioz wrote her letters 'full of affection and gratitude'. 'Whenever he has conquered the violence of this exalted mood (God grant that it come quickly!)', she wrote, 'I hope to be able to restore some peace to his soul. It would really seem to be my destiny to care for wounded hearts. It is something like the mission of a sister of charity, but I love it.'[63]

Although Berlioz was very ill and always in pain, he had another ten years to live. Back in Paris, Pauline comforted him. She was not alone; Princess Carolyne also ministered to his needs.[64]

Carvalho thought he could quickly repeat the triumph of *Orphée* with Pauline cast in another trouser role, the part of Leonora in Beethoven's *Fidelio*. This was not a success, for several reasons.[65]

Carvalho changed the story. Beethoven's opera of 1805, set in Spain, depicts despotism in the Age of the Enlightenment. The wife of an imprisoned 'democrat' disguises herself as a man and rescues her husband from secret death at the hands of the local tyrant. Carvalho's 1860 production was set in Italy and depicted despotism some three centuries earlier. Queen Isabella, in disguise, rescues the man she loves, the young Duke of Milan whose dukedom has been usurped by his wicked uncle.[66] This change in location and story was curiously tactless considering that French foreign policy in Italy was still in considerable disarray. Napoleon III wanted to help the Italian freedom fighters end the Pope's despotism. However, he was stymied because he depended on Roman Catholic support for his own throne.[67]

So the prospects were inauspicious on the first night, 5 May 1860. Pauline had difficulty sustaining the high notes and had trouble with the spoken dialogue. She received considerable criticism.[68]

Only eleven performances of *Fidelio* were given. The opera was withdrawn, the official reason being that Pauline Viardot had to go away.[69]

Pauline returned to the Théâtre-Lyrique for another season of *Orphée*. Carvalho's successor there wished to capitalise on her continuing popularity. So, during the first part of 1861, she experimented with excerpts from Gluck's other operas. Pauline, who was neither young nor enchanting, was not suited to the youthful parts of Armide and Iphigénie. However, the mature Alceste, in a story about conjugal love, suited her well.[70] According to Pauline's view of her own performance of extracts from *Alceste*, 'no such success had ever been seen in the hallowed hall of the Conservatoire'.[71] Maybe; but she was deluding herself if she thought she was operating other than on a short lease.

In the event it was the Opéra which signed her up, for 1,000 francs per performance, on the basis that she gave at least six opera performances per month, not necessarily in *Alceste*. Berlioz, who possibly was disappointed that Gluck's opera was being preferred to his own *Les Troyens*, tried to have the production stopped. He felt that his arm had been twisted over amending *Orphée*. He was increasingly concerned about the artistic integrity of what he was being asked to do; he did not approve of the changes necessary to adapt the soprano music for Pauline's contralto voice. He claimed that the amendments would be a desecration, analogous to changing the words and rhymes of one of the great classical dramatists.[72] There was an attempt to conciliate him, and he agreed to take an advisory role.

The production of Gluck's *Alceste* went ahead on 21 October 1861. This was Pauline's last triumph on stage. For many, including Berlioz, triumph it was.[73] He now claimed that he had to direct the 'whole thing'.

Berlioz's involvement with the production probably helped to oil the wheels so that his own opera finally reached the stage. However, Pauline's disappointing performance in *Fidelio* led him to realise that she was no longer his ideal Dido. His letters to her became less frequent. The friendship cooled.[74]

Pauline was not around when, in November 1863, part of Berlioz's *Les Troyens* was staged as *Les Troyens à Carthage*. This was a truncated version of the second half of the work. Pauline was neither Dido, nor in the audience. Berlioz's undertaking to her, one which he seems also to have given Rosine Stoltz, had been forgotten. 'I have made enemies of two friends, two pretenders to the throne of Carthage', he wrote. He added, cuttingly, 'Singers will not recognise the unremitting ravages of time'.[75]

Act Four

CHAPTER 21

Baden-Baden

Orphée really marked the end of Pauline's successful stage career. In early May 1863, after a final performance in Paris, it was announced that the Viardots were going to live in Baden-Baden.[1] Why move then? Why there?

It must have been clear to Pauline that her career as a performing singer was drawing rapidly to a close. Her voice was beginning to show signs of wear, perhaps not surprisingly because, at the time of *Fidelio,* she was singing three times a week. She had recently performed at 50 concerts in England.[2] She would soon be aged 42. In a year or so she would reach the age at which the noticeably worn voice of Pasta had been heard in St Petersburg two decades earlier. She did not want to go out like her.

Pauline was on the downward slope. We have just seen how selective Berlioz could be about his prima donnas. Verdi, who at the time was supreme, was particularly choosy. He demanded sopranos who were credible in their parts, both in looks and voice. Although Pauline was an exceptional dramatic actress, her looks and her tired voice did not stand her in good stead. Verdi could call the shots; on one day in London, his *La Traviata* was being staged at three theatres.[3]

Pauline was still getting paid well. Before the Opéra signed her up for *Alceste,* she had raised the fee which she was demanding from the Théâtre-Lyrique from 3,000 francs a month to 4,000 francs. This was not bad, considering that 40 per cent of the orchestra at the Opéra were paid less than 1,200 francs a year.[4] It was relatively trifling, if perhaps surprising, that a Belfast newspaper should give more publicity to Marietta Piccolomini, who was the 'niece' of a cardinal and a popular but inferior soprano. However, Pauline could not afford to ignore the acid reaction of *Le Figaro* which commented that, while Pauline's increased fee represented little enough for the tragédienne, it was a lot to pay for the singer.[5]

Pauline was rapidly being superannuated by a new generation of excellent divas and by a new market. Christine Nilsson, another Swede, who was the rival of Miolan-Carvalho for the role of Marguerite in *Faust*, was the 'first lady of the Opéra'. Célestine Galli-Marié was about to be chosen to become the star of Ambroise Thomas's long-running hit *Mignon*.[6] The public liked a new class of star, such as Hortense Schneider, the lead singer in Offenbach's *La Belle Helène* and in his *La Grande-Duchesse de Gérolstein* which Turgenev infinitely preferred to some of Gounod's work. Schneider had all the trappings of celebrity; she was under the protection of a racy, fast-living duke who, on one occasion, filled the grand piano at the Café Anglaise with champagne, in order to see if it could serve as an aquarium.[7]

Perhaps more galling, Marie Sax, the ignorant Eurydice from Pauline's own *Orphée*, was on her way to become another star of the Opéra, and indeed sang the part of Elisabeth in the sensational 1861 production of *Tannhäuser* which was disrupted by the catcalls of members of the Paris Jockey Club.[8]

Pauline wilted under the stresses and strains, not least the pressure to perform second-rate operas. Even when learning the part of Lady Macbeth, she wrote that she had a little theatre in her head where her little actors move. 'Even in my sleep, my private theatre pursues me', she said. 'It becomes unbearable at times.' Perhaps the relentless pressure was a reason why she did not choose to revert to her other potential career, that of a piano virtuoso;[9] besides, she might then be compared with Clara Schumann.

No, Pauline wanted to get away. Courtavenel no longer provided the magic or the space.[10] Cosmopolitan Baden-Baden might even provide a good place to find husbands for the young girls. The spa attracted high quality musicians. Clara Schumann now lived there when not away on tour, earning money to support her family following the illness and death of her husband. In the summer months Johannes Brahms, Clara's young would-be swain, took a house just outside. Among the regular Russian visitors was the supreme piano virtuoso, Anton Rubinstein. Baden-Baden was an ideal location in which Pauline herself could compose more songs, or some operettas perhaps; something subtler, even better, than the shows with which Offenbach was making such a sensation in Paris.

The extent to which politics entered the Viardots' thinking about making a move is not entirely clear. There were many niggling matters which would have caused the authorities to disapprove of them. Their circle of friends was, at the very least, mildly subversive. They had provided shelter at Courtavenel for the German political refugee Hermann Müller-Strübing who, some decades earlier, had spent five years in prison. Pauline was the dedicatee of Saint-Saëns' setting of *Les Châtiments* which was written in exile by Victor Hugo who was totally opposed to the Second Empire.[11]

Intelligent and reasonable people found the squalid society led by Napoleon III hard to stomach. It was not just the corruption – all past régimes manifested this and all future ones would – it was the attempt to disguise it, the spin, which got up their nose. The Empire 'dressed up its rottenness in such terms as progress, democracy and the like'.[12] Yet it seems improbable that antipathy to the régime was actually the cause of the Viardots' move. The authorities and the Viardots had tolerated each other for more than a decade, so there was no obvious reason suddenly to make a break. Pauline, who had recently appeared on the stage at the Opéra and in the salons of the leaders of 'society', was welcomed by the Establishment.[13] Besides, in the second decade of his rule, Napoleon III started making concessions, such as conceding the right to strike. So the political outlook, to the extent that it was a concern, was improving.

For the Viardots, it was simply time for a change. They had decided to move from France by the end of 1861. They spent much of the following summer prospecting Baden-Baden. They upped sticks and moved their centre of gravity; they did not return to France for eight years.[14] The place to which they moved was different but not much better. Queen Victoria regarded Baden-Baden as notorious, a 'little Paris', where nobody could mix in society 'without loss of character'.[15]

Pauline, who had performed in Baden-Baden several times, knew it well. Louis found the place most congenial, 'an oasis of peace and liberty'.[16] On 6 September 1862, the Viardots bought the site in Tiergartenweg (today

Fremersbergstrasse). This was above the leafy and charming park through which runs the Lichtenthalerallee, which was to Baden-Baden as Rotten Row was to Hyde Park in London. They rented a house while they built their own villa, in the alpine style. Louis encouraged Turgenev, who was contemplating a move to Germany, also to buy a villa there.[17]

The Viardots let the house in Paris for 10,500 francs per annum and removed the organ to Baden-Baden. As for the château of Courtavenel, Consuelo's Castle of the Giants, 'l'endroit le plus charmant de la terre',[18] the furniture was taken to Baden-Baden. Pauline gave a power of attorney to Dr Louis Frisson to handle the sale of the château. 'Le bon docteur Frisson', as Turgenev called him, was a great family friend of, and enthusiast* for, the Viardots. This dodgy doctor was also a property speculator of considerable commercial acumen, although medically perhaps he was rather less astute. He was subsequently prosecuted for practising medicine without a licence. Louise claimed that he was a swindler who destroyed Courtavenel, sold its materials and pocketed the cash.[19] However, Louise does not seem to have been fair.

An attempt was made to sell Courtavenel by auction. However, the bidding failed to reach the reserve, so Frisson sold it off piecemeal and without sentiment. A farm was sold for 48,000 francs. The timber was disposed of. The axe did not even spare Hermann the Chestnut and those other trees so much loved by Pauline and Turgenev, under which they had loved and read. The château was razed. However, Pauline retained the land, which was only sold shortly after Louis's death.[20]

Today, the idea of simply levelling a château seems almost inconceivable. However, large houses, the upkeep of which is very expensive indeed, have in the past often been pulled down or allowed to become derelict. The demand for châteaux is cyclical. It picked up again; the American soprano Adelina Patti created her castle about twenty miles to the north of Swansea in Wales in the late 1870s. In the early 1860s in France, the craze for châteaux was over. They were often pulled down to save tax, just as many such houses in Ireland, for example, had the roof removed as a means of avoiding the local land tax.[21]

*The enthusiasm was reciprocated, at least for Frisson's company and his medicine, if not his novels. Frisson stayed with the Viardots during the 1860s and took part in the portrait game. He may well have delivered Paul; in 1864, he delivered Louise of her son in Baden-Baden. Four years later, he attended Louis when he was ill.

Baden-Baden, where the Viardots now made their home, was the name given to seat of the Margraves of Baden. The town was given its double name in order to distinguish it from other Badens. The word 'Baden' means 'bath'.

The Margrave was one of the many German princelings who collectively comprised the Holy Roman Empire, the ancient agglomeration which was dominated, but not ruled, by the Habsburg Emperors in Vienna. The Baden family played their cards exceptionally well. They successfully married their daughter Princess Louisa Maria to Tsar Alexander I. When Napoleon I consolidated the German states, the Badens obtained more territory and were styled Grand Dukes. Their hereditary rule lasted until their principality was absorbed by the German Empire in 1870.[22]

The higgledy-piggledy Grand Ducal capital, with its castle above, is on the edge of the Black Forest, eighteen miles from Karlsruhe. It was an attractive place with its 'green trees, the neat white houses of the pretty town, and the grand mountains towering above'.[23] The influx of an enormous number of French, German, Russian and English visitors,[24] who poured in to enjoy the spa and its facilities, was quite recent. The remains of Roman baths were 'discovered' in the 1840s. A Pump Room was built[25] to exploit the 29 hot springs, which belched from the castle rock at the rate of 90 gallons a minute. The visitor was dispensed a hot, almost too hot, liquid which tasted sufficiently salty and rich in minerals to provide confidence that there was some medical benefit to be derived from imbibing it.[26]

There was a strong Russian presence because of the connection with Tsar Alexander. Russians were often to be seen frequenting the casino whose owners, Bénazet and his nephew, promoted horse-racing, balls, fireworks, and other diversions for their patrons. In the mid-1860s, the Prince of Wales* gambled, attended the races and bought jewellery there, in contravention of explicit instructions from his mother to keep away.[27] For the more cultured, or those seeking culture, there were concerts, opera and periodic appearances by the Comédie-Française. Gounod's very successful light opera *La Colombe* was premièred there. The première of Berlioz's *Béatrice et Bénédict* took place at the opening season of Bénazet's theatre

* When performing before the Prince of Wales in London, Paul Viardot mistook court dress for the livery of a flunkey, and duly sent the Duke of Westminster to fetch him a glass of water.

which had very recently been built.[28] Last but not least, there was also good shooting for Louis in the Black Forest.

Baden-Baden 1870: Didie, Pauline and Marianne, standing, with (seated) their friend Jeanne Pomey

Of course, not everybody was attracted to Baden. Liszt disliked it. 'I should not know what to do in such places, except be bored to death and stupidly spend more money than elsewhere',[29] he wrote.

Turgenev was somewhat jaundiced in his opinion of Baden-Baden. He described the general impression of brightness and elation which 'even the painted and powdered faces of the Parisian *demi-monde* could not destroy. The Pavilion orchestra played now a medley from *Traviata*, now a Strauss waltz, now a Russian romance arranged for the band by its conductor.' He continued, 'Around the green tables in the casino were to be found the familiar faces, with that stupified, greedy and rapacious expression, and that furtive look which the gambling fever imprints upon the most aristocratic features.'[30]

The visitors came from *monde* as well as *demi-monde*. As one walked through the park, along the fashionable Lichtenthalerallee, one could bump into the militaristic King of Prussia, unaccompanied, out for a stroll, nonchalantly wearing a straw hat and carrying a cane. A few moments later, one might spy Cora Pearl from Plymouth, the notoriously promiscuous Paris courtesan, the possessor of perfect breasts for those privileged to see them.[31] 'Heavens! Who's that monster?' cried one of Turgenev's characters as she drew attention 'to a jaunting car in which reclined a red-haired pug-nosed woman dressed in gaudy colours and displaying her lilac stockings for all to see. 'Why, that's the celebrated Ma'mselle Cora, a Parisian celebrity', was the answer. The dialogue continued: 'What? That fright? Why, but she's very ugly.' 'That does not make any difference.'[32]

We have wondered why this place attracted Pauline. What of Turgenev? Although his relations with Pauline had gone up and down in recent years, he had continued to follow her. In November 1862, she visited him in his flat in Paris and in his manuscript book she drew a five-pointed star, a magic figure which possibly indicated some pledge of affection. One writer has suggested that Pauline lured Turgenev to Baden-Baden because she was about to publish her Russian songs and needed a famous name to endorse them.[33] Indeed, this was a very prolific period for her compositions. In 1864, she published *Twelve Poems of Pushkin, Fet and Turgenev set to music by Pauline Viardot-Garcia*. In 1869, *Five poems of Lermontov and Turgenev* appeared. However, it seems infinitely more likely that, despite his view of the place, Turgenev now had a good opportunity to settle close to his beloved. It was that opportunity upon which he capitalised.

He first took lodgings in 277 Schillerstrasse in the town centre. There, he was joined by Paulinette and Mrs Innis. There, his landlady looked after him with motherly care. In 1864, he bought almost four acres above[34] the Viardots' house* and built his own villa. Building began immediately, but was stretched out over three years as a consequence of Turgenev's financial position. It cost 50,000 francs to build the house in the Louis XIII style, a design which perhaps represented a gesture of opposition to the Second Empire. The cost was financed with help from Louis. A small private

*The Viardots' house was destroyed, but Turgenev's remains.

theatre and concert hall were built at the end of the Viardots' garden (see Plate 12). They were finally inaugurated on 13 August 1869, with a performance of an operetta which Pauline composed to words by Turgenev, *Le Dernier sorcier*.[35] The performance was attended by Pauline's aunt and her cousin Antonia, and also, perhaps surprisingly, by Grisi and Mario, an indication that the hatchet had been buried. Manuel, Pauline's brother, came. He was still up to his usual tricks and had turned up in Baden unannounced. In order to give his sister a bit of a surprise, he appeared in drag. Turgenev's pointer was also not going to miss the fun, so it terrorised the cat population.[36]

Pauline was in her element. With her grace and elegance – she was always very well dressed – she became one of the leading hostesses. Her Saturday salons were honoured by the cream of 'society', even by royalty. Queen Augusta of Prussia, the mother of the Grand-Duchess of Baden, was a visitor and became quite a friend.[37] Bismarck and his army chief Helmut von Moltke were sometimes to be seen at the Viardot villa, as was Richard Wagner. Clara Schumann tells us, with heavy irony, that even Baden's visiting international royalty felt it an honour to be invited to Pauline's parties. In some ways, she was right. Pauline's visitors included King Leopold I of the Belgians, the King of Holland, the Grand Duke of Saxe-Weimar and Crown Prince Fritz. The formidable King Wilhelm, who could only bear to listen to military marches, stood at the back and tried not to attract attention on the few occasions when he came.[38]

On the outskirts of the town, in the area actually called Lichtenthal, Schumann's widow lived by the river in a modest cottage furnished with three grand pianos. Some way beyond, Johannes Brahms took his summer home on the side of a mountain, where he had magnificent views up a tree-lined valley. A few years before, Pauline had expressed a rather jaundiced view about Brahms when Clara played some of his music, 'which neither pleased nor interested her'. Among the works which Brahms worked on in Baden were his *Requiem* which was first performed in 1868, the First and Second Symphonies, and the glorious *Alto Rhapsody*, of which Pauline gave the first performance in Jena on 3 March 1870.[39]

Of a different order was a birthday serenade provided by a choir of Pauline's pupils, led by Brahms. This was performed under Pauline's bedroom window at dawn on 18 July 1869.[40] We might speculate that the idea provided a model for Brahms' sworn enemy Wagner when, a year later, he organised *The Siegfried Idyll* to be performed on the stairs outside the bedroom of Cosima his wife.[41] The Viardot version either went spectacularly wrong or, more probably, provided an opportunity for yet another Viardot practical joke.

According to one account, the dawn chorus, whose performance was doubtless magical, was chased away by the butler who emptied a bucket of cold water on them. More probably, Pauline and Louis were having a lie-in because they had been up late the night before. The performance of the serenade elicited no response. Silence. The then-agile Johannes leapt onto the balcony and led his choir in through the window so that the singers could deposit their bouquets of flowers. A sleepy Madame Viardot shuffled down the stairs and asked what the hell was going on; Louis had said that he thought he heard the dogs howling. Soon everyone was smiling, if not laughing. The event concluded when the choir sang their pieces again and ended with a rousing 'Happy Birthday!'[42]

Clara Schumann, still sorrowing for the loss of her husband, continued to eke out her own living as a virtuoso pianist, a role in which she had received some support from Pauline. But battered as she was by life's experience, Clara found the Viardots' 'sparkling sophisticated home' somewhat overwhelming.[43] 'There is always a sense of restlessness', she wrote. 'Callers drop in every minute, or Pauline suddenly remembers that she has a letter to write, and then one sits for hours without having got any pleasure from her or from others.'[44]

Clara had experienced enough of life's tribulations to be down-to-earth. Her relationship with Pauline was 'always cordial'. They were often on the same platform together. She enjoyed listening to Pauline's operettas. However, they lived in a different world and Clara knew she was on the B-list. This became very obvious at the time of Pauline's official house-warming of her 'Palace of Arts', as she liked to call it, at the end of October 1864. Clara told Brahms that 'to the first ceremony, she invited High Society (the Queen of Prussia etc.) when she naturally did not want me. Afterwards she had a reception for the *hoi polloi* for which I was considered good enough.'[46] Clara thus missed the master of ceremonies announcing the Prussian Queen's lady-in-waiting ('La dame d'honneur'), as 'Madame Tonnerre'.[47]

Clara Schumann

Brahms

Clara Schumann was born on 13 September 1819. She was a prodigy who by the age of twenty had already become one of the leading pianists in Europe. A former law student, Robert Schumann was a pupil of her father, the distinguished piano teacher Friedrich Wieck. After a wild youth, Robert, who in behaviour and style was the perfect Romantic, married Clara against her father's fierce opposition. She continued her successful career. To a great extent, Robert's career as a pianist, composer, journalist and teacher was conducted in her shadow. His mental health deteriorated. In early 1854, he was fished out of the Rhine at Düsseldorf. He was taken to an asylum near Bonn, where he died on 29 July 1856. To support herself and her seven children,[45] Clara travelled around Europe giving her concert performances. She championed Robert's works and also herself composed vocal, choral, chamber and piano works. During Schumann's insanity, Clara was greatly helped by Brahms, who died on 3 April 1897, less than a year after Clara, who then lived in Frankfurt.

All this seemed understandably vulgar, indeed tasteless, to someone with Clara's refinement. Long ago, she had damned Pauline for her deplorable penchant for Italian music and now she criticised her for being more concerned with vocal effect than with the underlying meaning of the songs she sang.[48] For a Schumann, this was a capital offence. The observation lies uneasily with Pauline's reputation for purity of style. We may suspect that Pauline had now developed some of that loudness which we associate with celebrity. However, neither Pauline nor Clara seemed entirely blameless to a certain actress, once England's answer to Rachel, and a most distinguished Desdemona and Juliet in her day. She felt overwhelmed by both Pauline and Clara. 'How one longs for a little simplicity and repose in Viardot! She fatigues you with power. Madame Schumann plays too forcibly; and oh, how ungraceful, ungainly, her motions are!'[49]

Clara, perhaps harshly, also did not think much of the musical arrangements which Pauline prepared for her pupils and family to perform. On one occasion, she had to listen to a 'tasteless setting of Gounod's *Ave Maria*, arranged for organ, harp, violins and three women bawling *unisono*'. Clara was sufficiently disgusted to leave the house 'bristling with indignation'. She disappeared on her winter tour without saying goodbye. Perhaps Clara, who set a very high standard indeed, was hyper-critical. However, we sense that Pauline appeared to convey the trappings and tinsel of the parvenu, at least to someone who was bound to be jealous. On the one hand, Clara said that a life like Pauline's would not suit her. On the other, she wrote to Brahms about the Viardots' splendid organ in the music room. 'Oh why can't I have such an organ? How sacred it would be to me!' Clara, no doubt sarcastically, thought of emigrating to America so as to be able to earn enough to buy one.[50]

In less exalted moments, the Viardot ménage enjoyed bourgeois activities such as 'the exchange of literary conceits, parlour games and intellectual pastimes.' The family would play Turgenev's favourite game of portraits, in which, as we have seen, the participants would separately think of a caption for a sketch drawn by one of the players. They would then amuse themselves by comparing the results.[51]

These games must have been a pleasant diversion from and for Louis who, now in his sixties, was generally silent and unsociable and kept out of the way.

Like many who live to a considerable age, Louis's health was not good.

At one stage, Dickens sent him *The Pickwick Papers* to cheer him up, which the book cannot have failed to do.[52] We must be careful, however, of superannuating Louis. He had twenty years of his life left, much longer than Dickens. He was still writing about weighty subjects such as copyright, and against religion. He also retained his considerable sense of humour. In a talk on the arts, he envisaged a government of musicians. Beethoven would be Generalissimo, Handel the Minister of Culture, Bach the Minister for Justice; Gluck would have the Foreign Ministry, Weber Agriculture and Forestry. Haydn would be the Chamberlain in charge of Court festivities, and Rossini would be Crown Jeweller. Mozart would be King.[53] Maybe Pauline helped him prepare his speech.

Louis Viardot

Louis happened to dislike socialising. He would toil away in the background, occasionally to emerge and converse, or to make a terse contribution to the portrait game.[54] His relationship with his wife is revealed in his preface to the *Apology of an Unbeliever*, surely one of the most extraordinary inter-marital communications ever published. 'To P, Baden-Baden, November 1866', he wrote. 'It has happened to us sometimes, in the course of conversation, to touch upon the great questions of Philosophy. It is not a good plan. Conversation is necessarily broken up by digressions, by questions and answers. One loses continually the line of thought and reasoning.'

Louis proceeds, in this quotation taken verbatim from the London edition of the book: 'I desire to begin and to continue the conversation in order to enunciate, in a few concise paragraphs, my opinion on these subjects … I promise not to be as clear as I shall be brief, so clear as to be understood by a child – that would be insulting to you – but that I will put aside all the apparatus of learning and keep to the simple and familiar language of common sense. Once more it is a conversation which I ask of you; but one speaker only will talk and without interruption.' And he signs this 'LV.'[55]

It must have been essential for Pauline to find some diversion from this intense intellect. She composed light operettas: *Trop de Femmes*, *L'Ogre* and *Le Dernier sorcier*. One entitled *Le Miroir* never reached the boards.[56] These operettas gave the family enormous fun and they also provided useful stage experience for Pauline's pupils. Even Louis emerged to direct and prompt. The first full 'season' was in 1867, which saw the premières of both *Le Dernier sorcier* and *Trop de Femmes*. These took place in the salon of Turgenev's as yet unoccupied villa, and were performed several times.

The lead role in *L'Ogre*, which was first performed on 24 May 1868, was mimed by Turgenev, with someone in the wings singing the music for him.[57] Turgenev's other star roles included the Pasha in *Trop de Femmes*. For *Le Dernier sorcier*, on one occasion,* he donned an absurd fancy dress, wig and false beard to play the part of Krakamiche, a wizard who has lost his powers of sorcery. The elves delude him into thinking that his magic

*Usually starring as Krakamiche was a great friend, Louis Pomey, who translated Schubert's *Lieder* for Pauline. On her writing table, she had a photograph of Pomey and one of Turgenev. One expert suspects that Pomey may have been Turgenev's half-brother, the product of one of his mother's trips to Italy.[58]

powers will be restored. Claudie starred as the Queen of the Elves and Marianne was a principal Elf. The elves also organise the betrothal of the wizard's daughter Stella, played by a pupil, to Prince Lélio, played by Louise who was recently back from Cape Town. Paul played the wizard's comical servant Perlimpinpin, once a giant, now a dwarf.[59] Pauline accompanied on the piano. They must have had enormous fun.

Turgenev also wrote a scenario for an opera set in the Alps for Brahms to compose, although nothing came of this.[60]

Pauline's cartoon of her operettas

The Viardots' royal acquaintances asked for Pauline to arrange special performances of her operettas. A gala performance was laid on for the Prussian royal family. A more ambitious staging of *Le Dernier sorcier*, translated into German and with a chamber orchestra accompaniment, took place subsequently at the Grand-Ducal court in Weimar. This was arranged to celebrate the birthday of the Grand-Duchess, a sister of the Tsar. The work which was originally scheduled for that occasion had been Wagner's

Die Meistersinger. However, it proved too difficult to produce. Pauline's operetta was adapted in a rush; she had only written the vocal and piano score for it. Eduard Lassen orchestrated it and made some misguided 'corrections'. He was a Dane who became court director of music in Weimar after Liszt had resigned the post. Together with Pauline's operetta, Lassen's *Le Captif* was performed.[61]

Turgenev had ambitions for Pauline to develop a second career as a composer. Yet she was unwittingly about to overreach herself. The Weimar performance was indeed judged a success, even though court etiquette precluded applause; it led to a production in Karlsruhe in January 1870. This, however, was not well-received, possibly on account of personal animosities, but also because Pauline's operetta may have been seen as an irreverent send-up of Wagner's *Das Rheingold.* In any event, a local newspaper recorded that 'the most famous writers can write nonsense, the most excellent singers can write ear-splitting music'.[62] For the avoidance of doubt, the reference was to Turgenev's and Pauline's work, not Wagner's.

Clara Schumann was genuinely impressed by Pauline's operettas. 'I have heard each of them three times, and always with equal pleasure. It is all so cleverly written, so dainty, so light, so finished, and so full of humour – it really is wonderful', she exclaimed to Brahms. 'The children are fascinating. Paul really has a genius for comedy. I found fresh confirmation that she is the most gifted woman I have ever known', Clara said. 'When I saw her sitting at the piano and managing everything with such perfect ease, my heart melted within me, and I could have clasped her in my arms.'[63]

Liszt, in a less euphoric moment, thought Pauline's works were 'pretty and even distinguished'.[64] However, Turgenev's Russian friends were horrified to find him, their idol, not only writing the words, but acting. We can imagine the scene at the Royal Gala. Turgenev, spreadeagled on the floor, raises his eyes only to behold staring at him the glowering po-face of Vicky, who combined in her exalted person the British Princess Royal and the Crown Princess of Prussia. Yet despite the way people frowned on acting, Turgenev was not the only great novelist to enjoy amateur dramatics. Dickens staged several productions in London, albeit of more serious works. Dickens's dramatics involved intimacies with one of his actresses. They fell passionately in love.[65] What the stuffy Russians would have made of the behaviour of the English novelist whose works they admired greatly, we do not know.

During the Baden period, Turgenev came and went. He visited Paris to see Paulinette. His literary friends, such as the Goncourts and Flaubert, enjoyed his company at Magny's restaurant where 'the gentle giant's' brilliance as a raconteur provided several anecdotes, many suitably titillating, for the Goncourts to record in their *Journal.* He also dealt with the publishing of his works and Pauline's compositions. On one such occasion, he took an organ pipe with him for Cavaillé-Coll to repair. He also went to the Paris Exposition of 1867.[66]

During one of these visits, Turgenev attended the 'toilette' and the public guillotining of Troppmann, a notorious criminal who had murdered a family of eight. Turgenev told George Sand that he could not bear to watch the blade fall.[67] He did however write a letter to Didie about it, and also wrote an essay about it in which he expressed his revulsion for capital punishment.

Public executions were normal at the time. Tolstoy attended one and was revolted by it. Dickens and Thackeray were relatively unperturbed after watching the hanging at Newgate of a valet who had cut his employer's throat.[68] Dickens was struck by the sensual way in which the female corpse swung when the Bermondsey murderers, whose crime was committed at the time of *Le Prophète,* were jointly hanged in 1849.[69] Ten thousand people attended this unusual husband-and-wife spectacle. Similarly, there was a vast and ghoulish crowd at the Troppman event.

On a happier note, on one of these visits to Paris Turgenev met the Emperor's mistress, Countess Castiglione. To reward her for her favours, the Emperor reputedly gave her a pearl necklace costing 422,000 francs plus 50,000 a month pin money. Turgenev thought she looked like a tart. She had a high coiffure which was crowned with a whole pheasant. His trips provided a good opportunity to get ideas for the design of the operetta productions. When in Paris, he could buy the fancy dress, costumes, beards and wigs.[70] The Countess may have given him some ideas for fancy dress design.

In some years Turgenev also went to Russia for a month or two, to see his publishers and to attend to his affairs generally. A visit in 1867 was necessary to sort out the chaos at the estate which was going to wrack and ruin, with the yield dwindling alarmingly. Turgenev had provided Paulinette's dowry; he had his property commitments in Baden-Baden.[71] He needed more cash. His uncle Nicholas had been in charge and had lost financial control, and the estate was yielding around a fifth of its potential income.[72] Nicholas had also tried to frustrate Turgenev's attempts at implementing the terms of the Emancipation of the serfs, who in any case regarded their master as a convenient milk-cow. When the uncle was sacked, he responded furiously. He seized his nephew's assets which included the Baden-Baden villa. Turgenev had hastily to sell it to the Viardots and lease it back in order to protect his position.[73]

With the arrival of the railway, Spasskoye became much more accessible. The decree sanctioning the construction of the Moscow-Oryol line was issued in mid-1864. After this, workers and convicts built the line, with the construction work making travel at the time very difficult.[74] The railway passed through populated territory, so there was much litigation about the acquisition of land. The single track from Moscow reached Serpukhov in 1866 (a two-hour journey today). Tula was reached in the following year.[75] The first train arrived in Oryol on 28 August 1868. Now, Turgenev could travel in style, 'lying back on the velvet cushions of a first-class compartment'. This represented a considerable improvement on the 'blockhaus ambulant, six in a row on a hard bench, among the pipes and cigars, so that we felt like smoked ham', a description which Louis once used to describe third-class travel.[76]

In March 1867, when Turgenev went to fire his uncle, he could only get as far as Serpukhov by train. He had bronchitis, and could not bear the thought of the confrontation. He turned back and left his agent to deal with the uncle who eventually was mollified with compensation of 20,000 silver roubles plus the coach and horses and other bits and pieces.*[77] In the following year, Turgenev went by rail as far as Tula. From there he changed to a sledge which was 'old and uncomfortable, and pulled along the dreadful roads by half-dead horses'.[78]

It is surprising that Pauline never went to Spasskoye, especially now that travel was relatively easy. In 1868, Turgenev spoke to his steward about a planned visit for the Viardots for the following year. They planned in which room each member of the family, including Louis, would sleep.

*Uncle Nicholas died aged 86, in 1881. Turgenev seems to have remained fond of him.

However, this visit never came about.[79] Perhaps that says something about distances, something about Pauline's other activities and her teaching programme, and something about her relationship with Turgenev. Perhaps the Franco-Prussian War just came in the way.

One of Turgenev's trips to Russia was rather sinister. As we know, Turgenev was well acquainted with Alexander Herzen, the radical writer and publisher of the contentious newspaper *The Bell.* They had first met at Belinsky's house twenty years before, and kept up with each other whether in London or Paris. Herzen nursed Turgenev in Paris, when he was suffering from one of his many ailments.

When in London in May 1862, Turgenev saw Herzen and met Bakunin and Ogaryov, a poet and publicist. They discussed Russia's future in the wake of the Edict of Emancipation. Turgenev's views, as exemplified in *Fathers and Sons*, were less radical than Herzen's and very different from the far more revolutionary views of the others. Turgenev was keen to achieve change by peaceful means.

The Emancipation was badly received. The consequent disturbances led to a crackdown on political dissent; the London dissidents were a particular focus of concern for the Russian authorities.[80] This led to the trial of London Propagandists, known as the Case of the Thirty-Two.

Turgenev was politically quite active, as his meetings in the Isle of Wight indicated. The authorities got wind of his London meetings; Herzen's correspondence with Bakunin, which referred to Turgenev, was intercepted on the Austro-Hungarian border.[81] Turgenev was summoned to appear before a committee of the Senate in St Petersburg. Had he refused to go, his assets would have been confiscated.

Fortunately this enquiry, which concerned him for much of 1863, the year in which Russia was absorbed with the rebellion against its authority in Poland, passed off quietly. Turgenev first had to respond to a questionnaire. Subsequently he had to appear personally, in the first fortnight of 1864.

Turgenev's activities on behalf of the London agitators had largely centred around getting Bakunin's wife to England from Siberia.[82] Turgenev's treatment by the authorities was favourable from the outset. The Russian ambassador in Paris assisted him; the chief of police and the military governor of St Petersburg seemed well disposed towards him; the Senate committee treated him in a friendly manner. It may have helped that not only was Turgenev a 'high-profile person', but also one of the members of the committee of enquiry had known Pushkin and Gogol.[83] At the end of the fortnight, Turgenev was allowed to leave Russia again to return to Baden-Baden.

While away, Turgenev dreamt of the cosy scene he had left behind; Pauline making music, Louis dozing in the corner, the children drawing. His own circumstances, had they taken a turn for the worse, would have been considerably different. Nikolay Chernyshevsky, the outspoken radical who worked on *The Contemporary*, was exiled to Siberia a fortnight before Turgenev was exonerated. There he wrote an answer to Turgenev's *Fathers and Sons*, called *What is to be done?*, a book which Lenin admired greatly.[84]

Back in Baden-Baden, Pauline taught and composed. She also published the *Ecole Classique de Chant*, comprising extracts from composers' works which she had annotated. In earlier times Pauline had disliked teaching. However, she now took in female pupils[85] from all over Europe who lived *en pension* in the town. They kept the Viardot household 'vibrant with youthful activity'. The atmosphere was noticeably light-hearted and carefree. 'In her house everything is as merry as if there were no sorrow in the world', said Clara Schumann.[86] Presumably Louis was tucked away at this moment.

Pauline continued to perform, particularly in *Orphée* and *Le Prophète*. She appeared on the platform for concerts at the Leipzig Gewandhaus and in other cities around Germany.[87] Saint-Saëns considered that she went on performing in public for far too long. 'For several years, she presented the sorry spectacle of genius contending with adversity', he said. He described her voice as 'broken, stubborn, uneven and intermittent'. 'An entire generation knew her only in a guise unworthy of her', he wrote. 'She sang roles which she should never have undertaken had she wanted to preserve her voice.' Pauline recognised this herself. 'Don't do as I did', she once told a pupil. 'I wanted to sing everything and I ruined my voice.'[88] Saint-Saëns was recording his impressions, with hindsight, in the early 1920s. It would be interesting to know precisely when he felt that she should have retired. Yet his conclusion, one applicable to so many singers even today, was clear and devastating.

Pauline made very brief visits to Paris. In May 1864 she went to Brussels, where Madame Garcia died. Pauline was very upset. After the funeral, she could not stop weeping.[89]

—

The first years at Baden-Baden were a relatively fallow period for Turgenev's literary activity. He was distracted by the problems at Spasskoye, the Senate enquiry and his building activity. Between the autumn of 1861 and the end of 1865, he wrote a few stories such as 'Phantoms', 'Enough', 'The Dog', and a short lecture on Shakespeare, but little else. Later in the decade, he wrote 'The Brigadier' and 'Lieutenant Yergunov' which were published in 1868. 'A Hapless Girl' followed in 1869, 'A Strange Story' in 1870. He also translated, with Louis Viardot, *Eugene Onegin* and many other works by Pushkin.[90]

His principal novel of the 1860s was *Smoke* which was published in 1867. He began it soon after the publication of *Fathers and Sons.* It represented a fierce caricature of Russian society in Baden-Baden and of his own literary critics.[91] For example, he depicted the dilettante Count, said to be profoundly musical, who divinely performs songs at the piano but 'cannot in fact play two notes correctly without fumbling at random on the keys'. He describes the Prince, 'the friend of religion and the people' who had made a fortune selling vodka adulterated with belladonna; the Princess, 'who would have been irresistible, if she did not so strongly resemble a stout country washerwoman'; 'the brilliant General who had conquered somebody and subjugated something, but who, once off the parade ground, was at a loss to know how to fit in and what to do'. There were 'the young lions, fashionably turned out in the best clothes from London, their coiffure perfectly parted and their whiskers dropping down to their shoulders. Each was in search of an easy-going woman, but would not have had a clue what to do if he found one.' 'That's Baden!' Turgenev wrote. 'Everybody congregates there like cockroaches behind a stove.'[92]

Besides lampooning the visitors to Baden-Baden, Turgenev, in *Smoke*, was trenchantly provocative. He described a group of Russians all holding forth, a veritable Tower of Babel, about the future of Russia 'I kept wanting to ask those gentlemen what they were making such a fuss about. The funny thing is that they had not a clue themselves. They are all excellent, but, when you work it out, they don't add up to a row of beans. The ingredients are first-class, but the dish is uneatable.'[93] This was hardly palatable for his critics.

The main action in *Smoke* takes place within a fortnight[94] and concerns Litvinov, a young man, who is in Baden-Baden awaiting the arrival of his fiancée, Tatyana.* He encounters and is seduced by a former fiancée, the capricious, self-centred and extremely clever Irina. She is married to a general whose superficial 'vague liberalism' had not prevented him from flogging 50 rioting peasants. Her circle of friends 'understand nothing, feel for nothing; they've no intelligence even, nothing but tact and cunning; Music, Poetry and Art are all equally remote from them.'[95]

Litvinov and Irina plan to elope. Meanwhile, Tatyana arrives with her 'good, absurd, generous,' aunt. Litvinov confesses his Fall, so Tatyana and the aunt push off. Then Irina gets cold feet. She suggests that, instead of eloping, Litvinov should return to live in St Petersburg where 'we will find something for you to do'. Self-respect vanishes. He stands 'in the debris of his moral collapse'. When, on his own, he leaves Baden-Baden, the smoke from the train blows past his carriage. 'Suddenly the past seemed like smoke to him. His whole life, his life in Russia – everything human, but chiefly everything Russian – all smoke and steam.'[96] He returns to Russia and his farm which he tends. Eventually he visits Tatyana; and the reader is left to assume that they actually live happily ever after.

Of course, just as happens today, Litvinov's revolutionary friends end up in comfortable bourgeois jobs. Turgenev is devastating about the 'piss and wind' of all these so-called revolutionaries, the windbags and charlatans of Young Russia, and the 'Slav nature which analyses everything with force and brilliancy, and ends so often by doing nothing'.[97] Russians worry away at the future of Russia in the same way that boys chew a piece of india-rubber, but with the same result. Turgenev does not pull his punches. 'Russia for ten whole centuries has originated nothing in Government, the Arts and Sciences and even in manufactures', he writes. 'Even Russia's

*Tatyana is supposed to be based on Olga Turgenev, the cousin with whom Turgenev had a romance in mid-1854. Irina is primarily modelled on a mistress of Alexander II, but may have some characteristics of Pauline.

famous products, the knout, the shoes woven from bark, the samovar were not invented by us.' Yet the Sandwich Islanders have invented their own peculiar canoes and javelins.

Turgenev wades in deeply and bitterly. 'Russian Art, Russian skills, indeed! I recognise Russian bombast and Russian feebleness, but Russian fine art, I've never come across; the notion is simply laughable.'

Even Glinka, reputed to be the first 'Russian' composer, the composer of *A Life for the Tsar*, has been oversold. 'Nobody doubts that he was a truly remarkable musician, who circumstances and whose own limitations prevented from becoming the founder of Russian opera. But no, they have to hype him up into a kind of Napoleon of music and pretend that other nations have failed to produce anything comparable. They spin some rubbish about a "sublime" production of a "great vintage" work, which in fact is just a pitiable imitation of something by a second-rate foreign composer, and I mean second-rate, because the second-rate are the easiest to imitate.'[98]

The story of *Smoke* is powerful and sensual. Its political content was devastating. A good ten per cent of the book is taken up with various pro-Western remarks made by a subsidiary character. The Slavophile view of the distinctive nature of Russian culture was demolished. Turgenev argued that the complete Westernisation of Russia was the only way forward if the country was to progress. Russia's past and present achievements, if any, insofar as their origin was not from the West, were dismissed.[99]

This book caused a fury across the political spectrum in Russia. Even before publication, Turgenev's publisher Katkov had demanded cuts and expressed difficulty with the character of Irina.[100] There were some heated exchanges and the author was required to compromise, which, although not unusual for an author, is perhaps surprising in the case of a writer of such distinction. The traditionalists ostracised Turgenev. At the other end of the spectrum, Turgenev's friend the poet Fet was aghast; Tolstoy thought the book objectionable;[101] Herzen was furious. He described Turgenev as 'a white-haired Magdalen of the male sex who could not sleep at night for thinking that the Emperor might not have heard of her repentance'.[102]

None was more enraged than Dostoyevsky.

CHAPTER 22

DOSTOYEVSKY

'FRANKLY, I NEVER liked the man personally', Dostoyevsky wrote of a character he based on Turgenev. 'I also dislike the aristocratic buffoonery of his embrace, whereby he makes as if to kiss your cheek, but then proffers his own. What appalling self-importance.'[1]

Dostoyevsky and Turgenev had known each other for a long time. They met in the early days at *The Contemporary*. They got along well then. Turgenev used to pull Dostoyevsky's leg.[2] To begin with, Dostoyevsky was an effusive admirer of Turgenev who he regarded as 'a poet, a great talent'. 'You cannot doubt the sincere regard I feel for you', Dostoyevsky told Turgenev in late 1861. He liked *Fathers and Sons*, and he took Turgenev's side in various disputes with *The Contemporary*. However, just as Dostoyevsky changed his views about Belinsky who became, in the writer's opinion, a 'shit' and a 'stinking dung beetle',[3] this friendship with Turgenev could not last.

By the end of the 1860s, Turgenev and Dostoyevsky were irreconcilable. At one stage, they tried to cooperate; Turgenev sent his short story 'Phantoms' for Dostoyevsky to publish in his journal. However, the journal collapsed financially, and that was the end of it.

The viewpoints of Turgenev and Dostoyevsky were totally different, as we shall see. Also, their styles were poles apart, with Dostoyevsky 'indifferent to natural scenery, being exclusively obsessed with human beings and their behaviour'. Turgenev, after Dostoyevsky was dead, accused him of sadism,[4] an accusation with which some readers of the lengthy *The Brothers Karamazov* may have some sympathy.

Before turning to the extraordinary meeting between Dostoyevsky and Turgenev in Baden-Baden in June 1867, we shall consider Dostoyevsky's fearful background which was so completely different from the comfortable, plush, dandified youth which Turgenev enjoyed.

Dostoyevsky

Feodor Dostoyevsky was a few months younger than Pauline. He was the son of a middle-class doctor. He was born on 11 November 1821 at his father's hospital in Moscow. When he was sixteen, around the time his mother died of tuberculosis, Dostoyevsky entered the army's Engineering Academy. A couple of years later, his father was murdered by his serfs,[5] an event which his son would reflect in *The Brothers Karamazov*, where the old man is murdered by a serf who is his illegitimate son.

Dostoyevsky worked in the War Ministry until 1844, when he resigned his commission. His literary ability was noticed by Nekrasov, the proprietor of *The Contemporary*, and by Belinsky who converted him to socialism and atheism. Despite early literary success, he failed to live up to his promise.

Meanwhile, he became beholden to his publisher who lent him money. He also started to suffer from epilepsy.[6]

Dostoyevsky attended Friday gatherings of a group led by an official of the Foreign Ministry called Petrashevtsy, who a few years earlier had published a pocket dictionary of foreign words. This provided an ideal medium in which to elucidate radical ideas.[7] The Petrashevtsy meetings were infiltrated by an undercover police agent. Dostoyevsky was arrested and accused of plotting to acquire a printing press. He was also accused of reciting Belinsky's vitriolic *Letter to Gogol* of 1847 and of failing to report its dissemination. In this, Belinsky accused Gogol of betraying the Russian people by advocating submission to the Church and the state.

The Tsar had become sufficiently rattled about the political situation that, recently, he had introduced some severe anti-revolutionary legislation. The death penalty was prescribed for those tainted with sedition, for any attempt to alter the prevailing system of government, and for failure to denounce. Even a casual discussion group might be regarded by the authorities as a nest of traitors.[8]

Dostoyevsky found himself caught by this legislation. In 1849, after eight months in solitary confinement, he was taken with some others from St Peter and St Paul Fortress to a square to be shot.

Dostoyevsky described what the experience must have been like for the condemned man. 'At the beginning of his journey to the scaffold, he sits in the cart and feels that he has infinite life before him. The cart moves on and on, the houses recede behind him, and it's still a long way to the turning into the next street. He glares boldly to the right and left at all those thousands of callously curious faces, their eyes riveted on him. The cart turns into another street. Not to worry! there is still a whole street ahead. He imagines that the journey will go on for ever. And so to the very end, and into the square itself.'[9] Then, 'there is no torture in the world more terrible'. Unlike for an ordinary victim, say of murder, there is not so much as a vestige of hope. Death is absolutely inevitable, just a matter of time. There is no escape; the execution, the judicial murder, is certain.[10]

Clad in his shroud, counting down the now very few moments left to him, his brain throbbing like a steam-engine at full throttle, Dostoyevsky looked on as the first batch was lined up. When the squad took aim, an officer galloped up waving a document which stated that the sentences were commuted. Mock executions had a deterrent effect.

Dostoyevsky's sentence was commuted to four years in prison in Siberia, followed by an unspecified period of compulsory military service. On Christmas morning, shackled in fetters, he was put on a sledge for the 2,000-mile journey far beyond the Ural Mountains, to Omsk. He was imprisoned with common criminals and deafened by the never-ending clanging of the fetters which they all wore. The only book allowed to him was a copy of the Gospels. This was provided by the wives of those imprisoned after the 1825 Decembrist uprising who had, remarkably, accompanied their husbands into captivity. However, when in the sick bay, Dostoyevsky managed to read some novels by Dickens. Needless to say, he was filled with despair at the thought of being 'shut in a coffin, buried alive for four years', and being unable to write during that time. However, for the novelist of the future, this experience of Russia's lower depths was invaluable.[11]

Dostoyevsky's recollections, 'somewhat sensationalised',[12] were subsequently published in his documentary study, *Memoirs from the House of the Dead.* He recalls the dull stifling days 'as monotonous as drops of water falling from the roof after rain'. He describes the fetters weighing between eight and twelve pounds, the half-shaved heads, the interminable, thin, watery cabbage soup, the illicit trafficking in vodka. Dostoyevsky found it particularly hard to handle the resentment felt by the other felons for a member of the so-called 'nobility' in their midst.[13]

The book condemns the sadism of the prison governor and the futility of 'one of the ulcers of society', the corporal punishments. These were regular and normal, although he seems to have avoided the experience himself. Many of the inmates of the hospital were recovering from this brutal treatment; 500 strokes, 1,000 strokes, 4,000 strokes, the running of the gauntlet. Nobody could endure a thousand strokes at a time. So, after a spell in hospital to allow the back to heal, the convict would be discharged only to hear, on the following day, the executioner again shout 'Hold tight I'm going to flay you'. The process would begin once more, and many died as a result. Other hospital inmates were genuinely ill. The consumptives, the dying, wasted men, still wore their fetters. As the writer poignantly observes, each dying man must have had a mother.[14]

The scene in the prison bath is a portrayal of Hell. A hundred men were crammed into a room twelve paces by twelve for 'Steam that half blinded the eyes, soot, filth, a press so thick that there was nowhere to put one's foot down'. The dirty water from those who were standing trickled onto the heads of those sitting hunched up below. The heat made the scars from the floggings stand out clearly so that all the backs seemed newly flayed. Everybody was almost in a state of intoxication, they were high.[15]

In March 1854, Dostoyevsky was freed as a settler to serve in the army at Semipalatinsk, now in Kazakhstan, 500 miles south-east of Omsk. He was eventually allowed to resume writing. Five years later, he was permitted to reside in European Russia, although he was only allowed back to St Petersburg in December 1859. Even then, he was under secret surveillance by the police.

Dostoyevsky next worked as a journalist on a magazine which he founded. Then, in 1861–2, the publication of the *Memoirs from the House of the Dead* made him very prominent. In 1863, at the time of a rebellion in Poland, his magazine was closed down because it was thought to be supporting Polish culture over Russian culture. Another journal launched to attack the Russian socialist movement also collapsed.[16]

Dostoyevsky's first wife, whom he had married in Siberia in 1857, died of tuberculosis.[17] Meanwhile, Dostoyevsky had gone to Paris, chased a succession of mistresses and indulged in wanton gambling at various resorts, such as Baden-Baden, Wiesbaden and Bad Ems nearby.[18] He proposed to three women in two years.[19]

To pay for his lifestyle and the cost of supporting his wife's son by a previous marriage, Dostoyevsky mortgaged the copyright in his existing works to his publisher. The agreement included a penalty clause. If he failed to deliver a new novel by the beginning of November 1866, the publisher would be entitled to all future works, the writer's livelihood, for nine years for free. Dostoyevsky also borrowed from the Society of Needy Authors. Turgenev, from whom he requested 100 thalers, lent 50, the equivalent of around 60 silver roubles at the time.[20] Turgenev forgot that he had halved the request. This caused friction later, when it came to be repaid.[21]

Dostoyevsky had already been working on *Crime and Punishment*,[22] an immensely powerful, terrifyingly elemental story of social deprivation, murder and psychological disease. It has eluded consensus from its interpreters to this day. The publication of the first instalments during early 1866 was a literary sensation,[23] even if the political event of the year was an assassination attempt on Alexander II. To finish the book, and to write the additional novel required by his publisher, Dostoyevsky hired a shorthand assistant half his age, Anna Grigoryevna. They had only four weeks left, but they delivered *The Gambler* with two hours to spare.

Not surprisingly, *The Gambler*, out of which Prokofiev made an opera, is relatively short. It is largely set in Roulettenburg and its centrepiece is the compulsive gambling, 'a most foolish and imprudent pursuit', of a Granny. Although presumed and desired dead, she turns up out of the blue and manages to lose virtually her entire wealth, to the consternation of her voracious dependants who were expecting to inherit it from her. 'As sure as I am alive, I'll win back', she cries as she carries on 'like a man on a sledge accelerating down a snow-covered mountain'.[24]

Dostoyevsky and Anna Grigoryevna married in February 1867. Because of his own debts, the Dostoyevskys had to leave Russia, so for four years from April 1867 the couple lived abroad.[25] There, mainly in Dresden, Geneva and Florence, he wrote *The Idiot, The Eternal Husband* and much of *The Devils*. In *The Idiot* he describes the onset of one of the epileptic fits of which he had personal experience. Suddenly, in the midst of spiritual darkness and oppression, there was a flash of light in his brain and all his vital forces began working at their highest tension; then his mind and his heart were suffused with great light and all his anxieties were relieved. In the last unendurable second, he could understand the saying 'There shall be no more time'. He heard his own scream. There was total darkness.[26]

Dostoyevsky gave up chasing mistresses. However, his chronic gambling mania periodically surged, at least until April 1871 when he stopped playing the tables. He had had a dream in which his father told him to stop.[27]

During July and most of August 1867, Dostoyevsky, who disliked *Smoke* intensely, was in Baden-Baden losing on the tables. To settle his debts, Anna even had to pawn her wedding ring and clothes.

Dostoyevsky still owed Turgenev the 50 thalers. Courtesy demanded that the borrower call on the creditor.[28] This meeting was unlikely to go smoothly, because Dostoyevsky regarded Turgenev as one of those 'drones and sluggards who spend their idle lives abroad, in summer at the waters and in winter in Paris'.[29] Moreover, Turgenev represented Russian liberalism, which he considered to be not so much an attack on the existing order of things as an attack on the very essence of things: not so much an attack on the Russian political system, but on Russia itself. In Dostoyevsky's view, liberals such as Turgenev not only derided Russia for its failures but delighted in them. 'He hates and beats his own Mother', Dostoyevsky thought.

The courtesy visit to Turgenev in his villa took place about a week after Dostoyevsky's arrival. An episode in Dostoyevsky's *The Devils* is based on this meeting, and we will draw on this, with two important caveats. First of all, abbreviation dilutes the devastating character assassination so successfully achieved by the author. Secondly, the caricature comes from a novel. It is fictitious, at least insofar as the detail is concerned. Yet, for us, the meeting and the caricature of Karmazinov which follows usefully illustrate how Turgenev was perceived by his many foes. It shows what a contentious figure he had become, not least because Pauline was his muse; it also shows the complex which Dostoyevsky had, not surprisingly, developed from life's experience.

Dostoyevsky would have us think that when he arrived at the villa, Turgenev was eating his morning cutlet, and being served by a footman who was turned out in a frock coat, soft, noiseless boots and gloves. Turgenev rose, wiped his mouth with a napkin. With a blissful expression he came to exchange kisses with Dostoyevsky, 'in the way Russians do, if they are very famous'. Both their cheeks just touched lightly.

We are led to believe that Turgenev sat down on the sofa and charmingly indicated an armchair in which his uncouth visitor proceeded to sprawl. Turgenev at last offered him something to eat, some lunch. The offer was made with that air which implied that Turgenev expected a polite refusal. When his visitor, however, assented, 'a shade of offended surprise darkened the face of the host, but only for an instant'. Turgenev rang nervously for the servant. 'In spite of all his breeding, he raised his voice scornfully as he ordered a second lunch to be served. "What will you have, a cutlet or coffee?" he asked.' 'A cutlet and coffee', Dostoyevsky answered. 'Tell him to bring some more wine; I'm starving.'

Turgenev was wearing a wadded jacket with pearl buttons. Although it was warm in the room, Turgenev's knees were covered by a rug which trailed to the floor. Seeing this, his visitor asked if he was unwell. 'No, not unwell, but I'm afraid of being so in this climate', answered Turgenev in his shrill voice, with its agreeable aristocratic lisp.[30]

So much, apart from the shrill voice, is fiction. In reality, when the conversation turned to Turgenev's views on Russia and his admiration of Germany, it became heated. Dostoyevsky advised Turgenev to acquire a telescope with which, from Germany, he could observe what was going on in his distant motherland. Turgenev blew up. When Dostoyevsky said that the Germans were thieves and scoundrels, Turgenev apparently responded that he regarded himself now as a German and found Dostoyevsky's remarks offensive. Still, they parted courteously.[31]

Dostoyevsky's Later Life

Anna, Dostoyevsky's second wife, had considerable business ability and was his salvation. On his return to Russia in July 1871, she persuaded his creditors that their interest lay in him having a steady income, rather than languishing in a debtor's prison. By 1881, his debt was paid off. Anna started publishing *The Devils* from home. She undertook the administration and eventually she ran a small mail order business. With the sole aid of an errand boy, they produced a magazine. In May 1878, one of their sons suddenly died; Dostoyevsky was devastated. He went on a pilgrimage to the Optina Pustyn' monastery. This provided the model for *The Brothers Karamazov* which was a tremendous success.[32] He died in St Petersburg on 9 February 1881.

Convention required Turgenev to return the call. However, he arranged for his card to be delivered when Dostoyevsky was still in bed. When Dostoyevsky was at the station leaving for Switzerland they saw, but did not acknowledge, each other.[33]

Dostoyevsky told the story of the lunchtime meeting in a letter, extracts from which found their way to a historical journal. When Turgenev heard of this, he was concerned that Dostoyevsky might be wishing to get him into trouble with the Russian authorities. He wrote to the editor giving his account of what had taken place at the meeting and saying that he was sure that Dostoyevsky had gone mad.[34]

Dostoyevsky's *The Devils*, or *The Possessed* as the novel was sometimes called, which was published four years after the meeting, continues its unmerciful personal attack on Turgenev in the character of Karmazinov, a 'vain, spoilt, gentleman who was so offensively unapproachable to all but the elect'. Karmazinov has been living in Karlsruhe, a few miles from Baden-Baden, for the last seven years, taking an interest in the water treatment facilities which he thought more important than Mother Russia.[35]

The setting for Dostoyevsky's attack on Turgenev is a ridiculous, yet fictional, charity fête which is being organised by the wife of the provincial governor in aid of the governesses of the province. The event was to start with a literary matinée and end with a ball.[36]

At the literary matinée Turgenev, alias Karmazinov, 'the cleverest man in Russia', 'the great literary genius',[37] is going to read one of his latest 'most exquisite literary inspirations', called *Merci.* This is a send-up of Turgenev's extremely depressing 'Enough'. In this short story of fifteen pages, subtitled 'Fragment from the Diary of a Dead Artist', the superfluous artist folds 'his useless arms on his empty breast to preserve the last, the sole merit which is accessible to him, the merit of recognising his own insignificance'. It concludes 'No … no … It is enough … enough … enough … The rest is silence.'[38]

Dostoyevsky's story of the matinée is littered with dry humour. Echoes of it are heard today. There was a concern that the food was going to absorb the budget and there would be nothing left for the governesses. All that the attendees actually wanted was a large quantity of free refreshment. To increase the subscriptions, it was rumoured that Mr Karmazinov might read his *Merci* in the costume of a governess.[39]

The reading itself dragged on for a whole hour and was an utter disaster. Dostoyevsky suggests that it would have saved the situation if Karmazinov had 'read a short tale such has he had written in the past, overelaborate, that is, and affected, but sometimes witty'. But no! We hear how he delivered a pompous oration which would have stupified even a St Petersburg audience. The first part was read with a sort of 'melancholy condescension. The subject? God knows! The most pretentious piffle. Even the leading intellects of the province could not make head or tail of it. They listened to the second part simply out of politeness.'[40]

Karmazinov, with his shrill, somewhat feminine and honeyed voice, began his reading. With 'the affected lisp of a born gentleman', he talked about his first kiss. 'Those kisses were somehow different from those of ordinary mortals. There were always some gorse bushes nearby with fancy botanical names. The tree under which the couple sat was of an orange colour, and the sky was tinted with purple, such as no mortal had ever seen.'[41]

The sarcastic Dostoyevsky then satirises the style of Turgenev's 'Phantoms', an erotic fantasy, a dream whose narrator is improbably and suddenly transported to Rome, to Paris, even to the Blackgang Chine in the rugged cliffside of the Isle of Wight which Turgenev knew from his summer holiday there.[42] Dostoyevsky also takes his Karmazinov to Germany where, suddenly, he beholds Pompey – or maybe it's Cassius? – on the eve of battle. 'A wood-nymph then squeaks in the bushes. Gluck plays a violin among the rushes.' But the scene again changes completely. The great genius is crossing the Volga in a thaw. On he drones. The genius falls through the ice. You imagine that he was drowned? No chance. Karmazinov just wrote this so that 'at his last gasp, he might catch sight of a bit of ice the size of a pea, but pure and crystal as a frozen tear, in which Germany, no, the sky of Germany, was reflected.'[43] It is absurd, and meant to be.

Thus, Mr Karmazinov, that is Turgenev in Dostoyevsky's fictional account, 'made a perfect ass of himself'. Despite some heckling, 'he went on lisping, mumbling and appealing to the audience to applaud him'. 'Praise me, praise me more and more, I like it enormously',[44] he declared.

This merciless stuff is more than just light relief. The episode is deliberately comic, almost in a Shakespearian way, to contrast with the sickening crescendo of violence depicted in the rest of the book, where everything is nasty. We read about theft, cold-blooded murder, a town fire, childbirth, the lynching of a beautiful rich 'radiant, carelessly gay and happy'[45] girl. The stage is littered with bodies at the end. It is horrifying; the author would have made it worse. When the novel was being serialised, the publisher refused to include some text about the rape of an eleven-year-old child who commits suicide. Her violator, aware of what she is doing, makes no attempt to save her.[46]

Dostoyevsky in *The Devils* grimly anticipates revolution. However, his message is positive. Russia will be great; first, however, there must be a great bloodletting catharsis. 'One or two generations of vice are essential now. Monstrous, abject vice by which man is transformed into a loathsome, cruel and selfish wretch – that's what we need! And, what is more, a little 'fresh blood' so that we may get accustomed to it.'[47]

'Well, there will be an upheaval such as the world has never seen before. Russia will be overwhelmed with darkness, and the earth will weep for its old gods.'[48] As with the Gadarene swine in the Bible,[49] these devils would enter us in the same way as they entered the pigs. Raving and possessed, we shall rush headlong from the cliffs into the sea. 'It will serve us damn well right, for that is all that we are fit for. We shall all be drowned. But the sick man will be healed and sit at the feet of Jesus, and gaze on him with amazement'.[50]

Turgenev, of course, continued to deny the slander implicit in the character of Karmazinov. To a friend, he wrote that Dostoyevsky came to see him, not to repay his loan, but to abuse him about *Smoke* which he thought should be burnt by the public executioner. He repeated that he had not the slightest doubt that Dostoyevsky had gone completely off his head.

There was a real-life sequel to Karmazinov. In the summer of 1880, Turgenev and Dostoyevsky attended the unveiling of the Pushkin Memorial, then at the Tver Barrier, now the centre of Moscow. Tolstoy wisely declined the invitation, although Turgenev had been to Tolstoy's estate Yasnaya Polyana in order to try to persuade him to attend.[51]

Many famous foreign writers were invited to the ceremonies. Alfred Tennyson, the English Poet Laureate, sent a message of regret. Turgenev, on behalf of the organising committee, also wrote to ask George Eliot to come. He recognised that she would be unable to accept. He seemed mainly interested in having a telegram from her to read out at the formal dinner.[52] Turgenev took along to the ceremonies one of his most priceless possessions, Pushkin's signet ring.*[53]

Sensing that there might be some row between Slavophiles and Westerners, window space overlooking the monument was priced at up to 50 roubles a seat. The ceremony went off relatively quietly, as did the church service and the readings at the University, where Dostoyevsky was worried that a claque had been organised to support Turgenev.

*Pushkin's signet ring, with its cornelian stone and motto 'Simkha son of the esteemed Rabbi Joseph the Elder of blessed memory' had been given to Turgenev by the son of Pushkin's precursor, the poet Zhukovsky. Although donated to Russia by Pauline after Turgenev's death, it has since been lost.

The climax came at the Hall of the Nobility, the location in years to come of the Stalinist show trials. Turgenev's speech was well received, although Dostoyevsky did not like it. He felt that although gushing, Turgenev had not gushed enough.

The audience became almost hysterical about Dostoyevsky's own speech which was 'more emotional and less scholarly'.[54] It largely centred on *Eugene Onegin*, 'that immortal and unequalled poem'.[55] One Dostoyevsky biographer has said that rarely has a national inferiority complex been clothed in rhetoric so splendid. It is 'a compelling yet deplorable document'.[56] His peroration, implicitly if not explicitly critical of Turgenev, was: 'Pushkin sounds a belief in the Russian character, in its spiritual might. If there is belief, there is hope also, the great hope for the people of Russia.'[57] The applause was overwhelming.

Early in the speech, Dostoyevsky said that Tatyana, the girl jilted by Eugene Onegin, was the apotheosis of the Russian woman. Never had so beautiful or positive a type of Russian woman been created, save perhaps for Liza in Turgenev's *Nest of the Gentry*.[58] With this, Turgenev, supremely Karmazinov-like, is said to have blown him a kiss across the hall.[59]

The two embraced on the stage. Seven months later, Dostoyevsky died.

CHAPTER 23

Escape

All the fun and games in the operettas at Baden-Baden lasted only a few years. We return now to the end of June 1870, when the graceful life was suddenly interrupted by the Franco-Prussian War. The Viardots escaped to London. Although the armistice at the end of the following January brought the war to a close, the revolutionary Paris Commune supervened. For a few months while this lasted, the outlook got no better. By then, the Viardots were among a congregation of French émigrés, which included Gounod, who sought asylum in London.

Turgenev had predicted the beginning of the end of the Second Empire over three years earlier in early 1867. He thought that, once the Great Exhibition was over, if the Emperor wanted to keep his throne he would have to do something desperate. Turgenev expected the reactionary régime to go to war against Prussia, the symbol of progress. He thought that the Russians, surprisingly for them, would be wholly on the side of the Prussians.[1]

But for many, the Second Empire seemed stable and unshakeable. And on 30 June 1870, the French premier felt sufficiently confident to announce that 'at no epoch was the peace of Europe more assured'. However, as a British premier later explained, 'A week is a long time in politics'.[2]

A couple of days after the French premier's claim, the Spanish military government offered the rickety Spanish throne to a German prince. This was the latest development in Spanish turbulence which dated back to the time of Louis Viardot's 'national service'. France, which was already concerned about the growing strength of Prussia, did not want to be surrounded by Germans. The French government insisted that the Prince should refuse to accept the throne. Instead of allowing the Prussians to withdraw gracefully, which they seemed prepared to do, the French foreign minister cabled to his ambassador instructing him to demand a formal guarantee that Prussia would not seek to appoint its candidate.

On 13 July, the King of Prussia received the ambassador in Bad Ems, a spa on the Rhine which was frequented by Offenbach and Dostoyevsky. Pauline's acquaintance refused the demand and forwarded it by telegram to his chancellor, Bismarck. Having suitably strengthened the wording, Bismarck gave the provocative document to the press. There was German outrage at the French arrogance. Two days later, France declared war with the intention of giving the Prussians a thrashing. The Franco-Prussian War began. 'À Berlin', shouted the French. Their premier, who was also Liszt's son-in-law, said that he entered the war 'with a light heart'.[3]

The French were the largest contingent in Baden-Baden. Suddenly, within a few days, they found themselves cast as the enemy. There was chaos and panic. The station was besieged by people wanting to leave. On 17 July, a rumour spread that the French, who won some immediate military successes, were about to break through from Strasbourg to Baden. Pauline sent the children some twenty miles eastwards through the Black Forest to Wildbad; Louis, in a rage, shut himself up in his room. Pauline's 49th birthday on 18 July, normally a day for much celebration, was a sombre event. It was only a year since Brahms had led his early morning serenade.[4]

Louis-Napoléon's successes in his wars against the Austrians in Italy had promoted a sense of complacency. Empress Eugénie sent him off to the north-east of France, saying 'Louis, fais bien ton devoir', 'do your duty'.[5] However, the Prussians were much more efficient than the French. They had a better fighting force. The Emperor, with his 39 generals, 2,700 officers and 84,000 men, was surrounded at Sedan in the Ardennes. On the afternoon of 1 September, the whole lot capitulated.[6] It was a humiliation from which France has never quite recovered.

The Parisians expected the Prussians to besiege their city imminently. By 5 September, King Wilhelm was at Rheims. Ten days after that, the encircling movement around the fortifications of Paris began. Two days later, Prussian guns were trained over the city. Paris then was a formidable place to besiege. It was surrounded by a wall, 30 feet high with a moat 10 feet wide, along ground which is only too familiar to those who today find themselves making their way around the boulevard Péripherique. Beyond, at a distance of 1–3 miles, there then lay a chain of sixteen powerful forts which filled out a circumference of 40 miles. One of these, which guarded the city's western approaches, was perched on Mont Valérien overlooking Paris,[7] and was close to Gounod's country home at Saint-Cloud.

The city held out through a freezing winter. Early in October, the residents began to eat horsemeat, which had been introduced by Parisian butchers a few years earlier as cheap provender for the poor. By mid-November, they had begun to eat cats, dogs and rats. According to one contemporary American calculation, 65,000 horses, 5,000 cats and 1,200 dogs, but only 300 rats, were eaten during the whole siege.[8]

Fear of the consequences deterred the French government from recognising that defeat was inevitable. Eventually, on 28 January 1871, Paris capitulated and the siege of around 130 days was over.[9] Meanwhile, at Versailles, Bismarck had seized the opportunity to have Pauline's acquaintance proclaimed Kaiser.

The outlook in Paris went from bad to worse. Soon after the German victory parade on 1 March, the city erupted. This insurrection was to be known as the Paris Commune. The government decamped to Versailles, and Paris was again besieged, this time by Frenchmen. Turgenev, in Russia, was appalled, and feared that France would become like Mexico or be partitioned like Poland.[10]

A couple of months later, on 21 May, government troops got through an unguarded gate. Barricades went up. As the government forces passed inwards, the retreating Communards set the city on fire. The Archbishop of Paris, the second such to die in upheavals in Paris during the 19th century, was murdered with other hostages. On Whitsunday morning, 28 May, when the Archbishop's corpse was found, 147 men were taken to Père Lachaise cemetery and shot. The retribution was severe. Anyone with a gun was shot. Anyone with blackened hands was assumed to have been involved in incendiary operations and shot. In this 'semaine sanglante',

20,000 citizens were killed. In London, *The Times* recorded: 'So far as we can recollect, there has been nothing like it in history'.[11]

Apart from the siege of Paris, the main theatre of the Franco-Prussian War was in Alsace and Lorraine, in the north-east, on the border with Germany. The chief town[12] in Alsace is Strasbourg,* which is only around 40 miles from Baden-Baden. During the early part of the war, the cannon fire could be heard from Baden-Baden.[14]

Pauline was no admirer of Napoleon III. Like Turgenev and Brahms, she supported the Germans.[15] For Turgenev, the war represented 'civilisation against the barbarians. Bonapartism must be shown the errors of its ways.' He was delighted 'to witness the plunge into the sewer of that wretched scum and his cronies'. When the Prussians allowed Napoleon to retire to England, Turgenev wondered why they were being so lenient 'with the creature'. The ex-Emperor deserved to be sent to Cayenne and 'be eaten alive by the lice'.[16]

At first, the Viardots tried to stay in Baden-Baden. Pauline and her girls joined in the charitable groups which provided clothes for the war-wounded and so forth. However, it comes as no surprise that Pauline, a French national, found herself in an increasingly difficult position. Indeed, life for French residents in Baden-Baden had become tricky even before the conflict began. Outside the Viardots' house, there were demonstrations and a certain amount of cat-calling. Turgenev's enthusiasm for the Germans waned when he saw their bellicose attitude; besides, his son-in-law, Paulinette's husband, was financially ruined by the war.[17]

Soon, Pauline and her family thought it best to escape to London. Turgenev took Pauline and the two girls to Ostend, where he waved them off on 21 October before returning to his villa. Louis stayed put for another three weeks, then he and Turgenev set off to London. For the moment, Paul remained behind with Louis's sister, the neurotic, sanctimonious, amusingly dull Aunt Berthe.[18]

Turgenev later returned to the deserted resort. From there he sent the

*Strasbourg is around 100 miles from Metz (in Lorraine), which is 90 miles from Sedan, almost in a straight line. Although Sedan fell at the beginning of September 1870, Strasbourg held out until the end of the month and Metz until the end of October.[13]

Viardots news of servants, dogs and Berthe.[19] He then went to Berlin on his way to Russia.

Sentiment in the Prussian capital naturally turned against a prominent Frenchwoman such as Pauline. This was despite the fact that, less than a month before the war broke out, Turgenev told Pauline that he had heard that the Queen of Prussia 'loved her greatly'.[20]

'There was something terrible in an arrival in London. The dusky, smoky, far-arching vault of the station, the strange, livid light, the dense dark, pushing crowd' must have seemed an awful contrast to leafy, provincial Baden-Baden. On their arrival in London, the Viardots lodged in Seymour Street and subsequently at 30 Devonshire Place.[21] Many French émigrés and distinguished acquaintances, such as Saint-Saëns, Gounod and Louis Blanc, congregated in London.

'The street-lamps, in the thick, brown air, looked weak and red in the gathering dusk in the London streets – the hurrying cabs, the lighted shops, the flaring stalls, the dark, shining dampness of everything.' London, with its 'dingy dignities', was still shrouded in the 'national aroma' of 'fog and beer and soot'. It still seemed inhospitable.[22] However, it was rather different at this time from the city of *Oliver Twist*, where Pauline had first performed some three decades earlier. The Thames was no longer the open sewer it used to be. Thirty-seven acres had been reclaimed to create the Victoria Embankment; and the world's first underground line had been opened between Paddington and Kings Cross stations in January 1863. At the time when the French refugees arrived, the District Line from South Kensington was being extended from Blackfriars to Mansion House under the newly created Queen Victoria Street. Yet the massive construction works were nothing like on the scale of the systematic clearance and rebuilding by which Baron Haussmann, the prefect of the Seine, had transformed Paris into a showcase for the Imperial régime. There, 20,000 houses had been demolished and 40,000 new ones built.[23]

London was becoming much more like the city we recognise today. However, there was still the most appalling filth and wretchedness. A French historian and humanist said that the area around the London Docks, the Canary Wharf of today, was far worse than the poor quarters of Marseilles and Paris.[24]

It was a difficult and tough time for the Viardots. The refugees' first predicament was financial. Like others in their situation, they were short of cash; the Viardots' property was tied up in Baden-Baden and France. Turgenev arranged the sale of one of Louis's Rembrandts to a Russian Grand-Duchess. Pauline's brother Manuel, who lived in London, was able to help a bit and find pupils. Clara Schumann told Brahms that she nearly broke into tears when she saw Pauline 'teaching third-rate pupils in shabby London lodgings'.[25] Pauline had indeed fallen from a pinnacle.

However, Pauline was not reduced to doing the housework. She had a cook, a governess and two housemaids on her staff. Had she wanted to, she could have taken up the Rubinstein brothers' separate offers* to work at the Moscow and St Petersburg Conservatoires. Instead, she stayed in England where she took part in concerts and oratorio. She also gave her lessons, dreary work. Her financial predicament must have been particularly worrying at her age, because her revenue-earning potential was now severely limited. Her health was affected. We hear that she had difficulty shaking off some catarrh which she developed; this occasionally stopped her singing. Some of her concerts, such as one in March in Liverpool, were less than successful, although a concert in Manchester went well.[26]

The Viardots had some good friends in London, such as Henry Chorley, the music critic. Somehow, Pauline managed to resume her salons which were held on Saturday evenings. She even managed to put on a production of *Le Dernier sorcier* in 30 Devonshire Place in mid-February. This was attended by George Eliot, Robert Browning, Charles Gounod, the highly admired painter Frederic Leighton and Manuel, Pauline's brother. Other luminaries who attended the salons were the Pre-Raphaelite painters Edward Burne-Jones, Dante Gabriel Rossetti and Ford Madox Brown. At one of George Eliot's Sunday lunches, which went on until 6pm, Pauline sang 'divinely'.[27] Dickens they could not see: he was in Westminster Abbey, 'the great Valhalla by the Thames'.[28] He had died on 9 June 1870, a few weeks before the political events which gave rise directly to the war. He was only in his 58th year, but was exhausted by his travelling and lecturing.[29]

Paul was installed at a school in Regent's Park. The normal routine had been for the whole Viardot ménage, including Turgenev, to move to

*They offered her 5,000 roubles for the seven months of the winter. She could have supplemented this with lessons at 25 roubles per hour. At that time, the petite Adelina Patti, five foot tall, but possibly the highest opera earner of the century, was earning 40,000 roubles in Moscow.

Karlruhe in the off-season, so that Claudie could study painting and Paul could go to school there. The carefully manicured boys in north London found their new colleague from Karlsruhe somewhat unkempt. Yet Paul learnt to play cricket on Primrose Hill. He also discovered that idleness was not to be tolerated and could lead to a sharp rap on the knuckles from the headmaster. Even if young Viardot and young Carvalho were not in the first eleven, they were the undisputed stars in the school play. Some after-hours coaching from their mothers saw to that.[30]

Paul

Turgenev, being Russian, could easily have remained in Baden-Baden. However, he had to follow his muse. In March he made a trip to Russia, where he gave readings similar to those which Dickens used to give with such financial success. After his return in April, he settled in 16 Beaumont Street, Marylebone.[31] In fact, his life was centred at the Viardots' residence in Devonshire Place.

Turgenev was able to help, particularly with the children. He looked for a publisher for Pauline's next volume of songs, although he secretly paid for them to be published himself.[32] There was even a false rumour that Pauline had died. 'I've just written to Turgenev. He must be shattered',[33] George Sand told a friend. Premature deaths, or at least the reporting of them, seem to have been a frequent occurrence. Nine months later, Turgenev himself found that Chorley had published an obituary of him.[34] Ironically, Chorley himself, sad and lonely, was about to die.

One of the casualties of the Franco-Prussian War was Dr Frisson who was still trying to dispose of bits of Courtavenel. The area around the estate was overrun by soldiers from Bavaria and Württemberg who at first were welcomed by some as liberators. Frisson, however, led a resistance movement. Irregulars bearing arms were automatically condemned to death.[35]

There is a tale that on his way to his prison Frisson managed to get a message, hidden in a hollowed-out apple, to Pauline who went to the Prussian Queen and pleaded for his life. However, given the nature of communications at the time, it is improbable that there would have been sufficient time to organise this before the doctor was despatched. He somehow obtained his freedom; he then supported the Commune. After its fall, he had to escape to the north and to England. He was allowed back under various amnesties, but died in 1882.[36]

Among the war refugees in London was Gounod. Wounds are healed by the passage of time and by the need to pull together in adversity. The Gounod and Viardot families became friends again and visited each other. Gounod gave some help to Paul.[37] We need to catch up with the story of this chameleon-like composer, in the intervening years.

Gounod's father-in-law died shortly after his marriage to Anna, the wedding which, for the Viardots, had been so contentious. The happy couple were fortunate to inherit the Zimmermanns' country house at Saint-Cloud in the former parc de Montretout, near the château which the brother of Louis XIV had built for himself.[38] Even if *Sapho* had been unfortunate, Gounod had now married an heiress and fallen on his feet.

Gounod had learnt that there were more fruitful sources of money than antique subjects such as *Sapho* and *Ulysse*. 'Ambition forced him to ignore both taste and refinement'. In 1852, he was offered Scribe's libretto of *La Nonne sanglante* which, despite its appealing title, had already been hawked around seven composers. Gounod's setting was a success at the box-office. That it ran only for eleven performances was attributable to the disruption caused by a change of directorship at the Opéra rather than to the failure of the work. Meanwhile, Gounod's strengths as a master of religious music were demonstrated by the *Messe solennelle de Sainte-Cécile*, which was first performed in November 1855.[39]

Gounod wrote an opera based on Molière's play *Le Bourgeois gentilhomme*. He planned to write a 'Faust' which Léon Carvalho was prepared to stage. However, a Faust with music was about to be put on by another impresario, so Carvalho asked Gounod to defer his version. He asked him first to write an opera based on the story in another of Molière's plays, *Le Médecin malgré lui*.

Gounod's *Faust* was premièred in January 1858. Caroline Miolan-Carvalho sang Marguerite and also took the lead in Gounod's *Mireille* and in his *Roméo et Juliette* in 1864 and 1867 respectively.[40]

Gounod in old age

In these operas, Gounod presented the Paris public with something new; a lighter and brighter style, more intimate and poetic than the grandiose operas of Meyerbeer, with their massive staging.[41] Caroline – who a respected composer described as Léon's 'terrible wife, Oh! Yes, terrible' – was a singer of doubtful taste. Adored by her fans, she contentedly mutilated the music of composers such as Mozart,[42] but fitted ideally into Gounod's roles.

Gounod's formula was a great success. *Faust* ran for 59 performances in its first year. It had a hundred successive performances,[43] and it was soon being performed all over the world. Until the 1940s, when it yielded to Bizet's *Carmen, Faust* was the most popular of all operas in London.[44]

Faust is 'basically a simple love story flavoured with demoniac elements'.[45] We cannot doubt its accessible lyricism and attractiveness to an audience. Even Berlioz was enthusiastic about it. It became Queen Victoria's favourite opera.[46] Empress Eugénie was so enthusiastic that she even suggested that Gounod and she should write a ballet together. This was indeed a most interesting proposition, but sadly nothing came of this partnership.[47]

Gounod's *Ave Maria* of 1859, which became very popular in the salons, also helped his popularity enormously. His 'distinctive blend of piety and hypocrisy, of high thinking and vulgarity, was one that increasingly puzzled the young Bizet', who in the 1860s did hack work for him.[48]

Turgenev, whose musical taste was not always wholly 'reliable',* described Gounod's opera *Mireille* as a 'fiasco'. He thoroughly disliked the first two acts, and said the work represented 'Halévy de 4ème ordre'. Thus, he was rather disconcerted when a cheery Gounod invited him to dinner to discuss the work. One way or another, Gounod must have got the message, as he subsequently revised *Mireille* and cut it down to three acts.[50]

The production of *Roméo et Juliette* in 1867 coincided with the Exposition Universelle. The opera was extremely popular and drew full houses at 90 successive performances. Gounod's other works benefited from its reflected glory, particularly its four duets. *Roméo et Juliette* 'represented a peak of success that Gounod was never to reach again'. Turgenev, perhaps jaundiced by memories of his one-time rival, found it very disappointing.[51]

*For example, Turgenev wrote that Berlioz's opera *Les Troyens à Carthage* was a case of impotence, of a mountain labouring and a little mouse being born; Berlioz only succeeded when he was writing something dreamy, languid, excitable and sensual.[49]

The French government responded to public opinion. Gounod was awarded the Légion d'honneur, he was invited to stay with the Emperor at Compiègne and he was elected to the coveted position of a member of the Institut, the distinguished body which included the most honoured French composers.[52] But popular success is not synonymous with lasting critical acclaim.

Like many celebrities, Gounod had the commercial sense to write his Memoirs early in life. He completed them just after the success of his *Faust*. He could dismiss his earlier failure with *Sapho*. 'A dramatic work always has, or nearly so, all the success that it deserves with the public', the 40-year-old would-be sage observed. 'The author and the public are reciprocally called to instruct each other in matters of Art. The public instructs the author by showing its discernment and approval of the true; and the author teaches the public by initiating it into the elements and conditions of the beautiful'.[53] Even Louis Viardot could not have bettered this pomposity.

Gounod's recognition of the important interaction between commerce and aesthetics was surprisingly perspicacious for someone who was chronically mentally unstable. In 1856, he had a breakdown when out riding at Saint-Cloud. His family sent him to Dr Blanche's fashionable clinic at Passy. 'Poor Gounod's gone mad', observed Berlioz. By mid-October Gounod was back at home at work. In 1863, he had to return to the clinic.[54] His charm and his fluctuations between the sacred and the profane were the two characteristics which he shared with Liszt. However, Liszt,[55] whose stature was immeasurable, was always sane.

At the outbreak of war, Gounod evacuated his family to Varangeville near Dieppe. After this, the Gounods moved to Blackheath near London, at first lodging with a friend of Anna's mother, Mrs Louisa Brown, then at 8 Morden Road, near the railway station. Later, they moved to 9 Park Place, near Regent's Park.[56]

The Gounod house at Saint-Cloud was threatened by the German invasion, so the composer wrote to the Prussian Crown Prince who had been Louise Viardot's childhood playmate. Gounod drew the royal attention to the German roots of his art. The Crown Prince, unaware that, at the same time, the sincere Monsieur Gounod was comparing the Germans graphically to Iron Age barbarians,[57] had his house sealed off. He presumably overlooked the fact that Gounod was the composer of a *Prière pour l'Empéreur et la Famille Impériale*,[58] and *A la Frontière*.

The sealing off of the house in Saint-Cloud did not stop some fierce fighting in the area. On the day after the Kaiser was proclaimed at Versailles in the Hall of Mirrors, a Breton regiment took a stand less than 50 yards from Gounod's front door. Also, the fort at Mont Valérien nearby was the pivotal point during the French Government's attack on the city at the time of the Commune.[59]

The Viardots had really dropped out of Gounod's colourful life. Their re-entry into London coincides with his meeting Mrs Georgina Weldon. This took place at the home of Sir Julius Benedict, the conductor whose hospitality, some 30 years earlier, had been the setting for Liszt's attempt to warn Pauline off her friendship with George Sand.*[60] Now, when the charming Gounod saw Mrs Weldon, he went to the piano and played his song 'A une jeune fille'. Shortly afterwards, he heard her singing Mendelssohn's 'Hear my Prayer' and admired the purity of her voice. The profane and the sacred again.

Gounod had not lost his propensity for being unable to resist a pretty woman or schoolgirl. Age was no impediment. He was 52 and Georgina was 35. Although flamboyant, emotional and passionate, she was however the type of woman who 'acts with a chasteness and propriety as definite as the clang of an iron door barring the way'.[61] It seems that Gounod's relationship with her must have been totally chaste, because even those who assume that Pauline was Turgenev's mistress say that it was.[62]

Indeed, we have to be wary of saying anything untoward about this extraordinary feminist. Georgina thrived on litigation, which her nephew surprisingly attributed to her Welsh temperament. In 1883, at her peak, there were 25 cases of *Weldon v Someone*.[63] A couple of years later, a series was published entitled *The Great Composers*, which recounted some of the scurrilous things that the Paris papers had printed about her friendship

*Benedict was born in Stuttgart, the son of a Jewish banker. He composed the opera *The Lily of Killarney*, which was 'still perhaps sometimes to be heard in provincial towns', according to a view expressed in the middle of the twentieth century.

with Gounod. This led to an action between her and Routledge, the publishers, and W.H. Smith and Son. She was complimented by the Lord Chief Justice for her reasonableness in settling the case on the court room steps for £250 from each of the defendants. However, as she died in 1914, even if her ghost were to rise up it could not now bring an action.[64]

Georgina had been born in Clapham on 24 May 1837. Her father was Morgan Thomas, a rich barrister who preferred to dabble in farming and politics. Her mother, who was musical, lived in Italy where Georgina was brought up. She was presented at court as Georgina Treherne, because her father had by then decided to take the name of an ancestor who fought in the English victory at Crécy in 1346.

When Georgina married the impecunious Harry Weldon, her father cut her off. The Weldons then lived at Beaumaris in Anglesey, although Georgina spent a lot of time in London. 'Throughout the early years of the 1860s, she sang for her supper in the houses of the nobility and appeared publicly in oratorio and operetta.'[65]

Harry was appointed to the ceremonial office of Herald.[66] The Weldons settled at Dickens's old house in Tavistock Square, the fine town house of eighteen rooms with a garden with a mulberry tree in it.[67] Here, Georgina set up her National Training School of Music, a combination of an orphanage and a music school. The house was stocked with 'children, maids, governesses and endless dogs'.[68]

After 'the old man', as Harry Weldon called Gounod, had known Georgina for three months, he became besotted. He moved into the house in Tavistock Square, where she lived. He turned down an offer to become head of the Paris Conservatoire, a most prestigious appointment.[69] Anna Gounod was discarded and sent back to France with Jean, their son.

Not surprisingly, Gounod's mental health continued to be precarious. He took Georgina to Paris to sing *Gallia*, an oratorio which had been premièred at the new Royal Albert Hall for the London International Exhibition of 1871. Georgina's appearance in Paris naturally caused great friction with Anna Gounod, such that Gounod had yet another breakdown.

Back in Tavistock House, Gounod and Georgina had blazing rows. Occasionally he stormed out, regardless of the climate outside. For Gounod, the year 1872 was particularly turbulent. In May of that year, he had a row with the Albert Hall management who were being criticised for promoting a foreign conductor, one tainted with a whiff of scandal. The management was also concerned that Gounod's programmes featured too many of his own works.[70]

The storm got worse. That autumn, Gounod received a writ for libel from Novello, his publishers, who he had accused of having conspired with other publishers. Gounod claimed in the press that they had 'mulcted' him and that the head of Novello, Littleton, had swindled him out of his royalties. It seems that Gounod had been provoked by Novello's publication of his song 'La siesta' with a second-rate English translation, and by his perception, or more likely Georgina's, that she was getting insufficient recognition. Gounod foolishly ignored his counsel's advice and would not retract. The case before Mr Justice Denman and a Special Jury was reported in Novello's journal, *The Musical Times*. The lawyers of course had great fun. Counsel asked Gounod 'Are you by profession a musical composer?' After Gounod replied 'I think I am', the judge interjected 'I know you are'. At the end of Georgina's brief examination, she expostulated 'Why do you not ask me more questions?'. Counsel was brisk: 'I will ask you this question "Will you have the great kindness to step out of the box?"'

Gounod lost. Novellos had suffered little if anything from the libel, so the damages were nominal, £2 plus the costs. Had Georgina not gone into the witness box, the damages would have been £500, according to counsel.[71] Gounod responded like the vehement Mr Samuel Pickwick: 'You may try, and try, and try again, but not one farthing of costs or damages do you ever get from me, if I spend the rest of my existence in a debtor's prison.' Had his mother-in-law Madame Zimmermann not paid up, Gounod also would also have found himself in the Fleet.[72]

Gounod would not let go, and wrote to the Paris *Figaro* insinuating that the plaintiff had dropped the claim. Three months after the hearing, *The Musical Times* printed a notice contradicting this. Gounod was clearly deranged. In March 1874, he became very ill again. He went to convalesce in St Leonards, an English winter watering place on the Channel coast, a London-super-Mare where the seafront and a 'multitude of cheap comforts and conveniences offered a kind of resumé of middle-class English civilisation'.[73] We may wonder what Gounod thought of the 'hand organs and German bands, the nurse-maids and British babies' which adorned the seafront, or what he made of the 'ladies and gentlemen of leisure – looking rather embarrassed with it and trying rather unsuccessfully to get rid of it'. Eventually, Dr Blanche rescued him and fetched him back to his clinic at Passy. There was a happy outcome. In October 1874, Gounod was reconciled with his wife.[74]

The sequel is bizarre. Georgina, who separated from Harry, had relied on Gounod to finance her National Training School. She refused to return Gounod's possessions, but instead sent him a bill for £9,787.5s.9d.[75] This was an enormous amount. Dickens had sold Tavistock House for only 2,000 guineas ten years before. Like all litigation, the case dragged on. In 1884, judgement was given in Georgina's favour for a record sum of £11,640 for secretarial work, board and lodging, and damages for libels.

Georgina dressed up in prison clothes

At the time, Georgina was about to be taken to Newgate for calling Jules Rivière, the French conductor of a ladies' choir which she trained, a fraudulent bankrupt.[76] Georgina had nothing to lose from her litigation: she found the jails conducive to getting on with her role in life, being controversial. When in Holloway, she was soon exchanging photographs with the matron. When she was released after 37 days, she left the jail riding in a barouche with four horses. She apparently led a procession, through Piccadilly to London's Green Park, where resolutions were put and acclaimed by a crowd 'estimated' to number 17,000 people. Everything to do with Georgina was exaggerated.[77]

Because Georgina could not get judgement against Gounod in France, she attempted to seize his United Kingdom royalties. These were substantial. The receipts from the first performance of *Mors et Vita* in August 1885 amounted to £25,000. Three years earlier, Birmingham Festival had offered Gounod £4,000 to conduct the first performance of *La Rédemption.* Georgina was unsuccessful in her attempt to seize the royalties and get paid. However, Gounod could never again appear in England without risking imprisonment. So he could not attend a Royal Command performance of *Mors et Vita.* When his solicitor tried to remonstrate with Georgina, she sent him away telling him not to be so impudent.[78]

Safely back in Paris, Gounod divided his time between his rather ugly house in Saint-Cloud[79] and his newly-constructed, opulent residence, with its grandiose organ room, in 20 Place Malesherbes.*[80] He had an amazing facility to compose. The opera *Cinq-Mars* was completed only 26 days after he received the libretto. It has been said that 'masses, prayers, motets and canticles dripped from him as the rain from heaven'.[81]

Gounod was greatly venerated as 'the incarnation of modern French music', an epithet which seems odd with hindsight. However, his water-coloured lyricism did have a considerable impact on the prominent French composers of the period, such as Bizet and Massenet. His influence on English choral music was also considerable, even if not always beneficial.[82]

*This corner house has been replaced by a modern office block.

Cartoon of old Gounod

Sir Charles Stanford, the distinguished Anglo-Irish musician, averred that Gounod's religious works were 'sufficiently sentimental temporarily to capture the unthinking part of the English public, appealing alike to Catholics, Anglicans and the Salvation Army'.[83] Stanford was at least more polite than his compatriot, the novelist George Moore, who claimed that

Gounod was 'a base soul who went about pouring a kind of bath water melody down the back of every woman he met'.[84]

Gounod gave interviews to the press, contributed to a symposium on the breastfeeding of newborn infants, and occasionally performed music with Pauline. He was irrepressible. But when he was asked why he had not become a priest, he said that he did not think he had the moral strength to take confession from women. Despite the obvious weaknesses in his character, he was devoid of any ill will.[85]

The Viardots and Gounods had indeed patched up their differences. Paul Viardot, who had not been born at the time of Gounod's marriage and the bust-up with the Viardots, was a contemporary and friend of Gounod's son and had fond memories of the old man. Paul was impressed by Gounod's memory and by his immense charm which, like his music, he regarded as spiritual, passionate and mystical.[86]

There was a revival of *Sapho* in spring 1884. Gounod was offered, but did not accept, a million francs to go on tour to the USA.[87] In 1891, after some bronchitis, he suffered from heart trouble and temporary paralysis of one side of his body. He died on 17 October 1893. There was a state funeral at La Madeleine before the burial at Auteuil.

Georgina too had seemed unstoppable. 'The heroine of a hundred legal fights, her name was known from John o'Groats to Lands End.' A letter could reach her with the simple address 'The Mrs Weldon, London'.[88] She had been the subject of an abortive kidnapping attempt at Tavistock House, when some doctors tried to abduct her to a lunatic asylum. As a consequence of this episode which was straight out of, even inspired by, Wilkie Collin's *The Woman in White*, she took up the cause of lunacy reform.[89] She also acted in plays aimed at promoting the cause of feminism. Indeed, it has been claimed that that her advocacy of the restitution of conjugal rights led to the

Married Woman's Property Act 1882, which enabled a married woman to retain and exercise her own rights over her property.[90]

A less contentious cause was Pears Soap. She appeared in an advertisement for this product with the caption: 'I am 50 today but thanks to Pears soap my complexion is only 17.' Nowadays, she would presumably sell treatments for the avoidance of wrinkles.

Surely, this was a bizarre twist to the life of the composer who Pauline had promoted, with *Sapho,* all those years ago.

CHAPTER 24

The Nest in Paris

The disruption in Paris caused by the Franco-Prussian War and the Commune only lasted nine months. The Government forces defeated the Commune and repressed it with great brutality. During June 1871, the situation began to settle down surprisingly quickly. The Viardots left England at the end of July, and Turgenev accompanied them back to France. Shortly afterwards, he went back to London and on to Edinburgh for the centenary of Sir Walter Scott's birth. The Viardots had a short holiday in Boulogne; from there, they returned to Baden-Baden. However, they no longer found themselves welcome. The gossips spread it about that, during the war, Pauline had slandered the Baden family and Prussian royalty.[1]

When in Scotland, Turgenev went grouse shooting. His efforts were not entirely successful. He missed his first nine birds and, with 50 shots, only killed 22. However, the lunch was excellent and he had a good time on the moors. Robert Browning was there at the time. Turgenev did not like him. He found his handshake to be like an electric shock. He also considered the very successful poet to be a self-satisfied bore.[2] Browning was indeed curious, and has been called 'one of the most difficult poets to assess'. The American-born novelist Henry James described him as 'a poet without a lyre', and when Browning was buried in Westminster Abbey, he commented that although he could be found where a good many oddities and great writers were entombed, 'none of the odd ones have been so great and none of the great ones so odd'.[3]

After his Scottish visit, Turgenev joined the Viardots in Baden-Baden where they were selling up. Turgenev was keen that the property be sold. Fortunately, Baden had not been overrun as feared, so Louis's valuable pictures by Velasquez, Guardi and Ribera, were unharmed, as was the organ. However, the villa was sold at a great loss compared to the money which had been invested in it.[4]

The Viardots returned to Paris, 'that city of aimless prattling, of trivial cares and innumerable handshakes',[5] and set themselves up in their house in the rue de Douai. Pauline taught and resumed her twice weekly salons. We can picture her from the description by Henry James who was visiting Paris in 1875. She was 'a most fascinating and interesting woman, ugly, yet also very handsome, or, in the French sense, *très-belle*'.[6] She made occasional concert appearances. She entered into the musical life of the capital which saw a flowering of music in the period after the war.[7] We think of the works of Saint-Saëns, Lalo, D'Indy, Chabrier and Dukas, and of the Concerts Colonne and Lamoureux. We think of the songs of Duparc, Debussy and Fauré.

In 1870–71, Turgenev wrote a novella, *Spring Torrents.* There is not much in this about the Russian social issues which so obsessed his contemporaries. However, there is much that seems to touch on his relationship with Pauline, sufficiently so that he departed from his usual practice of showing works in advance to her.[8] The story is about a middle-aged man, Sanin, who recalled a youthful romance with Gemma, an Italian girl whose mother ran a pastry shop in Frankfurt. He fought a duel on Gemma's behalf and they became engaged. Before he could marry her, he needed to raise money by selling his Russian estates. He encountered a former schoolfriend who suggested an alternative. Maria Nikolayevna, his fascinating nouveau riche wife, would oblige by making him a loan. And oblige she did.

The debtor and creditor went on a wild, erotic and improbably fantastic ride into the mountains. At one stage, she twisted his hair with all ten fingers, in a manner reminiscent of the maid who had seduced Turgenev when a teenager.[9] 'She stood erect and smiled triumphantly. Her eyes glared fiercely, sated with success. The hawk with its talons dug into a captured bird has such eyes.'[10] 'I will go wherever you go, and I will stay with you until you drive me away', Sanin declared. In *Smoke*, the predatress wanted to take her conquest back to St Petersburg as a toyboy.[11] Here, in *Spring Torrents*, Maria Nikolayevna whisked Sanin, who represented just another of her conquests and chattels, away to Paris.

Yet again, Turgenev describes how sex enslaves a man. He portrays its destructive force. Happy, lasting, mutual love seems, to him, but an illusion.[12]

In the rue de Douai, the Viardots occupied the ground floor, the drawing-room, the dining-room. The organ, with its roundel on which Pauline was depicted as Saint Cecilia, was returned to the music room. Louis's pictures were hung in the picture gallery. He continued to add to his collection. One, a nude, was hidden behind a curtain for the sake of decency. Turgenev also made acquisitions. He bought a picture of a nude entitled *La Courtisane*. He renamed it *La Charmeuse*.[13]

The Viardots were surrounded by exceptional talent. The painter Edgar Degas, who today we remember especially for his pictures of ballet dancers, lived nearby, as did Paulinette's piano teacher Georges Bizet, the composer of *Carmen*. Not far away was the apartment in which Bizet's father-in-law Fromental Halévy, the composer of *La Juive*, had lived. Near there, Gounod also resided until he moved to the Place Malesherbes.[14]

Up the hill of Montmartre, the foundation stone for the basilica of Sacré-Coeur, the city's expiation for the Commune, was laid in June 1875. Horses and carts dragged materials up the hill, from which many of the old windmills were removed. The construction was slow and continued throughout the remainder of the Viardots' residence in the rue de Douai. The blessing of the dome cross only took place at the turn of the century. The Basilica was finally consecrated after the Great War, in 1919.[15]

In August 1871, Turgenev wrote to the Viardots asking if they had any 'chambres à louer', since these might be less expensive for him than a hotel.[16] The answer was 'Oui'. So, from November of that year, Turgenev created a small apartment for himself on the top floor of the house, with his bedroom, studio and library. When he was at home, he dined with the Viardots. Despite the terms of his approach, according to Louise, Turgenev never contributed to the expenses of the house. This seems surprising as the Viardots' financial circumstances are thought to have become relatively straitened at this time. Although Paris attracted masses of aspiring singers prepared to pay for lessons, the income from Pauline's teaching seems to have been modest. In any case, it was far less than she had earned in her heyday.[17]

Louise's comment was churlish, because Turgenev was devoted to the family and supported them in many ways, personally and financially. He would sometimes leave a dinner party because his 'ladies' needed escorting to the opera or the theatre. He would refuse invitations so as not to miss an evening with them, perhaps reading or playing cards. He was keen to provide a dowry for Didie, 'Chère, bien-aimée et adorée Didie de mon coeur'.[18] He wrote many letters to her, some of which, when it comes to expressions of endearment, compete with those which he wrote to her mother. He began to put aside capital for the dowry in the summer of 1868, and by March 1871, he had accumulated the considerable sum of 80,000 francs[19] of which around a fifth was invested in Russian railway stock. Louis, whose sense of patriotism may have been eclipsing his normal financial prudence, thought it might be appropriate to invest some with the French government who were borrowing heavily to pay the enormous indemnity owed to the Prussians under the terms of the peace. Turgenev sensibly advised caution on this.[20]

Meanwhile, it would be wholly wrong to imagine that Louis was parked away on a chair in a corner of the house in the rue de Douai. He went out shooting and sent his trophies to friends such as George Sand.[21] His literary activities continued apace. He was commissioned to write two books on sculpture and paintings. These, he said, constituted a distillation of his five-volume series *Musées d'Europe*, which were then available in their third edition at 3 francs 50 cents each. However, the new books, which were illustrated with wood engravings, provided something to read at home, whereas the earlier publications were more suitable for the traveller. His books display the immense breadth of his knowledge, and also show that, when he had been with Pauline on tour, he had been to all the significant art galleries and collections, from Windsor to St Petersburg.

Les Merveilles de la Sculpture was translated into English and published in 1873 in the *Illustrated Library of Wonders* series. The translator feels bound to apologise for Louis's attitude to England, where he can find no single work worth mentioning by a native sculptor.[22] 'In mourning over our short-comings, and ridiculing our public monuments', moaned the translator, 'the author has omitted to mention the works of Gibson, Bailey, Mac-Dowell, Foley, Bell, Marshall, Woolner, and other equally eminent sculptors'.[23] In a book which starts with ancient Egypt, this may seem pardonable, but Louis could have desisted from regurgitating the description of the Hyde Park Corner statue of the Duke of Wellington, no hero for the French, as 'Punch mounted on Balaam's ass'.[24] Modern English sculpture is insignificant, according to Louis, whereas modern French sculpture is in the first rank among nations.

Much the same sentiments pervade *Les Merveilles de la Peinture*. The first volume of this was published in London as *Wonders of Italian Art*, the second as *Wonders of European Art*. These titles facilitate the omission of the chapter on the English school, about which the translator suggests a volume may follow subsequently. This was wishful thinking: in the French version, Louis wrings his hands and says that, despite all his ties of affection for England, he can find no such thing as an English school.[25] There were some portrait painters such as Reynolds and Gainsborough, and there was Turner about whom Louis was ambivalent. For him, the English are best in watercolour. Even Landseer's dogs and stags are preferable in the black and white engravings in which they are popularised rather than in the original.

If the Viardot anti-Britishness shines through Louis's writings, so does his republicanism. When writing about monuments, he cannot resist a dig at those whom accident or birth have called to the throne.[26] Indeed, Louis continued to be highly regarded in politics, and his house in the rue de Douai was at one stage considered a suitable place in which to try to arrange an accord between two bitterly rival politicians, Gambetta and Grévy.[27]

Upstairs in that house, Turgenev had his flat which he stuffed from wall to wall with his books and other possessions.[28] His collection of paintings included landscape pictures by Théodore Rousseau and Corot. He had a marble bas-relief of Pauline and a cast of her hands. The walls also boasted a considerable number of hunting trophies, skins, reindeer heads and so forth. He installed an acoustic tube leading to the music room, where

Pauline gave singing lessons, so that he could hear her voice more clearly.[29]

He was apt to be gloomy and depressed. 'Midnight … Downstairs my poor friend is singing something or other in her completely cracked voice … and in my heart it is darker than a dark night', he noted in his diary in 1877. 'It is as if the grave were hurrying to swallow me up.' 'My dear fellow, we are both crocks from a broken vessel', he told a friend.[30]

Turgenev in middle age

Actually, it was not as bad as that. Dressed in a Caucasian jacket with red lapels, Turgenev would sprawl on his large divan and receive Russian visitors who came to seek his support. Everybody was impressed by the presence of this distinguished, tall, strong, white-haired man with a beard.[31] Maupassant described him as 'a giant with a head of silver, as one would say in a fairy tale. He had long white hair, large white eyebrows and a large white beard – but truly silver white, all shining, all illuminated by reflections. Amidst all this whiteness, a good, serene face, with rather strong features – a real head of the River God pouring forth his waves, or better still, the head of the Eternal Father.' Maupassant also said that he was 'quite incredibly innocent, this novelist genius who had travelled far and wide. He showed stupefaction even, when confronted with things which would have appeared simple to a Paris schoolboy'.[32]

George Moore, the man of letters from County Mayo, said that Turgenev's hair was 'as white as Croagh Patrick's peak after a fall of snow'.[33] Edmond de Goncourt described him as 'that gentle giant and kindly savage with his white hair falling over his eyes and the deep lines which mark his forehead from temple to temple like a furrow made by the plough'. He gave the impression of being a big child. 'It is difficult to imagine a less pompous celebrity', or a less vain one.[34]

Turgenev in old age

However, many of the Russians seem to have regarded him as somewhat patronising, even supercilious, with a tendency to hold forth on the subject of art. While the Russian view may give credence to the Dostoyevsky caricature, Turgenev did much good work helping the applicants for his patronage, and would organise dinner parties for his visitors at which he tried to introduce them to buyers and critics. Once such applicant was the leading Russian portrait painter Ilya Repin. Pauline, however, disliked Repin's work. She required him to alter his portrait of Turgenev many times before she was satisfied with it.[35]

Another, the Russian landscape painter Vasily Polenov, gave Turgenev a painting of a Moscow courtyard which he hung in his study until he died (Plate 3).[36] Turgenev was so impressed by some paintings by Kuindzhi that he tried to have them exhibited in France. In the case of one such painting, he even went to the French Customs to make the necessary arrangements, although, in the event, its owner would not allow it to leave Russia.[37]

Pauline arranged concerts for Russian causes, such as the foundation of a Russian library in Paris. However, most Russians still regarded her as a tyrannical mistress who detained Turgenev from Russia. Many of them thought, or wanted to think, that his bachelor rooms were deliberately allowed to become shabby and dusty. When they visited him there, the sound of Pauline teaching down below reminded them of her dominant influence over him. There had long been rumours of her, imperious in her middle age, bossing him and sending him on errands, and of Louis making him carry his hunting bags. Turgenev's critics may not have realised that, possibly, he liked to be dominated,[38] or at the very least mothered. Also, it was only polite to offer to carry the bags of a gentleman who was over eighteen years older than oneself.

Turgenev continued to go to Russia regularly to deal with business matters relating to his publications and with Spasskoye. By the end of the decade, he was being given a celebrity welcome in St Petersburg and Moscow, so that a somewhat anxious Pauline feared he might want to remain there.[39]

Turgenev continued his involvement with a literary dining club whose regular members, The Five, now comprised, as well as him, Flaubert, Edmond de Goncourt, Zola and Daudet. Originally, it was intended that the club should meet monthly, although the gatherings were actually less frequent.[40]

Turgenev enthralled and enchanted his colleagues. The gathering may have been ostensibly highbrow but often the conversation was not. Filthy stories about their sex lives abound in these sessions, as do many titillating anecdotes such as the response of the English poet Algernon Swinburne, when asked by Turgenev what original and improbable experience he would most enjoy. Swinburne's answer was to take St Genevieve at prayer, her most passionate and ecstatic moment, and to do so with her tacit approval. Turgenev can hardly have realised that his stories would do the rounds and that Goncourt and others would record his exploits for posterity. Occasionally, Turgenev was asked about Pauline and probed about her sexuality. It is interesting that his friends needed to ask and that the issue was one which they thought they could raise.[41]

The Goncourts described Turgenev's 'combination of innocence and shrewdness'. 'He looks like a druid or the kindly old monk in *Romeo and Juliet*', they noted in their journal. 'He is handsome, but in an awe-inspiring impressive way … there is the blue of the heavens in Turgenev's eyes'.[42] Turgenev, the Russian bear, must have seemed relatively tame compared to many of these friends who were very wild. Flaubert, his protégé Guy de Maupassant, and Daudet all definitely contracted syphilis,[43] a disease which Edmond de Goncourt, whose inclinations were different, was less likely to catch.

On Thursdays, Pauline resumed her musical soirées which were held in the music room. For the Thursday audiences, she limited herself to chamber music. Tea and cakes were provided, rather than the champagne and cold buffet which was more usually served at Paris salons. Typically, Claudie and Marianne would perform duets; Paul might play on the violin which Turgenev had given him. At the end Pauline performed, often accompanied on the organ or the piano, by Saint-Saëns[44] or Fauré.

On Sundays, the atmosphere was completely different and light-hearted. There were charades and readings by Turgenev. They played games such as forfeits.

When Henry James arrived in Paris, he sought out Turgenev. Within a few weeks, he had attended some of Pauline's Thursdays and her Sundays *'en famille'*. He described the experience in a letter to his father. He wrote that the Thursday musical parties 'are rigidly musical and to me, therefore, rigidly boresome, especially as she herself sings very little. I stood the other night on my legs for three hours (from 11 till 2) in a suffocating room, listening to an interminable fiddling'. We may guess that he was listening to Paul playing the family's favourite, the *Duets for Piano and Violin*, by Reber, one of Paul's teachers. Henry James's only consolation was that standing next to him was the leading illustrator and printmaker in Paris, Gustave Doré. James added that 'when Mme Viardot does sing, it is superb'. He described her singing an extract from *Alceste* as 'the finest piece of musical declamation, of a gently tragic sort, that I can conceive'.[45]

Henry James Jr. was born in New York in 1843. His father was a highly regarded philosopher who brought him to Europe as a boy. The young man preferred reading his favourite authors to studying at Harvard Law School. He soon became recognised as a leading writer of short stories. In 1875–6, he lived in Paris and worked on his novel *The American.* He then moved to London where he became part of the social circle. When dining with Maupassant in London, he was shocked when his guest asked him to get him a pretty girl who had just entered the restaurant. He wrote twenty novels, 112 short stories including *The Turn of the Screw*, many plays and other works. The delightful *Washington Square* and more verbose but much hailed masterpiece *The Portrait of a Lady* were published in 1880 and 1881; and *The Bostonians*, more a satire on feminism than a picture of Boston, around five years later. His recurring theme is the interaction between the older European culture and the newer culture of America. He became a British subject in 1915 and died in London in the following year, having been much honoured.

Saint-Saëns was an ideal participant in the Sunday frivolities. He was very comical. He spoke with a pronounced lisp and had staccato gestures. Like Louis, he had a lengthy hooked nose on which he wore a pince-nez. He sang a good falsetto and he could easily parody a singer's mannerisms, such as a tendency to sing out of tune. He would sing Marguerite's 'Jewel Song' from Gounod's *Faust*, wearing blond plaits, his bearded face framed by a blue and white bonnet.[48] The effect must have been very comical.

Camille Saint-Saëns, who Liszt said was the greatest organist in the world, is now best remembered for the *Carnaval des animaux* (including 'The Swan', the Third (Organ) Symphony, his *Danse Macabre* and *Samson et Dalila*. He was born in Paris in October 1835 and brought up by his dominant mother and aunt.[46] When he was ten, he made his concert début, offering as an encore to play from memory any one of Beethoven's piano concertos. At 22, he was appointed organist at the fashionable La Madeleine. Subsequently, a large bequest enabled him to leave and devote his time to composition. At 40, he married a girl half his age. Their two-year-old son was killed by falling out of a fourth floor window; their other son died of pneumonia six weeks later. Three years afterwards, he abandoned his wife. He travelled as far as French Indo-China, the USA (where he played before President Roosevelt), Scandinavia and Ceylon; Algeria was a favourite, and he was a frequent visitor to England. He died in Algiers in December 1921, aged 85. He was increasingly out-of-date in his own style and intolerant of new styles.[47]

There was one evening when Turgenev, in the role of a medical professor, demonstrated the dissection of a corpse – Saint-Saëns wearing pink tights – who had expired from an excessive growth of the nose. When 'the professor' wielded the knife, an 'English medical student' swooned into the arms of the 'corpse', who had arranged the event so as to achieve just that objective.[49] Even if some may regard Turgenev as gloomy and Saint-Saëns as stuffy, their sense of humour was in proportion to the size of the Viardot and Saint-Saëns nose, which was enormous.

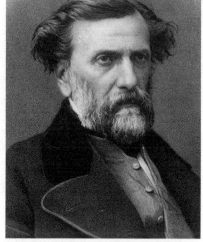

Ernest Renan

Ambroise Thomas

Gounod and the novelist Gustave Flaubert were sometimes present for this tomfoolery, as was César Franck who watched with amusement but did not take part. The obese Ernest Renan, the historian and controversial theologian, would jump over a handkerchief. In a game reminiscent of ducking for apples at Halloween, Renan would try to grab, with his mouth, a ring placed on top of a pile of flour, only to find his large belly covered in white.[50]

Another frequent guest was Ambroise Thomas, a palaeolithic composer whose pleasing but commonplace *Mignon* was commercially one of the most successful operas there has ever been.[51] Thomas's lengthy, melodious and lightweight *Hamlet* may occasionally be heard today. It was very successful. Unusually, Napoleon III and Eugénie lasted the full performance of it. Indeed Thomas became so distinguished that he was the first musician to be awarded the Grand Cross of the Légion d'Honneur.[52]

Fauré described how, at the Viardot salon, 'Turgenev was the great panjandrum himself, handsome and with a gentleness that was even more attractive.'[53] Henry James, however, was scathing about this 'usual Sunday evening occupation' possibly because, for a Protestant, Sunday should be devoted to religious observance.[54] He told his father that the Viardots' 'Sundays seem rather dingy and calculated to remind one of Concord historical games etc.' 'But', continued the American, 'it was both strange and sweet to see poor Turgenev acting charades of the most extravagant description, dressed out in old shawls and masks, going on all fours etc. The good faith with which Turgenev, at his age and with his glories, can go into them is a striking example of that spontaneity which Europeans have and we have not.' How quickly national characteristics can be reversed! Henry James concludes: 'Fancy Longfellow,* Lowell or Charles Norton doing the like and every Sunday evening!'[55]

Despite Henry James's strictures and his concern that Turgenev did not live 'like a gentleman', the *ménage* was now clearly part of the Establishment, the 'great and the good'. The Viardots' portraits by Alexis Kharlamov were exhibited in the Paris Salon of 1875. Turgenev supported Paris charities which raised money for Russia, and was fêted in Moscow and St Petersburg.[56] Oxford University awarded him an honorary doctorate. The citation praised him for his role in advancing the cause of the Russian serfs. We may wonder what Henry James made of Turgenev's sensible suggestion that his scarlet doctoral gown could be useful for the charades at the rue de Douai.[57]

Pauline's main occupation was to teach. In Paris, teaching singing was developing into a thriving industry which was largely fed by foreigners, several of whom came from the USA, and many of whom were aspirants with virtually no chance of success or understanding of the effort that

*The supremely popular Henry Longfellow wrote the ballad about 'Paul Revere's Ride' in which he recalled the hero who warned of the impending raid at Concord, a town twenty miles from Boston, where the first blood was shed in the War of Independence. Today, Longfellow is also remembered particularly for *The Song of Hiawatha*, 'The Wreck of the Hesperus' and 'Evangeline'. James R. Lowell was another very popular poet and was US ambassador to London. Norton was a teacher at Harvard and translator of the works of Dante.

success demanded. Among the teachers there were charlatans at one end of the scale, and teachers like Pauline at the other. She could be selective about who she took on.

Being in her fifties, she was on the periphery of the mainstream musical activity going on in Paris at the time. This was considerable. Many believed that, for too long, French music had been subservient to foreign music. Following the war, German music was unpopular. Under the leadership of Saint-Saëns, the Société Nationale de Musique was founded in 1871 for encouraging and performing new music by French composers. Works were democratically selected by the voting committee that met on Sundays at the house of Romain Bussine, the professor of singing at the Conservatoire. When not hosting his committee, Bussine was, likely as not, taking part in Pauline's Sunday frivolities. Gabriel Fauré became secretary in 1874. Many of the composers of the period, such as Fauré himself, Duparc, Chabrier and even Debussy, owed their first hearings to this initiative by Saint-Saëns.[58]

For a short time, Pauline taught at the conservatoire,[59] where she was appointed professor of singing in October 1871. However, by 1875, she had resigned. She was annoyed that one of her pupils had been passed over for a prize; she took exception to the teaching methods whereby a pupil was required to be taught by several professors rather than just by one. She also disliked the way the conservatoire was encouraging its pupils to compose in the style of the light opera, with which its rigidly conservative director, Ambroise Thomas, the bane of adventurous composers, had been so successful.[60] Perhaps surprisingly, Pauline also resigned as a member of the Société Nationale. One can sympathise that, as an occupant of the centre ground of the musical spectrum, Pauline might feel uncomfortable about the tug-of-war to which her art form was increasingly being subjected. In 1880, she published her own primer, *Une heure d'étude*.[61]

Despite Turgenev's bitter remark about the way in which age was affecting her voice, Pauline still performed in public occasionally. Although critical of her, Saint-Saëns, a far more reliable witness, said that her voice actually had an Indian summer. It seems to have retained its strength, except in the middle register. She appeared at charity concerts and at salons including some held at the Russian Embassy. Her performance of Schubert's *Erlkönig*, accompanied by Saint-Saëns, at the first of the Concerts Colonne, made a particular impression.[62]

The Music Room at the Viardots' house in the rue de Douai

Pauline helped to launch Jules Massenet whose *Marie Magdeleine* was first performed on Good Friday 1873. At one of Pauline's salons, Massenet had played a portion of the work which had been rejected by Jules Etienne Pasdeloup, who had been the leading conductor before 1870. The up-and-coming Edouard Colonne, who was superseding Pasdeloup, was prepared to perform it with Pauline singing the part of Méryem, the title role.[63] *Marie Magdeleine* was a work in Gounod's style. The composer Vincent d'Indy remarked on its 'eroticism, discreet and quasi-religious'. Not for nothing did Massenet have the sobriquet 'La fille de Gounod'.[64] Saint-Saëns was more supportive. He described *Marie Magdeleine* as 'the most audacious experiment' since *L'Enfance du Christ* of Berlioz.[65]

There were less serious ventures. Pauline played the piano for the first performance of *Gabriella di Vergy*, a satire on Italian opera which Saint-Saëns wrote for a chamber music society of former students at the Imperial

Jules Massenet, the son of a manufacturer of scythes, was born in Saint-Etienne to the south-west of Lyon in 1842. He won the Prix de Rome. After his success with *Le Roi de Lahore* in 1877, his production line extruded a succession of well over 30 popular operas, so he became enormously rich. *Manon* made him France's most popular composer in the last decades of the century. Today, we also remember his *Werther*. He taught composition at the Conservatoire and was greatly honoured in his time. Most French composers of his era were influenced by him, either through attraction or repulsion.[66] He died in Paris in 1912.

Military Academy. This met at the Salle de l'Horticulture, amid test tubes and botanical drawings. 'At the close, the heroine, having been served the heart of her lover by the enraged husband, seizes a dagger and contemplates suicide, with much dithering over "yes" and "no". Finally she stabs herself and expires.'[67]

However, Pauline could take a hard, even hard-hearted, attitude to requests from individuals to help out at concerts. Grisi's somewhat impoverished cousin, the 'widow' of Théophile Gautier, was given the brush-off when she asked Pauline to take part in a benefit concert being held on her behalf.[68]

Saint-Saëns composed *Samson & Dalila* for Pauline and dedicated it to her. This opera about yet another seductive predatress is the only one of the composer's thirteen operas to last. Pauline never performed Dalila in public. Because the opera was about a biblical subject, Saint-Saëns had difficulty getting it staged. Pauline sang it in a fully-costumed private performance in 1874, which, as chance would have it, was actually to be the last operatic performance of her life.[69] How wonderful it would have been to hear her sing *Amour! Viens, aider ma Faiblesse* and *Printemps qui commence!*

For the Viardots, now that the war and the Commune were over, France provided an attractive place in which to retire. After the Commune, the septuagenarian and archetypal bourgeois 'Monsieur Thiers', as he was called, lifted the country from its knees and ran it with a conservative administration. Loans raised to pay off the war indemnity were oversubscribed thirteen times. By the end of September 1873, the last German soldier had left French soil, for the time being at least.

Thiers was followed by Marshal MacMahon, the Duc de Magenta, a devout Catholic and conservative. There was a 'passionate desire for virtue' and a surge in religious enthusiasm with which Massenet's *Marie Magdeleine* was consistent. There was thus considerable support for building the Sacré-Coeur basilica, and for the places of great pilgrimage such as Lourdes. Turgenev did not approve of MacMahon, or the government's clerical tendency. He continued to worry that France might be going the way of Mexico and Spain. The Viardots were not church supporters. Louis was at most an agnostic; Pauline mentions God and 'our loving Father' in her letters to Rietz. She was also godmother to the children of various of her tenants and members of her staff. However, her religion, whatever it was, was not of the conventional kind.[70]

We may assume that, on balance, the Viardots approved of the backlash against religion that was in full swing by the time that the Host was first displayed in Sacré-Coeur in 1885. There were calls for the dominant position of the Church to be reversed. Unauthorised religious orders, not least the Jesuits, were required to disband within three months. Legislation severely curtailed the involvement of the Church in schools, hospitals, charities and the armed services. The 'Godless school' was introduced. These steps were extremely divisive and led to considerable civil disorder and indeed hardship.[71] Religion in schools is still a very touchy subject in France to this day.

Although, or perhaps because, France was run by a succession of 'largely grey mediocrities',[72] it gradually slipped into La Belle Epoque. It motored ahead economically, even though it was declining relative to other countries. The empire mushroomed, principally in Indo-China and Africa. The bourgeois enjoyed the pleasures of the music hall and cabaret depicted by Toulouse-Lautrec, as well as the benefits of decent sanitation and the supply of gas and electricity. The Exhibition of 1889, which endowed Paris with the Eiffel Tower, attracted 25 million visitors. The centenary of the Revolution was celebrated with a banquet for all the mayors of France at which 15,000 people sat down to table. Apparently 45,000 bottles of wine, three per head, were opened.[73]

The political backdrop to La Belle Epoque was wobbly. There were some 60 governments between 1870 and 1914.[74] Occasional attempts to restore the monarchy floundered. The candidates, the leading one being Chambord, the grandson of Charles X, were not strong. The death of the Prince Imperial, the son of Napoleon III, put an end to Bonapartism.

Still, there was a potent desire for *revanche*, for a strong leader who would recover Alsace and Lorraine which had been raped* by Germany in the Franco-Prussian War. Pauline would have been reminded of this every time she crossed the Place de la Concorde where, until 1918, the statue representing Strasbourg was draped in black crêpe.[75] At one moment, such a strong man seemed to be emerging in the guise of the self-publicist war minister, General Boulanger, who had great electoral success. The crowd roared 'A l'Elysee'. However, the government held its nerve. Threatened with arrest, Boulanger fled with his mistress to Belgium where, a couple of years later, he committed suicide.[76]

Prosperity is usually accompanied by violence from the underclass who feel deprived, or from 'anarchists' who reject it. The apartment of a salon

*Others had held a different view, not least the essayist Thomas Carlyle who contentiously argued that the Germans were just taking back what had previously belonged to them. For him France, in the guise of its monarchs such as Louis XIV, had been 'insolent, rapacious, insatiable, unappeasable, continually aggressive'. He had no sympathy for 'vapouring, vainglorious, gesticulating, quarrelsome, restless and over-sensitive France'.

hostess and painter, a friend of Saint-Saëns, was robbed and set on fire. The composer Vincent D'Indy found a note pinned to the conductor's rostrum saying 'Death to the aristocrats. Next time we will finish you off'.[77] In 1893, a bomb exploded close to La Madeleine and damaged the offices of Durand, the music publishers. Also in 1893, there was an attempt to blow up the Chamber of Deputies. President Carnot was assassinated with a six-inch knife in the following year.[78]

There were the usual scandals as well. The son-in-law of one President was accused of trafficking in honours and abusing the presidential facilities. There was a row about the construction of the Panama Canal, where the costs were both massively underestimated and inflated by apparently excessive charges by banks and publicity agents. There were accusations of paying bribes to parliamentarians.[79] For several years in the mid-1890s, the nation was divided over the most notorious and persistent scandal, in which Alfred Dreyfus was wrongfully convicted of treason. It was alleged that he had leaked military information to the Germans. Emile Zola famously intervened to defend Dreyfus with his open letter *J'accuse* in which he denounced both government and army. He was prosecuted for libel and had to flee to England. Gounod was a Dreyfusard, and we may assume that the Viardots also supported the case for the Jewish army officer.

There were catastrophes. In 1887 a fire at the Opéra-Comique, caused by sparks on torn gauze scenery, took over 70 lives. Ambroise Thomas's *Mignon* was being performed at the time. Carvalho, the director, who was Pauline's friend and the impresario of *Orphée*, took the blame and was condemned to three months in prison.

The Viardots, who had earlier become so dependent on the British for their income, must have been intrigued by the souring in Anglo-French relations. In 1893, the British ambassador in Paris described the attitude of all classes towards Great Britain as one of 'animosity and bitter dislike'. In 1898, there was a crisis when the British demanded the withdrawal of a French expeditionary force at Fashoda in the Sudan. This was a significant blow to French prestige. France took the side of the Boers in the Boer War. Some anti-British propaganda during this period was so forceful that the Germans had copies of it distributed when they occupied France in the Second World War. Reasonable relations with France were resumed, but only for a time, with the Entente Cordiale in 1905.[80]

We have seen that the Viardot circle included Saint-Saëns' protégé Gabriel Fauré. Although Fauré was self-effacing and unambitious,[81] his swarthy looks, his dark and dreamy eyes, and 'amazing, unsurpassable charm',[82] made him exceptionally attractive to women. He was good fun. He described himself, despite the saccharine piety of his *Requiem*, as 'an incorrigible religious defaulter'. One of his first jobs was to be an organist in Rennes in Brittany. However, the curé sacked him for smoking in the porch during sermons. The priest had earlier objected to him arriving for an early service wearing evening dress straight from the night before. His accompaniment of the church scene in Gounod's *Faust* at a local theatre also got him into trouble.[83]

Pauline's drawing of Fauré and Didie playing a duet.
It is sometimes thought to be Fauré and Marianne.

Fauré showed his appreciation of the Viardots by dedicating songs to Pauline, such as 'La Chanson du pêcheur' of 1872, and a 'Barcarolle' of 1873. He dedicated several works to other members of the family, works such as the first Violin Sonata which was dedicated to Paul, and the duets which he wrote for Claudie and Marianne.[84]

Gabriel Fauré, who has been described as 'the most complete musician France had ever possessed', and 'the greatest master of French song',[85] was born on 12 May 1845 in Pamiers, just north of the Pyrenees, where his father was a headmaster. When he was eight, he was sent to Paris to a school for children destined to be organists and choirmasters. An early work was *Cantique de Jean Racine* (1865). He was successively on the staff at several Paris churches. He fought in the Franco-Prussian War. During the Commune, he escaped to Lausanne and then London. Back in Paris, he worked for Saint-Saëns at La Madeleine, where he became chief organist in June 1896. His duties left him little time for composition, except in the summer months. Despite the style of his *Requiem*, Fauré became increasingly associated with the avant-garde. In 1905, following an uproar when Ravel was rejected for the Prix de Rome, Fauré was appointed director of the Conservatoire, where he gained a reputation for ruthlessness. He retired in 1920, beset by deafness and distorted hearing. He died in Paris on 24 November 1924.[86]

In July 1877, Fauré became engaged to Marianne. Perhaps she was attracted by his soft and beautiful voice, his melancholy punctuated with occasional naughty gaiety. Those were attributes so typical of the Viardot *ménage*. In the following month Fauré went to Cauterets, in the Pyrenees near Lourdes, to take a cure for his chronic migraine. He sent his fiancée 35 letters; sometimes he wrote twice daily. The letters, which he kept until the end of his life, are surprisingly formal. However, it was difficult for him to say anything interesting, let alone romantic, about the monotonous life he was leading, other than to wish that he could hear Marianne sing over a telephone. He writes that he has heard of defeats in the Russo-Turkish War which must be of great concern to Turgenev. He has also heard of the death of Thiers the politician, and has read that there had been a storm in the English Channel near where Marianne was staying. When he had to rush back to play at the service at La Madeleine he found himself locked out of his apartment. Oh, his doctor likes the operettas of Offenbach and Lecoq. There is little or nothing about passionate love in this pedestrian prose. Maybe this was suitably consistent with the Viardot character.[87]

After around three months, Marianne broke the engagement off. Fauré himself was worried that he might have been too ardent, too 'turbulent' and 'ombrageux' in his wooing. Or perhaps he was just insufficiently ambitious as a composer.[88] Maybe, having lived far from home deep in southern France from the age of eight, Fauré was 'constantly searching for a female figure in which there were maternal elements, a role which Marianne felt unable to sustain'.[89] One suspects that underneath the light-heartedness and even superficial exuberance and warmth of the Viardots, there was the statuesque frigidity reminiscent of the figures which we see on a Greek vase. This frigidity was not limited to Louis.

Fauré was greatly upset at his rejection. It has been suggested[90] that his *Requiem* was actually more an elegy for Marianne than a requiem for the dead. Maybe. However, Fauré himself said that, oppressed by accompanying countless funeral services, he wanted to portray death as a peaceful deliverance rather than a grand drama or expression of pious hope.[91] Five years after his breakup with Marianne, Fauré married the daughter of a sculptor. The marriage was unhappy and he had many extra-marital affairs.

Marianne later married Victor Alphonse Duvernoy, once a prodigy, then a composer, pianist and teacher at the Conservatoire.[92] The roll-call of witnesses at the wedding gives an indication of who the Viardot family friends were. Obviously, it included Turgenev. There was also the director of the Conservatoire, Ambroise Thomas; and there was Charles Gounod who was by then *persona grata* again. Hatchets had been buried, and Gounod was regarded as a close personal friend.

Eleven months after the wedding, the Duvernoys provided Pauline with another grandchild, Suzanne.[93]

CHAPTER 25

FLAUBERT

TURGENEV HAD A wide circle of literary friends and contacts in Paris. He was asked to be Vice-President of the International Literature Congress which met there in June 1878. It was not a happy experience for him. The President and hero of the Congress was Victor Hugo, whom Turgenev disliked and whose work he despised. Turgenev's short speech at the Congress was criticised by many in the Russian contingent, who thought that he should have given weight to the Russianness[1] of Russian literature, rather than emphasising the debt which it owed to the French. A familiar theme.

Within the literary circle, Turgenev's closest friend was Gustave Flaubert,[2] the author of *Madame Bovary*, the novel which caused such controversy when it was published. Turgenev and Flaubert had first met at a literary gathering in the early 1860s. However, their friendship really only blossomed at the end of the decade[3] when he told George Sand 'Apart from you and Turgenev, I know not a single mortal to whom I can pour out my heart about matters which are most dear to me'.[4] Flaubert had become friendly with George after she published a sympathetic review of his novel *Salammbô*.[5]

Turgenev and Flaubert would dine with other members of the Five, Edmond de Goncourt, Daudet and Zola. Turgenev would visit the florid Flaubert in Croisset, near Rouen. There he would find this vast, crude man, a larger-than-life character, a workaholic who had a horror of exercise. He was 'le gros Flaubert, tout rouge, vêtu de rouge, dans une chambre rouge'.[6]

Turgenev translated two of Flaubert's *Trois Contes* into Russian, 'La

Légende de Saint Julien l'Hospitalier' and the exotic 'Hérodias'. Flaubert improved a French version of a Pushkin short story which had been translated by Turgenev.[7]

Gustave Flaubert

Once the Viardots returned to Paris after the end of the Commune, it was not long before they, Turgenev, Flaubert and Pauline's great friend from the 1840s, George Sand, came together. In March 1872, Flaubert told her 'I have made the acquaintance of your old friend Mme Viardot who I find very pleasant'. Flaubert started attending soirées at Pauline's. They all were to be found at the theatre together.[8] A little coterie had been formed.

Gustave Flaubert was born on 12 December 1821, in Rouen where his father was a prominent doctor. He began his literary career while a schoolboy. At the age of fourteen, he had developed a passion for a much older woman. He was on a family holiday at the fashionable resort of Trouville, on the English Channel coast. The woman was the luscious, curvaceous Elisa Schlésinger, the wife of a successful businessman, the proprietor of La

Gazette Musicale. Flaubert used her as a model for a character in *The Memoirs of a Madman.* This is a brief tale in which Flaubert's sexual longing for the unattainable woman is surprisingly precocious, and his vivid imagery gives the reader a taste of his style to come.[9]

Flaubert went to Paris to study law. He evokes the atmosphere in one of his novels, where he makes plain his lack of enthusiasm for the subject. 'Three hundred bareheaded youths filled an amphitheatre where an old man in a red gown held forth in a monotone. A flock of quill-pens could be heard scratching on paper. The atmosphere was reminiscent of a schoolroom, with the same dusty smell, the same sort of chair, the same tedium'.[10] Flaubert gave up his studies on the grounds of ill health, probably an early form of the epilepsy which he later suffered from.

When Flaubert was 24, his father died of blood poisoning having nicked himself with a scalpel, coincidentally the fate of the key character in Turgenev's *Fathers and Sons.* His sister also died, in the same year, following childbirth. After these sad events, Flaubert became a kind of surrogate father to his niece.[11] He took her to live with him and his dominant mother at Croisset, his mother's 'pretty homestead situated half way up a hill on the banks of the Seine'. The house was noticeably damp, so it aggravated the rheumatism from which Turgenev thought he suffered. This was perhaps not surprising, because Rouen has been described as the 'chamber-pot of France'.[12]

For us, the first part of Flaubert's life was dull, although for him it was relieved by occasional tours in France, Italy and the Middle East, and his more frequent forays into brothels. According to his best friend, Flaubert was 'a splendid companion over a bottle or a whore'. He bragged at a Goncourt dinner how on entering a brothel, he would select the ugliest girl and, with his cigar hanging from his mouth, would have her there and then in front of his friends. Other than impressing them, he reached the age of 30 having achieved absolutely nothing.[13]

Soon after his father and sister died, Flaubert visited a sculptor, James Pradier. He wanted him to create a bust of the dead girl. Pradier was a fashionable sculptor, particularly of the female nude, a state in which his notorious wife often found herself. On this occasion however, the beautiful Louise Colet was posing for the artist. Thus Flaubert, nine years her junior, began an affair with Louise.[14]

Louise Colet was a poet and feminist, a formidable woman who had tried to stab a gossip columnist who had slandered her about a baby she had probably provided to the Minister of Education. It is hard to know what she saw in Flaubert and why their affair lasted nine years. He would not invite her to Croisset. Their intermittent and steamy relationship was conducted in hotels or during very rare visits by him to Paris. Any thought of marriage horrified him; not surprisingly, Louise eventually got fed up. She went off, at first with Pauline's first admirer Alfred de Musset, now old and ailing, and then with France's other leading poet Alfred de Vigny. Both these partners were infinitely more distinguished for their literary abilities than her previous lover was at the time. They may also have been more satisfying. Flaubert apparently had a preference for *coitus interruptus.*[15]

Louise Colet

Before leaving for a tour abroad in 1849, Flaubert read his draft of *La Tentation de Saint Antoine* to some friends who condemned it out of hand. One suggested that, instead, he should write a novel based on the recent case of a country doctor in Normandy who died of grief after being cuckolded and ruined by his wife. This case struck a chord with Flaubert, as did the reports of the wife of his sculptor who had eventually been cast out as a fallen woman.[16] Flaubert, from very early in his life, could not abide the hypocritical attitude of the bourgeois.

It took Flaubert almost five years to write the sensational *Madame Bovary* which Turgenev regarded as 'indisputably the most remarkable work of modern French literature'.[17] Flaubert was almost aged 35 when the six instalments began to appear in *La Revue de Paris* during the autumn of 1856. Emma Bovary, bored, is married to a bourgeois country doctor whose conversation is 'as flat as a pavement'. Sex is 'a habit like any other, a dessert to look forward to after a humdrum dinner'. 'Why in the world did I get married?' she asks herself.[18]

Emma lets herself be seduced by a rich local landowner, while out riding with him. 'I have a lover' she tells herself, relishing the thought 'as if she were experiencing a second puberty'.[19] After the landowner terminates the affair, she begins one with a legal clerk in Rouen. Emma's appetite for sex with her two lovers increases to fever pitch, almost in proportion to her growing contempt for and dislike of the husband whose career and life she proceeds to wreck. In the end, she has no option but to do away with herself. Henry James found a useful moral in the story whose full title, he suggested, should be 'Madame Bovary, or, the Consequences of Misconduct'.[20] He went so far as to suggest, tongue in cheek, that the book would make suitable reading for Sunday school. There is truth in his jest, because the actual cause of Emma Bovary's downfall is the financial profligacy which accompanies her insatiable and raw craving for extra-marital sex.

Flaubert leaves little to the imagination in describing Emma's adultery; not just the act, but its destructive force.[21] When the instalments of *Madame Bovary* appeared in *La Revue de Paris*, there were howls of scandal and accusations of immorality.

After three warnings a publication could be suspended and then suppressed. The publisher's attempts to make the published instalments acceptable to the authorities were resisted by Flaubert, although he had to capitulate. Nevertheless, the authorities, who had been 'watching' the journal for some time, struck. They summoned the author, publisher and printer to face charges of 'grossly offending against public morality, religion and decency'. 'Who are the readers of *Madame Bovary*?' asked the public prosecutor. 'Men concerned with social and political economy? No', he declared. 'The readers are young girls and married women.' The prosecutor's hobby was later rumoured to be the writing of pornographic verses.[22]

Flaubert was represented by excellent counsel. The case against him, which was heard in January 1857, was dismissed. However, the author was reprimanded and reminded that 'the mission of literature should be to enrich and refresh the mind by elevating the understanding and refining morals'. He was lucky. The same tribunal convicted Baudelaire on a similar charge six months later. By the end of the year, there were adaptations of *Madame Bovary* running in two theatres of Paris.[23]

Flaubert's next novel, in complete contrast, was *Salammbô*, which was exotic in style and truly horrifying in content. It is set during an uprising in around 240 BC, when the Carthaginians failed to pay the wages due to their mercenary army. As a historical novel, *Salammbô* is evocative in a way in which no other novel before had been. The story is notable for its sadistic violence. Children are roasted alive[24] in an attempt to appease the gods; an entire army is trapped in a valley and reduced to cannibalism; those left provide a tasty morsel for lions. The book reeks of priestly perfume, the smell of blood, the odour of corpses, many of which, whether human or leonine, are crucified.

Salammbô, the high priestess who is destined to be wedded to one of the generals allied to the Carthaginians, falls instead for the leader of the mercenaries. After their annihilation, he is forced to stagger a bloody gauntlet between his dungeon and Salammbô's wedding feast. He arrives, falls dead, his heart is ripped out. She poisons herself. It is horrific.

Salammbô is like a piece of great modern art. Its impressionistic style might have had more immediate impact with the public if it had not found itself competing with Victor Hugo's novel *Les Misérables*, which appeared around the same time.[25] The two books are about as different as can be imagined. In Flaubert's far shorter novel, one-third the length of Hugo's, the reader is gripped by sheer horror. In Hugo's much easier thriller, the reader's attention is held for 1,200 pages by wondering whether Jean Valjean, an escaped convict, will ultimately be caught. This underlying theme enables Hugo to drive inexorably forward his stories of love, murder, violence, prison escape and insurrection on the barricades.

The distinguished critic Sainte-Beuve said that, for fear of seeming mawkish and like a snivelling bourgeois, Flaubert had deliberately gone to the other extreme; he had produced something atrocious.[26] *Salammbô* was a cruel book. Flaubert seemed to think that it was a sign of virility to appear to be devoid of feeling.[27] Others were more charitable. Gautier said that it was not a history book, nor a novel, but an epic poem.[28] Maupassant described it as 'a kind of opera in prose'.[29]

Salammbô surprised Flaubert's critics because like many of his works it was very unusual. The volume entitled *Trois Contes*, which was published at the end of his life, was more straightforward and successful. This comprises three short stories which demonstrate different aspects of his talent. As well as the two translated by Turgenev, the book includes 'Un coeur simple', Flaubert's story about unalloyed affection. This could verge on the whimsical if his tale were not so delightful. A simple-minded house servant seeks an object on whom to bestow her pure and boundless love. Death or other circumstances get in the way as she seeks to transfer it from one human to another. Eventually her love settles on a parrot which, even in death, can be stuffed and provide an object on which to focus her affection.

Before this Flaubert had published, in 1869, *L'Éducation sentimentale* which grew out of his unpublished, pubescent story *The Memoirs of a Madman.* Flaubert, being a perfectionist, wrote and re-wrote, so that many of his books took a very long time to emerge. Nevertheless, his public found *L'Éducation sentimentale* difficult and it failed to sell well.

Flaubert's friend Maxime Du Camp, who had been sent a draft of *L'Éducation sentimentale* for comment, sent him a frosty critique. Not only was Flaubert's grammar often conspicuously faulty, a criticism which was made about several of his works, including *Madame Bovary.*[30] Du Camp also said that Flaubert's style was poor and, as a result, he was often incomprehensible. Nevertheless, he was to be congratulated on his *tour de force* in writing a book with 'no subject, no plot and featureless characters'. The title should be 'Les Gens médiocres',[31] 'Mediocrity'.

Du Camp was not alone in his criticism. Henry James excoriated the novel. It was mechanical and inanimate, 'elaborately and massively dreary', he said. Reading it was 'like masticating ashes and sawdust'. 'The book is, in a single word, a dead one'. 'That a novel should have a certain charm seems to us the most rudimentary of principles', continued James, 'and there is no more character in this laborious monument to a treacherous ideal than there is perfume in a gravel heap'.[32] Contrary views were also expressed, notably by the novelist Emile Zola who said that *L'Éducation sentimentale* was the only true historical novel he knew.[33]

For us, again, its story has a particular resonance. It is set against the upheavals in Paris of the 1840s and 1850s. It portrays the infatuation of a sentimental romantic youth for his ideal woman, whose husband is considerably older. When the young man, Frédéric, takes the opportunity to try to seduce her, the atmosphere becomes extremely chilly. She puts him down promptly once he makes his opening gambit.

Frédéric asks languidly whether she accepted that 'a man may love ... a woman'. 'If she's free to marry, he may marry her. When she belongs to another, he should leave her alone', Madame Arnoux, the ideal woman, replies. We can experience bliss, she explains, 'but it is never to be found in falsehood, anxiety or remorse'. When the youth suggests that all that is irrelevant, provided their love is sublime, she puts him down again. 'L'experience est trop coûteuse', 'the price is too high', she retorts. When he suggests that it follows that virtue and cowardice are identical, she responds: 'I should prefer to use the expression clear-sightedness. Even for women who overlook duty or religion, mere good sense may be enough'.[34]

The youth relieves his lust in the fleshpots of Paris with a courtesan who has attributes of La Présidente who, we may recall, was the model who George Sand's son-in-law used for his sculpture of 'The Woman bitten by a Snake' (see picture on p. 207).[35] Flaubert's Madame Arnoux was, as we know, modelled on Elisa Schlésinger. However, for us, the model could equally have been the ideal woman of the author's great friend Turgenev. That was, Pauline Viardot.

Flaubert's first encounter with Pauline, a quarter of a century earlier, had not been promising. It arose on a visit he made to the 'dungeons deep and old' in the castle made notorious by Byron in his poem 'The Prisoner of Chillon'. Chillon stands on Lake Geneva near Montreux, and is one of Switzerland's best-known monuments, not least because of Byron's fable. Byron tells of seven prisoners of conscience incarcerated there. 'Below the surface of the lake, the dark vault lies wherein we lay; we heard it ripple night and day.' In this 'living grave', each prisoner was chained to a column. Only one prisoner survived, totally broken by grief and his circumstances. By the time he was freed, he said 'it was at length the same to me fettered or fetterless to be'. 'Even I regained my freedom with a sigh'. On one of the columns, Flaubert saw Byron's name inscribed.

Flaubert was understandably outraged when he saw that Victor Hugo and George Sand had left their graffiti on the column. 'One would have to be very daring or very stupid to write one's name in such a place after Byron', he wrote. 'It gave me an appalling impression of them. I thought they had more taste.' Flaubert was particularly scathing about an inscription, written in pencil: 'Mme Viardot, née Pauline Garcia'. He said that, when he saw that, he fell about laughing. 'Mme Viardot née Garcia dreaming of the misfortunes poetised by the master and wanting the public to know about it – it was utterly grotesque.'[36] With hindsight, few would question Flaubert's conclusion, even if George Sand, who should have known better, may have set Pauline a very bad example on this occasion.

However, Flaubert, who was a very keen musician,[37] did enjoy a performance of *Le Prophète* just before he left for a tour of Egypt. He said that he came away 'refreshed, bedazzled and full of life'.[38]

Yet twenty or so years after this, Flaubert still did not particularly warm to Pauline who he thought had 'une nature bien curieuse'.[39] By that, presumably he meant that she was an odd sort of woman, not his type. Soon, however, he became part of her circle through his friendship with George Sand and Turgenev.

And Flaubert recognised her artistic merit when he heard her sing at one of her salons. 'I greatly missed you at the Viardots a fortnight ago', he wrote to Sand. 'She sang arias from *Iphigénie en Aulide*. I can't tell you how beautiful it was – soul-stirring, utterly sublime. What an artist that woman is! Such emotions console one for existing'.[40] A couple of months later, he complained that he could not detect 'the slightest sign of life from the

Muscovite!' He continued, 'I wrote to him a while ago at his address in the rue de Douai. Why this silence? Has Madame Viardot eaten him?'[41]

In spring 1872, Flaubert wrote to George Sand. 'Mme Viardot, Turgenev and I have a plan – to visit you at Nohant in July. Will this little dream be realised?' he asked. George was still enthusiastic about the 'Diva Paulita'. I forget everything when Pauline Viardot sings', she wrote.[42]

George Sand

The thought of Turgenev and Flaubert in the same carriage – together they weighed 35 stone – caused some mirth, if not apprehension, in the Berry château.[43] In the event, Flaubert's visit was delayed until September of the following year, although Pauline herself did go there that summer.

It had been a quarter of a century since Pauline's last visit to Nohant. She sang, to Sand's astonishment, many of the Berrichon songs which she had learnt in the Chopin days. Sand was overcome. 'What a day, what emotion, what musical penetration' she noted in her diary'.[44] The teenager Paul said that Sand at this time was like an adorable granny, a source of great joy. She got up at lunchtime, said little, did less, and chain-smoked poor quality cigarettes made more of dust than leaf. Even in her old age George would bathe in the River Indre.[45] She would think wistfully of those who had bathed there in the past; Pauline and her mother, Chopin, Delacroix ... 'We would even swim at night', she wrote. 'They are all dead, except for Madame Viardot and me.'[46]

The old friendship was revived. The Viardots followed up their visit by sending Christmas presents to Nohant: there were toys for George's grandchildren, a monkey which played the harp, a toy cow which could be filled with milk and some miniature items for Maurice to use in the puppet theatre which was his obsession.[47]

In January 1873 Pauline held a party at the rue de Douai at which she dressed up as a 16th century noblewoman; Turgenev was an ogre and Flaubert was a chef wearing an apron and round hat. One of George Sand's friends noted that 'nothing could be funnier than the author of *Salammbô* carrying trays of refreshments like a flunky in an upper-class home'.[48]

Pauline and Turgenev went again to Nohant at Easter. Flaubert accompanied them this time.[49] Turgenev demonstrated the mazurka. 'Turgenev loves noise and gaiety. He's as childish as we are', George wrote.[50] Paul Viardot played the violin; Maurice put on shows in the puppet theatre. Solange came to dinner and danced. Flaubert, however, irritated George by pontificating about literature, so much so that 'the great Muscovite', as she called him, who she found more interesting, could not get a word in. She found Turgenev charming, although sometimes extremely unwell.[51]

We might think that, back in Paris, old Louis was wrapped up in blankets. If so, the cause would not have been infirmity. He had just returned from a shoot with Turgenev at Rougemont, where Paulinette lived, and where the shooting was better than at Nohant. He sent some venison for them all to eat.[52]

Flaubert had continued to look after his orphaned niece whom he had adopted when his sister died. He pushed her into an unhappy marriage with a timber importer who was ostensibly very rich. In the mid-1870s, the merchant got into financial difficulties. Flaubert used his own assets to defer the inevitable bankruptcy. It was at this time that he took special consolation from the friendship of Turgenev, George Sand and the young Guy de Maupassant. Turgenev must have noticed the similarity between the circumstances of the timber importer and those of his own son-in-law, the glass manufacturer. To help Flaubert financially Turgenev tried, although without success, to get him a job in one of the Paris libraries.[53]

Guy de Maupassant's uncle, his mother's brother, was a great friend of Flaubert who took a fatherly interest in him and introduced him to his circle of literary friends. Maupassant was born into the minor aristocracy near Dieppe in 1850. He fought in the Franco-Prussian War, and began to train as a lawyer. He entered the civil service. In 1880, Maupassant's reputation was made by his short story 'Boule de Suif' ('Ball of Fat') which tells of the abuse of a prostitute by the hypocritical bourgeois at the time of the Franco-Prussian War. His subsequent stories, around 300, which depicted France in the two decades after the war, made him very rich. He also wrote several novels, some travel books and poetry. He enjoyed rowing, swimming and frequenting prostitutes. He died of syphilis in 1893 aged 42. He had earlier tried to commit suicide.

The friendship with George Sand was about to come to an end. On 8 June 1876, when Pauline was just about to leave for Nohant, George died.[54] Pauline sent a wreath of yellow flowers in which was picked out, in black letters, the single word 'Consuelo'.[55]

'What a brave man she was, and what a good woman', was Turgenev's epitaph.[56] George was indeed remarkable; and her massive achievement tends to be overshadowed by her extraordinary behaviour. Robert and Elizabeth Browning, who themselves had defied convention by eloping, provided an interesting interpretation. They thought that Sand was the victim of her uncontrollable sensual appetite, a sin no more reprehensible than gluttony or intemperance. 'I pity her, more than I blame her', said Elizabeth Browning. 'Her mind is none the less godlike.'[57] This perception is entirely consistent with Pauline's. Passion evaporates, sensual appetite wears off. For Pauline, friendship was infinitely more important than passion,[58] as we know.

Four years after George's death, on 8 May 1880, it was Flaubert's turn. He died suddenly in Croisset. It seems that he had an epileptic fit. Maupassant informed Turgenev, who was in Russia. 'I wrote on the day of the calamity to Mme Viardot, asking her to tell you, because I did not know your address in Russia', he said. 'I preferred you to learn this sad news from friends, rather than from a newspaper.'[59]

Flaubert was so large that his gravedigger miscalculated. His coffin had to be lowered at an angle. Surely, the mourner's nightmare.[60]

CHAPTER 26

BOUGIVAL

BECAUSE THE CHÂTEAU at Courtavenel had been destroyed, the Viardots no longer had a summer residence. So, in May 1875,[1] jointly with Turgenev, they bought a country house called Les Frênes, the Ash Trees. This was just outside Bougival, about five miles from Versailles; today, it is within sight of the towers of La Défense.

Bougival was idyllic and was frequented by the Impressionists (see Plate 6). The house, which was built around 1800, sits up a hill and is approached by a very steep drive which winds its way through some fine trees. We are told that fountains and statues decorated the gardens[2] and 'there were natural springs in the grounds, and the air was full of the sound of water cascading in little streams over rocks across lawns, and among clumps of fuchsias and begonias'.[3] Below is the broad curve of the Seine with a long island in its middle. On the river, 'the tanned and knotted play of male biceps gleamed and glistened under the hot sun. Silken parasols, like strange, aquatic flowers, red and green, blue and yellow, glowed in the sternsheets'.[4]

The Viardots' house had once been owned by Empress Joséphine.[5] Subsequently, a parfumier and a doctor lived in it. Nearby, their neighbour from Paris, Bizet, also had a house, as did some of Turgenev's relations.

The Viardots had already summered in Bougival, at a house closer to the church.[6] When Les Frênes came up for sale, they thought that it was too small. However, provided Turgenev built a place for himself in the grounds, rather like he had done next door in Baden-Baden, the property would be suitable. They bought it for 180,000 francs.[7]

Pauline was no longer earning much, so the Viardots were dependent on her savings and investments to provide their income. Therefore Turgenev contributed at least a third of the capital with which to buy and renovate Les Frênes (see Plate 11).[8] The cost considerably strained his resources. His Russian income continued to be depleted by incompetent, rapacious and possibly fraudulent stewards, which was not unusual where a landlord was absent.[9] The successor to the improvident Uncle Nicholas lost him enormous amounts. Also, a bequest which Turgenev inherited from his brother who died in January 1879 provided only around half of what he had expected to receive. There were bitter arguments with his brother's widow over his portion. As a result of all this, he had less money than he had expected and he had to sell his pictures in order to raise the necessary cash. The sale, in which he realised about half what he had paid for them,[10] was not a success. He described it as 'a disaster of the order of Sedan'.[11]

The chalet which Turgenev had built for himself, in the Swiss style, is a few yards above the house. To reach it, one continues on up a steep path. With his chronic gout, this arrangement was hardly ideal. Yet, from his desk in his upstairs study, where he was surrounded by his books and the busts of his heroes Beethoven and Pushkin, Turgenev had a wonderful view over the trees to the Seine and beyond. From the balcony outside his bedroom, he could look out over Les Frênes itself, towards his beloved. It is not surprising that he told Didie that, for him, the place was like 'La Mecque pour les Musulmans'.[12]

The Viardots spent the winters in Paris and the summers in Bougival. We can picture their serene but largely uneventful life there. A visitor recalls that Turgenev would not normally emerge in the morning. If he did take a meal, it was just some strong tea from the samovar. Pauline taught in the morning. In the afternoon, around 3 pm, they would all congregate in the study. They would then quietly get on with whatever they had to do. Sometimes Louise, who Fauré called 'la prodigieuse muse des Frênes', might read aloud a French work or an English novel. A favourite was *Daniel Deronda* by George Eliot, which was published in instalments in early 1876. The book runs to 700 pages, so we may assume that Louise only chose the brilliantly dramatic chapters, of which there are several, to declaim. That they could understand the text shows how proficient the family must have been in the use of English. (Presumably they took in their stride one of its central themes, that which concerns the deeply unhappy marriage with which a woman is forced to cope. Had she possessed the ability to realise her ambition to achieve independence by becoming a star singer, she would have avoided this). Turgenev, although often gouty and depressed, livened up these activities by making occasional amusing comments.[13]

Claudie Viardot, Didie, set up her easel in Turgenev's study. She was very talented at painting and worked away at it while he wrote. She had large eyes which were blue like Turgenev's. She was prettier than her mother.[14] No wonder Turgenev adored her.

A year or so earlier, on 6 March 1874, Claudie married, at the age of 22, Georges Chamerot, a master printer and the son of a shooting friend of Louis Viardot. Nine months later, after an extremely difficult confinement which she only just survived, she gave birth to her first daughter Jeanne. Turgenev adored the child and wrote children's stories for her.[15]

We shall see that Turgenev, who was now aged nearly 60, had a partiality for much younger women, those in their twenties and early thirties. This, together with the tone of his correspondence with Didie, lends support to the theory that he had an affair with her during the 1870s. He was of course the oldest friend of the family, and a familiar, god-paternal and avuncular style was to be expected. But one does not have to look far to find phrases – for example, the ambiguity about where he wishes to bestow his kisses, 'sur ton joli front que tu as grand tort de cacher'[16] – which seem unduly colourful and support the theory that, on his part, the relationship was sexual. But whether or not it was sexual on her part is altogether another matter. The fact that her second daughter Marcelle looked, in old age, exactly like Turgenev lends considerable weight to the theory that it was.*

Marcelle was born almost five years after Didie gave birth to Jeanne. In 1885 the Chamerots had a son, Raymond, who like so many young men of that generation would be killed in the Great War. He fell with many others on 6 July 1915 near La Targette, just to the north of Arras, about fifteen miles from Douai. The French suffered horrific casualties when making a vain attempt to take a ridge which dominated a coal-mining district.[17]

*When in the 1960s Pauline's biographer April FitzLyon visited Didie's daughter Marcelle, she found a 'Turgenev in a skirt', a description which has also been applied to Paulinette.

As before, Pauline's own family hangers-on were never very far away from her home. Her half-brother Joaquin would come and sponge off them. Sometimes visitors came who needed entertaining. When Nikolay Rubinstein turned up with a Russian Grand Duke, Paul Viardot took them to a 'dance' held for rowers. Perhaps this was a euphemism for highly disreputable goings-on, the drinking, shouting, singing, dancing, held in a marquee on a large raft in a backwater of the river. Maupassant described the clientèle, the strong stench of upper-crust debauchery, the shady speculators, the third-rate journalists, the pox-eaten rakes, and the women on the lookout for the evening's prey. This would have been home territory to Rubinstein who must have enjoyed his visit enormously.[18]

Pauline, who was now in her fifties, had retired from her full-time performing and teaching career. Turgenev, however, was in the full flow of his work as a writer. He went back several times to Russia, where he dealt with his publishers and did 'research' for a novel on which he was working. Following the example set by Dickens, he gave readings of his works.[19]

He was greatly honoured. He was invited to a reunion dinner by the Committee for the Emancipation, an honour which he attributed to his authorship of the *Sketches from a Hunter's Album*, in which he took great pride. It was around this time that he made the claim that the Tsar had indicated that the book had been an important factor in his decision to implement the legislation. This surprising claim, even though based on a remark by the Russian ambassador, seems particularly uncharacteristic, given that Turgenev had a reputation for modesty and unpretentiousness, characteristics which particularly struck Henry James. Maupassant agreed that Turgenev pushed 'modesty to the point of humility'.[20]

Turgenev was often laid up with illness; often, although not always, it was gout. One evening in St Petersburg, he was at a salon at which the leading Russian composers were present: Rubinstein, Rimsky-Korsakov, Borodin, and a red-faced Mussorgsky whose *Boris Godunov* was premièred that year.[21]

While Anton Rubinstein was playing, Turgenev began to feel spasms. Soon, he was doubled up with pain and was sweating profusely. The other guests were terrified that he had caught the dreaded cholera. It is fortunate, at least for Russian music and literature, that he had not. However, an imperial physician told Turgenev that there was nothing wrong with him and that he had another 30 years to live. The doctor advised him to continue his frequent visits to the spa at Carlsbad and imbibe the waters. However, within a week, Turgenev had an attack of gout which gave him tremendous pain at night. He sent Pauline drawings of his swollen knee.[22]

Eventually, Turgenev was able to go off to Spasskoye. There the house itself was let to a neighbour whose son moved into the big house and also acted as manager. At last, Turgenev had found someone who could run the estate efficiently.[23] He began to lose interest in the place.

In a letter to Didie, Turgenev drew this picture of himself with gout

For over six years, up to its publication in the January and February 1877 editions of the *European Herald*, Turgenev worked on his longest novel, *Virgin Soil*. George Eliot was lukewarm towards it, and Henry James regarded it as 'inferior to other works'. Thus, it is criticised by many recent experts who find fault with its lack of passion. They take exception to its political aspects.[24] They also criticise Turgenev's failure realistically to depict characters of which he did not have real-life experience.[25]

The novel actually makes an interesting and entertaining read. It was deliberately topical. It reflects a specific phenomenon of 1874 when the Russian intelligentsia headed into the countryside in order to rouse the slumbering rural masses, a step which Herzen had once advocated. The countryside swarmed with around 2–3,000 crusading nobles, teachers, lawyers, physicians and students who 'went to the people'.[26] Despite the men growing their hair long, the women cropping their hair, and both sexes smoking a great deal,[27] the movement was a failure. The Russian peasant was just not interested.

In Turgenev's novel, the young Nezhdanov was appointed tutor to the son of a liberal but ambitious privy councillor and his icily beautiful wife. The politician Sipyagin possessed that mandarin type of lofty compassion and fastidious condescension so characteristic of the higher official. His self-centred[28] wife thrived on the strength of her 'inaccessibility, her impregnable virtue, and the gracious way with which she submitted to the legitimate caresses of her well-bred and polished spouse'.[29]

Madame Sipyagin had a brother who lived on a 600-acre run-down estate a few miles away. He was left-wing, 'obstinate and dauntless to desperation'. He was destined for the Sipyagins' relatively plain and penniless niece Marianna who survived on their charity. Marianna was a nihilist, came from a disgraced family, and smoked.[30]

The tutor Nezhdanov eloped with Marianna. They took shelter in a cotton factory. They joined a movement similar to the real one which 'Went to the People'. The servant who was provided to look after Marianna was doubtful. 'How young and helpless you are, you two. It makes my heart ache. You have taken upon yourselves a burden much too heavy for your shoulders', she said. 'You will scour pots, and pluck chickens; and so, who knows, maybe you will save your country', said the factory manager, Turgenev's more practical hero who preferred slow, orderly change.[31] Marianna appreciated that they were 'really acting a sort of farce'.[32]

When Nezhdanov tried to make friends with the peasants, one of them assumed that the pamphlet which he was distributing was about religion and refused to take it. 'Another took it for his children because of the picture on the cover; a third threatened him with a poker. A fourth took one, although it was obvious that he did not understand a single word of what it was about.'[33] The peasants plied Nezhdanov with alcohol, so he returned, blind drunk, to the factory and Marianna. 'It's hard for an aesthete to be brought in contact with real life', he explained.[34]

Mme Sipyagin's brother intended a more active form of disruption. However, he was beaten up by the peasants who then turned him over to the authorities. The attempt to 'go to the people' was a failure. The disillusioned Nezhdanov shot himself. But he came round for long enough to bestow Marianna on the factory manager, and say 'Failed again'. Then he expired. He was another, the last, of Turgenev's superfluous men.[35] Of course Sipyagin's career progressed, despite the embarrassment over his brother-in-law's activities. Madame Sipyagin 'patronised the Arts, gave musical soirées, and organised soup-kitchens'.[36]

By reflecting the conditions in Russia, Turgenev perhaps hoped that *Virgin Soil* could strike a chord with the younger generation.[37] However, his devastating criticisms, not least his exposure of the absurdity of the agitation, annoyed his radical readers. The conservatives were also angry. They disliked the notion of Marianna as an upper-class revolutionary, and thought her character improbable.

How wrong they were. In real life, a noble's daughter, Vera Zasulich, shot the Governor of St Petersburg in 1878 for having a student revolutionary flogged.[38] The jury acquitted her, to the dismay of the authorities. Turgenev illustrated the two polarised points of view in a short story in which he described a similar girl who is intent on becoming a terrorist. 'Fool', commented one person; 'Saint', said another.[39]

The underground political agitation was well under way and would continue, as Turgenev knew it would. In Russia, from autumn 1879 to spring 1881, 'the terrorists waged a relentless duel with the government'. Russia was not alone. In the USA, President Garfield was shot.[40]

In 1879, there were three attempts to kill the Tsar. Anarchists tried to blow up the Imperial train on the railway line which goes past Spasskoye. In the following year, the dining-room at the Winter Palace was blown up.[41] Turgenev, who was in St Petersburg at the time, regarded this as deplorable. He wrote a letter to Pauline in which he said that there was 'une véritable panique' as people started fleeing the city. However, a performance of Glinka's *A Life for the Tsar* was duly put on at the Opera. Turgenev attended, and the audience demonstrated their loyalty to the royal family by requiring the national anthem to be repeated eleven times. The less privileged populace was reassured by a parade of loyal soldiers in front of the Palace.[42]

After less than a fortnight, there was an attempt to shoot the Prime Minister, Loris-Melikov. Turgenev was in the crowd[43] when the would-be assassin was summarily executed, within a couple of days of the crime.

Repression did not stop the terrorists. In March 1881, Tsar Alexander II was at last successfully assassinated. The first bomb killed a child; the Tsar went to investigate and was killed by the second bomb.*[44] The attempt succeeded despite considerable security arrangements. Only a month earlier Pauline's son, who was in St Petersburg for concerts organised by the Rubinsteins, had seen the Tsar's cavalcade passing by. All bystanders were roughly huddled away to the back streets by his security entourage.[45]

Five conspirators, including a woman, were publicly executed for the crime.[46] There were mixed views in intellectual circles about how justified this tyrannicide was. This was so especially in England, then sufficiently self-confident to be a safe haven for anarchists and others who did not accept the legitimacy of the ruling regime. A correspondent to *The Times* wrote that tyrannicide was 'the sublimest of murders'.[47] One highly-born and highly-educated English poet, Algernon Swinburne, whose poem 'Ave atque Vale' English schoolchildren used to recite, reckoned that the Tsar had been properly condemned and executed.[48] One wonders what these people would have made of a 'war on terror'.

Not surprisingly, the Russian censors had trouble with *Virgin Soil*. The first of the two volumes gave them less difficulty. However, the second was only approved with the chairman exercising his casting vote. He said that, if originally he had known the entire contents, he would have banned the book completely.[49]

Within a few weeks of publication, the authorities arrested 52 revolutionaries, including eighteen women, for spreading propaganda in Moscow

*In 1914, when Archduke Franz-Ferdinand was assassinated at Sarajevo, the first attempt failed, but the terrorists were successful when he returned later to visit the site.

factories. As a consequence, *Virgin Soil* became an international bestseller in France, England and the USA.[50]

This was to be Turgenev's last novel although, at the time of his death, he seems to have been thinking of writing a further one. His seventh novel was intended to demonstrate the moral superiority of the Russian revolutionary socialist compared with the French equivalent.[51]

Turgenev continued to work on other pieces and he assembled several *Prose Poems*; tiny, miniature stories and observations. He recommended that these should be read one at a time – one today, another tomorrow – rather than through as a whole. Many of these are concerned with death.[52] In one, he dreams of the end of the world, of a tidal wave engulfing the earth. Gasping for breath, he awakes. In another, addressed to Pauline, he asked that she should not visit his tomb, but should read a favourite passage from a book which they used to read together, and thus recall him who loved her so deeply and so tenderly.[53]

It is possible that around the time of *Virgin Soil*, Turgenev contemplated going into politics. He was in touch with some revolutionaries who were based in Paris at the time. He was under the impression that they had become moderate, deserved support, and he might have some useful role to play. Nothing came of this. Perhaps it was just as well; Bakunin regarded Turgenev as a political nitwit.[54]

CHAPTER 27

THE FISHERMAN

FOR THE LAST years of his life, Turgenev resided in France, either in Bougival or in the Viardots' house in the rue de Douai. The storms had subsided and he could enjoy a 'quiet happiness in which passion played no part, in the vicinity and company of the woman he loved'.[1]

Pauline felt responsible for looking after him. He needed mothering and she loved doing this. But it was not easy. He was very impractical and unpunctual. He was also 'prone to indiscreet eating and drinking'.[2] Although he was still only aged around 60, he was 'aging, weary, morose and gout-ridden'.[3] Worse, he suffered from periodic bouts of depression. He was terrified of cholera, and even more so of death. He was looking increasingly ancient, far beyond his years. He was obsessed with his age and he believed that life was behind him.[4]

Turgenev's fear of illness and death suddenly became a terrible reality. In *On the Eve*, he described how Death is like a fisherman who catches a fish in his net. He leaves it for a bit, as it swims and flaps in the water. He will haul it in, when it suits him.[5] He did.

Meanwhile, Turgenev had continued to enjoy the company of women, and he did not confine his interest to Pauline or the attractive Didie. During his periodic visits to Russia to deal with business matters, Turgenev's state of premature senility did not prevent him enjoying an Indian summer chasing the ladies. This activity was but a flash in the pan, although it caused Pauline much irritation.

Occasionally he had enjoyed 'associations of a quasi-erotic nature with women in which physical relations played no part', although he might have fantasised that they would. Around 1860 there was Madame Markovich, a Ukrainian writer who Pauline described as 'votre grosse Petite-Russienne'.[6]

Vrevskaya goes to war

In the early 1870s, Turgenev befriended the widow of a general killed in the Caucasus.[7] This was Baroness Julia Vrevskaya, a 'good-looking woman of thirty-two' who had been widowed very shortly after her marriage. Pauline labelled her 'La Veuve de Malabar', possibly because, as an attractive widow in St Petersburg society, she felt very unsettled and wanted to go to India. Turgenev saw her at Spasskoye, where they were near neighbours. Twice, she came to stay. They also met at Carlsbad and in Paris.[8]

Vrevskaya chased after him. Turgenev, true to character, wrote to her to say that he had wanted her. But he did not wish to marry her, yet he knew that she would never consent to an affair. The disappointed Baroness went off as a nurse to Romania and Bulgaria for the Russo-Turkish war. There, as a kind of Florence Nightingale, she worked bravely in appalling conditions.[9] She insisted on going to the front which was very dangerous indeed. She caught typhus and died. After this, Turgenev wrote a *Prose Poem* in which he said that it grieved him to think that nobody was present at her deathbed to thank her for her self-sacrifice, or even to pay homage to her dead body. He added, touchingly, 'I know that she recoiled from any show of gratitude, because it embarrassed her.'[10]

The Russo-Turkish War 1877–8

For governments to Russia's west, the survival of the Sultan's decaying régime provided an important obstacle to the extension of Russian power. However, their support entailed propping up a notorious régime. Insurrections in the Balkans, particularly in Bulgaria, were repressed by the Turks with a brutality 'at which Hell itself might almost blush', according to William Gladstone who demanded that the Turks be expelled 'bag and baggage'.

Britain was somewhat hamstrung when in April 1877 the Russians declared war on Turkey, ostensibly to defend the Christian Slavs. The 'ill commanded' Russians invaded Bulgaria where they were checked by the Turks, in various defeats to which Fauré refers in his letters to Marianne. However, in mid-winter the Russians traversed the Shipka Pass through the Eastern Balkans and reached the suburbs of Constantinople. The Sultan declared that the Russians would have to pass over his dead body to enter the city. But he had a British ship standing by to rescue him.

The Peace of San Stefano which the Russians imposed was unacceptable to Britain, where belligerence had reached fever pitch with the refrain 'We don't want to fight, but, by Jingo, if we do, We've got the men, we've got the ships, we've got the money too'. This crisis was defused by the Russians agreeing to the Congress of Berlin, where Russia was forced to climb down. After this, Disraeli, the British Prime Minister, claimed he had negotiated 'Peace with Honour'. Russian public opinion responded negatively. However, a major European war had been averted and a catchphrase created for Neville Chamberlain to repeat some 60 years later.[11]

Savina

Perhaps more 'serious' was Turgenev's infatuation with Maria Gavrilovna Savina, a 25-year-old actress who played Vera in the 1879 St Petersburg production of *A Month in the Country.* He had seen Savina in the year of her début, five years earlier, in a bad play which was badly acted, although she stood out as an exception. Her intelligence, prettiness, figure and soubrette naughtiness provided masses of sex appeal. This was tempered, however, by her nasal voice which was reminiscent of a Russian chambermaid at full volume.[12]

In 1880, Savina was invalided out of *A Month in the Country* after she damaged her shoulder in a fall. Turgenev went to see her. A month later, he saw her perform in *La Dame aux Camélias.* 'Beaucoup de talent et de chaleur', he wrote, while he said that the other actors were bad.[13]

Turgenev invited Savina to stay at Spasskoye. However, she could not afford the time. When she was on her way from Moscow to Odessa, he met her on the train at Mtsensk and travelled the short distance on to Oryol. He did not dare kiss her. The next day, he wrote to her speculating on the scandal which would have arisen had he abducted her, as he had felt inclined to do. 'I am profoundly regretful that that wonderful night should be lost forever', he said.[14] It was a kind of fantasy.

In 1881, Maria Savina did join Turgenev for four days at a house party he held at Spasskoye. During this visit, he took pleasure in watching her bathe in the lake. He read the assembled company 'The Song of Triumphant Love' which is about the enduring, hypnotic and consuming power of love.[15]

Turgenev kept writing to Savina; he suggested that they abscond to Italy together. This was absurd. At the time when he kissed her on the lips during her Spasskoye visit, she was already engaged to the man who was to become her second husband. She came to Paris at the end of March 1881. Turgenev visited her and helped find her a doctor. He obtained a cast of her hands, just as he obtained a cast of Pauline's hands.[16] He wrote to Savina, sometimes quite erotic letters, almost to the end of his life. Their relationship was unconsummated.[17]

Pauline was irritated when she heard of Turgenev's trysts. She was particularly jealous of Baroness Vrevskaya, we may surmise, because with her background she could actually constitute a serious competitor.[18]

As well as visiting Russia, Turgenev went away on shooting parties with friends and acquaintances in England. In 1878, he went partridge shooting at Six Mile Bottom in Cambridgeshire, six miles from Newmarket, a shoot which today still has an excellent reputation. The landowner was a friend of George Eliot and her partner G.H. Lewes. Also present was a former master at Eton, Oscar Browning, who had been sacked for preferring the classroom to the playing-fields and for paying too much attention to the boys. In the evening, Turgenev entertained the assembled company 'in his slow broken English'. He also read poems by Pushkin. George Eliot and Turgenev toasted and complimented each other.[19]

A couple of years later, after again shooting in Cambridgeshire, a banquet was arranged for him in London. This was organised by his English translator, William Ralston, a former librarian at the British Museum who had visited him in Spasskoye.[20] The banquet was attended by sixteen of the top literary people in the the country, such as Anthony Trollope, the author of *Barchester Towers*; R. D. Blackmore who wrote *Lorna Doone*; and George du Maurier, the illustrator for *Punch* and grandfather of Daphne. Also at the table were William Morris, the designer artist and craftsman, and Leslie Stephen, the first editor of the *Dictionary of National Biography* and father of the painter Vanessa Bell and the novelist Virginia Woolf. What a gathering! How one envies the waiters at it.

Because the event was arranged at short notice, Thomas Hardy, Wilkie Collins and Browning sent their apologies, as did Tennyson who suggested that Turgenev should visit his country house on his way home to France.[21]

In March 1881, Pauline and Turgenev attended Nikolay Rubinstein's funeral at the Russian Church in Paris.[22] During Turgenev's trip to Russia a few months later, he began to feel a severe pain in the shoulder. However, for the six months after his return, he enjoyed good health and went again to England to shoot and to be fêted by the literary establishment, as we have just seen.[23]

In March 1882, the Viardot *ménage* experienced that moment, familiar to many, when the barometer which had been pointing at 'set fair', suddenly lurches to the left. Marianne had a very difficult confinement. Louis had a stroke. Paulinette escaped with her two children and took refuge in Switzerland.[24]

For the next twelve months, Pauline devoted herself to looking after her husband who she loved so dearly,[25] getting him up, putting him by the window, reading the newspapers to him. In the last three months of his life, she only left his side to give the occasional singing lesson.[26]

The pressures on her increased because, in early April, Turgenev also became very ill. On Savina's birthday, he trudged along to her place in Paris with a couple of pot plants. On this occasion, he began to suffer acute and alarming pain under the collarbone and in his shoulder and chest. So, plans to go to Russia in the summer were deferred. He never returned there. The pain increased and would not go away, and apart from a few brief moments of remission[27] he was in nothing less than intense agony. Except when dosed with morphine, he had little uninterrupted sleep for the remaining seventeen months of his life.

The doctors thought that Turgenev had angina pectoris, chest pains which are usually caused by the narrowing of the coronary arteries.[28] All sorts of treatments were prescribed by a variety of experts, some of them the top, fashionable, most expensive doctors in Paris. He was given an intense form of heat treatment on his back, known as ignipuncture. Surgical instrument makers supplied and devised, sometimes with the victim's assistance, items intended to provide relief. There was a harness and a 'chaîne galvanique', which was a belt made of copper and zinc, attached to electric batteries. There was a copper brace whose inventor advocated pulmonary gymnastics, including singing, declamation and playing the horn, as a cure for respiratory troubles. There were other imaginative instruments, such as a contraption which shot 36 needle tips into the place where it was applied. Turgenev was also advised to drink twelve glasses of milk a day which was kindly supplied by his Franco-Russian relatives who had a cow. However, he found any position painful and described himself as nothing but an oyster.[29]

In the summer,[30] Turgenev was taken to Bougival. He worked at correcting the proofs of an edition of his complete works. He corresponded with Paulinette, who was still in Switzerland, about her precarious situation and reminded her of the absolute imperative of lying low. He also peremptorily insisted that she stop demanding money, stop being so sorry for herself, and begin to show some affection for Pauline who had been so good to her. In very different tones, he also found time to write a kindly letter to his granddaughter Jeanne. He congratulated her on her English and French, and hoped that next time she would write to him in German. Jeanne will have been too young to appreciate his irony when he wrote that she should be grateful to her mother for encouraging her with her languages. Paulinette's appalling grammar was one of his sorrows.[31]

Meanwhile, Pauline had to deflect visitors, and she was criticised for this. To keep an enquirer away, the concierge said that Turgenev was dangerously ill. The person was a journalist. When Turgenev read the newspaper report which said this, he suffered a relapse. From that day on, Pauline had to censor the papers before he got them.[32] The melancholy mood was occasionally alleviated, for example when Pauline's pupils put on *Le Dernier sorcier*, or the family played a game of whist in which Turgenev participated.

In the late autumn, Turgenev returned to Paris with Henry James.[33] Towards the end of the year, Turgenev noticed an apparently new development in the pubic area, the alarming enlargement of the remains of a carbuncle. This had originally been removed three decades before, shortly after he had been chasing after some Polish woman.[34] Before Christmas he consulted his doctor, and in mid-January he had an operation to remove the lump which was now as large as a plum. An incision was made sixteen centimetres long. Apart from a little local chilling with ether, he had no anaesthetic. The operation lasted twelve minutes. He needed to divert his mind from the pain as the steel cut in. So, he imagined himself dining with his literary friends. He tried to encapsulate the exact words he would use to tell them how it felt.[35] It seemed rather like a knife cutting a banana, he told Edmond de Goncourt.[36] This nonchalance succeeded. Pauline told her son that Turgenev did not even say 'ouf', that is, the French equivalent of 'ow'.[37]

Today, we must admire the toughness of earlier generations. As well as Turgenev, other writers illustrate this fortitude. Forty years earlier, without anaesthetic, Dickens's rectum was opened up and held apart by a surgical appliance, while tissue was cut away and the sides of the rectal wall were sewn together. An excruciating operation was experienced by Samuel Pepys when a stone, almost the size of a tennis ball, was removed from his bladder. The novelist Fanny Burney survived a mastectomy of the right breast in 1811.[38]

Their operations succeeded, as possibly did Turgenev's as far as the lump was concerned. However, by the end of January 1883, Turgenev was in dreadful pain from his 'former complaint'. 'Le pauvre Tourguéneff est dans un état pitoyable', Pauline wrote.[39] It was not long before he was shrieking with agony. The doctors became concerned that he was being given dangerously large doses of morphine. He, however, took no notice because he just wanted to die. Given his pain threshold, it must have been truly awful. He began cursing Pauline. At one moment, according to Louise, he tore off the knob of the bell-pull and threw it at her, shouting 'Ha! Voilà Lady Macbeth'.[40]

He had experienced hallucinations for some time. They got worse. He suffered from persecution mania, he thought he was being poisoned, and he seemed to be going insane. He thought he was under attack from Assyrian soldiers. He threatened to grab a brick from the walls of Nineveh and hurl it at his doctor. His behaviour was very distressing for all around him. Pauline managed to keep a sense of humour. When he asked her to throw him out of the window, she replied 'But you are too big and heavy, my dear Turgenev! Besides, it would hurt you!'[41]

Turgenev went back to Bougival at the beginning of May 1883. As he left the house in the rue de Douai, the octogenarian and ever-learned Louis Viardot emerged onto the landing. There, he gave the gladiators' salute, 'Ave Tourguéneff, morituri se salutant'.* 'Hail, Turgenev, those about to die salute each other'.[43] All those stags, bears, wolves and other game were about to have their revenge. On 5 May 1883, Louis Viardot died.

Louis was taken the few hundred yards to the Montmartre cemetery, where he was buried in a civil ceremony. Louis was an unbeliever to the end, even though, much to Turgenev's amusement, he used to litter his conversation with expressions such as ' Si Dios quiere', 'God-willing'.[44] The thoughts with which Louis had wrestled, during what he himself described as his 'long, honourable and studious life', had destroyed, piece by piece, all the edifice of conventional belief and reduced him, 'like Montaigne, to a state where he had nothing whereon to lay his head but the "pillow of doubt"'. Devotion to humanity had become Louis's God. There was 'no better sacrifice to offer to Humanity than an honest and laborious life'.[45]

Pauline was distraught. Louise, their daughter, later wrote that her father's death was the one great sorrow of her mother's life. She was so frantic with grief that she tried to throw herself out of a window. For weeks she had to be carefully watched.[46]

After her husband's funeral, Pauline had to move out to Bougival to look after Turgenev who was now so emaciated and weak. He continued to

*'Ave Caesar, morituri te salutant' was the salute given by gladiators at the start of their fight.[42]

long for death. Tempers occasionally became frayed. 'I have seen too many old men in my time, too many dead ones too', his literary cronies reported Pauline as saying.[47] However, Turgenev was able to dictate to her the short article 'A Fire at Sea', about that experience in his youth when he escaped from the burning ship. He was also able to arrange for Pauline's son-in-law Alphonse Duvernoy, the composer, to meet a Ukrainian friend about a possible libretto.

Turgenev's carer, at first, was Mademoiselle Arnholt who had been governess for Claudie and Marianne since the Baden-Baden days and was the subject of some naughty stories invented by Turgenev in his correspondence with Claudie. The kind-hearted Arnholt, when required to dilute the morphine with distilled water, occasionally thought it better to dilute it with the cherry-laurel drops prescribed as a laxative. Towards the end, Mademoiselle Arnholt was assisted, for a time, by Tata Herzen, the daughter of Alexander.[48]

As we know, five years earlier, Turgenev had made peace with Tolstoy after the rupture in their tempestuous relations which had lasted seventeen years. On 9 July, in one brief moment of remission, Turgenev wrote to Tolstoy, urging him to return to literature and give up all his philosophy.[49]

Five days after writing to Tolstoy, Turgenev was in appalling agony again.[50] At his bedside, the loyal Pauline watched from 7 am until he dozed off in the middle of the morning. She returned in the afternoon. Towards the end, she stayed for the night.

About a fortnight before his death, during a short remission, Turgenev dictated his last work, 'Une Fin', to Pauline. He longed for a release and even asked Maupassant to provide him with a revolver.[51]

Suffering so, Turgenev can have had little chance to recall the calm and controlled end which he had predicted for himself in one of his *Prose Poems* just a few years before. 'What shall I be thinking?' he had asked. 'I shall try to occupy myself with some trifle so as to take my mind off the threatening gloom, stretching out black in front of me.'[52]

Monday 3 September 1883. In his delirium, he seemed to be saying something unintelligible about Alexander II, the Tsar whose compliment on his contribution to the Emancipation made him so proud. His last words, as those around him paled into the distance, were 'Farewell my dear ones, my whitish ones'. Mademoiselle Arnholt moistened his parched tongue. He died in the presence of Pauline, Didie and Marianne and their husbands, among others. Turgenev's only child Paulinette, from whom he was estranged, was still in Switzerland. Although she was sent her monthly allowance on the day before he died, she was only told on the day of his death that it was imminent.[53]

Pauline was stricken with grief.

The family asked for an autopsy. This reported that, although Turgenev had displayed symptoms of angina pectoris, the actual cause of death was a large and destructive cancer in the lower spine. No wonder he had been in such terrible pain and could not move. Whether this was in some way related to his sexual misdemeanours we shall never know.[54] The days before Turgenev died, when at times he seemed to be insane, must have seemed like a horror scene from Dr Blanche's well-known clinic in Passy. As Pauline reflected on the last seventeen months of sheer hell, she might just have thought how wise she had been to resist his blandishments and entreaties all those years ago.

He was seen off at the Gare du Nord.[55] He was taken to St Petersburg, where he was buried on 9 October in the Volkov cemetery, close to Belinsky to whom he had dedicated *Fathers and Sons*. He did not think himself worthy of being buried at the feet of Pushkin.[56]

Turgenev was not religious. He said one could no more love God than love gravity or electricity. However, he told Countess Lambert that he regretted that he could not enjoy the solace which those who believe in religion obtain.[57]

Didie and her husband Georges Chamerot, who acted as Turgenev's executor, went to the funeral, as did Marianne and Alphonse Duvernoy. The ceremony took place in the presence of representatives of the Imperial government, the intelligentsia and worker's organisations. It was 'perhaps the first and last occasion on which these groups peacefully met in Russia'. There was a large police presence because the authorities were twitchy about such a large gathering.[58]

It had suited the fisherman to haul him in.

Last Act

Biographers face the problem that the twilight years of their subject are almost invariably relatively dull. There is often an imbalance between the early years which are full of interest and activity, and the humdrum later years. For some subjects, the transition starts earlier than for others. With a bit of luck, however, a macabre death scene provides some relief and an opportunity for the author. However, we have had that.

Nevertheless, we have been fortunate to get as far as we have. The biography on the programme for the first performance of Brahms's *Alto Rhapsody* and the Massenet *Marie Magdeleine* would today be crammed with credits which wearisomely listed each platform on which Pauline had appeared and each teacher with whom she could claim to have studied. Yet if it had not been for her friendship with Turgenev, whose star rose almost as her career subsided, the prestigious credits reflecting her public life would virtually have come to a halt in the 1860s. That was when the Viardots retired to Baden-Baden.

After the death of Louis and Turgenev, Pauline was as lonely as surviving spouses usually are. When, in the following year, she met Clara Schumann in Frankfurt, she told her that they were the two oldest friends of the century.[1] Saint-Saëns recorded that Pauline 'was very sad; her pupils are gone, she is alone in the world and feels cruelly the void left by her husband and Turgenev'.[2] Yet she had almost 27 years of her life still to live.

In the immediate aftermath of Turgenev's death, Pauline was embroiled in a row about his will. Although he had indicated that he wanted his friend Annenkov, the literary critic, to be at least his literary executor, his intentions were not precise. By a will made in the middle of the June before he died, Turgenev left everything to Pauline. Steps were taken to ensure that the Russian assets would go to her as well.[3] Pauline was, as we know, always alive to money matters.

However, she immediately faced threats on several fronts. The Russian literary establishment, who resented, indeed loathed, her were furious about Turgenev's dispositions. Fet, the poet, claimed that Turgenev had finally realised his dream of being trodden face down in the mud under Pauline's heel.[4] Some Russian cousins, one a niece of Fet, emerged from the woodwork to claim the estate at Spasskoye, as they were entitled to do under Russian law. The claim was successful. A settlement was eventually made in 1887, whereby Pauline received 25,000 silver roubles together with a further 600 roubles for some of the contents. The Russian estate was valued at 165,000 roubles, then the equivalent of around 412,500 francs.[5]

A bizarre challenge came from Gaston Bruère who, though estranged, was legally still in charge of Paulinette's affairs. Gaston's potential to cause disruption had worried Turgenev considerably. The annuity arrangements for Paulinette, whereby payments were channelled through Pauline, reflected his concerns. His forebodings were fully justified.

Within three days of Paulinette's father's death, Gaston tried to assume and claim Turgenev's tenant's rights over the flat at the top of the Viardots' house in the rue de Douai. As a consequence, the magistrates sealed up the whole house, so that Pauline found that she could not even get into her own home. When she did obtain access, Gaston accused her of interfering with the property by moving items out of Turgenev's flat; he thus claimed his right to all of Turgenev's assets which were spread over the remainder of the house. Gaston's mother, the cause of much trouble in Paulinette's marriage, also intervened and made a claim. For a time, magistrates' seals were affixed to Pauline's property such as her Pleyel piano. It was almost eighteen months before this dispute was finally resolved in her favour.

Les Frênes was sold in 1884, as was the house in the rue de Douai, both so replete with memories, the recent ones particularly unpleasant. The organ was sold for 7,000 francs to the church of Notre-Dame in Melun, south of Paris. The townhouse was sold for 400,000 francs[6] and was soon pulled down. From 1884 Pauline lived in an apartment in the Boulevard Saint-Germain, on the Left Bank overlooking the Seine, almost next to the Assemblée Nationale.[7] This was around the corner from the basilica of Sainte-Clotilde, where, until his death in 1890, César Franck was still the organist.

Pauline

Not surprisingly, Pauline was enraged by the legal action over Turgenev's estate and the badmouthing from the Russians. And, not least, she was furious with her son Paul who sided with the Bruères.[8] A considerable amount of ill-will developed between them all. So, although Annenkov was to get the papers, he mainly received some Russian material which he took away with him to Berlin. Pauline later gave some of Turgenev's effects, including Pushkin's signet ring, to a museum in Russia. Most of these things have now disappeared.

The whereabouts of much of Pauline's correspondence with Turgenev is also a mystery. She had made many moves, from Courtavenel, from Baden-Baden, from the house in the rue de Douai. On each occasion, she may have cleared out documents which she considered were personal to her, but which are important to us.[9]

Some of the correspondence with Turgenev did turn up. Various items connected with him appear occasionally at auctions. At first Pauline, through Chamerot, denied that any letters had ever been lost and threatened to sue if they were published. In 1897, she at last agreed to review a series of letters. She authorised some for publication, she made excisions and withdrew others.[10] Of the first twenty letters which she saw, Pauline rejected three outright; from the next 25 she rejected nine, and made deletions in others. Everything 'of a private character' was cut.[11]

Detractors can easily jump to the conclusion that Pauline was slashing away in an attempt to remove anything prurient. While this may be so, one may equally wonder whether she would have really have been so desperately concerned about what had happened half a century before. It is possible that she was merely applying a principle, to which she apparently strongly adhered, that although she had once been a public figure, her life was private, as was that of Turgenev.[12] This is a point of view which we recognise today and about which opinions differ.

Turgenev had a habit of writing ruthless and unflattering opinions of contemporaries, friends and events, some of which we have noticed. In that sense, the letters were intended for private view. Pauline may have thought that they should remain so.[13] She also cut out text which revealed Turgenev's musical taste which she rightly did not regard as particularly admirable.[14]

Despite Saint-Saëns's assertion to the contrary, Pauline did have pupils, for example Clara Butt, a young Sussex girl* who would subsequently become 'famous'.[15] Pauline could claim credit for the first Kundry in *Parsifal*, the first Geneviève in *Pelléas et Mélisande*. She died just a few months before her pupil starred as the first Marschallin in *Der Rosenkavalier*.

She continued to teach until she was 80.[16] Louise gave her a white poodle who she tried to teach to sing, but without success. The dog, which took up a position under the grand piano, would emerge in anger when a pupil sang out of tune.[17]

Pauline told one pupil that she was 'as happy as one can be when one's heart is profoundly sad'. However, seeing her grandchildren, such as Paul's daughter, learning to play music must have given her enormous pleasure.[18]

*The Royal Albert Hall was said to have been built in anticipation of the gigantic Dame Clara with her trombone-like sound. A critique of an 1894 performance of Handel's *Israel in Egypt* recorded that she had 'lately been studying under Mme Viardot to some purpose though for far too short a time'. Butt apparently gave a very poor performance of 'Their land brought forth frogs' but was better in 'Thou shalt bring them in'.

Clara Butt

Pauline also composed new works and republished earlier ones. She had published something in almost every year of her adult life. When she did not, there was usually a reason, such as the disruption caused by the Franco-Prussian War.[19] In that dreadful year of death, 1883, she published Handel's funereal *Largo*, arranged for voice accompanied by piano with cello or violin. In subsequent years, songs poured forth, including a setting for voice of Brahms's *Hungarian Dances.*

In 1886, she laid on a performance of Saint-Saëns' *Carnaval des animaux* for Liszt. In the following year, she organized a concert of Russian music at which Balakirev's *Islamey* was performed.[20] One wonders if she remembered Turgenev's typically astringent assessment of this composer after he met him, 'kein Talent, doch ein Character','No talent, but a character'.[21]

The twentieth anniversary of the Weimar performance of *Le Dernier sorcier* was celebrated in April 1889 with a performance, together with that of *Trop de femmes.* They were staged in Pauline's flat. When she was 75, she wrote music for a pantomime *Au Japon.* In 1904, she composed and assembled the music for *Cendrillon*, for which she also wrote the words. This is a delightful three-act chamber operetta using the story of Cinderella; it is accompanied on the piano and lasts about an hour; a recording of it from January 2000 is published by Opera Rara.[22]

Pauline maintained her energetic pace until she was aged 85.

Through all this, Pauline remained 'enchanting' yet sufficiently formidable for Tchaikovsky to be 'apprehensive'[23] about the lunch which he had arranged to have with her. He set forth in a thunderstorm and got soaked to the skin. As was often the case, Tchaikovsky was in Paris on a drunken and homosexual binge.[24]

Pauline in old age

Pauline showed Tchaikovsky her priceless manuscript of *Don Giovanni.* 'I cannot express the feeling which overwhelmed me as I examined that sacred relic', he told his patron back in Russia. 'It was just as if I had shaken hands with Mozart himself, and chatted with him.'[25]

Around two years later, when he was in Paris as part of a concert tour, Tchaikovsky visited her many times. He heard her singing beautifully. Before he left for London, he attended the anniversary performance of *Le Dernier sorcier* at Pauline's.[26]

Sir Charles Stanford, the Anglo-Irish composer, was invited to dinner by Pauline; he described her as looking just like 'a French Marquise of the old régime'.[27] We can imagine her, elderly, upright and autocratic; but, as ever, she was capable of great charm and enthusiasm. She had risen many ranks since Marie d'Agoult had called her 'une demoiselle du très grand monde'.[28]

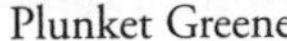

Plunket Greene

Sir Charles Stanford

Pauline wanted to meet another distinguished Irishman, the singer Plunket Greene who was celebrated especially for his performances of oratorio, such as *Messiah* and *The Dream of Gerontius.* His wife was the daughter of Sir Hubert Parry, the composer of *Jerusalem.* Pauline, being over 80 at the time, was unable to get to the concert at which Greene was performing. He was invited in towards the end of dinner. When the bell rang, she called her butler to fetch a salver, some glasses and some champagne. She had him throw open the double doors of the drawing room in which Greene was waiting. In a theatrical gesture, from a very theatrical lady, she swooped into the drawing-room, curtseyed to Greene, presented him with a glass. They duly toasted each other 'with the reverence which one great artist has for another'. Stanford made a comment which reminds us that we really have reached the 20th century. 'I inwardly wished for a Kodak', he wrote.[29]

Pauline was awarded the Légion d'honneur in 1901. In that year, she was visited by Reynaldo Hahn who wanted to establish an authentic French text for *Don Giovanni.* He found Pauline full of life and enthusiasm, despite her failing sight. 'She took immediate charge of the interview', he recorded. 'They tell me you're Spanish', Pauline told the Venezuela-born composer and conductor, having launched into Andalusian dialect at great speed. Hahn, who was well known in the salons for his songs and his attractive voice,[30] really wanted to spend the time talking about the Mozart manuscript. However, Pauline insisted on hearing him sing. She listened, approved of his performance and the simplicity of his style. Then, they got down to discussing her interpretation of the role of Donna Anna.

As the years wore on, Pauline usually had a sketch book or some needlework in her hands. Her sight continued to deteriorate with cataract, and her hearing went. Mademoiselle Arnholt stayed as her companion, but when she died her place was taken by a former pupil, Mademoiselle Mathilde de Nogueiras, whose father had been the Portuguese ambassador in Paris. A private performance of *Cendrillon* was held in her apartment. In the last years, Mademoiselle de Nogueiras lived with Pauline and tended her night and day.[31]

Friends who used to visit Pauline died off. Ernest Renan died in 1892, his wife two years later; Jules Simon, the former Prime Minister who had been a frequent visitor to Courtavenel, died in 1896. In 1906, her brother Manuel Garcia died in London aged 101.[32] Her son-in-law Alphonse Duvernoy died in the following year.

Increasingly she was on her own. Like many elderly people, Pauline read and wrote. In 1907, she wrote a letter to Turgenev's old friend, the artist Pietsch, in which she recommended a pupil and told him that she was working on a history of the song in France.[33]

She was awake for much of the night; she could count the hours striking on the clock at the Palais Bourbon.[34] She reminisced about her parents, about her brilliant ebullient father, and about Maria whose life had been cut so tragically short. Many of those whom she had known were now but history to the next generations, names such as Alfred de Musset, George Sand, George's son Bouli, Delacroix, Scheffer, Gounod, Berlioz, Rietz, Turgenev. All were dead, some many years ago. Tuberculosis had taken away both Chopin, Chip-chip, and Rachel her contemporary, around half a century before.

Musset had been really dreadful, hadn't he? She was lucky to escape from him. Was not there a quip that, when he missed meetings at the Académie Française, some members complained 'Musset s'absente trop', while others explained 'Il s'absinthe trop'?[35]

And Rachel who, together with Pauline, had shown such great promise. Pauline's mind will surely have wandered back to the time of her Paris début at the Théâtre de la Renaissance, after which Musset published his poem welcoming, applauding, hailing those two young hearts, both bursting with ancient poetry, both blessed by the gods. That two such geniuses were of even age came as no surprise to him. For they both were born of the Muse who guards the sacred fire. He urged them to obey fearlessly the true principles of their Art, and to pour forth its treasure, in fullest measure:

O jeunes coeurs remplis d'antique poésie,
Soyez les bienvenus, enfants aimés des dieux !
Vous avez le même âge et le même génie
    La douce clarté soit bénie
    Que vous ramenez dans nos yeux !

    Allez, que le bonheur vous suive!
Ce n'est pas du hasard un caprice inconstant
    Qui vous fit naître au même instant.
Votre mère ici-bas, c'est la Muse attentive
Qui sur le feu sacré veille éternellement.

Obéïssez sans crainte au dieu qui vous inspire.
Ignorez, s'il se peut, que nous parlons de vous.
Ces plaintes, ces accords, ces pleurs, ce frais sourire,
    Tous vos trésors, donnez-les nous:
    Chantez, enfants, laissez-nous dire.[36]

Pauline had been so nervous in that first *Otello*, when she sang Rossini's Desdemona, a colossal part for a seventeen-year-old. However, 'en un quart d'heure, une belle destinée fut ouverte'.[37] 'What will become of Pauline Garcia', Musset had asked. 'There is no doubt, her success is assured. Whatever she does, she can only achieve greater things.'[38]

Such promise! Of course, she knew that, in appearance, she was never remotely as fascinating as Rachel, who immediately became a star.

For Pauline, it had been an uphill struggle to climb her way to professional and financial security. Once she was at the top, her life, at times, was sheer drudgery. She had had to be tough, even ruthless. Fortunately, Louis was around to look after her business affairs. Funny old Loulou with his big nose. She was so fond of him. He had loved her so dearly. He was so learned. He it was that ensured that she had not ended her life like Mario who died in somewhat straitened circumstances in Rome;[39] or worse, that Rosine Stoltz, who had died a batty recluse in a flat in the Avenue de l'Opéra, a 'Princesse' who left behind hardly enough money to pay for a proper funeral.[40]

Pauline knew that the final tragedy of lyric artists, certainly in those days, is that they leave no audible or lasting legacy.[41] Would she ever be remembered except as someone who had nurtured, developed and sustained her beloved, innocent Turgenev, the big baby for whom she had acted as a mother substitute? She herself had inspired him, and their relationship had had such a profound and lasting influence on his works.[42] She had not just been some adjunct. Without their relationship, without its extraordinary complexity, Turgenev's works would have had no source.

She had dominated him, and he had loved it. He adored her.[43] She had wanted to be 'a sister of charity with a mission' and she had achieved it. Had not the leading historian of the century called her 'la bonne, la charitable, la sainte Garcia-Viardot', a superior form of humanity, the most noble type of woman of which he could dream?[44] She had cared for several 'wounded hearts': Turgenev, Berlioz, Scheffer, Louis. Yet Turgenev was special. Without her, that great author would never have existed. In that sense, their relationship was unique.

As a singer, had she really fulfilled her artistic destiny? She had certainly obeyed fearlessly 'the God who had inspired her' and preached her Art. Countless people had benefited. She had excelled in many leading roles in works by Mozart, Rossini, Donizetti, Bellini; all great works, great composers. With Fidès, she had established the contralto as an operatic heroine during the 19th century. Yet those first nights in *Le Prophète*, *Sapho*, *Orphée*, and those countless appearances strutting and fretting 'her hour upon the stage' and platform,[45] what did they add up to? Probably they, and the rest, signified nothing.

Meyerbeer, Gounod, Gluck ... the first two were not in the top rank. Nor was she herself, perhaps. Indeed, the contralto had quickly been supplanted by noisy sopranos. And certainly when it came to immortality, Turgenev would survive longer, as would even the curiously eccentric Gounod.[46]

She had had to contend with Grisi, Stoltz and the others. Her voice, her instrument, had not been as naturally beautiful as Grisi's. However, in musicianship and learning, she outclassed them all. Camille Saint-Saëns would praise her 'astonishing versatility in style', and say that 'what made her even more captivating than her talent as a singer was her personality'.[47] Musset had put his finger on it. He said that she possessed the secret of really great artists: 'avant d'exprimer, elle sent'. Before opening that large mouth of hers, she felt the music in her heart.[48]

She would endure in the memory of those who knew her. If all else failed, she would forever be associated with her bequest of the manuscript of *Don Giovanni* to the Conservatoire.

So, it was not all depressing; besides, they had had such enormous fun with their practical jokes, at the Théâtre des Pommes de Terre and on those hilarious Sunday evenings. She also had her large and growing family to visit and enjoy, and to provide consolation.[49] Claudie, Didie, Ivan's darling, painted beautifully. Had she not been commended by the great English painter of classical scenes, Frederic Leighton? Marianne sang well. Even Louise. Had not Gounod described her as 'a remarkable musical composer'?[50]

However, she had to admit that it was Paul, the violin virtuoso, who had really inherited her talent, as well as Louis's big nose.[51] It was a pity that she and Paul had fallen out again. Paul resented working in her shadow, even being complimented on being her son.[52] She did not like his wife. 'That boy cannot stop getting himself into deep water', she had said.[53]

By the time of her death, she had three grandsons, four granddaughters, and four great-grandchildren of which the oldest was already ten. The eighteen months before Pauline died were full of family events which had enlarged the family. Marcelle, Claudie's daughter who looked uncannily like Turgenev, got married and had a son; Paul had a child by his second wife.[54]

The nights passed quickly. The Palais Bourbon clock seemed to strike every five minutes rather than every hour.[55] Fortunately, she had managed to deal with the correspondence.

The First Act of *Orphée* ended with thundering applause as Pauline made her exit, following a virtuoso aria with the recurring line 'Je vais braver le trépas', I will confront Death. This aria had a stupendous, breathtaking coloratura cadenza, the arpeggios culminating in a two-octave chromatic scale from middle C up to top C and down again.

There was no such drama for Pauline just over half a century later. She died in Paris on Wednesday 18 May 1910. Two days before, she apparently said 'I have two days left to live'.[56] After this, she said little more, except that she seemed to converse with some of those people from her past.

Louise, the daughter whose difficult character and unhappy life was so much the responsibility of her successful, proud mother, described the end. Her mother 'dozed off in her comfortable armchair. At three in the morning, she passed away without waking. Her cheeks seemed rosy and her lips bore a contented smile.'[57]

Louise concluded, surely with great generosity and much experience: 'Thus a peaceful death closed and crowned a life of hard work, success and happiness'.[58] 'May death deal with us all as gently and kindly as with her.'[59]

Pauline's last word had apparently been 'Norma',[60] the name of Bellini's druid priestess who sacrificed herself for love. This was a role in which Pauline never felt that she had been entirely successful. Last words are unlikely to be rational. She had been caring, motherly and inspirational, but she had never really sacrificed herself to Louis and Turgenev. They sacrificed themselves entirely to her. George Sand recognised this; she said that Pauline had the egoism required of a first-class artist.[61] However, as the man who had adored her so much has told us, 'Great are the mysteries of human life, and the most inaccessible of these mysteries is Love'.[62]

The obituary in *The Times* that Thursday stated: 'Her personal qualities were of a high order and her kindness to beginners in the ranks of her profession was proverbial'. The notice was printed next to information about a meeting of aviators hoping to fly the 42 km from Angers to Saumur and enjoy a prize fund of 50,000 francs.

The fact that all the columns of *The Times* were lined in black had nothing to do with Pauline, or an aristocratic polo player who had blown his brains out, or an aviator who had crashed in France. Nor was the mourning meant for the 130 men and boys entombed in the appalling Whitehaven mining disaster in Cumberland. It was for King Edward VII whose funeral was on the same day as Pauline's.[63]

Two days after her death, the funeral service for Pauline's earthly remains was held around the corner at Sainte-Clotilde. The 'Pie Jesu' from the *Requiem* by Fauré, who had so nearly become her son-in-law, was sung, among other works. Pauline was buried in the cemetery at the foot of the hill of Montmartre, next to Louis. The graveyard is close to the house in the rue de Douai in which she had lived and where so much music had been made. Camille Saint-Saëns and Jules Massenet gave orations.[64]

Pauline entered the Elysian Fields, and passed the Shades, to the sublime sound of Gluck's melodies, without sorrow, without joy.[65] Many years before, she had told her great confidant Julius Rietz that she had 'the firm conviction that the soul is immortal, and that all loves will one day be united … the great loves, whatever be their nature, provided that they have made themselves worthy of it'.[66]

Turgenev did not believe in immortality, but at a number of moments of great tenderness he told Pauline of the consolation to be derived from the thought of lying for eternity next to the one whom one has loved. He was reminded of the Song by Robert Burns:

John Anderson, my jo,* John,
  We clamb the hill thegither;
And mony a canty day, John,
  We've had wi' ane anither:
Now we maun totter down, John,
  But hand in hand we'll go
And sleep thegither at the foot,
  John Anderson, my jo.[67]

* My love

That was not to be. They were not to lie together at the foot of life's hill. Although located on the map, Pauline's tomb in the Montmartre cemetery is difficult to find among all the others. To find that of her 'bien, cher Tourguéneff, mon cher ami',[68] her spirit, her phantom, would have to fly some 1,500 miles.

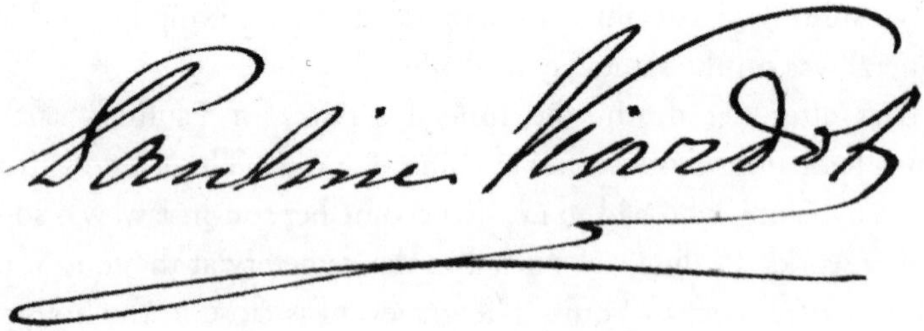

References

Preface (pp. xiii–xv)

1 Goncharov (trans. D. Magarshack), *Oblomov* (London: Penguin, 1954), p. 241; I. Turgenev (trans. and intro. I. Berlin), *A Month in the Country* (London: Penguin, 1981), p. 33; M. Lermontov (trans. P. Foote), *A Hero of Our Time* (London: Penguin, 2001), p. 3.
2 N. Žekulin, 'The story of an operetta', *Le Dernier Sorcier and Ivan Turgenev* (Munich: Verlag Otto Sagner, 1989), p. 1.
3 P. Waddington, *A Modest Little Banquet at the Arts Club* (New Zealand: Pinehaven, 2001), p. 1.
4 *History Today*, October 2004, p. 6; *History Today*, June 2005, p. 21.
5 F. Dostoyevsky, *The Idiot* (Ware, Herts: Wordsworth Classics, 1996), Part IV, ch. 1, p. 431.
6 P. Waddington, 'Some Gleanings on Turgenev and his International Connections', *New Zealand Slavonic Journal*, 1983, p. 190.
7 D. Magarshack, *Turgenev, a Life* (London: Faber & Faber, 1954), p. 51.
8 P. Mansel, *Paris between Empires, 1814–1852* (London: John Murray, 2001), p. 320 – a view attributed to the Marquis de Custine.
9 H. Granjard and A. Zviguilsky, *Lettres Inédites à Pauline Viardot et à sa famille* (Paris: Editions de l'Age de l'Homme, 1972), p. 157.
10 Ibid., p. xi.
11 R. Poole, 'Making up for Lost Time', *History Today*, December 1999, pp. 40–46; *Encyclopaedia Britannica*, ninth edition, vol. IV, p. 671; M. Fainsod, *How Russia is Ruled* (Cambridge, MA: Harvard University Press, 1963), p. 9; P. Waddington, *Turgenev and England* (London: Macmillan, 1980), p. x.
12 *Oxford Book of Quotations*, third edition (Oxford: OUP, 1985).
13 I. Turgenev (trans. Isabel Hapgood), *Lieutenant Ergúnoff* (1867), (Freeport New York: Books for Libraries Press, 1971), p. 45.

Overture (pp. 1–8)

1 *The Times*, 11 July 1849 (84 degrees Fahrenheit in the shade, 109 degrees in the sun at Greenwich).
2 D.G. Rossetti in P. Waddington, *Russian interests of the Rossetti Family* (New Zealand: Pinehaven, 1998), p. 4.
3 C. Woodham-Smith, *The Great Hunger* (London: First Four Square Edition, 1994), pp. 372, 374, 376, 379, 413.
4 *Illustrated London News* (*ILN*), 7 July 1849, 21 July 1849; *The Times*, 18 July 1849, 28 July 1849.
5 C. Woodham-Smith, op. cit., p. 382.
6 In May: G. St Aubyn, *Queen Victoria, a Portrait* (London: Sinclair-Stevenson, 1991), p. 163.
7 *The Times*, 17 July 1849 (court circular), 18 July 1849.
8 Ibid., 18 July 1849.
9 *ILN*, 28 July 1849, p. 55.
10 *The Times*, 4 July 1849; 13 June 1849.
11 *ILN*, 21 April 1849.
12 *The Times*, 11 July 1849.
13 *ILN*, 11 August 1849.
14 *The Times*, 25 July 1849.
15 B. Rees, *Camille Saint-Saëns, A Life* (London: Chatto & Windus, 1999), p. 203; P. Waddington, 'Dickens, Pauline Viardot and Turgenev: a Study in Mutual Admiration', *New Zealand Slavonic Journal*, 1974, no. 2, p. 56; P. Waddington, *A letter of W.M. Thackeray to Louis Viardot* (New Zealand: Pinehaven, 1998); S. Rutherford, *The Prima Donna and Opera 1815–1930* (Cambridge: Cambridge University Press, 2006), p. 62. The dramatic poem was 'Armgart'.
16 C.V. Stanford & C. Forsyth, *A History of Music* (New York: Macmillan, 1917) p. 279; *New Grove Dictionary of Music and Musicians* (London: Macmillan, 1980), vol. 12, p. 253, Meyerbeer (H. Becker).
17 M. Curtiss, *Bizet and his World* (London: Secker and Warburg, 1959), p. 147; *New Grove*, vol. 12, p. 253 (H. Becker).
18 L. Davies, *César Franck and his Circle* (London: Barrie and Jenkins, 1970), p. 24.
19 M. Curtiss, *Bizet and his World* (London: Secker and Warburg, 1959), p. 147
20 T. Marix-Spire, *Lettres inédites de George Sand et de Pauline Viardot 1839–1849*, 'le plus beau génie de femme de nôtre époque' (Paris: Nouvelles Editions, 1959) pp. 10, 13.
21 A. FitzLyon, *The Price of Genius, a life of*

Pauline Viardot (London: John Calder, 1964), p. 355; G. Dulong, *Pauline Viardot Tragédienne Lyrique* (Bougival: Association d'Amis d'Ivan Tourguéniev, Pauline Viardot et Maria Malibran), p. 139.

22 P. Waddington, 'Dickens, Pauline Viardot and Turgenev: a study in Mutual Admiration', *New Zealand Slavonic Journal*, 1974, no. 2, p. 64; H. Granjard and A. Zviguilsky, *Ivan Tourguénev, Lettres inédites à Pauline Viardot et à sa famille* (Paris: Editions l'Age d'Homme, 1972), p. 163; P. Ackroyd, *Dickens* (London: Sinclair Stevenson, 1990), p. 919.

23 P. Waddington, 'Dickens, Pauline Viardot and Turgenev', op. cit., p. 66; J. Forster, *The Life of Charles Dickens* (London: Chapman & Hall, 1874), pt III, p. 115 (footnote); S. Rutherford, op. cit., p. 52. Bernhardt said that Pauline was 'the finest actress she had ever seen'.

24 *Musical Quarterly*, 1915, vol. I, p. 352.

25 N. Žekulin, *The story of an operetta, Le Dernier sorcier and Ivan Turgenev* (Munich: Verlag Otto Sagner, 1989), p. 30.

26 Manuel's pupil Mathilde Marchesi, a most influential and distinguished teacher in Vienna and Paris, taught Melba, and so on. Harold Bruder, 'Manuel Garcia the Elder, his School and his Legacy', *Opera Quarterly*, vol. 13, no. 4, 1997, pp. 38, 42; *New Grove*, vol. 11, p. 658, Marchesi (Elizabeth Forbes).

27 Daniel Barenboim, first BBC Reith lecture, 2006.

28 *New Grove*, vol. 19, p. 694, Viardot (A. FitzLyon); A. FitzLyon, *The Price of Genius*, op. cit. (London: John Calder, 1964), p. 298.

29 P. Waddington, 'Dickens, Pauline Viardot and Turgenev', p. 61; P. Waddington, *A Modest Little Banquet at the Arts Club* (Pinehaven, New Zealand, 2001), pp. 13, 40.

30 R. Freeborn, *Turgenev, the novelist's novelist* (Oxford: Oxford University Press, 1960), pp. 18, 19.

31 Sir I. Berlin, Romanes lecture 1970, 'Fathers and Children', from I. Turgenev (trans. R. Edmonds), *Fathers and Sons* (London: Penguin, 1965 and 1970), pp. 9, 35.

32 Ibid. p. 9; subtle, the view of Wilkie Collins, P. Waddington, *A Modest Little Banquet at the Arts Club* (Pinehaven, New Zealand, 2001), p. 9; clever, P. Waddington, *Turgenev and England* (London: Macmillan, 1980), pp. 2, 3.

33 Sir I. Berlin, op. cit., p. 9.

34 L. Schapiro, *Turgenev, his Life and Times* (Oxford: OUP, 1978), p. 152.

35 H. James, Jr., *French Poets and Novelists* (London: Macmillan, 1878), p. 270.

36 H. James, Jr., op. cit., p. 318.

37 V.S. Pritchett, *The Gentle Barbarian, The Life and Work of Turgenev* (London: Chatto & Windus, 1977), p. 7.

38 D. Magarshack, *Turgenev, a Life* (London: Faber & Faber, 1954), pp. 12, 15; V.S. Pritchett, op. cit., p. 1; Mr Kyril FitzLyon would argue that the incident was an accident.

39 R. Hingley, *Dostoyevsky, his life and work* (London: Paul Elek Ltd, 1978), p. 37.

40 A. FitzLyon, *The Price of Genius*, pp. 191, 208.

41 R. Freeborn in his introduction to I. Turgenev (trans. and intro. R. Freeborn), *First Love and Other Stories* (Oxford: OUP, 1999), p. 14; Ibid., p. 32.

42 E. Zola (trans M. Mauldon), *L'Assommoir* (Oxford: Oxford University Press, 1995), ch. 11, p. 376; ch. 8, p. 243.

43 G. Weldon, *My Orphanage and Gounod in England* (London: London Music and Art Association, 1882), p. 96.

44 *The Whistle*, quoted in H.Troyat (trans. N. Amphoux), *Turgenev* (London: W.H. Allen, 1989), p. 70.

45 L. Hudson, and B. Jacot, *Intimate relations, the natural history of desire* (Yale, London 1995), which quotes K. Wellings et al., *Sexual Behaviour in Britain* (Penguin, 1994). The actual figures were 79 per cent of men and 84 per cent of women.

46 I. Turgenev (trans. D. Noyes), 'A Month in the Country', in *Masterpieces of the Russian Drama* (London: D. Appleton & Co, 1933), p. 316.

Chapter 1. The Garcias (pp. 11–27)

1 A. FitzLyon, *The Price of Genius, a life of Pauline Viardot* (London: John Calder, 1964), p. 15; *The Book of Saints* sixth edition (London: A & C Black, 1989), p. 484.

2 P. Barbier, *Opera in Paris 1800–1850* (Oregon: Amadeus Press, 1995), p. 169.

3 C. Saint-Saëns (trans. E.G. Rich), *Musical Memories* (London: Murray, 1921), p. 146.

4 *New Grove Dictionary of Music and Musicians* (London: Macmillan, 1980), vol. 7, p. 152,

Garcia (A. FitzLyon); I. Turgenev (trans. L. Schapiro), *Spring Torrents* (London: Penguin, 1980), p. 27.

5 *New Grove*, op. cit., vol. 7, p. 152, Garcia (A. FitzLyon); A. FitzLyon, *Maria Malibran – Diva of the Romantic Age* (London: Souvenir Press, 1987), p. 23.

6 A. FitzLyon, *The Price of Genius*, op. cit., p. 16, and A. FitzLyon, *Maria Malibran*, op. cit., p. 24; G. Sand's *Consuelo* would support the case that 'elle était de bon sang espagnol, sans doute mauresque à l'origine'; G. Sand (trans. Fayette Robinson), *Consuelo* (New York: Stringer and Townsend, 1851), p. 4, and N. Savy (ed.), George Sand, *Consuelo, La Comtesse de Rudolstadt* (Paris: Editions Robert Laffont SA, 2004), p. 38. The interest which the Viardot family took in George Eliot's *Daniel Deronda* (see p. 402) might be relevant to the Jewish connection.

7 G. Dulong, *Pauline Viardot Tragédienne Lyrique* (Bougival: Association des Amis d'Ivan Tourguéniev Pauline Viardot et Maria Malibran, 1987), p. 12; L. Héritte-Viardot (trans. E.S. Bucheim), *Memories and Adventures* (London: Mills & Boon, 1913), p. 5; Pauline told her daughter Louise about this in 1908.

8 *New Grove*, op. cit., vol. 11, p. 577, Malibran (Elizabeth Forbes).

9 *Musical Quarterly*, 1915, p. 532: he could do everything 'depuis cuisine jusqu'à opéra'; L. Héritte-Viardot (trans. E.S. Bucheim), *Memories and Adventures* (London: Mills & Boon, 1913), p. 5.

10 A. FitzLyon, *Maria Malibran*, op. cit., p. 28; Comtesse Merlin, *Maria Malibran* (London: Henry Colburn, 1840), p. 142.

11 A. FitzLyon, *Maria Malibran*, op. cit., pp. 26, 105; P. Waddington, 'Some Gleanings on Turgenev and his International Connections', *New Zealand Slavonic Journal*, 1983, p. 217.

12 A FitzLyon, *Maria Malibran*, op. cit., p. 25.

13 T. Marix-Spire, *Lettres inédites de George Sand et de Pauline Viardot 1839–1849* (Paris: Nouvelles Editions, 1959), p. 259.

14 A. FitzLyon, *Maria Malibran*, op. cit., p. 27; *The New Oxford Companion to Music* (Oxford: Oxford University Press, 1984), p. 1382.

15 A. FitzLyon, *Maria Malibran*, op. cit., p. 39, 105; G. Dulong, op. cit., p. 13.

16 H.F. Chorley, *Thirty years' Musical Recollections* (London: Hurst & Blackett, 1862), vol. I, p. 8.

17 R.D. Owen, *Threading My Way* (London: Trübner, 1874), p. 229; A. FitzLyon, op. cit., *The Price of Genius*, p. 21; A. FitzLyon, *Maria Malibran*, op. cit., p. 34.

18 R.D. Owen, op. cit., p. 229; A. FitzLyon, *The Price of Genius*, op. cit., p. 22; *Encyclopaedia Britannica*, ninth edition, vol. XVIII, p. 87 (Owen).

19 R.B. Nye and J.A. Mopurgo, *A History of the United States* (Harmondsworth: Penguin, 1965), pp. 345–8, 358, 361. The figure for the price of plots is dated 1820, minimum acreage, minimum price.

20 H. James, Jr, *Washington Square* (London: Penguin Classics, 2000), pp. 28, 40, 50; *Encyclopaedia Britannica*, Standard Millennium edition.

21 *New Grove*, op. cit., vol. 5, p. 237, Da Ponte (R. Angermüller).

22 S. Hodges, *Lorenzo da Ponte* (University of Wisconsin Press, 2002), p. 191; G. Dulong, op. cit., p. 13. A fashionable doctor might expect to earn, say, $20,000 per year ($3,333 for two months), for example Dr Sloper in H. James, Jr, *Washington Square*, op. cit., p. 37.

23 A. FitzLyon, *Maria Malibran*, op. cit., p. 38; *Encyclopaedia Britannica*, Standard Millennium edition, op. cit.; B. Weinreb and C. Hibbert, *London Encyclopaedia* (London: Macmillan, 1993), p. 210.

24 A. FitzLyon, *Maria Malibran*, op. cit., pp. 40, 44; A. FitzLyon, *The Price of Genius*, op. cit., p. 23; Eugène Malibran's letters are in the Bougival museum.

25 J. McPherson, *Battle Cry of Freedom* (New York: Oxford University Press, 1988), p. 26.

26 A. FitzLyon, *Maria Malibran*, op. cit., pp. 51, 59–63; *Encyclopaedia Britannica*, ninth edition, vol. X, p. 117.

27 C. Gowan, *France from the Regent to the Romantics* (London: Harrap, 1961), p. 242

28 H.F. Chorley: *Thirty years' Musical Recollections*, op. cit., vol. I, p. 8.

29 A. FitzLyon, *Maria Malibran*, op. cit., pp. 73, 39, 80.

30 W. Kuhe, *My musical recollections* (London: Richard Bentley, 1896), p. 185.

31 J. Harding, *Gounod* (London: George Allen & Unwin Ltd, 1973), p. 28.

32 A. FitzLyon, *Maria Malibran*, op. cit., p. 80.

33 The figure of 600,000 francs comes from Comtesse Merlin, *Maria Malibran* (London: Henry Colburn, 1840), p. 161; the price of a

mansion in 1826, 350,000 francs, is taken from P. Mansel, *Paris Between Empires, 1814–1852* (London: John Murray, 2001), p. 309.

34 Comtesse Merlin, op. cit., pp. 79, 117; the English comparison is from D. Thomson, *England in the Nineteenth Century* (Harmondsworth: Pelican, 1964), p. 17.

35 S. Hodges, op. cit., p. 191; *New Grove*, op. cit., vol. 12, p. 241 (Mexico City).

36 E.C. Clayton, *Queens of Song* (London: Smith Elder & Co, 1863), vol. II, p. 237.

37 *Encyclopaedia Britannica*, 9th Edition, vol. XVI, p. 221.

38 *Musical Quarterly*, vol. I, 1915, p. 528; E.C. Clayton, op. cit., vol. II, p. 237. The incident took place near Tepeyagualo.

39 'grand manteau à carreaux écossais': *Musical Quarterly*, vol. I, 1915, p. 525.

40 Ibid., vol. I, 1915, p. 528.

41 E.C. Clayton, op. cit., vol. II, p. 238.

42 *Musical Quarterly*, op. cit,. vol. I, 1915, pp. 526, 532, letter dated 21 January 1859.

43 A. FitzLyon, *The Price of Genius*, op. cit., p. 18; A. FitzLyon, *Maria Malibran*, p. 31; C. Saint-Saëns (trans. E.G. Rich), *Musical Memories* (London: Murray, 1921), p. 146.

44 A. FitzLyon, *Maria Malibran*, op. cit., pp. 184, 210; *Musical Quarterly*, op. cit., vol. I, 1915, pp. 532, 542.

45 L. Héritte-Viardot, op. cit., p.14.

46 E.C. Clayton, op. cit., vol. II, p. 239.

47 A. FitzLyon, *The Price of Genius*, op. cit., p. 29; A. FitzLyon, *Maria Malibran*, op. cit., p. 105; H. Bruder, 'Manuel Garcia the Elder, his School and his Legacy' *Opera Quarterly*, vol. 13, no. 4, 1997, p. 21.

48 E.C. Clayton, op. cit., vol. II, p. 239.

49 Comtesse Merlin, op. cit., pp. 17, 28.

50 P. Mansel, op. cit., pp. 283, 284.

51 E.C. Clayton, op. cit., vol. II, p. 241.

52 A. FitzLyon, *The Price of Genius*, op. cit., p. 37.

53 F-J. Fétis, *Biographie Universelle des Musiciens*, second edition (Paris, 1884), vol. VI, p. 130.

54 In 1832 (21 Sept), a few months after Manuel's death, Liszt wrote asking his mother to visit Mme Garcia: A. Williams, *Franz Liszt, selected letters* (Oxford: Clarendon Press, 1998), pp. 8, 1001.

55 According to Comtesse d'Agoult. D. Ollivier (ed.), *Correspondance de Liszt et de la Comtesse d'Agoult* (Paris: Editions Bernard Grasset, 1933–4), vol. I, p. 380; R. Bolster, *Marie d'Agoult, the Rebel Countess* (New Haven and London: Yale University Press, 2000), p. 128.

56 She said this after hearing him in Weimar in 1858: A.Williams, op. cit., p. 1001.

57 *Musical Quarterly* 1915, vol. I, p. 364.

58 *Cahiers Ivan Tourguéniev, Pauline Viardot, Maria Malibran* (*Cahiers*) (Bougival: Association des Amis d'Ivan Tourguéniev, Pauline Viardot et Maria Malibran), vol. 2, pp. 91, 94; A. FitzLyon, *Maria Malibran*, op. cit., p. 67.

59 Comtesse Merlin, op. cit., p. 105.

60 A. FitzLyon, *Maria Malibran*, op. cit., p. 119.

61 Comtesse Merlin, op. cit., p. 163 and letter in Appendix.

62 A. FitzLyon, *Maria Malibran*, op. cit., p. 166.

62 Ibid., p.112; the friend was the Comtesse de Sparre, daughter of Naldi the buffo tenor. She lived in the château de Brizay: Comtesse Merlin, op. cit., pp. 85, 149.

64 *The New Oxford Companion to Music*, op. cit., p. 1383.

65 Comtesse Merlin, op. cit., p. 158.

66 A. FitzLyon, *Maria Malibran*, op. cit., pp. 156, 167, 169; A. FitzLyon, *The Price of Genius*, op. cit., p. 36.

67 Comtesse Merlin, op. cit., pp. 14, 66, 120,131; A. FitzLyon, *Maria Malibran*, op. cit., pp. 173, 108.

68 E.C. Clayton, op. cit., p. 211.

69 B. Lumley, *Reminiscences of the Opera* (London: Hurst and Blackett, 1864), p. 8.

70 A. FitzLyon, *Maria Malibran*, op. cit., pp. 174, 182; J. Harding, *Gounod* (London: George Allen & Unwin Ltd, 1973), p. 48.

71 She gave Bellini two miniatures which she had painted herself, one of him and one of her, which are now in Catania museum. 'They were only to meet again twice': *Catania Bellini Museum Guide* (Catania, 1998), p. 80; A. FitzLyon, *Maria Malibran*, op. cit., pp. 118, 175, 176, 181, 191, 205.

72 For the two carnival seasons 1835–6, 1836–7 and for the autumn seasons of 1835, 1836 and 1837, she was paid 420,000 francs. A. FitzLyon, *Maria Malibran*, op. cit., p. 186; P. Ackroyd, *Dickens* (London: Sinclair Stevenson, 1990), pp. 155, 157.

73 P. Ackroyd, op. cit., pp. 67, 79.

74 Comtesse Merlin, op. cit., around p. 160; A.

FitzLyon, *Maria Malibran*, op. cit,. pp. 144, 199; *Cahiers*, op. cit., 2, p. 96.
75 The marriage was celebrated in March 1836; the accident was in July: A. FitzLyon, *Maria Malibran*, op. cit., p. 212; *Lancet*, Wellcome Library for the History and Understanding of Medicine, 1836. The Belgian concerts were in Liège and Lille: *Cahiers*, op. cit., no. 20, p. 145 (Gosselin).
76 A. FitzLyon, *Maria Malibran*, op. cit., p. 221.
77 *Lancet*, op. cit., 18 March 1837, p. 894; *Lancet*, 6 February 1836, pp. 788, 840; *Lancet report of London Medical Society*, 10 October 1836, p. 143; the zenith of homeopathy was in the 1870s and 1880s. See H. James, *The Bostonians* (London: Penguin Classics, 2000), pp. 281, 395.
78 *Lancet*, op. cit., 12 November 1836, p. 268.
79 A. FitzLyon, *Maria Malibran*, op. cit., p. 227.
80 Ibid., pp. 219, 236, 243.
81 Ibid., p. 245.
82 *New Grove*, op. cit., vol. 5, p. 204, Dance; *Encyclopaedia Britannica*, ninth edition, vol. XXIII, p. 21; Duvernay – information supplied by Professor Patrick Waddington.
83 R. Barham, *The Ingoldsby Legends, or Mirth and Marvels* (London: Richard Bentley and Son, 1882), p. 190; *Encyclopaedia Britannica*, ninth edition, vol. 3, p. 374 (Barham). I am particularly grateful to Mr Jonathan Price for this reference.
84 'N'était pas hier qu'à la fleur de ton âge, tu traversais l'Europe, une lyre à la main'. Stanza X.
85 H. F. Chorley, *Thirty years' Musical Recollections*, op. cit., vol. 1, pp. 10, 11; Comtesse Merlin, op. cit., p. 98.
86 H.F. Chorley, op. cit., p. 15.
87 A. FitzLyon, *Maria Malibran*, op. cit., p. 248.
88 June 1837: A. FitzLyon, *Maria Malibran*, op. cit., p. 251.
89 A. FitzLyon, *The Price of Genius*, op. cit., pp. 37, 38; T. Marix-Spire (ed.), *Lettres inédites de George Sand et de Pauline Viardot*, op. cit., p. 21.

Chapter 2. The Stage (pp. 29–40)

1 *Encyclopaedia Britannica*, Standard Millennium edition; W. G. Atwood, *The Lioness and the Little One – The Liaison of George Sand and Frederic Chopin* (New York, NY: Columbia University Press, 1980), p. 65; Salon: E. Zola (trans. M. Mauldon), *L'Assommoir* (Oxford: Oxford University Press, 1995), p. 444.
2 W.G. Atwood, op. cit., p. 66; R. Somerset-Ward, *Angels and Monsters* (New Haven and London: Yale University Press, 2004), p. 162; The diva was Caroline Branchu: Ibid., pp. 121, 130, 163.
3 B. Lumley, *Reminiscences of the Opera* (London: Hurst and Blackett, 1864), p. 230.
4 P. Barbier, *Opera in Paris 1800–1850* (Oregon: Amadeus Press, 1995), p. 72.
5 Ibid., pp. 76, 77.
6 J. Harding, *Gounod* (London: George Allen & Unwin Ltd, 1973), p. 84; P. Barbier, op. cit., p. 38.
7 A. FitzLyon, *Maria Malibran – Diva of the Romantic Age* (London: Souvenir Press, 1987), p. 151; P. Barbier, op. cit., p. 8.
8 A. FitzLyon, *The Price of Genius, a life of Pauline Viardot* (London: John Calder, 1964), p. 237.
9 C.V. Stanford and C. Forsyth, *A History of Music* (New York: Macmillan, 1917), pp. 275, 276.
10 P. Barbier. op. cit., pp. 16, 18.
11 G. Sand (trans. Fayette Robinson), *Consuelo* (New York: Stringer and Townsend, 1851), p. 211. Sand attributes the remark to Empress Maria Theresa.
12 *Revue des Deux Mondes*, vol. XXI, p. 582, a comment by G. Sand.
13 P. Barbier, op. cit., p. 51.
14 Ibid., pp. 41, 42; for the importance of the foot, see A. Pushkin (trans. C. Johnston, Preface J. Bayley, Notes M. Basker), *Eugene Onegin* (London: Penguin, 2003), ch. 1, stanza XXXII.
15 A. FitzLyon, *Maria Malibran*, op. cit., p. 19.
16 E.C. Clayton, *Queens of Song* (London: Smith Elder & Co, 1863), p. 94.
17 H.F. Chorley, *Thirty years' Musical Recollections* (London: Hurst & Blackett, 1862), vol. II, p. 50.
18 T. Marix-Spire, *Lettres inédites de George Sand et de Pauline Viardot 1839–1849* (Paris: Nouvelles Editions, 1959), p. 51; J. Chissell, Schumann (London: J.M. Dent, 1977), p. 195.
19 *New Grove Dictionary of Music and Musicians* (London: Macmillan, 1980), vol. 18, p. 169, Stoltz (Elizabeth Forbes).
20 P. Barbier, op. cit., p. 158; A. FitzLyon, *Maria Malibran*, op. cit., p. 98.
21 N. Savy (ed.), G. Sand, *Consuelo, La Comtesse de Rudolstadt* (Paris: Editions Robert Laffont SA, 2004), p. 922.

22 A. FitzLyon, *Maria Malibran*, op. cit., p. 126; *Encyclopaedia Britannica*, ninth edition, vol. XVI (Molière), p. 630.
23 E.C. Clayton, op. cit., pp. 80, 90, 204; *New Grove*, op. cit., vol. 11, p. 689, Mario (Elizabeth Forbes); A. FitzLyon, *Maria Malibran*, op. cit., p. 101.
23 *New Grove*, op. cit., vol. 17, p. 528, Sontag (J. Warrack); E.C. Clayton, op. cit., p. 204.
24 Maupassant's reference to a student from the Conservatoire is from *The Olive Grove* in (trans. G. Hopkins), *Short Stories* (London: The Folio Society, 1959), p. 279. 'C'est extraordinaire ce que votre femme est distinguée, pour une femme d'artiste': Paul Viardot, *Souvenirs d'un Artiste* (Paris: Librairie Fischbacher SA, 1910), p. 292.
25 P. Ackroyd, *Dickens* (London: Sinclair Stevenson, 1990), p. 1075.
26 'Quel monde que notre monde à l'Opéra ... Quelles intrigues! Toutes ces rivalités! Toutes ces haines! ... C'est vraiment plus curieux de jour en jour': T. Marix-Spire, *Lettres inédites de George Sand*, op. cit., pp. 34, 35.
27 P. Barbier, op. cit., p.181.
28 'S'embrouiller parmi les comparses'; 'Une actrice vertueuse était un phênomène impossible à admettre ou tout au moins fatigant à respecter ... La chasteté et le désinteressement sont les plus grands ennemis de la fortune d'une femme de théâtre' Rudolstadt: N. Savy, *Consuelo*, pp. 1114, 1115.
29 *Daily Telegraph*, 12 January 2006, p. 25. The tenor was Franco Corelli, and the opera was *Turandot*.
30 H.F. Chorley, op. cit., vol. II, p. 87.
31 'On se défend comme on peut': Gustave Bord, *Rosina Stoltz* (*Victoire Noël*), (Paris: Henri Daragon, 1909), p. 90.
32 T. Marix-Spire, *Lettres inédites de George Sand*, op. cit., p. 37.
33 G. Bord, op. cit., p. 23.
34 Comtesse Merlin, *Maria Malibran* (London: Henry Colburn, 1840), p. 47.
35 G. Bord, op. cit., p. 97.
36 R. Somerset-Ward, op. cit., pp. 174, 177; G. Bord, op. cit., pp. 75, 120.
37 'pour en faire du suif': G. Bord, op. cit., p. 81.
38 Ibid., pp. 142, 145,165; *Encyclopaedia Britannica*, ninth edition, vol. 1, p. 471; the pension was payable 'provided he never set foot in France': G. Bord, op. cit., p. 19.
39 G. Bord, op. cit., pp. 148, 160.
40 Ibid., pp. 16, 137, 138, 149.
41 Ibid., pp 20, 21, 77.
42 A. FitzLyon, *Maria Malibran*, op. cit., pp. 202, 232.
43 H.G. Hewlett, *Memoirs of Henry Fothergill Chorley* (London: Richard Bentley and Son, 1873), vol. I p. 297.
44 *New Grove*, op. cit., vol. 7, p. 642, Grassini (E. Forbes); E.C. Clayton, op. cit., pp. 187, 192, 190; W. Kuhe, *My musical recollections* (London: Richard Bentley, 1896), p. 38.
45 R. Somerset-Ward, op. cit., p. 142.
46 H.F. Chorley, op. cit., vol. II, p. 23. The *Illustrated London News*, on 19 May 1855, p. 495, noted that Grisi was back, having retired the previous year; it stated that Mario was 'greater than ever'.
47 R. Somerset-Ward, op. cit., p. 144; *New Grove*, op. cit., vol. 11, p. 689, Mario (Elizabeth Forbes).
48 W. Kuhe, op. cit., p. 199.
49 'Le type le plus pur et le plus parfait de la beauté grecque': T. Marix-Spire, *Lettres inédites de George Sand*, op. cit., p. 33; G. Sand, 'Le Théâtre-Italien et Mlle Pauline Garcia', *Revue des Deux Mondes*, vol. XXI, p. 584.
50 L Héritte-Viardot (trans. E.S. Bucheim), *Memories and Adventures* (London: Mills & Boon, 1913), p. 88.
51 A. de Musset (ed. L Sèche): *Correspondance* (Société du Mercure de France, 1907), p. 156.
52 G. Dulong, *Pauline Viardot Tragédienne Lyrique* (Bougival: Association des Amis d'Ivan Tourguéniev Pauline Viardot et Maria Malibran, 1987), p. 24; Elizabeth Forbes in *New Grove*, op cit., vol. 7, p. 737; *New Grove*, op. cit., vol. 11, p. 689 (Elizabeth Forbes); W. Kuhe, op. cit., 201.
53 R. Somerset-Ward, op. cit., p. 143.
54 *New Grove*, op. cit., vol. 18, p. 516, Tacchinardi-Persiani (Francesco Bussi); the father was Tacchinardi; E.C. Clayton, op. cit., pp. 257, 264.
55 'une méchante femme': A. Zviguilsky (ed.), *Ivan Tourguénev: Nouvelle Correspondance inédite* (Paris: Librairie des Cinq Continents, 1971), p. 21.
56 'Elle a fait un geste qui m'a rappelé une des femmes de chambre de ma mère, l'être le plus froidement méchant que je connaisse': Ibid., p. 21.
57 R. Somerset-Ward, op. cit., pp. 145, 146.

CHAPTER 3. MUSSET (pp. 41–53)

1 L. Vallas (trans. H. Foss), *César Franck* (London: Harrap, 1951), pp. 16, 84, 49; rumours of marriage: *Cahiers Ivan Tourguéniev, Pauline Viardot, Maria Malibran* (Bougival: Association des Amis d'Ivan Tourguéniev Pauline Viardot et Maria Malibran), no. 20, p. 128 (Borchard).

2 E.C. Clayton, *Queens of Song* (London: Smith Elder & Co, 1863), vol. II, p. 244.

3 B. Kendall-Davies, *The Life and Work of Pauline Viardot-Garcia* (London: Cambridge Scholars Press, 2003), vol. I, 'The years of fame', pp. 24, 25, 29; A. FitzLyon, *The Price of Genius, a life of Pauline Viardot* (London: John Calder, 1964), p. 43; *Cahiers*, op. cit., no. 20, p. 128 (Borchard); Ibid., pp. 128, 130, 131, 136. The songs were 'Nine Heine Songs of the Liederkreis', Op. 24.

4 *Cahiers*, op. cit., no. 20, p. 132 (Borchard); A. de Musset, 'Concert de Mademoiselle Garcia', *Revue des Deux Mondes*, vol. XVII, p. 110; G. Dulong, *Pauline Viardot Tragédienne Lyrique* (Paris: Association des Amis d'Ivan Tourgueniev, Pauline Viardot et Maria Malibran, 1987), p. 20.

5 G. Dulong, op. cit., p. 28; the comment on style was one later made by Annenkov, see L. Schapiro, *Turgenev, his Life and Times* (Oxford: Oxford University Press, 1978), p. 103; S. Rutherford, *The Prima Donna and Opera 1815–1930* (Cambridge: Cambridge University Press, 2006), p. 178.

6 P. Waddington, 'Turgenev's relations with H.F. Chorley', *New Zealand Slavonic Journal*, no. 2, 1978), p. 27.

7 H.F. Chorley, *Thirty years' Musical Recollections* (London: Hurst & Blackett, 1862), vol. II, pp. 45, 48.

8 A. FitzLyon, *The Price of Genius*, op. cit., p. 63; H.F. Chorley (ed. E. Newman), *Thirty years' Musical Recollections* (New York: Alfred Knopf, 1926), pp. 231–232.

9 A. FitzLyon, *The Price of Genius*, op. cit., p. 66; see letter to Clara in *Cahiers*, op. cit., no. 20, p. 133 (Borchard).

10 T. Marix-Spire, *Lettres inédites de George Sand et de Pauline Viardot 1839–1849* (Nouvelles Editions), p. 15; A. FitzLyon, *The Price of Genius*, op. cit., p. 68; G. Dulong, op. cit., p. 31.

11 P. Mansel, *Paris between Empires, 1814–1852* (London: John Murray, 2001), p. 133.

12 Ibid., p. 126.

13 Comtesse D'Agoult, *Mes Souvenirs* (Paris: Calmann-Lévy, 1880), p. 303.

14 'Quelques maisons plus modestes': Ibid., p. 303.

15 F. Lestringant, *Alfred de Musset* (Flammarion, 1999), pp. 144, 321, 355, 353; A. FitzLyon, *The Price of Genius*, op. cit., p. 44. Mme Jaubert's maiden name was Caroline d'Alton-Shée.

16 *Encyclopaedia Britannica*, ninth edition, vol. XVII, pp. 111, 112 (W.H. Pollock).

17 C. Gowan, *France from the Regent to the Romantics* (London: Harrap, 1961), p. 246; M. Steen, *The Lives and Times of the Great Composers* (Cambridge: Icon, 2003), p. 378; F. Lestringant, op. cit., pp. 315, 321.

18 A. FitzLyon, *The Price of Genius*, op. cit., p. 45.

19 W. Karénine, *George Sand sa Vie et ses Oeuvres* (Paris: Paul Ollendorff, 1899), vol. III, pp. 212, 213.

20 A. FitzLyon, *The Price of Genius*, op. cit., p. 48; A. de Musset (ed. L Sèche), *Correspondance* (Société du Mercure de France, 1907), p. 156; A. de Musset, 'Concert de Mademoiselle Garcia', *Revue des Deux Mondes*, vol. XVII, p. 115.

21 A. de Musset, *Oeuvres Posthumes* (Paris: Alphonse Lemerre, 1845), letter of 17 December 1938.

22 *Encyclopaedia Britannica*, Standard Millennium edition.

23 Asparagus: B. Lumley, *Reminiscences of the Opera* (London: Hurst and Blackett, 1864), p. 52.

24 *The Times Literary Supplement*, London 5 May 2006, p. 20.

25 H.G. Hewlett, *Memoirs of Henry Fothergill Chorley* (London: Richard Bentley and Son, 1873), vol. I, p. 266 (the word is indeed 'listening').

26 Sir T. Martin, *Helena Faucit (Lady Martin)* (Edinburgh and London: William Blackwood and Sons, 1900), p. 81.

27 A. de Musset, *Correspondance*, op. cit., p. 156; A. de Musset: 'Concert de Mademoiselle Garcia', op. cit., p. 115.

28 A de Musset, *Oeuvres Posthumes*, op. cit, p. 61, 'Un souper chez Mademoiselle Rachel'; A. de Musset, *Correspondance*, op. cit., p.156; A. FitzLyon, *The Price of Genius*, op. cit., p50.

29 A. de Musset, in *Revue des Deux Mondes*, vol. XVII, p. 110.

30 A. de Musset, 'Débuts de Mademoiselle Pauline Garcia', *Revue des Deux Mondes*, vol. XX, p. 439.
31 Ibid., p. 437; A. FitzLyon, *Maria Malibran – Diva of the Romantic Age* (London: Souvenir Press, 1987), p. 138, quoting *Revue des Deux Mondes*, 1 January 1839. Musset's description was 'une jeune fille qui aime naïvement'.
32 S. Rutherford, *The Prima Donna and Opera 1815–1930* (Cambridge: Cambridge University Press, 2006), p. 207 et seq., p. 257.
33 A. de Musset, *Correspondance*, op. cit., p. 199; A. de Musset 'Débuts de Mademoiselle Pauline Garcia', op. cit., p. 435. Musset's description was 'elle débute comme bien d'autres voudraient finir'.
34 W. Karénine, op. cit., vol. III, p. 213; A. FitzLyon, *The Price of Genius*, op. cit., p. 61. Pauline told one of Karénine's friends this material about Musset.
35 G. Dulong, op. cit., p. 17.
36 A. FitzLyon, *The Price of Genius*, op. cit., p. 61; W. Karénine, vol. III pp. 212, 213; T. Marix-Spire, *Lettres inédites de George Sand*, op. cit., p. 22; W. Karénine, op. cit., vol. II, p. 17. Pauline talked of his 'paupières (eyelids) rouges, sans cils (eyelashes) et qu'il n'avait pas de sourcils'.
37 C.V. Stanford, *Pages from an Unwritten Diary* (London: Edward Arnold, 1914), p. 66.
38 A. de Musset, *Correspondance*, op. cit., p. 159, 160; G. Dulong, op. cit., p.37; A. FitzLyon, *The Price of Genius*, op. cit., pp. 57, 59.
39 A. de Musset, *Oeuvres Posthumes*, op. cit.; F. Lestringant, op. cit., pp. 403, 411.
40 *Revue des Deux Mondes*, vol. XXVIII, December 1841, p. 851.
41 A. Hedley (trans.), *Selected Correspondence of Fryderyk Chopin* (London: Heinemann, 1962); L. Héritte-Viardot, *Une famille de grands musiciens* (Paris: Librairie Stock, 1922), p. 20; T. Marix-Spire, op. cit.; *Musical Quarterly*, 1945; I. Turgenev (ed. E. Halpérine-Kaminsky), *Lettres à Madame Viardot* (Paris: Bibliothèque-Charpentier, 1907), 20 November 1846, p. 3.
42 N. Reich, *Clara Schumann, the Artist and the Woman* (Cornell University, 2001), p. 209; L. Héritte-Viardot, *Une famille de grands musiciens* (Paris: Librairie Stock, 1922), p. 20; W. Kuhe, *My musical recollections* (London: Richard Bentley, 1896), p. 187; J. Chissell, *Clara Schumann: a Dedicated Spirit* (London: Hamish Hamilton, 1983), p. 59.
43 A. FitzLyon, *The Price of Genius*, op. cit., p. 52; *Revue des Deux Mondes*, 1 January 1939; also A. de Musset, *Oeuvres Complètes, Poésies*, p. 400.
44 T. Marix-Spire, *Lettres inédites de George Sand*, op. cit., p. 29; A. FitzLyon, *The Price of Genius*, op. cit., p. 66.
45 Bériot was helping to launch Clara in Paris at the time. Clara, with a chaperone, was staying in the same hotel in Paris as Pauline and her mother. This was the visit which Clara's father had let her make unaccompanied by him in order to make her appreciate how dependent on him she was. J. Chissell, *Clara Schumann*, op. cit., pp. 63, 64; B. Kendall-Davies, *The Life and Work of Pauline Viardot-Garcia* (London: Cambridge Scholars Press, 2003), vol. I 'The years of fame', p. 52; J. Chissell, *Schumann* (London: J.M. Dent, 1977), p. 45.
46 J. Chissell, *Clara Schumann*, op. cit., p. 59; *Ovid Heroines* (trans. Daryl Hine) (New Haven: Yale University Press, 1991), pp. 151, 152.
47 T. Marix-Spire, *Lettres inédites de George Sand*, op. cit., p. 14; Marie d'Agoult, 26 February 1840, in D. Ollivier (ed.), *Correspondance de Liszt et de la Comtesse d'Agoult* (Paris: Editions Bernard Grasset, 1933–34), vol. I, p. 399.
48 L Héritte-Viardot, *Une famille de grands musiciens* (Paris: Librairie Stock, 1922) p. 20; P. Waddington, *Courtavenel, the History of an Artists' Nest and its Role in the Life of Turgenev* (*PhD Thesis*, Queen's University Belfast, The British Library, British Thesis Service, spring 1972), p. 272.
49 A. FitzLyon, *The Price of Genius*, op. cit., pp. 71, 312, 433; C.V. Stanford, op. cit., p. 287; E. de Goncourt, *Journal* (Paris, 1887–96), 3 June 1862, vol. I, p. 1083; Ibid., 10 October 1887, vol. III, p. 712; Ibid., vol. IV, p. 485. The Goncourts were crudely obsessed with the connection between female singers, especially Pauline, and male sexuality. Edmond persuaded himself that successful women, such as Sand and Viardot, had genitals the size of men's. 'Je dirais crûment être persuadé que, si on avait fait l'autopsie des femmes ayant un talent original, comme Mme Sand, Mme Viardot etc, on trouverait chez elles des parties génitales se rapprochant de l'homme, des clitoris un peu parents de nos verges'.
50 The King's son was the Prince de Joinville: P. Mansel, op. cit., p. 293. The English actress was Helena Faucit: Sir T Martin, *Helena Faucit*

(Lady Martin) (Edinburgh and London: William Blackwood and Sons, 1900), p. 81.
51 A. de Musset, 'Concert de Mademoiselle Garcia', *Revue des Deux Mondes*, vol. XVII, p. 111.
52 A. FitzLyon, *The Price of Genius*, op. cit., p. 70; T. Marix-Spire, *Lettres inédites de George Sand*, op. cit., p. 14; C. Saint-Saëns (trans. E.G. Rich), *Musical Memories* (London: Murray, 1921), p. 146; K. Hughes, *George Eliot, The Last Victorian* (London: The Fourth Estate, 1998), pp. 2, 119.
53 'Qui joue avec dédain de son public', 23 November 1839: D. Ollivier, op. cit., vol. I, p. 297; G. Dulong, op. cit., p. 32; A. FitzLyon, *The Price of Genius*, op. cit., p. 71; H. Troyat (trans. N. Amphoux), *Turgenev* (London: W.H. Allen, 1989), p. 56. Examples of D'Agoult's views may be found in D. Ollivier, op. cit., vol. I, p. 399, 26 February 1840; Ibid., vol. II, p.154, 15 June 1841.
54 D. Cairns, *Berlioz: Servitude and Greatness* (London: Penguin, 2000), p. 635.
55 V.S. Pritchett, *The Gentle Barbarian, The Life and Work of Turgenev* (London: Chatto & Windus, 1977), p. 36, quoting Heine; A. FitzLyon, *The Price of Genius*, op. cit., p. 223.
56 V.S. Pritchett, op. cit., pp. 36, 37.
57 J. Harding, *Saint-Saëns and his Circle* (London: Chapman & Hall, 1965), p. 41; C. Saint-Saëns, op. cit., p. 145. Saint-Saëns first played for Pauline in 1849.
58 E.C. Clayton, op. cit., vol. II, p. 254; R. Somerset-Ward, *Angels and Monsters* (New Haven and London: Yale University Press, 2004), p. 131; J. Harding, op. cit., p. 60; C. Saint-Saëns, op. cit., p.145. Clara Schumann said the voice was amazingly powerful: *Cahiers*, op. cit., vol. 20, p. 138.
59 C. Saint-Saëns, op. cit., p. 145; T. Marix-Spire, *Lettres inédites de George Sand*, op. cit., p. 27 quoting *Revue de Paris.*
60 Kalmus vocal score, p. 270.
61 G. Dulong, op. cit., p. 19. Clayton said bottom F to top C (E.C. Clayton, op. cit., vol. II, p. 242); Rietz wrote that it covered more than three octaves, from Bass C to F in alt. (*Musical Quarterly*, vol. I, 1915, p. 350).
62 L. Héritte-Viardot, op. cit., p. 14.
63 A. FitzLyon, *Maria Malibran*, op. cit., p.189; A. FitzLyon, *The Price of Genius*, op. cit., p. 64; L. Schapiro, *Turgenev, his Life and Times* (Oxford: OUP, 1978), p. 103; R. Somerset-Ward, op. cit., pp. 123, 145, 193–196.
64 Gerald Moore described Ferrier's top A. G. Moore, *Am I too loud?* (London: Hamish Hamilton, 1962), p. 152.
65 A. FitzLyon, *The Price of Genius*, op. cit., p. 73.
66 Ibid., p. 69; T. Marix-Spire, *Lettres inédites de George Sand*, op. cit., p. 29; her costume which was praised by Théodore Gautier.
67 A. FitzLyon, *The Price of Genius*, op. cit., pp. 66, 113; T. Marix-Spire, *Lettres inédites de George Sand*, op. cit., p. 116; E.C. Clayton, op. cit., vol. II, pp. 248, 254.
68 H.F. Chorley, *Thirty years' Musical Recollections* (London: Hurst & Blackett, 1862), p. 302.
69 A. FitzLyon, *The Price of Genius*, op. cit., p. 75.

CHAPTER 4. GEORGE (pp. 55–66)

1 R. Jordan, *George Sand* (London: Constable, 1976), p. xiv; P. Waddington, *Turgenev and George Sand: An Improbable Entente* (Victoria University Press, 1981), p. 13; P. Waddington, *Courtavenel, the History of an Artists' Nest and its Role in the Life of Turgenev* (*PhD Thesis*, Queen's University Belfast, The British Library, British Thesis Service, spring 1972), p. 108.
2 W.G. Atwood, *The Lioness and the Little One – The Liaison of George Sand and Frederic Chopin* (New York, NY: Columbia University Press, 1980), p. x.
3 J. Forster, *The Life of Charles Dickens* (London: Chapman & Hall, 1874), p. 309; A. FitzLyon, *The Price of Genius*, op. cit., pp. 75, 77; T. Marix-Spire, *Lettres inédites de George Sand et de Pauline Viardot 1839–1849* (Paris: Nouvelles Editions, 1959), pp. 11, 169.
4 T. Marix-Spire, *Lettres inédites de George Sand*, op. cit., p. 91; *Encyclopaedia Britannica,* ninth edition, vol. IX, p. 25.
5 'J'aime assez le génie; mais quand il est joint à la bonté, je me prosterne devant lui': T. Marix-Spire, *Lettres inédites de George Sand*, op. cit., p. 91; B Jack, *George Sand: A Woman's Life Writ Large* (London: Chatto & Windus, 1999), p. 1.
6 Ibid., pp. 5, 168; R. Jordan, op. cit., pp. 2, 4; W.G. Atwood, op. cit., p. 11.
7 'Voir sans regarder': Comtesse D'Agoult, *Mes Souvenirs* (Paris: Calmann-Lévy, 1880), p. 208.
8 'Intrépide amazone': Ibid., pp. 207, 208; R. Jordan, op. cit., p. xiv.

9 P. Waddington, 'Dickens, Pauline Viardot and Turgenev: a Study in Mutual Admiration', *New Zealand Slavonic Journal*, no. 2, 1974, p. 58.
10 T. Marix-Spire, *Lettres inédites de George Sand*, op. cit., pp. 123, 124; G. Flaubert, *Sentimental Education*, pt 2, ch. 1, p. 113.
11 Caisse nationale des monuments historiques et des sites, *George Sand in Paris*, Berry and Creuse.
12 Musée de la Vie Romantique, *General Guide* (Paris-Musées, 1992), p. 31; Paul Viardot called it 'la vaste maison, quasi-château'. Paul Viardot, *Souvenirs d'un Artiste* (Paris: Librairie Fischbacher SA, 1910), p. 40.
13 B. Jack, op. cit., pp. 110, 318; G. Sand, *Correspondance* (Paris: Editions de Georges Lubin, Editions Garnier Frères, 1969), vol. VI, p. 43 (mid-February 1843).
14 W.G. Atwood, op. cit., p. 18; R. Jordan, op. cit., p. 26; B. Jack, op. cit., pp, 133, 150.
15 B. Jack, op. cit, pp. 157, 158, 185; R. Jordan, op. cit., p. 53.
16 B. Jack, op. cit., p. 212.
17 P. Raby, *Fair Ophelia: A Life of Harriet Smithson Berlioz* (Cambridge: Cambridge University Press, 1982), pp. 148, 149; G. Sand (ed. T. Bodin), *Lettres Retrouvées* (Paris: Gallimard, 2004), p. 90: 'c'était pas une femme comme vous, cétait tout le contraire dans un certain sens'. *Encyclopaedia Britannica,* Standard Millennium edition (Vigny).
18 R. Bosco, *The Brownings and Mrs Kinney* (Browning Institute Studies, no. 4, 1976), p. 70.
19 B. Jack, op. cit., p. 254; W.G. Atwood, op. cit., p. 43.
20 T. Marix-Spire, *Lettres inédites de George Sand*, op. cit., pp. 94, 99, 102.
21 T. Marix-Spire, *Lettres inédites de George Sand*, op. cit., pp. 100, 115, 137. Flaubert's niece called him Nounou: G. Wall, *Flaubert, a Life* (London: Faber and Faber, 2001), p. 263.
22 D. Ollivier (ed.), *Correspondance de Liszt et de la Comtesse d'Agoult* (Paris: Editions Bernard Grasset, 1933–34), vol. I, pp. 246, 322. 23 November 1838, and also around November 1839. (Ollivier was a member of D'Agoult's family so perhaps shared her views.) On 10 October 1887, questions were asked about Pauline's tastes and whether she was really of the feminine sex: E. de Goncourt, *Journal*, Paris 1887, vol. III, p. 712.
23 'amour sacré que j'ai pour mon fils et ma fille': T. Marix-Spire, *Lettres inédites de George Sand*, op. cit., p. 18.
24 G. Dulong, *Pauline Viardot Tragédienne Lyrique* (Bougival: Association des Amis d'Ivan Tourguéniev Pauline Viardot et Maria Malibran), p. 47.
25 *Cahiers de Alfred Musset Etudes et Documents sur Alfred de Musset et son Temps*, publiés par la Société Alfred de Musset, I, January 1934, p. 29; A. de Musset (ed. L Sèche): *Correspondance*, Société du Mercure de France, 1907, p. 220; A. FitzLyon, *The Price of Genius*, op. cit., p. 87; E. Henriot, *Alfred de Musset* (Paris, 1928), p. 217.
26 T. Marix-Spire, *Lettres inédites de George Sand*, op. cit., p. 94; B. Jack, op. cit., p. 288.
27 T. Marix-Spire, *Lettres inédites de George Sand*, op. cit., p. 131.
28 *Musical Quarterly*, vol. I, 1915, p. 374. She recommends 'the first part', which we may assume to be *Consuelo* as opposed to *La Comtesse.* She adds 'I shall see if you can discover the other similarity with me'.
29 G. Sand (trans. Fayette Robinson), *Consuelo* (New York: Stringer and Townsend, 1851), p. 221.
30 *Great Expectations* was published in 36 consecutive numbers: P. Ackroyd, *Dickens* (London: Sinclair Stevenson, 1990), p. 888. Occasionally, this led Dickens to pad out (Ibid., pp. 963, 1056).
31 W. Karénine, *George Sand sa Vie et ses Oeuvres* (Paris: Paul Ollendorff, 1899), vol. III, p. 333. The singer was Gertrude-Elisabeth Mara (1749–1833). E. Anderson, *The Letters of Mozart and his Family* (London: Macmillan, 1966), 24 November 1780, pp. 660, 668, 671; *The New Oxford Companion to Music* (Oxford: Oxford University Press, 1984), p. 306; *New Grove Dictionary of Music and Musicians* (London: Macmillan, 1980), vol. 11, p. 638 (J. Marshall).
32 G. Sand, *Consuelo*, op. cit., p. 18; N. Savy (ed.), *George Sand: Consuelo, La Comtesse de Rudolstadt* (Paris: Editions Robert Laffont SA, 2004), p. 75.
33 R. Somerset-Ward, *Angels and Monsters* (New Haven and London: Yale University Press, 2004), p. 43.
34 G. Sand, *Consuelo*, op. cit., p. 9; 'tu aimes la gloire, rien que la gloire, et pour toi seul'; N. Savy, op. cit., p. 50.
35 G. Sand, *Consuelo*, op. cit., p. 140; Turgenev

used the word 'insupportable'. A. Zviguilsky (ed.), *Ivan Tourguénev: Nouvelle Correspondance inédite* (Paris: Librairie des Cinq Continents, 1971), p. 30.
36 'Te voilà donc enfin trouvée' – N. Savy, op. cit., p. 217.
37 G. Sand, *Consuelo*, op. cit., pp. 69, 109.
38 Ibid., pp. 133, 140.
39 Ibid., p. 145.
40 Ibid., pp. 179, 184, 185; A. FitzLyon, *The Price of Genius*, op. cit., pp. 118, 119.
41 G. Sand, *Consuelo*, op. cit., p. 219.
42 Ibid., pp. 216, 249, 252.
43 W. Karénine, op. cit., vol. III, pp. 212, 333, 358; R. Locke, *Music, Musicians and the Saint-Simonians* (Chicago: University of Chicago Press, 1986), pp. 46, 49.
44 N. Savy, op. cit., p. 772; A. FitzLyon, *Maria Malibran – Diva of the Romantic Age* (London: Souvenir Press, 1987), p. 139; G. Sand, *Consuelo*, op. cit., p. 219.
45 N. Savy, op. cit., p. 742.
46 She calls Frederick 'dur, violent et profondément égoïste', N. Savy, op. cit., pp. 740, 747.
47 Ibid., pp. 919, 922, 931. Her 'chasteté ne se sentait ni affrayée ni souillée par ses caresses'.
48 Ibid., p. 994; A. Zviguilsky (ed.), op. cit., p. 193
49 N. Savy, op. cit., pp. 1858, 1069, 1088, 1143.
50 B. Jack, op. cit., p. 293; A FitzLyon, *Maria Malibran*, op cit., p. 139. This view is confirmed by the head of the George Sand Association à propos the two novels together with Sand's autobiography – *The Economist*, 31 July 2004, p. 76.
51 A. Zviguilsky (ed.), op. cit., p. 38.
52 P. Waddington, *Turgenev and George Sand: An Improbable Entente* (Victoria University Press, 1981), p. 39.
53 N. Savy, op. cit., pp. 994, 1005, 1010, 1083, 1102, 1112; Sand regarded marriage as 'le tombeau de l'amour; une prostitution jurée', N. Savy, op. cit., p. 1099.
54 G. Sand, *Consuelo*, op. cit., pp. 124, 204; A. FitzLyon, *Maria Malibran*, op. cit., p. 139.
55 This was on 10 May 1841: he refers to George's 'amour du tripotage et des cancans, déplorable manque de sincérité ... [Pauline] finit par me dire « Je ne suis d'ailleurs pas très liée avec Mme Sand »': D. Ollivier (ed.), op. cit., vol. II, p. 134.
56 P. Waddington, *Turgenev and George Sand: An Improbable Entente* (Wellington: Victoria University Press, 1981). The dialogue apparently went as follows: 'Je ferai connaître votre conduite.' 'Et moi, je sculpterai votre cul. Tout le monde le reconnaîtra.'
57 Ibid., pp. 22, 46, 85, 100, 103.

Chapter 5. Louis (pp. 67–81)

1 A. FitzLyon, *The Price of Genius, a life of Pauline Viardot* (London: John Calder, 1964), p. 75; M. L'Hôpital, *Louis Viardot, Mémoires de l'Académie des Sciences* (Dijon: Arts et Belles-Lettres de Dijon, 1954), p. 28.
2 A. FitzLyon, *Maria Malibran – Diva of the Romantic Age* (London: Souvenir Press, 1987), p. 107; Comtesse Merlin, *Maria Malibran* (London: Henry Colburn, 1840), p. 147; T. Marix-Spire, *Lettres inédites de George Sand et de Pauline Viardot 1839–1849* (Paris: Nouvelles Editions, 1959), p. 23.
3 G. Dulong, *Pauline Viardot Tragédienne Lyrique* (Bougival: Association des Amis d'Ivan Tourguéniev Pauline Viardot et Maria Malibran, 1987), p. 39; V.S. Pritchett, *The Gentle Barbarian, The Life and Work of Turgenev* (London: Chatto & Windus, 1977), pp. 39, 40; A. FitzLyon, *The Price of Genius*, op. cit., p. 83.
4 A. FitzLyon, *Maria Malibran*, op. cit., p. 119; F. Lestringant, *Alfred de Musset* (Paris: Flammarion, 1999), p. 354; L Héritte-Viardot, *Une famille de grands musiciens* (Paris: Librairie Stock, 1922), p. 31; A. FitzLyon, *The Price of Genius*, op. cit., pp. 80, 85; T. Marix-Spire, *Lettres inédites de George Sand*, op. cit., p. 23.
5 *Musical Quarterly*, vol. I, 1915, p. 367; T. Marix-Spire, *Lettres inédites de George Sand*, op. cit., p. 65; A. FitzLyon, *The Price of Genius*, op. cit., p. 131.
6 L. Héritte-Viardot, op. cit., p. 31; *Musical Quarterly*, vol. I, 1915, 'Das kindische Element fehlt, die Frische des Gemüths', p. 358.
7 L. Héritte-Viardot, op. cit., p. 31; L. Viardot, *Souvenirs de Chasse dans toute l'Europe* (Paris: Editions Pygmalion, 1985), p. 67.
8 *Musical Quarterly* 1916, p. 546; A. Zviguilsky (ed.), *Ivan Tourguénev: Nouvelle Correspondance inédite* (Paris: Librairie des Cinq Continents, 1971), p. 90; J. Forster, *The Life of Charles Dickens* (London: Chapman & Hall, 1874), vol. III, p. 116.
9 A. Zviguilsky (ed.), op. cit., vol. II p. 115.
10 His history of the Moors was published in

1833, according to the British Library catalogue. *L'Ingénieux Hidalgo Don Quichotte de la Manche traduit et annoté par Louis Viardot* was published by Dubochet et Cie in Paris; volume 1 in 1836 (740 pages); volume 2 in 1837 (754 pages). *Les Nouvelles de Miguel de Cervantès Saavedra traduites et annotées pas Louis Viardot* was published by Dubochet et Cie in Paris in 1838. *Der sinnreiche Junker Don Quixote von la Mancha aus dem Spanien übersezt mit dem Leben von Miguel Cervantes nach Viardot* was published in Stuttgart: volume 1 in 1837 (730 pages), volume 2 in 1838 (864 pages). *La Fille du Capitaine, roman traduit du russe par Louis Viardot*, was published in Paris by Hachette in 1869.

11 L. Viardot, *Apology of an Unbeliever*, translated from the Third Edition (London: Trübner & Co, 1869), Introduction.

12 L. Viardot, *Souvenirs de Chasse dans toute l'Europe* (Paris: Editions Pygmalion, 1985), pp. 15, 18, 233, 270.

13 G. Sand, *Correspondance* (Paris: Editions de Georges Lubin, Editions Garnier Frères, 1969), vol. 9, p. 82. Dr Zviguilsky told the author that M. Mazon was the source of the information about tricycles. Louis is described as a well-known art critic in the preface to L. Viardot, *Wonders of Sculpture* (New York: Scribner, Armstrong, and Company, 1873)

14 M. L'Hôpital, *Louis Viardot, Mémoires de l'Académie des Sciences* (Dijon: Arts et Belles-Lettres de Dijon, 1954), p. 35.

15 L. Héritte-Viardot (trans. E.S. Bucheim), *Memories and Adventures* (London: Mills & Boon, 1913), p. 18.

16 This occurred in the mid-1850s: H. Granjard and A. Zviguilsky, *Ivan Tourguénev, Lettres inédites à Pauline Viardot et à sa famille* (Paris: Editions l'Age d'Homme, 1972), pp. 77, 78.

17 A. FitzLyon, *The Price of Genius*, op. cit., p. 80; 'il ne rêve que carnage': T. Marix-Spire, *Lettres inédites de George Sand*, op. cit., pp. 114, 124; V.S. Pritchett, op. cit., p. 41.

18 L. Viardot, *Souvenirs de Chasse*, op. cit., pp. 106, 107, 151, 299, 265; A. Zviguilsky (ed.), pp. 164, 177; H. Granjard and A. Zviguilsky, *Ivan Tourguénev, Lettres inédites à Pauline Viardot et à sa famille* (Paris: Editions l'Age d'Homme, 1972), p. 36.

19 L. Viardot, *Souvenirs de Chasse*, op. cit., pp. 100, 184.

20 Ibid., pp. 144, 151, 232, 252, 321, 327, 329, 357, 359. Apparently, the King had killed five birds with two bullets (Ibid., op. cit., p. 284).

21 Ibid., p. 297; T. Marix-Spire, *Lettres inédites de George Sand*, op. cit., p. 22; M. L'Hôpital, op. cit., p. 28.

22 P. Mansel, *Paris between Empires, 1814–1852* (London: John Murray, 2001), p. 183.

23 A. FitzLyon, *The Price of Genius*, op. cit, p. 85; G. Dulong, op. cit., p. 39.

24 J.P.T. Bury, *France 1814–1940* (London: Methuen, 1969), p. 60; T. Marix-Spire, *Lettres inédites de George Sand*, op. cit., p. 23.

25 C. Jones, *The Cambridge Illustrated History of France* (Cambridge: Cambridge University Press, 1994), p. 202.

26 P. Mansel, op. cit., pp. 386, 387.

27 T. Marix-Spire, *Lettres inédites de George Sand*, op. cit., p. 24; M. L'Hôpital, op. cit., p. 29; G. Sand (ed. T. Bodin), *Lettres Retrouvées* (Paris: Gallimard, 2004), p. 34. The paper on tariffs was published in 1841: T. Marix-Spire, op. cit, p. 114.

28 P. Mansel, op. cit., pp. 285, 287, 288, 289. The later attempt was on 25 June 1836: Ibid., p. 290.

29 L. Viardot, *Souvenirs de Chasse*, op. cit., p. 327.

30 *New Grove Dictionary of Music and Musicians* (London: Macmillan, 1980), vol. 3, p. 842, Carvalho (H. Rosenthal). The Odéon fire was in 1799: N. Simeone, *Paris – A Musical Gazetteer* (New Haven and London: Yale University Press, 2000), p. 204. Gaslight: R. Somerset-Ward, *Angels and Monsters* (New Haven and London: Yale University Press, 2004), p. 169.

31 E.C. Clayton, *Queens of Song* (London: Smith Elder & Co, 1863), p. 200.

32 N. Simeone, op. cit., p. 187.

33 C. Saint-Saëns (trans. E.G. Rich), *Musical Memories* (London: Murray, 1921), p. 147; *Cahiers Ivan Tourguéniev, Pauline Viardot, Maria Malibran* (Bougival: Association des Amis d'Ivan Tourguéniev Pauline Viardot et Maria Malibran), 2, p. 90; L Héritte-Viardot, op. cit., p. 31. Music festivals gave Louis 'une épouvantable indigestion musicale': L. Viardot, *Souvenirs de Chasse*, op. cit., p. 342.

34 G. Dulong, op. cit., pp. 30, 40.

35 G. Sand, 'Le Théâtre-Italien et Mlle Pauline Garcia', *Revue des Deux Mondes*, vol. XXI,

p. 582; G. Dulong, op. cit., p. 30; A. FitzLyon, *The Price of Genius*, op. cit., p. 67.
36 'The Olive Grove', from G. de Maupassant (trans. G. Hopkins), *Short Stories* (London: The Folio Society, 1959), p. 279.
37 F. Lestringant, *Alfred de Musset* (Paris: Flammarion, 1999), p. 419; A. FitzLyon, *The Price of Genius*, op. cit., p. 79.
38 P. Bloom (ed.), *Music in Paris in the Eighteen Thirties* (New York: Pendragon Press, 1987), p. 17; the author was told about Mme Garcia's attitude by Dr Zviguilsky.
39 N. Simeone, op. cit., p. 265.
40 V. Hugo, *Les Misérables* (Brussels: A. Lacroix, Verboekheven, 1862), Part V, book 6, ch. 1, pp. 94, 95.
41 P. Bloom (ed.), op. cit., p. 17.
42 T. Marix-Spire, *Lettres inédites de George Sand*, op. cit., p. 24.
43 A. FitzLyon, *The Price of Genius*, op. cit., pp. 83, 303.
44 M. L'Hôpital, op. cit., p. 31; B. Jack, *George Sand: A Woman's Life Writ Large* (London: Chatto & Windus, 1999), p. 290.
45 C. Jones, op. cit., p. 240; P. Mansel, op. cit., p. 314.
46 E.C. Clayton, op. cit., vol. II, p. 249.
47 G. Dulong, op. cit., p. 41; M. Steen, *The Lives and Times of the Great Composers* (Cambridge: Icon, 2003), p. 15; Musée Municipal de l'Ecole de Barbizon, *Landscape painters at Barbizon 1825–1827*, 1989, p. 20; *Encyclopaedia Britannica*, ninth edition, vol. XIII, p. 160.
48 A. FitzLyon, *The Price of Genius*, op. cit., p. 89; C. Gounod (trans. A. Crocker), *Memoirs of an Artist* (Chicago: Rand McNally & Company, 1895), pp. 79, 124, 137, 138.
49 T. Marix-Spire, *Lettres inédites de George Sand*, op. cit., pp. 160, 219; I. Turgenev (trans. T.S. Perry), *Virgin Soil* (London: Ward, Lock & Co, pre-1880), pp. 24, 46, 51, 57 (the aunt, Anna Zaharovna, is supposed to be similar to Berthe); A. Zviguilsky (ed.), *Ivan Tourguénev: Nouvelle Correspondance inédite* (Paris: Librairie des Cinq Continents, 1971), p. 24 (the dog was a Carlin, even then an almost extinct breed); P. Waddington, *Courtavenel, the History of an Artists' Nest and its Role in the Life of Turgenev* (*PhD Thesis*, Queen's University Belfast, The British Library, British Thesis Service, spring 1972), p. 111.
50 G. Dulong, op. cit., p. 42; G. Bord, *Rosina Stoltz* (*Victoire Noël*) (Paris: Henri Daragon, 1909), pp. 77, 112.
51 P. Mansel, op. cit., pp. 322, 326.
52 Liszt to Marie d'Agoult, 1 December 1840: D. Ollivier (ed.), *Correspondance de Liszt et de la Comtesse d'Agoult* (Paris: Editions Bernard Grasset, 1933–34), vol. II, p. 58; G. Dulong, op. cit., pp. 42, 43; T. Marix-Spire, *Lettres inédites de George Sand*, op. cit., p. 38.
53 A. FitzLyon, *The Price of Genius*, op. cit., p. 279.
54 'Affreusement laide, mais si je la revoyais, j'en deviendrais amoureux fou': *Musical Quarterly* 1915, vol. I, p. 363.
55 A. FitzLyon, *The Price of Genius*, op. cit., p. 95; Mrs Grote, *Memoirs of the Life of Ary Scheffer* (London: John Murray, 1860), p. 66.
56 L. Viardot, *Wonders of European Art* (London: Sampson Low, Son, and Marston, 1871), p. 298.
57 Musée de la Vie Romantique, *General Guide* (Paris-Musées, 1992), p. 7; Mrs Grote, op. cit., pp. 4, 132.
58 Mrs Grote, op. cit., pp. 16, 20, 32, 34, 63, 74.
59 Musée de la Vie Romantique, *General Guide*, op. cit., p. 18.
60 *Encyclopaedia Britannica*, ninth edition, vol. 21, p. 389.
61 Maison Atelier de Théodore Rousseau at Barbizon.
62 A leaflet available in Musée de la Vie Romantique, December 1999; Mrs Grote, op. cit., p. 140. £1,000: P. Ackroyd, *Dickens* (London: Sinclair Stevenson, 1990), p. 478; O'Connor: *Illustrated London News*, 25 August 1849, p. 135.
63 *Musical Quarterly*, vol. I, 1915, p. 364.
64 Musée de la Vie Romantique leaflet.
65 'Bienfaisant': *Musical Quarterly*, vol. I, 1915, p. 364.

Chapter 6. Tours (pp. 83–96)

1 'precipités dans l'espace': T. Marix-Spire, *Lettres inédites de George Sand et de Pauline Viardot 1839–1849* (Nouvelles Editions), p. 115.
2 L. Viardot, *Souvenirs de Chasse dans toute l'Europe* (Paris: Editions Pygmalion, 1985), p. 56; V. Hugo (trans. N. Denny), *Les Misérables* (London: Penguin, 1982), p. 389.

3 This was until 1844: B. Weinreb and C. Hibbert, *London Encyclopaedia* (London: Macmillan, 1993), p. 265.
4 P. Ackroyd, *Dickens* (London: Sinclair Stevenson, 1990), p. 539; *Encyclopaedia Britannica,* ninth edition, vol. XX, p. 246.
5 In 1848, 1852, 1856: A. Zviguilsky (ed.), op. cit., p. 87; L. Viardot, *Souvenirs de chasse,* op. cit., p. 336.
6 G.M. Trevelyan, *English Social History* (London: Longmans, 1946), p. 531; D. Thomson, *England in the Nineteenth Century* (Harmondsworth: Pelican, 1964), p. 32, quoting Cobden.
7 *Encyclopaedia Britannica,* ninth edition, vol. XX, pp. 224, 251.
8 F. Dostoyevsky, *The Idiot* (Ware, Herts: Wordsworth Classics, 1996), part 3, ch. 4, p. 350.
9 *Encyclopaedia Britannica,* ninth edition, vol. XVIII, p. 839.
10 W. Collins, *The Woman in White* (Oxford: Oxford University Press, 1996), part 2, ch. 1, p. 201; A. Zviguilsky (ed.), *Ivan Tourguénev: Nouvelle Correspondance inédite* (Paris: Librairie des Cinq Continents, 1971), p. 159.
11 *Encyclopaedia Britannica,* Standard Millennium edition; J. Ridley, *Napoléon III and Eugénie* (London: Constable, 1979), p. 204; A. Zviguilsky (ed.), op. cit., pp. 191, 123.
12 C.V. Stanford and C. Forsyth, *A History of Music* (New York: Macmillan, 1917), p. 269.
13 *Illustrated London News,* 17 June 1865, p. 591. Around the time of the Staplehurst disaster, there were also gory disasters near Chester and near Bristol.
14 December 1849: B. Lumley, *Reminiscences of the Opera* (London: Hurst and Blackett, 1864), p. 262.
15 L. Héritte-Viardot (trans. E.S. Bucheim), *Memories and Adventures* (London: Mills & Boon, 1913), p. 244.
16 The accident was in June 1865: P. Ackroyd, op. cit., p. 960; *Illustrated London News,* 17 June 1865, p. 571; P. Waddington, 'Dickens, Pauline Viardot and Turgenev: a Study in Mutual Admiration', *New Zealand Slavonic Journal,* no. 2, 1974, p. 66. Pauline's accident is referred to in *Cahiers Ivan Tourguéniev, Pauline Viardot, Maria Malibran* (Bougival: Association des Amis d'Ivan Tourguéniev Pauline Viardot et Maria Malibran), no. 20, p. 135 (Borchard).
17 L.Viardot, *Souvenirs de Chasse,* op. cit., p. 74. The Faucits' journey took four hours – see Sir T. Martin, *Helena Faucit* (*Lady Martin*) (Edinburgh and London: William Blackwood and Sons, 1900), p. 133.
18 A. FitzLyon, *The Price of Genius, a life of Pauline Viardot* (London: John Calder, 1964), p. 96; T. Marix-Spire, *Lettres inédites de George Sand,* op. cit., p. 115; G. Dulong, *Pauline Viardot Tragédienne Lyrique* (Bougival: Association des Amis d'Ivan Tourguéniev Pauline Viardot et Maria Malibran), p. 53; D. Ollivier (ed.), *Correspondance de Liszt et de la Comtesse d'Agoult* (Paris: Editions Bernard Grasset, 1933–34), vol. II, p. 154. 'Un vrai duel, et le public l'attend avec grande impatience': T. Marix-Spire, *Lettres inédites de George Sand,* op. cit., pp. 101, 102.
19 P. Mansel, *Constantinople* (London: Penguin, 1997), p. 342. 'Hell is a city much like London'; Byron, *Beppo,* stanza 43.
20 C. Dickens, *Bleak House* (published 1853) (London: Pan Books, 1976), ch. 1; the word 'aits' has been replaced with 'eyots', and 'kennel' with 'gutter'.
21 C. Dickens, *Sketches by Boz* (London: Chapman and Hall), 'Scenes', ch. 2.
22 P. Ackroyd, op. cit., pp. 381, 383, 384.
23 C. Dickens, *Sketches by Boz,* op. cit., 'Scenes', ch. 2.
24 Mrs Grote, *Memoirs of the Life of Ary Scheffer* (London: John Murray, 1860), pp. 85, 140; *History Today,* vol. 54, 11 November 2004, p. 43; M. Mainwaring (ed.), *Ivan Turgenev, the Portrait Game* (London: Chatto and Windus, 1973), p. 133. 'Proud, insolent' was a criticism of Ary Scheffer: Mrs Grote, op. cit., pp. 85, 140.
25 T. Marix-Spire, *Lettres inédites de George Sand,* op. cit., pp. 101, 110, 111.
26 'Une obéisance si servile, une si lâche soumission aux plus puériles exigencies de l'habitude': L. Viardot, *Souvenirs de Chasse,* op. cit., pp. 73, 74.
27 'Se mette volontairement dans la servitude des usages qu'elle s'impose': Ibid., p. 74.
28 T. Marix-Spire, *Lettres inédites de George Sand,* op. cit., p. 102; A. Zviguilsky (ed.), op. cit., p. 82; P. Waddington, *Turgenev and England* (London: Macmillan, 1980), p. 4.
29 Chopin's letter to J. Fontana, 20 August 184: B. Eisler, *Chopin's Funeral* (London: Little, Brown, 2003), p. 91; A. Hedley (revised M.E.J. Brown), *Chopin* (London: J.M. Dent, 1947),

p. 200; A. FitzLyon, *The Price of Genius*, op. cit., p. 104.
30 T. Marix-Spire, *Lettres inédites de George Sand*, op. cit., pp. 124, 126. See ibid., p. 129 for bits on Gloucester; L. Viardot, *Souvenirs de Chasse*, op. cit., p. 356.
31 T. Marix-Spire, *Lettres inédites de George Sand*, op. cit., p. 128; A. FitzLyon, *The Price of Genius*, op. cit., p. 106. For 'celebrity', she actually uses the expression in English 'celebrated singer': *Musical Quarterly* 1915, vol. I, p. 532.
32 L. Viardot, *Souvenirs de Chasse*, op. cit., pp. 291, 341.
33 T. Marix-Spire, *Lettres inédites de George Sand*, op. cit., p. 115; R. Locke, *Music, Musicians and the Saint-Simonians* (Chicago: University of Chicago Press, 1986), p. 5.
34 R. Locke, op. cit., pp. 6, 71, 10, 227; J. Ridley, *Garibaldi* (London: Constable, 1974), p. 23.
35 *Encyclopaedia Britannica,* ninth edition, vol. XIV, p. 471.
36 R. Locke, op. cit., pp. 49, 57, 67.
37 G Sand (trans. Fayette Robinson), *Consuelo* (New York: Stringer and Townsend, 1851), p. 109.
38 B. Eisler, op. cit., p. 80; T. Marix-Spire, *Lettres inédites de George Sand*, op. cit., p. 96.
39 The Arc was inaugurated in 1836: P. Mansel, *Paris between Empires 1814–1852* (London: John Murray, 2001), p. 282.
40 There were 600,000 people: Ibid., p. 370 (the temperature was 14 degrees below zero).
41 H. Weinstock, *Donizetti and the World of Opera* (London: Methuen, 1964), p. 172; T. Marix-Spire, *Lettres inédites de George Sand*, op. cit., pp. 40, 104.
42 T. Marix-Spire, *Lettres inédites de George Sand*, op. cit., p. 146
43 L. Héritte-Viardot, op. cit., pp. 18, 19.
44 C. Saint-Saëns (trans. E.G. Rich) *Musical Memories* (London: Murray, 1921), pp. 147, 148; A. FitzLyon, *The Price of Genius*, op. cit., pp. 110, 130; L. Héritte-Viardot, op. cit., p. 61.
45 T. Marix-Spire. op. cit., pp. 145, 149, 154; E.C. Clayton, *Queens of Song* (London: Smith Elder & Co, 1863), vol. II, p. 250.
46 T. Marix-Spire, *Lettres inédites de George Sand*, op. cit., p.150; *Encyclopaedia Britannica,* ninth edition, vol. XXII, p. 345.
47 T. Marix-Spire, *Lettres inédites de George Sand*, op. cit., p. 155.
48 Although the note on page 44 of T. Marix-Spire, *Lettres inédites de George Sand*, op. cit., records 'la femme du tout puissant ambassadeur d'Angleterre', Pauline herself (ibid., p. 155), records 'la femme ou maîtresse du sécretaire l'ambassade'.
49 'La première, la seule, la grande, la vraie cantatrice': T. Marix-Spire, *Lettres inédites de George Sand*, op. cit., p. 159, 168. 'La prêtresse de l'idéal en musique et vous avez pour mission de le répandre' (to be an evangelist): Ibid., p. 43.
50 A. FitzLyon, *The Price of Genius*, op. cit., p. 125; October to 24 March; T. Marix-Spire, *Lettres inédites de George Sand*, op. cit., p. 168.
51 T. Marix-Spire, *Lettres inédites de George Sand*, op. cit., pp. 48, 49 A. FitzLyon, *The Price of Genius*, op. cit., p. 123.
52 T. Marix-Spire, *Lettres inédites de George Sand*, op. cit., pp. 56, 51.
53 *Revue des Deux Mondes*, vol. XXXII, p. 860; G. Dulong, op. cit., p. 57.
54 The *Revue Indépendante* was founded in November 1841; *Encyclopaedia Britannica,* ninth edition, vol. XIV, p. 471.
55 M. L'Hôpital, *Louis Viardot, Mémoires de l'Académie des Sciences* (Dijon: Arts et Belles-Lettres de Dijon, 1954), p. 33; A. FitzLyon, *The Price of Genius*, op. cit., p. 128.
56 21 January 1843, A. Hedley, op. cit., p. 227. The portrait of the La Baronne de Rothschild is dated 1848: *Encyclopaedia Britannica,* Standard Millennium edition.
57 T. Marix-Spire, *Lettres inédites de George Sand*, op. cit., pp. 170, 172, 173, 174, 175, 185; A. FitzLyon, *The Price of Genius*, op. cit., p. 462
58 T. Marix-Spire, *Lettres inédites de George Sand*, op. cit., pp. 178, 18
59 L. Viardot, *Souvenirs de Chasse*, op. cit., pp. 79, 85, 86.
60 T. Marix-Spire, *Lettres inédites de George Sand*, op. cit., p. 180; Comtesse Merlin, *Maria Malibran* (London: Henry Colburn, 1840), p. 14; E.C. Clayton, op. cit., p. 197.
61 G. Bord, *Rosina Stoltz* (Victoire Noël) (Paris: Henri Daragon, 1909), p.149.
62 She was in Vienna during April 1843–1July.
63 Meyerbeer was appointed in June 1842; *New Grove Dictionary of Music and Musicians* (London: Macmillan, 1980), vol. 12, p. 250: Meyerbeer (Heinz Becker).
64 Ibid., vol. 18, p. 19: Spontini (Dennis Libby); also *Grove's Dictionary of Music and*

Musicians, 5th edition (ed. E. Blom), vol. 8, p. 24.
65 T. Marix-Spire, *Lettres inédites de George Sand*, op. cit., pp. 181–182.
67 Ibid., pp. 183, 187.
68 On 2 October 1843: Chopin to Auguste Léo, A. Hedley (trans.), *Selected Correspondence of Fryderyk Chopin* (London: Heinemann, 1962), p. 229.
69 A. FitzLyon, *The Price of Genius*, op. cit., p. 135; T. Marix-Spire, *Lettres inédites de George Sand*, op. cit., p. 187.

Chapter 7. Russia (pp. 99–120)

1 I. Goncharov (trans. D. Magarshack), *Oblomov* (London: Penguin, 1954), p. 393; R. Somerset-Ward, *Angels and Monsters* (New Haven and London: Yale University Press, 2004), p. 122; G. Dulong, *Pauline Viardot Tragédienne Lyrique* (Bougival: Association des Amis d'Ivan Tourguéniev Pauline Viardot et Maria Malibran), p. 61.
2 The Director was Field Marshal Prince Volkonsky (1776–1852); this was not Tolstoy's grandfather. A. FitzLyon, *Price of Genius, a Life of Pauline Viardot* (London: John Calder, 1964), p. 146.
3 *Grove Dictionary of Music and Musicians* (London: Macmillan, 1980), vol. 18, p. 556: Tamburini (Elizabeth Forbes); H. Granjard and A. Zviguilsky, *Ivan Tourguénev, Lettres inédites à Pauline Viardot et à sa famille* (Paris: Editions l'Age d'Homme, 1972), p. 20.
4 *New Grove*, op. cit., vol. 14, p. 287: Pasta (Elizabeth Forbes); M. Steen, *The Lives and Times of the Great Composers* (Cambridge: Icon, 2003), p. 640; *New Grove*, op. cit., vol. 11, p. 41: Liszt (H. Searle). Another special case would be Sontag, who followed her husband on his diplomatic missions – *New Grove*, op. cit., vol. 17, p. 528, Sontag (J. Warrack).
5 G. Dulong, op. cit., p. 58.
6 They were paper rouble fees, suggest Professor Patrick Waddington and Dulong. This makes sense. The season was (per G. Dulong, op. cit., p. 58) from 1 November to 20 February, sixteen weeks. As a rough check, say, she performed four times a week (a maximum); that would be around 60 performances, or 830 roubles per performance. There were 3.5 assignats to the silver rouble (A. Seljak, article for www.moneymuseum.com, *Zum Geld und Kreditsystem in Russland vom Kiever Reich bis 1897*, p. 18), giving 240 silver roubles per performance. According to Seljak's table (A. Seljak, *Ivan Turgenev's Ökonomien* (Zurich: University of Basel, Pano Verlag, 2004), p. 489), that would be £90, which compares with the 100 guineas a night Jullien offered her in London, or Bunn's offer to Jenny Lind of £40 per performance later in the decade. Malibran was paid 2,775 for 24 performances in 1835, an average of £115 (A. FitzLyon, *Maria Malibran – Diva of the Romantic Age* (London: Souvenir Press, 1987), p. 186). It would be improbable that Pauline would have received silver roubles, 3.5 times as much.
7 L. Tolstoy (trans. L. and A. Maude), *War and Peace* (London: OUP, 1933), Book VIII, ch. IX, p. 204; the immovable property of a merchant in 1843/44 was on average 16,139 silver roubles (see A. Seljak, *Ivan Turgenev's Ökonomien*, op. cit., p. 493), that is equivalent to 56,500 assignats. This comparison is supplied very tentatively, and the author is most grateful to Prof Seljak for his help on this. Director: L. Tolstoy, *Anna Karenina*, op. cit., Part VII, ch. 17, p. 752; Pushkin's salary: *Encyclopaedia Britannica*, ninth edition, vol. XIX, p. 649. Professor Seljak considers this to be probably designated in assignats.
8 G. Dulong, op. cit., p. 73.
9 The company director figures are later in the century, in the 1870s, when the founding partner of a bank might earn 50,000 roubles, the bank director be paid 12,000 roubles and a company director 17,000: L. Tolstoy, (trans. R. Edmonds), *Anna Karenin* (Harmondsworth: Penguin, 1954), Part VII, ch. 17, p. 752; advice received from Professor Seljak suggests that these figures would be silver roubles, so the author has multiplied by 3.5, although this being in 1870 there were no assignats at the time.
10 In 1839: G. Dulong, op. cit., p. 30.
11 In the first half of 1843: G. Kennan, *The Marquis de Custine and his Russia in 1839* (London: Hutchinson, 1972), pp vii, 95.
12 The mugging was in the autumn of 1824: Ibid., pp. vii, 3, 5, 6, 98, 99.
13 P. Ackroyd, *Dickens* (London: Sinclair Stevenson, 1990), p. 376.
14 I. Evans, *A Short History of English Literature* (Harmondsworth: Penguin, 1963), p. 179.
15 P. Mansel, *Paris between Empires 1814–1852* (London: John Murray, 2001), p. 351.

16 Marquis de Custine (foreword by D.J. Boorstin), *Empire of the Czar* (New York: Anchor Books, 1989), p. xviii.
17 Marquis de Custine,(ed. and trans. P.P. Kohler), *Journey for our Time* (London: George Prior), p. 138. 'Not yet civilised': Ibid., vol. I, p. 196; 'regimented tartars': Ibid., p. 74, 14 July 1839.
18 *Encyclopaedia Britannica,* ninth edition, vol. XXI, pp. 191, 193.
19 F. Dostoyevsky, *The Double* (London: Hesperus Press, 2004), ch. 5, p. 40.
20 *Encyclopaedia Britannica,* ninth edition, vol. XXI, p. 191 (fifteen degrees Fahrenheit); Ibid., vol. XVIII, p. 274; H. Granjard and A. Zviguilsky, op. cit., p. 35.
21 The Moskva was then ice-bound from the second week in November to the second week in April. (*Encyclopaedia Britannica,* ninth edition, vol. XVI, p. 858). And the Neva at St Petersburg, about a week later. (Ibid., vol. XXI, p. 191).
22 I. Goncharov, *Oblomov,* op. cit., p. 333.
23 A. Zviguilsky (ed.), *Ivan Tourguénev: Nouvelle Correspondance inédite* (Paris: Librairie des Cinq Continents, 1971), p. 135 (eight degrees Fahrenheit); Snow – Ibid., p. 202; I. Turgenev, *Phantoms,* ch. 22, p. 46, in I. Turgenev (trans. Isabel Hapgood), *First Love and other stories* (New York: Charles Scribner's Sons, 1923); H. Granjard and A. Zviguilsky, op. cit., p. 147; Marquis de Custine, *Journey for our Time,* op. cit., p. 103, 22 July 1839.
24 *Encyclopaedia Britannica,* ninth edition, vol. XVIII, p. 274: during the winter of 1829–30.
25 'St Petersburg without the court is a desert': Marquis de Custine, op. cit., p. 133, 1 August 1839; L. Tolstoy, *Anna Karenina,* op. cit., pt 1, ch. 14, p. 65; A. Pushkin (trans. C. Johnston, Preface J. Bayley, Notes M. Basker), *Eugene Onegin* (London: Penguin, 2003), ch. 2, pp. xi, xii; Ibid., ch. 3, p. ii; A.N. Wilson, *Tolstoy* (London: Hamish Hamilton, 1988), p. 54; *Marquis de Custine* (ed. and trans. P.P. Kohler), *Journey for our Time* (London: George Prior), p. 237.
26 L. Tolstoy, *Anna Karenina,* op. cit., pp. 142, 317; I. Goncharov, *Oblomov,* pt III, ch. 5.
27 L. Tolstoy, *Anna Karenina,* op. cit., pt II, ch. 4, pt IV, ch. 4; dinner at 4.30pm – F. Dostoyevsky, *The Idiot* (Ware, Herts: Wordsworth Classics, 1996), pt I, ch 8.
28 L. Tolstoy, *Anna Karenina,* op. cit., pt 1, ch. 17, pt II, ch. 6, pt IV, ch. 9; I. Turgenev, *Virgin Soil,* pt I, ch. 19; A. Pushkin, *Eugene Onegin,* op. cit., ch. 2, p. iii.
29 *Encyclopaedia Britannica,* ninth edition, vol. XXI, p. 67.
30 L. Viardot, *Souvenirs de chasse dans toute l'Europe* (Paris: Editions Pygmalion, 1985), p. 129: 91 versts in six hours. A verst is 3,500 feet, about two-thirds of a mile, slightly more than a kilometre. (*Chambers* and *Concise Oxford English Dictionaries*). The horses could do 54 versts in one stage 'et sans prendre haleine'. A stage in England (mid-1830s) might be fifteen miles long, and 15mph was a chase at high speed. C. Dickens, *The Pickwick Papers* (Oxford: Oxford University Press, World Classics, 1988), Book IV, ch. 9.
31 F. Dostoyevsky, *The Brothers Karamazov,* Book 8, ch. 6; the same for a rake, Anatole Kuryagin, in L. Tolstoy (trans. L. and A. Maude), *War and Peace* (London: OUP, 1933), Book VIII, ch. 16, where Tver to Moscow took seven hours.
32 L. Viardot, *Souvenirs de Chasse,* op. cit., p. 235; Marquis de Custine, *Journey for our Time,* op. cit., pp. 138, 220, 1 August 1839; Marquis de Custine, *The Empire of the Czar* (London: Longman Brown Green and Longmans, 1843), vol. I, p. 123.
33 T. Marix-Spire, *Lettres inédites de George Sand et de Pauline Viardot 1839–1849* (Paris: Nouvelles Editions, 1959), pp. 188, 194; Marquis de Custine, *Journey for our Time,* op. cit., p. 50. B. Kendall-Davies, *The Life and Work of Pauline Viardot-Garcia* (London: Cambridge Scholars Press, 2003), vol. I, 'The years of fame', p. 167, records that they called in on the Chopin family and performed at one of Mme Chopin's Thursday salons.
34 J. Chissell, *Clara Schumann: a Dedicated Spirit* (London: Hamish Hamilton, 1983), p. 89; L. Viardot, *Souvenirs de Chasse,* op. cit., p. 151.
35 H. Berlioz (trans. R. and E. Holmes), *Autobiography of Hector Berlioz* (London: Macmillan, 1884), pp. 262, 263. He arrived in February 1847. Sheepskin-lined overcoat – F. Dostoyevsky, *The Idiot,* op. cit., pt 1, ch. 1: Myshkin's journey was late November.
36 Marquis de Custine, *Journey for our Time,* op. cit., pp. 137–9.
37 L. Viardot, *Souvenirs de Chasse,* op. cit., p.110.

38 Marquis de Custine, *Journey for our Time*, op. cit., pp. 52, 82, 103, 289, 302.
39 L. Tolstoy, *War and Peace*, op. cit., Book VIII, ch. 3; Marquis de Custine, *Journey for our Time*, op. cit., p. 55; Marquis de Custine, *The Empire of the Czar* (London: Longman Brown Green and Longmans, 1843), vol. I, p. 195.
40 Marquis de Custine, *Journey for our Time*, op. cit., p. 81, 15 July 1839.
41 Marquis de Custine, *The Empire of the Czar* (London: Longman Brown Green and Longmans, 1843), vol. I, p. 220; Marquis de Custine, *Journey for our Time*, op. cit., pp. 57, 85, 114, 118. See also L. Tolstoy, *War and Peace*, op. cit., Book III, ch. 10, and Book III, ch. 15.
42 Lack of practical knowledge – F. Dostoyevsky, *The Idiot*, op. cit., part 3, ch. 1; H. Seton-Watson, *The Russian Empire 1801–1917* (Oxford: Clarendon Press, 1988), pp. 14, 239.
43 For 12,000 roubles, many times his stipend: R. Hingley, *Dostoyevsky, his life and work* (London: Paul Elek Ltd, 1978), p. 24.
44 Belinsky, quoted in *Encyclopaedia Britannica,* Standard Millennium edition (History of Russia Education and Intellectual Life).
45 Marquis de Custine, *Journey for our Time*, op. cit., p. 167. The percentages for 1897 were Orthodox 69 per cent, Roman Catholic 9 per cent: H. Seton-Watson, op. cit., p. 534.
46 Marquis de Custine, *Journey for our Time*, op. cit., p.111; in L. Tolstoy, *War and Peace*, op. cit., vol. III, book 12, ch. 11, Pierre is made to watch the execution of fellow prisoners accused of incendiarism.
47 R. Hingley, op. cit., pp. 72, 73, 74.
48 Marquis de Custine, *Journey for our Time*, pp. 222, 224.
49 The nobility totalled 604,000 in 1858: H. Seton-Watson, op. cit., p. 240; at end of XVIIIc, D. Saunders, *Russia in the Age of Reaction and Reform* (London: Longman, 1992), pp. 16, 18. The percentage was 84 per cent in 1837.
50 A. Walker, *Franz Liszt, Vol. 1, The Virtuoso Years 1811–47* (London: Faber and Faber, 1983), p. 26.
51 *Encyclopaedia Britannica,* ninth edition, vol. XVI, p. 858; I. Turgenev (trans. Isabel Hapgood), *On the Eve* (Freeport, New York: Books for Libraries Press, 1971), ch. 22, and 'A Strange Story', in I. Turgenev (trans. Isabel Hapgood), *The Brigadier and other stories* (Freeport, New York: Books for Libraries Press, 1971); L. Tolstoy, *Anna Karenina*, op. cit., Pt. 7, ch. 7, Pt. 3, ch. 26. The author is most grateful to Mr Kyril FitzLyon, whose ancestors were Marshals, and who escaped from Russia in 1922, for enlightening him about the nature of this gentry class in Russia.
52 A. Pushkin, *Eugene Onegin*, op. cit., ch. 3, p. 26. ch. 5 p. 25; ch. 6 pp. 1, 15; L. Tolstoy, *War and Peace*, op. cit., Book VIII, ch. 3; L. Tolstoy (trans. R. Edmonds), *Anna Karenin* (Harmondsworth: Penguin, 1954), pt IV, ch. 1; I. Turgenev, *Virgin Soil*, op. cit., pt I, ch. 8, pt I ch. 9, pt I, ch. 20; Ibid., pt II, ch. 23.
53 Marquis de Custine, *Journey for Our Time*, op. cit., p. 116; I. Turgenev, *Nest of Gentlefolk*, ch. XII, ch. XIII; F. Dostoyevsky (trans. C. Garnett, introduction G.S. Morson), *The Gambler* (New York: The Modern Library, 2003), ch. 3, p. 25.
54 Princess Helène, circumstantially: L. Tolstoy, *War and Peace*, op. cit., Book XII, ch. 2.
55 L Tolstoy, *Anna Karenina*, op. cit., pt VI, ch. 22, p. 660.
56 Ibid., pt VII, ch. 2.
57 I. Goncharov, *Oblomov*, op. cit., pt II, ch. 3, ch. 4.
58 L. Tolstoy, *War and Peace*, op. cit., Book I ch. 2, ch. 26: Princess Mary, and the little princess when she went to have her baby and die.
59 I. Goncharov, *Oblomov*, op. cit., pt I, ch. 4; Pt I ch. 9
60 I. Turgenev, *First Love*, ch. 1.
61 I. Turgenev, *Virgin Soil*, op. cit., pt I, ch. 19.
62 I. Turgenev, *On the Eve*, op. cit., ch. 22.
63 I. Goncharov, Oblomov, op. cit., pt I, ch. 8; pt I, ch. 9.
64 Ibid., pt II, ch. 4
65 L. Tolstoy, *War and Peace*, op. cit., Book III ch. 3.
66 Separate caste – F. Dostoyevsky, *The Idiot*, op. cit., part 3 ch. 1; 'Progenitors' – H. Seton-Watson, op. cit., p. 362; B. Waller (ed.), *Themes in Modern European History 1830–1890* (London: Unwin Hyman, 1990), p. 165; Impoverished – Marmaladov, the former titular councillor in F. Dostoyevsky (trans. D. McDuff), *Crime and Punishment* (London: Penguin, 2003), Part 1, ch. 2 and passim; some exceptionally rich women married into the nobility – F. Dostoyevsky, *The Idiot*, op. cit., pt 1, ch. xvi.
67 T. Marix-Spire, *Lettres inédites de George Sand et de Pauline Viardot 1839–1849* (Paris:

Nouvelles Editions, 1959), p. 218; H. Seton-Watson, op. cit., p. 29.

68 B. Waller, op. cit., p. 165; L. Tolstoy, *Anna Karenina*, op. cit., Book 2, pt 3, ch. 26, ch. 27; I. Turgenev; *Punin and Baburin*, in *The Brigadier and other stories* (trans. Isabel Hapgood) (Freeport, New York: Books for Libraries Press, 1971); I. Turgenev, *Virgin Soil*, op. cit., pt I, ch. 11.

69 'Women he despised from the depth of his soul': I. Turgenev (trans. Richard Freeborn), *Sketches from a Hunter's Album* (London: Penguin, 1967 and 1990), 'Khor and Kalinych', p. 26; 'The women were standing up waiting on them': L. Tolstoy, *Anna Karenina*, op. cit., pt III, ch. 25; I. Goncharov, *Oblomov*, op. cit., pt I, ch. 9; Black monk and hare – A. Pushkin, *Eugene Onegin*, op. cit., ch. 5, p. 6.

70 L. Tolstoy, *Anna Karenina*, op. cit., pt III, ch. 27, p. 354.

71 I. Turgenev (trans. E. Schuyler), *Fathers and Sons* (London: Ward, Lock & Co, 1883), ch. 9, in which the text, approved by Turgenev, states 'the Russian peasant would skin God'. It does not matter for us if this is not true; it was the impression at the time.

72 L. Viardot, *Souvenirs de Chasse*, op cit., p. 118; R. Hingley, *Dostoyevsky, his life and work* (London: Paul Elek Ltd, 1978). pp. 35, 37; D. Saunders, *Russia in the Age of Reaction and Reform* (London: Longman, 1992), pp. 8, 9. The information on the sister-in-law was provided by Herzen. P. Waddington, 'Some Gleanings on Turgenev and his International Connections', *New Zealand Slavonic Journal*, 1983, p. 200.

73 Marquis de Custine, *Journey for our Time*, op. cit., p. 146; Marquis de Custine, *The Empire of the Czar* (London: Longman Brown Green and Longmans, 1843), vol. II, p. 181; L. Tolstoy, *Anna Karenina*, op. cit., pt III, ch. 26. English servant girls also all had 'fat noses and hard cheeks' – W. Collins, *The Woman in White* (Oxford: Oxford University Press, 1996), pt II, ch. 10.

74 M. Lermontov (trans. P. Foote), *A Hero of Our Time* (London: Penguin, 2001), pt II, ch. 1 (Taman).

75 Marquis de Custine, *Empire of the Czar*, op. cit., pp. 378, 498.

76 A.N. Wilson, *Tolstoy* (London: Hamish Hamilton, 1988), pp. 55, 58, 74, 184, 195; F. Dostoyevsky, *The Brothers Karamazov*, op. cit., pt I, Book III, ch. 8, p. 180; 'The Inn', from I. Turgenev (ed. D Borovsky), *Stories in Poems and Prose* (Moscow: Progress Publishers, 1982), p. 51.

77 D. Thomson, *England in the Nineteenth Century* (Harmondsworth: Pelican, 1964), p. 88.

78 The Jamaican date was August 1838; the Emancipation Act was in 1833.

79 Slavery today: *The Times Literary Supplement*, London, 3 March 2006, p. 3; French dates and Caribbean: *History Today*, July 2005, p. 19; *History Today*, March 2007, pp. 20–29.

80 P. McPhee, *A Social History of France 1780–1880* (London: Routledge, 1992), pp. 144–146, 149. The penniless statistics are for 1824.

81 Abandoned babies: in 1846, 12.8 per cent of babies, 22.7 per cent 30 years earlier. Children below fourteen in Mulhouse, in 1835. P. McPhee, op. cit., pp. 144, 145,.

82 63 per cent of men, 48 per cent of women and 25 per cent of children in Lille: P. McPhee, op. cit., pp. 145, 146; death or injury – E. Zola (trans. M. Mauldon), *L'Assommoir* (Oxford: Oxford University Press, 1995), passim.

83 D. Saunders, op. cit., pp. 104, 108.

84 L. Viardot, *Souvenirs de Chasse*, op. cit., p. 118.

85 Marquis de Custine, *Journey for our Time*, op. cit., pp. 120, 121, 134; L. Tolstoy, *War and Peace*, op. cit., Book I, ch. 10; A.N. Wilson, op. cit., p. 111.

86 Marquis de Custine, *Journey for our Time*, op. cit., p. 120.

87 Ibid., p. 128; *Encyclopaedia Britannica*, ninth edition, vol. XIX, p. 649; A. Thomson, 'The Final Agony of Alexander Pushkin', *New Zealand Slavonic Journal*, winter 1975, no. 1, passim. The first Duke of Wellington, then Prime Minister, fought a duel with Lord Winchilsea in March 1829 over a matter related to Catholic Emancipation.

88 Note (by M. Basker) from A. Pushkin, *Eugene Onegin*, op. cit., p. 252, and J. Bayley's Preface; *Encyclopaedia Britannica*, ninth edition, vol. XIX, p. 649.

89 M. Lermontov, 'Princess Mary', in M. Lermontov, *A Hero of our Time*, op. cit., pt II, ch. 2.

90 *Encyclopaedia Britannica*, ninth edition, vol. XIV, p. 471; Introduction to M. Lermontov (trans. P. Foote), *A Hero of Our Time* (London:

Penguin, 2001); L. Kelly, *Lermontov, a tragedy in the Caucasus* (London: Robin Clark, 1983), pp. 166, 178.
91 A. Zviguilsky (ed.), *Ivan Tourguénev: Nouvelle Correspondance inédite* (Paris: Librairie des Cinq Continents, 1971), p. 216; Marquis de Custine, op. cit., p. 211.
92 F. Dostoyevsky, *Crime and Punishment*, op. cit., Part I ch. 1, Part II ch. 1; J. Westwood, *Endurance and Endeavour* (Oxford, 2002), p. 172. Figures for end of 19th century.
93 M. Lermontov, *A Hero of our Time*, op. cit., pt II, ch. 3 ('The Fatalist'); L. Tolstoy, *War and Peace*, op. cit., Book IV, ch. 13; Book V, ch. 15; Book VII, ch. 8; R. Hingley, op. cit., pp. 130, 145.
94 I. Turgenev, 'Khor and Kalinych', in I. Turgenev (trans. Richard Freeborn), *Sketches from a Hunter's Album* (London: Penguin, 1967 and 1990), pp. 19, 27; I. Goncharov, *Oblomov*, op. cit., p. 117; A. Zviguilsky (ed.), op. cit., p. 167; I. Turgenev, *On the Eve*, op. cit., ch. 2.
95 L. Tolstoy, *War and Peace*, op. cit., Book VII ch. 9; A. Pushkin, *Eugene Onegin*, op. cit., ch. 5 p. iv.
96 L. Viardot, *Souvenirs de Chasse*, op. cit., p. 133.
97 In winter: I. Turgenev (trans. F. Abbott), *Annals from a Sportsman* (New York: Henry Holt & Co, 1885), p. 311; A. Zviguilsky (ed.), op. cit., p. 128; The skylarks: I. Turgenev, *Annals from a Sportsman*, op. cit., p. 389; I. Turgenev (trans. R. Freeborn), *Sketches from a Hunter's Album*, op. cit., p. 389.
98 I. Turgenev, ibid., pp. 305–307.
99 I. Turgenev, *Virgin Soil* (trans. T.S. Perry), *Virgin Soil* (London: Ward, Lock & Co, pre-1880), pt II, ch. 23 p. 180.
100 Ibid., pt II, ch. 24; No better off – Ibid., pt II, ch. 24; no spiritual peace – F. Dostoyevsky, *The Idiot*, op. cit., pt 3, ch. 4.
101 A. Chekhov (trans. C. Garnett), *The Cherry Orchard and other Plays* (London: Chatto and Windus, 1935), passim.
102 Marquis de Custine, *Journey for our Time*, op. cit., p. 58 (12 July 1849), p.109 (23 July 1849), p. 156 (2 August 1849).
103 R. Freeborn, *Turgenev, the novelist's novelist* (Oxford: Oxford University Press, 1960), p. 97; M. Fainsod, *How Russia is Ruled* (Cambridge, MA: Harvard University Press, 1963), p. 7; I. Turgenev, *Nest of the Gentry*, op. cit., ch. 33.
104 I. Goncharov, *Oblomov*, op. cit., passim.
105 In 1897, 69 per cent were Orthodox, 9 per cent were Roman Catholic: H. Seton-Watson, op. cit., p. 534.
106 M. Steen, *The Lives and Times of the Great Composers* (Cambridge: Icon, 2003), p. 639; M. Fainsod, op. cit., p. 7; R. Freeborn, op. cit., p. 85.
107 A. FitzLyon, *The Price of Genius*, op. cit., p.149; G. Dulong, op. cit., p. 62.
108 D. Magarshack, *Turgenev, a Life* (London: Faber & Faber, 1954), p. 78; A. FitzLyon, *The Price of Genius*, op. cit., p. 150.
109 I. Turgenev, *On the Eve*, op. cit., ch. 15.
110 Marquis de Custine (ed. and trans. P.P. Kohler), *Journey for our Time* (London: George Prior), p. 82, 15 July 1839; Marquis de Custine, *The Empire of the Czar* (London: Longman Brown Green and Longmans, 1843), vol. I p. 192, vol. I, p. 265.
111 T. Marix-Spire, *Lettres inédites de George Sand*, op. cit., p. 193; Marquis de Custine, *The Empire of the Czar*, 1843, op. cit., vol. I, p. 193.
112 Marquis de Custine, *Journey for our Time*, op. cit., p. 81; Marquis de Custine, *The Empire of the Czar*, 1843, op. cit., vol. I, p. 220.
113 F. Dostoyevsky, *The Double* (London: Hesperus Press, 2004), pp. 40, 43.
114 T. Marix-Spire, *Lettres inédites de George Sand*, op. cit., pp. 194, 198; A.N. Wilson, op. cit., p. 136; L. Tolstoy, *War and Peace*, Book VIII, ch. 8, p. 198.
115 Ibid., Book VIII, ch. 10, p.199.
116 A. FitzLyon, *The Price of Genius*, op. cit., p. 156.
117 T. Marix-Spire, *Lettres inédites de George Sand*, op. cit., pp. 192, 193.
118 Ibid., pp. 200, 208; A. FitzLyon, *The Price of Genius*, op. cit., p. 172; G. Sand (ed. T. Bodin), *Lettres Retrouvées* (Paris: Gallimard, 2004), pp. 53–55.
119 L. Viardot, *Souvenirs de Chasse*, op. cit., p. 107, pp. 124–126.
120 Ibid., pp. 107, 119, 121, 122, 124, 125. In the second shoot there were 200: Ibid., p. 143.
121 'et pouvant dormer comme sur une ottomane doucement bercée': Ibid., pp. 130, 237, 235.
122 I. Turgenev, *Virgin Soil*, op. cit., ch. 19.
123 I. Turgenev, *A Strange Story*, op. cit., p. 245; L. Tolstoy (trans. Rochelle S. Townsend), *Anna Karenina* (published 1873–6, also London:

J.M. Dent Everyman edition, 1912), Pt. I, ch. 10.
124 P. Waddington, 'The Role of Courtavenel in the Life and Work of Turgenev', from *Issues in Russian Literature before 1917*, selected papers of the Third World Congress for Soviet and East European Studies (Colombus, Ohio: Slavica Publishers Inc, 1989), p. 108. H. Troyat (trans. N. Amphoux), *Turgenev* (London: W.H. Allen, 1989), p. 20; D. Magarshack, op. cit., p. 81. 28 Oct old style (OS) = 9 November new style (NS), H. Granjard and A. Zviguilsky, op. cit., p. 42; P. Waddington, *A Modest Little Banquet at the Arts Club* (Pinehaven, New Zealand, 2001), p. 14; V.S. Pritchett, *The Gentle Barbarian, The Life and Work of Turgenev* (London: Chatto & Windus, 1977), p. 18; E. de Goncourt, *Journal* (Paris, 1887–96), vol. I, p. 1241.
125 H. Granjard and A. Zviguilsky, op. cit., pp. 42, 148. Pauline's début was on 22 October (OS); Louis met Turgenev on 28 October (OS) and Turgenev met Pauline on 1 November (OS) per P. Waddington, *Turgenev and Pauline Viardot, An Unofficial Marriage* (Canadian Slavonic Papers, vol. XXVI, no. 1, March 1984), p. 44.; D. Magarshack, op. cit., pp. 11, 81; A. Zviguilsky (ed.), op. cit., p. 57.
126 I. Turgenev (trans. I. and T. Litvinov), *Three Short Novels* (Moscow: Foreign Language Publishing House, no date but around 1980), p. 230; A. Zviguilsky (ed.), op. cit., p. 229; *The Poetical Works of Robert Burns* (London and New York: Frederick Warne and Co).

CHAPTER 8. FIRST LOVE (pp. 121–131)

1 P. Waddington, *Turgenev and Pauline Viardot, An Unofficial Marriage* (Canadian Slavonic Papers, vol. XXVI, no. 1, March 1984), p. 44; see also L. Schapiro, *Turgenev, his Life and Times* (Oxford: OUP, 1978), pp. 24, 55, 194. See R.D. Blackmore, author of *Lorna Doone*, in P. Waddington, *A Modest Little Banquet at the Arts Club* (Pinehaven, New Zealand, 2001), p. 25.
2 V.S. Pritchett, *The Gentle Barbarian, The Life and Work of Turgenev* (London: Chatto & Windus, 1977), p. 31; P. Waddington, *Turgenev and George Sand: An Improbable Entente* (Victoria University Press, 1981), p. 20. I. Goncharov (trans. D. Magarshack), *Oblomov* (London: Penguin, 1954), Pt. I, ch. 2. The linguist and ethnographer was Vladimir Ivanovich Dal' (1801–1872) according to Professor Patrick Waddington.
3 V.S. Pritchett, op. cit., p. 32.
4 D. Magarshack, *Turgenev, a Life* (London: Faber & Faber, 1954), p. 41; H. Troyat (trans. N. Amphoux), *Turgenev* (London: W.H. Allen, 1989), pp. 115, 123; V.S. Pritchett, op. cit., p. 18.
5 D. Magarshack, op. cit., p. 18; A. Zviguilsky (ed.), *Ivan Tourguénev: Nouvelle Correspondance inédite* (Paris: Librairie des Cinq Continents, 1971), pp. 49, 52; I. Turgenev (trans. Richard Freeborn), *Home of the Gentry* (London: Penguin, London 1970, ch. 11; I. Turgenev (trans. Isabel Hapgood), *On the Eve* (Freeport, New York: Books for Libraries Press, 1971), ch. 8.
6 R. Freeborn, *Turgenev, the novelist's novelist* (Oxford: Oxford University Press, 1960), p. 3.
7 R. Freeborn, op. cit., p. 3; I. Turgenev (trans. Isabel Hapgood), *First Love and other stories* (New York: Charles Scribner's Sons, 1923), p. 6; I. Turgenev (trans. I. and T. Litvinov), *Three Short Novels* (Moscow: Foreign Language Publishing House, no date but around 1980), p. 92. H. Troyat, op. cit., p. 6; I. Turgenev, *On the Eve*, op. cit., ch. 22; the father's picture hangs at Spasskoye.
8 V.S. Pritchett, op. cit., p. 7; H. Troyat, op. cit., p. 3.
9 P. Waddington, *Turgenev's Mortal Illness from its Origins to the Autopsy* (Pinehaven, New Zealand: Whirinaki Press, 1999), p. 3; V.S. Pritchett, op. cit., p. 6; D. Magarshack, op. cit., p. 16; H. Troyat, op. cit., p. 1; L. Schapiro, op. cit., p. 2.
10 V.S. Pritchett, op. cit., p. 218, quoting *Virgin Soil*; L. Tolstoy (trans. L. and A. Maude), *War and Peace* (London: OUP, 1933), Book XV, ch. 12.
11 'Qui ne m'inspire aucun sentiment sympathique': H. Granjard and A. Zviguilsky, *Ivan Tourguénev, Lettres inédites à Pauline Viardot et à sa famille* (Paris: Editions l'Age d'Homme, 1972), p. 273.
12 I. Turgenev (trans. Isabel Hapgood), *The Brigadier and other stories* (Freeport, New York: Books for Libraries), ch. 13; I. Turgenev (trans. W. Ralston), *Liza* (London: Chapman & Hall, 1869), vol. I, p. 150; D. Magarshack, op. cit., p. 11. Such violence was not confined to Russia: the pugilistic Marquess of Queensberry, bane of Oscar Wilde, had an 18th-century ancestor who killed a boy and roasted him on a spit, according to L. McKinstry, *Rosebery,*

Statesman in Turmoil (London: John Murray, 2005), p. 352.
13 I. Turgenev, 'Farmer Ovsyanikov', in I. Turgenev (trans. Richard Freeborn), *Sketches from a Hunter's Album* (London: Penguin, 1967 and 1990).
14 D. Magarshack, op. cit., pp. 12, 13; Sir Isaiah Berlin, Romanes lecture 1970, 'Fathers and Children', from I. Turgenev (trans. R. Edmonds), *Fathers and Sons* (London: Penguin, 1965 and 1970), p. 15; 'The Brigadier', ch. 13, in I. Turgenev (trans. Isabel Hapgood), *The Brigadier and other stories* (Freeport, New York: Books for Libraries Press, 1971).
15 V.S. Pritchett, op. cit., pp. 3, 71; *Encyclopaedia Britannica*, Standard Millennium edition.
16 I. Turgenev (trans. Rosemary Edmonds), *Fathers and Sons* (London: Penguin, 1965 and 1970), ch. 4, pp. 17; D. Magarshack, op. cit., p. 54; I. Turgenev (trans. E. Schuyler), *Fathers and Sons* (London: Ward, Lock & Co, 1883), ch. 8, p. 76. The fire was in 1840 – G. Dulong, *Pauline Viardot Tragédienne Lyrique* (Bougival: Association des Amis d'Ivan Tourguéniev Pauline Viardot et Maria Malibran), p. 68.
17 V.S. Pritchett, op. cit., pp. 3–5; G. Dulong, op. cit., p. 66; H. Troyat, op. cit., p. 2; D. Magarshack, op. cit., p. 15; L. Schapiro, op. cit., p. 11; L. Tolstoy, *War and Peace*, op. cit., Book I, ch. 27. See 'Mumu' in I. Turgenev (trans. R. Freeborn), *First Love and other stories* (Oxford: OUP 1999. The National Gallery, London, *Russian Landscape*, the Exhibition Guide for *Russian Landscape in the Age of Tolstoy*, July 2004, p. 153.
18 H. Granjard and A. Zviguilsky, op. cit., pp. 23, 25, 48; A. Zviguilsky (ed.), *Ivan Tourguénev: Nouvelle Correspondance inédite* (Paris: Librairie des Cinq Continents, 1971), p. 50; I. Turgenev (ed. E. Halpérine-Kaminsky), *Lettres à Madame Viardot* (Paris: Bibliothèque-Charpentier, 1907), 13 January 1851, p. 145. A.N. Wilson, *Tolstoy* (London: Hamish Hamilton, 1988), pp. 150, 279; H. Troyat, op. cit., p. 26. The daughter was Bogdanovich Loutovinova Varvara Nikolaïevna.
19 D. Magarshack, op. cit., p. 35; A.N.Wilson, op. cit., p. 43; V.S. Pritchett, op. cit., p. 1; R. Baldick (ed.), *Pages from the Goncourt Journal* (Oxford: Oxford University Press, 1978), p. 235; Schapiro suggests that this is apochryphal (L. Schapiro, op. cit., p. 11).
20 I. Turgenev, *Lettres à Madame Viardot*, op. cit., 24 May 1853, p. 174; I. Turgenev (trans. Hugh Aplin, foreword by Simon Callow), *Faust and Yakov Pasynkov* (London: Hesperus Press, 2003), first letter.
21 The lady of the house in 'Mumu' is supposed to be based on Varvara Petrovna; see I. Turgenev, *First Love and other stories*, op. cit., pp. 75, 86; V.S. Pritchett, op. cit., pp. 9, 11.
22 D. Magarshack, op. cit., p. 27; H. Troyat, op. cit., p. 5; he was taught by various teachers including a poet, Klyushnikov.
23 H. Troyat, op. cit., p. 7; R. Freeborn, op. cit., p. 23.
24 In May 1838; H. Troyat, op. cit., p. 11; H. Aplin in intro to 'Faust', p. xiii, in I. Turgenev (trans. Isabel Hapgood), *First Love and other stories*, op. cit; D. Magarshack, op. cit., p. 44.
25 D. Magarshack, op. cit., p. 46; H. Granjard and A. Zviguilsky, op. cit., p. 209.
26 I. Turgenev, *First Love and other stories*, op. cit., ch. 7, p. 162. In *War and Peace*, op. cit., the young Count Petya Rostov has a personal serf in attendance, Book VII, ch. 9.
27 V.S. Pritchett, op. cit., p. 25; L. Schapiro, op. cit., p. 18; P. Waddington, *Turgenev and Pauline Viardot, An Unofficial Marriage*, op. cit., p. 47. The lady died in spring 1839: D. Magarshack, op. cit., p. 48.
28 L. Schapiro, critical essay 'Spring Torrents, Its Place and Significance in the Life and Work of I.S. Turgenev', in I. Turgenev (trans. L Schapiro), *Spring Torrents* (London: Penguin, 1980), p. 193; P. Waddington, *Turgenev and England* (London: Macmillan, 1980), p. 8; R. Freeborn, op. cit., p. 8; F. Randall, *Vissarion Belinsky* (Newtonville, Mass: Oriental Research Partners, 1987), p. 17.
29 *New Grove Dictionary of Music and Musicians* (London: Macmillan, 1980), vol. 12, p. 246, Meyerbeer (H. Becker); D. Magarshack, op. cit., p. 46; R. Cardinal, *German Romantics in Context* (London: Studio Vista, 1975), p. 144; *Encyclopaedia Britannica*, ninth edition, vol. XII, p. 343; L. Schapiro, *Turgenev, his Life and Times* (Oxford: OUP, 1978), p. 193. 'The last man who knew everything' is quoted from Daniel Johnson in *The Times Literary Supplement*, London, 22 July 2005.
30 *Encyclopaedia Britannica*, Standard Millennium edition.
31 R. Freeborn, op. cit., p. 2; *Cahiers Ivan Tourguéniev, Pauline Viardot, Maria Malibran*

(Bougival: Association des Amis d'Ivan Tourguéniev Pauline Viardot et Maria Malibran), no. 20, pp. 39, 61.
32 A. Zviguilsky (ed.), op. cit., p. 44; D. Magarshack, op. cit., p. 53; R. Freeborn, op. cit., p. 2.
33 R. Freeborn, op. cit., p. 11; V.S. Pritchett, op. cit., p. 26; H. Troyat, op. cit., pp. 17, 18; L. Schapiro, *Turgenev, his Life and Times* (Oxford: OUP, 1978), p. 28; F. Randall, op. cit., p. 21.
34 L. Schapiro, *Critical essay*, op. cit., p. 195. As wih Asya in *Asya*, Maria Nikolevna in *Spring Torrents* and Irina in *Smoke*.
35 D. Magarshack., op. cit., pp. 54, 56.
36 *Encyclopaedia Britannica,* Standard Millennium edition; R. Freeborn, op. cit., pp. 11, 13, 15, 82; R. Hingley, *Dostoyevsky, his life and work* (London: Paul Elek Ltd, 1978), p. 47; L. Schapiro, *Turgenev*, op. cit., p. 39; F. Randall, op. cit., p. 6; D. Magarshack, op. cit., p. 72; H. Troyat, op. cit., p. 24.
37 The daughter was born in May 1842: G. Dulong, op. cit., p. 69.
38 D. Magarshack, op. cit., pp. 56, 80.
39 V.S. Pritchett, op. cit., p.40; A. FitzLyon, *The Price of Genius, a life of Pauline Viardot* (London: John Calder, 1964), p. 162; P. Waddington, *Courtavenel, the History of an Artists' Nest and its Role in the Life of Turgenev* (*PhD Thesis*, Queen's University Belfast, The British Library, British Thesis Service, spring 1972), p. 30; G. Dulong, op. cit., p. 64; A. FitzLyon, *The Price of Genius*, op. cit., p. 164. The author received information on the Four Paws from Mr Kyril FitzLyon.
40 I. Turgenev, *A Correspondence in First Love and other stories* (trans. I. Hapgood), op. cit., p. 166.
41 R. Freeborn, op. cit., p. 12.
42 Professor Patrick Waddington suggests that he may have started to coach her in Russian from the second season.
43 J. Chissell, *Clara Schumann: a Dedicated Spirit* (London: Hamish Hamilton, 1983), p. 89.
44 A. FitzLyon, *The Price of Genius*, op. cit., p. 165.
45 Marquis de Custine (ed. and trans. P.P. Kohler), *Journey for our Time* (London: George Prior), pp. 226, 237 and Resumé.
46 Marquis de Custine (foreword by D.J. Boorstin), *Empire of the Czar* (New York: Anchor Books, 1989), p. 586.
47 T. Marix-Spire, *Lettres inédites de George Sand et de Pauline Viardot 1839–1849* (Paris: Nouvelles Editions, 1959), pp. 195, 197.
48 'Le pauvre être que l'on nomme empereur. C'est un malheureux idiot qu'il faut traiter comme un enfant' : Ibid., pp. 171, 172.
49 'Voilà les grandes sources d'iniquités, voilà les forces vives de la destruction.' G. Sand, *La Comtesse de Rudolstadt* (Paris: Calmann-Lévy), pp. 994, 1083. T. Marix-Spire, *Lettres inédites de George Sand*, op. cit., p.65.
50 'Une fluxion de poitrine' H. Granjard and A. Zviguilsky, op. cit., p. 3.
51 P. Waddington, 'Turgenev and Gounod, Rival Strangers in the Viardots' Country Nest', *New Zealand Slavonic Journal*, no. 1, 1976, p. 31; I. Turgenev, *Lettres à Madame Viardot*, op. cit., 26 March 1867 and 20 June 1868, pp. 211, 240; P. Waddington, *Turgenev's Mortal Illness from its Origins to the Autopsy*, op. cit., p. 3 etc.
52 R. Freeborn, op. cit., p. 39; A. Zviguilsky (ed.), op. cit., pp. 5, 99, 112, 238, 243; H. and A. Zviguilsky, op. cit., pp. 154, 174, 188, 203.
53 T. Marix-Spire, *Lettres inédites de George Sand*, op. cit., pp. 187, 202.

Chapter 9. From Courtavenel to Moscow (pp. 133–144)

1 T. Marix-Spire, *Lettres inédites de George Sand et de Pauline Viardot 1839–1849* (Paris: Nouvelles Editions, 1959), pp. 204, 207; P. Waddington, *Courtavenel, the History of an Artists' Nest and its Role in the Life of Turgenev* (*PhD Thesis*, Queen's University Belfast, The British Library, British Thesis Service, spring 1972), pp. 2, 16,17, 83; P. Waddington, 'The Role of Courtavenel in the Life and Work of Turgenev', from *Issues in Russian Literature before 1917*, selected papers of the Third World Congress for Soviet and East European Studies (Colombus, Ohio: Slavica Publishers Inc, 1989), p. 108. The estate comprised 39 hectares, 40 ares and 13 centiares: B. Kendall-Davies, *The Life and Work of Pauline Viardot-Garcia*, vol. I, 'The years of fame' (London: Cambridge Scholars Press, 2003), p. 184.
2 T. Marix-Spire, *Lettres inédites de George Sand*, op. cit., p. 165.
3 P. Waddington, 'The strange history of Dr F. and the dismantling of Courtavenel', *Modern Language Review*, vol. 65, 1970, pp. 333, 335.

4 D. Magarshack, *Turgenev, a Life* (London: Faber & Faber, 1954), p. 110; T. Marix-Spire, *Lettres inédites de George Sand*, op. cit., p. 205; P. Waddington, *The Role of Courtavenel*, op. cit., p. 108; V.S. Pritchett, *The Gentle Barbarian, The Life and Work of Turgenev* (London: Chatto & Windus, 1977), p. 44.
5 L. Frieda, *Catherine de Medici* (London: Weidenfeld and Nicolson, 2003), p. 202.
6 T. Marix-Spire, *Lettres inédites de George Sand*, op. cit., p. 211; P. Waddington, *PhD Thesis*, op. cit., pp. 262, 265, 353; B. Kendall-Davies, op. cit., p. xi; L. Frieda, *Catherine de Medici* (London: Weidenfeld and Nicolson, 2003), p. 202; D. Magarshack, op. cit., p. 111; *Paul Viardot, Souvenirs d'un Artiste* (Paris: Librairie Fischbacher SA, 1910), p. 3. 'Some people don't like a moat', said Ld Warburton in H. James, Jr., *The Portrait of a Lady* (London: Penguin Classics, 2000), p. 163.
7 T. Marix-Spire, *Lettres inédites de George Sand*, op. cit., pp. 199, 207; G. Sand (ed. T. Bodin), *Lettres Retrouvées* (Paris: Gallimard, 2004), p. 54.
8 T. Marix-Spire, *Lettres inédites de George Sand*, op. cit., pp. 210, 211, 214; A. FitzLyon, *The Price of Genius, a life of Pauline Viardot* (London: John Calder, 1964), p. 172.
9 T. Marix-Spire, *Lettres inédites de George Sand*, op. cit., pp. 203, 207; A. FitzLyon, *The Price of Genius*, op. cit., p. 171; I. Turgenev, *Lettres à Madame Viardot* (ed. E. Halpérine-Kaminsky), *Lettres à Madame Viardot* (Paris: Bibliothèque-Charpentier, 1907), p. 84.
10 P. Waddington, *PhD Thesis*, op. cit., pp. 20, 56; A. Zviguilsky (ed.), *Ivan Tourguénev: Nouvelle Correspondance inédite* (Paris: Librairie des Cinq Continents, 1971), p. 24; H. Granjard and A. Zviguilsky, *Ivan Tourguénev, Lettres inédites à Pauline Viardot et à sa famille* (Paris: Editions l'Age d'Homme, 1972), p. 13; T. Marix-Spire, *Lettres inédites de George Sand*, op. cit., pp. 74, 227; P. Waddington, *The Role of Courtavenel*, op. cit., p. 111; *New Grove Dictionary of Music and Musicians* (London: Macmillan, 1980), vol. 20, p. 48. Vivier (R. Morley-Pegge/H. Fitzpatrick).
11 A. Zviguilsky (ed.), op. cit., p. 19; D. Magarshack, op. cit., p. 111; I. Turgenev (trans. R. Freeborn), *Rudin* (London: Penguin, 1975), ch. 2; L. Héritte-Viardot, *Une famille de grands musiciens* (Paris: Librairie Stock, 1922), p. 29; P. Waddington, 'Two Months in the Country', *New Zealand Slavonic Journal*, no. 11, winter 1973, p. 33.
12 P. Waddington, *PhD Thesis*, op. cit., pp. 46, 60; C. Santley, *Reminscences of my Life* (London: Pitman, 1909), p. 282;
13 'One of the greatest singing teachers ever', according to April Fitzlyon in A. FitzLyon, *The Price of Genius*, op. cit., p. 459. 'Nicola Porpora': according to H.S Holland and W.S Rockstro, *Jenny Lind the Artist* (London: John Murray, 1891), p. 115; also C. Santley, op. cit., p. 281.
14 W. Kuhe, *My musical recollections* (London: Richard Bentley, 1896), p. 188; T. Marix-Spire, *Lettres inédites de George Sand*, op. cit., p. 259; L. Héritte-Viardot, op. cit., pp. 2, 257.
15 T. Marix-Spire, *Lettres inédites de George Sand*, op. cit., pp. 144, 277; P. Waddington, PhD Thesis, op. cit., p. 46.
16 L. Héritte-Viardot, op. cit. , pp. 66, 67; A. FitzLyon, *The Price of Genius*, op. cit., p. 306.
17 G. Dulong, *Pauline Viardot Tragédienne Lyrique* (Bougival: Association des Amis d'Ivan Tourguéniev Pauline Viardot et Maria Malibran), p.114.
18 He was born on 30 June 1823: B. Jack, *George Sand: A Woman's Life Writ Large* (London: Chatto & Windus, 1999), p. 115; P. Waddington, *PhD Thesis*, op. cit., pp. 18, 19.
19 B. Eisler, *Chopin's Funeral* (London: Little, Brown, 2003), p. 124; G. Sand (ed. T. Bodin), *Lettres Retrouvées* (Paris: Gallimard, 2004), p. 34; T. Marix-Spire, *Lettres inédites de George Sand*, op. cit., p. 199; B. Jack, op. cit., p. 296; J. Brault, *Une Contemporaine: Biographie et Intrigues de George Sand avec une lettre d'elle et une de M. Dudevant* (Paris: en vente Rue des Marais-Saint-Germain 6, 1848)
20 G. Sand, *Correspondance* (Paris: Editions de Georges Lubin, Editions Garnier Frères, 1969), Tome VI, p. 632; B. Kendall-Davies, op. cit., p. 191; H. Granjard and A. Zviguilsky, op. cit., p. 206.
21 P. Bloom (ed.), *Music in Paris in the Eighteen Thirties* (New York: Pendragon Press, 1987), p. 17 (J. Barzun); Balzac's *Père Goriot* passim.
22 B. Jack, op. cit., p. 296: G. Sand, *Correspondance*, op. cit., p. 800, letter of 20 February 1845 from Sand to Blanc is justification for the affair.
23 'Maurice a été pour moi ce qu'il est toujours, parfait', G. Sand, *Lettres retrouvées*, op. cit., p. 71.
24 B. Kendall-Davies, op. cit., p. 283; G. Sand,

Lettres retrouvées, op. cit., p. 90. Writing of Dorval on her death, George said to Pauline 'ce nétait pas une femme comme vous, c'était tout le contraire dans un certain sens'.

25 'Elle n'a fait que courir les bois et danser la bourrée tout le temps qu'elle a passé ici', G. Sand, *Correspondance*, op. cit., Tome VI 1843–Juin 1845, letter of 2 October 1843, number 2715, p. 243 to Charlotte Marliani, also p. 287.

26 'Souffrant ... Pour écuyer'; G. Sand, *Lettres Retrouvées*, op. cit., p. 55, 11 August 1844.

27 Ibid., pp. 55, 69.

28 T. Marix-Spire, *Lettres inédites de George Sand*, op. cit., p. 211.

29 'Nous nous sommes promis d'avoir du courage. Je ne puis en dire davantage dans ce moment'.

30 'Ecrivez-moi bientôt, à double entente, si c'est possible, en addressant la lettre à la direction impériale des Théâtres de Pétersburg', G. Sand, *Correspondance*, op. cit., Tome VI 1843–Juin 1845, letter of 20 October 1844 from Pauline, p. 632.

31 A. FitzLyon, *The Price of Genius*, op. cit., p. 100.

32 *Musical Quarterly* 1915, vol. 1, p. 536. This was a remark she made to Rietz.

33 January 1859: *Musical Quarterly*, vol. I, 1915, p. 532 (author's translation).

34 Musée de la Vie Romantique, *General Guide* (Paris-Musées, 1992), pp. 14, 43; anonymous letter – information at Maison Atelier de Théodore Rousseau in Barbizon; R. Jordan, *George Sand* (London: Constable, 1976), p. 243, G. Sand, *Lettres Retrouvées*, op. cit., p. 70.

35 G. Sand, *Lettres Retrouvées*, op. cit., p. 70.

36 T. Marix-Spire, *Lettres inédites de George Sand*, op. cit., p. 243.

37 Golaud, in Act V Scene 1 of Debussy's *Pelléas et Mélisande*. 'Experts' – Dr Zviguilsky told the author that M. Georges Lubin had told him that he regretted that such a letter, which almost certainly was sent to Lina, was missing.

38 Source: Grant Meekings based on H. Dufour's biography of Sand.

39 T. Marix-Spire, *Lettres inédites de George Sand*, op. cit., p. 215; A. FitzLyon, *Maria Malibran – Diva of the Romantic Age* (London: Souvenir Press, 1987), p. 248.

40 T. Marix-Spire, *Lettres inédites de George Sand*, op. cit., p. 215.

41 Ibid., p. 218; *Encyclopaedia Britannica*, ninth edition, vol. XX, p. 251. Although a line between St Petersburg and Tsarskoe Selo was built in 1837, the St Petersburg to Moscow line only opened in 1851. By 1867, it had heated carriages (A. Zviguilsky (ed.), op. cit., p. 146).

42 Marquis de Custine (ed. and trans. P.P. Kohler), *Journey for our Time* (London: George Prior), pp. 163, 165, 169, 223; Marquis de Custine, *The Empire of the Czar* (London: Longman Brown Green and Longmans, 1843), vol. II, p. 279; Marquis de Custine (foreword by D.J. Boorstin), *Empire of the Czar* (New York: Anchor Books, 1989), pp. 361, 362. A league was approx. three miles – per *Concise Oxford Dictionary*.

43 Marquis de Custine, *The Empire of the Czar* (London: Longman Brown Green and Longmans, 1843), vol. II, p. 284; I. Turgenev, *Púnin and Babúrin* (1874), in *The Brigadier and other stories* (trans. I. Hapgood) (Freeport, New York: Books for Libraries Press, 1971), p. 325; Marquis de Custine (ed. and trans. P.P. Kohler), p. 208.

44 Ibid., pp. 170, 171; Marquis de Custine, *The Empire of the Czar*, 1843, op. cit., vol. II, pp. 287, 288.

45 A. FitzLyon, *The Price of Genius*, op. cit., p. 186; A. Zviguilsky (ed.), op. cit., p. 49.

46 T. Marix-Spire, *Lettres inédites de George Sand*, op. cit., p. 219; L. Tolstoy (trans. Rochelle S. Townsend), *Anna Karenina* (published 1873–6, also London: J.M. Dent Everyman edition, 1912), pt 7, ch. 20, ch. 22; G. Dulong, op. cit., p.76.

47 A. Hedley (revised M.E.J. Brown), *Chopin* (London: J.M. Dent, 1947), p. 247. She left 12 June 1845.

48 Ibid., pp. 249, 250.

49 T. Marix-Spire, *Lettres inédites de George Sand*, op. cit., p. 220.

50 In August 1845. Ibid., pp. 221, 222; D. Cairns, *Berlioz: Servitude and Greatness* (Penguin: London 2000), p. 328.

51 P. Waddington, 'Pauline Viardot-Garcia as Berlioz's Counselor and Physician', *Musical Quarterly*, vol. LIX, no. 3, July 1973, p. 382.

52 *The New Oxford Companion to Music* (Oxford: Oxford University Press, 1984), p. 673 – this was published in Brussels 1835–44; *New Grove*, op. cit., vol. 6, p. 513; A. Zviguilsky (ed.), p. 255. A. FitzLyon, *The Price of Genius*,

op. cit., p. 18; T. Marix-Spire, *Lettres inédites de George Sand*, op. cit., p.25.
53 A. Hedley, op. cit., p. 254.

Chapter 10. Circe (pp. 145–152)

1 This was in 1845. A. Zviguilsky (ed.), *Ivan Tourguénev: Nouvelle Correspondance inédite* (Paris: Librairie des Cinq Continents, 1971), p. 299.
2 L. Schapiro, *Turgenev, his Life and Times* (Oxford: OUP, 1978), p. 49; P. Waddington, 'Turgenev's relations with H.F. Chorley', New *Zealand Slavonic Journal*, no. 2, 1978, p. 27; P. Waddington, *Turgenev and George Sand: An Improbable Entente* (Victoria University Press, 1981), p. 22.
3 A. FitzLyon, *The Price of Genius, a life of Pauline Viardot* (London: John Calder, 1964), p. 191; D. Magarshack, *Turgenev, a Life* (London: Faber & Faber, 1954), p. 83.
4 V.S. Pritchett, *The Gentle Barbarian, The Life and Work of Turgenev* (London: Chatto & Windus, 1977), p. 41.
5 This was in 1845: L. Schapiro, op. cit., p. 49.
6 G. Dulong, *Pauline Viardot Tragédienne Lyrique* (Bougival: Association des Amis d'Ivan Tourguéniev Pauline Viardot et Maria Malibran), p. 86; A. Zviguilsky (ed.), op. cit., p. 6; V.S. Pritchett, op. cit., p. 45.
7 A. FitzLyon, *The Price of Genius*, op. cit., pp. 192, 193; T. Marix-Spire, *Lettres inédites de George Sand et de Pauline Viardot 1839–1849* (Nouvelles Editions), p. 227; L. Viardot, *Souvenirs de chasse dans toute l'Europe* (Paris: Editions Pygmalion, 1985), p. 216; *Black's Medical Dictionary*, 39th edition (London: A&C Black, 1999), p. 589; L. Héritte-Viardot, *Une famille de grands musiciens* (Paris: Librairie Stock, 1922), p. 22.
8 A. Zviguilsky (ed.), op. cit., p. 7; A. Pushkin (trans. C. Johnston, Preface J. Bayley, Notes M. Basker), *Eugene Onegin* (London: Penguin, 2003), ch. 7, pp.34. 35; L. Viardot, *Souvenirs de Chasse*, op. cit., p. 198. 'Un dégel est une véritable calamité': Ibid., p. 130. And St Petersburg ran short of the frozen food which had amply fed it (ibid., p. 131).
9 L. Tolstoy (trans. Rochelle S. Townsend), *Anna Karenina* (published 1873–6); London: J.M. Dent Everyman edition, 1912), pt III, ch. 25.
10 I. Turgenev, *A Strange Story*, in trans. I. Hapgood), *The Brigadier and other stories* (Freeport, New York: Books for Libraries Press, 1971), p. 267; Marquis de Custine, *The Empire of the Czar* (London: Longman Brown Green and Longmans, 1843), vol. II, p. 177; A. Pushkin, *Eugene Onegin*, op. cit., ch. 7, p. 34.
11 L. Viardot, *Souvenirs de Chasse*, op. cit., pp. 222, 223, 228, 229, 233, 234.
12 L. Héritte-Viardot, op. cit., p. 27; A. FitzLyon, *The Price of Genius*, op. cit., p.195; A. Zviguilsky (ed.), op. cit., p. 6. The opera was by Otto Nicolai; the admirer in May 1846 was Solovoï.
13 'ils m'aideront à me représenter plus vivement ce qui me vient bien souvent à l'esprit', A. Zviguilsky (ed.), op. cit., p. 6.
14 'Je crois vous voir dans votre petit cabinet': Ibid., p. 8.
15 L. Schapiro, op. cit., p. 70.
16 P. Waddington, *Courtavenel, the History of an Artists' Nest and its Role in the Life of Turgenev* (*PhD Thesis*, Queen's University Belfast, The British Library, British Thesis Service, spring 1972), p. 90; D. Magarshack, *Turgenev, a Life* (London: Faber & Faber, 1954), p. 110; A. FitzLyon, *The Price of Genius*, pp. 269, 196.
17 *Der sinnreiche Junker Don Quixote von la Mancha aus dem Spanien übersezt (sic) mit dem Leben von Miguel Cervantes nach Viardot*, Stuttgart, 1837.
18 A. Hedley (revised M.E.J. Brown), *Chopin* (London: J.M. Dent, 1947), p. 263; T. Marix-Spire, *Lettres inédites de George Sand et de Pauline Viardot 1839–1849* (Nouvelles Editions), p. 225. On 1 May 1846, Sand told Maurice about a party at Chopin's rooms; those present included Prince and Princess Czartorysky, Delacroix, Louis Blanc, Pauline and Louis Viardot.
19 May 1846: T. Marix-Spire, *Lettres inédites de George Sand*, op. cit., p. 223. 'Si j'ai commis quelque faute, châtiez-moi', and 'un sentiment de clarté dans le Coeur': Ibid., p.224.
20 ' Il me semble que je vois plus clair, que je sens plus clair, que je respire plus clair': Ibid., p. 224.
21 'Un serrement au Coeur assez pénible', 'coûte que coûte': A. Zviguilsky (ed.), op. cit., pp. 9, 10–12, 50; G. Dulong, op. cit., p. 87.
22 T. Marix-Spire, *Lettres inédites de George Sand*, op. cit., pp. 229, 233, 235; G. Dulong, op. cit., p. 79.
23 'Les publics allemands sont toujours horrible-

ment froids pour les débutants': T. Marix-Spire, *Lettres inédites de George Sand*, op. cit., p. 234.
24 Ibid., pp. 232, 235.
25 L. Viardot, *Souvenirs de Chasse*, op. cit., p. 298.
26 Ibid., pp. 255, 261.
27 R Freeborn, *Turgenev, the novelist's novelist* (Oxford: Oxford University Press, 1960), p. 37; A.N. Wilson, *Tolstoy* (London: Hamish Hamilton, 1988), p. 96; A. Thomson, 'The Final Agony of Alexander Pushkin', *New Zealand Slavonic Journal*, winter 1975, no. 1, p. 2. *The Contemporary* was called *Sovremennik*.
28 L. Schapiro, op. cit., p. 104; A.N.Wilson, op. cit., p. 96; H. Granjard and A. Zviguilsky, *Ivan Tourgénev, Lettres inédites à Pauline Viardot et à sa famille* (Paris: Editions l'Age d'Homme, 1972), p. 91; A. FitzLyon, *The Price of Genius*, op. cit., p. 205.
29 R. Freeborn's introduction to I. Turgenev, (trans. Richard Freeborn), *Sketches from a Hunter's Album* (London: Penguin, 1967 and 1990), p. 2; R. Freeborn, *Turgenev, the novelist's novelist* (Oxford: Oxford University Press, 1960), p. 2.
30 Ibid., p. 28.
31 E. de Goncourt (trans. Belloc and Shedlock), *Journal* (London: Heinemann, 1895), vol. 5, p. 24, 2 March 1872.
32 L. Schapiro, op. cit., p. 66; R. Freeborn, op. cit., pp. 29, 30.
33 I. Turgenev (trans. L. Schapiro), *Spring Torrents* (London: Penguin, 1980), ch. 42.
34 G. Dulong, op. cit., p. 87; A. FitzLyon, *The Price of Genius*, op. cit., p. 211; A. Zviguilsky (ed.), op. cit., p. 113.
35 A. FitzLyon, *The Price of Genius*, op. cit., pp. 208, 218; V.S. Pritchett, *The Gentle Barbarian, The Life and Work of Turgenev* (London: Chatto & Windus, 1977), p. 49; P. Waddington, 'The Role of Courtavenel in the Life and Work of Turgenev', from *Issues in Russian Literature before 1917*, selected papers of the Third World Congress for Soviet and East European Studies (Colombus, Ohio: Slavica Publishers Inc, 1989), pp. 113, 114.
36 D. Magarshack, op. cit., p. 146; Schapiro refers to 'the enormous influence exercised over him [Turgenev] by the strong-willed Pauline Viardot'. Turgenev regarded himself as soft-willed, even a coward: L. Schapiro, op. cit., p. 219.
37 A. FitzLyon, *The Price of Genius*, op. cit., p. 217.
38 T. Marix-Spire, *Lettres inédites de George Sand*, op. cit., p.243.
39 Turgenev first met Pietsch in Berlin in 1847: L. Schapiro, op. cit., p. 57; A. FitzLyon, *The Price of Genius*, op. cit., p. 210.
40 A. Zviguilsky (ed.), op. cit., p. 19; Waddington, *PhD Thesis*, op. cit., p. 77; A. FitzLyon, *The Price of Genius*, op. cit., pp. 210, 256, 257; B. Jack, *Sand: A Woman's Life Writ Large* (London: Chatto & Windus, 1999), p. 321.
41 A. FitzLyon, *The Price of Genius*, op. cit., p. 220, 221 I. Turgenev (ed. E. Halpérine-Kaminsky), *Lettres à Madame Viardot* (Paris: Bibliothèque-Charpentier, 1907), 8 and 14 December 1847, pp. 17, 19; A. Zviguilsky (ed.), op. cit., p. 16. In the museum at Bougival there is an escritoire in which Pauline kept Turgenev's letters.
42 E.C. Clayton, *Queens of Song* (London: Smith Elder & Co, 1863), vol. II, p. 252.
43 1847: J. Chissell, *Clara Schumann: a Dedicated Spirit* (London: Hamish Hamilton, 1983), p. 100; A. FitzLyon, *The Price of Genius*, op. cit., p. 211. There had been a disastrous performance on 17 February, the one at which Clara said she was in agonies and thought she would sink into the ground. Pauline refused to take part in the repeat performance.
44 A. FitzLyon, *The Price of Genius*, op. cit., pp. 211, 223.
45 Lind as Berthe, as early as 1842: H.S. Holland and W.S. Rockstro, *Jenny Lind the Artist* (London: John Murray, 1891), p. 144; A. FitzLyon, *The Price of Genius*, op. cit., p.238.
46 G. Bord, *Rosina Stoltz* (Victoire Noël) (Paris: Henri Daragon, 1909), p. 118.
47 T. Marix-Spire, *Lettres inédites de George Sand*, op. cit., p. 242.

Chapter 11. London and Paris (pp. 153–167)

1 B. Lumley, *Reminiscences of the Opera* (London: Hurst and Blackett, 1864), p.155.
2 Ibid., p.170.
3 D. Cairns, *Berlioz: Servitude and Greatness* (Penguin: London 2000), p. 394.
4 *Illustrated London News*, 9 June 1849.
5 A. Carse, *The Life of Jullien* (Cambridge: W. Heffer & Sons Ltd, 1951), p. 20.

6 Ibid., pp. 19, 23, 32, 34; *New Grove Dictionary of Music and Musicians* (London: Macmillan, 1980), vol. 9, p. 748, Jullien (Keith Horner). The battle was said to be at Navarino.
7 A. Carse, op. cit., p. 13; The Paris concerts were led by Philippe Musard.
8 Ibid., pp. 4, 11; *New Grove,* op. cit., vol. 9, p. 748. Jullien (Keith Horner).
9 A. Carse, op. cit., pp. 40, 54.
10 *New Grove,* op. cit., vol. 11, p. 205; *The Times,* 13 June 1849.
11 *New Grove,* op. cit., vol. 9, p. 748, Jullien (Keith Horner).
12 B. Lumley, op. cit., p. 10; Comtesse Merlin, *Maria Malibran* (London: Henry Colburn, 1840), p. 108.
13 In 1840: A. FitzLyon, *The Price of Genius, a life of Pauline Viardot* (London: John Calder, 1964), p. 146.
14 The impresario was Laporte; B. Lumley, op. cit., p. 14.
15 Ibid., pp. 156, 133.
16 G. St Aubyn, *Queen Victoria, a Portrait* (London: Sinclair-Stevenson, 1991), p. 47.
17 B. Lumley, op. cit., pp. 157, 180.
18 H.S. Holland and W.S. Rockstro, *Jenny Lind the Artist* (London: John Murray, 1891), p.274.
19 P. Waddington, in *The Times Literary Supplement,* London, 1 January 1970, p. 16.
20 G. Byron, *Don Juan,* Canto I, stanza 108.
21 H.S. Holland and W.S. Rockstro, op. cit., vol. I, p. 235.
22 W.S. Blunt, *On Wings of Song* (London: Hamish Hamilton, 1974), p. 247.
23 H.S. Holland and W.S. Rockstro, op. cit., p. 198.
24 W. Kuhe, *My musical recollections* (London: Richard Bentley, 1896), pp. 71, 74; P. Waddington, *Courtavenel, the History of an Artists' Nest and its Role in the Life of Turgenev* (*PhD Thesis,* QUB, The British Library, British Thesis Service, spring 1972), p. 59; H.S. Holland and W.S. Rockstro, op. cit., pp. 110, 114; *New Grove,* op. cit., vol. 10, p. 865, Lind (Elizabeth Forbes). Lind donated to charity a whole week's proceeds of a provincial tour. Pauline's view comes from G. Dulong, *Pauline Viardot Tragédienne Lyrique* (Bougival: Association des Amis d'Ivan Tourguéniev Pauline Viardot et Maria Malibran), p. 77.
25 H.S. Holland and W.S. Rockstro, op. cit., vol. I, p. 296.
26 Ibid., vol. II, pp. 40, 298; B. Lumley, op. cit., p. 178.
27 B. Lumley, op. cit., p. 170.
28 W.S. Blunt, op. cit., p. 255.
29 B. Lumley, op. cit., p. 182
30 W. Kuhe, op. cit., pp. 65, 69.
31 B. Lumley, op. cit., pp. 185, 187; Ibid., p. 208.
32 Ibid., p. 192; Verdi's reputation – *Illustrated London News,* 19 May 1855, p. 488.
33 A. Zviguilsky (ed.), *Ivan Tourguénev: Nouvelle Correspondance inédite* (Paris: Librairie des Cinq Continents, 1971), pp. 13, 14.
34 'La taille colossale et la voix tonnante du suprême basse': A. de Musset in *Revue des Deux Mondes,* vol. XVII, p. 849; R. Somerset-Ward, *Angels and Monsters* (New Haven and London: Yale University Press, 2004), p. 202.
35 A. Zviguilsky (ed.), op. cit., p. 13.
36 L. Héritte-Viardot (trans. E.S. Bucheim), *Memories and Adventures* (London: Mills & Boon, 1913), p. 64; G. Dulong, op. cit., p. 81.
37 *Illustrated London News,* 29 January 1848, p. 56.
38 B. Lumley, op. cit., pp. 191, 220.
39 Ibid., pp. 187, 232.
40 The conductor and Lind supporter, Julius Benedict; T. Marix-Spire, *Lettres inédites de George Sand et de Pauline Viardot 1839–1849* (Nouvelles Editions), pp. 244, 252; J.P.T. Bury, *France 1814–1940* (London: Methuen, 1969). D. Cairns, op. cit., p. 408.
41 'Elle ne peut pas, il est vrai, m'empêcher d'avoir du succès quand je chante, mais elle s'arrange pour m'empêcher de chanter aussi souvent que la Direction même le voudrait par des maladies subites qui sont guéries le lendemain – ou en n'apprenant pas par coeur des rôles qu'ils ont joué toute leur vie': T. Marix-Spire, *Lettres inédites de George Sand,* op. cit., p. 251.
42 'Je vous dirai en quatre mots que j'ai une vraie *lega italiana* contre moi': Ibid., p. 251.
43 A. Hedley (revised M.E.J. Brown), *Chopin* (London: J.M. Dent, 1947), p. 321.
44 *Illustrated London News,* 13 May 1848, pp. 312, 315.
45 Ibid., 29 May 1848, p. 329.
46 Ibid., 17 June 1848, p. 392.
47 L. Melitz, *Opera Goer's Complete Guide* (London: J.M. Dent, 1925), p. 147; G. Dulong, op. cit., p.98.

48 B. Lumley, op. cit., pp. 190, 243; A. FitzLyon, *The Price of Genius*, op. cit., p.227.
49 Demar Irvine, *Massenet, a Chronicle of his Life and Times* (New York: Amadeus Press, 1994). P. Waddington, *PhD Thesis*, op. cit., p. 184.
50 *Illustrated London News*, 28 April 1848, p. 281.
51 Ibid., 15 April 1948, pp. 239, 240.
52 Ibid., 22 April 1848, p. 255; C. Woodham-Smith, *The Great Hunger* (London: First Four Square Edition, 1994), pp. 65, 351–6.
53 *Illustrated London News*, 22 April 1848; 6 May 1848; 27 May 1848.
54 Ibid., 22 April 1848, p. 255.
55 Ibid., 1 July 1848, p. 416.
56 P. Mansel, *Paris between Empires* 1814–1852 (London: John Murray, 2001), pp. 395, 396; G. Wall, *Flaubert, a Life* (London: Faber and Faber, 2001), p. 147.
57 G. Flaubert (trans. D.F. Hannigan), *Sentimental Education* (London: H.S. Nichols Ltd Publishers, 1898), pt II, ch. 6 and pt III, ch. 1; C. Jones, *The Cambridge Illustrated History of France* (Cambridge: Cambridge University Press, 1994), p. 209; P. Mansel, op. cit., p. 406.
58 J.P.T. Bury, op. cit., p. 72; C. Jones, op. cit., p. 210; B. Jack, *George Sand: A Woman's Life Writ Large* (London: Chatto & Windus, 1999), p. 307.
59 L. Viardot, *Souvenirs de chasse dans toute l'Europe* (Paris: Editions Pygmalion, 1985), p. 296; whether or not Louis was in Prussia is not certain. H. Troyat (trans. N. Amphoux), *Turgenev* (London: W.H. Allen, 1989), p. 30.
60 T. Marix-Spire, *Lettres inédites de George Sand*, op. cit., p. 245.
61 Ibid., pp. 246, 249.
62 Ibid., pp. 248, 250.
63 P. Mansel, op. cit., p. 412; T. Marix-Spire, *Lettres inédites de George Sand*, op. cit., p. 251, 253; B. Jack, op. cit., pp. 313, 314.
64 A. Hedley, op. cit., pp. 315, 316, 324, 331.
65 A. FitzLyon, *The Price of Genius*, op. cit., p. 229; P. Waddington, *The Musical Works of Pauline Viardot-Garcia* (Pinehaven, New Zealand: Whirinaki Press, 2004), p. 11; A. Hedley, op. cit., pp. 316, 322, also F. Chopin, letter of 13 May 1848 to Gryzmala.
66 'Si pleine de cette belle vie variée que les artistes seuls peuvent connaître': T. Marix-Spire, *Lettres inédites de George Sand*, op. cit., p.256.
67 P. Waddington, 'Some Gleanings on Turgenev and his International Connections', *New Zealand Slavonic Journal*, 1983, p. 210.
68 T. Marix-Spire, *Lettres inédites de George Sand*, op. cit., pp. 255, 263, 273 (6 April 1849); The number in the street changed with the passage of time.
69 G. de Maupassant (trans. G. Hopkins), *Short Stories* (London: The Folio Society, 1959); G. Flaubert, op. cit., pt I, ch. 6. N. Simeone, *Paris – A Musical Gazetteer* (New Haven and London: Yale University Press, 2000), p. 156.
70 E. Zola (trans. M. Mauldon), *L'Assommoir* (Oxford: Oxford University Press, 1995), ch. 6, 8, 10, 11; *Musée de Montmartre, Bals et Cabarets au temps de Bruant et Lautrec* (Paris: Editions le Vieux Montmartre, 2002), p. 8.
71 Goncourt, E. et J. de (trans. L. Tancock), *Germinie Lacerteux* (Harmondsworth: Penguin, 1984), ch. 12, p. 60.
72 T. Marix-Spire, op. cit., pp.255, 263; A. Zviguilsky (ed.), op. cit., p. 35. The Moulin Rouge was opened in 1889: Musée de Montmartre, op. cit., pp. 8, 29.
73 P. Waddington, 'Dickens, Pauline Viardot and Turgenev: a Study in Mutual Admiration', *New Zealand Slavonic Journal*, no. 2, p. 57; Musée Tourguéniev, (par Tamara Zviguilsky), *Guide* (Corlet Condé-sur-Noireau, 1993), p. 44; D. Magarshack, *Turgenev, a Life* (London: Faber & Faber, 1954), p. 268.
74 P. Waddington, 'Some Gleanings on Turgenev and his International Connections', *New Zealand Slavonic Journal*, 1983, where there is a map of the ground plan.
75 'Sur un terrain qui servait à la culture des artichauts': T. Marix-Spire, *Lettres inédites de George Sand*, op. cit., p. 263; *Paul Viardot, Souvenirs d'un Artiste* (Paris: Librairie SA, 1910), p. 8.
76 P. Waddington, *Some Gleanings*, op. cit., p. 211.
77 T. Marix-Spire, *Lettres inédites de George Sand*, op. cit., p. 256.
78 G. Flaubert, *Sentimental Education*, op. cit., pt III, ch. 1.
79 T. Marix-Spire, *Lettres inédites de George Sand*, op. cit., pp. 256, 259; G. Flaubert, op. cit., p. 373.
80 The figures vary according to source: C. Jones, op. cit., p. 211; J.P.T. Bury, op. cit., p. 79; P. Mansel, op. cit., p. 412.
81 P. Mansel, op. cit., p. 414.
82 J.P.T. Bury, op. cit., p. 89.

83 P. Mansel, op. cit., p. 422.
84 J.P.T. Bury, op. cit., p. 127.

CHAPTER 12. *LE PROPHÈTE* (pp. 169–180)

1 A. FitzLyon, *The Price of Genius, a life of Pauline Viardot* (London: John Calder, 1964), p. 243.
2 C.V. Stanford and C. Forsyth, *A History of Music* (New York: Macmillan, 1917), p. 275; H. Lacombe, *The Keys to French Opera in the nineteenth century* (London: University of California Press, 2001), p. 26.
3 H. Lacombe, op. cit., p. 26.
4 Pauline Viardot told Stanford this: C.V. Stanford and C. Forsyth, op. cit., p. 276; C.V. Stanford, *Pages from an Unwritten Diary* (London: Edward Arnold, 1914), p. 286.
5 C.V. Stanford, *Pages from an Unwritten Diary*, op. cit., p. 286; G. Dulong, *Pauline Viardot Tragédienne Lyrique* (Bougival: Association des Amis d'Ivan Tourguéniev Pauline Viardot et Maria Malibran), p. 98.
6 R. Somerset-Ward, *Angels and Monsters* (New Haven and London: Yale University Press, 2004), p. 169.
7 G. Dulong, op. cit., pp. 98, 99; *Illustrated London News*, 21 April 1849, p. 258; A. Hedley (revised M.E.J. Brown), *Chopin* (London: J.M. Dent, 1947), p. 357.
8 *Illustrated London News*, 28 July 1849, p. 55; Ibid., 21 April 1849, p. 258; L. Melitz, *Opera Goer's Complete Guide* (London: J.M. Dent, 1925), p. 308.
9 *Illustrated London News*, 21 April 1849, p. 258.
10 P. Waddington, 'Turgenev's relations with H.F. Chorley', *New Zealand Slavonic Journal*, no. 2, 1978, p. 28; 'Siddonian in dignity' – *Illustrated London News*, 21 April 1849, p. 258.
11 T. Marix-Spire, *Lettres inédites de George Sand et de Pauline Viardot 1839–1849* (Nouvelles Editions), p. 274; A. FitzLyon, *The Price of Genius*, op. cit., p. 245; C.V. Stanford, *Pages from an Unwritten Diary*, op. cit., p. 286.
12 *Illustrated London News*, 21 April 1849.
13 W. Kuhe, *My musical recollections* (London: Richard Bentley, 1896), p. 185.
14 A. FitzLyon, *The Price of Genius*, op. cit., p. 244; B. Rees, *Camille Saint-Saëns, A Life* (London: Chatto & Windus, 1999), p. 203; H.F. Chorley, *Thirty years' Musical Recollections* (London: Hurst & Blackett, 1862), pt II, p. 102.
15 J.P.T. Bury, *France 1814–1940* (London: Methuen, 1969), p. 83; G. Dulong, op. cit., p. 100.
16 *Illustrated London News*, 21 April 1849, p. 258.
17 G. Dulong, op. cit., p. 101; *Illustrated London News*, 28 April 1849, p. 55.
18 *The Times*, 25 May 1849.
19 *The Times*, 13 June 1849, 26 June 1849, 30 June 1849; 4 July 1849.
20 *The Times*, 11 July 1849; *Illustrated London News*, 14 July 1849.
21 *Illustrated London News*, 28 July 1849, p. 55.
22 Ibid., 11 August 1849, p. 74:
23 *New Grove Dictionary of Music and Musicians* (London: Macmillan, 1980), vol. 17, p. 528, Sontag (J Warrack); E.C. Clayton, *Queens of Song* (London: Smith Elder & Co, 1863), p. 90; A. FitzLyon, *Maria Malibran – Diva of the Romantic Age* (London: Souvenir Press, 1987), p. 101.
24 *The Times*, 25 July 1849; *Illustrated London News*, 28 July 1849, p. 55. Sontag was praised for her performance in *La Sonnambula*.
25 E.C. Clayton, op. cit., p. 88.
26 Ibid, pp. 83, 88; a pilgrimage – *Illustrated London News*, 7 July 1849; Sontag was born in January 1806. The British Ambassador was Earl Clanwilliam.
27 *Illustrated London News*, 11 August 1849, p. 102; Ibid., 25 August 1849, p. 135.
28 T. Marix-Spire, *Lettres inédites de George Sand*, op. cit., p. 287; B. Weinreb and C. Hibbert, *London Encyclopaedia* (London: Macmillan, 1993), p. 505. G. Dulong, op. cit., pp. 30, 102; *New Grove*, op. cit., vol. 20, p. 145 (Wagner).
29 T. Marix-Spire, *Lettres inédites de George Sand*, op. cit., p. 283.
30 B. Waller (ed.), *Themes in Modern European History 1830–1890* (London: Unwin Hyman, 1990), p. 162; H. Seton-Watson, *The Russian Empire 1801–1917* (Oxford: Clarendon Press, 1988), p. 276; L. Schapiro, *Turgenev, his Life and Times* (Oxford: OUP, 1978), p. 79.
31 H. Granjard and A. Zviguilsky, *Ivan Tourgénev, Lettres inédites à Pauline Viardot et à sa famille* (Paris: Editions l'Age d'Homme, 1972), pp. 222, xxiv; P. Waddington, 'The Role of Courtavenel in the Life and Work of Turgenev', from *Issues in Russian Literature before*

1917, selected papers of the Third World Congress for Soviet and East European Studies (Colombus, Ohio: Slavica Publishers Inc, 1989), p. 113; P. Waddington, *Courtavenel, the History of an Artists' Nest and its Role in the Life of Turgenev* (*PhD Thesis*, Queen's University Belfast, The British Library, British Thesis Service, spring 1972), p. 74.

32 Turgenev had been a regular visitor to Herzen's Paris apartment: L. Schapiro, op. cit., p. 61; P. Waddington, *PhD Thesis*, op. cit., p. 75.

33 A. Herzen (trans. C. Garnett), *My Past and Thoughts, the Memoirs of Alexander Herzen* (London: Chatto and Windus, 1974), p. 348; also *Memoirs of Alexander Herzen* (trans. C. Garnett) (Chatto and Windus 1924 edition), p. 41.

34 H. Granjard and A. Zviguilsky, op. cit., p. 44; A. FitzLyon, *The Price of Genius*, op. cit., p. 276.

35 V.S. Pritchett, *The Gentle Barbarian, The Life and Work of Turgenev* (London: Chatto & Windus, 1977), p. 64; A. FitzLyon, *The Price of Genius*, op. cit., p. 243.

36 L. Schapiro, op. cit., pp. 75, 76.

37 I. Turgenev (trans. and intro. by Sir Isaiah Berlin), *A Month in the Country* (London: Penguin, 1981), p. 124 (Appendix); H. Granjard and A. Zviguilsky, op. cit., p.44.

38 Sir Isaiah Berlin's introduction to I. Turgenev, *A Month in the Country*, op. cit.

39 Sir Isaiah Berlin's introduction to I. Turgenev, *A Month in the Country*, op. cit.

40 A. FitzLyon, *The Price of Genius*, op. cit., p. 259; L. Schapiro, op. cit., p.76.

41 L. Schapiro, op. cit., p. 187.

42 R. Freeborn in introduction to I. Turgenev (trans. R. Freeborn), *Rudin* (London: Penguin, 1975), p. 9; R. Freeborn in introduction to I. Turgenev (trans. R. Freeborn), *First Love and other stories* (Oxford: Oxford University Press, 1999), pp. 12, 32; R. Freeborn, *Turgenev, the novelist's novelist* (Oxford: Oxford University Press, 1960), p. 20; P. Foote in introduction to M. Lermontov (trans. P. Foote), *A Hero of Our Time* (London: Penguin, 2001), p. xvii.

43 I. Turgenev, *First Love and other stories*, op. cit., pp. 13, 32, 33, 72.

44 I. Turgenev, *Virgin Soil*, pt II, ch. 37.

45 He arrived 13 June 1849: P. Waddington, *PhD Thesis*, op. cit., p. 86; P. Waddington, 'Two Months in the Country', *New Zealand Slavonic Journal*, no. 11, winter 1973, p. 32; A. FitzLyon, *The Price of Genius*, op. cit., p. 255; P. Waddington, *PhD Thesis*, op. cit., p. 139; I. Turgenev (ed. E. Halpérine-Kaminsky), *Lettres à Madame Viardot* (Paris: Bibliothèque-Charpentier, 1907), 29 July 1849, p. 115.

46 G. Dulong, op. cit., p. 100; P. Waddington, 'Turgenev's relations with H.F. Chorley', op. cit., p. 27; P. Ackroyd, *Dickens* (London: Sinclair Stevenson, 1990), p. 540.

47 P. Waddington, *Turgenev and Pauline Viardot, An Unofficial Marriage* (Canadian Slavonic Papers, vol. XXVI, no. 1, March 1984), p. 49; *Musical Quarterly* 1916, p. 44; D. Cairns, *Berlioz: Servitude and Greatness* (Penguin: London 2000), p. 635.

48 A. FitzLyon, *The Price of Genius*, op. cit., p. 252; P. Waddington, *Two Months in the Country*, op. cit., pp. 32, 39; I. Turgenev, *Lettres à Madame Viardot*, op. cit., July 1849, p. 109; A. Zviguilsky (ed.), *Ivan Tourguénev: Nouvelle Correspondance inédite* (Paris: Librairie des Cinq Continents, 1971), p. 26.

49 P. Waddington, *Two Months in the Country*, op. cit., p. 30; I. Turgenev, *Lettres à Madame Viardot*, op. cit., 30 July 1849, p. 116.

50 A. Zviguilsky (ed.), op. cit., p. 31; P. Waddington, *Two Months in the Country*, op. cit., pp. 30, 43; P. Waddington, 'Dickens, Pauline Viardot and Turgenev: a Study in Mutual Admiration', *New Zealand Slavonic Journal*, no. 2, 1974, p. 59.

51 A. FitzLyon, *The Price of Genius*, op. cit., p. 258; J. Samson, *Chopin* (Oxford: OUP, 1998), p. 260.

52 Turgenev – Prof. Patrick Waddington.

53 B. Eisler, *Chopin's Funeral* (London: Little, Brown, 2003), p. 7; J. Samson, op. cit., p. 282; *I Corinthians*, ch. 14, v. 34.

54 J. Samson, op. cit., p. 282; Letter of Gryzmala, October 1849: A. Hedley (trans.), *Selected Correspondence of Fryderyk Chopin* (London: Heinemann, 1962), p. 335; A. FitzLyon, *The Price of Genius*, op. cit., p. 132.

55 Letter of Gryzmala, October 1849: A. Hedley, op. cit., p.335.

Chapter 13. Gounod and Sapho (pp. 183–203)

1 P. Waddington, 'Turgenev and Gounod, Rival Strangers in the Viardots' Country Nest', *New Zealand Slavonic Journal*, no. 1, 1976, p. 14.

2 J. Harding, *Gounod* (London: George Allen & Unwin Ltd, 1973), p. 14.
3 A. FitzLyon, *The Price of Genius, a life of Pauline Viardot* (London: John Calder, 1964), p. 89; G. Dulong, *Pauline Viardot Tragédienne Lyrique* (Bougival: Association des Amis d'Ivan Tourguéniev Pauline Viardot et Maria Malibran), p. 41.
4 He was aged 47. J. Harding, op. cit., pp. 17, 18.
5 J.P.T. Bury, *France 1814–1940* (London: Methuen, 1969), p. 298; P. Mansel, *Paris between Empires 1814–1852* (London: John Murray, 2001), p. 166.
6 J. Harding, op. cit., p. 22.
7 Ibid., p.23; B. Rees, Camille Saint-Saëns, *A Life* (London: Chatto & Windus, 1999), pp. 30, 45.
8 J. Harding, op. cit., pp. 28, 34.
9 J. Harding, op. cit., pp. 18, 37, 39, 40; T. Marix-Spire (trans. E. Huntress), *Gounod and his first interpreter, Pauline Viardot* (Musical Quarterly, vol. 31, 1945); C. Gounod (trans. A. Crocker), *Memoirs of an Artist* (Chicago: Rand McNally & Company, 1895), p. 93; *Souvenirs d'un Artiste* (Paris: Librairie Fischbacher SA, 1910), p. 67.
10 C. Gounod, op. cit., p. 79; *New Grove Dictionary of Music and Musicians* (London: Macmillan, 1980), vol. 7, p. 581, Gounod (Martin Cooper).
11 J. Harding, op. cit., pp. 42, 46, 47, 49; C. Gounod, op. cit., p. 150.
12 J. Harding, op. cit., pp. 41, 51; C. Gounod, op. cit., p. 158.
13 T. Marix Spire in *Musical Quarterly* 1945, op. cit.; *New Grove*, op. cit., vol. 7, p. 581, Gounod (Martin Cooper); J. Harding, op. cit., pp. 54, 56.
14 P. Waddington, 'Turgenev and Gounod, Rival Strangers', op. cit., p. 11. The mutual friend was François Seghers, a cellist and an enthusiast for avant-garde music. P. Waddington, 'Turgenev and George Eliot, a literary friendship', *Modern Language Review*, vol. 66, 1971, p. 757; C. Gounod, op. cit., p.169.
15 J. Harding, op. cit., p. 62; H. Lacombe, *The Keys to French Opera in the nineteenth century* (London: University of California Press, 2001), p. 210. The Director was Nestor Roqueplan.
16 They included in 1838 Liszt and Marie d'Agoult, and later E. de Goncourt. D. Ollivier (ed.), *Correspondance de Liszt et de la Comtesse d'Agoult* (Paris: Editions Bernard Grasset, 1933–34), pt I, p. 246; E. de Goncourt, *Journal* (Paris, 1887), vol. IV, p. 485.
17 C. Gounod, op. cit., p. 171; P. Waddington, 'Turgenev and Gounod, Rival Strangers', op cit., p. 15; S. Huebner, *The Operas of Charles Gounod* (Oxford: Clarendon Press, 1990), p. 27; A. FitzLyon, *The Price of Genius*, op. cit., p. 261; A. Zviguilsky (ed.), op. cit., p. 37.
18 A. Zviguilsky (ed.), *Ivan Tourguénev: Nouvelle Correspondance inédite* (Paris: Librairie des Cinq Continents, 1971), 7 May 1850, pp. 38, 40, 41; I Turgenev (ed. E. Halpérine-Kaminsky), *Lettres à Madame Viardot* (Paris: Bibliothèque-Charpentier, 1907), 19 June 1849, p. 78.
19 *Musical Quarterly*, vol. 31, 1945; A. FitzLyon, *The Price of Genius*, op. cit., p. 261; *Lettres inédites de George Sand*, op. cit; *Musical Quarterly*, vol. 31, 1945, pp. 198, 207.
20 C. Gounod, op. cit., pp. 174, 175; J. Harding, op. cit., p. 97; B. Rees, op. cit., p. 85.
21 T. Marix-Spire, *Lettres inédites de George Sand*, op. cit; *Musical Quarterly*, vol. 31, 1945; A. Zviguilsky (ed.), op. cit., p. 39.
22 A. Zviguilsky (ed.), op. cit., pp. 39, 40; L. Héritte-Viardot, *Une famille de grands musiciens* (Paris: Librairie Stock, 1922), p. 42.
23 L. Héritte-Viardot, op. cit., pp. 69, 70; P. Waddington, *Courtavenel, the History of an Artists' Nest and its Role in the Life of Turgenev* (*PhD Thesis*, Queen's University Belfast, The British Library, British Thesis Service, spring 1972), pp. 64, 283; *New Grove*, op. cit., vol. 1, p. 645, Artôt (Harold Rosenthal).
24 L. Héritte-Viardot, op. cit.. p. 73; P. Waddington, *PhD Thesis*, op. cit., p. 57. The guest was Vivier.
25 P. Waddington, *PhD Thesis*, op,. cit., pp. 44, 57; P. Waddington, *Turgenev and George Sand: An Improbable Entente* (Victoria University Press, 1981), p. 24; L. Héritte-Viardot, op. cit., p. 70. The officer possibly was Solovoï.
26 L. Héritte-Viardot, op. cit., p. 72.
27 P. Waddington, 'Two Months in the Country', *New Zealand Slavonic Journal*, no. 11, winter 1973, p. 34; I. Turgenev (ed. E. Halpérine-Kaminsky), *Lettres à Madame Viardot* (Paris: Bibliothèque-Charpentier, 1907), p. 72.
28 H. Macdonald (ed.) (trans. R. Nicholls), *Selected Letters of Berlioz* (London: Faber and Faber, 1995). Letter to Pauline Viardot, 30 September 1850.
29 A. Zviguilsky (ed.), op. cit., p. 59.

Publication was between 1847 and 1851, and a collected edition in August 1852.

30 D. Magarshack, *Turgenev, a Life* (London: Faber & Faber, 1954), p. 142

31 G. Dulong, op. cit., p. 110; A. Seljak, *Ivan Turgenev's Ökonomien* (Zurich: University of Basel, Pano Verlag, 2004), p. 98.

32 H. Granjard and A. Zviguilsky, Ivan Tourgénev, *Lettres inédites à Pauline Viardot et à sa famille* (Paris: Editions l'Age d'Homme, 1972), p. 23 – 17 June 1850; P. Waddington, 'Turgenev and Gounod, Rival Strangers', op. cit., p. 23.

33 A. FitzLyon, *The Price of Genius*, op. cit., p. 263; A. Zviguilsky (ed.), op. cit., pp. 40, 43, 49, 50.

34 H. Granjard and A. Zviguilsky, op. cit., pp. 31, 36, 48; H. Troyat (trans. N. Amphoux), *Turgenev* (London: W.H. Allen, 1989), p. 38; The property was 18 versts away. The row was in August.

35 H. Troyat, op. cit., p.39; G. Dulong, op. cit., p. 110; H. Granjard and A. Zviguilsky, op. cit., p.45; A. FitzLyon, *The Price of Genius*, op. cit., p. 275; A. Zviguilsky (ed.), op. cit., p. 50; L. Schapiro, *Turgenev, his Life and Times* (Oxford: OUP, 1978), p. 81.

36 L. Schapiro, op. cit., pp. 95, 107; A. Seljak, op. cit., p. 110.

37 L. Schapiro, op. cit., p. 109; H. Granjard and A. Zviguilsky, op. cit., p. 54

38 L. Schapiro, op. cit., pp. 95, 139; A. Zviguilsky (ed.), op. cit., p. 94.

39 P. Waddington, 'Turgenev and Gounod, Rival Strangers', op. cit., p. 23.

40 S. Huebner, op. cit., p. 30.

41 *Encyclopaedia Britannica,* ninth edition, vol. XXI, p. 302

42 Ovid, *Heroines* X (Sappho to Phaon).

43 G. Dulong, op. cit., p. 107.

44 S. Huebner, op. cit., p. 190.

45 J. Harding, op. cit., p. 218.

46 C. Jones, *The Cambridge Illustrated History of France* (Cambridge: Cambridge University Press, 1994), p. 211.

47 J. Ridley, *Napoléon III and Eugénie* (London: Constable, 1979), pp. 180, 279.

48 Ibid., pp. 180, 279; J.P.T. Bury, *France 1814–1940* (London: Methuen, 1969), p. 85.

49 S. Huebner, op. cit., p. 31.

50 For example, 'Que les bras se lèvent pour les maux soufferts; A défaut de glaive, brandissons nos fers'.

51 According to Gautier: S. Huebner, op. cit., p. 31.

52 G. Dulong, op. cit., p. 106.

53 T. Marix-Spire (ed.), *Lettres inédites de George Sand et de Pauline Viardot 1839–1849* (Paris: Nouvelles Editions Latines, 1959); *Musical Quarterly* 1945, p. 299.

54 S. Huebner, op. cit., p. 33; *Musical Quarterly*, 1945, p. 299 reports 2,677 francs taken on the first night, 1,432 francs on the second and 1,177 francs on the third, consistent with Gounod (Paris: Librairie Ch. Delagrave, 1911), p. 124, which adds that the 238 costumes cost 3,597 francs.

55 C. Gounod, op. cit., p. 177; S. Huebner, op. cit., p. 190. 'Mutilée pour rendre sa durée compatible avec la dignité du ballet de Vert-Vert'; Pauline's part was sung by Mademoiselle Masson; Prod'homme et Dandelot, op. cit., p. 130.

56 *The Times*, 11 August 1851; *Musical World*, 16 August 1851, p. 513.

57 T. Marix-Spire, *Lettres inédites de George Sand*, op. cit., p. 78; Prod'homme et Dandelot, op. cit., p. 123. 'Madame Viardot ne chante plus; chaque note qui sort de sa voix intelligente est un cri déchirant ... Son organe brisée n'a plus aucun charme'.

58 H.F. Chorley, *Thirty years' Musical Recollections* (London: Hurst & Blackett, 1862), p. 11.

59 P. Waddington, *PhD Thesis*, op. cit., pp. 198, 203.

60 'Déjà àprès de sa fin, et chantant faux tout le temps': Prod'homme et Dandelot, op. cit., vol. 1, p. 130; T. Marix-Spire, *Lettres inédites de George Sand*, op. cit., *Musical Quarterly* 1945, p. 316.

61 A. FitzLyon, *The Price of Genius*, op. cit., p. 277.

62 L. Viardot, *Souvenirs de Chasse dans toute l'Europe*, Editions Pygmalion, Paris 1985, p. 358, 360, 361, 364. B. Kendall-Davies, *The Life and Work of Pauline Viardot-Garcia*, vol. I 'The years of fame' (London: Cambridge Scholars Press, 2003), p. 323.

63 A. Zviguilsky (ed.), op. cit., p. 29; *Encyclopaedia Britannica,* Standard Millennium edition.

64 B. Weinreb and C. Hibbert, *London Encyclopaedia* (London: Macmillan, 1993), p. 505.

65 It was held on 8 August 1849: P. Waddington, 'Turgenev's relations with H.F. Chorley', *New Zealand Slavonic Journal*, no. 2,

1978, p. 28.
66 G. Dulong, op. cit., p. 108.
67 B. Rees, op. cit., pp. 63, 107, 122; A. FitzLyon, *The Price of Genius*, op. cit., p. 302; L. Héritte-Viardot, op. cit., p. 42.
68 J.P.T. Bury, op. cit., p. 86; P. Mansel, *Paris between Empires 1814–1852* (London: John Murray, 2001), p. 419. Figures vary slightly.
69 *Encyclopaedia Britannica*, ninth edition, vol. XIV, p. 471; H. Granjard and A. Zviguilsky, op. cit., p. 52; B. Kendall-Davies, op. cit., pp. 311, 316.
70 L. Viardot, *Souvenirs de chasse dans toute l'Europe* (Paris: Editions Pygmalion, 1985), pp. 380, 383.
71 P. Waddington, *The Musical Works of Pauline Viardot-Garcia* (Pinehaven, New Zealand: Whirinaki Press, 2004), p. 11; G. Dulong, op. cit., p. 109.
72 G. Dulong, op. cit., pp. 109, 129.
73 P. Waddington, *PhD Thesis*, op. cit., p. 207.
74 T. Marix-Spire (trans. E. Huntress), *Gounod and his first interpreter, Pauline Viardot* (*Musical Quarterly*, vol. 31, 1945), pp. 299–317; *Cahiers Ivan Tourguéniev, Pauline Viardot, Maria Malibran* (Bougival: Association des Amis d'Ivan Tourguéniev Pauline Viardot et Maria Malibran), no. 20, p. 139.
75 A. FitzLyon, *The Price of Genius*, op. cit., p. 275.
76 *New Grove*, op. cit., vol. 20, p. 690, Zimmermann (Frédéric Robert); C. Gounod, op. cit., p. 182; B. Rees, op. cit., p. 30.
77 J. Harding, op. cit., pp. 74, 76.
78 It had been founded in 1833: Ibid., p. 77.
79 T. Marix-Spire, *Lettres inédites de George Sand*, op. cit., *Musical Quarterly* 1945, p. 309; information from Professor Waddington.
80 J. Harding, op. cit., p. 76; G. Weldon, *My Orphanage and Gounod in England* (London: London Music and Art Association, 1882), p. 96.
81 A. FitzLyon, *The Price of Genius*, op. cit., p. 287; P. Treherne, *A Plaintiff in Person* (Heinemann, 1923), p. 35.
82 *Lettres inédites de George Sand*, *Musical Quarterly* 1945 p. 303; A. Zviguilsky (ed.), op. cit., pp. 68, 73; G. Sand (ed. T. Bodin), *Lettres Retrouvées* (Paris: Gallimard, 2004), p. 115.
83 C. Gounod, op. cit., pp. 183, 189; *New Grove*, op. cit., vol. 7, p. 581, Gounod (Martin Cooper).
84 B. Kendall-Davies, op. cit., p. 323.
85 A. Zviguilsky (ed.), op. cit., p. 230.
86 Ibid., pp. 101, 103.
87 A. FitzLyon, *The Price of Genius*, op. cit., p. 277; the blank is between 27 July and 4 October: L. Schapiro, op. cit., p.102.
88 A. Zviguilsky (ed.), op. cit., p. 121
89 M. Curtiss, *Unpublished Letters by Georges Bizet* (*Musical Quarterly*, vol. 36, 1950), p. 395.
90 A. FitzLyon, *The Price of Genius*, op. cit., p. 274.
91 T. Marix-Spire, *Lettres inédites de George Sand*, op cit., *Musical Quarterly* 1945, p. 316; A. FitzLyon, *The Price of Genius*, op. cit., p. 275; *My Orphanage and Gounod in England* (London: London Music and Art Association, 1882), p. 96.
92 G. Sand, *Lettres retrouvées*, op. cit., p. 115
93 The sentence was handed down in May 1880; B. Thompson, *A Monkey among Crocodiles* (London: HarperCollins, 2000), pp. 101, 234, 235, 267; J. Harding, op. cit., p. 210.
94 B. Kendall-Davies, op. cit., p. 312; A. Zviguilsky (ed.), op. cit., vol. II, p. xiv; T. Marix-Spire, *Lettres inédites de George Sand*, op. cit., p. 78.
95 Letter dated 11 January 1852: H. Granjard and A. Zviguilsky, op. cit., p. 56.

Chapter 14. Children (pp. 205–220)

1 B. Jack, George Sand: A Woman's Life Writ Large (London: Chatto & Windus, 1999), pp. 93, 119, 149. The student was Stéphane de Grandsagne (1802–1845).
2 Comtesse D'Agoult (D. Stern), *Mémoires 1833–1854* (Paris: Calmann-Lévy, 1927), p. 82.
3 F. Dostoyevsky, *The Idiot* (Ware, Herts: Wordsworth Classics, 1996), pt 3, ch. 1.
4 B. Jack. op. cit., p. 275.
5 D'Agoult, op. cit., p. 209; T. Marix-Spire, *Lettres inédites de George Sand et de Pauline Viardot 1839–1849* (Nouvelles Editions), p. 137; B. Jack, op. cit., pp. 296, 335.
6 G. Dulong, *Pauline Viardot Tragédienne Lyrique* (Bougival: Association des Amis d'Ivan Tourguéniev Pauline Viardot et Maria Malibran), p. 47; P. Waddington, Courtavenel, the History of an Artists' Nest and its Role in the Life of Turgenev (*PhD Thesis*, Queen's University Belfast, The British Library, British Thesis Service, spring 1972), p. 32.

7 Exhibition guide, *George Sand, Une Nature d'Artiste, Exposition du Bicentenaire de sa Naissance*, Paris-Musées, 2004, pp. 60, 61; R. Baldick (ed.), *Pages from the Goncourt Journal* (Oxford: Oxford University Press, 1978), p. 98, 16 April 1864.

8 B. Jack, op. cit., pp. 299, 300; T. Marix-Spire, *Lettres inédites de George Sand*, op. cit., p. 272; A. Hedley (revised M.E.J. Brown), *Chopin* (London: J.M. Dent, 1947), p. 298.

9 The child lived ftom 28 February to 6 March. Musée de la Vie Romantique exhibition guide, 2004: Sand family tree.

10 B. Jack, op. cit., p. 324.

11 Ibid., p. 327.

12 W. Karénine, *George Sand sa Vie et ses Oeuvres* (Paris: Paul Ollendorff, 1899), vol. III, p. 612, 24 April 1852.

13 B. Jack, op. cit., pp. 327, 329, 330, 355.

14 R. Jordan, *George Sand* (London: Constable, 1976), p. 335. Musée de la Vie Romantique exhibition guide, 2004: Sand family tree.

15 P. Waddington, *Turgenev and George Sand: An Improbable Entente* (Victoria University Press, 1981), p. 37.

16 L. Héritte-Viardot (trans. E.S. Bucheim), *Memories and Adventures* (London: Mills & Boon, 1913)

17 A. FitzLyon, *The Price of Genius, a life of Pauline Viardot* (London: John Calder, 1964), pp.132, 133; T. Marix-Spire, *Lettres inédites de George Sand*, op. cit., pp. 174, 185.

18 Mrs Grote, *Memoirs of the Life of Ary Scheffer* (London: John Murray, 1860), p. 68; Musée de la Vie Romantique, *General Guide* (Paris-Musées, 1992), p. 8; M. Kirlew, *Famous Sisters of Great Men* (London: Thos Nelson, 1905); R. Chadbourne, *Ernest Renan* (New York: Twayne Publishers Inc, 1968), pp. 132, 135.

19 L. Héritte-Viardot, op. cit., p. 37; Mrs Grote, op. cit., p. 49.

20 T. Marix-Spire, *Lettres inédites de George Sand*, op. cit., pp. 257–259; L. Héritte-Viardot, op. cit., p. 26.

21 A. FitzLyon, *The Price of Genius*, op. cit., p.204; G. Dulong, op. cit., p. 79.

22 L. Héritte-Viardot, op. cit., pp. 29, 42.

23 T. Marix-Spire, *Lettres inédites de George Sand*, op. cit., p. 244 (June 1847).

24 Les manières un peu 'je n'en fiche pas mal' – I. Turgenev (ed. E. Halpérine-Kaminsky), *Lettres à Madame Viardot* (Paris: Bibliothèque-Charpentier, 1907), p. 127; L. Héritte-Viardot, op. cit., p. 33.

25 L. Héritte-Viardot, op. cit., pp. 23, 88, 98.

26 Ibid., p. 172; G. Dulong, op. cit., p. 152, however, implies that it was not entirely according to their liking.

27 L. Héritte-Viardot, op. cit., p. 113.

28 A. Zviguilsky (ed.), *Ivan Tourguénev: Nouvelle Correspondance inédite* (Paris: Librairie des Cinq Continents, 1971), pp. 121, 123, 249.

29 L. Héritte-Viardot, op. cit., p. 139.

30 Diamonds were discovered there in 1867. The collective suicide took place in 1857: *Encyclopaedia Britannica*, ninth edition, vol. V, p. 45.

31 L. Héritte-Viardot, op. cit., pp. 130, 133.

32 H. Granjard and A. Zviguilsky, *Ivan Tourgénev, Lettres inédites à Pauline Viardot et à sa famille* (Paris: Editions l'Age d'Homme, 1972), pp. 127, 128, 131, 139, 141.

33 Ibid., pp. 130–133.

34 Ibid., pp. 126, 128, 130. 'Quel caractère que cette Louise et comment est-il possible qu'elle soit votre fille': Ibid., p. 126.

35 Ibid., pp. 217, 218, 250. For *Lindora* (Weimar, 1879), see T. Marix-Spire, *Lettres inédites de George Sand*, op. cit., p. 265.

36 W. Karénine, op. cit., vol. III, p. 214.

37 Letter of 26 May 1879 to Princess Carolyne; A. Williams, *Franz Liszt, selected letters* (Oxford: Clarendon Press, 1998), p. 841.

38 A. Zviguilsky (ed.), op. cit., p. 142; H. Granjard and A. Zviguilsky, op. cit., pp. 169, 170. 'D'une conduite irréprochable mais d'un caractère impossible, excentrique et brusque': A. Zviguilsky (ed.), op. cit., p. 185.

39 A. Zviguilsky (ed.), op. cit., p. 188.

40 Ibid., p. 129; information on Loulou from Dr Zviguilsky (who had obtained it from Jacques-Paul Viardot).

41 Ibid., p. 52.

42 A. FitzLyon, *The Price of Genius*, op. cit., p. 119; A. Zviguilsky (ed.), op. cit., pp. 53, 62, 77, 79; H. Granjard and A. Zviguilsky, op. cit., p. 50, 79. Paulinette's mother died in 1875. A. Zviguilsky (ed.), op. cit., p. 52.

43 H. Granjard and A. Zviguilsky, op. cit., pp. 40, 41.

44 Ibid., pp. 36,40, 47

45 I. Turgenev (trans. I. and T. Litvinov), *Three Short Novels* (Moscow: Foreign Language Publishing House, no date but around 1980), pp. 38.

46 'tant mieux si *notre* fille est bonne et aimante': H. Granjard and A. Zviguilsky, op. cit., p. 46.
47 Ibid., pp. 43, 37. 'Une petite sauvage, timide et mal élevée.'
48 Ibid., p. 37.
49 V. Hugo, *Les Misérables* (Brussels: A. Lacroix, Verboekheven, 1862), pt II, book IV, ch. 3.
50 *Cahiers Ivan Tourguéniev, Pauline Viardot, Maria Malibran* (Bougival: Association des Amis d'Ivan Tourguéniev Pauline Viardot et Maria Malibran), vol.12, pp. 63, 73.
51 A. Zviguilsky (ed.), op. cit., pp. 66, 77; *Cahiers*, op. cit., vol. 12, pp. 12, 26, 30; G. Dulong, op. cit., pp. 111, 147.
52 'Elle a un très bon coeur, la fillette, et je pense souvent à elle avec beacucoup d'affection': A. Zviguilsky (ed.), op. cit, p. 90.
53 *Cahiers*, op. cit., vol. 12, p. 28; W. Karénine, op. cit., vol. III, p. 612
54 Renard was at 14, rue Ménilmontant: A. Zviguilsky (ed.), op. cit., p. 62; H. Granjard and A. Zviguilsky, op. cit., pp. 39, 53, 68.
55 H. Granjard and A. Zviguilsky, op. cit., p. 71. Harang is also spelt Harend and Hareng. She was at 16, rue de Berlin.
56 P. Waddington, 'The Role of Courtavenel in the Life and Work of Turgenev', from *Issues in Russian Literature before 1917*, selected papers of the Third World Congress for Soviet and East European Studies (Colombus, Ohio: Slavica Publishers Inc, 1989), p. 119.
57 H. Granjard and A. Zviguilsky, op. cit., p. 82; A. Zviguilsky (ed.), op. cit., pp. 95, 97.
58 *Cahiers*, op. cit., vol. 12, pp. 28, 32, 33; G. Dulong, op. cit., p. 147.
59 A. Zviguilsky (ed.), op. cit., p. 119; D. Saunders, *Russia in the Age of Reaction and Reform* (London: Longman, 1992), p. 108; H. Granjard and A. Zviguilsky, op. cit., pp. 89, 107. L. Schapiro, *Turgenev, his Life and Times* (Oxford: OUP, 1978), p. 241.
60 P. Waddington, *PhD Thesis*, op. cit., p. 395; *Cahiers*, op. cit., vol. 12, p. 33; P. Waddington, *Turgenev and England* (London: Macmillan, 1980), p. 94; H. Troyat (trans. N. Amphoux), *Turgenev* (London: W.H. Allen, 1989), p. 81.
61 H. Granjard and A. Zviguilsky, op. cit., p. 121.
62 A. Zviguilsky (ed.), op. cit., pp. 113, 119; H. Granjard and A. Zviguilsky, op. cit., p. 106; *Cahiers*, op. cit., vol. 12, p. 38. The official was called Pinet.
63 A. Zviguilsky (ed.), op. cit., pp. 137, 138; P. Waddington, *Turgenev and England*, op. cit., p. 20; G. Dulong, op. cit., p.147. The civil ceremony was on 23 February; the church ceremony on 25 February.
64 The glassworks were established in 1798; the château was built in c. 1615 in the style of Louis XIII. Information at St Jean Froidmental church.
65 *Encyclopaedia Britannica*, ninth edition, vol. XIV, p. 809.
66 H. Granjard and A. Zviguilsky, op. cit., p. 124; *Cahiers*, op. cit., vol. 12, p. 39.
67 H. Granjard and A. Zviguilsky, op. cit., p. 124; G. Dulong, op. cit., p. 147; L. Schapiro, op. cit., p. 194.
68 This was in 1881: (trans. G. Hopkins), *Short Stories* (London: The Folio Society, 1959), p. 69. Gervaise, the heroine of Zola's *L'Assommoir*, earned up to three francs a day as a skilled laundry worker in Paris and worked hard at a five-day week. A husband (roofer) and wife earned nine francs a day between them. E. Zola (trans. M. Mauldon), *L'Assommoir* (Oxford: Oxford University Press, 1995), ch. 4, pp. 96, 108.
69 *Cahiers*, op. cit., vol. 12, p. 40.
70 H. Granjard and A. Zviguilsky, op. cit., pp. 97, 124; A. Zviguilsky (ed.), op. cit., pp. 137, 138; *Cahiers*, op. cit., vol. 12, p. 41.
71 A. Zviguilsky (ed.), op. cit., p. 137; H. Granjard and A. Zviguilsky, op. cit., pp. 144, 161; *Cahiers*, op. cit., vol. 12, pp. 40, 43, 72.
72 P. Waddington, 'Turgenev and George Eliot, a literary friendship', *Modern Language Review*, vol. 66, 1971, p. 229. A. Zviguilsky (ed.), op. cit., p. 141; H. Granjard and A. Zviguilsky, op. cit., p. 124; *Cahiers*, op. cit.,vol. 12, pp. 47–49. *Encyclopaedia Britannica*, ninth edition, vol. V, pp. 434, 438.
73 A. FitzLyon, *The Price of Genius*, op. cit., p. 38; *Cahiers*, op. cit., vol. 12, pp. 49, 50, 51.
74 L. Schapiro, op. cit., p. 133.
75 A. FitzLyon, *The Price of Genius*, op. cit., p. 453; P. Waddington, 'Turgenev's Last Will and Testament', *New Zealand Slavonic Journal*, no. 2, 1974, p. 41 et seq.
76 L. Schapiro, op. cit., p.323.
77 A. FitzLyon, *The Price of Genius*, op. cit., p. 209.

CHAPTER 15. ARREST (pp. 221–233)

1 I. Turgenev (trans. W Ralston), *Liza* (London: Chapman & Hall, 1869), vol. I, ch. 19, p. 180. This records Lavretsky's return to Vasilyevskoye. The book was written in 1858.
2 G. Dulong, *Pauline Viardot Tragédienne Lyrique* (Bougival: Association des Amis d'Ivan Tourguéniev Pauline Viardot et Maria Malibran), p. 111.
3 H. Granjard and A. Zviguilsky, *Ivan Tourgénev, Lettres inédites à Pauline Viardot et à sa famille* (Paris: Editions l'Age d'Homme, 1972), p. 49.
4 A. Zviguilsky (ed.), *Ivan Tourguénev: Nouvelle Correspondance inédite* (Paris: Librairie des Cinq Continents, 1971), p. 65.
5 Ibid., p. 65; L. Schapiro, *Turgenev, his Life and Times* (Oxford: OUP, 1978), p. 92.
6 L. Schapiro, op. cit., p. 92.
7 Ibid., p. 92
8 V.S. Pritchett, *The Gentle Barbarian, The Life and Work of Turgenev* (London: Chatto & Windus, 1977), p. 77.
9 Ibid., p. 78.
10 Ibid., p. 78; H. Granjard and A. Zviguilsky, p. 56.
11 Turgenev told this to the Goncourts on 2 March 1872: E. de Goncourt, *Journal*, Paris 1887, vol. 5, p. 24.
12 H. Troyat (trans. N. Amphoux), *Turgenev* (London: W.H. Allen, 1989), p. 43; P. Waddington, *Turgenev and England* (London: Macmillan, 1980), p. 87. Turgenev described how he kept fit in a letter to Flaubert, 24 January 1879.
13 D. Magarshack, *Turgenev, a Life* (London: Faber & Faber, 1954), p. 138.
14 V.S. Pritchett, op. cit., p. 79; D. Magarshack, op. cit., p. 140.
15 L. Schapiro, op. cit., pp. 93, 104, 107; H. Granjard and A. Zviguilsky, op. cit., p. 70; D. Magarshack, op. cit., p. 142; A. Zviguilsky (ed.), op. cit., p. 65.
16 H. Troyat, op. cit., p. 45. For large bags see L. McKinstry, *Rosebery, Statesman in Turmoil* (John Murray, 2005) pp. 127, 183.
17 H. Troyat, op. cit., p. 45; H. Granjard and A. Zviguilsky, op. cit., pp. 42, 67. Information also taken from the author's visit to Spasskoye. Although the manager had the same name as the poet with whose first wife Turgenev had had a dalliance during his studies in Berlin, they were different: L. Schapiro,op. cit., pp. 95, 381.
18 A. Seljak, *Ivan Turgenev's Ökonomien* (Zurich: University of Basel, Pano Verlag, 2004), p. 201.
19 H. Granjard and A. Zviguilsky, op. cit., p. 62; I. Turgenev (trans. Isabel Hapgood), *On the Eve* (Freeport, New York: Books for Libraries Press, 1971), ch. 5.
20 D. Magarshack, op. cit., p. 141.
21 H. Troyat, op. cit., p. 46; H. Granjard and A. Zviguilsky, op. cit., pp. 7, 8; A. Zviguilsky (ed.), op. cit., pp. 89, 237.
22 L. Tolstoy (trans. Rochelle S. Townsend), *Anna Karenina* (published 1873–6, also London: J.M. Dent Everyman edition, 1912), part II, ch. 14.
23 'From my early youth I had had a passion for chess'; I. Turgenev, *A Hapless Girl*, ch. 2, in I. Turgenev (trans. I. Hapgood), *The Brigadier and other stories* (Freeport, New York: Books for Libraries Press, 1971); H. Granjard and A. Zviguilsky, op. cit., p. 133; R. Freeborn in introduction to I. Turgenev (trans. R. Freeborn), *Rudin* (London: Penguin, 1975), p. 10.
24 L. Tolstoy, *Anna Karenina*, op. cit., part II, ch. 14.
25 L. Schapiro, op. cit., pp. 100, 109; V.S. Pritchett, op. cit., p. 84. The affair was between 1851 and 1853.
26 Information provided by Professor Patrick Waddington.
27 V.S. Pritchett, op. cit., p. 83; L. Schapiro, op. cit., p. 100. The interpretation was suggested by Professor Waddington.
28 P. Waddington, *Courtavenel, the History of an Artists' Nest and its Role in the Life of Turgenev* (*PhD Thesis*, Queen's University Belfast, The British Library, British Thesis Service, spring 1972), p. 255.
29 *Encyclopaedia Britannica*, ninth edition, vol. XX, p. 251; Ibid., vol. XVI p. 856; A. FitzLyon, *The Price of Genius, a life of Pauline Viardot* (London: John Calder, 1964), p. 295. The line was opened in 1851.
30 G. Dulong, op. cit., p. 112.
31 A. FitzLyon, *The Price of Genius*, op. cit., p.295; Magarshack, for example, questions whether this visit actually took place. G. Dulong, op. cit., p. 112 is ambivalent. L. Schapiro, op. cit., at p. 102 supports the view that the journey was made. Professor Patrick Waddington believes that there is no doubt. There is also Turgenev's letter of 21 July, when

he writes that 'nothing is impossible on this earth: witness ...' and Herzen's reference to it, see H. Granjard and A. Zviguilsky, op. cit., pp. 66, 67.

32 P. Waddington, *PhD Thesis*, op. cit., p. 255.

33 *Musical Quarterly* 1915, vol. 1, p. 530.

34 A. FitzLyon, *The Price of Genius*, op. cit., p. 300.

35 Turgenev writing about Lieutenant Yergunov: I. Turgenev (trans. I Hapgood), *The Brigadier and other stories*, op. cit., p. 44. In France, people would say that snow had fallen on his head: Musée Tourguéniev (par Tamara Zviguilsky), *Guide* (Corlet Condé-sur-Noireau, 1993), p. 44.

36 A. FitzLyon, *The Price of Genius*, op. cit., p. 300; G. Dulong, op. cit., pp. 129, 130.

37 T.J.Walsh, *Second Empire Opera* (London: Calder, 1981), p. 111.

38 G. Dulong, op. cit., p. 130.

39 *The Times Literary Supplement*, London, 8 February 2007, p. 20.

40 *Illustrated London News*, 19 May 1855, p. 495.

41 G. Dulong, op. cit., p. 130.

42 G. St Aubyn, *Queen Victoria, a Portrait* (London: Sinclair-Stevenson, 1991), p. 298; *Illustrated London News*, 19 May 1855. p. 495.

43 *Illustrated London News*, 19 May 1855; Ibid., 26 May 1855, p. 510.

44 G. Dulong, op. cit., pp. 130, 131.

45 D. Cairns, *Berlioz: Servitude and Greatness* (Penguin: London 2000), p. 586.

46 H. Seton-Watson, *The Russian Empire 1801–1917* (Oxford: Clarendon Press, 1988), p. 320; I. Turgenev, *On the Eve*, op. cit., ch. 14.

47 H. Granjard and A. Zviguilsky, op. cit., p. 69; H. Seton-Watson, op. cit., p. 326.

48 A. Zviguilsky (ed.), op. cit., p. 79.

49 J. Hannavy, 'Crimea in the Round', *History Today*, vol. 54, September 2004, pp. 40–45; H. Seton-Watson, op. cit., p. 328.

50 H. Granjard and A. Zviguilsky, op. cit., p. 62; R. Freeborn, *Turgenev, the novelist's novelist* (Oxford: Oxford University Press, 1960), pp. 38, 41; A. Zviguilsky (ed.), op. cit., p. 67.

51 R. Freeborn in introduction to I. Turgenev (trans. R. Freeborn), *Rudin* (London: Penguin, 1975), p. 12; D. Magarshack, op. cit., p. 149.

52 According to Lezhnev, in I. Turgenev (trans. R. Freeborn), *Rudin*, op. cit., ch. 6.

53 I. Turgenev (trans. R. Freeborn), *Rudin*, op. cit., ch. 6, p. 85.

54 Edward Garnett, cited in R. Freeborn, *Turgenev, the novelist's novelist* (Oxford: Oxford University Press, 1960), p. 81.

55 I. Turgenev, *Dimitri Roudine* (London: Ward Lock & Co, c. 1880), ch. 3, pp. 66, 67, 68.

56 Ibid., ch. 5, pp. 67, 76, 87.

57 Ibid., ch. 6, pp. 8, 11.

58 Ibid. ch. 9, pp. 178, 180, 184.

59 D. Magarshack, op. cit., p. 150.

60 R. Freeborn in introduction to I. Turgenev, *Rudin*, op. cit., p. 15.

61 I. Turgenev, *Rudin*, op. cit., Epilogue.

62 This took place in 1855: A. FitzLyon, *The Price of Genius*, op. cit., p. 279.

63 P. Waddington, 'Dickens, Pauline Viardot and Turgenev: a Study in Mutual Admiration', *New Zealand Slavonic Journal*, No. 2, 1974, p. 56; P. Ackroyd, *Dickens* (London: Sinclair Stevenson, 1990), p. 750.

64 P. Ackroyd, op. cit., p. 17; P. Waddington, *Dickens, Pauline Viardot and Turgenev*, op. cit., p. 56; P. Waddington, 'Turgenev and George Eliot, a literary friendship', *Modern Language Review*, vol. 66, 1971, p. 752.

65 P. Ackroyd, op. cit., pp. 64, 86, 113, 140, 163, 223, 261, 265, 267, 414, 549, 998.

66 P. Waddington, *Turgenev and England* (London: Macmillan, 1980), p. 177.

67 P. Ackroyd, op. cit., pp. 683, 784, 804–807, 836, 979, 834, 926, 950.

68 L. Héritte-Viardot (trans. E.S. Bucheim), *Memories and Adventures* (London: Mills & Boon, 1913), p. 65.

69 L. Héritte-Viardot, op. cit., p. 65; P. Ackroyd, op. cit., pp. 149, 474, 832, 948.

70 P. Ackroyd, op. cit., p. 750; C. Dickens, *The Cricket on the Hearth* (London: Chapman and Hall), 'chirp the first, second and third', pp. 82, 98, 107.

71 P. Ackroyd, op. cit., p. 485. *The Times* also called it 'the babblings of genius in its premature dotage'.

72 P. Waddington, *Dickens, Pauline Viardot and Turgenev*, op. cit., p. 57.

73 The dinner was on 10 January 1856; P. Ackroyd, op. cit., p. 236.

74 P. Ackroyd, op. cit., pp. 222, 829; J. Forster, *The Life of Charles Dickens* (London: Chapman & Hall, 1874), part III, p. 116.

75 J. Forster, op. cit., part III, p. 116; T. Marix-Spire, *Lettres inédites de George Sand et de Pauline Viardot 1839–1849* (Nouvelles Editions), p. 263;

P. Ackroyd, op. cit., pp. 222, 223. Dickens wrote on 12 January 1856.
76 J. Forster, op. cit., part III, p. 116.
77 P. Waddington, 'Some Gleanings on Turgenev and his International Connections', *New Zealand Slavonic Journal*, 1983, p. 211.
78 V.S. Pritchett, op. cit., p. 50.
79 H. Troyat, op. cit., p. 58, V.S. Pritchett, op. cit., p. 51; *Musical Quarterly*, vol. I, 1915, p. 548. Sources can be found in P. Waddington, *PhD Thesis*, op. cit., p. 312, where Waddington calls Scheffer's candidature 'preposterous'.
80 For example, Goya's portraits of the 'The Naked Maja' and 'The Clothed Maja' in the Prado. The 'Portrait of a Man' by Goya in the Museum of Fine Arts, Boston, was known at one time as a portrait of Manuel Garcia (see Plate 7).
81 *Musical Quarterly*, vol. I, 1915, p. 364.
82 Sjeng Scheijen article in National Gallery, London, *Russian Landscape, the Exhibition Guide for Russian Landscape in the Age of Tolstoy*, July 2004, p. 93. That Repin (b. August 1844) was under fourteen when Scheffer (d. June 1858) died perhaps suggests that at least there is some conflation of ideas here.
83 H. Troyat, op. cit., p. 58.
84 *Musical Quarterly* 1915, vol. I, p. 362.
85 A. FitzLyon, *The Price of Genius*, op. cit., p. 279.
86 Mrs Grote, *Memoirs of the Life of Ary Scheffer* (London: John Murray, 1860), pp. 85, 90, 91, 95; P. Mansel, *Paris between Empires 1814–1852* (London: John Murray, 2001), p. 376.
87 Mrs Grote, op. cit., p. 113; *Encyclopaedia Britannica*, ninth edition, vol. XXI, p. 389.
88 P. Waddington, *Dickens, Pauline Viardot and Turgenev*, op. cit., p. 56.

Chapter 16. Tolstoy (pp. 235–244)

1 E. de Goncourt, *Journal* (Paris: 1887), 8 February 1865; H. Seton-Watson, *The Russian Empire 1801–1917* (Oxford: Clarendon Press, 1988), pp. 327, 331.
2 V.S. Pritchett, *The Gentle Barbarian, The Life and Work of Turgenev* (London: Chatto & Windus, 1977), p. 83, assumed that the son was Turgenev's, which Professor Waddington says there are no grounds for assuming.
3 The Russian girl from Sorrento (Chouchou) – *Cahiers Ivan Tourguéniev, Pauline Viardot, Maria Malibran* (Bougival: Association des Amis d'Ivan Tourguéniev Pauline Viardot et Maria Malibran), vol. 20, pp. 37–41, E. de Goncourt, *Journal*, op. cit., vol. X, pp. 80–81.
4 Yasnaya Polyana Guide, p. 94.
5 A.N. Wilson, *Tolstoy* (London: Hamish Hamilton, 1988), p. 270.
6 H. Troyat (trans. N. Amphoux), *Turgenev* (London: W.H. Allen, 1989), p. 49; A.N. Wilson, op. cit., pp. 55, 184.
7 G. Dulong, *Pauline Viardot Tragédienne Lyrique* (Bougival: Association des Amis d'Ivan Tourguéniev Pauline Viardot et Maria Malibran), p. 114.
8 I. Turgenev, *Faust*, 3rd letter.
9 Ibid., 9th letter.
10 Ibid., 2nd letter; also introduction to I. Turgenev (trans. Hugh Aplin, Foreword by Simon Callow), *Faust and Yakov Pasynkov* (London: Hesperus Press, 2003), p. xv.
11 *Faust*, 9th letter.
12 A.N. Wilson, op. cit., pp. 188, 270; Ibid., pp. 149, 194, 270, 506. In August 1857, she announced she was coming to stay. The viscount with whom she had an affair around 1861–1862 was Victor Hector de Kleen.
13 A.N. Wilson, op. cit., pp. 291, 510, 506.
14 A.N. Wilson, op. cit., pp. 598, 510; Ibid., p. 196. Dickens also had a fraught marriage, which was terminated after 22 years and after Catherine, his wife, had borne ten children. He treated her abominably and seemed to prefer her two sisters, one dead, the other alive, and an actress, Nelly Ternan. P. Ackroyd, *Dickens* (London: Sinclair Stevenson, 1990), pp. 815, 655, 915, 938, 991, 1021.
15 A.N. Wilson, op. cit., p. 514.
16 I. Evans, *A Short History of English Literature* (Harmondsworth: Penguin, 1963), p. 182; Virginia Woolf said so: *Encyclopaedia Britannica*, Standard Millennium edition.
17 Marquis de Custine (ed. and trans. P.P. Kohler), *Journey for our Time* (London: George Prior, 1980), p. 186 (page two of 11 August).
18 Ibid., p. 186; A.N. Wilson, op. cit., pp. 15, 38.
19 A.N. Wilson, op. cit., p. 48.
20 Ibid., pp. 80, 85, 103, 105, 108, 109, 139.
21 Ibid., pp. 74, 154, 188. Recently, staff at Yasnaya Polyana did not accept that he needed the money to pay off his debts.
22 A. FitzLyon, *The Price of Genius, a life of Pauline Viardot* (London: John Calder, 1964),

p. 317. The visit about genital trouble was on 3 April 1857. Their Paris frolics were in 1857–1858.
23 A.N. Wilson, op. cit., p. 146.
24 Moscow Museum Guide, p. 31; confirmed in A. Edwards, *Sonya* (London: Hodder & Stoughton, 1981)
25 A.N. Wilson, op. cit., p. 197.
26 Levin in L. Tolstoy (trans. Rochelle S. Townsend), *Anna Karenina* (published 1873–6, also London: J.M. Dent Everyman edition, 1912), part 4, ch. 16.
27 A.N. Wilson, op. cit., p. 167.
28 V.S. Pritchett, *The Gentle Barbarian, The Life and Work of Turgenev* (London: Chatto & Windus, 1977), p. 143.
29 A.N. Wilson, op. cit., pp. 126, 167.
30 P. Waddington, *Turgenev's Mortal Illness from its Origins to the Autopsy* (Pinehaven, New Zealand: Whirinaki Press, 1999), p. 5; H. Troyat (trans. N. Amphoux), *Turgenev* (London: W.H. Allen, 1989), pp.52, 59; A.N. Wilson, op. cit., p. 147.
31 D. Magarshack, *Turgenev, a Life* (London: Faber & Faber, 1954), p. 155; A.N. Wilson, op. cit., p. 126. The St Petersburg frolic was in 1855.
32 H. Troyat, op. cit., p. 53; P. Waddington, *Turgenev and George Sand: An Improbable Entente* (Victoria University Press, 1981), p. 39; L. Schapiro, critical essay 'Spring Torrents, Its Place and Significance in the Life and Work of I.S. Turgenev' in I. Turgenev (trans. L. Schapiro), *Spring Torrents* (London: Penguin, 1980), p. 113.
33 L. Schapiro, *Turgenev, his Life and Times* (Oxford: OUP, 1978), p. 131; H. Troyat, op. cit., p. 53; D. Magarshack, op. cit., p.156; V.S. Pritchett, op. cit., p. 108. Turgenev wrote from Courtavenel in September 1856.
34 A. Zviguilsky (ed.), *Ivan Tourguénev: Nouvelle Correspondance inédite* (Paris: Librairie des Cinq Continents, 1971), p. 136; H. Troyat, op. cit., pp. 72, 176; L. Schapiro, op. cit., p. 173.
35 H. Troyat, op. cit., pp. 74, 75; V.S. Pritchett, op. cit., p.141.
36 A.N. Wilson, op. cit., p.475; H. Troyat, op. cit., pp. 87, 125; *Encyclopaedia Britannica*, Standard Millennium edition. This was in a letter dated 1/13 October 1878.
37 H. Troyat, op. cit., p. 95; L. Tolstoy (trans. L. and A. Maude), *War and Peace* (London: OUP, 1933), Book X. His heroes gradually appreciate the meaning of life, the insignificance of 'greatness', and the still greater unimportance of death, an event which no living person can understand or explain. *War and Peace*, Book XIV, ch. 14; Ibid., Book III, ch. 19; Ibid., Book IV, ch. 15.
38 A.N. Wilson, op. cit., p. 478; Yasnaya Polyana, *Guide*, pp. 50, 92; Tolstoy Museum Khamovniki, *Guide* (Moscow, 1994), p. 19.
39 Yasnaya Polyana *Guide*, pp. 35, 86; Moscow Guide, pp. 3, 22–24; A.N. Wilson, op. cit., pp. 61, 345, 481. During the author's visit, there were copies of Haydn and Beethoven duets on the piano at the Moscow museum.
40 A.N. Wilson, op. cit., p.310; Moscow Guide, p. 19.
41 A.N. Wilson, op. cit., pp. 6, 257, 348, 376, 388, 406, 430.
42 Ibid., pp. 233, 335, 422, 425, 368; Moscow Guide, p. 29; Yasnaya Polyana Guide, p. 40.
43 A.N. Wilson, op. cit., pp. 501, 507.
44 Ibid., p. 508.
45 Ibid., p. 298; H. Troyat, op. cit., p.122.
46 H. Troyat, op. cit., pp. 122, 123, 147. He stayed in 1881.
47 A.N. Wilson, op. cit., p. 298; H. Troyat, op. cit., p. 147; V.S. Pritchett, op. cit., p. 228.
48 H. Troyat, op. cit., p. 73.
49 Ibid., p. 151; A.N. Wilson, op. cit., p. 336.

Chapter 17. Reunion? (pp. 245–260)

1 A. Zviguilsky (ed.), *Ivan Tourguénev: Nouvelle Correspondance inédite* (Paris: Librairie des Cinq Continents, 1971), pp. 81, 83.
2 *The Times*, 6 March 1856. The fire was on Wednesday 5 March 1856.
3 V.S. Pritchett, *The Gentle Barbarian, The Life and Work of Turgenev* (London: Chatto & Windus, 1977), p. 108.
4 M. Mainwaring (ed.), *Ivan Turgenev, the Portrait Game* (London: Chatto and Windus, 1973), pp. 12, 18; V.S. Pritchett, op. cit., p. 109; *Turgenev, his Life and Times* (Oxford: OUP, 1978), p. 128; P. Waddington, 'The strange history of Dr F. and the dismantling of Courtavenel', *Modern Language Review*, vol. 65, 1970, p. 338.
5 D. Magarshack, *Turgenev, a Life* (London: Faber & Faber, 1954), p. 164. This was according to Fet.
6 G. Dulong, *Pauline Viardot Tragédienne*

Lyrique (Bougival: Association des Amis d'Ivan Tourguéniev, Pauline Viardot et Maria Malibran), pp. 114, 115.
7 A. FitzLyon, *The Price of Genius, a life of Pauline Viardot* (London: John Calder, 1964), p. 312 (according to his friend the poet and essayist Polonsky).
8 G. Dulong, op. cit., p.114; D. Magarshack, op. cit., p.166.
9 P. Waddington, 'The Role of Courtavenel in the Life and Work of Turgenev', from *Issues in Russian Literature before 1917*, selected papers of the Third World Congress for Soviet and East European Studies (Colombus, Ohio: Slavica Publishers Inc, 1989), p. 120.
10 This was in May 1857.
11 H. Granjard and A. Zviguilsky, *Ivan Tourgénev, Lettres inédites à Pauline Viardot et à sa famille* (Paris: Editions l'Age d'Homme, 1972), p. 75; A. Zviguilsky (ed.), op. cit., p. 87; H. Troyat (trans. N. Amphoux), *Turgenev* (London: W.H. Allen, 1989), p. 60.
12 P. Ackroyd, *Dickens* (London: Sinclair Stevenson, 1990), p. 301.
13 J. Morrow, *Thomas Carlyle* (London: Hambledon, 2006), p. 149.
14 A. Zviguilsky (ed.), op. cit., p. 83; P. Waddington, *Turgenev and England* (London: Macmillan, 1980), p. 46. The clergyman was The Rev. Charles Merivale, later Dean of Ely; the Vienna-Constantinople journey was done by George John Shaw-Lefevre.
15 Information based on Palace of Westminster and Big Ben websites.
16 P. Ackroyd, op. cit. p. 202.
17 A. Zviguilsky (ed.), op. cit., p. 87; *Hansard*, 9 June 1857, p. 1454. Palmerston, being an Irish Peer, sat in the Commons.
18 A. Zviguilsky (ed.), op. cit., p. 87.
19 The *Illustrated London News* of 23 May 1857 refers to the mutiny by the native troops in India, but a leader only appeared on 4 July (p. 1), and in *The Times* on 29 June (which referred to the details of the Indian Mutiny having come by telegraph, and 'it was less alarming than was originally thought'. The Meerut mutiny began on 10 May; Lucknow began on 30 May and Cawnpore on 4 June). Lord Granville replied to Ellenborough, a former Governor-General, about telegraphic information. *Hansard*, 9 June 1857, p. 1398.
20 'Un peu trop calme et gentleman pour un artiste': H. Granjard and A. Zviguilsky, op. cit., pp. 74., 75; *The New Oxford Companion to Music* (Oxford: Oxford University Press, 1984), p. 1858.
21 *Dictionary of National Biography 2004*, vol. 55, p. 323 (G Boase, D Washbrook).
22 A. Zviguilsky (ed.), op. cit., pp. 85, 86; C. Woodham-Smith, *The Great Hunger* (London: First Four Square Edition, 1994), pp.53, 411. The revelations were in May 1857: *Encyclopaedia Britannica*, Standard Millennium edition.
23 C. Woodham Smith, op. cit., pp. 53, 411; *Dictionary of National Biography 2004*, vol. 55, p. 323.
24 C. Woodham-Smith, op. cit., p. 54.
25 A. Zviguilsky (ed.), op. cit., vol. I, p. 86. 'Cathédrale admirable, une des plus belles que j'ai vues – une pureté de lignes admirable'.
26 Ibid., vol. I, p. 86.
27 *Encyclopaedia Britannica*, Standard Millennium edition. However, in P. Waddington, *A Modest Little Banquet at the Arts Club* (Pinehaven, New Zealand, 2001), p. 27, it is suggested that Turgenev had read no Trollope.
28 C. Woodham-Smith, op. cit., p. 53; A. Zviguilsky (ed.), op. cit., p. 85.
29 A. Zviguilsky (ed.), op. cit., vol. I, p. 86; I. Turgenev (ed. E. Halpérine-Kaminsky), *Lettres à Madame Viardot* (Paris: Bibliothèque-Charpentier, 1907), 4 July 1849 et seq., pp. 87, 99, 107.
30 H. Troyat, op. cit., p. 60.
31 Quoted in I. Turgenev (trans. R.Freeborn), *First Love and other stories* (Oxford: OUP 1999), intro p. 16.
32 I. Turgenev, *Asya* (in *First Love and other stories*, op. cit.), ch. 1, ch. 4; D. Magarshack,op. cit., p. 172.
33 I. Turgenev, *Asya*, op. cit., ch. 8, ch. 14.
34 I. Turgenev (trans. I. and T. Litvinov), *Three Short Novels* (Moscow: Foreign Language Publishing House, no date but around 1980), p. 38.
35 I. Turgenev, *Asya*, op. cit., ch. 3, c. 4.
36 Ibid., ch. 12, 21, 22.
37 I. Turgenev, *Three Short Novels*, op. cit., p. 64.
38 I. Turgenev, *First Love and other stories*, op. cit., introduction by Richard Freeborn, p. 17.
39 *Encyclopaedia Britannica*, Standard Millennium edition; R. Freeborn, *Turgenev, the novelist's novelist* (Oxford: Oxford University Press, 1960), pp. 98, 99.

40 R. Freeborn, *Turgenev, the novelist's novelist*, op. cit., p. 3.
41 Introduction to *Asya*, p. 17 in I. Turgenev, *First Love and other stories*, op. cit.
42 Introduction to *Asya*, p. 16 in I. Turgenev, *First Love and other stories*, op. cit; D. Magarshack, op. cit., p. 201.
43 H. Granjard and A. Zviguilsky, op. cit., pp. 75, 76; V.S. Pritchett, op. cit., p. 114.
44 P. Ackroyd, op. cit., p. 677.
45 This was in October 1857, G. Dulong, op. cit., p. 115; A. Zviguilsky (ed.), op. cit., p. 90.
46 'La créature la plus ravissante que nous ayons jamais vue': H. Granjard and A. Zviguilsky, op. cit., p. 77.
47 G. Dulong, op. cit., p. 115.
48 A. Zviguilsky (ed.), op. cit., p. 93.
49 *Musical Quarterly* 1915, vol. I, p. 532; *Musical Quarterly* 1915, vol. I, pp. 532, 542. She referred to 'Travail de nègre', and 'Mon métier de nègre'. This was in January 1859.
50 L. Héritte-Viardot (trans. E.S. Bucheim), *Memories and Adventures* (London: Mills & Boon, 1913); A. FitzLyon, *The Price of Genius*, op. cit., p. 341; *Musical Quarterly* 1915, vol. I, p. 550.
51 G. Dulong, op. cit., p. 133.
52 C. Santley, *Reminscences of my Life* (London: Pitman, 1909), p. 302.
53 *Musical Quarterly* 1915, vol. I, p. 550; G. Dulong, op. cit., p. 132; H.F. Chorley (ed. E. Newman), *Thirty years' Musical Recollections* (New York: Alfred Knopf, 1926), p. 395.
54 *Musical Quarterly* 1915, vol. I, pp. 540, 550; L. Héritte-Viardot, op. cit., p. 97.
55 *Musical Quarterly* 1915, vol. I, p. 550.
56 L. Héritte-Viardot, op. cit., pp. 95, 103.
57 *New Grove Dictionary of Music and Musicians* (London: Macmillan, 1980), vol. 13, p. 431, Nourrit (P. Sand).
58 P. Waddington, *Courtavenel, the History of an Artists' Nest and its Role in the Life of Turgenev* (*PhD Thesis*, Queen's University Belfast, The British Library, British Thesis Service, spring 1972), p. 48.
59 Chekhov, *The Seagull*, Act I, in A. Chekhov (trans. C. Garnett), *The Cherry Orchard and Other Plays* (London: Chatto and Windus, 1935).
60 A. Walker, *Franz Liszt, Vol 1, The Virtuoso Years 1811–47* (London: Faber and Faber, 1983), pp. 157, 167.
61 T. Marix-Spire, *Lettres inédites de George Sand et de Pauline Viardot 1839–1849* (Nouvelles Editions), pp. 18, 43; Sand saw her as 'la prêtresse de l'idéal en musique et vous avez pour mission de le répandre (to be an evangelist)'.
62 G. Sand (trans. Fayette Robinson), *Consuelo* (New York: Stringer and Townsend, 1851), ch. 55, p. 118. (It is disadvantageous that Sand chooses to attribute these important and deep thoughts to Albert who is such an improbable character in the novel.)
63 G. Sand, *Consuelo*, op. cit., ch. 55, p. 118.
64 G. Flaubert, *Sentimental Education*, part 1, ch. 4.
65 I. Turgenev (trans. E. Schimanskaya), *Poems in Prose* (London: Lindsay Drummond, 1945), p. 62.
66 *New Grove*, op. cit., vol. 14, Pasta (Elizabeth Forbes), p. 287
67 W. Kuhe, *My musical recollections* (London: Richard Bentley, 1896), p. 115; 'Its state of utter ruin on the night in question passes description', according to Chorley. H.G. Hewlett, *Memoirs of Henry Fothergill Chorley* (London: Richard Bentley and Son, 1873), vol. II, pp. 207, 208.
68 'D'une part, cela a été un repos pour mon coeur un peu fatigué de l'expression d'un amour qu'il ne peut partager, et de l'autre l'absence ne fait que fortifier mon amitié, mon estime et mon grand respect pour cet homme si noble et si dévoué qui donnerait sa vie pour satisfaire le moindre de mes caprices, si j'en avais.' *Musical Quarterly* 1915, p. 548.
69 Six leagues = twenty miles approx. *Musical Quarterly* 1915, vol. I, p. 550.
70 P. Waddington, 'Dickens, Pauline Viardot and Turgenev: a Study in Mutual Admiration', *New Zealand Slavonic Journal*, No. 2, 1974, p. 63.
71 A. Williams, *Franz Liszt, selected letters* (Oxford: Clarendon Press, 1998), p. 471; A. FitzLyon, *The Price of Genius*, op. cit., p. 337; *Musical Quarterly*, vol. I, 1915, pp. 358, 360.
72 *Musical Quarterly*, vol. I, 1915, pp. 364, 366, 544.
73 A. FitzLyon, *The Price of Genius*, op. cit, pp. 154, 164, 325; P. Waddington, *PhD Thesis*, op. cit., p. 333.
74 A. FitzLyon, *The Price of Genius*, op. cit., p. 327.
75 P. Waddington, *PhD Thesis*, op. cit., p. 333; P. Waddington, *The Role of Courtavenel in the*

Life and Work of Turgenev, op. cit., p. 124.
76 J. Chissell, *Schumann* (London: J.M. Dent, 1977), pp. 67, 69; *New Grove*, op. cit., vol. 16, pp. 12, 13, Rietz (A. Mell).
77 *Musical Quarterly*, vol. I, 1915, pp. 354, 532. The cantata was 'Vom grossen Alten'.
78 *Musical Quarterly*, vol. I, 1915, pp. 526, 530, 540; A. FitzLyon, *The Price of Genius*, op. cit., p. 329.
79 'Ich liebe Sie mit der innigsten, tiefsten, wahrsten, warmsten, sonnenhellsten Liebe, die eine Freundin für ihren Freund je empfunden hat.' Note the use of Sie rather than Dich. *Musical Quarterly*, vol. I, 1915, p. 536.
80 H. Granjard and A. Zviguilsky, op. cit., p. 71; A. Zviguilsky (ed.), op. cit., p. 131; *Musical Quarterly*, vol. I, 1915, p. 58.
81 H. Granjard and A. Zviguilsky, op. cit., pp. 81, 83.
82 L. Schapiro, *Turgenev, his Life and Times* (Oxford: OUP, 1978), p. 144; A. FitzLyon, *The Price of Genius*, op. cit., pp. 331, 356; H. Troyat, op. cit., p. 54.
83 H. Granjard and A. Zviguilsky, op. cit., pp. 81, 83.
84 D. Magarshack, op. cit., p. 172; H. Granjard and A. Zviguilsky, op. cit., p. 77; L. Héritte-Viardot, op. cit., p. 77.
85 'L'épanouissement de l'être': the story, told on 2 March 1872, comes from E. de Goncourt, *Journal*, Paris 1891, vol. 5, p. 26.
86 V.S Pritchett, op. cit., p. 117.
87 G. Dulong, op. cit., p. 115; H. Granjard and A. Zviguilsky, op. cit., pp. xvi, 80, 88; H. Troyat, op. cit., p. 63.
88 A. FitzLyon, *The Price of Genius*, op. cit., p. 343.

Chapter 18. Consummation? (pp. 261–280)

1 V.S. Pritchett, *The Gentle Barbarian, The Life and Work of Turgenev* (London: Chatto & Windus, 1977), p. 112; Mr Kyril FitzLyon told the author that the rift completely split the family.
2 H. Granjard and A. Zviguilsky, *Ivan Tourgénev, Lettres inédites à Pauline Viardot et à sa famille* (Paris: Editions l'Age d'Homme, 1972), pp. 42, 159, 194.
3 He told this to Nekrasov, in Spring 1857: L. Schapiro, *Turgenev, his Life and Times* (Oxford: OUP, 1978), p. 129.
4 He wrote this on 3/15 January 1857: A. FitzLyon, *The Price of Genius, a life of Pauline Viardot* (London: John Calder, 1964), p. 320.
5 Written on 9/21 July 1850, 'Il ne se passe pas de nuit que je ne vous voie en rêve': A. Zviguilsky (ed.), *Ivan Tourguénev: Nouvelle Correspondance inédite* (Paris: Librairie des Cinq Continents, 1971), pp. 51, 69.
6 The locket is in the Museum at Bougival.
7 'Three Encounters' from I. Turgenev (ed. D. Borovsky), *Stories in Poems and Prose* (Moscow: Progress Publishers, 1982), p. 26.
8 A. Zviguilsky (ed.), op. cit., p. 54.
9 L. Schapiro, op. cit., p. 122; A. Zviguilsky (ed.), op. cit., pp. 32, 347; A. FitzLyon, *The Price of Genius*, op. cit., p. 250.
10 A. Pushkin (trans. C. Johnston, Preface J. Bayley, Notes M. Basker) *Eugene Onegin* (London: Penguin, 2003), ch. 1, xxxii; V. Hugo, *Les Misérables*, part III, book 2, ch. 8; 'Homer', *History Today*, vol. 55, 3 March 2005, p. 29.
11 I. Goncharov (trans. D. Magarshack), *Oblomov* (London: Penguin, 1954), pt IV, ch. 1; G. Flaubert, *L'Education Sentimentale* (Paris: Flammarion, 1985), pt I, ch. 5.
12 I. Goncharov, *Oblomov*, op. cit., p. 259.
13 There are countless references; see J. Harding, *Saint-Saëns and his Circle* (London: Chapman & Hall, 1965), p. 57; J. Harding, *Gounod* (London: George Allen & Unwin Ltd, 1973), pp. 61, 63; B. Thompson, *A Monkey among Crocodiles* (London: HarperCollins, 2000), p. 101; article by Sjeng Scheijen in The National Gallery, London, *Russian Landscape, the Exhibition Guide for Russian Landscape in the Age of Tolstoy*, July 2004, p. 93.
14 This is a point which has been emphasised to the author by Professor Patrick Waddington.
15 A. FitzLyon, *The Price of Genius*, op. cit., p. 208. L. Schapiro, *Turgenev, his Life and Times* (Oxford: OUP, 1978), p. 43.
16 A. FitzLyon, *The Price of Genius*, op. cit., p. 277.
17 Ibid., p. 277; D. Magarshack, *Turgenev, a Life* (London: Faber & Faber, 1954), p. 117.
18 I. Turgenev (ed. E. Halpérine-Kaminsky), *Lettres à Madame Viardot* (Paris: Bibliothèque-Charpentier, 1907), 13 August 1849, p. 119.
19 I. Turgenev (ed. D. Borovsky), *Three Encounters* from *Stories in Poems and Prose*

(Moscow: Progress Publishers, 1982), p. 29. According to P. Waddington, 'Two Months in the Country', *New Zealand Slavonic Journal*, no. 11, winter 1973, on 12 August 1849 Turgenev himself had a similar dream.

20 H. Troyat (trans. N. Amphoux), *Turgenev* (London: W.H. Allen, 1989), p. 56; G. Dulong, *Pauline Viardot Tragédienne Lyrique* (Bougival: Association des Amis d'Ivan Tourguéniev Pauline Viardot et Maria Malibran), p. 113; P. Waddington, 'Turgenev's relations with H.F. Chorley', *New Zealand Slavonic Journal*, no. 2, 1978, p. 28; A. FitzLyon, *The Price of Genius*, op. cit., p. 313.

21 L. Schapiro, op. cit., p. 147; I. Turgenev, *Lettres à Madame Viardot*, op. cit., 28 July 1849, p. 113.

22 D. Magarshack, *Turgenev, a Life* (London: Faber & Faber, 1954), p.171.

23 From *Asya* in I. Turgenev (trans. R. Freeborn), *First Love and other stories* (Oxford: OUP 1999), p. 107.

24 I. Turgenev (trans. I. and T. Litvinov), *Three Short Novels* (Moscow: Foreign Language Publishing House, no date but around 1980), p. 10.

25 This was written in January 1859: *Musical Quarterly*, vol. I, 1915, p. 532.

26 *Musical Quarterly*, vol. I, 1915, p. 548; T. Marix-Spire, *Lettres inédites de George Sand et de Pauline Viardot 1839–1849* (Nouvelles Editions), p. 225.

27 I. Turgenev (trans. Isabel Hapgood), *On the Eve* (Freeport, New York: Books for Libraries Press, 1971), ch. 27, p. 205.

28 Letter to Countess Lambert from Paris: A. FitzLyon, *The Price of Genius*, op. cit., p. 364.

29 L. Schapiro, op. cit., p. 192.

30 P. Mansel, *Paris between Empires 1814–1852* (London: John Murray, 2001), p. 46; R.A. Nye, 'Sex and sexuality in France since 1800', in *Sexual Cultures in Europe* (ed. F.X. Eder), p. 100; E.. Zola (trans. M. Mauldon), *L'Assommoir* (Oxford: Oxford University Press, 1995), ch. 1.

31 C. Jones, *The Cambridge Illustrated History of France* (Cambridge: Cambridge University Press, 1994), p. 240; R.A. Nye, op. cit., p. 94.

32 *Musical Quarterly*, vol. I, 1915, p. 532; also see *Consuelo*, who was only Bohemian by profession and 'as a manner of speaking'. She was Spanish, with a tinge of the Moresco: N. Savy (ed.), *George Sand: Consuelo, La Comtesse de Rudolstadt* (Paris: Editions Robert Laffont SA, 2004), pp. 36, 38.

33 S. Rutherford, *The Prima Donna and Opera 1815–1930* (Cambridge: Cambridge University Press, 2006), p. 42.

34 The figures are for 1840; P. McPhee, *A Social History of France 1780–1880* (London: Routledge, 1992), p. 202; Fantine's experience of 'the desperate alternative of starving to death or a life of vice' is referred to in E. Zola, Rentafoil from E. Zola (trans. and intro. D. Parmée), *The Attack on the Mill and other stories* (Oxford: Oxford University Press, 1984).

35 Figures for 1816–1831: P. McPhee, op. cit., pp. 142, 202; J. Richardson, *The Courtesans – the demi-monde in 19th century France* (London: Weidenfeld & Nicolson, 1967); E. Zola: *L'Assommoir*, op. cit., ch. 8, p. 238; G. de Maupassant (trans. G. Hopkins), *The Sign*, in *Short Stories* (London: The Folio Society, 1959), p. 208; A. Horne, *The Fall of Paris* (London: Macmillan, 1965), p.19.

36 J. Richardson, op. cit., pp. 1, 166.

37 G. Wall, *Flaubert, a Life* (London: Faber and Faber, 2001), p. 74.

38 *Encyclopaedia Britannica*, Standard Millennium edition.

39 R.A. Nye, op. cit., p. 91.

40 G. de Maupassant (trans. G. Hopkins), 'The Sign', in *Short Stories* (London: The Folio Society, 1959), p. 205.

41 G. de Maupassant, *An Adventure in Paris*, in *Short Stories*, op. cit., pp. 82, 83.

42 G. Flaubert, *Madame Bovary* (Oxford: Oxford University Press, 2004), pt III. ch. 6, p. 251: 'Elle se promettait continuellement, pour son prochain voyage, une félicité profonde; puis elle s'avouait ne rien sentir d'extraordinaire ... Elle se déshabillait brutalement, arrachant le lacet mince de son corset, qui sifflait autour de ses hanches comme une couleuvre qui glisse.'

43 L. Tolstoy (trans. Rochelle S. Townsend), *Anna Karenina* (published 1873–6, also London: J.M. Dent Everyman edition, 1912), pt II, ch. 27. The drawing-room could be used: see G. de Maupassant, *The Sign*, in *Short Stories*, op. cit., p. 207.

44 *The Times Literary Supplement*, London, 15 April 2005.

45 C. Hibbert, *Edward VII* (London: Allen Lane, 1976), p. 89; A. Leslie, *Edwardians in Love* (London: Arrow Books, 1972), p.16.

46 See also H. Granjard and A. Zviguilsky, op. cit., p. 155; young girls believe it is the beginning of the end.
47 *Black's Medical Dictionary*, (London: A&C Black, 1999), p. 455; see desciption of this for lower classes in E. & J. Goncourt, *Germinie Lacerteux*, ch. 20; L. Tolstoy, *Anna Karenina*, pt IV, ch. 17.
48 *Black's Medical Dictionary*, op. cit., 'Safe Period', pp. 479, 117.
49 G. Wall, op. cit., p. 207; F. Lestringant, *Alfred de Musset* (Paris: Flammarion, 1999), p. 321.
50 A. McLaren, *A History of Contraception* (Oxford: Blackwell, 1990), pp. 157, 158, 184.
51 J.H. Palmer, *Individual, Family and National Poverty* (London: E. Truelove, 1875), pp. 15, 16.
52 A. McLaren, op. cit., p. 184.
53 Ibid., p. 157; P. Waddington, *Courtavenel, the History of an Artists' Nest and its Role in the Life of Turgenev* (*PhD Thesis*, Queen's University Belfast, The British Library, British Thesis Service, spring 1972), p. 292; G. Dulong, op. cit., p. 95; F. Dostoyevsky (trans. D. McDuff), *Crime and Punishment* (London: Penguin, 2003) passim.
54 'There is no shortage of the easy virtues in Africa – the place swarms with them.' *Marocca* (set in Algeria), in G. de Maupassant, *Short Stories*, op. cit., p. 141.
55 P. Waddington, 'Turgenev and Gounod, Rival Strangers in the Viardots' Country Nest', *New Zealand Slavonic Journal*, no. 1, 1976, pp. 12, 19; P. Waddington, *Turgenev's Mortal Illness from its Origins to the Autopsy* (Pinehaven, New Zealand: Whirinaki Press, 1999), pp. 5, 68; D. Magarshack, op. cit., p. 158.
56 O. Friedrich, *Olympia – Paris in the Age of Manet* (London: Aurum Press, 1992), p. 281; *Black's Medical Dictionary*, op. cit., p. 532; Emma Hardy's health is described in *Times Literary Supplement*, 8 December 2006, p. 12, with cautionary comment thereon in subsequent letters, 15 December 2006, p. 17 etc.; E. de Goncourt, *Journal* (Paris, 1887), pt II, ch. 117.
57 O. Friedrich, op. cit., p. 282.
58 G. Flaubert (trans. A. Krailsheimer), *Bouvard et Pécuchet* (Harmondsworth: Penguin, 1976), at end of ch. 7; 'L'enfer sous un jupon'.
59 *In the Spring* (written in 1881), in G de Maupassant, *The Complete Short Stories* (London: Cassell, 1970), vol. I, p. 225; G. de Maupassant (trans. G. Hopkins), *In the Spring*, in *Short Stories* (London: The Folio Society, 1959), p, 90.
60 R.A. Nye, op. cit., p. 99; E. Zola (trans. D. Parmée), *Nana* (Oxford: Oxford University Press, 1998), ch. 13.
61 It was used in thirteen marriages per 1000, McPhee, op. cit., p. 208.
62 P. McPhee, op. cit., pp. 65, 96, 213, 266, 278. The riot was in 1879.
63 L. Tolstoy (trans. Rochelle S. Townsend), *Anna Karenina* (published 1873–6, also London: J.M. Dent Everyman edition, 1912), pt 2, ch. xi, p. 145.
64 L. Tolstoy, *Anna Karenina*, op. cit., pt II, ch. 11, p. 165. (Turgenev thoroughly disliked Anna Karenina: *Cahiers Ivan Tourguéniev, Pauline Viardot, Maria Malibran* (Bougival : Association des Amis d'Ivan Tourguéniev Pauline Viardot et Maria Malibran), no. 2, p. 32; one may wonder why.)
65 L. Tolstoy, *Anna Karenina*, op. cit., pt II, ch. 27; pt IV, ch. 3; pt V, ch. 27; pt VII, ch. 28.
66 G. de Maupassant (trans. G. Hopkins), *An Adventure in Paris*, in *Short Stories* (London: The Folio Society, 1959), p. 88.
67 G. de Maupassant, *The Story of a Farm Girl*, in *The Complete Short Stories* (London: Cassell, 1970), vol. I, p. 93.
68 L. Schapiro, op. cit., p. 100.
69 Comtesse Merlin, *Maria Malibran* (London: Henry Colburn, 1840), pp. 98, 149.
70 G. Dulong, op. cit., p. 88.
71 S. Rutherford, *The Prima Donna and Opera 1815–1930* (Cambridge: Cambridge University Press, 2006), p. 194. Verdi's wife was Giuseppina Strepponi.
72 P. Waddington, *PhD Thesis*, op. cit., p.47; Pauline's lecture to Clara, *Cahiers*, op. cit., vol. 20, pp. 136, 137 (Borchard).
73 P. Waddington, 'Turgenev and Pauline Viardot, An Unofficial Marriage', *Canadian Slavonic Papers*, vol. XXVI, no. 1, March 1984, p. 51; G. Dulong, op. cit., pp. 47, 95.
74 Rietz letters, op. cit., p. 548.
75 H. James, Jr, *The Portrait of a Lady* (London: Penguin Classics, 2000), p. 549.
76 F. Lestringant, *Alfred de Musset* (Paris: Flammarion, 1999), pp. 400, 403.
77 G. Sand, *Correspondance* (Paris: Editions de Georges Lubin, Editions Garnier Frères, 1969), Tome VI, 1843 – Juin 1845, letter of 17 September 1843, number 2708.

78 N. Savy (ed.), *George Sand: Consuelo, La Comtesse de Rudolstadt* (Paris: Editions Robert Laffont SA, 2004), p. 100; A. FitzLyon, *Maria Malibran – Diva of the Romantic Age* (London: Souvenir Press, 1987), p. 139.
79 'Hat Festigkeit und Ausdauer meinem schwungvollen Herz gegeben': *Musical Quarterly*, vol. I, 1915, p. 374.
80 P. Waddington, *PhD Thesis*, op. cit., p. 207.
81 Ibid., pp. 30, 333; A. FitzLyon, op. cit., p. 164.
82 P. Waddington, *A Modest Little Banquet at the Arts Club* (Pinehaven, New Zealand, 2001), p.14; T. Marix-Spire, *Lettres inédites de George Sand*, op. cit., p. 349; G. Dulong, op. cit., p. 148.
83 The friend was Botkin: P. Waddington, *PhD Thesis*, op. cit., p. 306.
84 A. Zviguilsky (ed.), op. cit., p. 126; see also loan of 400 francs in 1849: P. Waddington, *PhD Thesis*, op. cit., p. 139, and 500 francs in 1850: Ibid., p.154.
85 P. Waddington, 'Turgenev's Last Will and Testament', *New Zealand Slavonic Journal*, no. 2, 1974, p. 39.
86 P. Waddington, *PhD Thesis*, op. cit., p. 165.
87 P. Waddington, 'The Role of Courtavenel in the Life and Work of Turgenev', from *Issues in Russian Literature before 1917*, selected papers of the Third World Congress for Soviet and East European Studies (Colombus, Ohio: Slavica Publishers Inc, 1989), p. 108.
88 23 January/4 February: A. Zviguilsky (ed.), op. cit., vol. II, p. 113.
89 G. de Maupassant (trans. G. Hopkins), *One Evening*, in *Short Stories* (London: The Folio Society, 1959), p. 263.
90 G. Dulong, op. cit., p. 152; A. Zviguilsky (ed.), op. cit., p. 192.
91 P. Waddington, 'Two Months in the Country', *New Zealand Slavonic Journal*, no 11, winter 1973, p. 37.
92 I. Turgenev (trans. Richard Freeborn), *Sketches from a Hunter's Album* (London: Penguin, 1967 and 1990), *The Meeting*, p. 266.
93 P. Waddington, 'Turgenev's relations with H.F. Chorley', *New Zealand Slavonic Journal*, no. 2, 1978, p. 27; I. Turgenev (ed. E. Halpérine-Kaminsky), *Lettres à Madame Viardot* (Paris: Bibliothèque-Charpentier, 1907), p. 72 et seq.
94 P. Waddington, *Turgenev and Pauline Viardot, An Unofficial Marriage*, op. cit., p. 49; the suggested date, 1852, comes from Professor Waddington.
95 P. Waddington, *PhD Thesis*, op. cit., p. 41.
96 L. Schapiro, op. cit., p. 286.
97 P. Waddington, 'Two Months in the Country', op. cit., p. 36; Turgenev and trees: I. Turgenev, *Lettres à Madame Viardot*, op. cit., 14 July 1849, p. 108.
98 R. Jenkins, *Gladstone* (London: Macmillan, 1995), p. 107. P. Ackroyd, *Dickens* (London: Sinclair Stevenson, 1990), pp. 587, 727.
99 P. Waddington, *Turgenev and Pauline Viardot, An Unofficial Marriage*, op. cit., p. 62; see also H. James, Jr, *The Portrait of a Lady*, op. cit., p. 502, which provides a good example of the use of the phrase 'making love' in the 19th century.
100 P. Waddington, *PhD Thesis*, op. cit., p. 87: Maurice was at Courtavenel until around 16 June, and Pauline arrived in London. Pauline had arrived in London by 11 July per *The Times.*
101 A. Zviguilsky (ed.), op. cit., p. 347; H. Granjard and A. Zviguilsky, op. cit., p. 30; P. Waddington, *Turgenev and Pauline Viardot, An Unofficial Marriage*, op. cit., p. 62; I. Turgenev, *Lettres à Madame Viardot*, op. cit. (16 August 1849), p. 123.
102 R. Freeborn in introduction to I. Turgenev (trans. R. Freeborn), *First Love and other stories* (Oxford: OUP 1999), p. 14.
103 Ibid., p. 33.
104 A.N. Wilson, *Tolstoy* (London: Hamish Hamilton, 1988), p. 139.
105 The words of Vronsky, in L. Tolstoy (trans. Rochelle S. Townsend), *Anna Karenina* (published 1873–6, also London: J.M. Dent Everyman edition, 1912), pt 1, ch. xvii, p. 59; see also E. Zola (trans. and intro. R. Buss), *Thérèse Raquin* (Penguin, 2004; also Paris: Bibliothèque Charpentier, 1890), pp. 35, 39, 41.
106 L. Schapiro, critical essay 'Spring Torrents, Its Place and Significance in the Life and Work of I.S. Turgenev' in I. Turgenev (trans. L. Schapiro), *Spring Torrents* (London: Penguin, 1980), p. 201.
107 A. FitzLyon, *The Price of Genius*, op. cit., pp. 250, 251, 252; L. Schapiro, critical essay on *Spring Torrents*, op. cit., p. 199, 214. FitzLyon heard Turgenev's view of sex from a Baron, who

heard it from a Princess, who heard it from Turgenev (according to Kyril FitzLyon).

108 I. Turgenev, *Smoke*, ch. 17; R. Freeborn, *Turgenev, the novelist's novelist* (Oxford: Oxford University Press, 1960), p. 44; I. Turgenev (trans. and intro. by Isaiah Berlin), *A Month in the Country* (London: Penguin, 1981), appendix, p. 127.

109 *Cahiers*, op. cit., vol. 2, p. 33.

110 Regarding paternity, see A. FitzLyon, *The Price of Genius*, op. cit., p. 314.

111 G. Dulong, op. cit., p. 88 et seq, 109; D. Magarshack, op. cit., pp. 172, 173. Schapiro regards it as 'extremely implausible': L. Schapiro, op. cit., p. 130.

112 A. Zviguilsky (ed.), op. cit., vol. I, p. 88; vol. II, p. 16.

113 Professor Patrick Waddington's suggestion.

114 A. FitzLyon, *The Price of Genius*, op. cit., pp. 319, 321.

115 G. Dulong, op. cit., p. 88; D. Magarshack, op. cit., p. 171; A. FitzLyon, *The Price of Genius*, op. cit., p. 316.

116 The comment was made in 1867: P. Waddington, *Turgenev and Pauline Viardot, An Unofficial Marriage*, op. cit., p. 52.

117 Ibid., p. 49.

118 L. Tolstoy, *Anna Karenina*, op. cit., pt IV, ch. 12, p. 419.

119 H. Granjard and A. Zviguilsky, op. cit., p. xxix; A. Zviguilsky (ed.), op. cit., p. 140.

120 'Ich kann sogar ein Liebesverhältnis der Art hochschätzen und 100 mal der heuchlerischen Tugend einer ungetreuen Gattin vorziehen', *Musical Quarterly*, vol. I, 1915, p. 363.

121 'Il n'y avait pas d'amitié': From Dublin, 20 February 1859: Ibid., p. 540. 'Celle là est une passion qui ne peut pas décroître. C'est la plus belle de toutes.'

122 R. Freeborn, op. cit., p. 12.

123 H. Troyat, op. cit., p. 97.

124 For example, Paul suggests that Dickens was one of the visitors to the Viardots' London residence in 1870–1871. Dickens had died on 9 June 1870 in his home, Gad's Hill, near Chatham, before the Viardots moved to England.

125 E. Zola, *Thérèse Raquin* (Paris: Bibliotheque Charpentier, 1890), ch. v, ch. vii.

126 E. de Goncourt, *Journal* (Paris, 1887), 28 February 1882.

127 I. Turgenev (trans. Isabel Hapgood), *First Love and other stories* (New York: Charles Scribner's Sons, 1923), *Phantoms*, p. 24.

128 Ibid., *Phantoms*, p. 25.

129 R. Freeborn, op. cit., p. 12.

Chapter 19. Turgenev Triumphant (pp. 281–290)

1 I. Turgenev (trans. Isabel Hapgood), *On the Eve* (Freeport, New York: Books for Libraries Press, 1971), ch. 27.

2 D. Magarshack, *Turgenev, a Life* (London: Faber & Faber, 1954), p. 187; H. Granjard and A. Zviguilsky, *Ivan Tourgénev, Lettres inédites à Pauline Viardot et à sa famille* (Paris: Editions l'Age d'Homme, 1972), pp. 84, 90; A. Seljak, *Ivan Turgenev's Ökonomien* (Zurich: University of Basel, Pano Verlag, 2004), p. 492; R. Freeborn, *Turgenev, the novelist's novelist* (Oxford: Oxford University Press, 1960), p. 83, 130.

3 Introduction by R. Freeborn in I. Turgenev (trans. Richard Freeborn), *Home of the Gentry* (London: Penguin, London 1970), p. 13.

4 L. Schapiro, *Turgenev, his Life and Times* (Oxford: OUP, 1978), p. 151. I. Turgenev, *Home of the Gentry*, op. cit., ch. 27, ch. 31.

5 I. Turgenev, *Home of the Gentry*, op. cit., ch. 34 and Epilogue.

6 Ibid., ch. 36, ch. 42, ch. 45.

7 Ibid., Epilogue.

8 I. Turgenev (trans. W Ralston), *Liza* (London: Chapman & Hall, 1869), vol. II, p. 231.

9 'One can but point': I. Turgenev, *Home of the Gentry*, op. cit., Epilogue; W.B. Yeats's tombstone, Drumcliffe Churchyard, citing Yeats's Under Ben Bulben.

10 R. Freeborn, introduction to I. Turgenev, *Home of the Gentry*, op. cit., p. 14; A. FitzLyon, *The Price of Genius, a life of Pauline Viardot* (London: John Calder, 1964), p. 332.

11 V.S. Pritchett, *The Gentle Barbarian, The Life and Work of Turgenev* (London: Chatto & Windus, 1977), p. 126; L. Schapiro, *Turgenev, his Life and Times* (Oxford: OUP, 1978), p. 153.

12 I. Turgenev, *On the Eve*, op. cit., ch. 3, ch. 22, 23.

13 H. Troyat (trans. N. Amphoux), *Turgenev* (London: W.H. Allen, 1989), p. 116.

14 I. Turgenev, *On the Eve*, op. cit., ch. 28.

15 Ibid., ch. 33.

16 Ibid., ch. 30.

17 V.S. Pritchett, op. cit., p. 131; R. Freeborn,

Turgenev, the novelist's novelist, op. cit., p. xi.
18 V.S. Pritchett, op. cit., p. 132; L. Schapiro, op. cit., p. 170.
19 R. Freeborn introduction to *Home of the Gentry*, op cit. pp. 15, 18.
20 I. Turgenev (trans. Isabel Hapgood), 'First Love', in *First Love and other stories* (New York: Charles Scribner's Sons, 1923), ch. 1.
21 I. Turgenev, *First Love and other stories*, op. cit., ch. 9, ch. 16.
22 I. Turgenev, *First Love*, op. cit., ch. 1, ch. 21, ch. 22.
23 D. Magarshack, op. cit., p. 51.
24 R. Freeborn, introduction to *Home of the Gentry*, op. cit., p. 19.
25 I. Turgenev, *On the Eve*, op. cit., ch. 33.
26 P. Waddington, 'Turgenev's relations with H.F. Chorley', *New Zealand Slavonic Journal*, no. 2, 1978, p. 35; H.G. Hewlett, *Memoirs of Henry Fothergill Chorley* (London: Richard Bentley and Son, 1873), vol. I, pp. 5, 274.
27 V.S. Pritchett, op. cit., p. 134; A. Zviguilsky (ed.), *Ivan Tourguénev: Nouvelle Correspondance inédite* (Paris: Librairie des Cinq Continents, 1971), vol. II, pp. 115, 116.
28 *Encyclopaedia Britannica*, ninth edition, vol. 24, p. 162.
29 H. James, Jr, *English Hours* (Oxford: Oxford University Press, 1981), 'English Vignettes', p. 143; P. Waddington, *Turgenev and England* (London: Macmillan, 1980), p. 105.
30 V.S. Pritchett, op. cit., p. 145; L. Schapiro, op. cit., p. 174.
31 R. Freeborn, *Turgenev, the novelist's novelist*, op. cit., p. 75.
32 Sir Isaiah Berlin, Romanes lecture 1970, *Fathers and Children*, from Turgenev, I. (trans. R. Edmonds), *Fathers and Sons* (London: Penguin, 1965 and 1970), p. 31.
33 L. Schapiro, op. cit., p. 182; A. Zviguilsky (ed.), op. cit., pp. 100, 102.
34 V.S. Pritchett, op. cit., p. 153; R. Freeborn, op. cit., p. 98; Sir I. Berlin, op. cit., pp. 27, 29, 30; L. Schapiro, op. cit., p. 182.
35 I. Turgenev (trans. E. Schuyler), *Fathers and Sons* (London: Ward, Lock & Co, 1883), ch. 5; Sir I. Berlin, op. cit., p. 27.
36 Sir I. Berlin, op. cit., p. 35. Turgenev even went so far as to keep his own diary recording how he imagined Bazarov would respond to daily events – L. Schapiro, op. cit., p. 185.
37 I. Turgenev, *Fathers and Sons*, op. cit., ch. 18; A. Zviguilsky (ed.), op. cit., p. 101.
38 I. Turgenev, *Fathers and Sons*, op. cit., ch. 11, ch. 17.
39 R. Freeborn, op. cit., p. 10.
40 I. Turgenev, *Fathers and Sons*, op. cit., ch. 19.
41 Ibid., ch. 4, ch. 5, ch. 23; P. Waddington, *The Origins and Composition of Turgenev's Novel 'Dym' (Smoke) as seen from his first Sketches* (Pinehaven, New Zealand: Whirinaki Press, 1998), p. 4.
42 R. Freeborn, op. cit., p. 135; L. Schapiro, op. cit., p. 185.
43 V.S. Pritchett, op. cit., p. 153.
44 R. Freeborn, op. cit., pp. 34, 126; *Encyclopaedia Britannica*, Standard Millennium edition; I. Goncharov (trans. D. Magarshack), *Oblomov* (London: Penguin, 1954), p. 4.
45 F. Dostoyevsky (trans. A.R. MacAndrew), *The Brothers Karamazov* (New York: Bantam Classic, 1970), ch. 2, p. 11. The character is Peter Miusov.
46 Ibid., ch. 2, p. 12.
47 R. Freeborn, op. cit., pp. 48, 132, 180; P. Waddington, op. cit., p. 28.
48 R. Freeborn, op. cit., p. 132; P. Waddington, 'Turgenev's relations with H.F. Chorley', *New Zealand Slavonic Journal*, no. 2, 1978, p. 34.
49 P. Ackroyd, *Dickens* (London: Sinclair Stevenson, 1990), p. 911.
50 H. James, Jr, *French Poets and Novelists* (London: Macmillan, 1878), p. 309.
51 E. Gombrich, *The Story of Art* (London: Phaidon, 1963), p. 383; *Landscape painters at Barbizon 1825–1827* (Musée Municipal de l'Ecole de Barbizon, 1989); V. Pomarède and G. de Wallens, *Corot Extraordinary Landscapes* (Paris: Gallimard, 1996)
52 R. Freeborn, op. cit., p. 176.
53 E. de Goncourt, *Journal* (Paris, 1887), vol. III, p. 712, vol. VII, p. 216. Goncourt's adjective was 'paysagiste'.
54 R. Freeborn, op. cit., pp. 27, 51, 56, 60, 63, 69; H. James, Jr, *The Portrait of a Lady* (London: Penguin Classics, 2000), preface, p. 43.
55 A.N. Wilson, *Tolstoy* (London: Hamish Hamilton, 1988), p. 307.
56 V.S. Pritchett, op. cit., p. 86; R. Freeborn, op. cit., pp. 1, 46, 179; D. Magarshack, op. cit., p. 64.
57 P. Waddington, *Turgenev and England*, op. cit., pp. 2, 3.
58 A.N. Wilson, op. cit., pp. 307, 327.

CHAPTER 20. PAULINE TRIUMPHANT, *ORPHÉE* (pp. 291–305)

1 D. Cairns, *Berlioz: Servitude and Greatness* (Penguin: London 2000), p. 639.

2 T. Marix-Spire, *Lettres inédites de George Sand et de Pauline Viardot 1839–1849* (Nouvelles Editions), p. 80.

3 *Musical Quarterly*, vol. I, 1915, p. 370, 30 December 1858.

4 J. Ridley, *Napoléon III and Eugénie* (London: Constable, 1979), pp. 140, 199, 324, 331; O. Friedrich, *Olympia – Paris in the Age of Manet* (London: Aurum Press, 1992), pp. 45, 135; A. Horne, *The Fall of Paris* (London: Macmillan, 1965), pp. 4, 23; A. Faris, *Jacques Offenbach* (London: Faber and Faber, 1980), p. 55; E. Zola (trans. D. Parmée), *Nana* (Oxford: Oxford University Press, 1998), ch. 7.

5 J. Richardson, *The Courtesans – the demi-monde in 19th century France* (London: Weidenfeld & Nicolson, 1967), pp. 62, 58; 191. S. Kracauer, *Offenbach and the Paris of his Time* (London: Constable, 1937), pp.17, 16; A. Faris, op. cit., p. 142; E. Zola, *Nana*, op. cit., ch.12. S. Kracauer, op. cit., p.191.

6 S. Kracauer, op. cit., pp.17, 16, 191; A. Faris, op. cit., p. 142; E. Zola, *Nana*, op. cit., ch. 12.

7 B. Rees, *Camille Saint-Saëns, A Life* (London: Chatto & Windus, 1999) p.130; J. Richardson, op. cit., p. 54; A. Horne, op. cit., p. 7; O. Friedrich, op. cit., p. 191; A. Faris, o. cit., p. 132; E. Zola, *Nana*, op. cit., ch. 11.

8 E. Zola (trans. M. Mauldon), *L'Assommoir* (Oxford: Oxford University Press, 1995), ch. 4, ch. 5, ch. 11.

9 The sign painter is Gautruche in E. et J. de Goncourt (trans. L Tancock), *Germinie Lacerteux* (Harmondsworth: Penguin, 1984), ch. 8, p. 39; E. Zola, *L'Assommoir*, op. cit., ch. 4 (The wages of a nailsmith were cut from twelve francs to nine francs, then to seven francs).

10 O. Friedrich, op. cit., p. 138; P. McPhee, *A Social History of France 1780–1880* (London: Routledge, 1992), p. 205; *The Times Literary Supplement*, London, 27 April 2001, p. 12; A. Horne, op. cit., p. 25.

11 V. Hugo, *Les Misérables* (Brussels: A. Lacroix, Verboekheven, 1862), pt 2, book 8, ch. 7.

12 E. Zola, *L'Assommoir*, op. cit., ch. 1.

13 E. and J. de Goncourt, *Germinie Lacerteux*, op. cit., ch. 31, ch. 63.

14 A. FitzLyon, *The Price of Genius, a life of Pauline Viardot* (London: John Calder, 1964), p. 336; P. Waddington, *Courtavenel, the History of an Artists' Nest and its Role in the Life of Turgenev* (*PhD Thesis*, Queen's University Belfast, The British Library, British Thesis Service, spring 1972), p. 117.

15 B. Rees, op. cit., p. 74; P. Waddington, 'Some Gleanings on Turgenev and his International Connections', *New Zealand Slavonic Journal*, 1983, pp. 215, 255; A. FitzLyon, *The Price of Genius*, op. cit., p. 338; P. Waddington, *PhD Thesis*, op. cit., p. 176.

16 C. Saint-Saëns (trans. E.G. Rich), *Musical Memories* (London: Murray, 1921), p. 148.

17 L. Héritte-Viardot (trans. E.S. Bucheim), *Memories and Adventures* (London: Mills & Boon, 1913), pp. 48, 49; Manin was a converted Jew whose grandparents changed their name to that of the last Doge when they converted. (*The Times Literary Supplement*, London, 6 January 2006, p. 7.)

18 Mrs Grote, *Memoirs of the Life of Ary Scheffer* (London: John Murray, 1860), p. 121; Manin was buried in the Scheffer family tomb.

19 L. Héritte-Viardot, op. cit., p. 48; H.G. Hewlett, *Memoirs of Henry Fothergill Chorley* (London: Richard Bentley and Son, 1873), vol. II, p. 264.

20 P. Waddington, *Turgenev and George Sand: An Improbable Entente* (Victoria University Press, 1981), p. 53; L. Héritte-Viardot, op. cit., pp. 44, 45.

21 G. Flaubert, *Sentimental Education*, pt 1, ch. 4.

22 A. FitzLyon, *The Price of Genius*, op. cit., p. 339.

23 *Musical Quarterly*, vol. I, 1915, pp. 378, 379.

24 L. Héritte-Viardot, op. cit., p. 52; M. Curtiss, 'Bizet, Offenbach and Rossini', *Musical Quarterly*, 1954, p. 356.

25 *Musical Quarterly*, vol. I, 1915, p. 378. 'Une masse de méchants petits Musikanten de quatre sous.'

26 *Cahiers Ivan Tourguéniev, Pauline Viardot, Maria Malibran* (Bougival: Association des Amis d'Ivan Tourguéniev Pauline Viardot et Maria Malibran), vol. 2, p. 39; M. L'Hôpital, *Louis Viardot, Mémoires de l'Académie des Sciences* (Dijon : Arts et Belles-Lettres de Dijon, 1954), p. 38.

27 T. Marix-Spire, *Lettres inédites de George Sand*, op. cit.; *Musical Quarterly* 1945; A. FitzLyon, *The Price of Genius*, op. cit., pp. 340, 506; *Cahiers*, op. cit., vol. 2, p. 39.
28 In 1896, W. Kuhe, *My musical recollections* (London: Richard Bentley, 1896), p. 187.
29 *Cahiers*, op. cit., vol. 2, p. 39; A. FitzLyon, *The Price of Genius*, op. cit., p. 340.
30 B. Rees, op. cit., p. 93. He spells it 'cocoa'.
31 M. Curtiss, *Bizet and his World* (London: Secker and Warburg, 1959), p. 356; H. Weinstock, *Donizetti and the World of Opera* (London: Methuen, 1964), pp. 284, 346; A. FitzLyon, *The Price of Genius*, op. cit., pp. 358; Paul Viardot, *Souvenirs d'un Artiste* (Paris: Librairie Fischbacher SA, 1910), p. 16.
32 A. FitzLyon, *The Price of Genius*, op. cit., p. 358; D. Cairns, op. cit., p. 632; F. Lestringant, Alfred de Musset (Flammarion, 1999), p. 534. The 10,000 francs can be seen in the display cabinet 17 at the Richard-Wagner-Museum, Bayreuth. The uncle was Count Nesselrode who for over a third of a century had been foreign minister.
33 Paul Viardot, op. cit., p. 16; F. Lestringant, op. cit., pp. 453, 534.
34 *Musical Quarterly* 1915, vol. 1, p. 546. 'Quelle assomonte monotonie, quelle ennuyeuse laideur.'
35 I. Turgenev (ed. E. Halpérine-Kaminsky), *Lettres à Madame Viardot* (Paris: Bibliothèque-Charpentier, 1907), p. 238.
36 N. Žekulin, *The story of an operetta, Le Dernier sorcier and Ivan Turgenev* (Munich: Verlag Otto Sagner, 1989), p. 32; H. Granjard and A. Zviguilsky, *Ivan Tourguénev, Lettres inédites à Pauline Viardot et à sa famille* (Paris: Editions l'Age d'Homme, 1972), pp. 147, 152; G. Dulong, *Pauline Viardot Tragédienne Lyrique* (Bougival: Association des Amis d'Ivan Tourguéniev Pauline Viardot et Maria Malibran), p. 171.
37 A. FitzLyon, *The Price of Genius*, op. cit., p. 358.
38 *New Grove Dictionary of Music and Musicians* (London: Macmillan, 1980), vol. 3, p. 841, Caroline Carvalho (Harold Rosenthal); G. Dulong, op. cit., p.136.
39 *Musical Quarterly* 1916, p. 32; D. Cairns, op. cit., p. 638.
40 G. Dulong, op. cit., p. 137.
41 A. FitzLyon, *The Price of Genius*, op. cit., p. 55; P. Waddington, *PhD Thesis*, op. cit., p. 260; D. Cairns, op. cit., p. 633.
42 H. Lacombe, *The Keys to French Opera in the Nineteenth Century* (London: University of California Press, 2001), p. 42.
43 G. Dulong, op. cit., p. 138; *Musical Quarterly* 1916, p. 35.
44 D. Cairns, op. cit., pp. 632, 642; B. Rees, op. cit., p..86; Paul Viardot, op. cit., p. 4.
45 G. Dulong, op. cit., p. 135; A. Williams, *Franz Liszt, selected letters* (Oxford: Clarendon Press, 1998), p. 481, 484 (27 October 1859) to Princess Carolyne, 'The Les Troyens soirée at Pauline's is in very good taste.'
46 D. Cairns, op. cit., p. 632.
47 T. J. Walsh, *Second Empire Opera* (London: Calder, 1981), p. 111.
48 This is according to Dr Zviguilsky.
49 *Musical Quarterly* 1916, p. 46; G. Dulong, op. cit., p. 139; A. FitzLyon in *New Grove*, op. cit., vol. 19, p. 694; G. Dulong, op. cit., p.139.
50 H.F. Chorley, *Thirty years' Musical Recollections* (London: Hurst & Blackett, 1862), vol. II, pp. 55, 57, 58, 60.
51 *Musical Quarterly* 1915, vol. I, p. 352.
52 C. Dupêchez, *Marie d'Agoult* (Paris: P. Lon, 1994), p. 264. 'Le chant et le jeu de Mme Viardot ont dépassé pour moi toute attente. Je n'ai jamais rien vu, pas même Rachel, qui approchât de cette beauté plastique, et de cette liberté dans le sentiment de l'antique ... Elle m'a fait contamment penser aux beaux bas-reliefs et vas grecs'.
53 D. Cairns, op. cit., p. 639; R. Somerset-Ward, *Angels and Monsters* (New Haven and London: Yale University Press, 2004), p. 186; A. FitzLyon, *The Price of Genius*, op. cit., p. 355.
54 L. Héritte-Viardot, op. cit., p. 103; A. Faris, op. cit., pp. 100, 190. The première was on 21 October 1858, and it was still running at the Bouffes in 1862–63.
55 Demar Irvine, *Massenet, a Chronicle of his Life and Times* (New York: Amadeus Press, 1994); A. FitzLyon, *The Price of Genius*, op. cit., p. 356; G. Dulong, op. cit., pp. 140, 141; A. Zviguilsky (ed.), *Ivan Tourguénev: Nouvelle Correspondance inédite* (Paris: Librairie des Cinq Continents, 1971), p. 99; *Musical Quarterly* 1916, vol. II, p. 52. The 121st performance was on 21 June 1861.
56 D. Cairns, op. cit., p. 643.
57 A. FitzLyon, *The Price of Genius*, op. cit., p. 438; P. Waddington, 'Pauline Viardot-Garcia

as Berlioz's Counselor and Physician' (*Musical Quarterly*, vol. LIX, no. 3, July 1973), p. 384.
58 D. Cairns, op. cit., p.635.
59 D. Cairns, op. cit., pp. 233, 681.
60 *Musical Quarterly* 1916 p. 40. 'Mais j'espère que cette espèce d'accès de fièvre chaude de mon pauvre ami B passera sans malheurs ni scènes violentes.'
61 D. Cairns, op. cit., p. 635.
62 A. FitzLyon, *The Price of Genius*, op. cit., p. 347; D. Cairns, op. cit., pp. 634, 635.
63 D. Cairns, op. cit., p. 635; *Musical Quarterly* 1916, p. 44.
64 D. Cairns, op. cit., p. 648; P. Waddington, *Pauline Viardot-Garcia as Berlioz's Counselor and Physician*, op. cit., p. 394.
65 A. FitzLyon, *The Price of Genius*, op. cit., p. 356.
66 T.J. Walsh, op. cit., p. 123. Florestan was Gian Galeazzo Sforza; Pizarro was Ludovico Sforza.
67 G. Dulong, op. cit., p. 140; J.P.T. Bury, *France 1814–1940* (London: Methuen, 1969), p. 97.
68 T.J Walsh, op. cit., p. 124.
69 Ibid., pp. 126, 312.
70 G. Dulong, op. cit., p.142.
71 *Musical Quarterly* 1916, p. 56.
72 G. Dulong, op. cit., p.142; D. Cairns, op. cit., pp. 675, 676.
73 P. Waddington, *Pauline Viardot-Garcia as Berlioz's Counselor and Physician*, op. cit., p. 56.
74 D. Cairns, op. cit., pp. 664, 666, 677.
75 Ibid., p. 703; P. Waddington, *Pauline Viardot-Garcia as Berlioz's Counselor and Physician*, op. cit., p. 397. The soprano was Mme Charton-Demeur, who had given a private performance for Berlioz some time before.

Chapter 21. Baden-Baden (pp. 309–330)

1 G. Dulong, *Pauline Viardot Tragédienne Lyrique* (Bougival: Association des Amis d'Ivan Tourguéniev Pauline Viardot et Maria Malibran), p. 144.
2 *Musical Quarterly*, vol. I, 1915 (Rietz letters), p. 351; H. Granjard and A. Zviguilsky, Ivan Tourgénev, *Lettres inédites à Pauline Viardot et à sa famille* (Paris: Editions l'Age d'Homme, 1972), pp. 85, 90.
3 G. Dulong, op. cit., p. 145; R. Somerset-Ward, *Angels and Monsters* (New Haven and London: Yale University Press, 2004), pp. 196, 210, 223. The relevant day was 25 May 1858.
4 T.J.Walsh, *Second Empire Opera* (London: Calder, 1981), p. 197. The figures represent annual pay for 34 out of 84 members in 1864/5.
5 P. Waddington, 'Dickens, Pauline Viardot and Turgenev: a Study in Mutual Admiration', *New Zealand Slavonic Journal*, No. 2, 1974, p. 63; T.J. Walsh, op. cit., p. 135; S. Rutherford, *The Prima Donna and Opera 1815–1930* (Cambridge: Cambridge University Press, 2006), p. 82. The opinion on Piccolomini's ability is attributed to Chorley: see *New Grove Dictionary of Music and Musicians* (London: Macmillan, 1980), vol. 14, p. 730, Piccolomini (Elizabeth Forbes).
6 R. Somerset-Ward, op. cit., pp. 182, 184; *The New Oxford Companion to Music* (Oxford: Oxford University Press, 1984), p. 1818. Mignon had over 1,000 performances in under 30 years.
7 *Cahiers Ivan Tourguéniev, Pauline Viardot, Maria Malibran* (Bougival: Association des Amis d'Ivan Tourguéniev Pauline Viardot et Maria Malibran), vol. 12, p. 70; S. Kracauer, *Offenbach and the Paris of his time* (London: Constable, 1937), pp. 210, 234; A. Faris, *Jacques Offenbach* (London: Faber and Faber, 1980), p. 117. The Duc de Gramont-Caderousse, the father of her son, is alleged to have been a gambler, a champion jockey, and to have killed a man in a duel.
8 R. Somerset-Ward, op. cit., p. 186; The Tannhäuser programme is on display in cabinet 17 at the Richard-Wagner-Museum, Bayreuth.
9 Rietz Letters, op. cit., p. 532; C. Saint-Saëns (trans. E.G. Rich), *Musical Memories* (London: Murray, 1921), p. 152.
10 P. Waddington, 'The Role of Courtavenel in the Life and Work of Turgenev', from *Issues in Russian Literature before 1917*, selected papers of the Third World Congress for Soviet and East European Studies (Colombus, Ohio: Slavica Publishers Inc, 1989), p. 127.
11 B. Rees, *Camille Saint-Saëns, A Life* (London: Chatto & Windus, 1999), pp. 107, 122; G. Dulong, op. cit., p. 105; H. Granjard and A. Zviguilsky, op. cit., p. 19.
12 E & J de Goncourt (trans. L. Tancock), *Germinie Lacerteux* (Harmondsworth: Penguin, 1984), p. 8. The comment is Tancock's.
13 G. Dulong, op. cit., p. 145.
14 P. Waddington, 'The strange history of Dr F.

and the dismantling of Courtavenel', *Modern Language Review*, vol. 65, 1970, p. 340; P. Waddington, *The Role of Courtavenel in the Life and Work of Turgenev*, op. cit., p. 127; P. Waddington, *Dickens, Pauline Viardot and Turgenev: a Study in Mutual Admiration*, op. cit., p. 66.

15 C. Hibbert, *Edward VII* (London: Allen Lane, 1976), p. 89. She shared the phrase with the first Duke of Wellington who said that 'the gentlemen!!! of the press are so demoralised that nobody can approach them without incurring the risk of loss of character' – *History Today*, November 2002, vol. 52 (11), p. 30.

16 A. FitzLyon, *The Price of Genius, a life of Pauline Viardot* (London: John Calder, 1964), p. 371; M. L'Hôpital, *Louis Viardot, Mémoires de l'Académie des Sciences* (Dijon: Arts et Belles-Lettres de Dijon, 1954), p. 31.

17 R. and K. Hofmann, *Johannes Brahms in Baden-Baden* (Baden-Baden: Brahmsgesellschaft, 1996), p. 18; H. Troyat (trans. N. Amphoux), *Turgenev* (London: W.H. Allen, 1989), p. 79; G. Dulong, op. cit., p. 148.

18 V.S. Pritchett, *The Gentle Barbarian, The Life and Work of Turgenev* (London: Chatto & Windus, 1977), p. 159; P. Waddington, 'Some Gleanings on Turgenev and his International Connections', *New Zealand Slavonic Journal*, 1983; H. Granjard and A. Zviguilsky, op. cit., p. 88.

19 A. Zviguilsky (ed.), *Ivan Tourguénev: Nouvelle Correspondance inédite* (Paris: Librairie des Cinq Continents, 1971), pp. 124, 129; H. Granjard and A. Zviguilsky, op. cit., p. 191; M. Mainwaring (ed.), *Ivan Turgenev, the Portrait Game* (London: Chatto and Windus, 1973), pp. 124, 132; G. Dulong, op. cit., p. 158; L. Héritte-Viardot (trans. E.S. Bucheim), *Memories and Adventures* (London: Mills & Boon, 1913), p. 74; P. Waddington, The strange history of Dr F. and the dismantling of Courtavenel, op. cit., passim.

20 P. Waddington, 'Two Months in the Country', *New Zealand Slavonic Journal*, no. 11, winter 1973, p. 36; P. Waddington, 'The strange history of Dr F. and the dismantling of Courtavenel', op. cit., p. 352. The tree was called after Hermann and Dorothea, a work by Goethe which they had read together.

21 R. Somerset-Ward, op. cit., p. 157; P. Waddington, 'The strange history of Dr F. and the dismantling of Courtavenel', op. cit., p. 342. Patti's castle was at Craig-y-nos.

22 *Encyclopaedia Britannica*, ninth edition, vol. 1, p. 492; vol. III, p. 226.

23 I. Turgenev (trans. W. West), *Smoke* (London: Ward Lock & Co, 1872), ch. 1.

24 R. and K. Hofmann, op. cit., p. 18. N. Žekulin, *The story of an operetta, Le Dernier sorcier and Ivan Turgenev* (Munich: Verlag Otto Sagner, 1989), at p. 8, records that the town of 8,000 had an influx of 40,000 visitors per annum.

25 *Encyclopaedia Britannica*, ninth edition, vol. III, p. 226. The Pump Room was built in 1842.

26 Information obtained during author's visit. The temperature varies from 115–153 degrees Fahrenheit.

27 Paul Viardot, *Souvenirs d'un Artiste* (Paris: Librairie Fischbacher SA, 1910), p. 152; C. Hibbert, op. cit., p. 89.

28 *New Grove*, op. cit., vol. VII, p. 587, Gounod (Dennis Libby); *New Grove*, op. cit., vol. 2, p. 602, Berlioz (H. Macdonald).

29 A. Williams, *Franz Liszt, selected letters* (Oxford: Clarendon Press, 1998), p.785. He wrote this on 25 July 1875 to Princess Carolyne.

30 I. Turgenev (trans. W. West), *Smoke* (London: Ward Lock & Co, 1872), p. 4.

31 Paul Viardot, op. cit., p. 11; J. Richardson, *The Courtesans – the demi-monde in 19th century France* (London: Weidenfeld & Nicolson, 1967), p. 51.

32 Turgenev, *Smoke*, op. cit., ch. 18, p. 141.

33 P. Waddington, *The Origins and Composition of Turgenev's Novel 'Dym' (Smoke) as seen from his first Sketches* (Pinehaven, New Zealand: Whirinaki Press, 1998), pp. 2, 5; V.S. Pritchett, op. cit., p. 160.

34 V.S. Pritchett, op. cit., p. 160; G. Dulong, op. cit., p. 148; L. Schapiro, *Turgenev, his Life and Times* (Oxford: OUP, 1978), p. 192.

35 N. Žekulin, op. cit., p. 13; H. Troyat, op. cit., p. 86; G. Dulong, op. cit., p. 148; H. Granjard and A. Zviguilsky, op. cit., p. 151; A. Zviguilsky (ed.), op. cit., p. 251. A. Zviguilsky (ed.), op. cit., pp. 97, 249; H. Granjard and A. Zviguilsky, op. cit., p. 249; N. Žekulin, op. cit., pp. 7, 16.

36 A. Zviguilsky (ed.), op. cit., p. 251; N. Žekulin, op. cit., pp. 17, 47; L. Héritte-Viardot, op. cit., p. 112.

37 A. FitzLyon, *The Price of Genius*, op. cit., p. 392; J. Chissell, *Clara Schumann: a Dedicated*

Spirit (London: Hamish Hamilton, 1983), p. 158; N. Žekulin, op. cit., p. 18.

38 G. Dulong, op. cit., p. 154; L. Schapiro, op. cit., p. 191; J. Chissell, op. cit., p. 158; Paul Viardot, op. cit., p. 14; H. Granjard and A. Zviguilsky, op. cit., p. 165.

39 B. Litzmann (trans. G. Hadow), *Clara Schumann, an Artist's Life* (London: Macmillian, 1913), vol. II, p. 217; *Musical Quarterly*, vol. I, 1915, p. 538; A. FitzLyon, *The Price of Genius*, op. cit., pp. 381, 406.

40 P. Waddington, 'Turgenev's Scenario for Brahms', *New Zealand Slavonic Journal*, 1982, pp. 1–16, p. 2.

41 The Idyll was performed on Christmas morning 1870, *The New Oxford Companion to Music* (Oxford: Oxford University Press, 1984), p. 1686.

42 N. Žekulin, op. cit., pp. 46, 87–90.

43 J. Chissell, op. cit., p. 150; *Cahiers*, op. cit., no. 20, p. 141.

44 B. Litzmann, op. cit., p. 203. She recorded this on 24 March 1862.

45 J. Chissell, *Schumann* (London: J.M. Dent, 1977), p. 77.

46 J. Chissell, *Clara Schumann: a Dedicated Spirit* (London: Hamish Hamilton, 1983), p. 158.

47 A. Zviguilsky (ed.), op. cit., p.177; Paul Viardot, op. cit., p. 14.

48 N.B. Reich, *Clara Schumann, the Artist and the Woman* (Cornell University, 2001); *Cahiers*, op. cit., vol. 20, pp. 137, 138.

49 Professor Waddington has supplied this anecdote of 23 September 1867: Sir T. Martin, *Helena Faucit* (*Lady Martin*) (Edinburgh and London: William Blackwood and Sons, 1900), pp. 143, 262, 291. Helena Faucit is the actress referred to in the text. Chorley also thought Clara Schumann a 'masterly' pianist but 'perhaps a little wanting in grace and dignity' – H.G. Hewlett, *Memoirs of Henry Fothergill Chorley* (London: Richard Bentley and Son, 1873), vol. I, p. 325.

50 J. Chissell, *Clara Schumann: a Dedicated Spirit*, op. cit., pp.150, 158, 159.

51 V.S. Pritchett, op. cit., p. 200; P. Waddington, *The strange history of Dr F. and the dismantling of Courtavenel*, op. cit., p. 338.

52 A. FitzLyon, *The Price of Genius*, op. cit., p. 392; P. Waddington, 'Dickens, Pauline Viardot and Turgenev: a Study in Mutual Admiration', *New Zealand Slavonic Journal*, no. 2, 1974, p. 68.

53 M. L'Hôpital, op. cit., pp. 37, 38.

54 L. Héritte-Viardot, op. cit., p. 31; M. Mainwaring, op. cit., p. 103.

55 L. Viardot, *Apology of an Unbeliever*, translated from the Third Edition (London: Trübner & Co, 1869), Introduction.

56 L. Schapiro, op. cit., p. 224.

57 N. Žekulin, op. cit., pp. 14, 17, 47, 49, 72; H. Granjard and A. Zviguilsky, op. cit., p. 146.

58 N. Žekulin, op. cit., p. 15; The expert to whom reference is made is Professeur Zviguilsky.

59 G. Dulong, op. cit., p. 156; A. FitzLyon, *The Price of Genius*, op. cit., p.396; N. Žekulin, op. cit., pp. iv, 15.

60 P. Waddington, *Turgenev's Scenario for Brahms*, op. cit., p. 6; I am indebted to Professor Žekulin for clarification of the dates of the premières of these operettas, about which there seems to have been some confusion in the past. He has also established that Brahms was not involved at the première of *Le Dernier Sorcier* as had previously been thought.

61 L. Kelly, *Lermontov, a tragedy in the Caucasus* (London: Robin Clark, 1983), p. 187; A. Williams, op. cit., pp. 699, 974.

62 N. Žekulin, op. cit., pp. 38, 43, 55.

63 B. Litzmann, op. cit., vol. II, p. 255. Letter to Brahms, 3 October 1867.

64 A. Williams, op. cit., p. 699. Liszt's comment was on 4 February 1869.

65 H. Granjard and A. Zviguilsky, op. cit., pp. 155, 158; P. Ackroyd, *Dickens* (London: Sinclair Stevenson, 1990), p. 789. The actress was Ellen Ternan.

66 E. de Goncourt (trans. Belloc and Shedlock), *Journal* (London: Heinemann, 1895), vol. I, p. 261; E. de Goncourt, *Journal* (Paris: 1887), vol. II, p. 95; *Cahiers*, op. cit., vol. 20, p. 29; H. Granjard and A. Zviguilsky, op. cit., pp. 121, 122, 138.

67 P. Waddington, *Turgenev and George Sand: An Improbable Entente* (Victoria University Press, 1981), p. 49; A. Zviguilsky (ed.), op. cit., p. 252. The visit was in 1870.

68 A.N. Wilson, *Tolstoy* (London: Hamish Hamilton, 1988), p. 146; F. Dostoyevsky, *The Idiot* (Ware, Herts: Wordsworth Classics, 1996) passim. P. Ackroyd, op. cit., pp. 312, 313. The Tolstoy experience was in April 1857; this Dickens experience was in 1840.

69 P. Ackroyd, op. cit., p. 574. This was the execution of the Mannings. In England, after 1868,

executions were carried out within the prison.

70 O. Friedrich, *Olympia – Paris in the Age of Manet* (London: Aurum Press, 1992), p.18; A. Zviguilsky (ed.), op. cit., pp. 151, 135; G. Dulong, op. cit., p. 150.

71 V.S. Pritchett, op. cit., pp. 182, 185; L. Schapiro, op. cit., p. 194. He went in 1865, 1867 and 1868.

72 G. Dulong, op. cit., p. 149; I. Turgenev (ed. E. Halpérine-Kaminsky), *Lettres à Madame Viardot* (Paris: Bibliothèque-Charpentier, 1907), 26 March 1867, p. 212. The estate which should have yielded 25,000 roubles per annum was producing only 5,500 roubles: L. Schapiro, op. cit., p. 107.

73 L. Schapiro, op. cit., p. 221; V.S. Pritchett, op. cit., p. 183.

74 I. Turgenev, *Lettres à Madame Viardot*, op. cit., 29 March 1867, p. 215.

75 H. Granjard and A. Zviguilsky, op. cit., p. 150.

76 I. Turgenev (trans. T.S. Perry), *Virgin Soil* (London: Ward, Lock & Co, pre-1880), pt 1, ch. 4; L. Viardot, *Souvenirs de Chasse dans toute l'Europe* (Paris: Editions Pygmalion, 1985), p. 269.

77 L. Schapiro, op. cit., p. 222; A. Seljak, op. cit., p. 218. H. Granjard and A. Zviguilsky, op. cit., p. 228.

78 A. Zviguilsky (ed.), op. cit., p. 160. 'Une vieille voiture incommode, sur des chemins affreux, avec des chevaux à demi morts.'

79 A. Zviguilsky (ed.), op. cit., p.163; I. Turgenev, *Lettres à Madame Viardot*, op. cit., 25 June 1868, p. 235.

80 P. Waddington, *The Origins and Composition of Turgenev's Novel 'Dym' (Smoke) as seen from his first Sketches*, op. cit., p. 3; L. Schapiro, op. cit., pp. 178, 203.

81 V.S. Pritchett, op. cit., p. 163. This was in July 1862.

82 L. Schapiro, op. cit., p. 199.

83 A. Zviguilsky (ed.), op. cit., pp. 105, 108; I. Turgenev, *Lettres à Madame Viardot*, op. cit., 7 January 1864 p. 194.

84 G. Dulong, op. cit., p. 148; R. Freeborn, *Turgenev, the novelist's novelist* (Oxford: Oxford University Press, 1960), p. 141; L. Schapiro, op. cit., p. 188.

85 P. Waddington, *PhD Thesis*, op. cit., p. 280; A. FitzLyon, *The Price of Genius*, op. cit., p. 381.

86 N.B. Reich, op. cit., p. 133; J. Chissell, op. cit., p. 158.

87 G. Dulong, op. cit., pp. 148, 156; A. Zviguilsky (ed.), op. cit., p. 111.

88 C. Saint-Saëns (trans. E.G. Rich), *Musical Memories* (London: Murray, 1921), p. 153.

89 H. Granjard and A. Zviguilsky, op. cit., p. 121; A. FitzLyon, *The Price of Genius*, op. cit., p. 393. She died on 10 May 1864.

90 L. Schapiro, op. cit., pp. 207, 218; Musée Tourguéniev (par Tamara Zviguilsky), *Guide* (Corlet Condé-sur-Noireau, 1993), p. 32.

91 V.S. Pritchett, op. cit., p. 168.

92 These quotations from *Smoke* are taken from I. Turgenev (trans. W. West), *Smoke* (London: Ward Lock & Co, 1872), ch. 1, and I. Turgenev, *Fumée* (Paris: J. Hetzel, 1868), ch. 1, ch. 3.

93 I. Turgenev, *Fumée*, op. cit., ch. 5.

94 R. Freeborn, op. cit., p. 142. The action takes place between 10 and 22 August.

95 I. Turgenev, *Smoke*, op. cit., chs 2, 3, 12, 13 16, 17, 19; P. Waddington, *The Origins and Composition of Turgenev's Novel 'Dym' (Smoke) as seen from his first Sketches*, op. cit., p. 26. D. Magarshack, *Turgenev, a Life* (London: Faber & Faber, 1954), p. 147.

96 I. Turgenev, *Smoke*, op. cit., ch. 20, ch. 18, 25, 26; V.S. Pritchett, op. cit, p. 174.

97 E. Garnett's introduction to I. Turgenev (trans. Constance Garnett), *Smoke* (USA: Turtle Point Press, 1995), p. vi.

98 I. Turgenev, *Smoke*, op. cit., ch. 5, ch. 14.

99 L. Schapiro, op. cit., pp. 211, 212.

100 Ibid., p. 212.

101 I. Turgenev, *Lettres à Madame Viardot*, op. cit., March 1867, pp. 225–230; H. Troyat, op. cit., p. 93

102 Sir Isaiah Berlin, Romanes lecture 1970, *Fathers and Children*, from Turgenev, I. (trans. R. Edmonds), *Fathers and Sons* (London: Penguin, 1965 and 1970), p. 43.

Chapter 22. Dostoyevsky (pp. 331–342)

1 R. Hingley, *Dostoyevsky, his life and work* (London: Paul Elek Ltd, 1978), p. 131.

2 D. Magarshack, *Turgenev, a Life* (London: Faber & Faber, 1954), p. 86.

3 R. Hingley, op. cit., pp. 56, 152, 163; L. Schapiro, *Turgenev, his Life and Times* (Oxford: OUP, 1978), pp. 50, 169, 188.

4 R. Hingley, op. cit., pp. 82, 196.

5 Ibid., pp. 29, 37.
6 Ibid., pp. 46, 47, 53, 54, 57, 58.
7 H. Seton-Watson, *The Russian Empire 1801–1917* (Oxford: Clarendon Press, 1988), p. 276.
8 R. Hingley, op. cit., pp. 61, 62; L. Schapiro, op. cit., p. 59.
9 F. Dostoyevsky, *The Brothers Karamazov*, Book 12, ch. 9.
10 F. Dostoyevsky, *The Idiot* (Ware, Herts: Wordsworth Classics, 1996), Part 1, ch. 2, ch. 5. In *War and Peace*, Pierre is made to watch the execution of fellow prisoners accused of incendiarism. L. Tolstoy (trans. L. and A. Maude), *War and Peace* (London: OUP, 1933), Book 12, ch. 11.
11 R. Hingley, op. cit., pp. 16, 71, 72, 75, 76, 81, 92.
12 R. Hingley in introduction to F. Dostoyevsky (trans. J. Coulson), *Memoirs from the House of the Dead* (Oxford, Oxford University Press, 2001).
13 F. Dostoyevsky, *Memoirs from the House of the Dead*, op. cit., Part 1, ch. 2, ch. 5, ch. 6, ch. 7, ch. 11; Part 2, ch. 1 ch. 5, ch. 7, ch. 9.
14 Ibid., Part 2, ch. 1, ch. 3.
15 Ibid., Part 1, ch. 9.
16 R. Hingley in introduction to F. Dostoyevsky, *Memoirs from the House of the Dead*, op. cit.; R. Hingley, *Dostoyevsky, his life and work* (London: Paul Elek Ltd, 1978), pp. 87, 90, 104.
17 R. Hingley, *Dostoyevsky, his life and work* (London: Paul Elek Ltd, 1978), p. 103. She died in April 1864.
18 Ibid., p. 100.
19 F. Dostoyevsky (trans. C Garnett, introduction G.S. Morson), *The Gambler* (New York: The Modern Library, 2003), introduction by G.S. Morson, p. xii.
20 R. Hingley, op. cit., pp. 106, 107.
21 L. Schapiro, op. cit., p. 216.
22 R. Hingley, op. cit., pp. 108, 124.
23 F. Dostoyevsky (trans. D. McDuff), *Crime and Punishment* (London: Penguin, 2003), introduction by D. McDuff, p. x.
24 F. Dostoyevsky, *The Gambler*, op. cit., ch. 1, ch. 12, ch. 13.
25 R. Hingley, op. cit., pp. 126, 146.
26 F. Dostoyevsky, *The Idiot*, op. cit., part 2, ch. 5.
27 R. Hingley, op. cit., pp. 130, 131, 146.
28 F. Dostoyevsky, *The Idiot*, op. cit., part 3, ch. 1; R. Hingley, op. cit., p. 131.
29 F. Dostoyevsky, *The Idiot*, op. cit., part 2, ch. 8; D. Magarshack's introduction to F. Dostoyevsky (trans. D. Magarshack), *The Devils* (London: Penguin, 1971), p. xvi.
30 F. Dostoyevsky (trans. D. Magarshack), *The Devils* (London: Penguin, 1971), pt 2, ch. 6, section 5.
31 R. Hingley, op. cit., p. 132; D. Magarshack's introduction to F. Dostoyevsky, *The Devils*, op. cit., p. xv.
32 R. Hingley, op. cit., pp. 162, 183, 185, 186, 187.
33 D. Magarshack's introduction to F. Dostoyevsky, *The Devils*, op. cit., p. xvi.
34 Ibid., p. xvi.
35 F. Dostoyevsky, *The Devils*, op. cit., pt 2, ch. 5, p. 10. (The translations are based on F. Dostoyevsky (trans. D. Magarshack), *The Brothers Karamazov* (Harmondsworth: Penguin, 1958), and F. Dostoyevsky (trans. C. Garnett), *The Possessed* (London and Toronto: J.M. Dent, 1931)).
36 F. Dostoyevsky, *The Devils*, op. cit., pt 3, ch. 1, section 2.
37 Ibid., part 2, ch. 6, section 5; Ibid., pt 3, ch. 1, section 3.
38 I. Turgenev (trans. Isabel Hapgood), *First Love and other stories* (New York: Charles Scribner's Sons, 1923), pp. 313, 322.
39 F. Dostoyevsky, *The Devils*, op. cit., pt 3, ch. 1, section 1, 2.
40 Ibid., part 3, ch. 1, section 3; Ibid., ch. 2, section 2.
41 Ibid., part 2, ch. 6, section 5; Ibid., part 3, ch. 1, section 3.
42 I. Turgenev (trans. Isabel Hapgood), *First Love and other stories*, op. cit., p. 17.
43 F. Dostoyevsky, *The Devils*, op. cit., pt 3, ch. 1, section 3.
44 Ibid., part 3, ch. 2, section 2; pt 3, ch. 1, section 3.
45 Ibid., pt 3, ch. 3, section 3.
46 F. Dostoyevsky, *The Devils*, op. cit., Appendix; Stavrogin's Confession; R. Hingley, op. cit., p. 157. Information also received from Professor Patrick Waddington.
47 F. Dostoyevsky, *The Devils*, op. cit., pt 2, ch. 8.
48 Ibid., pt 2, ch. 8.
49 Luke ch. 8, vv. 32–36.
50 This was said by old Mr Verkhovensky in F. Dostoyevsky, *The Devils*, op. cit., pt 3, ch. 7, section 2.

51 *Encyclopaedia Britannica,* ninth edition, vol. XIX, p. 649; H. Troyat (trans. N. Amphoux), *Turgenev* (London: W.H. Allen, 1989), pp. 136, 141.
52 P. Waddington, 'Turgenev and George Eliot, a literary friendship', *Modern Language Review,* vol. 66, 1971, p. 758.
53 P. Waddington, 'Turgenev's Last Will and Testament', *New Zealand Slavonic Journal,* no. 2, 1974, p. 62.
54 R. Freeborn, op. cit., p. 178.
55 F. Dostoyevsky (trans. S. Koteliansky and J. Middleton Murry), *The Pushkin Speech* (Unwin Books, 1960), p. 52.
56 R. Hingley, op. cit., p. 203.
57 F. Dostoyevsky, *The Pushkin Speech,* op. cit., p. 53.
58 Ibid., p. 48.
59 R. Hingley, op. cit., p. 198.

CHAPTER 23. ESCAPE (pp. 343–361)

1 I. Turgenev (ed. E. Halpérine-Kaminsky), *Lettres à Madame Viardot* (Paris: Bibliothèque-Charpentier, 1907), 28 and 29 March 1867, pp. 214, 226.
2 A. Zviguilsky (ed.), *Ivan Tourguénev: Nouvelle Correspondance inédite* (Paris: Librairie des Cinq Continents, 1971), p. 171; J. Ridley, *Napoléon III and Eugénie* (London: Constable, 1979), p. 557. The quotation is attributed to Harold Wilson; *Oxford Dictionary of Quotations* (third edition).
3 J.P.T. Bury, *France 1814–1940* (London: Methuen, 1969), p. 113.
4 U. Lange-Brachmann and J. Draheim (ed.), *Pauline Viardot in Baden Baden und Karlsruhe* (Baden-Baden: Nomos Verlaggesellschaft, 1999), p. 63.
5 A. Horne, *The Fall of Paris* (London: Macmillan, 1965), p. 47.
6 J.P.T. Bury, op. cit., p. 114.
7 A. Horne, op. cit., pp. 63, 75, 77.
8 Ibid., pp. 177, 178.
9 J.P.T. Bury, op. cit., p. 127; A. Horne, op. cit., p. 242.
10 A. Zviguilsky (ed.), op. cit., p. 190; G. Dulong, *Pauline Viardot Tragédienne Lyrique* (Bougival: Association des Amis d'Ivan Tourguéniev Pauline Viardot et Maria Malibran), p. 157.
11 A. Horne, op. cit., pp. 366, 415, 417.
12 *Encyclopaedia Britannica,* ninth edition, vol. 22, p. 588.
13 A. Horne, op. cit., p. 106.
14 H. Troyat (trans. N. Amphoux), *Turgenev* (London: W.H. Allen, 1989), p. 99.
15 V.S. Pritchett, *The Gentle Barbarian, The Life and Work of Turgenev* (London: Chatto & Windus, 1977), p. 187; P. Waddington, 'Turgenev's Scenario for Brahms', *New Zealand Slavonic Journal,* 1982, pp. 1–16, p. 5.
16 H. Troyat, op. cit., p. 100.
17 L. Schapiro, *Turgenev, his Life and Times* (Oxford: OUP, 1978), p. 230; N. Žekulin, *The story of an operetta, Le Dernier sorcier and Ivan Turgenev* (Munich: Verlag Otto Sagner, 1989), p. 67; P. Waddington, *Turgenev and England* (London: Macmillan, 1980), p. 141; H. Troyat, op. cit., pp. 100, 101.
18 A. Zviguilsky (ed.), op. cit., pp. 175, 176; N. Žekulin, op. cit., p. 67; H. Granjard and A. Zviguilsky, *Ivan Tourgénev, Lettres inédites à Pauline Viardot et à sa famille* (Paris: Editions l'Age d'Homme, 1972), pp. 128, 158; P. Waddington, *Turgenev and England,* op. cit., p. 141.
19 A. Zviguilsky (ed.), op. cit., pp. 177, 178.
20 A. Zviguilsky (ed.), op. cit., p. 182; H. Granjard and A. Zviguilsky, op. cit., p. 165. 'Je sais qu'elle vous aime bien.'
21 H. James, Jr, *The Portrait of a Lady* (London: Penguin Classics, 2000), p. 549; A. Zviguilsky (ed.), op. cit., pp. 175, 181.
22 H. James, Jr, *The Portrait of a Lady,* op. cit., pp. 372, 194; Paul Viardot, *Souvenirs d'un Artiste* (Paris: Librairie Fischbacher SA, 1910), p. 21.
23 B. Weinreb and C. Hibbert, *London Encyclopaedia* (London: Macmillan, 1993), pp. 227, 512, 91; J.P.T. Bury, op. cit., p. 108; C. Jones, *The Cambridge Illustrated History of France* (Cambridge: Cambridge University Press, 1994), p. 214; A. Horne, op. cit., p. 20.
24 H. James, Jr, *The Portrait of a Lady,* op. cit., pp. 217, 241. The French historian was H. Taine, quoted in P. Ackroyd, *Dickens* (London: Sinclair Stevenson, 1990), p. 940.
25 A. Zviguilsky (ed.), op. cit., p. 179; A. FitzLyon, *The Price of Genius, a life of Pauline Viardot* (London: John Calder, 1964), p. 409; J. Chissell, *Clara Schumann: a Dedicated Spirit* (London: Hamish Hamilton, 1983), p. 166; U. Lange-Brachmann and J. Draheim (ed.), op. cit., p. 63. The Grand-Duchess was the influential Elena Pavlovna, the patron of Anton Rubinstein among many others – G. Dulong, op. cit., p. 158.

26 P. Waddington, *Turgenev and England*, op. cit., p. 143; H. Granjard and A. Zviguilsky, op. cit., p. 173; A. FitzLyon, op. cit., p. 409; A. Zviguilsky (ed.), op. cit., pp. 187, 325. R. Somerset-Ward, *Angels and Monsters* (New Haven and London: Yale University Press, 2004), pp. 153, 156; H. Granjard and A. Zviguilsky, op. cit., pp. 173, 177.
27 A. Zviguilsky (ed.), op. cit., p. 249; N. Žekulin, op. cit., p. 67; P. Waddington, *Russian Interests of the Rossetti Family* (Pinehaven, New Zealand, 1998), p. 11; P. Waddington, 'Turgenev and George Eliot, a literary friendship', *Modern Language Review*, vol. 66, 1971, p. 48.
28 H. James, Jr, *English Hours* (Oxford: OUP, 1981, first published 1905) 'Browning in Westminster Abbey', p. 33.
29 P. Waddington, 'Dickens, Pauline Viardot and Turgenev: a Study in Mutual Admiration', *New Zealand Slavonic Journal*, no. 2, 1974, p. 68. Some suggest that they saw Dickens. Paul Viardot, wrongly, wrote that Dickens was one of the visitors to Devonshire Place.
30 G. Dulong, op. cit., p. 148; Paul Viardot, *Souvenirs d'un Artiste* (Paris: Librairie Fischbacher SA, 1910), p. 21.
31 D. Magarshack, *Turgenev, a Life* (London: Faber & Faber, 1954), p. 265.
32 V.S. Pritchett, op. cit., p. 188.
33 F. Steegmuller and B. Bray (trans.), *Flaubert-Sand, the Correspondence* (Hammersmith: Harvill, 1993), p. 228.
34 P. Waddington, 'Turgenev's relations with H.F. Chorley', *New Zealand Slavonic Journal*, no. 2, 1978, p. 38.
35 E. Zola (trans. and intro. D. Parmée), 'The Attack on the Mill', in *The Attack on the Mill and other stories* (Oxford: Oxford University Press, 1984).
36 G. Dulong, op. cit., p. 158; P. Waddington, 'The strange history of Dr F. and the dismantling of Courtavenel', *Modern Language Review*, vol. 65, 1970.
37 M. L'Hôpital, *Louis Viardot, Mémoires de l'Académie des Sciences* (Dijon: Arts et Belles-Lettres de Dijon, 1954), p. 31 A. FitzLyon, op. cit., p. 409.
38 J. Harding, *Gounod* (London: George Allen & Unwin Ltd, 1973), p. 83.
39 J. Harding, op. cit., pp. 85, 87, 92; *New Grove Dictionary of Music and Musicians* (London: Macmillan, 1980), vol. 17, p. 89, Scribe (C.N. Smith).
40 *New Grove*, op. cit., vol. 7, p. 582, Gounod (Martin Cooper). Marie Miolan-Carvalho changed her name to Caroline on marrying Léon: *New Grove*, op. cit., vol. 3, p. 840, Carvalho (H. Rosenthal).
41 J. Harding, op. cit., pp. 106, 114, 130.
42 Ibid., pp. 106, 130; T.J. Walsh, *Second Empire Opera* (London: Calder, 1981), p. 90. She mutilated the part of Cherubino. The composer was Reynaldo Hahn, later an acquaintance of Pauline.
43 J. Harding, op. cit., pp. 104, 112.
44 Covent Garden Programme, October 2004, p. 46.
45 J. Harding, op. cit., p. 108.
46 *New Grove*, op. cit., vol. 7, p. 583, Gounod (Martin Cooper).
47 J. Harding, op. cit., p. 121.
48 Ibid., pp. 80, 81.
49 'Une sorte de rêverie languissante, nerveuse et sensuelle': H. Granjard and A. Zviguilsky, op. cit., p. 95.
50 H. Granjard and A. Zviguilsky, op. cit., pp. xiv, 113, 114.
51 J. Harding, op. cit., pp. 145, 147; H. Granjard and A. Zviguilsky, op. cit., p. 137.
52 J. Harding, op. cit., p. 148. His appointment followed the death of Clapisson.
53 C. Gounod (trans. A. Crocker), *Memoirs of an Artist* (Chicago: Rand McNally & Company, 1895), pp. 177, 180.
54 J. Harding, op. cit., pp. 97, 133.
55 Paul Viardot, op. cit., pp. 178, 179.
56 J. Harding, op. cit., pp. 155, 156, 158.
57 *Musical Quarterly*, vol. 5, 1919, pp. 40–61 (Gounod Letters). Writing to his brother-in-law, Gounod called the Prussians 'a race of men still allied to the deformities of chaos and monstrosities of the Iron Age, who, instead of thrusting the iron into the soil for the benefit of humanity, thrust it into the hearts of men to gain possession of the soil'.
58 J. Harding, op. cit., p. 82.
59 A. Horne, op. cit., p. 232; *Encyclopaedia Britannica*, ninth edition, vol. XVIII, p. 294. A plaque near Gounod's house records: '19 janvier 1871. Ici résistèrent les mobiles Bretons sous les orders du Cdt de Lareinty'.
60 J. Harding, op. cit., p. 161. *The New Oxford Companion to Music* (Oxford: Oxford University Press, 1984), ninth edition.

61 J. Harding, op. cit., p. 168.
62 Ibid., pp. 168, 184, 63; B. Thompson, *A Monkey among Crocodiles* (London: HarperCollins, 2000), p. 107; *New Grove*, op. cit., vol. 7, p. 583, Gounod (Martin Cooper) refers to Georgina as Gounod's mistress.
63 P. Treherne, *A Plaintiff in Person* (Heinemann, 1923), pp. 4, 90.
64 P. Treherne, op. cit., pp. 110, 237. The case was in 1885. She died in January 1914.
65 J. Harding, op. cit., p. 164.
66 Rougedragon Poursuivant.
67 P. Ackroyd, *Dickens* (London: Sinclair Stevenson, 1990), pp. 634, 881. Dickens sold it in 1860. The description of the garden comes from P. Treherne, op cit. p. 24.
68 P. Treherne, op. cit., p. 31; *New Grove*, op. cit., vol. 7, p. 583, Gounod (Martin Cooper); J. Harding, op. cit., p. 165.
69 B. Thompson, op. cit., p. 108; J. Harding, op. cit., p.70.
70 B. Thompson, op. cit., p. 121; J. Harding, op. cit., p. 177.
71 P. Treherne, op. cit., p. 29.
72 C. Dickens, *The Pickwick Papers* (Oxford: Oxford University Press, World Classics, 1988), ch. XXXIV; J. Harding, op. cit., p. 178; The *Musical Times* report and quotes are from the 1 July 1873 edition, p. 143. In *Le Figaro*, Gounod said that the plaintiff had dropped the claim or knew who had settled it; The *Musical Times* notice, of 1 October 1973, p. 242, was to the effect that the full amount had been paid and Novellos did not know the name of who had settled it.
73 H James Jr, *English Hours*, op. cit., p. 156; J. Harding, op. cit., p.182.
74 N. Simeone, *Paris – A Musical Gazetteer* (New Haven and London: Yale University Press, 2000), p. 76. This was in 1874.
75 J. Harding, op. cit., p.186.
76 P. Treherne, op. cit., pp. 85, 86.
77 *The Strange Life of Georgina Weldon* (London: Chatto & Windus, 1959), p. 247; J. Harding, op. cit., p. 210. She was released on 22 September 1885.
78 P. Treherne, op. cit., p. 110; J. Harding, op. cit., pp. 208, 210.
79 There is a picture of the house on the wall outside no. 3, rue Gounod in Saint-Cloud. The original house has gone.
80 N. Simeone, op. cit., pp. 35, 77; J. Harding, op. cit., p. 203. He set up in Pl. Malesherbes in 1879.
81 *Musical Times*, 1 June 1877; J. Harding, op. cit., p. 213. The quality of the opera betrayed the speed of its composition.
82 J. Harding, op. cit., p. 205; *New Grove*, op. cit., vol. 7, p. 586, Gounod (M Cooper); E. Walker, *A History of Music in England* (Oxford: Clarendon Press, 1952), p. 399.
83 C.V. Stanford and C. Forsyth, *A History of Music* (New York: Macmillan, 1917), p. 279.
84 P. Treherne, op. cit., p. 26.
85 J. Harding, op. cit., pp. 206, 220; Paul Viardot, op. cit., p. 66. 'Son esprit était inépuisable, sans malveillance aucune, même vis-à-vis ses confrères.'
86 A. FitzLyon, op. cit., p. 41; P. Waddington, 'Some Gleanings on Turgenev and his International Connections', *New Zealand Slavonic Journal*, 1983, p. 218; Paul Viardot, op. cit., p. 65.
87 J. Harding, op. cit., p. 216.
88 P. Treherne, op. cit., pp. 96, 118.
89 Ibid., p. 54. She began this in 1878.
90 Ibid., pp. 57, 87; *Encyclopaedia Britannica*, ninth edition, vol. XXIV, p. 641.

Chapter 24. The Nest in Paris (pp. 363–384)

1 A. Horne, *The Fall of Paris* (London: Macmillan, 1965), p. 421; P. Waddington, *Turgenev and England* (London: Macmillan, 1980), p. 206; A. Zviguilsky (ed.), *Ivan Tourguénev: Nouvelle Correspondance inédite* (Paris: Librairie des Cinq Continents, 1971), pp. 194, 195; U. Lange-Brachmann and J. Draheim (ed.), *Pauline Viardot in Baden Baden und Karlsruhe* (Baden-Baden: Nomos Verlaggesellschaft, 1999), p. 63.
2 H. Granjard and A. Zviguilsky, *Ivan Tourgénev, Lettres inédites à Pauline Viardot et à sa famille* (Paris: Editions l'Age d'Homme, 1972), pp. 178, 181; P. Waddington, *A Modest Little Banquet at the Arts Club* (Pinehaven, New Zealand, 2001), p. 10.
3 I. Evans, *A Short History of English Literature* (Harmondsworth: Penguin, 1963), p. 66; D. Karlin's introduction to R. Browning, *Selected Poems* (London: Penguin, 1989), p.12.
4 G. Dulong, *Pauline Viardot Tragédienne Lyrique* (Bougival: Association des Amis d'Ivan

Tourguéniev Pauline Viardot et Maria Malibran), p. 159; A. Zviguilsky (ed.), op. cit., p. 191; H. Troyat (trans. N. Amphoux), *Turgenev* (London: W.H. Allen, 1989), p. 104; V.S. Pritchett, *The Gentle Barbarian, The Life and Work of Turgenev* (London: Chatto & Windus, 1977), p. 189; W. Kuhe, *My musical recollections* (London: Richard Bentley, 1896), p. 187.

5 G. de Maupassant (trans. G. Hopkins), *Short Stories* (London: The Folio Society, 1959), p. 250.

6 H. James, Jr (ed. P. Lubbock), *Letters of Henry James* (London: Macmillan, 1920), p. 45.

7 *New Grove Dictionary of Music and Musicians* (London: Macmillan, 1980), vol. 6, p. 751, France (Martin Cooper).

8 V.S. Pritchett, op. cit., p. 206; P. Waddington, *Turgenev's Seventh* (Pinehaven, New Zealand, 2003), p. 34; Leonard Schapiro's critical essay '*Spring Torrents*, Its Place and Significance in the Life and Work of I.S. Turgenev' (London: Penguin, 1980); I. Turgenev (trans. L. Schapiro), *Spring Torrents* (London: Penguin, 1980), p. 183; L. Schapiro, *Turgenev, his Life and Times* (Oxford: OUP, 1978), p. 251.

9 I. Turgenev, *Spring Torrents*, op. cit., p. 168.

10 I. Turgenev (trans. I. and T. Litvinov), *Three Short Novels* (Moscow: Foreign Language Publishing House, no date but around 1980), p. 297.

11 Ibid., p. 297.

12 L. Schapiro, *Turgenev, his Life and Times*, op. cit., p. 199.

13 Musée Tourguéniev (par Tamara Zviguilsky), *Guide* (Corlet Condé-sur-Noireau, 1993); A. Zviguilsky (ed.), op. cit., pp. 198, 256, 207.

14 N. Simeone, *Paris – A Musical Gazetteer* (New Haven and London: Yale University Press, 2000), pp. 35, 77; Bizet lived at number 22, Rue de Douai – see plaque on wall. Information on Degas from Professeur Zviguilsky. Halévy lived in the rue de La Rochefoucauld.

15 Musée de Montmartre, Bals et Cabarets au temps de Bruant et Lautrec (Paris: Editions le Vieux Montmartre, 2002). Also, information obtained during the author's visit. The blessing of the dome cross was in 1899.

16 H. Granjard and A. Zviguilsky, op. cit., p. xi.

17 H. Troyat, op. cit., p. 104; V.S. Pritchett, op. cit., pp. 190, 208; G. Dulong, op. cit., p. 164; A. FitzLyon, *The Price of Genius, a life of Pauline Viardot* (London: John Calder, 1964), p. 417; S. Rutherford, *The Prima Donna and Opera 1815–1930* (Cambridge: Cambridge University Press, 2006), p.90 et seq.

18 L. Schapiro, *Turgenev, his Life and Times*, op. cit., p. 244; H. Granjard and A. Zviguilsky, op. cit., pp. 273, 163.

19 L. Schapiro, *Turgenev, his Life and Times*, op. cit., p. 227; H. Granjard and A. Zviguilsky, op. cit., p. 150; P. Waddington, 'The strange history of Dr F. and the dismantling of Courtavenel', *Modern Language Review*, vol. 65, 1970, p. 336.

20 P. Waddington writing in *The Times Literary Supplement*, London, 1 January 1970, p. 16; A. Zviguilsky (ed.), op. cit., p. 190.

21 G. Dulong, op. cit., p. 163.

22 L Viardot, *Wonders of Sculpture* (New York: Scribner, Armstrong, and Company, 1873), p. 271.

23 Translator's note in L Viardot, *The Wonders of Sculpture*, op. cit.

24 L. Viardot, *The Wonders of Sculpture*, op. cit., p. 272.

25 L. Viardot, *Les Merveilles de la Peinture* (Paris: Libriarie Hachette, 1875), p. 249.

26 L.Viardot, *The Wonders of Sculpture*, op. cit., p. 274.

27 G. Dulong, op. cit., p. 163. This meeting was in 1877.

28 P. Waddington, 'Some Gleanings on Turgenev and his International Connections' *New Zealand Slavonic Journal*, 1983.

29 G. Dulong, op. cit., p. 164; H. Troyat, op. cit., pp. 102, 104; *Musée Tourguéniev Guide*, op. cit., p. 44; V.S. Pritchett, op. cit., p. 210.

30 A. FitzLyon, *The Price of Genius*, op. cit., p. 428; L. Schapiro, *Turgenev, his Life and Times*, op. cit., p. 271. This was in March 1877.

31 V.S. Pritchett, op. cit., p. 210; H. Granjard and A. Zviguilsky, op. cit., p. 201; P. Waddington, *A Modest Little Banquet at the Arts Club* (Pinehaven, New Zealand, 2001), p. 14; P. Waddington, *Russian interests of the Rossetti Family* (Pinehaven, New Zealand, 1998), p. 12.

32 L. Schapiro critical essay in I. Turgenev (trans. L. Schapiro), *Spring Torrents*, op. cit., p. 202.

33 P. Waddington, 'Some Gleanings', op. cit., p. 189.

34 E. de Goncourt (trans. Belloc and Shedlock), *Journal* (London: Heinemann, 1895), vol. II, p. 162; P. Waddington, *A Modest Little Banquet*, op. cit., p. 14; L. Schapiro,

Turgenev, his Life and Times (Oxford: OUP, 1978), pp. 109, 236.

35 The National Gallery, London, *Russian Landscape*, the Exhibition Guide for *Russian Landscape in the Age of Tolstoy*, July 2004, pp. 93, 96 (Sjeng Scheijen); L Schapiro, *Turgenev, his Life and Times*, op. cit., p. 242.

36 National Gallery London Exhibition Guide, op. cit., p. 96.

37 Ibid., p. 96.

38 V.S. Pritchett, op. cit., p. 210; G. Dulong, op. cit., p.166.

39 H. Granjard and A. Zviguilsky, op. cit., pp. 279, 328.

40 *Cahiers Ivan Tourguéniev, Pauline Viardot, Maria Malibran* (Bougival: Association des Amis d'Ivan Tourguéniev Pauline Viardot et Maria Malibran), vol. 20, p. 79; H. Troyat, op. cit., p. 110.

41 P. Waddington, *Turgenev and England*, op. cit., p. 192; E. de Goncourt, *Journal*, op. cit., vol. III, p. 712 (10 October 1887). The Swinburne story was very much third-hand, and may have come from Kharlamov who painted the portrait of Turgenev.

42 R. Baldick (ed.), *Pages from the Goncourt Journal* (Oxford: Oxford University Press, 1978), pp. 83, 197.

43 G. Wall, *Flaubert, a Life* (London: Faber and Faber, 2001), pp. 183, 222, 250, 278; *Encyclopaedia Britannica*, Standard Millennium edition.

44 L. Schapiro, *Turgenev, his Life and Times*, op. cit., p. 245; Paul Viardot, *Souvenirs d'un Artiste* (Paris: Librairie Fischbacher SA, 1910), p. 47; A. Zviguilsky (ed.), op. cit., p. xxix; C. Saint-Saëns (trans. E.G. Rich), *Musical Memories* (London: Murray, 1921), p. 148; A. FitzLyon, *The Price of Genius*, op. cit., p. 421.

45 C. Saint-Saëns, op. cit., p. 149; Paul Viardot, op. cit., p. 34; A. FitzLyon, *The Price of Genius*, op. cit., p. 420; Henry James, Jr (ed. P. Lubbock), *Letters of Henry James* (London: Macmillan, 1920), p. 45: 11 April 1876.

46 B. Rees, *Camille Saint-Saëns, A Life* (London: Chatto & Windus, 1999), p. 90; J. Harding, *Saint-Saëns and his Circle* (London: Chapman & Hall, 1965), p. 5; Paul Viardot was, however, charmed by the old lady – Paul Viardot, op. cit., p. 48.

47 B. Rees, op. cit., pp. 199, 216, 221, 371.

48 Ibid., pp. 93, 373; J. Harding, op. cit., p. 89.

49 J. Harding, op. cit., p. 57, Paul Viardot, op. cit., p. 54.

50 G. Dulong, op. cit., p. 162.

51 A. Zviguilsky (ed.), op. cit., p. 183; *New Grove*, op. cit., vol. 18, p. 774, Thomas (P. Robinson).

52 I. Turgenev (ed. E. Halpérine-Kaminsky), *Lettres à Madame Viardot* (Paris: Bibliothèque-Charpentier, 1907), 25 March 1868, p. 233; *The New Oxford Companion to Music* (Oxford: Oxford University Press, 1984), p. 1818; Review of performance at Covent Garden in 2003 (*The Times Literary Supplement*, London, 23 May 2003, p. 20).

53 R. Orledge, *Gabriel Fauré* (London: Eulenburg, 1979), p. 10.

54 Sunday games were prohibited at Blenheim Palace: see A. Mackenzie Stuart, *Consuelo & Alva* (London: HarperCollins, 2005).

55 H. James, Jr, *Letters*, op. cit., p. 45, 11 April 1876; L. Schapiro, *Turgenev, his Life and Times*, op. cit., p. 290; *Encyclopaedia Britannica*, ninth edition, *Encyclopaedia Britannica*, Standard Millennium edition.

56 L. Schapiro, *Turgenev, his Life and Times*, op. cit., pp. 240, 274, 293.

57 I. Turgenev (trans. Hugh Aplin, foreword by Simon Callow), *Faust and Yakov Pasynkov* (London: Hesperus Press, 2003), p. 91; V.S. Pritchett, op. cit., p. 231.

58 R. Orledge, op. cit., p. 9; Paul Viardot, op. cit., p. 53; B. Rees, op. cit., p. 165.

59 A. FitzLyon, *The Price of Genius*, op. cit., p. 437.

60 G. Dulong, op. cit., p. 160; *The New Oxford Companion to Music* (Oxford: Oxford University Press, 1984), p. 1818.

61 G. Dulong, op. cit., pp. 160, 162; *Cahiers*, op. cit., no. 2, p. 102; P. Waddington, *Three letters of Gustave Flaubert* (Pinehaven, New Zealand, 2000), p. 4.

62 P. Waddington, *The Musical Works of Pauline Viardot-Garcia* (Pinehaven, New Zealand: Whirinaki Press, 2004); S. Rutherford, *The Prima Donna and Opera 1815–1930* (Cambridge: Cambridge University Press, 2006), pp. 90 et seq.

63 A. FitzLyon, *The Price of Genius*, op. cit., p. 436; Demar Irvine, *Massenet, a Chronicle of his Life and Times* (New York: Amadeus Press, 1994), p. 71.

64 B. Rees, op. cit., p. 172; J. Harding, op. cit., p. 219.

65 B. Rees, op. cit., p. 172.
66 Demar Irvine, op. cit., p. 1; *New Grove*, op. cit., vol. 11, p. 801, Massenet (M. Cooper).
67 B. Rees, op. cit., p. 256.
68 P. Waddington, *Three letters*, op. cit., p. 3.
69 B. Rees, op. cit., pp. 140, 152, 210; G. Dulong, op. cit., p. 161; J. Harding, op. cit., pp. 102, 149; A. FitzLyon, *The Price of Genius*, op. cit., p. 459.
70 L. Schapiro, *Turgenev, his Life and Times*, op. cit., p. 272; P. Waddington, *Courtavenel, the History of an Artists' Nest and its Role in the Life of Turgenev* (*PhD Thesis*, Queen's University Belfast, The British Library, British Thesis Service, spring 1972), p. 67; L. Héritte-Viardot (trans. E.S. Bucheim), Memories and Adventures (London: Mills & Boon, 1913), p. 27; *Musical Quarterly*, vol. I, 1915, p. 542. Turgenev was horrified by the bloody side of Christianity: Turgenev, *Lettres à Madame Viardot*, op. cit., 19 October 1847, p. 10.
71 J.P.T. Bury, *France 1814–1940* (London: Methuen, 1969), p. 161.
72 C. Jones, *The Cambridge Illustrated History of France* (Cambridge: Cambridge University Press, 1994), p. 221.
73 Ibid., pp. 225, 227, 229, 230; J.P.T. Bury, op. cit., pp. 181, 206. France slipped (by 1914) to fourth place in the greatest industrial world powers.
74 C. Jones, op. cit., p. 221.
75 J.P.T. Bury, op. cit., pp. 131, 180. *The Times*, 18 November 1870.
76 J.P.T. Bury, op. cit., p. 180.
77 B. Rees, op. cit., p. 267.
78 Ibid., pp. 308, 314; C. Jones, op. cit., p. 238. The attempt was in 1893.
79 J.P.T. Bury, op. cit., p. 187.
80 B. Rees, op. cit., p. 268; *New Grove*, op. cit., vol. 3, p. 842, Carvalho (H. Rosenthal).
81 R. Orledge, op. cit., p. 10; A. FitzLyon, *The Price of Genius*, op. cit., p. 434; B. Rees, op. cit., p. 398.
82 Camille Bellaigue comments in G. Fauré (ed. C. Bellaigue), 'Lettres à une Fiancée', *Revue des deux mondes*, xlvi, 1928, pp. 911–943
83 B. Rees, op. cit., pp. 143, 150; *New Grove*, op. cit., vol. 6, p. 417, Fauré (J-M Nectoux).
84 R. Orledge, op. cit., pp. 279, 280.
85 R. Orledge, op. cit., p. 232; *New Grove*, op. cit., vol. 6, p. 423, Fauré (J-M Nectoux). An example would be *Clair de Lune.*
86 *New Grove*, op. cit., vol. 6, pp. 417–427, Fauré (J-M Nectoux).
87 G. Fauré, *Lettres à une Fiancée*, op. cit., pp. 911–943.
88 J. Barrie Jones (trans. and ed.), *Gabriel Fauré, A life in letters* (London: Batsford, 1988), pp. 5, 33; G. Fauré, *Lettres à une Fiancée*, op. cit., pp. 911–943. The suggestion that he was unambitious is from Camille Bellaigue in G. Fauré, *Lettres à une Fiancée*, op. cit.
89 B. Rees, op. cit., p. 206.
90 Camille Bellaigue's comments in G. Fauré, *Lettres à une Fiancée*, op. cit.
91 R. Orledge, op. cit., p. 113.
92 B. Rees, op. cit., p. 37; *New Grove*, op. cit., vol. 5, p. 763. P. Waddington, 'Some Gleanings', op. cit., p. 218. The wedding was on 5 April 1881.
93 A. Zviguilsky (ed.), op. cit., Appendix.

Chapter 25. Flaubert (pp. 385–397)

1 P. Waddington, 'Turgenev and the International Literary Congress of 1878', *New Zealand Slavonic Journal*, 1983.
2 L. Schapiro, *Turgenev, his Life and Times* (Oxford: OUP, 1978), p. 289. Turgenev told Marianne that after her family, and Annenkov, Flaubert was the man he loved the most.
3 L. Schapiro, op. cit., p. 206. The friendship blossomed from 1868: L. Schapiro, op. cit.
4 B. Jack, *George Sand: A Woman's Life Writ Large* (London: Chatto & Windus, 1999), p. 347; A. Jacobs (ed.), *Correspondance: Gustave Flaubert-George Sand* (Paris, 1981), p. 301.
5 G. Wall, *Flaubert, a Life* (London: Faber and Faber, 2001), p. 269.
6 Ibid., pp. 253, 286; E. de Goncourt, *Journal* (Paris, 1887), vol. II, p. 242; V.S. Pritchett, *The Gentle Barbarian, The Life and Work of Turgenev* (London: Chatto & Windus, 1977), p. 211.
7 L. Schapiro, op. cit., pp. 235, 289.
8 F. Steegmuller and B. Bray (trans.), *Flaubert-Sand, the Correspondence* (Hammersmith: Harvill, 1993), pp. 269, 303, 311, 391.
9 G. Flaubert (trans. R. Baldick), *Sentimental Education* (London: Penguin, 2004), introduction, p. xiii; G. Wall, op. cit., p. 43; G. Flaubert, *Memoirs of a Madman* (London: Hesperus Press, 2002), p. 40.
10 G. Flaubert, *L'Éducation Sentimentale* (Paris: Flammarion, 1985).

11 G. Wall, op. cit., p. 262.
12 E. de Goncourt (trans. Bellloc and Shedlock), *Journal* (London: Heinemann, 1895), vol. I, p. 239; P. Waddington, *Turgenev's Mortal Illness from its Origins to the Autopsy* (Pinehaven, New Zealand: Whirinaki Press, 1999), p. 7; G. de Maupassant (trans. G. Hopkins), *Short Stories* (London: The Folio Society, 1959), p. 95.
13 G. Wall, op. cit., pp. 75, 196; E. de Goncourt, *Journal*, op. cit., 9 May 1865.
14 F. Steegmuller, *The Letters of Gustave Flaubert Vols I & II 1830–1880* (London: Picador, 2001), p. 68. The studio was Pradier's.
15 G. Wall, op. cit., pp. 202, 207, 218, 220.
16 G. Flaubert, *Sentimental Education*, op. cit., p. 467.
17 P. Waddington, *Turgenev and England* (London: Macmillan, 1980), p. 74.
18 G. Wall, op. cit., pp. 197, 214, 227; G. Flaubert, *Madame Bovary* (Oxford: Oxford University Press, 2004), part 1, ch. 7.
19 G. Flaubert, *Madame Bovary*, op. cit., part 1, ch. 9.
20 H. James, Jr, *French Poets and Novelists* (London: Macmillan, 1878), p. 255.
21 G. Flaubert, *Madame Bovary*, op. cit., pt 3, ch. 5.
22 G. Wall, op. cit., pp. 229, 234, 235, 349.
23 Ibid., pp, 237, 241. C. Baudelaire (ed. W. Fowlie), *Les Fleurs du Mal* (New York: Bantam, 1964), p. 42. For example, 'Je plongerai ma tête amoureuse d'ivresse/dans ce noir océan où l'autre est enfermé.'
24 G. Wall, op. cit., p. 256.
25 Ibid., p. 252
26 G. Flaubert, *Oeuvres complète* (Paris, 1971–75), vol. 2, p. 431. 'Il cultive l'atrocité.'
27 Ibid. p. 431. 'Une preuve de sa force de paraître inhumain dans ses lèvres.'
28 Ibid. p. 455.
29 Maupassant's Preface to *Lettres de Gustave Flaubert à George Sand* (Paris: Charpentier, 1884): this is quoted in F. Steegmuller, op. cit., p. 332.
30 *The Times Literary Supplement*, London, 6 May 2005, p. 22.
31 G. Wall, op. cit., p. 301.
32 H. James, Jr, *French Poets and Novelists*, op. cit., pp. 258, 267.
33 G. Flaubert (trans. R. Baldick), *Sentimental Education* (London: Penguin, 2004), p. xxvii.
34 G. Flaubert (trans. D.F. Hannigan), Sentimental Education (London: H.S. Nichols Ltd Publishers, 1898), p. 391; G. Flaubert, *L'Education Sentimentale* (Paris: Flammarion, 1985), p. 69.
35 G. Flaubert (ed. Bruneau), *Correspondence* (Paris, 1973–1998), vol. IV, p. 1436.
36 Flaubert to Le Poittevin, from Geneva: F. Steegmuller and B. Bray (trans.), op. cit., pp. 53, 54; Lord Byron, *The Prisoner of Chillon and Other Poems 1816* (Menston: The Scholar Press, 1969), lines 48,114, 116–118, 373–374, 391–392. The visit was in May 1845.
37 Paul Viardot, *Souvenirs d'un Artiste* (Paris: Librairie Fischbacher SA, 1910), p. 126.
38 G. Wall, op. cit., p. 160. This was in autumn 1849.
39 P. Waddington, *Turgenev and George Sand: An Improbable Entente* (Victoria University Press, 1981), p. 53.
40 F. Steegmuller and B. Bray (trans.), op. cit., p. 344.
41 Ibid., p. 319.
42 Ibid., pp. 278, 345, 561.
43 P. Waddington, *Turgenev and George Sand*, op. cit., p. 74; F. Steegmuller and B. Bray (trans.), op. cit., pp. 562, 569.
44 B. Jack, *George Sand: A Woman's Life Writ Large* (London: Chatto & Windus, 1999), p. 350. G Sand (ed. Anne Chevereau), *Agendas* (Paris, 1992–1993), vol. V, p. 80.
45 Paul Viardot, op. cit., pp. 40, 42.
46 B. Jack, op. cit., 351; G. Sand, *Agendas*, op. cit., vol. V, p. 149.
47 P. Waddington, *Turgenev and George Sand*, op. cit., p. 69; G. Wall, op. cit., p. 305.
48 The friend was Edmond Plauchut, a regular at Nohant: P. Waddington, *Turgenev and George Sand*, op. cit., p. 70. This party was over New Year (1872–73). If it were not for the fact that Hérodias (in which John the Baptist's head is served up on a charger) was begun in 1876, one would have thought that Plauchut had referred to the wrong novel.
49 H. Granjard and A. Zviguilsky, *Ivan Tourgénev, Lettres inédites à Pauline Viardot et à sa famille* (Paris: Editions l'Age d'Homme, 1972), p. 193
50 B. Jack, op. cit., pp. 351, 355; G. Sand, *Agendas*, op. cit., vol. V, p. 228.
51 P. Waddington, *Turgenev and George Sand*, op. cit., p. 75; G. Wall, op. cit., p. 326; F.

Steegmuller and B. Bray (trans.), op. cit., p. 322.
52 P. Waddington, *Turgenev and George Sand*, op. cit., p. 75; see Paul Viardot, op. cit., p. 42 for poor shooting at Nohant.
53 G. Wall, op. cit., pp. 262, 332; L. Schapiro, op. cit., p. 289.
54 P. Waddington, *Turgenev and George Sand*, op. cit., p. 100. Sand died on 8 June 1876. Pauline referred to her kindness. 'What a heart of gold she had.' A. FitzLyon, *The Price of Genius, a life of Pauline Viardot* (London: John Calder, 1964), p. 425.
55 L. Guichard's introduction to G. Sand (trans. Fayette Robinson), *Consuelo* (New York: Stringer and Townsend, 1851): 'Pauline envoya une couronne où se lisait en lettres noires, sur un fond d'immortelles jaunes, ce nom: Consuelo. (Renseignement communiqué par Mme Aurore Sand.)'
56 B. Jack, op. cit., p. 363, *G. Flaubert, lettres à Tourguéneff* (Monaco, 1946), pp. 104–6.
57 R. Bosco, *The Brownings and Mrs Kinney* (Browning Institute Studies, no. 4, 1976), p. 70.
58 From Dublin, *Musical Quarterly*, vol. I, 1915, p. 540, 20 February 1859. 'Celle là est une passion qui ne peut pas décroître. C'est la plus belle de toutes.'
59 25 May 1880: Maupassant to Turgenev, in F. Steegmuller, *The Letters of Gustave Flaubert*, vols I & II 1830–1880, op. cit., p. 666.
60 G. Wall, op. cit., p. 345.

Chapter 26. Bougival (pp. 399–407)

1 A. Zviguilsky (ed.), *Ivan Tourguénev: Nouvelle Correspondance inédite* (Paris: Librairie des Cinq Continents, 1971), p. 222.
2 V.S. Pritchett, *The Gentle Barbarian, The Life and Work of Turgenev* (London: Chatto & Windus, 1977), p. 211.
3 D. Magarshack, *Turgenev, a Life* (London: Faber & Faber, 1954), p. 269.
4 G. de Maupassant (trans. G. Hopkins), *Short Stories* (London: The Folio Society, 1959), 'Paul's Mistress', p. 45.
5 Musée Tourguéniev (par Tamara Zviguilsky), *Guide* (Corlet Condé-sur-Noireau, 1993), p. 1.
6 A. Zviguilsky (ed.), op. cit., p. 199; H. Granjard and A. Zviguilsky, *Ivan Tourguénev, Lettres inédites à Pauline Viardot et à sa famille* (Paris: Editions l'Age d'Homme, 1972), p. 193.
7 G. Dulong, *Pauline Viardot Tragédienne Lyrique* (Bougival: Association des Amis d'Ivan Tourguéniev Pauline Viardot et Maria Malibran), p. 166.
8 D. Magarshack, op. cit., p. 269. L. Schapiro, *Turgenev, his Life and Times* (Oxford: OUP, 1978), p. 280, suggests that Turgenev's contribution to the purchase was at least one third of the value of the property.
9 P. Waddington, 'Turgenev's Last Will and Testament', *New Zealand Slavonic Journal*, no. 2, 1974, p. 40; A. Seljak, *Ivan Turgenev's Ökonomien* (Zurich: University of Basel, Pano Verlag, 2004), p. 235.
10 L. Schapiro, op. cit., p. 280; A. Seljak, op. cit., pp. 302, 304.
11 H. Troyat (trans. N. Amphoux), *Turgenev* (London: W.H. Allen, 1989), p. 121 – letter of 17/29 April 1878.
12 A. Zviguilsky (ed.), op. cit., p. 258.
13 A. FitzLyon, *The Price of Genius, a life of Pauline Viardot* (London: John Calder, 1964), p. 417; G. Fauré (ed. C. Bellaigue), 'Lettres à une Fiancée', *Revue des deux Mondes*, xlvi, année xcviii, p. 936; H. Troyat, op. cit., p. 119; Musée Tourguéniev (par Tamara Zviguilsky), *Guide* (Corlet Condé-sur-Noireau, 1993), p. 10; P. Waddington, 'Turgenev and George Eliot, a literary friendship', *Modern Language Review*, vol. 66, 1971.
14 Musée Tourguéniev, *Guide*, op. cit., p. 10; A. FitzLyon, *The Price of Genius*, op. cit., p. 433.
15 *Cahiers Ivan Tourguéniev, Pauline Viardot, Maria Malibran* (Bougival: Association des Amis d'Ivan Tourguéniev Pauline Viardot et Maria Malibran), vol. 2, p. 27; H. Granjard and A. Zviguilsky, op. cit., p. 277.
16 A. Zviguilsky (ed.), op. cit., I, p. 270; Mrs FitzLyon met Marcelle in the mid-1960s. The thought that the elder daughter Jeanne was Turgenev's child seems far-fetched. She was born 9 months plus a fortnight after her wedding to Georges Chamerot, the son of a shooting friend of Louis Viardot. Information from Mr Kyril FitzLyon.
17 A. Zviguilsky (ed.), op. cit., Appendix. The author is grateful to the Rev. Peter Hewlett-Smith for this information.
18 H. Granjard and A. Zviguilsky, op. cit., p. 275; Paul Viardot, *Souvenirs d'un Artiste* (Paris: Librairie Fischbacher SA, 1910), p. 90; G. de Maupassant, *Paul's Mistress*, op. cit., p. 46.
19 L. Schapiro, op. cit., p. 254; H. Granjard and A. Zviguilsky, op. cit., p. 133.

20 H. Granjard and A. Zviguilsky, op. cit., p. 220; E. de Goncourt, *Journal* (Paris, 1887), vol. 5, p. 24: 2 March 1872; *Cahiers*, op. cit., no. 17—18, p. 113; D. Magarshack, op. cit., p. 271.
21 A. Zviguilsky (ed.), op. cit., pp. 212, 213.
22 H. Granjard and A. Zviguilsky, op. cit., pp. 199, 202, 206, 210.
23 A. Zviguilsky (ed.), op. cit., pp. 214, 215; L. Schapiro, op. cit., pp. 254, 280, 302.
24 D. Magarshack, op. cit., p. 275; P. Waddington, 'Turgenev and George Eliot, a literary friendship', *Modern Language Review*, vol. 66, 1971, p. 754; R. Freeborn, *Turgenev, the novelist's novelist* (Oxford: Oxford University Press, 1960), p. 176. Henry James' comment comes from a letter to his sister, 8 April 1877.
25 Such as Insarov or, in *Virgin Soil*, Solomin; R. Freeborn, op. cit., p. 184.
26 L. Schapiro, op. cit., p. 259; R. Freeborn, op. cit., p. 167; M. Fainsod, *How Russia is Ruled* (Cambridge, MA: Harvard University Press, 1963), p. 14.
27 I. Turgenev (trans. Constance Garnett), *Virgin Soil* (New York: New York Review Book, 2000), p. vi.
28 Ibid., part 1, ch. 8, ch. 11, ch. 13, ch. 14; part 2, ch. 34.
29 Ibid., part 1, ch. 12
30 Ibid., part 1, ch. 6, ch. 10, ch. 11.
31 I. Turgenev (trans. T.S. Perry), *Virgin Soil* (London: Ward, Lock & Co, pre-1880), pt 2, ch. 27, p. 220.
32 I. Turgenev (trans. Constance Garnett), *Virgin Soil*, op. cit., part 2, ch. 29.
33 *Virgin Soil* (trans. T. S. Perry), Ward, Lock & Co London (pre 1880) pt 2 ch. 29, p. 232.
34 I. Turgenev (trans. T.S. Perry), *Virgin Soil*, op. cit., pt 2, ch. 29, p. 233.
35 I. Turgenev (trans. Constance Garnett), *Virgin Soil*, op. cit., introduction, p. ix, pt 2, ch. 36.
36 I. Turgenev (trans. T.S. Perry), *Virgin Soil*, op. cit., pt 2, p. 306.
37 R. Freeborn, op. cit., p. 176.
38 *Encyclopaedia Britannica,* Standard Millennium edition; H. Troyat, op. cit., p. 120. The *Brothers Karamazov* trial is supposed to be based on this trial – R. Freeborn, op. cit., p. 133.
39 I. Turgenev (ed. D. Borovsky), *Stories in Poems and Prose* (Moscow: Progress Publishers, 1982), p. 52.
40 I. Turgenev (trans. Constance Garnett), *Virgin Soil*, op. cit., pt 2, ch. 38; L. Schapiro, op. cit., pp. 277, 278; M. Fainsod, op. cit., p. 15. Garfield was shot in September 1881.
41 Moscow-Kursk railway: A. Zviguilsky (ed.), op. cit., p. 236. Winter Palace, on 17 February 1880: H. Granjard and A. Zviguilsky, op. cit., p. 219.
42 H. Granjard and A. Zviguilsky, op. cit., p. 219.
43 A. Zviguilsky (ed.), op. cit., p. 231; P. Waddington, *Turgenev and George Sand: An Improbable Entente* (Victoria University Press, 1981), pp. 49–51. The execution was on 5 March 1880.
44 L. Schapiro, op. cit., p. 287.
45 Paul Viardot, op. cit., p. 95.
46 *Encyclopaedia Britannica,* ninth edition, vol. XXI, p. 102.
47 The correspondent regarding the Orsini attack was W.M. Rossetti: P. Waddington, *Russian interests of the Rossetti Family* (Pinehaven, New Zealand, 1998), p. 25.
48 P. Waddington, *Turgenev and England* (London: Macmillan, 1980), p. 31.
49 V.S. Pritchett, op. cit., p. 216.
50 Introduction to I. Turgenev (trans. Constance Garnett), *Virgin Soil*, p. v; V.S. Pritchett, op. cit., p. 217; D. Magarshack, op. cit., p. 281
51 P. Waddington, *Turgenev's Seventh* (Pinehaven, New Zealand, 2003), p. 8.
52 Introduction to I. Turgenev (trans. E. Schimanskaya), *Poems in Prose* (London: Lindsay Drummond, 1945); L. Schapiro, op. cit., p. 286. Twenty-seven out of 69 are concerned with death.
53 I. Turgenev, *Poems in Prose*, op. cit., p. 13; L. Schapiro, op. cit., p. 286.
54 L. Schapiro, op. cit., pp. 175, 279.

Chapter 27. The Fisherman (pp. 409–419)

1 L. Schapiro, in his critical essay included in I. Turgenev (trans. L. Schapiro), *Spring Torrents* (London: Penguin, 1980), p. 216.
2 A. FitzLyon, *The Price of Genius, a life of Pauline Viardot* (London: John Calder, 1964), pp. 426, 429.
3 H. Troyat (trans. N. Amphoux), *Turgenev* (London: W.H. Allen, 1989), p. 116.
4 A. FitzLyon, *The Price of Genius*, op. cit., pp.

4. 26; L. Schapiro, *Turgenev, his Life and Times* (Oxford: OUP, 1978), pp. 203, 215.

5 I. Turgenev (trans. Isabel Hapgood), *On the Eve* (Freeport, New York: Books for Libraries Press, 1971), ch. 35.

6 L. Schapiro, op. cit., p. 214; H. Granjard and A. Zviguilsky, *Ivan Tourgénev, Lettres inédites à Pauline Viardot et à sa famille* (Paris: Editions l'Age d'Homme, 1972), p. xix; A. FitzLyon, *The Price of Genius*, op. cit., p. 378.

7 This was in 1873–77: H. Granjard and A. Zviguilsky, op. cit., p. 209; *Cahiers Ivan Tourguéniev, Pauline Viardot, Maria Malibran* (Bougival: Association des Amis d'Ivan Tourguéniev Pauline Viardot et Maria Malibran), no. 2, p. 24.

8 H. Granjard and A. Zviguilsky, op. cit., p. 207; *Cahiers*, op. cit., vol. 2, p. 24; D. Magarshack, *Turgenev, a Life* (London: Faber & Faber, 1954), p. 277; V.S. Pritchett, *The Gentle Barbarian, The Life and Work of Turgenev* (London: Chatto & Windus, 1977), p. 214.

9 V.S. Pritchett, op. cit., p. 214; *Cahiers*, op. cit., vol. 2, pp. 34, 35.

10 *Cahiers*, op. cit., vol. 2, p. 23; I. Turgenev (ed. D. Borovsky), *Stories in Poems and Prose* (Moscow: Progress Publishers, 1982), p. 412.

11 R. Jenkins, *Gladstone* (London: Macmillan, 1995), p. 403; *Encyclopaedia Britannica*, ninth edition, vol. XXIII, p. 652; B. Waller (ed.), *Themes in Modern European History 1830–1890* (London: Unwin Hyman, 1990), p. 177.

12 L. Schapiro, op. cit., p. 214; A. FitzLyon, *The Price of Genius*, op. cit., p. 432; A. Zviguilsky (ed.), *Ivan Tourguénev: Nouvelle Correspondance inédite* (Paris: Librairie des Cinq Continents, 1971), p. 202. Her début was in 1874: 'Figure jolie et intelligente, mais très méchante; voix affreuse sentant la fille de chambre russe à pleine nez.'

13 A. Zviguilsky (ed.), op. cit., pp. 229, 233.

14 H. Troyat, op. cit., pp. 137, 138.

15 Ibid., p. 144.

16 Ibid., pp. 149, 150; L. Schapiro, op. cit., pp. 300, 301; V.S. Pritchett, op. cit., p. 236.

17 P. Waddington, *Turgenev's Mortal Illness from its Origins to the Autopsy* (Pinehaven, New Zealand: Whirinaki Press, 1999), p. 9.

18 V.S. Pritchett, op. cit., p. 214.

19 P. Waddington, 'Turgenev and George Eliot, a literary friendship', *Modern Language Review*, vol. 66, 1971, p. 756. Six Mile Bottom was the home of W. Hall-Bullock.

20 Ralston visited him in the autumn of 1881: L. Schapiro, op. cit., p. 227.

21 P. Waddington, *A Modest Little Banquet at the Arts Club* (Pinehaven, New Zealand, 2001), passim.

22 D. Brown, *Tchaikovsky*, vol. III (London: Gollancz, 1986), p. 135. This was on 26 March 1881.

23 L. Schapiro, op. cit., p. 318.

24 P. Waddington, *Turgenev's Mortal Illness*, op. cit., p. 10.

25 P. Waddington, 'Turgenev's Last Will and Testament', *New Zealand Slavonic Journal*, no. 2, 1974, pp. 44, 59.

26 P. Waddington, 'Some Gleanings on Turgenev and his International Connections', *New Zealand Slavonic Journal*, 1983, p. 207.

27 P. Waddington, *Turgenev's Mortal Illness*, op. cit., pp. 11, 30, 33.

28 *Black's Medical Dictionary*, 39th edition (London: A&C Black, 1999), p. 29.

29 P. Waddington, *Turgenev's Mortal Illness*, op. cit., pp. 17, 19, 20, 22, 23, 26, 27; H. Troyat, op. cit., pp. 153, 154; A. FitzLyon, *The Price of Genius*, op. cit., p. 440.

30 1882.

31 H. Troyat, op. cit., p. 156; *Cahiers*, op. cit., vol. 12, pp. 52, 53.

32 A. FitzLyon, *The Price of Genius*, op. cit., p. 441.

33 L. Schapiro, op. cit., p. 321.

34 P. Waddington, *Turgenev's Mortal Illness*, op. cit., pp. 5, 35. The chasing was in 1855.

35 H. Troyat, op. cit., p. 156; G. Dulong, *Pauline Viardot Tragédienne Lyrique* (Bougival: Association des Amis d'Ivan Tourguéniev Pauline Viardot et Maria Malibran), p. 168; P. Waddington, 'Some Gleanings', op. cit., p. 206; P. Waddington, *Turgenev's Mortal Illness*, op. cit., pp. 6, 39.

36 E. de Goncourt, *Journal* (Paris, 1887), vol. 6, p. 256, 25 April 1883. 'Ainsi qu'un coûteau qui couperait une banane.'

37 P. Waddington, 'Some Gleanings', op. cit., p. 206.

38 P. Ackroyd, *Dickens* (London: Sinclair Stevenson, 1990), p. 336; C. Tomalin, *Samuel Pepys* (London: Viking, 2002), p. 63; C. Harman, *Fanny Burney* (London: HarperCollins, 2000), p. 304.

39 P. Waddington, 'Some Gleanings', op. cit., p. 207.

40 A. FitzLyon, *The Price of Genius*, op. cit.,

p. 443; L. Héritte-Viardot (trans. E.S. Bucheim), *Memories and Adventures* (London: Mills & Boon, 1913), p. 85.
41 P. Waddington, *Turgenev's Mortal Illness*, op. cit., pp. 9, 44, 47, 48, 53.
42 *Oxford Dictionary of Quotations*, Third Edition (Oxford: Oxford University Press, 1985), p. 10.
43 P. Waddington, 'Some Gleanings', op. cit., p. 207.
44 H. Troyat, op. cit., p. 158; A. Zviguilsky (ed.), op. cit., p. 218.
45 L. Viardot, *Apology of an Unbeliever*, translated from the Third Edition (London: Trübner & Co, 1869), Introduction, p. 77.
46 L. Héritte-Viardot, op. cit., p. 21.
47 E. de Goncourt, *Journal*, op. cit., vol. III, p. 263, 14 June 1883.
48 A. Zviguilsky (ed.), op. cit., pp. 249, 253; P. Waddington, *Turgenev's Mortal Illness*, op. cit., p. 50.
49 P. Waddington, *Turgenev's Mortal Illness*, op. cit., p. 53, and endnote p. 424; H. Troyat, op. cit., p. 158.
50 P. Waddington, *Turgenev's Mortal Illness*, op. cit., p. 54. This was by 14 July.
51 A. FitzLyon, *The Price of Genius*, op. cit., p. 447; G. Dulong, op. cit., p. 168.
52 I. Turgenev (trans. E. Schimanskaya), *Poems in Prose* (London: Lindsay Drummond, 1945), p. 57.
53 P. Waddington, *Turgenev's Mortal Illness*, op. cit., pp. 34, 58, 59, 68, 79; A. FitzLyon, *The Price of Genius*, op. cit., p. 449; H. Troyat, op. cit., p. 160.
54 P. Waddington, *Turgenev's Mortal Illness*, op. cit., pp. 68, 79.
55 Musée Tourguéniev (par Tamara Zviguilsky), *Guide* (Corlet Condé-sur-Noireau, 1993), p. 45.
56 Sir I. Berlin, Romanes lecture 1970, *Fathers and Children*, from I. Turgenev (trans. R. Edmonds), *Fathers and Sons* (London: Penguin, 1965 and 1970), p. 8; F. Randall, *Vissarion Belinsky* (Newtonville, Mass.: Oriental Research Partners, 1987), p. 26; G. Dulong, op. cit., p. 168.
57 A. Zviguilsky (ed.), op. cit., p. 241; L. Schapiro, op. cit., p. 146.
58 Sir I. Berlin, *Fathers and Children*, op. cit., p. 8; H. Troyat, op. cit., p. 161.

Last Act (pp. 421–434)

1 A. FitzLyon, *The Price of Genius, a life of Pauline Viardot* (London: John Calder, 1964), p. 458; N. Reich, *Clara Schumann, the Artist and the Woman* (Cornell University, 2001), p. 209.
2 B. Rees, *Camille Saint-Saëns, A Life* (London: Chatto & Windus, 1999), p. 254.
3 P. Waddington, *Turgenev's Mortal Illness from its Origins to the Autopsy* (Pinehaven, New Zealand: Whirinaki Press, 1999), p. 51; P. Waddington, 'Turgenev's Last Will and Testament', *New Zealand Slavonic Journal*, no. 2, 1974, p. 45.
4 P. Waddington, *Turgenev's Mortal Illness*, op. cit., p. 63.
5 P. Waddington, 'Turgenev's Last Will', op. cit., pp. 45–48. A. Seljak, *Ivan Turgenev's Ökonomien* (Zurich: University of Basel, Pano Verlag, 2004). Seljak suggests that they were silver roubles; his table on p. 490 gives an exchange rate of 2.50 francs to the rouble.
6 P. Waddington, 'Turgenev's Last Will', op. cit., pp. 48, 49; Information on Les Frênes from Professeur Zviguilsky.
7 243 boulevard Saint Germain, 7e; N. Simeone, *Paris – A Musical Gazetteer* (New Haven and London: Yale University Press, 2000), p. 145.
8 G. Dulong, *Pauline Viardot Tragédienne Lyrique* (Bougival: Association des Amis d'Ivan Tourguéniev Pauline Viardot et Maria Malibran), p. 170.
9 P. Waddington in *The Times Literary Supplement*, London, 1 January 1970, p. 16.
10 G. Dulong, op. cit., p. 175.
11 P. Waddington in *The Times Literary Supplement*, 1 January 1970, p. 16.
12 G. Dulong, op. cit., p. 176.
13 See Turgenev to Chorley in P. Waddington, 'Turgenev's relations with H.F. Chorley', *New Zealand Slavonic Journal*, no. 2, 1978, p. 29.
14 L. Schapiro, *Turgenev, his Life and Times* (Oxford: OUP, 1978), p. 192.
15 *The Times*, 23 November 1894. This was unearthed by Professor Waddington to whom the author is most grateful. *New Grove Dictionary of Music and Musicians* (London: Macmillan, 1980), vol. 3, p. 520, Butt (Fuller-Maitland, Colles, A. Porter).
16 Maria Brandt shared the role of Kundry in the Bayreuth 1882 première; Jeanne Gerville-Réache was the first Geneviève and Margaretha

Siems the first Marschallin. H. Bruder, 'Manuel Garcia the Elder, his School and his Legacy', *Opera Quarterly*, vol. 13, no. 4, 1997, p. 36.
17 L. Héritte-Viardot (trans. E.S. Bucheim), *Memories and Adventures* (London: Mills & Boon, 1913), p. 247.
18 A. FitzLyon, *The Price of Genius*, op. cit., p. 456.
19 P: Waddington, *The Musical Works of Pauline Viardot-Garcia* (Pinehaven, New Zealand: Whirinaki Press, 2004), passim.
20 G. Dulong, op. cit., p. 171; A. FitzLyon, *The Price of Genius*, op. cit., p. 461.
21 I. Turgenev (ed. E. Halpérine-Kaminsky), *Lettres à Madame Viardot* (Paris: Bibliothèque-Charpentier, 1907), 21 February 1871, p. 25.
22 G. Dulong, op. cit., p. 171; P. Waddington, *The Musical Works of Pauline Viardot-Garcia*, op. cit., passim.
23 W. Lakond (trans.), *The Diaries of Tchaikovsky* (Westport, CT: Greenwood Press, 1973), p. 82, 31 May 1886.
24 In 1876, when Tchaikovsky was in Paris, he wanted to be incognito, and the musical 'set', the Viardots, Saint-Saëns etc., to be unaware of his visit: D. Brown, *Tchaikovsky* (London: Gollancz, 1982), vol. II, p. 58.
25 31 May 1886: A. FitzLyon, *The Price of Genius*, op. cit., p. 457; also see W. Lakond, op. cit., p. 82; A. Holden, *Tchaikovsky* (London: Bantam Press, 1995) has the same sentiments but different words on p. 257.
26 W. Lakond, op. cit., pp. 237, 238, 269 (26 February 1888, 27 March 1889).
27 C.V. Stanford, *Pages from an Unwritten Diary* (London: Edward Arnold, 1914), p. 287.
28 G. Dulong, op. cit., p.32; A. FitzLyon, *The Price of Genius*, op. cit., p. 71.
29 *New Grove*, op. cit., vol. 7, p. 687, Greene (Fuller-Maitland); C.V. Stanford, op. cit., pp. 287, 288.
30 T.J. Walsh, *Second Empire Opera* (London: Calder, 1981), p. 90; *New Grove*, op. cit., vol. 8, p. 26, Hahn (A. Hoérée).
31 A. FitzLyon, *The Price of Genius*, op. cit., p. 461; A. Zviguilsky (ed.), *Ivan Tourguénev: Nouvelle Correspondance inédite* (Paris: Librairie des Cinq Continents, 1971), p. 249; G. Dulong, op. cit., p. 170; P. Waddington, *The Musical Works*, op. cit., p. 27; L. Héritte-Viardot, op. cit.; Paul Viardot, *Souvenirs d'un Artiste* (Paris: Librairie Fischbacher SA, 1910), p. 5.
32 A. FitzLyon, *The Price of Genius*, op. cit., p. 459.
33 G. Dulong, op. cit., pp. 171, 172.
34 Ibid., p. 171.
35 H. James, Jr, *French Poets and Novelists* (London: Macmillan, 1878), p. 23.
36 A. de Musset, 'Concert de Mademoiselle Garcia', *Revue des Deux Mondes*, vol. XVII, p. 110.
37 A. de Musset, 'Débuts de Mademoiselle Pauline Garcia', *Revue des Deux Mondes*, vol. XX, pp. 436, 440.
38 Ibid., p. 440. 'Que deviendra maintenant Pauline Garcia? Personne ne doubte de son avenir; son succès est certain, il est constaté; elle ne peut, quoi qu'elle fasse, que s'élever plus haut.'
39 W. Kuhe, *My musical recollections* (London: Richard Bentley, 1896), p.199.
40 G. Bord, *Rosina Stoltz* (*Victoire Noël*) (Paris: Henri Daragon, 1909), pp. 203, 207.
41 *Cahiers Ivan Tourguéniev, Pauline Viardot, Maria Malibran* (Bougival: Association des Amis d'Ivan Tourguéniev Pauline Viardot et Maria Malibran), vol. 2, p. 39.
42 P. Waddington, 'The Role of Courtavenel in the Life and Work of Turgenev', from *Issues in Russian Literature before 1917*, selected papers of the Third World Congress for Soviet and East European Studies (Colombus, Ohio: Slavica Publishers Inc, 1989), p. 120.
43 P. Waddington, *Turgenev and George Sand: An Improbable Entente* (Victoria University Press, 1981), p. 53. This was Flaubert's view.
44 *Musical Quarterly* 1916, p. 44; M. L'Hôpital, *Louis Viardot, Mémoires de l'Académie des Sciences* (Dijon: Arts et Belles-Lettres de Dijon, 1954), p. 32. The historian was Jules Michelet (1798–1874).
45 W. Shakespeare, *Macbeth*, Act 5, Scene 5, II 23–7.
46 H. Bruder, op. cit., p. 32.
47 C. Saint-Saëns (trans. E.G. Rich), *Musical Memories* (London: Murray, 1921), p. 151.
48 A. de Musset, *Concert de Mademoiselle Garcia*, op. cit., p. 111.
49 *Cahiers*, op. cit., vol. 2, p. 39. G. Dulong, op. cit., p. 171.
50 A. Zviguilsky (ed.), op. cit., pp. 254, 358, 254; C. Gounod (trans. A. Crocker), *Memoirs of an Artist* (Chicago: Rand McNally & Company, 1895), p. 173.
51 Paul Viardot, op. cit., p. 63.
52 Ibid. p. 297.

53 A. FitzLyon, *The Price of Genius*, op. cit., p. 456; H. Granjard and A. Zviguilsky, *Ivan Tourgénev, Lettres inédites à Pauline Viardot et à sa famille* (Paris: Editions l'Age d'Homme, 1972), p. xvi. She said this in 1880.
54 A. Zviguilsky (ed.), op. cit., Appendix. Marcelle looked like 'Turgenev in skirts', according to Mr Kyril FitzLyon, whose wife had met her.
55 G. Dulong, op. cit., p. 171.
56 L. Héritte-Viardot, *Une famille de grands musiciens* (Paris: Librairie Stock, 1922), p. 65. 'J'ai encore deux jours a vivre.'
57 Ibid., p. 65.
58 Ibid., p.65.
59 L. Héritte-Viardot, *Memories and Adventures*, op. cit., p. 253.
60 Ibid. p. 252.
61 A. FitzLyon, *The Price of Genius*, op. cit., pp. 303, 464.
62 I. Turgenev, *A Hapless Girl* (1868), in I. Turgenev (trans. Isabel Hapgood), *The Brigadier and other stories* (Freeport, New York: Books for Libraries Press, 1971), p. 45.
63 *The Times*, 18–20 May 1910.
64 G. Dulong, op. cit., p. 176; A. FitzLyon, *The Price of Genius*, op. cit., p. 465.
65 I. Turgenev (trans. E. Schimanskaya), *Poems in Prose* (London: Lindsay Drummond, 1945), p. 66 ('N.N.').
66 *Musical Quarterly*, vol. I, 1915, p. 371. 'Pourvu qu'ils s'en soient rendus dignes.'
687 A. Zviguilsky (ed.), op. cit., p. 229; *The Poetical Works of Robert Burns* (London and New York: Frederick Warne and Co.) The significance of this was pointed out to me by Professeur Zviguilsky.
68 A. Zviguilsky (ed.), op. cit., pp. 343, 350.

Sources

Author's note: My sources, to which I am entirely indebted, are considerable. Except as indicated below, I have not researched primary documentation. Any concern about this evaporated once I began to appreciate the sheer volume of data involved, and the improbability of my discovering any new facts: it is more important to understand the characters than to embark on a fruitless search for treasure. The book would never have been started had I not been inspired and led by April FitzLyon's exemplary work *The Price of Genius, a life of Pauline Viardot* (London: John Calder, 1964), and if Professors Waddington and Zviguilsky had not provided their excellent works.

Biography, Letters and Other Sources

Ackroyd, P., *Dickens* (London: Sinclair Stevenson, 1990)

Atwood, W.G., *The Lioness and the Little One – The Liaison of George Sand and Frederic Chopin* (New York, NY: Columbia University Press, 1980)

Baldick, R. (ed.), *Pages from the Goncourt Journal* (Oxford: Oxford University Press, 1978)

Barbier, P., *Opera in Paris 1800–1850* (Oregon: Amadeus Press, 1995)

Barbizon, *Landscape painters at Barbizon 1825–1827* (Musée Municipal de l'Ecole de Barbizon, 1989)

Barham, R., *The Ingoldsby Legends, or Mirth and Marvels* (London: Richard Bentley and Son, 1882)

Barrie Jones, J. (trans. and ed.), *Gabriel Fauré, A life in letters* (London: Batsford, 1988)

Berlin, Sir I., Romanes lecture 1970, 'Fathers and Children', from Turgenev, I. (trans. R. Edmonds), *Fathers and Sons* (London: Penguin, 1965 and 1970)

Berlioz, H. (trans. R. and E. Holmes), *Autobiography of Hector Berlioz* (London: Macmillan, 1884)

Bloom, P. (ed.), *Music in Paris in the Eighteen Thirties* (New York: Pendragon Press, 1987)

Blunt, W.S., *On Wings of Song* (London: Hamish Hamilton, 1974)

Bolster, R., *Marie d'Agoult, the Rebel Countess* (New Haven and London: Yale University Press, 2000)

Bord, G., *Rosina Stoltz* (*Victoire Noël*) (Paris: Henri Daragon, 1909)

Bosco, R., *The Brownings and Mrs Kinney* (Browning Institute Studies, no. 4, 1976)

Brault, J., *Une Contemporaine: Biographie et Intrigues de George Sand avec une lettre d'elle et une de M. Dudevant* (Paris: en vente Rue des Marais-Saint-Germain 6, 1848)

Brown, D., *Tchaikovsky*, vol. III (London: Gollancz, 1986)

Brown, F., *Zola, a Life* (London: Macmillan, 1995)

Bruder, H, 'Manuel Garcia the Elder, his School and his Legacy', *Opera Quarterly*, vol. 13, no. 4, 1997

Bury, J.P.T., *France 1814–1940* (London: Methuen, 1969)

Cahiers Ivan Tourguéniev, Pauline Viardot, Maria Malibran (Bougival: Association des Amis d'Ivan Tourguéniev Pauline Viardot et Maria Malibran)

Cairns, D, *Berlioz: Servitude and Greatness* (Penguin: London 2000)

Cardinal, R., *German Romantics in Context* (London: Studio Vista, 1975)

Carse, A., *The Life of Jullien* (Cambridge: W. Heffer & Sons Ltd, 1951)

Castillon du Perron, M. (trans. M. McLean), *Princess Mathilde* (London: Heinemann, 1956)

Catania Bellini Museum Guide (Catania, 1998)

Chadbourne, R.M., *Ernest Renan* (New York: Twayne Publishers Inc., 1968)

Chissell, J., *Clara Schumann: a Dedicated Spirit* (London: Hamish Hamilton, 1983)

Chissell, J., *Schumann* (London: J.M. Dent, 1977)

Chorley, H.F. (ed. E. Newman), *Thirty years' Musical Recollections* (New York: Alfred Knopf, 1926)

Chorley, H.F., *Thirty years' Musical Recollections* (London: Hurst & Blackett, 1862)

Clayton, E.C., *Queens of Song* (London: Smith Elder & Co, 1863)

Curtiss, M., 'Unpublished Letters by Georges Bizet', *Musical Quarterly*, vol. 36, 1950

Curtiss, M., B*izet and his World* (London: Secker and Warburg, 1959)

Curtiss, M., 'Bizet, Offenbach and Rossini', *Musical Quarterly*, 1954

Custine, Marquis de (ed. and trans. P.P. Kohler), *Journey for our Time* (London: George Prior, 1980)

Custine, Marquis de, *The Empire of the Czar* (London: Longman Brown Green and Longmans, 1843)

Custine, Marquis de (foreword by D.J. Boorstin), *Empire of the Czar* (New York: Anchor Books, 1989)

D'Agoult, Comtesse (D. Stern), *Mémoires 1833–1854* (Paris: Calmann-Lévy, 1927)

D'Agoult, Comtesse (D. Stern), *Mes Souvenirs* (Paris: Calmann-Lévy, 1880)

Davies, L., *César Franck and his Circle* (London: Barrie and Jenkins, 1970)

Dulong, G., *Pauline Viardot Tragédienne Lyrique* (Paris: Association des Amis d'Ivan Tourgueniev, Pauline Viardot et Maria Malibran, 1987)

Dupêchez, C., *Marie d'Agoult* (Paris: P. Lon, 1994)

Eisler, B., *Chopin's Funeral* (London: Little, Brown, 2003)

Evans, I., *A Short History of English Literature* (Harmondsworth: Penguin, 1963)

Fainsod, M., *How Russia is Ruled* (Cambridge, MA: Harvard University Press, 1963)

Faris, A., *Jacques Offenbach* (London: Faber and Faber, 1980)

Fétis, F-J., *Biographie universelle des Musiciens*, second edition (Paris, 1884)

FitzLyon, A., *Maria Malibran – Diva of the Romantic Age* (London: Souvenir Press, 1987)

FitzLyon, A., *The Price of Genius, a life of Pauline Viardot* (London: John Calder, 1964)

Flaubert, G. (ed. Bruneau), *Correspondence* (Paris, 1973–1998)

Forster, J., *The Life of Charles Dickens* (London: Chapman & Hall, 1874)

Frederick, K., *George Eliot – a biography* (London: HarperCollins, 1995)

Freeborn, R., *Turgenev, the novelist's novelist* (Oxford: Oxford University Press, 1960)

Frieda, L., *Catherine de Medici* (London: Weidenfeld and Nicolson, 2003)

Friedrich, O., *Olympia – Paris in the Age of Manet* (London: Aurum Press, 1992)

Gombrich, E., *The Story of Art* (London: Phaidon, 1963)

Goncourt, E. de (trans. Belloc and Shedlock), *Journal* (London: Heinemann, 1895)

Goncourt, E. de, *Journal* (Paris, 1887–96)

Goncourt, E. et J. de, *Journal, Mémoires de la vie littéraire* (Paris: Fouquelle, Flammarion, 1956)

Gounod, C. (trans. A. Crocker), *Memoirs of an Artist* (Chicago: Rand McNally & Company, 1895)

Gowan, C. D'O., *France from the Regent to the Romantics* (London: Harrap, 1961)

Granjard, H. and Zviguilsky, A., *Ivan Tourguénev, Lettres inédites à Pauline Viardot et à sa famille* (Paris: Editions l'Age d'Homme, 1972)

Grierson, E., *The Strange Life of Georgina Weldon* (London: Chatto & Windus, 1959)

Grote, Mrs, *Memoirs of the Life of Ary Scheffer* (London: John Murray, 1860)

Haight, G.S., *George Eliot, a biography* (Oxford: Oxford University Press, 1968)

Harding, J., *Gounod* (London: George Allen & Unwin Ltd, 1973)

Harding, J., *Saint-Saëns and his Circle* (London: Chapman & Hall, 1965)

Hearder, H., *Italy in the Age of the Risorgimento* (Harlow: Longman, 1983)

Hedley, A. (revised M.E.J. Brown), *Chopin* (London: J.M. Dent, 1974)

Hedley, A. (trans.), *Selected Correspondence of Fryderyk Chopin* (London: Heinemann, 1962)

Henriot, E., *Alfred de Musset* (Paris, 1928)

Héritte-Viardot, L., *Une famille de grands musiciens* (Paris: Librairie Stock, 1922)

Héritte-Viardot, L. (trans. E.S. Bucheim), *Memories and Adventures* (London: Mills & Boon, 1913)

Herzen, A. (trans. C. Garnett), *My Past and Thoughts, the Memoirs of Alexander Herzen* (London: Chatto and Windus, 1974)

Hewlett, H.G., *Memoirs of Henry Fothergill Chorley* (London: Richard Bentley and Son, 1873)

Hibbert, C., *Edward VII* (London: Allen Lane, 1976)

Hingley, R., *Dostoyevsky, his life and work* (London: Paul Elek Ltd, 1978)

Hodges, S., *Lorenzo da Ponte* (University of Wisconsin Press, 2002)

Hofmann, R. and K., *Johannes Brahms in Baden-Baden* (Baden-Baden: Brahmsgesellschaft, 1996)

Holland, H.S. and Rockstro, W.S., *Jenny Lind the Artist* (London: John Murray, 1891)

Horne, A., *The fall of Paris* (London: Macmillan, 1965)

Huebner, S., *The Operas of Charles Gounod* (Oxford: Clarendon Press, 1990)

Hughes, K., *George Eliot, The Last Victorian* (London: Fourth Estate, 1998)

Illustrated London News (sometimes abbreviated to *ILN*)

Irvine, D., *Massenet, a Chronicle of his Life and Times* (New York: Amadeus Press, 1994)
Irvine, Demar, *Massenet* (New York: Amadeus Press, 1997)
Jack, B., *George Sand: A Woman's Life Writ Large* (London: Chatto & Windus, 1999)
James, Henry Jr., *English Hours* (Oxford: Oxford University Press, 1981)
James, Henry Jr. (ed. P. Lubbock), *Letters of Henry James* (London: Macmillan, 1920)
James, Henry Jr., *French Poets and Novelists* (London: Macmillan, 1878)
Jenkins, R., *Gladstone* (London: Macmillan, 1995)
Jones, C., *The Cambridge Illustrated History of France* (Cambridge: Cambridge University Press, 1994)
Jordan, R., *George Sand* (London: Constable, 1976)
Karénine, W., *George Sand sa Vie et ses Oeuvres* (Paris: Paul Ollendorff, 1899)
Kelly, L., *Lermontov, a tragedy in the Caucasus* (London: Robin Clark, 1983)
Kendall-Davies, B., *The Life and Work of Pauline Viardot-Garcia,* vol. I 'The years of fame' (London: Cambridge Scholars Press, 2003)
Kennan, G., *The Marquis de Custine and his Russia in 1839* (London: Hutchinson, 1972)
Kirlew, M., *Famous Sisters of Great Men* (London: Thomas Nelson, 1905)
Kracauer, S., *Offenbach and the Paris of his time* (London: Constable, 1937)
Kuhe, W., *My musical recollections* (London: Richard Bentley, 1896)
L'Hôpital, M., 'Louis Viardot', in *Mémoires de l'Académie des Sciences* (Dijon: Arts et Belles-Lettres de Dijon, 1954)
Lacombe, H., *The Keys to French Opera in the nineteenth century* (Berkeley: University of California Press, 2001)
Lakond, W. (trans.), *The Diaries of Tchaikovsky* (Westport, CT: Greenwood Press, 1973)
Lancet, The
Lange-Brachmann, U. and Draheim, J. (ed.), *Pauline Viardot in Baden Baden und Karlsruhe* (Baden-Baden: Nomos Verlaggesellschaft, 1999)
Leslie, A., *Edwardians in Love* (London: Arrow Books, 1972)
Lestringant, F., *Alfred de Musset* (Flammarion, 1999)
Litzmann, B. (trans. G. Hadow), *Clara Schumann, an Artist's Life* (London: Macmillian, 1913)
Locke, R., *Music, Musicians and the Saint-Simonians* (Chicago: University of Chicago Press, 1986)
Lumley, B., *Reminiscences of the Opera* (London: Hurst and Blackett, 1864)
Macdonald, H. (ed.) (trans. R. Nicholls), *Selected Letters of Berlioz* (London: Faber and Faber, 1995)
MacDonald, M., *Brahms* (London: J.M. Dent, 1990)
Magarshack, D., *Turgenev, a Life* (London: Faber & Faber, 1954)
Mainwaring, M. (ed.), *Ivan Turgenev, the Portrait Game* (London: Chatto and Windus, 1973)
Mansel, P., *Paris between Empires 1814–1852* (London: John Murray, 2001)
Marix-Spire, T (ed.), *Lettres inédites de George Sand et de Pauline Viardot 1839–1849* (Paris: Nouvelles Editions Latines, 1959)
Marix-Spire, T. (trans. E. Huntress), 'Gounod and his first interpreter, Pauline Viardot', *Musical Quarterly,* vol. 31, 1945
Martin, T., *Helena Faucit (Lady Martin)*, (Edinburgh and London: William Blackwood and Sons, 1900)
McLaren, A., *A History of Contraception* (Oxford: Blackwell, 1990)
McPhee, P., *A Social History of France 1780–1880* (London: Routledge, 1992)
Melitz, L., *Opera Goer's Complete Guide* (London: J.M. Dent, 1925)
Merlin, Comtesse, *Maria Malibran* (London: Henry Colburn, 1840)
Musée de la Vie Romantique, *General Guide* (Paris: Paris-Musées, 1992)
Musée de Montmartre, *Bals et Cabarets au temps de Bruant et Lautrec* (Paris: Editions le Vieux Montmartre, 2002)
Musée Tourguéniev (par Tamara Zviguilsky), *Guide* (Corlet Condé-sur-Noireau, 1993)
Musset, A. de, 'Débuts de Mademoiselle Pauline Garcia', *Revue des Deux Mondes,* vol. XX
Musset, A. de, 'Concert de Mademoiselle Garcia', *Revue des Deux Mondes,* vol. XVII
Musset, A. de (ed. L. Sèche), *Correspondance* (Société du Mercure de France, 1907)

Musical Quarterly (sometimes abbreviated to *MQ*)
The National Gallery, London, *Russian Landscape*, the Exhibition Guide for *Russian Landscape in the Age of Tolstoy*, July 2004
New Grove Dictionary of Music and Musicians (ed. S. Sadie), (London: Macmillan, 1980)
New Oxford Companion to Music (ed. Denis Arnold) (Oxford: Oxford University Press, 1983)
New Oxford Companion to Music (Oxford: Oxford University Press, 1984)
Newman, E., *Memoirs of Hector Berlioz* (New York: Dover Publications, 1932)
Nye, R.B. and Mopurgo, J., *A History of the United States* (Harmondsworth: Penguin, 1965)
Nye, R.A. (ed. F.X. Eder), 'Sex and sexuality in France since 1800', in *Sexual Cultures in Europe* (Manchester: Manchester University Press, 1999)
Ollivier, D. (ed.), *Correspondance de Liszt et de la Comtesse d'Agoult* (Paris: Editions Bernard Grasset, 1933–4)
Orledge, R., *Gabriel Fauré* (London: Eulenburg, 1979)
Owen, Robert Dale, *Threading my Way* (London: Trübner, 1874)
Palmer, J.H., *Individual, Family and National Poverty* (London: E. Truelove, 1875)
Pomarède, V. and de Wallens, G., *Corot Extraordinary Landscapes* (Paris: Gallimard, 1996)
Pritchett, V.S., *The Gentle Barbarian, The Life and Work of Turgenev* (London: Chatto & Windus, 1977)
Prod'homme et Dandelot, *Gounod* (Paris: Librairie Ch. Delagrave, 1911)
Raby, P., *Fair Ophelia: A Life of Harriet Smithson Berlioz* (Cambridge: Cambridge University Press, 1982)
Randall, F., *Vissarion Belinsky* (Newtonville, Mass.: Oriental Research Partners, 1987)
Renan, E., *The Life of Jesus* (London: Watts & Co, 1945)
Rees, B., *Camille Saint-Saëns, A Life* (London: Chatto & Windus, 1999)
Reich, Nancy B., *Clara Schumann, the Artist and the Woman* (Cornell University, 2001)
Richardson, J., *The Courtesans – the demi-monde in 19th century France* (London: Weidenfeld & Nicolson, 1967)
Ridley, J., *Garibaldi* (London: Constable, 1974)
Ridley, J., *Napoléon III and Eugénie* (London: Constable, 1979)
Rutherford, S, *The Prima Donna and Opera 1815–1930* (Cambridge: Cambridge University Press, 2006)
Saint-Saëns, C. (trans. E.G. Rich) *Musical Memories* (London: John Murray, 1921)
Samson, J., *Chopin* (Oxford: Oxford University Press, 1998)
Sand, George, 'Le Théâtre-Italien et Mlle Pauline Garcia', *Revue des Deux Mondes*, vol. XXI
Sand, George, *Correspondance* (Paris: Editions de Georges Lubin, Editions Garnier Frères, 1969)
Sand, George (ed. T. Bodin), *Lettres Retrouvées* (Paris: Gallimard, 2004)
Santley, C., *Reminscences of my Life* (London: Pitman, 1909)
Saunders, D., *Russia in the Age of Reaction and Reform* (London: Longman, 1992)
Savy, N (ed.), *George Sand: Consuelo, La Comtesse de Rudolstadt* (Paris: Editions Robert Laffont SA, 2004)
Schapiro, L., critical essay 'Spring Torrents, Its Place and Significance in the Life and Work of I.S. Turgenev', in I. Turgenev, *Spring Torrents* (trans. L. Schapiro) (London: Penguin, 1980)
Schapiro, L., *Turgenev, his Life and Times* (Oxford: Oxford University Press, 1978)
Seljak, A., *Ivan Turgenev's Ökonomien* (Zurich: University of Basel, Pano Verlag, 2004)
Seljak, A. (ed. A. Guski & U. Schmid), *Zum Geld und Kreditsystem in Russland vom Kiever Reich bis 1897 in Literatur und Kommerz im Russland des 19 Jahrhunderts* (Zurich: University of Basel, Pano Verlag, 2004)
Seton-Watson, H., *The Russian Empire 1801–1917* (Oxford: Clarendon Press, 1988)
Simeone, N., *Paris – A Musical Gazetteer* (New Haven and London: Yale University Press, 2000)
Somerset-Ward, R., *Angels and Monsters* (New Haven and London: Yale University Press, 2004)
St Aubyn, G., *Queen Victoria, a Portrait* (London: Sinclair-Stevenson, 1991)
Stanford, C.V., *Pages from an Unwritten Diary* (London: Edward Arnold, 1914)

Stanford, C.V. and Forsyth, C., *A History of Music* (New York: Macmillan, 1917)
Steegmuller, F., and Bray, B. (trans.), *Flaubert-Sand, the Correspondence* (Hammersmith: Harvill, 1993)
Steegmuller, F., *The Letters of Gustave Flaubert Vols I & II 1830–1880* (London: Picador, 2001)
Steen, M., *The Lives and Times of the Great Composers* (Cambridge: Icon, 2003)
Thompson, B., *A Monkey among Crocodiles* (London: HarperCollins, 2000)
Thomson, A., 'The Final Agony of Alexander Pushkin', *New Zealand Slavonic Journal*, winter 1975, no. 1
Thomson, D., *England in the Nineteenth Century* (Harmondsworth: Pelican, 1964)
The Times Literary Supplement, London
Tolstoy Museum Khamovniki, *Guide* (Moscow, 1994)
Treherne, P., *A Plaintiff in Person* (London: Heinemann, 1923)
Trevelyan, G.M., *English Social History* (London: Longman, 1946)
Troyat, H. (trans. N. Amphoux), *Turgenev* (London: W.H. Allen, 1989)
Turgenev, I. (ed. E. Halpérine-Kaminsky), *Lettres à Madame Viardot* (Paris: Bibliothèque-Charpentier, 1907)
Vallas, L. (trans. H. Foss), *César Franck* (London: Harrap, 1951)
Viardot, L., *Apology of an Unbeliever, translated from the Third Edition* (London: Trübner & Co, 1869)
Viardot, L., *Souvenirs de Chasse dans toute l'Europe* (Paris: Editions Pygmalion, 1985)
Viardot, L., *Wonders of Sculpture* (New York: Scribner, Armstrong, and Company, 1873)
Viardot, L., *Wonders of European Art* (London: Sampson Low, Son, and Marston, 1871)
Viardot, L., *Les Merveilles de la Peinture* (Paris: Libriarie Hachette, 1875)
Viardot, Paul, *Souvenirs d'un Artiste* (Paris: Librairie Fischbacher SA, 1910)
Waddington, P., *Courtavenel, the History of an Artists' Nest and its Role in the Life of Turgenev* (*PhD Thesis*, Queen's University Belfast, The British Library, British Thesis Service, spring 1972)
Waddington, P., *Turgenev's Seventh* (Pinehaven, New Zealand: Whirinaki Press, 2003)
Waddington, P., 'Turgenev and the International Literary Congress of 1878', *New Zealand Slavonic Journal*, 1983
Waddington, P., 'Turgenev and Gounod, Rival Strangers in the Viardots' Country Nest', *New Zealand Slavonic Journal*, no. 1, 1976
Waddington, P., 'Two Months in the Country', *New Zealand Slavonic Journal*, no. 11, winter 1973
Waddington, P., *A letter of W.M. Thackeray to Louis Viardot* (Pinehaven, New Zealand: Whirinaki Press, 1998)
Waddington, P., *A Modest Little Banquet at the Arts Club* (Pinehaven, New Zealand: Whirinaki Press, 2001)
Waddington, P., 'Dickens, Pauline Viardot and Turgenev: a Study in Mutual Admiration', *New Zealand Slavonic Journal*, no. 2, 1974
Waddington, P., 'Pauline Viardot as Turgenev's censor', *The Times Literary Supplement*, 1 January 1970
Waddington, P., 'Pauline Viardot-Garcia as Berlioz's Counselor and Physician', *MQ*, vol. LIX, no. 3, July 1973
Waddington, P., *Russian interests of the Rossetti Family* (Pinehaven, New Zealand: Whirinaki Press, 1998)
Waddington, P., 'Some Gleanings on Turgenev and his International Connections', *New Zealand Slavonic Journal*, 1983
Waddington, P., *The Musical Works of Pauline Viardot-Garcia* (Pinehaven, New Zealand: Whirinaki Press, 2004)
Waddington, P., *The Origins and Composition of Turgenev's Novel 'Dym' (Smoke) as seen from his first Sketches* (Pinehaven, New Zealand: Whirinaki Press, 1998)
Waddington, P., 'The Role of Courtavenel in the Life and Work of Turgenev', in *Issues in Russian Literature before 1917*, selected papers of the Third World Congress for Soviet and East European Studies (Colombus, Ohio: Slavica Publishers Inc, 1989)
Waddington, P., 'The strange history of Dr F. and the dismantling of Courtavenel', *Modern Language Review*, vol. 65, 1970

Waddington, P., *Three letters of Gustave Flaubert* (Pinehaven, New Zealand: Whirinaki Press, 2000)
Waddington, P., *Turgenev and England* (London: Macmillan, 1980)
Waddington, P., 'Turgenev and George Eliot, a literary friendship', *Modern Language Review*, vol. 66, 1971
Waddington, P., *Turgenev and George Sand: An Improbable Entente* (Wellington: Victoria University Press, 1981)
Waddington, P., 'Turgenev and Pauline Viardot, An Unofficial Marriage', *Canadian Slavonic Papers*, vol. XXVI, no. 1, March 1984
Waddington, P., 'Turgenev's Last Will and Testament', *New Zealand Slavonic Journal*, no. 2, 1974
Waddington, P., *Turgenev's Mortal Illness from its Origins to the Autopsy* (Pinehaven, New Zealand: Whirinaki Press, 1999)
Waddington, P., 'Turgenev's relations with H.F. Chorley', *New Zealand Slavonic Journal*, no. 2, 1978
Waddington, P., 'Turgenev's Scenario for Brahms', *New Zealand Slavonic Journal*, 1982, pp. 1–16
Walker, A., *Franz Liszt, Vol 1, The Virtuoso Years 1811–47* (London: Faber and Faber, 1983)
Walker, A., *Franz Liszt, Vol II, The Weimar Years* (London: Faber and Faber, 1989)
Walker, E., *A History of Music in England* (Oxford: Clarendon Press, 1952)
Wall, G., *Flaubert, a Life* (London: Faber and Faber, 2001)
Waller, B. (ed.), *Themes in Modern European History 1830–1890* (London: Unwin Hyman, 1990)
Walsh, T.J., *Second Empire Opera* (London: John Calder, 1981)
Weinreb, B. and Hibbert, C., *London Encyclopaedia* (London: Macmillan, 1993)
Weinstock, H., *Donizetti and the World of Opera* (London: Methuen, 1964)
Weldon, G., *My Orphanage and Gounod in England* (London: London Music and Art Association, 1882)
Westwood, *J., Endurance and Endeavour* (Oxford, 2002)
Williams, A., *Franz Liszt, selected letters* (Oxford: Clarendon Press, 1998)
Wilson, A.N., *Tolstoy* (London: Hamish Hamilton, 1988)
Woodham-Smith, C., *The Great Hunger* (London: First Four Square Edition, 1994)
Žekulin, N., *The story of an operetta, Le Dernier sorcier and Ivan Turgenev* (Munich: Verlag Otto Sagner, 1989)
Zviguilsky, A. (ed.), *Ivan Tourguénev: Nouvelle correspondance inédite* (Paris: Librarie des Cinq Continents, 1971)
Zviguilsky, Tamara, *Le Musée Tourguéniev, Littérature, musique, peinture* (Bougival, 1993)

Novels, Plays and Poetry

For novels *et cetera* not originally in the English language, a variety of sources have been used.

Byron, Lord: *The Prisoner of Chillon and Other Poems 1816* (Menston: The Scolar Press, 1969)
Baudelaire, C. (ed. W. Fowlie), *Les Fleurs du Mal* (New York: Bantam, 1964)
Chekhov, A. (trans. C. Garnett), *The Cherry Orchard and other Plays* (London: Chatto and Windus, 1935)
Collins, W., *The Woman in White* (Oxford: Oxford University Press, 1996)
Dickens, C., *Sketches by Boz* (London: Chapman and Hall)
Dickens, C., *The Cricket on the Hearth* (London: Chapman and Hall)
Dickens, C., *Bleak House* (published 1853) (London: Pan Books, 1976)
Dickens, C., *The Pickwick Papers* (Oxford: Oxford University Press, World Classics, 1988)
Dostoyevsky, F. (trans. J. Coulson), *Memoirs from the House of the Dead* (Oxford, Oxford University Press, 2001)
Dostoyevsky, F. (trans. C. Garnett), *The Brothers Karamazov* (London: J.M. Dent, 1927)
Dostoyevsky, F. (trans. A.R. MacAndrew), *The Brothers Karamazov* (New York: Bantam Classic, 1970)
Dostoyevsky, F. (trans. D. Magarshack), *The Brothers Karamazov* (Harmondsworth: Penguin, 1958)
Dostoyevsky, F. (trans. D. McDuff), *Crime and Punishment* (London: Penguin, 2003)
Dostoyevsky, F. (trans. D. Magarshack), *The Devils* (London: Penguin, 1971)

Dostoyevsky, F. (trans. C. Garnett), *The Possessed* (London and Toronto: J.M. Dent, 1931)
Dostoyevsky, F. (trans. C Garnett, introduction G.S. Morson), *The Gambler* (New York: The Modern Library, 2003)
Dostoyevsky, F., *The Idiot* (Ware, Herts: Wordsworth Classics, 1996)
Dostoyevsky, F., *The Double* (London: Hesperus Press, 2004)
Flaubert, G. (trans. A. Krailsheimer), *Bouvard et Pécuchet* (Harmondsworth: Penguin, 1976)
Flaubert, G. (trans. R. Baldick), *Sentimental Education* (London: Penguin, 2004)
Flaubert, G. (trans. D.F. Hannigan), *Sentimental Education* (London: H.S. Nichols Ltd Publishers, 1898)
Flaubert, G., *L'Éducation Sentimentale* (Paris: Flammarion, 1985)
Flaubert, G., *Madame Bovary* (Oxford: Oxford University Press, 2004)
Flaubert, G., *Memoirs of a Madman* (London: Hesperus Press, 2002)
Goncharov, I. (trans. D. Magarshack), *Oblomov* (London: Penguin, 1954)
Goncourt, E. et J. de (trans. L. Tancock), *Germinie Lacerteux* (Harmondsworth: Penguin, 1984)
Hugo, V. (trans. N. Denny), *Les Misérables* (London: Penguin, 1982)
Hugo, V., *Les Misérables* (Brussels: A. Lacroix, Verboekheven, 1862)
James, Henry, Jr., *The Bostonians* (London: Penguin Classics, 2000)
James, Henry, Jr., *The Portrait of a Lady* (London: Penguin Classics, 2000)
James, Henry, Jr., *Washington Square* (London: Penguin Classics, 2003)
Lermontov, M. (trans. P. Foote), *A Hero of Our Time* (London: Penguin, 2001)
Maupassant, G de (trans. G. Hopkins), *Short Stories* (London: The Folio Society, 1959)
Maupassant, G de, *The Complete Short Stories* (London: Cassell, 1970)
Musset, A de, *Oeuvres Posthumes* (Paris: Alphonse Lemerre, 1845)
Pushkin, A. (trans. C. Johnston, Preface J. Bayley, Notes M. Basker), *Eugene Onegin* (London: Penguin, 2003)
Sand, G. (trans. Fayette Robinson), *Consuelo* (New York: Stringer and Townsend, 1851)
Sand, G., *La Comtesse de Rudolstadt* (Paris: Calmann-Lévy)
Tolstoy, L. (trans. L. and A. Maude), *War and Peace* (London: Oxford University Press, 1933)
Tolstoy, L. (trans. R. Edmonds), *Anna Karenin* (Harmondsworth: Penguin, 1954)
Tolstoy, L. (trans. Rochelle S. Townsend), *Anna Karenina* (1873–6)
Tolstoy, L., *Anna Karenina* (London: J.M. Dent, 1912)
Turgenev, I. (ed. D. Borovsky), *Stories in Poems and Prose* (Moscow: Progress Publishers, 1982)
Turgenev, I. (trans. and intro. Isaiah Berlin), *A Month in the Country* (London: Penguin, 1981)
Turgenev, I., *A Month in the Country*, in *Masterpieces of the Russian Drama* (trans. D. Noyes) (London: D. Appleton & Co, 1933)
Turgenev, I. (trans. L. Schapiro), *Spring Torrents* (London: Penguin, 1980)
Turgenev, I. (trans. I. Hapgood), *The Brigadier and other stories* (Freeport, New York: Books for Libraries Press, 1971) ('The Brigadier'; 'The Story of Lieutenant Ergunoff'; 'A Hapless Girl'; 'A Strange Story'; 'Punin and Baburin')
Turgenev, I. (trans. Rosemary Edmonds), *Fathers and Sons* (London: Penguin, 1965 and 1970)
Turgenev, I. (trans. E. Schuyler), *Fathers and Sons* (London: Ward, Lock & Co, 1883)
Turgenev, I. (trans. Hugh Aplin, Foreword by Simon Callow), *Faust and Yakov Pasynkov* (London: Hesperus Press, 2003)
Turgenev, I. (trans. Isabel Hapgood), *First Love and other stories* (New York: Charles Scribner's Sons, 1923) ('First Love'; 'A Correspondence'; 'The Region of Dead Calm'; 'It is Enough'; 'The Dog'; 'Phantoms: A Fantasy'; 'Yakoff Pasynkoff'; '"Faust" – a Story in Nine Letters; An Excursion to the Forest Belt')
Turgenev, I. (trans. R. Freeborn), *First Love and other stories* (Oxford: Oxford University Press, 1999) ('The Diary of a Superfluous Man'; 'Mumu'; 'Asya'; 'First Love'; 'King Lear of the Steppes'; 'The Song of Triumphant Love')
Turgenev, I. (trans. I. and T. Litvinov), *Three Short Novels* (Moscow: Foreign Language Publishing House, no date but around 1980)

Turgenev, I. (trans. Richard Freeborn), *Home of the Gentry* (London: Penguin, London 1970)
Turgenev, I. (trans. W. Ralston), *Liza* (London: Chapman & Hall, 1869)
Turgenev, I. (trans. Isabel Hapgood), *On the Eve* (Freeport, New York: Books for Libraries Press, 1971)
Turgenev, I. (trans. E. Schimanskaya), *Poems in Prose* (London: Lindsay Drummond, 1945)
Turgenev, I. (trans. R. Freeborn), *Rudin* (London: Penguin, 1975)
Turgenev, I., *Dimitri Roudine* (London: Ward Lock & Co, *c.* 1880)
Turgenev, I. (trans. Richard Freeborn), *Sketches from a Hunter's Album* (London: Penguin, 1967 and 1990)
Turgenev, I. (trans. F. Abbott), *Annals from a Sportsman* (New York: Henry Holt & Co, 1885)
Turgenev, I. (trans. Constance Garnett), *Smoke* (USA: Turtle Point Press, 1995)
Turgenev, I. (trans. W. West), *Smoke* (London: Ward Lock & Co, 1872)
Turgenev, I., *Fumée* (Paris: J. Hetzel, 1868)
Turgenev, I. (trans. Constance Garnett), *Virgin Soil* (New York: New York Review of Books, 2000)
Turgenev, I. (trans. T.S. Perry), *Virgin Soil* (London: Ward, Lock & Co, pre-1880)
Zola, E. (trans. M. Mauldon), *L'Assommoir* (Oxford: Oxford University Press, 1995)
Zola, E. (trans. D. Parmée), *Nana* (Oxford: Oxford University Press, 1998)
Zola, E. (trans. and intro. D. Parmée), *The Attack on the Mill and other stories* (Oxford: Oxford University Press, 1984)
Zola, E. (trans. and intro. R. Buss), *Thérèse Raquin* (Penguin, 2004; also Paris: Bibliothèque Charpentier, 1890)

Note on Money

Inflation, economic growth and technological advances cause money to be a poor measure of value. Monetary amounts, which are further complicated by the sensitivity of foreign exchange rates, are thus usually uninformative, even misleading, in a historical context unless there is some indication of the purchasing power. So, when monetary items arise, I have often provided, in the vicinity, the cost of another item with which comparison can be made. I will however give some tentative general information in this note.

Roubles pre-1850: Reference to the 'rouble' can be confusing. The time of the Viardots' arrival in Russia at the end of 1843 represents a particularly difficult moment, because a 70-year period during which silver roubles and paper roubles ('assignats') had run in parallel was coming to an end. Wars and the unpopularity of the paper currency had led to the depreciation of the assignat relative to silver coinage, whose purchasing power was itself subject to the fluctuating value of silver. At the beginning of the 1840s, when assignats were being phased out, the value of the silver rouble was fixed at 3.5 assignats.[1] From 1840, a new silver-backed rouble banknote was issued which, at the start, had parity with silver coinage.[2]

When reference is made to the 'rouble', it is often far from clear which denomination is being talked about. Louis must have found his banking transactions in Russia a nightmare. Rouble figures can be seriously misleading unless one knows what 'rouble' is being referred to. Pauline's first fee was around 50,000 'roubles'. Almost certainly this was expressed in assignats, and represented rather less than 15,000 silver coins or notes. In all his dealings Louis will have had to have been particularly careful to be clear whether he was talking about the silver currency, of which there were at the time four to the French franc,[3] or the assignats which in practice were only worth just above a franc. The same applies to the modern interpreter who unfortunately does not have a bank official to ask. All my comparisons in roubles have therefore to be treated with caution.

Roubles after 1850: During the Crimean war, the silver coinage returned in Russia. With the need to finance the war, the Polish uprising, the Emancipation, the Russo-Turkish War and, not least, the infrastructure, the paper banknote began to depreciate again. This coincided with Turgenev's financial woes as a landowner, and must have exacerbated them. In 1861 the value of the banknote had fallen to 0.89 of a silver rouble. An attempt to reform finances in 1863 led the banknote to fall from 0.95 to 0.84 in the following year. In 1866, it was 0.76; it recovered, but by 1879 it was down to 0.63.[4] In 1880, at the end of Turgenev's life, there was a further monetary crisis.

Turgenev's correspondence indicates the practical difficulties a foreigner living abroad faced as his currency depreciated.[5] By the time of his death, the rouble stood at 62 per cent of its value[6] in francs at around the time that he first met the Viardots, and much the same in sterling. The fairly relentless depreciation had mainly followed the end of the Crimean War, when Turgenev was mainly outside Russia.

In the mid-1850s, we hear of a horse being sold for 400 roubles, a dozen shirts being bought for 300 roubles, a fancy waistcoat for 40 roubles, and a pair of boots for 25 roubles. An artisan's salary was 10 roubles a month.[7] These items, we may assume, are expressed in the banknotes which at the time would have been worth less than 90 per cent of the silver rouble value. At the same time, an annual subscription to *The Contemporary* was 15 silver roubles.[8]

Sterling, francs and dollars: Thankfully, for the other currencies, the denomination is unambiguous. The exchange rates fluctuated. In mid-century, the pound sterling and French franc exchange rate was around £1 = 25 and £1 = 26 francs;[9] and we read that in 1867 it was £1 = 23.60 francs, whereas in 1870 it was £1 = 25.10 francs. For much of the 19th century, the US dollar was fixed at around £1 = US$4.44–$4.85, although, during the Civil War, it may have been as low as £1 = US$8.[10]

In London in 1858, Turgenev's lodgings in Holles Street, north of Oxford Street, cost £2 per week including breakfast and laundry.[11] In the 1860s an overcoat might cost £1.75, a suit £1.25 and a ton of coal £1.50. A labourer's wage was £0.75 per week.[12]

Inflation was a very different experience to that in the 20th century. UK prices dropped by around 29 per cent between 1820 and 1850; they rose by around 48 per cent between 1850 and 1873, with a surge in 1854–5; between 1874 and 1896 prices fell 33 per cent, and they rose 21 per cent between 1896 and 1914.[13] Price inflation in the second half of the 20th century was horrific. A price index, which stood at around 10 in the UK in 1914, was at 53 in 1962 and 670 in 2000.[14] Against this unstable background, readers craving for amounts to be expressed sensibly in modern currency will almost certainly be misled by the result.

In France around 1830, it cost Gounod's mother 3 francs 75 centimes to get a place in the stalls for a performance by Maria Malibran.[15] In the 1860s, we hear of 10 francs a day being an exceptionally good wage and a joint income of 9 francs a day equating to prosperity; a nice shawl might cost 7 francs, and a day's coal for the stove 0.75 francs.[16] In 1884, we hear of 400 francs being paid for evening dress for a reception at a government ministry; 40,000 francs being the ticket price for a real diamond necklace, with an imitation one only costing 500 francs. Two or three magnificent roses would cost 10 francs.[17] A man visiting 'Madame Tellier's Establishment' near Fécamp in Normandy around 1881 would also be charged 10 francs for a bottle of champagne.[18]

REFERENCES

1 A. Seljak (ed. A. Guski & U. Schmid), *Zum Geld und Kreditsystem in Russland vom Kiever Reich bis 1897 in Literatur und Kommerz im Russland des 19 Jahrhunderts* (Zurich: University of Basel, Pano Verlag, 2004), p. 49.

2 Ibid., p. 54.

3 H. Granjard and A. Zviguilsky, *Ivan Tourgénev, Lettres inédites à Pauline Viardot et à sa famille* (Paris: Editions l'Age d'Homme, 1972), p. 41.

4 A. Seljak, op. cit., pp. 54, 55.

5 H. Granjard and A. Zviguilsky, op. cit., pp. 96, 136. A different rate could be obtained in Paris and Frankfurt. Turgenev found himself getting only 3.47 in November 1863 and 3.36 in April 1867.

6 A. Seljak, *Ivan Turgenev's Ökonomien* (Zurich: University of Basel, Pano Verlag, 2004), p. 489. In 1844, the exchange rate was rouble = £0.3806, in 1856 it was £0.3809, and in 1883 it was £0.2372. The French franc rates were: 1844, rouble = 405.52 francs; in 1856 it was 398.44 francs; in 1883 it was 249.39. 62 per cent = (23.72/38.06), and (249.39/405.52), approx.

7 I. Goncharov (trans. D. Magarshack), *Oblomov* (London: Penguin, 1954), part 1, ch. 9, part 2, ch. 1.

8 A. Seljak, *Ivan Turgenev's Ökonomien*, op. cit., p. 493.

9 The author's source here is Professor Patrick Waddington; also in 1880, H. James, Jr, *The Portrait of a Lady* (London: Penguin Classics, 2000), p. 492.

10 G. Weldon, *My Orphanage and Gounod in England* (London: London Music and Art Association, 1882), p. 10; *Encyclopaedia Britannica*, ninth edition, vol. VIII, p. 789.

11 P. Waddington, *Turgenev and England* (London: Macmillan, 1980), p. 59.

12 H. Priestley, *The What it cost the Day before Yesterday Book* (Havant: Kenneth Mason, 1979)

13 J. Burnett, *A History of the Cost of Living* (Gregg Revivals Aldershot, Penguin 1969)

14 'Focus on Consumer Price Indices, August 2001' (London: Office for National Statistics, 2001), table 14.

15 C. Gounod (trans. A. Crocker), *Memoirs of an Artist* (Chicago: Rand McNally & Company, 1895), p. 40.

16 E. Zola (trans. M. Mauldon), *L'Assommoir* (Oxford: Oxford University Press, 1995), ch. 2, p. 52; ch. 4, pp. 96, 98.

17 G. de Maupassant (trans. G. Hopkins), 'An Adventure in Paris', in *Short Stories* (London: The Folio Society, 1959), pp. 194, 195.

18 G. de Maupassant, 'Madame Tellier's Establishment', in *Short Stories*, op cit., p. 138.

Some of the Others in the Cast

The contralto **Marietta Alboni** was a protégée of Rossini. She sang the part of Anzoleto in the first performance of Giordigiani's *Consuelo* in Prague, a role which may have added relish to her first meeting with Pauline. Her stage appearance did not equal her rich, luscious tones. A photograph of her leading in *La Cenerentola* shows that the Ugly Sisters did not keep Cinders short of food. Turgenev thought she was fat and useless as an actress.[1]

Désirée Artôt, the daughter of the professor of horn-playing at the Brussels Conservatoire, was a pupil and protégée of Pauline, and a participant in Turgenev's portrait game at Courtavenel. Like Pauline, her vocal range was very wide. Her international career began with her début as Fidès in *Le Prophète* in 1858. Ten years later Tchaikovsky, an unlikely suitor, proposed marriage, but she married a Spanish baritone instead.

Mikhail Bakunin was born in 1814. His credo, early on, was 'The passion for destruction is also a creative passion.' He was in Paris for the February 1848 insurrection. In his *Appeal to the Slavs*, he denounced the bourgeoisie and called for the overthrow of the Habsburg Empire and the creation of a free federation of Slav peoples in central Europe. He was imprisoned following the fighting in Dresden in 1849, the uprising in which Wagner participated. In 1857, Bakunin was exiled to Siberia. He escaped via Japan and the USA to London. On arrival there, his first words to Herzen were 'Are there any oysters here?'[2] He later settled in Switzerland, in penury. He joined the Communist First International, although he led his own fringe group and was eventually expelled. Pauline acted as a conduit for correspondence between Bakunin and George Sand.[3] He died in 1876, in Switzerland.

By the end of the century, the once celebrity reputation of **Michael Balfe** was in shreds. One commentator said that the only good number in his *Maid of Honour* was the tenor aria, 'In this Old Chair my Father sat'.[4] Another, damning him with faint praise, conceded that one might do worse than *The Bohemian Girl*, 'the rubbish is quite unpretentious and decent'; fortunately, while 'we go to sleep over his middle-class, tawdry melodies, we are not actively irritated by them'.[5]

Vissarion Belinsky, the son of a doctor and grandson of a priest, was born in 1811. Because he did not come from the 'nobility', he had 'an unusual moral stature';[6] he was regarded as a critic of total integrity.[7] After he was expelled from Moscow University, he was required to carry on him his certificate of expulsion. He was largely self-taught. He became a journalist. In 1847, he wrote his famous *Letter to Gogol*, in which he denounced Gogol for betraying the Russian people by advocating submission to Church and state. Belinsky died of tuberculosis in 1848. When the police chief, the head of the notorious 'Third Section', heard of his death, he declared 'Too bad, we would have sent him to a fortress and let him rot'.[8]

The languid and charming **Vincenzo Bellini** was born in Catania in Sicily in 1801. He was trained in Naples. His reputation was made with *Il Pirata* which was premièred in Milan in 1827. Both *La Sonnambula* and his greatest masterpiece, *Norma*, were produced in 1831. After meeting Maria Malibran, he returned to Paris, where *I Puritani*, with a star-studded cast, was a sensational success. He had broken with his long-standing mistress. Bellini became ill and died in September 1835, outside Paris, in circumstances which were surprisingly lonely and even suspicious.

Johannes Brahms, a gruff and difficult man, was born in Hamburg on 7 May 1833 into a poor family. He became a virtuoso concert pianist and eventually settled in Vienna. *Ein Deutsches Requiem* made him financially secure. He played, conducted and composed the wide range of works we know. He acted as the conscience of Classical style as opposed to the 'New German Music' style of Wagner and of Bruckner whom he victimised. He died on 3 April 1897, less than a year after his great friend Clara Schumann.

Turgenev met **Robert Browning** at the Viardots' Saturday receptions in London during the Franco-Prussian War. Browning was born in Camberwell in 1812. When he was 33, he telegraphed Elizabeth Barrett of Wimpole Street to say that he loved her poetry and loved her too. They eloped and were married despite the opposition of her dominant father. She died in 1861. Browning belatedly became established as one of the United Kingdom's most important literary figures with the publication of *The Ring and the Book*, a poem of 21,000 lines, based on a murder in Rome around 1700.[9] He died in Venice in 1889.

Once labelled as 'the greatest bore that a man could tolerate', **Thomas Carlyle** was an influential writer who was born into a poor farming family in Dumfriesshire in 1795 and died 85 years later. He progressed by writing articles for influential periodicals such as the *London Magazine*. He moved to London where he eventually became known as the 'Sage of Chelsea'. For him, writing was a means of promoting moral leadership about contemporary issues. He married a descendant of John Knox[10] and adopted a similar outspoken and fearless style. In his lectures on German literature and heroes, and in his writings on Oliver Cromwell, the French Revolution and Frederick the Great, he adopted an individualistic mixture of the illiberal and radical, while condemning the cant and superficiality of his times. Although his views on prison reform might perhaps resonate in some quarters today, his support for slavery, along with his opinions on race and the shortcomings of democracy, would not find favour. They were, however, contemporary.[11]

The French soprano **Jeanne Castellan**, who sang Berthe in *Le Prophète*, was criticised by Chorley who disliked her off-pitch and 'squeezed' tone. 'She could be only rated as a *prima donna* in a second class opera house,' he wrote. He said that she 'attempts such feats as only one born a Garcia can accomplish; she often fails signally, and never succeeds completely'.[12]

Anton Chekhov's exquisite short stories such as 'Lady with Lapdog' and his plays such as *The Seagull* began to appear in the 1890s. Chekhov, whose father had been a serf, was born in Taganrog on the Sea of Azov by the Crimea, on 29 January 1860. After the failure of his father's business, the family moved to Moscow where Chekhov graduated as a doctor, wrote sketches for magazines and provided for his family. In the last years of his short life, he suffered from tuberculosis and spent much time in Yalta or on the French Riviera. He died in July 1904, within six months of the first performance of *The Cherry Orchard.*

Frédéric Chopin was born about 30 miles to the west of Warsaw in 1810. In October 1831 he settled in Paris. Five years later, he began a long affair with George Sand which included spending the winter of 1838–9 in Majorca, where the *Raindrop Prélude* was composed. Chopin's health was deteriorating, making the stay particularly fraught. He and Sand returned to France where they lived together until family difficulties, including the jealousy of Maurice and the waywardness of Solange, contributed to the break-up of Chopin's relationship with George in 1847. Chopin's tuberculosis got worse. After a visit to England and Scotland, he returned to Paris, where he died on 17 October 1849, aged only 39.

Costa, later Sir Michael Costa, was born in Naples. He was the dominant conductor in London for five decades in the middle of the 19th century. He was also a composer. 'Good old Costa has sent me an oratorio score and a Stilton cheese,' commented the gourmet Gioachino Rossini. 'The cheese was very good.'[13] Pauline thought that Costa sacrificed music to the Golden Calf, 'that is, English taste. They require Cayenne pepper in all sorts of aliments, moral as well as physical'.[14]

Alphonse Daudet was born six weeks after Zola and also came from a reasonably prosperous family which fell on hard times. He too became a journalist. He also worked for the Duc de Morny, the right-hand man of Napoleon III. He wrote many novels but he is perhaps best remembered today for his short stories; for his *Lettres de mon Moulin* based on his experiences in Corsica; and the unsuccessful play *L'Arlésienne.* Daudet died suddenly in 1897, having long suffered in agony from pain in his spinal cord occasioned by venereal disease.

Eugène Delacroix, is perhaps best known for his picture of 1830, *Liberty leading the People*, the tricolour raised above the revolutionaries. He was probably the illegitimate son of Talleyrand, the bishop and statesman who managed to serve the Revolution, Napoleon I and the Restoration.[15] One nurse nearly burnt Eugène to death by dropping a candle into his cot; he was nearly drowned accidentally by another; he was nearly poisoned and he nearly hanged himself by mistake.[16] He survived to demonstrate his belief 'that colour was much more important than draughtsmanship, and imagination than knowledge'.[17] His pictures include *Massacre at Chios* and *The Death of Sardanapalus.* He was always welcome at Courtavenel.[18] He died in 1863.

Charles Dickens was born in Portsmouth on 7 February 1812. When he was a boy, his father, a naval pay clerk, spent some time in a debtor's prison and was subsequently always in debt. Dickens became a parliamentary reporter and later, briefly, the first editor of the *Daily News.*[19] *Pickwick* (1836–7) was followed by *Oliver Twist* (1837–8), the first of his social tracts. *Dombey & Son* overtook the salons of Moscow in 1847, where there was a 'Dickens mania'.[20] *David Copperfield* was translated into Russian around 1850. To Dickens, the audience at his popular readings was 'like potent wine'[21] and to ensure the potency he had to please it.[22] His domestic life was troubled and messy. He separated from his wife, and as well as adoring her sister, he fell for an actress. In 1870, at the age of 58, he died soon after collapsing at the dinner table.

The novels of **George Eliot**, the pseudonym for Mary Anne Evans, include *Adam Bede* (1859), *The Mill on the Floss* (1860) and *Middlemarch* (1870–71). She was born in the English Midlands in 1819, into a staunchly evangelical family. To her family's horror, she became a journalist, wrote about religion and rejected Christianity. The philosopher Herbert Spencer refused to marry her because she was too ugly.[23] However, the scholar and journalist G.H. Lewes, whose book on Goethe was one of Pauline's favourites, lived openly with Eliot.[24] Lewes could not obtain a divorce, having condoned his wife's adultery with a colleague. When Lewes and Eliot lived at The Priory, in Regent's Park, London, their Sunday afternoons were a feature of Victorian literary life. Lewes died in 1878. She survived him by two years. In the meantime, she married her financial adviser who was over twenty years younger than her.

César Franck was born in Liège on 10 December 1822. He was a fellow pupil, with Pauline, of Reicha.[25] He held a succession of positions as organist. He spent the last 30 years of his life as organist at the new basilica of Sainte-Clotilde. He was professor of organ at the Conservatoire, where his influence on the subsequent generation of composers was immense. He also taught Paul Viardot, Pauline's son.[26] His death on 8 November 1890 was precipitated by an accident with a horse-bus.

Mikhail Glinka, a noble from near Smolensk, was born in the summer of 1804. He laid the foundation for a Russian musical tradition with his operas *A Life for the Tsar* (1836) and *Ruslan and Lyudmila* (1842). Turgenev, in April 1836, said that he was simply bored by a performance of *The Life for the Tsar.* He met Glinka at a performance of Beethoven's Ninth Symphony twenty years later. Glinka died in February 1857.

Nikolay Gogol was born in 1809 at Sorochintsy, near Poltava in Ukraine. He came from the minor nobility, and obtained a post in the civil service. He wrote occasional articles for journals. Subsequently, he taught at a girls' school and was briefly assistant professor at St Petersburg University. *Evenings in a Farm near Dikanka*, published in 1831–2, first made his name. This was followed by his successful comedy of 1836, *The Government Inspector*, which exposed the corruption, and the alternate arrogance and servility, of the civil service. His skill as a humorist was further displayed in *Dead Souls* (1842), which was chiefly written in Italy but was never completed. He became increasingly ascetic and mystical. After a pilgrimage to Palestine he settled in Moscow, where he died in March 1852, aged nearly 43.[27]

The novelist **Ivan Aleksandrovich Goncharov** came from a merchant family. His *Oblomov*, published in 1859, was sometimes called a powerful condemnation of serfdom; however, it reads much more like a parody on the indolence of the nobility, and on idleness generally. He later joined the censorship department.

Today, **Edmond and Jules de Goncourt** are remembered for the prize annually awarded for French literature. Edmond was born in 1822, his brother eight years later. Their *Journal*, a helpful cocktail of fact, gossip and anecdote, was started in 1851 and continued until Edmond's death in 1896. Less well-known today are their influential and realistic novels for which they researched with great sympathy the world of the lower classes, and in which they show an almost modern understanding of human psychology.[28] 'The public likes false novels, this one is true. The public likes books which take them into high society; this one comes in from the street',[29] they said of *Germinie Lacerteux*, based on the pathetic and secret private life of their devoted and trusted housekeeper, nanny, companion, treasure. For 25 years Rose had been an adored and respected member of the family. Within five days of her death they learnt of her illegitimate children and how she had embezzled twenty per cent of the house-keeping money to finance her lovers and their sprees, her lust and her drink.[30] Jules died from syphilis in 1870. In the 1850s, the Goncourts were charged but acquitted of outrage against public morality for quoting some erotic material in an article.

Tolstoy thought **Alexander Herzen**, the illegitimate son of a 'nobleman', 'enchanting'. 'I have never met a more attractive man', he said.[31] 'He stood head and shoulders above all politicians of his own and of our time.' He was born in 1812. Over his lifetime, Herzen's views changed, making it possible for both liberals and socialists to claim his legacy. At first he supported the westernisers, although preferring a more anarchist approach than the liberal reformers. After the failure of the 1848 insurrection, he promoted the idea of a collectivist peasant commune as the way forward to socialism. In 1853 in London, out of reach of the censors, he founded a press. He edited a series of periodicals that were designed to be smuggled back to Russia, in particular the highly influential newspaper *The Bell*. He died in 1870 in Paris.

Although ostensibly the daughter of an elderly army officer from Ireland, **Augusta Holmès** may have been the child of the poet Alfred de Vigny. She had a deep contralto and her striking personality 'dominated the musical and literary salons of her day to an extraordinary extent'.[32] Together with Pauline, she was one of the few female composers in Paris. Her works were influenced by military bands. It was said that they were reminiscent of the last act of *Götterdämmerung*. In her later years, she took to drink. Saint-Saëns's Dalila was possibly inspired by her. To her, César Franck dedicated his well-known *Third Choral* for the organ.[33]

Each morning, so it was said, **Victor Hugo**, the romantic poet and novelist wrote 100 lines of verse or twenty pages of prose. He was born at Besançon, between Dijon and Switzerland, in 1802. His father was a general. He gave up law for literature, and *The Hunch-back of Notre-Dame* was published in 1831. He became involved in politics. During the Second Empire he lived in exile in the Channel Islands; he returned to Paris in 1871. He took a long time to write *Les Misérables* which was published in 1862: this was his thriller about those who, through no fault of their own, were the outcasts, the underdogs, the dregs of society. Hugo was highly venerated,[34] but not by Turgenev who disliked his works.[35] He died in Paris in 1885.

Luigi Lablache, the half-Irish, half-French bass, was famed for his 'colossal girth and thundering voice'. He was the first Don Pasquale. Louise Viardot said that he was the greatest comic actor and singer of the age.[36] He was born in Naples in 1794.

Felix Mendelssohn, although born in Hamburg on 3 February 1809, was brought up in Berlin. His grandfather was a distinguished Jewish philosopher, his father a rich banker, and his sister Fanny a distinguished musician in her own right. When only twenty, he revived Bach's *St Matthew Passion*, which had been dormant for a large proportion of the hundred years since it was composed. He was conductor at the Leipzig Gewandhaus where he gave the first performance of Schubert's *Great Symphony* in C major. Much of his work was in England, where his *Songs without Words* and his oratorios such as *Elijah* were particularly well received, not least by Queen Victoria. He died on 4 November 1847 aged only 38, his health having been weakened by overwork. Surprisingly, Turgenev thought Mendelssohn's music came more from the head than the heart.[37]

Prosper Mérimée, novelist, archaeologist, essayist, and writer of many letters, was born in Paris on 28 September 1803, and is remembered today particularly for his *Colomba* and *Carmen.* He became a senior civil servant and an inspector of historical monuments. He was a long-time friend of the mother of Empress Eugénie, and thus was very close to the imperial couple. Accordingly, he became a senator during the Second Empire, albeit somewhat unenthusiastically. That he 'liked a king's palace better than a philosopher's hovel'[38] did not enhance his reputation. The French regarded his manner, his indifference, sarcasm and scepticism, as being very English. His health was poor and he died in Cannes on 23 September 1870. He was interested in the Russian language and was a friend of Turgenev.[39]

Giuditta Pasta, for whom Bellini wrote *La Sonnambula*, was Jewish and was born in Milan in 1797. She was the outstanding soprano of the early 1830s. It was said that her genius as a tragedian surpassed her talent as a singer.[40] An English nobleman said 'other singers find themselves endowed with a voice and leave everything else to chance. This woman leaves nothing to chance and her success is therefore certain'.[41] She gave the Paris première of Rossini's Desdemona, and much of Donizetti's success may be attributed to her. She had to rebuild her fortune which she lost in a bank failure in Vienna.[42] She died in 1865.

Fanny Persiani, *la piccola Pasta*, was born in 1812 in Rome. She excelled in vocal embroidery, and her trills and flourishes were executed 'with the facility of a fairy threading pearls'. She was also 'diaphanous, dreamy, pathetic'[43] and became a leading exponent of the works of Bellini and Donizetti. She married the composer and impresario Giuseppe Persiani. She retired in the 1840s, managed the Théâtre-Italien briefly, and taught singing. She died in 1867.

Ernest Renan was born in 1823, the son of a ship-outfitter from Brittany. He trained for the priesthood, but gave up his vocation. He married Ary Scheffer's niece Cornélie, who had to compete with his sister Henriette to whom he was devoted. Henriette, who was twelve years older than her brother, died of malaria on a visit to the Middle East.[44] In the early 1860s, Renan was appointed to a Professorship in Semitic Languages. He was suspended after his inaugural lecture in which he referred to Jesus as 'a man so great that I would not wish to contradict those who, impressed by the unique character of his movement, call him God'. Sixty thousand copies of his *Vie de Jésus* were sold in the first six months after it was published in 1863. In this, he presents Jesus, a man in whom was condensed all that is good and elevated in our nature, as the leader of a small band who believed that the end of the world was imminent.[45] Renan questions the reality of the miracles, and takes a few swipes at the Establishment. The book was virulently opposed by the Church. He died in 1892.

Gioachino Rossini, born in Pesaro in 1792, was brought up mainly in Bologna. *The Barber of Seville* was premièred in Rome when he was only 23. At first a fiasco, it was subsequently supremely successful and Rossini became extremely wealthy. In the 1820s, he was appointed the Director at the Théâtre-Italien in Paris. After *William Tell*, in 1829, he suddenly stopped composing. He then settled mainly in Bologna. He composed little more for the rest of his life. He returned to Paris in 1855, where he lived in style until his death in 1868. Pauline sang in many of his operas and in the first, albeit private, performance of his *Stabat Mater*, one of his few works in the intervening years.

Giovanni Battista Rubini, born in 1794, 'a divine singer, but far too lazy an actor',[46] was a Rossini tenor with an unusually high range, the top of which was falsetto. In the 1820s, he had worked closely with Bellini to create *Il Pirata* and *I Puritani.* His 'Il mio tesoro' from *Don Giovanni* was particularly popular.[47]

The brothers **Anton and Nikolay Rubinstein**, both central figures in Russian musical life and education in the 19th century, figured greatly in Tchaikovsky's life. Anton, virtuoso pianist, womaniser, composer of the *Melody in F* and much besides, founded the St Petersburg Conservatoire; his brother Nikolay founded the Moscow Conservatoire. They, particularly Anton, were reviled by nationalist composers such as Mussorgsky. Turgenev thought Nikolay was a better and more accurate pianist, 'plus simplement et plus correctement', than Anton.[48]

In late 19th century England, **Charles Augustin Sainte-Beuve** was said to be 'the most notable critic of our time', maybe because his mother was half-English.[49] He was born in Boulogne in 1804. Like Berlioz, he studied medicine; however, he preferred journalism and writing poetry and novels. Journals such as the *Revue de Paris, Revue des deux Mondes, Le Constitutionnel* and *Le Moniteur* featured his work. The demands for his weekly articles, for example his *Causeries du Lundi*, involved relentlessly hard work. He was criticised for supporting the Empire, under which he became a senator. He benefited from the patronage of Princess Mathilde who was the daughter of King Jérome, the younger brother of Napoleon I. However, they fell out when Sainte-Beuve transferred to an Opposition newspaper. He presided at Wednesday literary lunches at Magny's restaurant, after which people would move on to Princess Mathilde's salon.[50] He was much admired for his grace and charm. He died in 1869 after an unsuccessful gallstone operation.

Henriette Sontag, 'La petite Allemande', the blonde Venus, 'the Nightingale of the North', was born in Coblenz in 1806. Aged eight, she sang the Queen of the Night's grand aria[51] from *The Magic Flute* which cannot have done much good to her voice. She was Weber's first Euryanthe and sang at the first performance of Beethoven's Ninth Symphony.[52] At one time, she was the mistress of Bériot. Her husband lost his fortune in the 1848 insurrection. To replenish it, she returned to the stage in London in 1849. She had lost neither her looks nor her voice, which she had preserved by daily practice. In 1852, she crossed the Atlantic. She died, two years later, of cholera in Mexico.[53]

Antonio Tamburini, a baritone, was born in 1800. His career began in Italy where he featured in many opera houses and in several Donizetti premières. In the 1830s, he was mainly in London and Paris. He retired to Nice, where he died in 1876.

Emile Zola was born in 1840 and brought up in Aix-en-Provence, where he went to the same school as Cézanne. They remained close friends until Zola portrayed him in a novel. Zola's father, an Italian civil engineer, died of pneumonia when Emile was only seven, and left the family in great poverty. His first important novel, his Crime and Punishment, *Thérèse Raquin*, a horror story of sex, murder and the psychological consequences, was published in 1867. It was denounced as 'a pool of filth and blood'.[54] He then began the *Rougon-Macquart* series of twenty loosely connected and very carefully researched novels, subtitled 'the Natural and Social History of a Family under the Second Empire', along the lines of Balzac's *La Comédie humaine.* Number seven, *L'Assommoir*, which Edmond de Goncourt thought had plagiarised his *Germinie Lacerteux*,[55] is a distressing story about a decent working-class woman's pathetic struggle and progressive descent into alcoholism and depravity. Number nine, *Nana*, tells of her daughter who became a whore, and number thirteen, *Germinal*, of her son's work in the coalmines. Zola died in 1902, asphyxiated by fumes from a blocked chimney – possibly someone took revenge for his prominent role in the Dreyfus case.

REFERENCES

1 I. Turgenev (ed. E. Halpérine-Kaminsky), *Lettres à Madame Viardot* (Paris: Bibliothèque-Charpentier, 1907), 8 December 1847, p. 14.
2 E. de Goncourt, *Journal* (Paris, 1887), vol. II, p. 284.
3 *Encyclopaedia Britannica,* Standard Millennium edition; A. FitzLyon, *The Price of Genius, a life of Pauline Viardot* (London: John Calder, 1964), p. 256.
4 W. Kuhe, *My musical recollections* (London: Richard Bentley, 1896), p. 89.
5 E. Walker, *A History of Music in England* (Oxford: Clarendon Press, 1952), pp. 292, 203.
6 R. Freeborn, *Turgenev, the novelist's novelist* (Oxford: Oxford University Press, 1960), pp. 12, 13.
7 L. Schapiro, *Turgenev, his Life and Times* (Oxford: Oxford University Press, 1978), p. 105.
8 F. Randall, *Vissarion Belinsky* (Newtonville, Mass.: Oriental Research Partners, 1987), pp. 5, 6, 16, 22.
9 H. James, Jr, *English Hours* (Oxford: Oxford University Press, 1981, first published 1905) 'Browning in Westminster Abbey', pp. 32, 33; D. Karlin's introduction to R. Browning, *Selected Poems* (London: Penguin, 1989), p. 11.
10 R. Cochrane (ed.), *The English Essayists* (London: William Nimmo, 1876), p. 520.
11 J. Morrow, *Thomas Carlyle* (London: Hambledon, 2006), pp. 32, 45, 130, 208, 211.
12 *New Grove Dictionary of Music and Musicians* (London: Macmillan, 1980), vol. 3, p. 866, Castellan (P. Robinson); H.F. Chorley, *Thirty years' Musical Recollections* (London: Hurst & Blackett, 1862), vol.I, p. 258.
13 *New Grove,* op. cit., vol. 4, p. 820, Costa (Keith Horner).
14 *Musical Quarterly,* vol. I, 1915, p. 538. Costa added a military band to the orchestra for his Crystal Palace concerts.
15 *Encyclopaedia Britannica,* Standard Millennium edition.
16 *Encyclopaedia Britannica,* ninth edition, vol. VII, p. 39 (Delacroix).
17 E. Gombrich, *The Story of Art* (London: Phaidon, 1963), p. 381.
18 Paul Viardot, *Souvenirs d'un Artiste* (Paris: Librairie Fischbacher SA, 1910), p. 5.
19 *Encyclopaedia Britannica,* Standard Millennium edition.
20 A.N. Wilson, *Tolstoy* (London: Hamish Hamilton, 1988), p. 86.
21 I. Evans, *A Short History of English Literature* (Harmondsworth: Penguin, 1963), p. 181.
22 Ibid., p. 181.
23 K. Hughes, *George Eliot, The Last Victorian* (London: Fourth Estate, 1998), pp. 2, 119.
24 P. Waddington, 'Turgenev and George Eliot, a literary friendship', *Modern Language Review,* vol. 66, 1971.
25 *New Grove,* op. cit., vol. 15, p. 696, Reicha, (P. Eliot Stone).
26 Paul Viardot, op. cit., p. 35.
27 *Encyclopaedia Britannica,* Standard Millennium edition; *Encyclopaedia Britannica,* ninth edition, vol. x, p. 738.
28 See E. and J. de Goncourt (trans. L. Tancock), *Germinie Lacerteux* (Harmondsworth: Penguin, 1984), ch. 69, p. 167: 'Mademoiselle de Varandeuil wondered whether the poor woman (Germinie) was as guilty as some others, whether she had chosen evil, whether life, circumstances, the misfortunes of her body and destiny had not made her into the creature she had been, a creature of love and pain ... suddenly she drew herself up – she was going to forgive!'
29 Ibid., Preface, 'Le public aime les romans faux; ce roman est un roman vrai. Il aime les livres qui font semblant d'aller dans le monde: ce livre vient de la rue.'
30 Ibid., p. 152; E. de Goncourt (trans. Bellloc and Shedlock), *Journal* (London: Heinemann, 1895), 22 and 31 July 1862; 16 and 21 August 1862.
31 A. Herzen (trans. C. Garnett), *My Past and Thoughts, the Memoirs of Alexander Herzen* (London: Chatto and Windus, 1974), p. xvi.
32 *New Grove,* op. cit., vol. 8, p. 654, Holmès (H. Macdonald).
33 J. Harding, *Saint-Saëns and his Circle* (London: Chapman & Hall, 1965), pp. 73–5; L. Davies, *César Franck and his Circle* (London: Barrie and Jenkins, 1970), p. 257; B. Rees, *Camille Saint-Saëns, A Life* (London: Chatto & Windus, 1999), p. 128.
34 Paul Viardot, op. cit., p. 34.
35 L. Schapiro, *Turgenev, his Life and Times* (Oxford: Oxford University Press, 1978), p. 237.
36 T. Marix-Spire, *Lettres inédites de George Sand et de Pauline Viardot 1839–1849* (Paris: Nouvelles Editions, 1959), p. 92. 'Le plus grand acteur comique et le plus parfait chanteur de notre époque.' A. de Musset, *Revue des Deux Mondes,* vol. xvii, p. 849.
37 I. Turgenev, *Lettres à Madame Viardot,* op. cit., p. 9, 19 November 1847.
38 *Encyclopaedia Britannica,* ninth edition, vol. XIV, p. 37.
39 *Encyclopaedia Britannica,* Standard Millennium edition; A. Zviguilsky (ed.), *Ivan Tourguénev: Nouvelle Correspondance inédite* (Paris: Librairie des Cinq Continents, 1971), p. 127; L. Schapiro, op. cit., p. 220.
40 E. Creathorne Clayton, *Queens of Song* (London: Smith Elder & Co, 1863), pp. 6, 11, 31.

41 Ibid., p. 4.

42 *New Grove*, op. cit., vol. 14, p. 287, Pasta (Elizabeth Forbes); E.C. Clayton, op. cit., p. 31.

43 Blaze in *Revue des Deux Mondes*, vol. XXXII, p. 860; *New Grove*, op. cit., vol. 18, p. 516, Tacchinardi-Persiani (Francesco Bussi).

44 M. Kirlew, F*amous Sisters of Great Men* (London: Thos Nelson, 1905); R.M. Chadbourne, *Ernest Renan* (New York: Twayne Publishers Inc, 1968), pp. 132, 135.

45 E. Renan, *The Life of Jesus* (London: Watts & Co, 1945), pp. ix, 227.

46 A. de Musset, 'Débuts de Mademoiselle Pauline Garcia', *Revue des Deux Mondes*, vol. XX, p. 439.

47 *New Grove*, op. cit., vol. 16, p.296, Rubini (Julian Budden); G. Sand, 'Le Théâtre-Italien et Mlle Pauline Garcia', *Revue des Deux Mondes*, vol. XXI, p. 580.

48 I. Turgenev, *Lettres à Madame Viardot*, op. cit., p. 218, 1 April 1867.

49 *Encyclopaedia Britannica*, ninth edition, vol. XXI, p. 162.

50 M. Castillon du Perron (trans. M. McLean), *Princess Mathilde* (London: Heinemann, 1956), pp. 169, 185.

51 E.C. Clayton, op. cit., pp. 80, 88.

52 A. FitzLyon, *Maria Malibran – Diva of the Romantic Age* (London: Souvenir Press, 1987), p. 69.

53 E.C. Clayton, op. cit., pp. 90, 98, 100; A. FitzLyon, *Maria Malibran*, op. cit., p.101; *New Grove*, op. cit., vol. 17, p. 528, Sontag (J. Warrack); W. Kuhe, op. cit., p. 115.

54 R. Buss in Introduction to E. Zola (trans. and intro. R. Buss), *Thérèse Raquin* (Penguin, 2004; also Paris: Bibliothèque Charpentier, 1890), Introduction, p. xiii.

55 E. de Goncourt, *Journal*, op. cit., 2 February 1879 and 7 July 1891.

Some Key Dates

10 February 1795	Ary Scheffer born at Dort, Holland
31 July 1800	Louis Viardot born in Dijon
11 December 1803	Berlioz born at La Côte-St-André near Grenoble
1 July 1804	George Sand born in Paris
1 March 1810	Chopin born near Warsaw
11 December 1810	Alfred de Musset born in Paris
7 February 1812	Dickens born in Portsmouth
28 December 1812	Julius Rietz born in Berlin
17 June 1818	Gounod born in Paris
9 November 1818	Turgenev born in Oryol
13 September 1819	Schumann's wife, Clara, born in Leipzig
20 February 1820	Rachel born in Switzerland
18 July 1821	Pauline Garcia born in Paris
11 November 1821	Dostoyevsky born in Moscow
12 December 1821	Flaubert born in Rouen
30 June 1823	Maurice (Dudevant) Sand born in Paris
29 November 1825	Garcia Italian opera season opened in New York
During 1828	Garcia family leaves Mexico City, and is attacked by robbers
9 September 1828	Leo Tolstoy born at Yasnaya Polyana
Spring 1829	Garcias arrive back in France
27–29 July 1830	*Les Trois Glorieuses*
2 June 1832	Pauline's father dies in Paris
1836	Gounod enters Paris Conservatoire
23 September 1836	Maria Malibran dies in Manchester
10 February 1837	Pushkin dies in St Petersburg
24 May 1837	Georgina Weldon born
13 December 1837	Pauline's first performance in public as a singer, in Brussels
12 June 1838	Rachel's debut at Théâtre-Français
15 December 1838	Pauline's first public concert in Paris, Théâtre de la Renaissance
January 1839	Musset's article about Pauline in *Revue des Deux Mondes*
Spring 1839	Pauline goes to London
9 May 1839	Pauline appears at Her Majesty's Theatre
8 October 1839	Paris opera debut; Pauline meets George Sand
November 1839	Another Musset article about Pauline in *Revue des Deux Mondes*
5 December 1839	Gounod leaves for Rome having won the Prix de Rome
18 April 1840	Pauline and Louis marry
February 1841	Pauline goes to London for season
29 July 1841	Lermontov killed in duel
14 December 1841	Louise born
February 1842–February 1844	*Consuelo* published in the *Revue Indépendante*
April 1842	Viardot tour of Spain
Early summer 1842	Paulinette born
Autumn 1842	Gounod leaves Rome for Germany
October 1842	Pauline appears opposite Grisi at Théâtre-Italien
December 1842	Louis defends Pauline from critical article in *Revue des Deux Mondes*
1843	Gounod takes up appointment as organist at the Eglise des Missions Etrangères
April 1843	Pauline appears in Vienna; Turgenev publishes *Parasha*

July 1843	Turgenev obtains minor civil service post; Pauline goes to Prague and Berlin
3 November 1843	Pauline appears on Russian stage
13 November 1843	Turgenev meets Pauline
March 1844	Pauline goes to Vienna
April 1844	The Viardots acquire the Château de Courtavenel
October 1844	Pauline back in St Petersburg
Holy Week 1845	The Viardots go to Moscow
April 1845	Turgenev resigns from job
June 1845	The Viardots back in France
August 1845	Pauline at Beethoven memorial concert
October 1845	Pauline returns to St Petersburg with Louise
February 1846	Pauline catches whooping cough, returns to France
Winter 1846	Pauline goes to Berlin
1846	Louis's *Souvenirs de Chasse* published
Autumn 1847	German tour
February 1848	Revolution in Paris
6 April 1848	Pauline's *La Jeune République* performed
May 1848	Pauline in *La Sonnambula* and *Les Huguenots* in London; Pauline performing with Chopin and Berlioz in London
7 June 1848	Belinsky dies
23-26 June 1848	The June Days
October 1848	Viardots acquire house in rue de Douai
16 April 1849	Paris première of Meyerbeer's *Le Prophète*
Summer 1849	Gounod introduced to Pauline; Turgenev ill, nursed by Herzen
12 July 1849	Turgenev arrives at Courtavenel for summer; Pauline in London for *Le Prophète*
17 October 1849	Chopin dies
1850	*Diary of a Superfluous Man*
Spring 1850	Pauline and Gounod work on *Sapho*; Turgenev finishes *A Month in the Country*
22 June 1850	Turgenev leaves for Russia
4 November 1850	Paulinette departs St Petersburg for Paris
28 November 1850	Turgenev's mother dies
16 April 1851	Première of *Sapho*
9 August 1851	London premiere of *Sapho*
2 December 1851	Louis-Napoléon coup d'état
May 1852	Turgenev informs Viardots of his arrest; Gounod marries
21 May 1852	Claudie born
May/June 1852	Row with Gounod about wedding present
15 January 1853	Pauline appears in St Petersburg
March/April 1853	Pauline goes to Moscow, without Louis. Turgenev visits Moscow
December 1853	Turgenev allowed to leave Spasskoye
15 March 1854	Marianne born
1855	Scheffer paints portrait of Dickens
10 May 1855	Pauline sings Azucena in London première of *Il Trovatore*
June/July 1855	*Rudin* written
1855/56	Turgenev meets Countess Lambert
Beginning of 1856	*Rudin* published
10 January 1856	Viardots give dinner party to introduce Dickens to George Sand
June-August 1856	*Faust* written
29 July 1856	Robert Schumann dies near Bonn

October 1856	Fet finds Turgenev frustrated at Courtavenel
Autumn 1856	Turgenev in apartment in Rue de Rivoli, ill with bladder problem
2 May 1857	Alfred de Musset dies in Paris
20 July 1857	Paul born, Turgenev tours around Europe
3 January 1858	Rachel dies
May 1858	Pauline touring, including British Isles
15 June 1858	Ary Scheffer dies
October 1858	*Nest of the Gentry* finished at Spasskoye
End 1858/ beginning 1859	Correspondence with Rietz begins; it peaks in 1859—60
January 1859	Pauline leaves Paris for London, and provincial tour
19 March 1859	Première of Gounod's *Faust*
July/August 1859	Turgenev visits Courtavenel, Pauline sings at Baden-Baden under Berlioz's direction
August 1859	First public performance of extract from Berlioz *Les Troyens*
September 1859	Berlioz at Courtavenel
18 November 1859	*Orphée* premiere
1860	*On the Eve* written
January–March 1860	*First Love* written
25 February 1860	44th performance of *Orphée*
February 1860	Private audition at Viardot house of Act II of *Tristan*
May 1860	Pauline performs in *Fidelio*
Spring 1861	Pauline gives two concerts at Conservatoire, excerpts from *Alceste*
21 June 1861	121st performance of *Orphée*
21 October 1861	First performance of *Alceste* revival
1861	Emancipation of the Serfs decreed
1862	Louise marries, *Fathers & Sons* published
24 April 1863	Pauline's farewell performance (*Orphée*) at Théâtre-Lyrique
4 November 1863	*Trojans at Carthage* staged in Paris
1863	The Viardots leave France for Baden-Baden, Turgenev settles in Schillerstrasse
10 May 1864	Pauline's mother dies
23 February 1865	Paulinette marries
1866	Both *War and Peace* and *Crime & Punishment* are serialized in *Ruskii Vestnik*
1867	*Smoke* published; Louise takes up job at St Petersburg; *Trop de Femmes*
September 1867	*Le Dernier sorcier* first staged
27 April 1867	Première of Gounod's *Roméo et Juliette*
28 June 1867	Dostoyevsky visits Turgenev in Baden-Baden
24 May 1868	*L'Ogre* first performed
13 November 1868	Rossini dies near Paris
8 March 1869	Berlioz dies in Paris
8 April 1869	*Le Dernier sorcier* performed in Weimar
3 March 1870	Pauline gives first public performance of Brahms's *Alto Rhapsody* at Jena
9 July 1870	Dickens dies, Gad's Hill
Mid-July 1870	Franco-Prussian War begins
1 September 1870	French capitulation at Sedan
21 October 1870	Pauline and daughters cross Channel to London
Mid-November 1870	Louis and Turgenev leave for London
28 January 1871	Paris capitulates
21 May 1871	Commune collapses
May 1871	Pauline reads of her own death in the papers

1872	Fauré introduced into Viardot circle
11 April 1873	Pauline in *Marie Magdeleine*
1874	Claudie gets engaged; Pauline plays Dalila in private performance
1875	Les Frênes in Bougival purchased
8 June 1876	George Sand dies
1877	Fauré and Marianne get engaged, and break up
1877	*Virgin Soil*
12 September 1877	Julius Rietz dies in Dresden
1879	Savina appears in *A Month in the Country*
8 May 1880	Flaubert dies, Croisset
9 February 1881	Dostoyevsky dies, St Petersburg
1882	Gounod's *La Rédemption*, London
Early March 1882	Louis has a stroke and nearly dies; Marianne has a difficult confinement, and Paulinette seeks refuge in Switzerland
April 1882	Turgenev falls very ill
Summer 1882	Turgenev spends summer at Bougival
November 1882	Turgenev returns to Paris from Bougival
January 1883	Turgenev has operation for removal of neuroma
Beginning of May 1883	Turgenev returns to Bougival
5 May 1883	Louis dies
9 July 1883	Turgenev writes final letter to Tolstoy
3 September 1883	Turgenev dies at Bougival
31 July 1886	Liszt dies in Bayreuth
1885	Gounod's *Mors et Vita,* London
1889	Maurice Sand dies at Nohant
17 October 1893	Gounod dies at St-Cloud
20 May 1896	Clara Schumann dies in Frankfurt
1899	Solange Sand dies
23 April 1904	*Cendrillon* performed
18 May 1910	Pauline dies in Paris

Acknowledgements

The author and publisher wish to thank the following for their permission to reprint copyright material:

Musical Quarterly, volume 1, 1915: Pauline Viardot-Garcia to Julian Rietz, G. Shirmer (copyright 1915 and 1916). Reproduced with permission of Oxford University Press.
A. FitzLyon, *The Price of Genius, a life of Pauline Viardot* (London: John Calder, 1964). Reproduced with permission of Mr Kyril FitzLyon.
Dr Alexandre Zviguilsky, with L'Association des Amis d'Ivan Tourguéniev, Pauline Viardot et Maria Malibran, Musée Ivan Tourguéniev, Bougival, France.
Professor Patrick Waddington, for permission to quote from his works as listed in References and Sources.

Picture Credits

c.p. = colour plate number, p. = page in text

c.p. 1, c.p. 12, c.p. 13, copyright © Stadtmuseum Baden-Baden, Germany.
c.p. 2, p. 80, p. 139, p. 208, copyright © Musée de la Vie Romantique/Roger-Viollet.
c.p. 3, copyright © State Russian Museum, St. Petersburg, Russia/The Bridgeman Art Library. Reproduced with permission of the Bridgeman Art Library.
c.p. 4, copyright © Tretyakov Gallery, Moscow, Russia/The Bridgeman Art Library. Reproduced with permission of the Bridgeman Art Library.
c.p. 5, copyright © Private Collection/The Bridgeman Art Library. Reproduced with permission of the Bridgeman Art Library.
c.p. 6, reproduced with permission of the Milwaukee Art Museum. Gift of Jane Bradley Pettit, photo by John Glembin.
c.p. 7, reproduced with permission of the Museum of Fine Arts, Boston. Bequest of John T. Spaulding, photograph © Museum of Fine Arts, Boston.
c.p. 8, reproduced with permission of the Museum of Art, Rhode Island School of Design, Museum Appropriation Fund. Photography by Erik Gould.
c.p. 9, reproduced with permission of Klassik Stiftung Weimar, Herzog Anna Amalia Bibliothek.
c.p. 10, copyright © National Portrait Gallery, London, UK/The Bridgeman Art Library. Reproduced with permission of the Bridgeman Art Library.
c.p. 11, p. 40, p. 87, p. 95, p. 122, p. 243, p. 314, p. 320, p. 369, p. 403, p. 410, p. 412, p. 423, L'Association des Amis d'Ivan Tourguéniev, Pauline Viardot et Maria Malibran, Musée Ivan Tourguéniev, Bougival, France. Reproduced with permission of Dr Alexandre Zviguilsky.
c.p. 14, p. 1, p. 351, p. 360, p. 373, p. 421, p. 425, p. 434, from the author's collection.
p. xii (1, 3), p. xvi, p. 12, p. 17, p. 23, p. 31, p. 32, p. 37, p. 39 (1, 2), p. 53, p. 151, p. 157, p. 174, p. 256, p. 258, p. 318 (1, 2), p. 359, p. 374 (2), p. 377, p. 378, p. 426, p. 427 (1, 2), reproduced with kind permission of the Royal College of Music, London.
p. 42, copyright © Crown Publishing.
p. 45, p. 58, p. 213, p. 357, p. 388, reproduced with permission of the British Library.
p. 60, p. 74, p. 120, p. 322, p. 382, *Aesculape*, 7–8 July 1955.
p. 46, reproduced courtesy of Archives Juives.
p. 76, copyright © The Cobbe Collection Trust, UK/The Bridgeman Art Library. Reproduced with permission of the Bridgeman Art Library.
p. 79, copyright © National Gallery of Victoria, Melbourne, Australia/The Bridgeman Art Library. Reproduced with permission of the Bridgeman Art Library.
p. 92, p. 124, reproduced with permission of Mrs Rosemary Steen.
p. 105, copyright © Private Collection/The Bridgeman Art Library. Reproduced with permission of the Bridgeman Art Library.

p. 112 (1), copyright © Tretyakov Gallery, Moscow, Russia/The Bridgeman Art Library. Reproduced with permission of the Bridgeman Art Library.
p. 112 (2), copyright © Private Collection/Ken Welsh/The Bridgeman Art Library. Reproduced with permission of the Bridgeman Art Library.
p. 134, p. 136, p. 189, p. 211, p. 237, p. 246, p. 259, p. 299, p. 349, p. 368, reproduced with permission of Professor Patrick Waddington.
p. 184, p. 301, from L. Héritte-Viardot, *Memories and Adventures* (London: Mills and Boon, 1913).
p. 186, copyright © Louvre, Paris, France/Lauros/Giraudon/The Bridgeman Art Library. Reproduced with permission of the Bridgeman Art Library.
p. 190, p. 202 (1, 2, with thanks to Richard Todd for his help on these items), p. 218, reproduced with permission of Professor Patrick Waddington, from *Courtavenel, the History of an Artists' Nest and its Role in the Life of Turgenev* (*PhD Thesis*, Queen's University Belfast, The British Library, British Thesis Service, spring 1972).
p. 199, reproduced by permission of The Art Institute of Chicago. Photography © The Art Institute of Chicago.
p. 207: copyright © Musée d'Orsay, Paris, France/Giraudon/The Bridgeman Art Library. Reproduced with permission of the Bridgeman Art Library.
p. 268, copyright © Wallraf Richartz Museum, Cologne, Germany/The Bridgeman Art Library. Reproduced with permission of the Bridgeman Art Library.
p. 294, reproduced with permission of Professor Patrick Waddington. With thanks to Richard Todd for his work on this item.
p. 332, copyright © Archives Larousse, Paris, France/Giraudon/The Bridgeman Art Library. Reproduced with permission of the Bridgeman Art Library.
p. 372, copyright © Private Collection/The Bridgeman Art Library. Reproduced with permission of the Bridgeman Art Library.
p. 374 (1), copyright © Bibliothèque des Arts Decoratifs, Paris, France/Archives Charmet/The Bridgeman Art Library.
p. 386, copyright © Château de Versailles, France/Lauros/Giraudon/The Bridgeman Art Library. Reproduced with permission of the Bridgeman Art Library.
p. 394, from *Guide*, La Maison de George Sand, Nohant, France.
p. 396, copyright © Private Collection/Ken Welsh/The Bridgeman Art Library. Reproduced with permission of the Bridgeman Art Library.

Every effort has been made to contact copyright holders for other extracts and images contained in this book.

Index

Black and white illustrations are indicated by page numbers in **bold**.